Visual Analysis of Humans

Thomas B. Moeslund · Adrian Hilton ·
Volker Krüger · Leonid Sigal

Editors

Visual Analysis of Humans

Looking at People

 Springer

Editors
Assoc. Prof. Thomas B. Moeslund
Department of Media Technology
Aalborg University
Niels Jernes Vej 14
Aalborg, 9220
Denmark
tbm@create.aau.dk

Assoc. Prof. Volker Krüger
Copenhagen Institute of Technology
Aalborg University
Lautrupvang 2B
Ballerup, 2750
Denmark
vok@cvmi.aau.dk

Prof. Adrian Hilton
Centre for Vision, Speech & Signal Proc.
University of Surrey
Guildford, Surrey, GU2 7XH
UK
a.hilton@surrey.ac.uk

Dr. Leonid Sigal
Disney Research
Forbes Avenue 615
Pittsburgh, PA 15213
USA
lsigal@disneyresearch.com

ISBN 978-0-85729-996-3   e-ISBN 978-0-85729-997-0
DOI 10.1007/978-0-85729-997-0
Springer London Dordrecht Heidelberg New York

British Library Cataloguing in Publication Data
A catalogue record for this book is available from the British Library

Library of Congress Control Number: 2011939266

Cover design: VTeX UAB, Lithuania

Printed on acid-free paper

Springer is part of Springer Science+Business Media (www.springer.com)

Foreword

Understanding human activity from video is one of the central problems in the field of computer vision. It is driven by a wide variety of applications in communications, entertainment, security, commerce and athletics. At its foundations are a set of fundamental computer vision problems that have largely driven the great progress that the field has made during the past few decades. In this book, the editors have assembled many of the world's leading authorities on video analysis of humans to assemble a comprehensive and authoritative set of chapters that cover both the core computer vision problems and the wide range of applications that solutions to these problems would enable.

The book is divided in four parts that cover detection and tracking of humans in video, measure human pose and movement from video, using these measurements to infer the activities that people are participating in, and finally describing the main applications areas that are based on these technologies. The book would be an excellent choice for a second graduate course on computer vision, or for a seminar on video analysis of human movement and activities. The combination of chapters that survey fundamental problems with others that go deeply into current approaches to topics provides the book with the excellent balance needed to support a well balanced course.

Part I, edited by Thomas B. Moeslund, focuses on problems associated with detecting and tracking people through camera networks. The chapter by Al Haj et al. discusses how multiple cameras can be cooperatively controlled so that people can both be tracked over large areas with cameras having wide fields of view and simultaneously imaged at high enough resolution with other cameras to analyze their activities. The next two chapters discuss two different approaches to detecting people in video. The chapter by Elgammal discusses background subtraction. Most simply, for a stationary camera one can detect moving objects by first building a model (an image) of an empty scene and then differencing that model with incoming video frames. Where the differences are high, movement has occurred. In reality, of course, things are much more complicated since the background can change over different time scales(due to wind load on vegetation, bodies of water in the scene, or the introduction of a new object into the background), the camera might be active (panning, for example, as in Chap. 1), and there are many nuisance variables like shadows and specular reflections that should be eliminated. And, even if background subtraction worked "perfectly" true scene motion can be due to not just human movements but movement of other object in the scene. The chapter by Leibe, then, discusses a more direct method for detecting humans based on matching models of what people look like directly to the images. These methods generally employ a sliding window algorithm in which features based on shape and texture are combined to construct a local representation that can be used by statistical inference models to perform detection. Such methods can be used even when the camera is moving in an unconstrained manner. Detecting people is especially challenging because of variations in body shape, clothing and posture. The chapter by Chellappa discusses method for face detection. It not only contains an excellent introduction to sliding window based methods for face detection, but also explains how contextual information and high level reasoning can be used to locate faces, augmenting purely local approaches. The chapter by Song et al. discusses tracking. Tracking is especially complicated in situations where the scene contains many moving people because there is inevitably inter-occlusion. The chapter discusses fundamental multi-object techniques based on particle filters and joint probabilistic data association filters, and then goes on to discuss tracking in camera networks. Finally the chapter by Ellis and Ferryman discusses the various datasets that have been collected that researchers regularly use to evaluate new algorithms for detection and tracking.

Part II, edited by Leonid Sigal, discusses problems related to determining the time-varying 3D pose of a person from video. These problems have been intensely investigated over the past fifteen years and enormous progress has been made on designing effective and efficient representations for human kinematics, shape representations that can be used to model a wide variety of human forms, expressive and compact mathematical modeling mechanisms for natural human motion that can be used both for tracking and activity recognition, and computationally efficient algorithms that can be used to solve the nonlinear optimization problems that arise in human pose estimation and tracking. The first chapter by Pons-Mill and Rosenhahn begins by introducing criteria that characterize the utility of a parameterization of human pose and motion, and then discusses the merits of alternative representations with respect to these criteria. This is concerned with the "skeletal" component of the human model, and the chapter then goes on to discuss approaches to modeling the shapes of body parts. Finally, they discuss particle tracking methods that from an initial estimate of pose in a video sequence can both improve that estimate and then track the pose through the sequence. This process is illustrated for the case where the person can be segmented from the background, so that the silhouette of the person in each frame is (approximately) available. In the second chapter, Fleet motivates and discusses the use of low-dimensional latent models in pose estimation and tracking. While the space of all physically achievable human poses and motions might be very large, the poses associated with typical activities like walking lie on much lower-dimensional manifolds. The challenge is to identify representations that can simultaneously and smoothly map many activities to low-dimensional pose and motion manifolds. Fleet's chapter discusses the Gaussian Process Latent Variable Model, along with a number of extensions to that model, that address this challenge. He also discusses the use of physics based models that, at least for well studied movements like walking, can be used to directly construct motion models to control tracking rather than learn them from large databases of examples. Ramanan provides an excellent introduction to parts based graphical models and methods to efficiently learn and solve for those models in images that can handle occlusion and appearance symmetries. Parts based models are especially relevant in situations where prior segmentation of a person from the background is not feasible—for example, for a video taken from a moving camera. They have been successfully applied to many object recognition problems; The chapter by Sminchisescu discusses methods that directly estimate (multi-valued) pose estimates from image measurements. Unlike the methods in the previous chapter that require complex search through the space of poses and motions, the methods here construct a direct mapping from images to poses (and motions). The main drawback of these algorithms is their limited ability to generalize to poses and motions not adequately represented in their training datasets. The approach described is a very general structure learning approach which is applicable to a wide variety of problems in computer vision. Finally, the chapter by Andriluka and Black discusses datasets for pose estimation and tracking as well as the criteria typically used by researchers to compare and evaluate algorithms.

Part III, edited by Volker Krüger, deals with the problems of representation and recognition of human (and vehicular) actions. For highly stylized or constrained actions (gestures, walking) one can approach the problem of recognizing them using, essentially, the same representations and recognition algorithms employed for static object detection and recognition. So, researchers have studied action recognition representations based on space time tubes of flow, or shape information captured by gradient histograms, or collections of local features such as 3D versions of SIFT, or "corners" on the 3D volume swept out by a dynamic human silhouette. All of these representations attempt to implicitly capture changing pose properties; however, for many actions it is sufficient to represent only the changing location of the person without regard to articulation—for example, to decide if one person is following another or if two people are approaching each other. The chapters by Wang, Nayak and Chowdhury contain complementary discussions of representations that can be used directly for appearance based action recognition. While Wang focuses on topic models as an inference model for activity recognition, Nayak et al. and Chowdhury contain surveys of other methods that have been frequently employed to represent, learn and recognize action classes, such as Hidden Markov Models or stochastic context free grammars. These more structured models are based on a decomposition of observations into motion "primitives" and the chapter by Kulic et al. discusses how these primitives might be represented and learned from examples. The chapter by Chowdhury also discusses the important problem of anomaly detection—finding instances of activities that are, in some way, performed differently from the norm. The problem of anomaly representation and detection is critical in many surveillance and safety applications (is a vehicle being driven erratically? has a pot been left on a stove too long?) and is starting to receive considerable attention in the

computer vision field. The chapter by Kjellström addresses the important problem
of how context can be used to simultaneously improve action and object recognition. Many objects, especially at low magnification, look similar—consider roughly
cylindrical objects like drinking glasses, flashlights, power screwdrivers. They are
very hard to distinguish from one another based solely on appearance; but they are
used in very different ways, so ambiguity about object class can be reduced through
recognition of movements associated with human interaction with an object. Sym-
metrically, the body movements associated with many actions looks similar, but can
be more easily differentiated by recognizing the objects that are used to perform the
action. Kjellström explains how this co-dependence can be represented and used to
construct more accurate vision systems. De la Torre's chapter covers the problem of
facial expression recognition. Scientists have been interested in the problem of how
and whether facial expressions reveal human internal state for over 150 years dating
back to seminal work by Duchenne and Darwin on the subject in the 19th century.
Paul Ekman's Facial Action Coding System (FACS) is an influential system to tax-
onimize people's facial expressions that has proven very useful to psychologists to
model human behavior. Within the computer vision there has been intensive efforts
to recognize and measure human facial expressions based on FACS and other models, and this chapter provides a comprehensive overview of the subject. Finally, Liu
et al. discuss datasets that have been collected to benchmark algorithms for human
activity recognition.

Finally, Part IV, edited by Adrian Hilton, contains articles describing some of
the most important applications of activity recognition. The chapter by Chellappa is
concerned with biometrics and discusses challenges and basic technical approaches
to problems including face recognition, iris recognition and person recognition from
gait. Human activity analysis to central to the design of monitoring systems for security and safety. Gong et al. discuss a variety of applications in surveillance including
intruder detection, monitor public spaces for safety violations (such as left bag detection), and crowd monitoring (to different between normal crowd behavior and
potentially disruptive behavior). Many of these applications depend on the ability of
the surveillance system to accurately track individual people in crowded conditions
for extended periods. Pellegrini's chapter discusses how simulation based motion
models of human walking behavior in moderately crowded situations can be used to
improve tracking of individuals. This is a relatively new area of research, and while
current methods do not provide significant improvements in tracking accuracy over
more classical methods, this is still an area with good potential to substantially improve tracking performance. Face and hand or body gesture recognition can be used
to build systems that allow people to control computer applications in novel and
natural ways, and Lin's chapter discusses fundamental methods for representing
and recognizing face gestures (gaze, head pose) and hand gestures. Pantic's chapter
addresses the interpretation of facial and body gestures in the context of human interactions with one another and their environment. They describe the exciting new
research area of social signal processing—for example, determining whether participants in a discussion are agreeing or disagreeing, if there is a natural leader,
or natural subgroups. The chapter provides a stimulating discussion of the basic

research problems and methodological issues in this emerging area. Another important application of face and gesture recognition is recognition of sign language, and the chapter by Cooper et al. contains an excellent introduction to this subject. While specialized devices like 3D data gloves can be used as input for hand sign language recognition systems, in typical situations where such devices are not available one has to address technically challenging problems of measuring hand geometry and motion from video. Additionally, sign languages are multi-modal—for example, they might include in addition to hand shape, arm motions and facial expressions. The chapter also discusses the research problems associated with developing systems for multi-modal sign recognition. Thomas's chapter discusses application in sports. Many applications require that players be tracked through the game—for example, to forensically determine how players react under different game conditions for strategy planning. Typically, these multi-agent tracking problems are addressed using multiple camera systems and one important practical problem that arises is controlling and calibrating these systems. The chapter by Grau discusses these multi-perspective vision problems in detail. Other applications require detailed tracking of a player's posture during play—for example to identify inefficiencies in a pitcher's throwing motions. There are many important applications of face and gesture analysis in the automotive industry—for example, determining the level of awareness of a driver, or where her attention is focused. The chapter by Tran and Trevedi summarizes the many ways that computer vision can be used to enhance driving safety and the approaches that researchers have employed to develop driver monitoring systems.

In summary, this is a timely collection of scholarly articles that simultaneously surveys foundations of human movement representation and analysis, illustrates these foundations in a variety of important applications and identifies many areas for fertile future research and development. The editors are to have congratulations on the exceptional job they did in organizing this volume.

College Park, USA   Larry Davis
May 2011

Preface

Over the course of the last 10–20 years the field of computer vision has been preoccupied with the problem of looking at people. Hundreds, if not thousands, of papers have been published on the subject that span people and face detection, pose estimation, tracking and activity recognition. This research focus has been motivated by the numerous potential application for visual analysis of people from human–computer interaction to security, assisted living and clinical analysis of movement. A number of specific and general surveys have been published on these topics, but the field is lacking one coherent text that introduces and gives a comprehensive review of progress and open-problems. To provide such an overview is the exact ambition of this book. The target audience is not only graduate students in the computer vision field, but also scholars, researchers and practitioners from other fields who have an interest in systems for visual analysis of humans and corresponding applications.

The book is a collection of chapters that are written specifically for this book by leading experts in the field. Chapters are organized into four parts.

Part I: Detection and Tracking (seven chapters),
Part II: Pose Estimation (six chapters),
Part III: Recognition of Action (seven chapters),
Part IV: Applications (ten chapters).

The first three parts focus on different methods and the last part presents a number of different applications. The first chapter in each book part is an introduction chapter setting the scene. To support the reading of the book an index and list of glossary terms can be found in the back of the book. We hope this guide to research on the visual analysis of people contributes to future progress in the field and successful commercial application as the science and technology advances.

The editors would like to thank the authors for the massive work they have put into the different chapters! Furthermore we would like to thank Simon Rees and Wayne Wheeler from Springer for valuable guidance during the entire process of putting this book together. And finally, we would like to thank the reviewers who have helped to ensure the high standard of this book: Saiad Ali, Tamim Asfour, Patrick Buehler, Bhaskar Chakraborty, Rama Chellappa, Amit K.

Roy Chowdhury, Helen Cooper, Frederic Devernay, Mert Dikmen, David Fleet, Andrew Gilbert, Shaogang Gong, Jordi Gonzàlez, Jean-Yves Guillemaut, Abhinav Gupta, Ivan Huerta, Joe Kilner, Hedvig Kjellström, Dana Kulic, Bastian Leibe, Haowei Liu, Sebastien Marcel, Steve Maybank, Vittorio Murino, Kamal Nasrollahi, Eng-Jon Ong, Maja Pantic, Vishal Patel, Nick Pears, Norman Poh, Bodo Rosenhahn, Imran Saleemi, Mubarak Shah, Cristian Sminchisescu, Josephine Sullivan, Tai-Peng Tian, Sergio Valastin, Liang Wang, David Windridge, Ming-Hsuan Yang.

Aalborg University, Denmark   Thomas B. Moeslund
University of Surrey, UK   Adrian Hilton
Aalborg University, Denmark   Volker Krüger
Disney Research, Pittsburgh, USA   Leonid Sigal
May 2011

Contents

Contributors

Mykhaylo Andriluka Max Planck Institute for Computer Science, Saarbrücken, Germany, andriluka@mpi-inf.mpg.de

Michael J. Black Max Planck Institute for Intelligent Systems, Tübingen, Germany, black@tuebingen.mpg.de; Department of Computer Science, Brown University, Providence, USA, black@cs.brown.edu

Liefeng Bo University of Washington, Seattle, USA, lfb@cs.washington.edu

Aaron Bobick Georgia Institute of Technology, Atlanta, GA, USA, afb@cc.gatech.edu

Richard Bowden University of Surrey, Guildford, GU2 7XH, UK, R.Bowden@surrey.ac.uk

Rama Chellappa Department of Electrical and Computer Engineering, and UMIACS, University of Maryland, College Park, MD 20742, USA, rama@umiacs.umd.edu

Jeffrey F. Cohn Department of Psychology, University of Pittsburgh, Pittsburgh, PA 15260, USA, jeffcohn@pitt.edu

Helen Cooper University of Surrey, Guildford, GU2 7XH, UK, H.M.Cooper@surrey.ac.uk

Roderick Cowie Psychology Dept., Queen University Belfast, Belfast, UK

Francesca D'Errico Dept. Of Education, University Roma Tre, Rome, Italy

Larry Davis College Park, USA

Ahmed Elgammal Rutgers University, New Brunswick, NJ, USA, elgammal@cs.rutgers.edu

Anna-Louise Ellis University of Reading, Whiteknights, Reading, UK, a.l.ellis@reading.ac.uk

Andreas Ess ETH Zürich, Zürich, Switzerland, aess@vision.ee.ethz.ch

Rogerio Feris IBM T.J. Watson Research Center, Hawthorn, NY 10532, USA, rsferis@ibm.com

Carles Fernández Computer Vision Center, Universitat Autònoma de Barcelona, Bellaterra 08193, Spain, perno@cvc.uab.es

James Ferryman University of Reading, Whiteknights, Reading, UK, j.m.ferryman@reading.ac.uk

David J. Fleet Department of Computer Science, University of Toronto, Toronto, Canada, fleet@cs.toronto.edu

Shaogang Gong Queen Mary University of London, London, E1 4NS, UK, sgg@eecs.qmul.ac.uk

Jordi Gonzàlez Computer Vision Center and Departament de Ciències de la Computació, Universitat Autònoma de Barcelona, Bellaterra 08193, Spain, jordi.gonzalez@uab.cat

Luc Van Gool ETH Zürich, Zürich, Switzerland, vangool@vision.ee.ethz.ch; KU Leuven, Leuven, Belgium

Raghuraman Gopalan Department of Electrical and Computer Engineering, University of Maryland, College Park, MD 20742, USA, raghuram@umiacs.umd.edu

Oliver Grau BBC Research & Development, 56 Wood Lane, London, UK, Oliver.Grau@bbc.co.uk

Murad Al Haj Computer Vision Center, Universitat Autònoma de Barcelona, Bellaterra 08193, Spain, malhaj@cvc.uab.es

Dirk Heylen EEMCS, University of Twente, Enschede, The Netherlands

Adrian Hilton Centre for Vision, Speech & Signal Processing, University of Surrey, Guildford, Surrey, GU2 7XH, UK, a.hilton@surrey.ac.uk

Brian Holt University of Surrey, Guildford, GU2 7XH, UK, B.Holt@surrey.ac.uk

Thomas Huang Beckman Institute, University of Illinois at Urbana-Champaign, 405 North Mathews Avenue, Urbana, IL 61801, USA, huang@ifp.uiuc.edu

Ivan Huerta Computer Vision Center, Universitat Autònoma de Barcelona, Bellaterra 08193, Spain, ivan.huerta@cvc.uab.es

Catalin Ionescu INS, University of Bonn, Bonn, Germany, catalin.ionescu@ins.uni-bonn.de

Atul Kanaujia ObjectVideo, Reston, VA, USA, atul.kanaujia@objectvideo.com

Hedvig Kjellström (Sidenbladh) CSC/CVAP, KTH, SE-100 44 Stockholm, Sweden, hedvig@kth.se

Volker Krüger Copenhagen Institute of Technology, Aalborg University, Lautrup-vang 2B, Ballerup, 2750, Denmark, vok@cvmi.aau.dk

Danica Kragic Centre for Autonomous Systems, Royal Institute of Technology – KTH, Stockholm, Sweden, dani@kth.se

Dana Kulić University of Waterloo, Waterloo, Canada, dkulic@ece.uwaterloo.ca

Vuong Le Beckman Institute, University of Illinois at Urbana-Champaign, 405 North Mathews Avenue, Urbana, IL 61801, USA, vuongle2@ifp.uiuc.edu

Bastian Leibe UMIC Research Centre, RWTH Aachen University, Aachen, Germany, leibe@umic.rwth-aachen.de

Dennis Lin Beckman Institute, University of Illinois at Urbana-Champaign, 405 North Mathews Avenue, Urbana, IL 61801, USA, djlin@ifp.uiuc.edu

Haowei Liu University of Washington, Seattle, WA 98195, USA, hwliu@uw.edu

Chen Change Loy Queen Mary University of London, London, E1 4NS, UK, ccloy@eecs.qmul.ac.uk

Marc Mehu Psychology Dept., University of Geneva, Geneva, Switzerland

Thomas B. Moeslund Department of Architecture, Design and Media Technology, Aalborg University, Niels Jernes Vej 14, Aalborg, 9220, Denmark, tbm@create.aau.dk

Nandita M. Nayak University of California, Riverside, 900 University Ave. Riverside, CA 92521, USA, nandita.nayak@email.ucr.edu

Maja Pantic Computing Dept., Imperial College London, London , UK, m.pantic@imperial.ac.uk; EEMCS, University of Twente, Enschede, The Netherlands

Vishal M. Patel Department of Electrical and Computer Engineering, Center for Automation Research, University of Maryland, College Park, MD 20742, USA, pvishalm@umiacs.umd.edu

Catherine Pelachaud CNRS, Paris, France

Stefano Pellegrini ETH Zürich, Zürich, Switzerland, stefpell@vision.ee.ethz.ch

Jaishanker K. Pillai Department of Electrical and Computer Engineering, Center for Automation Research, University of Maryland, College Park, MD 20742, USA, jsp@umiacs.umd.edu

Isabella Poggi Dept. Of Education, University Roma Tre, Rome, Italy

Gerard Pons-Moll Leibniz University, Hanover, Germany, pons@tnt.uni-hannover.de

Deva Ramanan Department of Computer Science, University of California, Irvine, USA, dramanan@ics.uci.edu

Xavier Roca Computer Vision Center and Departament de Ciències de la Computació, Universitat Autònoma de Barcelona, Bellaterra 08193, Spain, xavier.roca@uab.cat

Bodo Rosenhahn Leibniz University, Hanover, Germany, rosenhahn@tnt.uni-hannover.de

Amit K. Roy-Chowdhury University of California, Riverside, 900 University Ave. Riverside, CA 92521, USA, amitrc@ee.ucr.edu

Marc Schroeder DFKI, Saarbrucken, Germany

William R. Schwartz Institute of Computing, University of Campinas, Campinas-SP 13084-971, Brazil, wschwartz@liv.ic.unicam.br

Ricky J. Sethi University of California, Los Angeles, 4532 Boelter Hall, CA 90095-1596, USA, rickys@sethi.org; University of California, Los Angeles, 4532 Boelter Hall, CA 90095-1596, USA

Leonid Sigal Disney Research, Forbes Avenue 615, Pittsburgh, PA 15213, USA, lsigal@disneyresearch.com

Cristian Sminchisescu Institute for Numerical Simulation (INS), Faculty of Mathematics and Natural Science, University of Bonn, Bonn, Germany, cristian.sminchisescu@ins.uni-bonn.de; Institute for Mathematics of the Romanian Academy (IMAR), Bucharest, Romania

Bi Song University of California, Riverside, 900 University Ave. Riverside, CA 92521, USA, bsong@ee.ucr.edu

Ankur Srivastava Department of Electrical and Computer Engineering, and Institute for Systems Research, University of Maryland, College Park, MD 20742, USA, ankurs@umd.edu

Ming-Ting Sun University of Washington, Seattle, WA 98195, USA, mts@uw.edu

Graham Thomas BBC Research & Development, Centre House, 56 Wood Lane, London W12 7SB, UK, graham.thomas@bbc.co.uk

Fernando De la Torre Robotics Institute, Carnegie Mellon University, Pittsburgh, PA 15213, USA, ftorre@cs.cmu.edu

Cuong Tran Laboratory for Intelligent and Safe Automobiles (LISA), University of California at San Diego, San Diego, CA 92037, USA, cutran@ucsd.edu

Mohan Manubhai Trivedi Laboratory for Intelligent and Safe Automobiles (LISA), University of California at San Diego, San Diego, CA 92037, USA, mtrivedi@ucsd.edu

Alessandro Vinciarelli Computing Science Dept., University of Glasgow, Glasgow, UK, vincia@dcs.gla.acvi.uk; IDIAP Research Institute, Martigny, Switzerland

Xiaogang Wang Department of Electronic Engineering, Chinese University of Hong Kong, Hong Kong, China, xgwang@ee.cuhk.edu.hk

Tao Xiang Queen Mary University of London, London, E1 4NS, UK, txiang@eecs.qmul.ac.uk

Zhanwu Xiong Computer Vision Center and Departament de Ciències de la Computació, Universitat Autònoma de Barcelona, Bellaterra 08193, Spain, zhanwu@cvc.uab.es

Part I
Detection and Tracking

Chapter 1
Is There Anybody Out There?

Thomas B. Moeslund

Applications within the field of Looking at People only make sense when the ana-lyzed imagery contains one or more humans. The first step in such systems is there-fore to determine if one or more humans are present and where in the scene they are. This task is termed *detection* or *figure-ground segmentation*. Moreover, since many applications require a number of consecutive frames containing people in order to do any processing, e.g., in many activity recognition tasks, *tracking* of individuals is often a requirement. This part provides an overview of detection and tracking methods. On one hand this part can be seen as the foundation on which the rest of the book builds, but detection and tracking methods are also applicable in their own rights, e.g., face detectors available in most new compact cameras, chroma-keying used for TV and movie productions, and in different surveillance applications.

In general, robust solutions to the detection and tracking problems are yet to be seen, but a massive effort can be observed by the number of papers published about these and related problems. Within the last decade or so a number of novel concepts and methods have been put forward allowing the research field to move further up the ladder toward the goal of systems that are able to work independently of, for example, illumination and weather conditions. Some of the more influential ones are the HoG detector [7], Viola and Jones' face detector [18] and the particle filter. These are discussed a bit more below and more thoroughly in the other chapters in Part I, and in general used in other systems discussed throughout this book.

Besides better methods, recent advancements can also be traced back to the in-troduction of public benchmarking data for assessing detection and tracking algo-rithms. This has first of all provided researchers and practitioners large annotated data sets to train and test their methods on, but equally important, those public data

T.B. Moeslund (✉)
Department of Architecture, Design and Media Technology, Aalborg University, Aalborg, Denmark
e-mail: tbm@create.aau.dk

T.B. Moeslund et al. (eds.), *Visual Analysis of Humans*,
DOI 10.1007/978-0-85729-997-0_1, © Springer-Verlag London Limited 2011

sets have allowed for different methods to be directly comparable, since they now can train and test on the same data sets. Some conferences even introduce competitions on data sets defined just for that event. Chapter 7 will give an overview of such data sets and how to evaluate them.

A last aspect that has to helped boost research and applications utilizing detection and tracking, is the fact that many of the methods have been implemented in software and made freely available. Good examples are OpenCV [6] aimed at engineers and computer scientists and EyesWeb [1] aimed at less mathematical and algorithmic oriented scholars. Both have equipped a whole generation of students and researchers from different fields with powerful tools for building Looking at People systems.

1.1 Detection

Two overall approaches to detecting people exist: pixel-based and object-based. In the former, each pixel in the incoming frame is compared to a model for that pixel in order to assess whether the incoming pixel is foreground or background. Having done so for the entire image a silhouette of each human in the incoming frame is (in theory) present. In the latter approach a sliding window is translated and scaled to all possible locations in the input frame and for each window the likelihood of it containing a human is calculated. This type of method will result in a bounding box (the window) containing the human as opposed to the silhouette resulting from the former method. These approaches are discussed further below—but first a few words on image acquisition.

1.1.1 Data Acquisition

Before any figure-ground segmentation can commence the frames need to be captured. Many algorithms require the humans in the frames to be of a reasonable resolution, otherwise the methods will fail. Combining this with the normal outdoor situation where a camera needs to cover a large scene renders the dilemma of resolution versus coverage. Increasing the field-of-view of the camera will provide better coverage, but lower resolution. Using cameras with a bigger image sensor can help, but this results in other problems like increased price. Another solution is to include multiple cameras and have them cooperate. This introduces the problem of handover during tracking, calibration among the cameras and of course increased price and data logistics. Yet another solution is to use an active sensor that can pan, tilt and zoom-in as need be. More of these might be cooperating and perhaps controlled in a master-and-slave fashion. No matter how this is organized, controlling active sensors is by no means trivial—especially when the object in focus (the human) can perform unpredicted movement. Chapter 2 is concerned with these issues and provides a more in-depth discussion. Moreover, some hands-on experiments are given in that chapter.

1.1.2 Pixel-Based Detection

The notion of having a model of the background and comparing each pixel in the incoming frame to that model is intuitively sound. The approach, however, has a major drawback assuming the background is fixed. While this works well in some indoor setting, it is in general not valid in outdoor scenes. Here trees will move in the wind and the illumination and shadows will change due to clouds and/or the shifting position of the sun. Current research therefore focuses on different ways of modeling the pixels in the background model and how to update such models during runtime. Especially the introduction of multiple models for each pixel [11, 13] has allowed for successful and real-time figure-ground segmentation in many applications. Pixel-based methods basically detect pixels from a new/moving object in the scene and hence some processing is required to determine whether the pixels are from a human, a car or something else. To this end filtering and blob analysis are normally required. Blob analysis can use shape cues to detect non-human-like objects, but the problem of shadows cast by humans is hard to solve since the shape of such blobs are naturally human-like. Different types of context-reasoning are therefore involved when trying to detect and delete shadows, for example the current weather conditions [8] or the fact that a shadow will be "bluish" since most of its illumination comes from the blue sky [12, 15]. Chapter 3 will provide more details on these matters.

1.1.3 Object-Based Detection

The pixel-based methods often fail in situations where the background is far from static, due to for example a moving camera, or when multiple people are occluding each other. To handle these situations the figure-ground segmentation problem can be addressed by using object-based detectors where the entire human (or major body parts) are detected directly. Such methods are often said to be window-based since they operate by translating a window over the input frame and calculating the likelihood of the window containing a human. Two methods have had a profound impact on such object-based approaches. The first is the HoG detector [7], which is built on the notion that different object shapes (here the human) always produce edges in an image and that these edges are not randomly distributed. Chapter 4 will describe how this, and other similar descriptors, can be used to detect humans even in complicated scenes.

Another significant approach to finding the human (or rather the face of a human) is the pioneering work behind Viola and Jones's face detector [18]. It combines simple features with the notion of cascaded classifiers. From studies into the human visual system it is known that some contrast detection is performed in specialized cells in the human eye. These rather simple operations have been simulated in computer vision using simple binary templates. Many different templates can be defined and a constellation of these can detect the face. The tricky issue is learning which constellation of which templates that will do the job. Viola and Jones solved this complex learning problem by utilizing massive amount of positive and negative samples together with a cascade of simple classifiers. This idea was adapted from the field of machine learning and has afterwards been used in other computer vision subfields. In Chap. 5 Viola and Jones's face detector is introduced together with other issues related to face detection.

A major difference between the two approaches is that pixel-based methods detect whatever is moving, while object-based methods detect specific things using the prior knowledge about the foreground, hence the human. So, pixel-based methods require post processing, while object-based detectors can work on their own. Object-based detection methods produce a bounding box for each person in the frame. In contrast, pixel-based methods produce a silhouette for each person. What is preferred depends on the application. In controlled scenes, pixel-based methods work rather well, as seen in for example commercial chroma-keying systems, and can provide a very detailed segmentation and in a generally short processing time. But the object-based methods are in general better at detecting people in especially complicated scenes like outdoor settings with multiple occluding people and changing lighting conditions. The object-based methods are computational expensive, but with the introduction of for example GPU-based implementations this is less of a problem.

1.2 Tracking

Tracking is here defined as finding the temporal trajectory of an object through some state-space. The object would here often be the human but it could also be different body-parts as will be the case in Part II. The variables spanning the state-space are very often the 3D location parameters in the space or 2D locations on the image plane, but it could also be other parameters, e.g., color and shape. When tracking people we have in each a number of predictions and a number of new measurements. We need somehow to associate the measurements with the predictions in order to assign a tracking ID to each new measurement. This is in general known as the data association problem [5].

If we have a robust method for detecting people, then tracking is simply a matter of concatenating the output of the detector. This approach is known as tracking-by-detection and discussed in Chap. 4. Very often noisy and missing measurements will appear and the tracking-by-detection framework cannot stand alone. For the simple case where one person is tracked the Kalman filter framework has proven successful in combining predictions with noisy measurements. In the case of multiple people a multiple hypothesis approach will often form the tracking framework. These frameworks are seriously challenged in the case of unexpected events, such as new people entering the scene, people leaving the scene, people occluding each other, objects occluding people, and bad segmentation (false positive and false negative). To complicate matters even more, it is sometimes desired to track people across non-overlapping cameras. A general solution to these problems is still far away.

Detecting people entering and leaving can to some extent be handled using the context of the scene, e.g., the fact that people do not just materialize or vanish, but tend to use doors. Knowing the trajectories of the past can help foresee the future, i.e. predicting where to search for people in the next frame. It might not be possible to track people during an occlusion, but the trajectories of the people after the occlusion can be compared with predicted trajectories to resolve ambiguities. More generally we can have short-term trajectory fragments with a low probability of error and view the tracking problem as a matter of merging these. Such trajectory fragments are denoted tracklets and described in more detail in Chap. 6 together with a method for tracking across multiple cameras.

If people stay occluded for some time even the notion of merging tracklets fails. Also, sometimes a system needs to track people during interaction. In these cases an appearance model of each individual is learned and updated online. Tracking can then be handled using a pixel-based segmentation method where each pixel in the input frame is compared with the different predicted appearance models of the different people. Alternatively, a generic tracker like template matching [9], mean-shift [16] or level sets [17] can be applied. This is discussed further in Chap. 4. When occlusion becomes a permanent situation, the individual is hard to track and instead we can analyze the movement patterns of the group or crowd the individual belongs to. This makes sense in applications where the objective is to understand for example the flow of people in airports or at public gatherings like concerts or sport events. Chapter 6 will discuss tracking in relation to groups and crowds.

1.3 Future Trends in Detection and Tracking

Pixel-based methods are point-based by nature and information about the neighbor pixels do not come into play before the post-processing stage. Random fields (MRF, CRF) or other approached to incorporate the spatial context is therefore an interesting approach to enhance foreground segmentation. Another possible use of context is to incorporate knowledge on the environment. If the 3D static environment and illumination sources could be modeled, then information about the spectral reflection properties of each surface could allow for a perfect computer graphics rendering of the current background. Combining this with dynamic information such as the current level and direction of sun's illumination would provide for a very robust pixel-based method. As mentioned above, pixel-based methods are fast and work well when the background can be modeled and updated. Moreover, during partial occlusion, pixels-based methods can also have their merits. On the other hand, object-based methods can operate without any scene knowledge, but are slower and tend to fail during occlusions. It seems only natural to combine these approaches as they can complement each other [17]. More of this can be expected in the future.

The sensor type plays a major role in detection and tracking. For example, a standard color camera will stand very little chance of detecting and tracking a human in a pitch black scene, whereas a thermal camera will capture similar data no matter whether it is night or day. For exactly this reason infrared cameras (often with their own infrared lighting source) are becoming popular in surveillance scenarios and other applications where the detection can be solved in hardware or simple software. A good example of such an application is commercial motion capture equipment [4]. 3D sensing is another strategy that might play an important role in future acquisition systems. While different stereo solutions have been around for some time [14] a new type of compact 3D measurement devices are emerging, the time-of-flight cameras [2, 3]. They also provide 3D images of the scene, but using a more compact physical device. Data from 3D sensors can make detection a trivial task. The resolution and price of current time-of-flight cameras are still to be improved before becoming widely used in computer vision. Another 3D sensor with a much better resolution and lower price is the Kinect produced for Microsoft's Xbox. This technology is based on a structured light approach, where an infrared light pattern is cast onto the scene and picked up by a calibrated infrared camera. Such technology has a limited range of operation (usually less than 10 m) and requires that no other infrared light sources are present. But when these requirements are met the Kinect as such, and also the detecting and tracking software developed for the Xbox, seem like very good candidates for many looking at people systems. Current surveillance cameras often produce poor quality images due to issues like, low resolution, low frame-rate, poor colors and hard compression. Using better cameras and perhaps combining this with the new 3D capturing technologies is expected to help solve many of the ambiguity in both detection and tracking—especially in situations where occlusion is a problem.

Even though many data sets have been annotated and made publicly available, the detection and tracking communities still lack very long test data to see if the different algorithms can stand the test of time. It is very difficult to process a few minutes of videos and then conclude how the detector/tracker operates after being online 24/7/365. So far not many results on long sequences have been reported (1–2 days) [10] and results on longer periods of time are only evaluated qualitatively. What is needed is extremely long sequences, basically a whole year, to test the effects of the changing seasons.

References

1. http://www.infomus.org/eywmain.html [4]
2. http://www.mesa-imaging.ch/ [8]
3. http://www.pmdtec.com/ [8]
4. http://www.vicon.com [8]
5. Bar-Shalom, Y., Fortmann, T.E.: Tracking and Data Association. Academic Press, Boston (1988) [6]
6. Bradski, G., Kaehler, A.: Learning Opencv. O'Reilly Media Inc., Sebastopol (2008). http://oreilly.com/catalog/9780596516130 [4]
7. Dalal, N., Triggs, B.: Histograms of oriented gradients for human detection. In: IEEE Computer Vision and Pattern Recognition (2005) [3,5]

8. Doshi, A., Trivedi, M.M.: Satellite imagery based robust, adaptive background models and shadow suppression. J. VLSJ Signal Process. **1**(2), 119–132 (2007) [5]
9. Ferrari, V., Marin, M., Zisserman, A.: Progressive search space reduction for human pose estimation. In: IEEE Conference on Computer Vision and Pattern Recognition (2008) [7]
10. Fihl, P., Corlin, R., Park, S., Moeslund, T.B., Trivedi, M.M.: Tracking of individuals in very long video sequences. In: International Symposium on Visual Computing, Lake Tahoe, Nevada, USA (2006) [8]
11. Grimson, W.E.L., Stauffer, C.: Adaptive background mixture models for real-time tracking. In: IEEE Conference on Computer Vision and Pattern Recognition (1999) [5]
12. Huerta, I., Holte, M., Moeslund, T.B., Gonzàlez, J.: Detection and removal of chromatic moving shadows in surveillance scenarios. In: International Conference on Computer Vision, Kyoto, Japan (2009) [5]
13. Kim, K., Chalidabhongse, T.H., Harwood, D., Davis, L.: Background modeling and subtraction by codebook construction. In: International Conference on Image Processing (2004) [5]
14. Moeslund, T.B., Hilton, A., Krüger, V.: A survey of advances in vision-based human motion capture and analysis. Comput. Vis. Image Underst. **104**, 90–126 (2006) [8]
15. Prati, A., Mikic, I., Trivedi, M.M., Cucchiara, R.: Detecting moving shadows: Algorithms and evaluation. IEEE Trans. Pattern Anal. Mach. Intell. **25**(7), 918–923 (2003) [5]
16. Rother, C., Kolmogorov, V., Blake, A.: Grabcut: Interactive foreground extraction using iterated graph cuts. In: ACM SIGGRAPH (2004) [7]
17. Stalder, S., Grabner, H., Van Gool, L.: Cascaded confidence filter for improved tracking-by-detection. In: European Conference on Computer Vision (2010) [7]
18. Viola, P., Jones, M.: Rapid object detection using a boosted cascade of simple features. In: IEEE Computer Vision and Pattern Recognition, pp. 511–518 (2001) [3,5]

Chapter 2
Beyond the Static Camera: Issues and Trends in Active Vision

Murad Al Haj, Carles Fernández, Zhanwu Xiong, Ivan Huerta,
Jordi Gonzàlez, and Xavier Roca

Abstract Maximizing both the area coverage and the resolution per target is highly desirable in many applications of computer vision. However, with a limited number of cameras viewing a scene, the two objectives are contradictory. This chapter is dedicated to active vision systems, trying to achieve a trade-off between these two aims and examining the use of high-level reasoning in such scenarios. The chapter starts by introducing different approaches to active cameras configurations. Later, a single active camera system to track a moving object is developed, offering the reader first-hand understanding of the issues involved. Another section discusses practical considerations in building an active vision platform, taking as an example a multi-camera system developed for a European project. The last section of the chapter reflects upon the future trends of using semantic factors to drive smartly coordinated active systems.

M. Al Haj (✉) · C. Fernández · I. Huerta
Computer Vision Center, Universitat Autònoma de Barcelona, Bellaterra 08193, Spain
e-mail: malhaj@cvc.uab.es

C. Fernández
e-mail: perno@cvc.uab.es

I. Huerta
e-mail: ivan.huerta@cvc.uab.es

Z. Xiong · J. Gonzàlez · X. Roca
Computer Vision Center and Departament de Ciències de la Computació, Universitat Autònoma de Barcelona, Bellaterra 08193, Spain

Z. Xiong
e-mail: zhanwu@cvc.uab.es

J. Gonzàlez
e-mail: jordi.gonzalez@uab.cat

X. Roca
e-mail: xavier.roca@uab.cat

T.B. Moeslund et al. (eds.), *Visual Analysis of Humans*,
DOI 10.1007/978-0-85729-997-0_2, © Springer-Verlag London Limited 2011

2.1 Introduction

Many applications in the computer vision field benefit from high-resolution imagery. These include, but are not limited to, license-plate identification [4] and face recognition, where it has been observed that higher resolution improves accuracy [27]. For other applications, such as identifying people in surveillance videos, having highly zoomed images is a must. The problem with zoom control is that two opposing aims are desirable: the first one is obtaining a maximum resolution of the tracked object, whereas the second is minimizing the risk of losing this object. Therefore, zoom control can be thought of as a trade-off between the effective resolution per target and the desired coverage of the area of surveillance.

With a finite number of fixed sensors, there is a fundamental limit on the total area that can be observed. Thus, maximizing both the area of coverage and the resolution of each observed target requires an increase in the number of cameras. However, such an increase is highly costly in terms of installation and processing. Therefore, a system utilizing a smaller number of Pan–Tilt–Zoom (PTZ) cameras can be much more efficient if it is properly designed to overcome the obvious drawback of having less information about the target(s).

Toward this end, different works have investigated the use of PTZ cameras to address this problem of *actively* surveying a large area in an attempt to obtain high-quality imagery while maintaining coverage of the region [25]. Starting two decades ago, the area of active vision has been gaining much attention, in an attempt to: i) improve the quality of the acquired visual data by trying to keep a certain object at a desired scale, and ii) react to any changes in the scene dynamics that might risk the loss of the target.

Accurate reactive tracking of moving objects is a problem of both control and estimation. The speed at which the camera is adjusted must be a joint function of current camera position in pan, tilt and focal length, and the position of the tracked object in the 3D environment.

This chapter deals with active vision systems, offering the reader hands-on experience and insights into the problem. Section 2.2 discusses the different design alternatives for active cameras configurations, such as the autonomous camera approach, the master-slave approach and the active camera network approach, in addition to touching upon the advantages that environment reasoning lends to the problem. In Sect. 2.3, an autonomous camera system is designed, where the problem of jointly estimating the camera state and 3D object position is formulated as a Bayesian estimation problem and the joint state is estimated with an extended Kalman filter. The authors of this chapter had the opportunity to be part of a dedicated consortium working on a European project, called HERMES, where an integrated platform involving active cameras was built. Therefore, in Sect. 2.4, practical considerations involved in building real-time active camera systems are discussed taking the HERMES platform as a case study. This chapter is concluded in Sect. 2.5, where the lessons learned are summarized and the future directions are noted.

2.2 Active Camera Configurations

The interest in active camera systems started as early as two decades ago. Beginning in the late 1980s, Aloimonos et al. introduced the first general framework for active vision in order to improve the perceptual quality of tracking results [3]. Since then, numerous active camera systems have been developed. In this section, we take a look at different approaches for configuring these systems.

2.2.1 The Autonomous Camera Approach

Autonomous cameras are those that can self-direct in their surrounding environment. Recent work addressing this topic includes that of Denzler et al., where the motion of the tracked object is modeled using a Kalman filter. The camera focal length that minimizes the uncertainty in the state estimation is selected [12]. The authors used a stereo set-up, with two zoom cameras, to simplify the 3D estimation problem.

A newer approach is described by Tordoff et al., which tunes a constant velocity Kalman filter in order to ensure reactive zoom tracking while the focal length is varying [26]. Their approach correlates all the parameters of the filter with the focal length. However, they do not concentrate on the overall estimation problem, and their filter does not take into account any real-world object properties.

In the work by Nelson et al., a second rotating camera with fixed focal length is introduced in order to solve the problem of lost fixation [19].

The latter two works are primarily focused on zoom control and do not deal with total object-camera position estimation and its use in the control process. An attempt to join estimation and control in the same framework can be found in the work of Bagdanov et al., where a PTZ camera is used to actively track faces [5]. However, both the estimation and control models used are ad hoc, and the estimation approach is based on image features rather than 3D properties of the target being tracked.

2.2.2 The Master/Slave Approach

In a master/slave configuration, a supervising static camera is used to monitor a wide field of view and to track every moving target of interest. The position of each of these targets over time is then provided to a foveal camera, which tries to observe the targets at a higher resolution. Both the static and the active cameras are calibrated to a common reference, so that data coming from one of them can be easily projected onto the other, in order to coordinate the control of the active sensors.

Another possible use of the master/slave approach consists of a static (master) camera extracting visual features of an object of interest, while the active (slave) sensor uses these features to detect the desired object without the need of any training data. In this case, features should be invariant to illumination, viewpoint, color distribution and image resolution, and usually consist of any kind of coarse-to-fine region descriptors, as in [31].

The master/slave approach is a simple but effective formulation that has been repeatedly used for solving many active vision problems [16, 20, 31]. Nonetheless, the use of supervising cameras has the disadvantage of requiring a mapping of the image content to the active cameras. This mapping needs to be obtained from restricted camera placements, movements or observations extended over time [6, 13].

2.2.3 The Active Camera Network Approach

In recent years, interest has grown in building networks of active cameras and optional static cameras, in order to cover a large area while also providing high-resolution imagery of multiple targets [7, 11, 17, 21]. An active camera network is a scaling up of a basic active camera approach, which can be either an autonomous active camera or a master/slave configuration, depending on whether fixed master cameras are deployed or not.

Due to the fact that an active camera network involves multiple cameras and is usually required to accomplish multiple tasks, the challenges of this approach mainly arise from two aspects: i) *task assignment* and ii) *task hand-over*.

Task assignment is the problem of deciding which camera resources are to be allocated to which task, or in other words, the problem of camera scheduling. On the other hand, task hand-over describes model transferring from one camera to another.

Furthermore, like the master/slave configuration, active camera networks also require calibration information, as well as extensive networking infrastructure. Communications within such systems require clever networking algorithms for routing and decision making. Though theoretically appealing, active camera networks are expensive to build and maintain, and do not scale well.

2.2.4 Environmental Reasoning

In some cases, low-level approaches such as those described above are not enough to address ambitious applications requiring more complex strategies toward sensors collaboration. Smart coordination among camera sensors requires exploiting resources that are often related to artificial intelligence and symbolic models, including techniques for camera selection according to the given task, protocols for allocating such tasks, tools for reasoning about the environment and mechanisms to resolve conflicts.

Some examples in which such techniques are used to enhance the collaboration among sensors in a camera network include constraint satisfaction formulations [22], Situation Graph Tree (SGT) [14] and Petri net coordination models [29].

2.3 The Autonomous Camera: A Hands-on Experience

This section is aimed at providing the reader with a hands-on experience to develop an autonomous active camera system that is able to track a moving object, taking proper decisions on when to zoom in, to maximize the resolution, and when to zoom out, to minimize the risk of losing the object. It is dedicated to an exemplary system showing all the design decisions that has been taken in the process, namely the camera-world model, the estimation process and the control process. Some performance indicators of the system are shown at the end. This section is based on the paper "Reactive object tracking with a single PTZ camera" by Al Haj et al., which appeared in the 20th International Conference on Pattern Recognition [2], ©2010 IEEE.

2.3.1 Camera-World Model

We use a pinhole camera model as shown in Fig. 2.1. The camera center is located at the origin of the world coordinate system. The principal point is at the origin of the plane of projection at zero pan and tilt. The axis of projection is aligned with the z-axis.

The object being tracked is assumed to be a rigid rectangular patch perpendicular to the axis of projection. It is located at world position (X, Y, Z) with known width W and height H. It is important to note here that upper-case characters, (X, Y, Z, W, H), will be used to denote values in the real-world while lower-case characters, (x, y, w, h), will be used to denote values in the image projection plane.

Changes in camera orientation due to panning and tilting are modeled as pure rotations of the coordinate system:

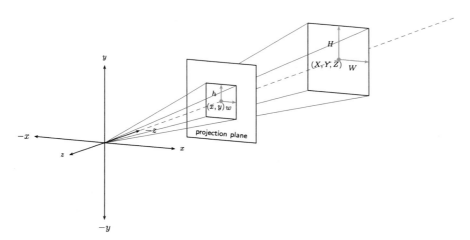

Fig. 2.1 The pinhole camera model with the camera positioned at the origin of the world coordinates

$$\mathbf{M}(\phi, \theta) = \begin{bmatrix} 1 & 0 & 0 \\ 0 & \cos\theta & -\sin\theta \\ 0 & \sin\theta & \cos\theta \end{bmatrix} \begin{bmatrix} \cos\phi & 0 & -\sin\phi \\ 0 & 1 & 0 \\ \sin\phi & 0 & \cos\phi \end{bmatrix}, \tag{2.1}$$

where ϕ and θ represent the pan and tilt angles, respectively.

We assume that the camera projection is reasonably approximated using equal scaling in the x and y directions (i.e. square pixels). The center of projection is also assumed to be at the origin of the world coordinate system. Then, the camera matrix, $\mathbf{N}$, is fully parameterized by the focal length parameter f:

$$\mathbf{N}(f) = \begin{bmatrix} f & 0 & 0 \\ 0 & f & 0 \\ 0 & 0 & 1 \end{bmatrix}. \tag{2.2}$$

The projection of the object at position $\mathbf{o} = [X, Y, Z]$ onto the plane of projection can now be written as

$$\mathbf{p}(\phi, \theta, f, \mathbf{o}) = \begin{bmatrix} \dfrac{X'}{Z'} & \dfrac{Y'}{Z'} \end{bmatrix}, \tag{2.3}$$

where X', Y' and Z' are given by the transformation

$$\begin{bmatrix} X' \\ Y' \\ Z' \end{bmatrix} = \mathbf{N}(f)\mathbf{M}(\phi, \theta)\mathbf{o}^\top. \tag{2.4}$$

The camera model relates the geometry and position of the tracked object in the 3D world to the internal camera parameters. In the next section, we describe how the estimation problem can be formulated.

2.3.2 Estimation

In this section we formulate the problem of jointly estimating the camera and world parameters in a recursive Bayesian filter framework.

At time t, the state configuration of the joint camera/object model is represented by the spatial coordinates of the tracked object in the real-world, the camera intrinsics and the velocities corresponding to the object position and camera intrinsics:

$$\mathbf{s}_t = [\mathbf{o}_t \,|\, \mathbf{c}_t \,|\, \dot{\mathbf{o}}_t \,|\, \dot{\mathbf{c}}_t]^\top, \tag{2.5}$$

where each component is defined by

$$\mathbf{o}_t = [X_t, Y_t, Z_t], \tag{2.6}$$

$$\mathbf{c}_t = [\phi_t, \theta_t, f_t], \tag{2.7}$$

$$\dot{\mathbf{o}}_t = [\dot{X}_t, \dot{Y}_t, \dot{Z}_t], \tag{2.8}$$

$$\dot{\mathbf{c}}_t = [\dot{\phi}_t, \dot{\theta}_t, \dot{f}_t]. \tag{2.9}$$

$[X_t, Y_t, Z_t]$ is the position of the planar patch in world coordinates at time t, and $[\phi_t, \theta_t, f_t]$ represent the camera pan angle, tilt angle and focal length at time t, respectively. The remaining elements, $[\dot{X}_t, \dot{Y}_t, \dot{Z}_t, \dot{\phi}_t, \dot{\theta}_t, \dot{f}_t]$, represent the velocities of the previously mentioned components.

From time $t-1$ to time t, the state is updated by the linear matrix $\mathbf{U}$:

$$\mathbf{s}_t = \mathbf{U}\mathbf{s}_{t-1} + \mathbf{v}_{t-1}, \tag{2.10}$$

where $\mathbf{U}$ is defined by

$$\mathbf{U} = \begin{bmatrix} \mathbf{I}_6 & \mathbf{I}_6 \\ \mathbf{0}_6 & \mathbf{I}_6 \end{bmatrix}, \tag{2.11}$$

and where $\mathbf{I}_n$ and $\mathbf{0}_n$ are the $n \times n$ identity and zero matrices, respectively. The term $\mathbf{v}_{t-1}$ in (2.10) is considered to be a zero-mean, Gaussian random variable adding noise to the system update.

At each time t, an observation $\mathbf{z}_t$ of the unknown system $\mathbf{s}_t$ is made:

$$\mathbf{z}_t = [x_t, y_t, w_t, h_t, \hat{\phi}_t, \hat{\theta}_t, \hat{f}_t], \tag{2.12}$$

where (x_t, y_t) is the center of the object in the image plane measured in pixels, (w_t, h_t) are the width and height of the object in the image plane, also measured in pixels, please refer again to Fig. 2.1. $(\hat{\phi}_t, \hat{\theta}_t, \hat{f}_t)$ are the camera parameters arriving from the camera imprecise measurements of the pan angle, tilt angle and focal length.

The measurement equation, against which the observation $\mathbf{z}_t$ is compared, is given by:

$$\mathbf{h}(\mathbf{s}_t) = \big[\mathbf{p}(\phi_t, \theta_t, f_t, \mathbf{o}_t) \,|\, \mathbf{p}(0, 0, f_t, [W, H, Z'_t]) \,|\, \mathbf{c}_t\big]^\top + \big[\mathbf{n}^o_t \,|\, \mathbf{n}^c_t\big]^\top, \tag{2.13}$$

where $\mathbf{n}^o_t$ and $\mathbf{n}^c_t$ are zero-mean Gaussian noise processes on the object and camera measurements, respectively. Z'_t is the projection of the depth Z_t in the new coordinate system resulting from the pan and tilt of the camera. $\mathbf{p}(\phi_t, \theta_t, f_t, \mathbf{o}_t)$ represents the projection of the object position $\mathbf{o}_t$ into the image plane and, similarly, $\mathbf{p}(0, 0, f_t, [W, H, Z'_t])$ is the projection of the known object size $W \times H$ into the image plane. The camera vector $\mathbf{c}_t$ consists of the pan angle, tilt angle and focal length, as estimated by the state vector.

Given the system update and measurement processes defined in (2.10) and (2.13), the Bayesian estimation problem is to find an estimate of the unknown state $\mathbf{s}_t$ that maximizes the posterior density $p(\mathbf{s}_t|\mathbf{z}_{1:t})$.

Toward this end, an Extended Kalman Filter (EKF) is used to recursively solve this estimation problem [28]. The EKF approximates the likelihood as a Gaussian density with argument $\mathbf{s}_t$, mean $\mathbf{m}_t$ and covariance $\mathbf{P}_t$:

$$p(\mathbf{s}_t|\mathbf{z}_{1:t}) \approx \mathcal{N}(\mathbf{s}_t; \mathbf{m}_t, \mathbf{P}_t). \tag{2.14}$$

Defining $\hat{\mathbf{H}}_t$ as a local linearization, given by the Jacobian, of the non-linear measurement function, $\mathbf{h}(\mathbf{s}_t)$:

$$\hat{\mathbf{H}}_t = \left. \frac{\partial \mathbf{h}(\mathbf{s}_t)}{\partial \mathbf{s}_t} \right|_{\mathbf{s}_t = \mathbf{m}_{t|t-1}}, \tag{2.15}$$

the update from time $t-1$ to time t is given by the set of equations

$$\mathbf{m}_{t|t-1} = \mathbf{U}\mathbf{m}_{t-1}, \tag{2.16}$$

$$\mathbf{P}_{t|t-1} = \mathbf{Q} + \mathbf{U}\mathbf{P}_{t-1}\mathbf{U}^{\top}, \tag{2.17}$$

$$\mathbf{m}_t = \mathbf{m}_{t|t-1} + \mathbf{K}_t\left(\mathbf{z}_t - \mathbf{h}(\mathbf{m}_{t|t-1})\right), \tag{2.18}$$

$$\mathbf{P}_t = \mathbf{P}_{t|t-1} - \mathbf{K}_t\hat{\mathbf{H}}_t\mathbf{P}_{t|t-1}, \tag{2.19}$$

$$\mathbf{S}_t = \hat{\mathbf{H}}_t\mathbf{P}_{t|t-1}\hat{\mathbf{H}}_t^{\top} + \mathbf{R}, \tag{2.20}$$

$$\mathbf{K}_t = \mathbf{P}_{t|t-1}\hat{\mathbf{H}}_t^{\top}\mathbf{S}_t^{-1}. \tag{2.21}$$

$\mathbf{S}_t$ is the covariance of the innovation term $\mathbf{z}_t - \mathbf{h}(\mathbf{m}_{t|t-1})$ and $\mathbf{K}_t$ is the Kalman gain. $\mathbf{Q}$ and $\mathbf{R}$ are the covariance of the Gaussian noise added to the system update and measurement, respectively.

2.3.3 Control

The estimated state outputted at each step of the filter is used to control the movement of the camera. Two PID controllers are used: one for controlling the pan and tilt and another one for the zoom. The control signal, outputted by a PID controller, is given by

$$\mathbf{u}(t) = K_p\mathbf{e}(t) + K_i \int_0^t \mathbf{e}(\tau)\, d\tau + K_d\frac{d}{dt}\mathbf{e}(t), \tag{2.22}$$

where $\mathbf{e}(t)$ is the error signal, K_p is the proportional gain, K_i is the integral gain and K_d is the derivative gain.

In our case, and at each time t, the *error in pan* is defined as the difference between the estimated pan angle and the estimated horizontal angle that the object forms with the world coordinate system, while the *error in tilt* is defined as the difference between the estimated tilt angle and the estimated vertical angle of the object:

$$e_{\text{pan}} = \arctan(X_t/Z_t) - \phi_t, \tag{2.23}$$

$$e_{\text{tilt}} = \arctan(Y_t/Z_t) - \theta_t. \tag{2.24}$$

The gains are experimentally set to: $K_p = 1$, $K_i = 0$ and $K_d = 0.2$.

To calculate the *error for the zoom controller*, we define the desired area D_a, which is the maximum area in pixels we aim to have and which is usually achieved when the object is static. The error is then defined, at each time t, as:

$$e_{\text{zoom}} = D_a - w_{\text{proj}} * h_{\text{proj}}, \tag{2.25}$$

where w_{proj} and h_{proj} are the projections of the width W and height H of the object in the image plane. The gains are experimentally set to: $K_p = 0.01$, $K_i = 0$ and $K_d = 0$.

The integral phase was bypassed in both controllers, by setting K_i to 0, because the output of the filter was found to be accurate at steady state, i.e. when the object is centered with maximum zoom.

The error e_{zoom} is considered only when both $|e_{\text{pan}}|$ and $|e_{\text{tilt}}|$ are constant or decreasing; otherwise, a zoom out operation is executed.

2.3.4 System Performance

In this section, we will show the reader the performance of the system on both simulated scenarios and live scenes of a PTZ camera. The simulated scenario consisted of a random motion of an object whose size is 10×10 cm, and the error was averaged over many runs. The camera used in the live scenes was an Axis 214 PTZ network camera.

2.3.4.1 Simulated Data

The error metric we used in all model parameters estimation is the root mean square deviation (RMSD) defined as:

$$\text{RMSD}(\eta_i) = \sqrt{E\big((\bar{\eta}_i - \eta_i)^2\big)}, \qquad (2.26)$$

where η_i is one of the model parameters, $[X, Y, Z, \phi, \theta, f, \dot{X}, \dot{Y}, \dot{Z}, \dot{\phi}_t, \dot{\theta}_t, \dot{f}_t]$, composing the state vector in (2.5), and $\bar{\eta}_i$ is the estimated model parameter. The expectation, E, is taken over the entire sequence. The RMSD is measured for several runs of the simulation (we used 100 runs in our experiments), and the average RMSD is used as a measure of estimation performance.

Figure 2.2a shows a box-and-whisker summary of the RMSD for a simulation where a moving object is tracked by a moving camera. In these experiments, we

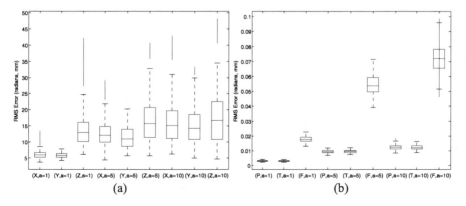

Fig. 2.2 a Error in 3D position parameters (X, Y, Z), measured in millimeters. **b** Error in pan angle, tilt angle and focal length. Angles are measured in radians, focal length in millimeters

simulate the motion the camera would execute due to corrections coming from the PID controllers described in the previous section. Also, some noise is introduced in the different state parameters. To investigate sensitivity to varying measurement noise, this value is scaled by a constant $a \in \{1, 5, 10\}$. Similar results can be seen in Fig. 2.2b for camera parameters estimation. From these figures, one can conclude that scaling the uncertainty, by $a = 5$ and $a = 10$, predictably scales the RMSD error as well as the spread (most notably in Z and f) and increases outliers. However, even with such increase, the estimates of both the object position and the camera parameters are very good.

2.3.4.2 Live Cameras

A commodity PTZ camera (Axis 214) was used for tracking different objects. Simple assumptions about object sizes were made: the cup tracked in Fig. 2.3 is assumed to be 8×12 cm, while the faces in Figs. 2.4 and 2.5 are assumed to be 18×18 cm. For the detection of the blue cup, a simple heuristics-based classifier for detecting blue regions in the normalized RGB colorspace was used; while for face detection, we used the method developed in [1]. The two red dots represent the center of the object and the upper left corner, outputted by the detection process. The green dots represent the projection of the estimates of the center and the bounding box position. The tracker was able to successfully follow the objects taking correct decisions on when to zoom in and when to zoom out.

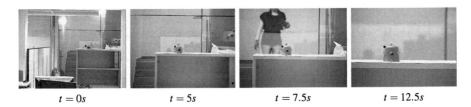

$t = 0s$ $\qquad$ $t = 5s$ $\qquad$ $t = 7.5s$ $\qquad$ $t = 12.5s$

Fig. 2.3 Reactive tracking of a stationary object

$t = 0s$ $\qquad$ $t = 5s$ $\qquad$ $t = 12.5s$ $\qquad$ $t = 32.5s$

Fig. 2.4 Reactive tracking of a moving face

$t = 0s$ $t = 5s$ $t = 12.5s$ $t = 32.5s$

Fig. 2.5 Another example of reactive face tracking

2.3.5 Closing Remarks

In this section, a method for reactive object tracking has been described. The system uses a single PTZ camera and jointly estimates, in a Bayesian framework, the orientation and focal length of the camera and the position of the tracked object in the 3D environment. The output of the estimation process is used to drive the control process, allowing the camera to reactively track the moving target. The main limitation of this method is that the EKF output is dependent on the detection, i.e. the measurement process; therefore, and although the method is tolerant to measurement noise, continuous erroneous detection leads to inaccurate tracking. Also, this method does not support multiple objects tracking. Other than that, the estimates are robust in the presence of camera motion and increased measurement noise.

2.4 Active Vision in Practice: A Case Study

Imagine a user communicating with a set of distributed PTZ cameras, as if they were humans reporting what they see. This would require converting a video stream into a textual description of temporal events. The user should, then, be able to request summaries of recent developments in chosen languages, to obtain responses to his questions for details, and to send commands, e.g., to zoom in on a particular body.

The challenge of building a cognitive system showing the aforementioned behavior involves addressing multiple research areas, such as computer vision, artificial intelligence and computational linguistics, to cite only a few. The term Human Sequence Evaluation (HSE) was coined to refer to this set of requirements, modules and flows of knowledge (numeric or semantic) that is essential for designing such a complex system [15]. As a result, HSE provided a theoretical framework upon which a European project called HERMES[1] was conceived and subsequently implemented thanks to the European Commission. HERMES was a consortium project that concentrated on extracting descriptions of people behavior from videos in re-

[1] http://www.hermes-project.eu

stricted discourse domains, such as pedestrians crossing inner-city roads, approaching or waiting at bus stops and even humans in indoor locations like halls or lobbies.

In this section, we present the resulting HERMES system that uses active cameras to help researchers in exploring a coherent evaluation of human movements and facial expressions across a wide variation of scale. The challenging objectives were the integration, demonstration and validation of different image processing techniques: in essence, the outputs of such techniques were pooled and integrated to build a coherent hardware and software system that can extract a subset of semantically meaningful behaviors from a scene.

To meet such objectives, the system uses active cameras to take high-resolution images of subjects, while still monitoring a large area in a manner similar to [24]. In such settings, the main issues tackled are:

- How to direct an active camera over a moving target while zooming on it. This process is referred to as foveation. Existing solutions to this problem only employ active tracking of motion and appearance to drive the camera motors [18].
- In the presence of several targets, how to select the most semantically relevant one to foveate on, according to a user-determined definition of relevance.

Solutions to this last problem select targets based on *Earliest Deadline First* policies, assigning higher relevance to those subjects that are going to leave the scene sooner [10]. Also, a solution based on the *Dynamic Traveling Salesperson Problem* has been proposed in [5]. While these approaches attempt to maximize the number of targets acquired over time, little effort has been made, yet, to maximize the quality, defined in semantically meaningful terms, of acquired images.

In the literature, active cameras are commonly used to provide a distribution of bodies and faces in the scene that can be exploited to select the best, most meaningful view. In [8], the technology to support tracking in a multiple-camera system is defined and is exploited for extracting and comparing the best view of each detected agent. Also, camera zoom allows active camera systems to supply imagery at the appropriate resolution for motion analysis of the human body and face, thus facilitating expression analysis [9, 30].

However, in our proposed framework the use of active sensors enhances the process of cognition via controlled responses to uncertain or ambiguous interpretations. In particular, the use of zoom provides a unification of interpretations at different resolutions, and bestows the ability to switch the sensing process between different streams in a controlled fashion. This integration of the cycle of *perception–knowledge acquisition–abstraction–reasoning–action generation* was also an interesting avenue of research.

In the rest of this section, we describe the resulting prototypical system that covers the aforementioned requirements. As a result, a slimmed-down demonstrator system, with both fixed and PTZ cameras, was able to generate natural language text based on activities of a particular agent (human or road vehicle) from schematic conceptual representations inferred using trajectory data.

2.4.1 Practical Considerations

An integrated hardware platform was designed, built and installed. This hardware platform consists of two high-speed cameras (one fixed and one PTZ) and three dedicated servers to host HERMES systems: for analysis of agent motion, active camera control and inferring high-level descriptions of agent behavior in the scene.

As noted before, the main objective of the HERMES project was set to improve active camera foveation ability by introducing semantics into active sensor guidance systems. This leads to the following specific sub-objectives:

- selecting the most appropriate low-level tracking techniques capable of focusing on specific aspects of agent motion like whole-body, limbs and face;
- constructing systems capable of classifying specific scene trajectories and human actions which form the basic attentive vocabulary for low-level scene description;
- improving active camera control systems to maximize the quality of acquired imagery based on low-level features;
- incorporating semantic feedback and requests from high-level scene description and reasoning into the active sensor control system, enabling it to acquire knowledge used for a robust and accurate description of the scene;
- designing active camera controllers capable of responding to uncertain or ambiguous interpretations;
- controlling active cameras in a manner that allows the analysis of three different degrees of human motion: agent, body and face, depending on the recognized behaviors;
- controlling active cameras to supply visual data while directing camera attention to those agents whose behaviors are deemed interesting.

These objectives allow a cognitive vision system to provide sensor data for each of the modules considered in HERMES, but more importantly, to bring all of the system modules together in a sensor perception/action cycle. Cooperating PTZ sensors enhance the process of cognition via controlled responses to uncertain or ambiguous interpretations. As a result, the use of zoom provides a unification for interpretations at different resolutions while exploiting the ability to switch the sensing process between different streams in a controlled fashion.

2.4.2 HERMES Hardware Platform

The HERMES-outdoor demonstrator platform was installed on top of the Computer Vision Center (CVC) building at the Universitat Autònoma de Barcelona, see Fig. 2.6. Based on a design of a demonstrator for indoor active surveillance scenarios [7], the demonstrator at CVC extends such a prototype to an outdoor scenario.

The hardware integration architecture is illustrated in Fig. 2.7. The hardware platform for the HERMES demonstrator consists of a fixed camera, another camera mounted in a pan/tilt platform and fitted with a zoom lens, three dedicated servers

Fig. 2.6 The view from atop
of the Computer Vision
Center

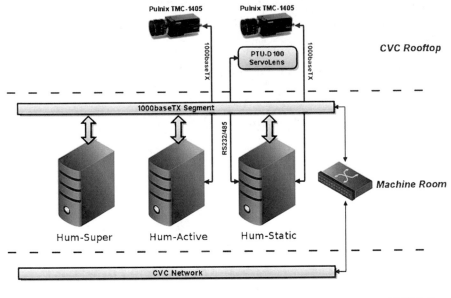

Fig. 2.7 The HERMES demonstrator hardware architecture

to provide raw computational power and a fast 10 Gb Ethernet switch. The main
components of the hardware infrastructure are:

Cameras Two Pulnix TMC-1405 cameras are used. These cameras are GigE-
compatible and deliver high-resolution images (1392 × 1040 pixels) at high framer-
ate (30 frames per second). Each camera is connected by a dedicated, 100base-TX
Ethernet connection to ensure constant, high-framerate streaming.

PTZ Platform One of the Pulnix cameras is mounted in a Directed Perception PTU-D100 pan/tilt platform that allows complete 360-degree pan and 180-degree tilt surveillance of the scene. The active camera is also fitted with a ServoLens zoom lens adjustable to focal lengths from 12.5 to 75 mm. Both the zoom lens and the PT platform are connected by direct RS-232/435 serial connections.

Compute Servers Three dedicated servers are used. Two of them are directly connected to the Pulnix cameras and are primarily dedicated to video acquisition. The third server is used for components not requiring direct access to the cameras, such as the supervisor tracker and SGT reasoning subsystems (explained later). These three machines are referred to as `hermes-super`, `hermes-fixed`, and `hermes-active` to emphasize their roles in the demonstrator platform.

Network Infrastructure The three servers are switched onto a 100baseTZ gigabit Ethernet segment in order to ensure the maximum possible bandwidth for communication among the demonstrator components.

2.4.3 HERMES Software Platform

Here we discuss the software integration of the demonstration platform. A modular software architecture was designed, see Fig. 2.8, which illustrates how the software components are distributed across the HERMES demonstrator machines.

The aim is to support a set of distributed static and PTZ cameras and visual tracking algorithms, together with a central supervisor unit. Each camera (and pan–tilt

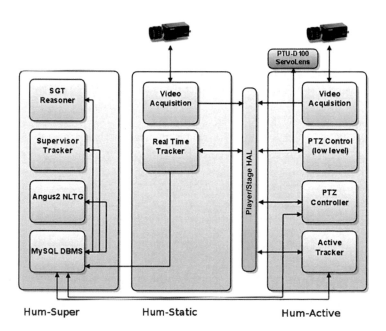

Fig. 2.8 The HERMES demonstrator software infrastructure

device) has a dedicated process and processor. Asynchronous interprocess communications and archiving of data are achieved in a simple and effective way via a central repository, implemented using a MySQL database. Visual tracking data from static views are stored dynamically into tables in the database via client calls to the SQL server. A supervisor process running on the SQL server determines if active zoom cameras should be dispatched to observe a particular target, and this message is sent via writing demands into another database table.

Video Acquisition Video acquisition is performed using the JAI Advanced Imaging SDK. Frames captured by the two cameras at high resolution (1392×1040 pixels) are scaled to the desired resolution (640×480 pixels) for processing. Scaled frames are made available to the Player/Stage architecture through a shared memory interface. Video is delivered to the HERMES demonstrator components at a constant 25 frames per second.

PTZ Controller The Directed Perception P/T platform and ServoLens zoom lens were integrated into the Player/Stage driver system. A custom driver for the ServoLens was created in order to control the zoom lens through the standard Player/Stage PTZ interface.

Real Time Tracker The Real Time Tracker (RTT) is one of the fundamental components in the demonstrator platform [23]. The RTT tracks multiple moving targets in the fixed camera view and writes its observations into a table on the MySQL server.

Supervisor Tracker A Supervisor Tracker (SVT) is responsible for performing data fusion, smoothing and association based on observations made by the RTT; it is also responsible for issuing commands for the PTZ controller to actively track targets in order to acquire high-resolution imagery of active targets in the area of surveillance.

SGT Reasoner In order to demonstrate high-level reasoning and to support generation of natural language text from surveillance scenes, a SGT traversal system was integrated into the demonstrator platform [14]. The SGT reasoner listens for fused, smoothed observations coming from the SVT and records its inferences in a dedicated table on the MySQL database.

Angus2 NLTG The Angus2 system for natural language text generation has been adapted to read inferences generated by SGT traversal from the database [14].

Player/Stage Hardware Abstraction Layer Integration and communication between low-level components in the demonstrator system is achieved through the use of the Player/Stage system which provides a level of abstraction, allowing the video consuming components to receive streaming video without having to deal with the low-level details of the camera device itself.

MySQL DBMS At a very fundamental and low level, communication between the high-level components of the demonstrator is accomplished through a central MySQL database.

A user interface for controlling the real-time demonstrator was also built, allowing the user to administer and monitor the components of the demonstrator platform, see Fig. 2.9.

Fig. 2.9 The GUI for the real-time active surveillance demonstrator

Working with images of size 640 × 480 pixels at 25 frames per second, our system can track up to 8 agents at a time. The PTZ camera can easily shift from one target to another; the time needed for the shift is between half a second and one second, depending on the angular distance between targets. The textual descriptions that can be generated include terms that describe status/gesture, such as: Run, Walk, Hand Wave, etc., and terms describing contextualized events, such as: Join, Appear, Disappear, Cross, Meet, Enter, etc.

The use of Player/Stage as an interface for low level modules and MySQL as an interface for high level modules was crucial to the success of the system.

2.5 Conclusions: Learning from the Past to Foresee the Future

The problem of covering relatively large scenarios with surveillance cameras, in such a manner that the targets of interest are captured with sufficient resolution, is still nowadays an open and active research field. Whereas camera networks are expensive and hard to manage and scale, active vision appears as a more natural solution to minimize the number of sensors while tackling the aforementioned goal.

Nevertheless, balancing the trade-off between area coverage and resolution per target calls for sensible techniques to control, integrate, and coordinate the possible passive and active components of an active vision system. Moreover, vision systems should be capable of providing human-interpretable descriptions of the occurrences being observed, and react according to certain policies. Thus, integrating the cameras with high-level semantic reasoning seems to be required for the intelligent capture and description of the interactions in a scene.

Toward extracting a semantic inference of what is happening in a scene and/or identifying semantically meaningful attentional factors, the possible future lines of research are:

- how the process of interpretation can be enhanced by PTZ sensors via semantic-based controlled responses to uncertain or ambiguous interpretations of human behaviors;
- how PTZ sensors can work on three different degrees of human motion analysis, i.e. agent, body and face, depending on the recognized behavior;
- how PTZ sensors can optimize transitions between these three degrees of resolution to supply visual data at the coarsest resolution, while subsequently directing the camera's attention to those agents deemed *interesting*;
- how the use of standard body and face detection algorithms can provide an attentional mechanism for controlling PTZ sensors.

The most interesting goal in the future is the control of zoom based on semantics and responding to uncertainty, in particular uncertainties and ambiguities due to high-level interpretations. Toward this goal, one could generate Natural Language descriptions for the active camera itself: a description and justification of what the camera is doing not only numerically but also semantically at a conceptual level.

In this context, semantics-driven control of active cameras will allow a computer vision system to better detect, track and reason about human motion using behavior models. Since these models are semantically rich, inference over them allows us to derive more meaningful targets toward which the active sensors should focus.

All in all, the automatic acquisition and exploitation of scene motion and context is compulsory to enhance the richness and expressiveness of semantic descriptions of human behaviors. By recognizing and labeling regions and objects associated with human activity, active systems will be able to reason about areas where humans are likely to be present and about the expected interactions with scene elements. Contextual reasoning will help to bridge the semantic gap by improving the ability to articulate high-level requests about human behaviors and send them to the active sensors acquiring low-level descriptions of the scene.

Acknowledgements   This work has been supported by the European Project FP6 HERMES IST-027110. The authors wish to thank the rest of the partners in the HERMES consortium, namely AVL at Oxford University, BiWi at ETH Zurich, CVMT at Aalborg University and IAKS at Universität Karlsruhe. Also, the authors acknowledge the support of the Spanish Research Programs Consolider-Ingenio 2010: MIPRCV (CSD200700018); Avanza I+D ViCoMo (TSI-020400-2009-133); CENIT-IMAGENIO 2010 SEGUR@; along with the Spanish projects TIN2009-14501-C02-01 and TIN2009-14501-C02-02. Moreover, Murad Al Haj acknowledges the support from the Generalitat de Catalunya through an AGAUR FI predoctoral grant (IUE/2658/2007).

References

1. Al Haj, M., Bagdanov, A.D., Gonzàlez, J., Roca, F.X.: Robust and efficient multipose face detection using skin color segmentation. In: Pattern Recognition and Image Analysis. Lecture Notes in Computer Science, vol. 5524, pp. 152–159. Springer, Berlin (2009) [20]
2. Al Haj, M., Bagdanov, A.D., Gonzàlez, J., Roca, F.X.: Reactive object tracking with a single PTZ camera. In: International Conference on Pattern Recognition, pp. 1690–1693 (2010) [15]
3. Aloimonos, J., Weiss, I., Bandyopadhyay, A.: Active vision. Int. J. Comput. Vis. 1(4), 333–356 (1988) [13]
4. Anagnostopoulos, C.K., Anagnostopoulos, I.E., Psoroulas, I.D., Kayafas, E.: License plate recognition from still images and video sequences: A survey. IEEE Trans. Intell. Transp. Syst. 9(3), 377–391 (2008) [12]
5. Bagdanov, A.D., Del Bimbo, A., Nunziati, W.: Improving evidential quality of surveillance imagery through active face tracking. In: International Conference on Pattern Recognition, pp. 1200–1203 (2006) [13,22]
6. Bashir, F., Porikli, F.: Collaborative tracking of objects in Eptz cameras. In: Visual Communications and Image Processing, vol. 6508, p. 2007 (2007) [14]
7. Bellotto, N., Sommerlade, E., Benfold, B., Bibby, C., Reid, I., Roth, D., Gool, L.V., Fernández, C., Gonzàlez, J.: A distributed camera system for multi-resolution surveillance. In: International Conference on Distributed Smart Cameras (ICDSC), Como, Italy (2009) [14, 23]
8. Calderara, S., Cucchiara, R., Prati, A.: Bayesian-competitive consistent labeling for people surveillance. IEEE Trans. Pattern Anal. Mach. Intell. 30(2), 354–360 (2008) [22]
9. Cohen, I., Sebe, N., Garg, A., Chen, L., Huang, T.S.: Facial expression recognition from video sequences: temporal and static modeling. Comput. Vis. Image Underst. 91(1–2), 160–187 (2003) [22]
10. Costello, C.J., Diehl, C.P., Banerjee, A., Fisher, H.: Scheduling an active camera to observe people. In: International Workshop on Video Surveillance and Sensor Networks (VSSN) (2004) [22]
11. Del Bimbo, A., Dini, F., Lisanti, G., Pernici, F.: Exploiting distinctive visual landmark maps in pan–tilt–zoom camera networks. Comput. Vis. Image Underst. 114(6), 611–623 (2010). http://www.micc.unifi.it/publications/2010/DDLP10/DDLP10.pdf [14]
12. Denzler, J., Zobel, M., Niemann, H.: Information theoretic focal length selection for real-time active 3-d object tracking. In: International Conference on Computer Vision, pp. 400–407. IEEE Comput. Soc., Los Alamitos (2003) [13]
13. Erdem, U.M., Sclaroff, S.: Look there! Predicting Where to look for motion in an active camera network. In: International Conference on Advanced Video and Signal-based Surveillance (AVSS), pp. 105–110. IEEE, New York (2006) [14]
14. Gerber, R., Nagel, H.-H.: Representation of occurrences for road vehicle traffic. Artif. Intell. 172(4–5), 351–391 (2008) [14,26]
15. Gonzàlez, J., Rowe, D., Varona, J., Roca, X.: Understanding dynamic scenes based on human sequence evaluation. Image Vis. Comput. 27(10), 1433–1444 (2009) [21]
16. Hampapur, A., Pankanti, S., Senior, A., Tian, Y.L., Brown, L., Bolle, R.: Face cataloger: Multi-scale imaging for relating identity to location. In: International Conference on Advanced Video and Signal-based Surveillance (AVSS), pp. 13–20. IEEE, New York (2003) [14]
17. Ilie, A., Welch, G., Macenko, M.: A stochastic quality metric for optimal control of active camera network configurations for 3D computer vision tasks. In: International Workshop on Multi-camera and Multi-modal Sensor Fusion Algorithms and Applications (M2SFA2), Marseille, France (2008) [14]
18. Murray, D.W., Bradshaw, K.J., McLauchlan, P.F., Reid, I.D., Sharkey, P.: Driving saccade to pursuit using image motion. Int. J. Comput. Vis. 16(3), 205–228 (1995) [22]
19. Nelson, E.D., Cockburn, J.C.: Dual camera zoom control: A study of zoom tracking stability. In: Proceedings of IEEE International Conference on Acoustics, Speech and Signal Processing. IEEE Comput. Soc., Los Alamitos (2007) [13]

20. Peixoto, P., Batista, J., Araujo, H.: A surveillance system combining peripheral and foveated motion tracking. In: International Conference on Pattern Recognition, vol. 1, pp. 574–577. IEEE, New York (2002) [14]

21. Qureshi, F.Z., Terzopoulos, D.: Surveillance in virtual reality: System design and multi-camera control. In: Computer Vision and Pattern Recognition, pp. 1–8 (2007) [14]

22. Qureshi, F.Z., Terzopoulos, D.: Multi-camera control through constraint satisfaction for persistent surveillance. In: International Conference on Advanced Video and Signal Based Surveillance (AVSS), pp. 211–218. IEEE, New York (2008) [14]

23. Roth, D., Koller-Meier, E., Rowe, D., Moeslund, T.B., Gool, L.V.: Event-based tracking evaluation metric. In: International Workshop on Motion and Video Computing (WMVC), Copper Mountain, Colorado, USA (2008) [26]

24. Smith, P., Shah, M., da Vitoria Lobo, N.: Integrating multiple levels of zoom to enable activity analysis. Comput. Vis. Image Underst. **103**(1), 33–51 (2006) [22]

25. Sommerlade, E., Reid, I.: Information-theoretic active scene exploration. In: Computer Vision and Pattern Recognition (2008) [12]

26. Tordoff, B.J., Murray, D.W.: A method of reactive zoom control from uncertainty in tracking. Comput. Vis. Image Underst. **105**(2), 131–144 (2007) [13]

27. Wang, J., Zhang, C., Shum, H.: Face image resolution versus face recognition performance based on two global methods. In: Asian Conference on Computer Vision (2004) [12]

28. Welch, G., Bishop, G.: An introduction to the Kalman filter. Technical report, University of North Carolina at Chapel Hill, Chapel Hill, NC, USA (1995) [17]

29. Wrede, S., Hanheide, M., Wachsmuth, S., Sagerer, G.: Integration and coordination in a cognitive vision system. In: International Conference on Computer Vision Systems (ICVS), IEEE Comput. Soc., Los Alamitos (2006) [14]

30. Zhang, Y., Ji, Q.: Facial expression understanding in image sequences using dynamic and active visual information fusion. In: International Conference on Computer Vision (2003) [22]

31. Zhou, X., Collins, R.T., Kanade, T., Metes, P.: A master-slave system to acquire biometric imagery of humans at distance. In: International Workshop on Video Surveillance (VS), pp. 113–120, ACM, New York (2003) [14]

Chapter 3
Figure-Ground Segmentation—Pixel-Based

Ahmed Elgammal

Abstract Background subtraction is a widely used concept to detect moving objects in videos taken from a static camera. In the last two decades several algorithms have been developed for background subtraction and were used in various important applications such as visual surveillance, sports video analysis, motion capture, etc. Various statistical approaches have been proposed to model scene background. In this chapter we review the concept and the practice in background subtraction. We discuss several basic statistical background subtraction models, including parametric Gaussian models and nonparametric models. We discuss the issue of shadow suppression, which is essential for human motion analysis applications. We also discuss approaches and tradeoffs for background maintenance, and point out many of the recent developments within the background subtraction paradigm.

3.1 Introduction

In many human motion analysis applications stationary cameras or pan-tilt-zoom (PTZ) cameras are used to monitor activities at outdoor or indoor sites. This is typical in visual surveillance systems as well as vision-based motion capture systems. Since the cameras are stationary, the detection of moving objects can be achieved by comparing each new frame with a representation of the scene background. This process is called *background subtraction* and the scene representation is called the *background model*. The scene here is assumed to be stationary or quasi stationary.

Typically, the background subtraction process forms the first stage in automated visual surveillance systems and motion capture applications. Results from background subtraction are used for further processing, such as tracking targets and understanding events. One main advantage of pixel-based detection using background subtraction is that the outcome is an accurate segmentation of the foreground regions from the scene background. For human subjects, the process gives accurate silhouettes of the human body, which can be further used for tracking, fitting body limbs, pose and posture estimation, etc. This is in contrast to classifier-based object-based

A. Elgammal (✉)
Rutgers University, New Brunswick, NJ, USA
e-mail: elgammal@cs.rutgers.edu

T.B. Moeslund et al. (eds.), *Visual Analysis of Humans*,
DOI 10.1007/978-0-85729-997-0_3, © Springer-Verlag London Limited 2011

detectors, which mainly decide whether a bounding box or a region in the image contains the object of interest or not, e.g. pedestrian detectors. Such object-based detectors will be discussed in the next chapter.

The concept of background modeling is rooted in photography since the 19th century where it was shown that film can be exposed for a period of time to capture the scene background without moving objects [14]. The use of background subtraction to detect moving objects is deeply rooted in image analysis and emanated from the concept of change detection, a process in which two images of the same scene taken at different time instances are compared, for example in Landsat Imagery, e.g. [8, 27].

The concept of background subtraction has been widely used since the early human motion analysis systems such as Pfinder [58], W4 [20], etc. Efficient and more sophisticated background subtraction algorithms that can address challenging situations have been developed since then. The success of these algorithms lead to the growth of many commercial applications, for example sports monitoring and automated visual surveillance industry. Unlike earlier background subtraction algorithms where the cameras and the scenes are assumed to be stationary, many approaches have been proposed to overcome these limitations, for example dealing with quasi-stationary scenes and moving cameras. We will discuss such approaches later in this chapter.

The organization of this chapter is as follows. Section 3.2 discusses some of the challenges in building a background model for detection. Section 3.3 discusses some of the basic and widely used background modeling techniques. Section 3.4 discusses how to deal with color information to avoid detecting shadows. Section 3.5 discusses the tradeoffs and challenges in updating background models. Section 3.6 discusses some background models that can deal with moving cameras. Finally in Sect. 3.7 we discuss further issues and point out to further readings in the subject.

3.2 Challenges in Scene Modeling

In any indoor or outdoor scene there are changes that occur over time to the scene background. It is important for any background model to be able to tolerate these changes, either by being invariant to them or by adapting to them. These changes can be local, affecting only parts of the background, or global affecting the entire background. The study of these changes is essential to understand the motivations behind different background subtraction techniques. Toyama et al. [56] identified a list of ten challenges that a background model has to overcome, and denoted them by *Moved objects, Time of day, Light switch, Waving trees, Camouflage, Bootstrapping, Foreground aperture, Sleeping person, Walking person, Shadows*. Elgammal et al. [12] classifies the possible changes in a scene background according to their source:

Illumination changes:

- Gradual change in illumination as might occur in outdoor scenes due to the change in the relative location of the sun during the day.

- Sudden change in illumination as might occur in an indoor environment by switching the lights on or off, or in an outdoor environment, e.g. a change between cloudy and sunny conditions.
- Shadows cast on the background by objects in the background itself (e.g., buildings and trees) or by moving foreground objects.

Motion changes:

- Global image motion due to small camera displacements. Despite the assumption that cameras are stationary, small camera displacements are common in outdoor situations due to wind load or other sources of motion, which causes global motion in the images.
- Motion in parts of the background. For example, tree branches moving with the wind, or rippling water.

Structural changes:

These are changes introduced to the background, including any change in the geometry or the appearance of the background of the scene introduced by targets. Such changes typically occur when something relatively permanent is introduced into the scene background. For example, if somebody moves (introduces) something from (to) the background, or if a car is parked in the scene or moved out of the scene, or if a person stays stationary in the scene for an extended period, etc. Toyama et al. [56] denoted these situations by "Moved Objects", "sleeping person" and "walking person" scenarios.

A central issue in building a representation for the scene background is what features to use for this representation or, in other words, what to model in the background. In the literature a variety of features have been used for background modeling including pixel-based features (pixel intensity, edges, disparity) and region based features (e.g., image block). The choice of the features affects how the background model will tolerate the changes in the scene and the granularity of the detected foreground objects.

Another fundamental issue in building a background representation is the choice of the statistical model that explains the observation at a given pixel or region in the scene. The choice of the proper model depends on the type of changes expected in the scene background. Such a choice highly affects the accuracy of the detection. Section 3.3 discusses some of the statistical models that are widely used in background modeling context. Beyond choosing the features and the statistical model, maintaining the background representation is another challenging issue, which we will discuss in Sect. 3.5.

3.3 Statistical Scene Modeling

In this section we will discuss some of the existing and widely used statistical background modeling approaches. For each model we will discuss how the model is initialized and how it is maintained. For simplicity of the discussion we will use pixel intensity as the observation. Instead, color or any other features can be used.

At the pixel level, the process of background subtraction can be formulated as followed: Given the intensity observed at a pixel at time t, denoted by x_t, we need to classify that pixel to either the background or foreground classes. This is a two class classification problem. However, since the intensity of a foreground pixel can arbitrary take any value, unless some further information about the foreground is available, we can just assume that the foreground distribution is uniform. Therefore, the problem reduces to a one class classification problem, i.e., modeling the distribution of the background class, which can be achieved if a history of background observations are available at that pixel. If the history observation is not purely coming from the background, i.e., foreground objects are present in the scene, the problem becomes more challenging.

3.3.1 Parametric Background Models

Pixel intensity is the most commonly used feature in background modeling. In a completely static scene, a simple noise model that can be used is an independent stationary additive Gaussian noise model [13]. According to that model, the noise distribution at a given pixel is a zero mean Gaussian distribution $N(0, \sigma^2)$, it follows that the observed intensity at that pixel is a random variable with a Gaussian distribution $N(\mu, \sigma^2)$. This Gaussian distribution model for the intensity value of a pixel is the underlying model for many background subtraction techniques and widely known as a single Gaussian background model. For the case of color images, a multivariate Gaussian is used. Typically, the color channels are assumed to be independent which reduces a multivariate Gaussian to a product of single Gaussians, one for each color channel. More discussion about dealing with color will be presented in Sect. 3.4.

Estimating the parameters for this model, i.e., learning the background model, reduces to estimating the mean and variance from history pixel observations. The background subtraction process in this case is a classifier that decides whether a new observation at that pixel comes form the learned background distribution. Assuming the foreground distribution is uniform, this amounts to putting a threshold on the tail of the Gaussian, i.e., the classification rule reduces to marking a pixel as foreground if

$$\|x_t - \hat{\mu}\| > k\hat{\sigma}, \tag{3.1}$$

where $\hat{\mu}$ and $\hat{\sigma}$ are the estimated mean and standard deviation and k is a threshold. The parameter σ can be even assumed to be the same for all pixels. So, literally, this simple model reduces to subtracting a background image B from each new frame I_t and checking the difference against a threshold. In such case the background image B is the mean of the history background frames.

This basic single Gaussian model can be made adaptive to slow changes in the scene (for example, gradual illumination changes) by recursively updating the mean with each new frame to maintain a background image,

$$B_t = \frac{t-1}{t} B_{t-1} + \frac{1}{t} I_t, \tag{3.2}$$

where $t \geq 1$. Obviously this update mechanism does not forget the history and, therefore, the effect of new images on the model tends to zero. This is not suitable when the goal is to adapt the model to illumination changes. Instead the mean and variance can be computed over a sliding window of time. However, a more practical and efficient solution is to recursively update the model via temporal blending, also known as exponential forgetting, i.e.

$$B_t = \alpha I_t + (1 - \alpha) B_{t-1}. \tag{3.3}$$

Here, B_t denotes the background image computed up to frame t. The parameter α controls the speed of forgetting old background information. This update equation is a low-pass filter with a gain factor α that effectively separates the slow temporal process (background) from the fast process (moving objects). Notice that the computed background image is no longer the sample mean over the history but captures the central tendency over time [16]. This basic adaptive model is used in systems such as the Pfinder [58]. In [30, 31, 34] variations of this recursive update was used after masking out the foreground regions.

Typically, in outdoor environments with moving trees and bushes, the scene background is not completely static. For example, one pixel can be the image of the sky in one frame, a tree leaf in another frame, a tree branch in a third frame and some mixture subsequently. In each situation the pixel will have a different intensity (color), so a single Gaussian assumption for the probability density function of the pixel intensity will not hold. Instead, a generalization based on a mixture of Gaussians has been used in [14, 17, 53] to model such variations. This model was first introduced in [14], where a mixture of three Gaussian distributions was used to model the pixel value for traffic surveillance applications. The pixel intensity was modeled as a weighted mixture of three Gaussian distributions corresponding to road, shadow and vehicle distribution. Fitting a MoG model can be achieved using the Expectation Maximization (EM) algorithm [6]. However, this is impractical for a real-time background subtraction application. An incremental EM algorithm [41] was used to learn and update the parameters of the model.

Stauffer and Grimson [17, 53] proposed a generalization to the previous approach. The intensity of a pixel is modeled by a mixture of K Gaussian distributions (K is a small number from 3 to 5). The mixture is weighted by the frequency with which each of the Gaussians explains the background. The probability that a certain pixel has intensity x_t at time t is estimated as

$$\Pr(x_t) = \sum_{i=1}^{K} w_{i,t} G(x_t, \mu_{i,t}, \Sigma_{i,t}), \tag{3.4}$$

where $w_{i,t}$, $\mu_{i,t}$, and $\Sigma_{i,t} = \sigma_{i,t} \mathbf{I}$ are the weight, mean, and covariance for the ith Gaussian mixture component at time t, respectively.

The parameters of the distributions are updated recursively using online K-means approximation. The mixture is weighted by the frequency with which each of the Gaussians explains the background, i.e., a new pixel value is checked against the existing K Gaussians and when a match is found the weight for that distribution is updated as follows:

$$w_{i,t} = (1 - \alpha)w_{i,t-1} + \alpha M(i,t), \tag{3.5}$$

where $M(i,t)$ is an indicator variable which is 1 if the ith component is matched, 0 otherwise. The parameter of the matched distributions are updated by

$$\mu_t = (1 - \rho)\mu_{t-1} + \rho x_t, \tag{3.6}$$

$$\sigma_t^2 = (1 - \rho)\sigma_{t-1}^2 + \rho(x_t - \mu_t)^T(x_t - \mu_t). \tag{3.7}$$

The parameters α and ρ are two learning rates. The K distributions are ordered based on w_j/σ_j^2 and the first B distributions are used as a model of the background of the scene where B is estimated as

$$B = \arg\min_b \left(\sum_{j=1}^{b} w_j > T \right). \tag{3.8}$$

The threshold T is the fraction of the total weight given to the background model. Background subtraction is performed by marking any pixel that is more that 2.5 standard deviations away from any of the B distributions as a foreground pixel.

The MoG background model was shown to perform very well in indoor and outdoor situations. Many variations have been suggested to the Stauffer and Grimson's model [53], e.g. [21, 28, 39]. The model also was used with in different feature spaces and/or with a subspace representations. Gao et al. [16] studied the statistical error characteristic of MoG background models.

3.3.2 Nonparametric Background Models

In outdoor scenes, typically there are wide range of variations, which can be very fast. Outdoor scenes usually contains dynamic areas such as waving trees and bushes, rippling water, ocean waves. Such fast variations are part of the scene background. Modeling such dynamics areas requires a more flexible representation of the background probability distribution at each pixel. This motivates the use of a non-parametric density estimator for background modeling [11].

A particular nonparametric technique that estimates the underlying density and is quite general is the Kernel Density Estimation (KDE) technique [7, 48]. Given a sample $S = \{x_i\}_{i=1,\dots,N}$ from a distribution with density function $p(x)$, an estimate $\hat{p}(x)$ of the density at x can be calculated using

$$\hat{p}(x) = \frac{1}{N} \sum_{i=1}^{N} K_\sigma(x - x_i), \tag{3.9}$$

where K_σ is a kernel function (sometimes called a "window" function) with a bandwidth (scale) σ such that $K_\sigma(t) = \frac{1}{\sigma} K(\frac{t}{\sigma})$. The kernel function K should satisfy $K(t) \geq 0$ and $\int K(t)\,dt = 1$. Kernel density estimators asymptotically converge to any density function with sufficient samples [7, 48]. In fact, all other nonparametric density estimation methods, e.g., histograms, can be shown to be asymptotically kernel methods [48]. This property makes these techniques quite general and applicable to many vision problems where the underlying density is not known [3, 9]. We can avoid having to store the complete data set by weighting a subset of the samples as

$$\hat{p}(x) = \sum_{x_i \in B} \alpha_i K_\sigma(x - x_i), \qquad (3.10)$$

where α_i are weighting coefficients that sum up to one and B is a sample subset. A good discussion of KDE techniques can be found in [48].

Elgammal et al. [11] introduced a background modeling approach based on kernel density estimation. Let $x_1, x_2, \ldots, x_N$ be a sample of intensity values for a pixel. Given this sample, we can obtain an estimate of the probability density function of the pixel intensity at any intensity value using kernel density estimation using (3.9). This estimate can be generalized to use color features or other high dimensional features by using kernel products as

$$\Pr(x_t) = \frac{1}{N} \sum_{i=1}^{N} \prod_{j=1}^{d} K_{\sigma_j}(x_{t_j} - x_{i_j}), \qquad (3.11)$$

where x_t is a d dimensional color feature at time t and K_{σ_j} is a kernel function with bandwidth σ_j in the jth color space dimension.

A variety of kernel functions with different properties have been used in the literature of nonparametric estimation. Typically kernel functions are symmetric and unimodal functions that fall off to zero rapidly away from the center, i.e., the kernel function should have finite local support and points beyond certain window will have no contribution. The Gaussian function is typically used as a kernel for its continuity, differentiability and locality properties although it violates the finite support criterion [9]. Note that choosing the Gaussian as a kernel function is different from fitting the distribution to a Gaussian model (normal distribution). Here, the Gaussian is only used as a function to weight the data points. Unlike parametric fitting of a MoG, kernel density estimation is a more general approach that does not assume any specific shape for the density function.

Using this probability estimate, the pixel is considered a foreground pixel if $\Pr(x_t) < th$, where the threshold th is a global threshold over all the image that can be adjusted to achieve a desired percentage of false positives. Practically, the probability estimation in (3.11) can be calculated in a very fast way using precalculated look-up tables for the kernel function values given the intensity value difference, $(x_t - x_i)$, and the kernel function bandwidth. Moreover, a partial evaluation of the sum in (3.11) is usually sufficient to surpass the threshold at most image pixels, since most of the image is typically from the background. This allows a real-time implementation of the approach.

(a)   (b)

Fig. 3.1 Example of probability estimation using a nonparametric model. **a** Original image. **b** Estimated probability image. Reproduced with permission from [11]

Since kernel density estimation is a general approach, the estimate of (3.9) can converge to any pixel intensity density function. Here the estimate is based on the most recent N samples used in the computation. Therefore, adaptation of the model can be achieved simply by adding new samples and ignoring older samples [11], i.e., using a sliding window over time. Figure 3.1b shows the estimated background probability where brighter pixels represent lower background probability pixels.

This nonparametric technique for background subtraction was introduced in [11] and has been tested for a wide variety of challenging background subtraction problems in a variety of setups and was found to be robust and adaptive. We refer the reader to [11] for details about the approach such as details about model adaptation and false detection suppression. Figure 3.2 shows two detection results for targets in a wooded area where tree branches move heavily and the target is highly occluded. Figure 3.3 top shows the detection results using an omni-directional camera. The targets are camouflaged and walking through the woods. Figure 3.3 bottom shows the detection result for a rainy day where the background model adapts to account for different rain and lighting conditions.

One major issue that needs to be addressed when using kernel density estimation technique is the choice of suitable kernel bandwidth (scale). Theoretically, as the number of samples reaches infinity, the choice of the bandwidth is insignificant and the estimate will approach the actual density. Practically, since only a finite number of samples are used and the computation must be performed in real time, the choice of suitable bandwidth is essential. a too small bandwidth will lead to a ragged density estimate, while a too wide bandwidth will lead to an over-smoothed density estimate [7, 9]. Since the expected variations in pixel intensity over time are different from one location to another in the image, a different kernel bandwidth is used for each pixel. Also, a different kernel bandwidth is used for each color channel. In [11] a procedure was proposed for estimating the kernel bandwidth for each pixel as a function of the median of absolute differences between consecutive frames. In [40] an adaptive approach for estimation of kernel bandwidth was proposed. Parag et al. [42] proposed an approach using boosting to evaluate different kernel bandwidth choices for bandwidth selection.

Fig. 3.2 Example background subtraction detection results: *Left*: original frames, *right*: detection results

3.3.2.1 KDE-Background Practice and Other Nonparametric Models

One of the drawbacks of the KDE background model is the requirement to store a large number of history samples for each pixel. In KDE literature many approaches was proposed to avoid storing a large number of samples. Within the context of background modeling, Piccardi and Jan [44] proposed an efficient mean-shift approach mean-shift to estimate the modes of a pixel's history PDF then a few number of Gaussians was used to model the PDF. Mean-shift is a nonparametric iterative mode seeking procedure [2, 4, 15]. With the same goal of reducing memory requirement, Han et al. [19] proposed a sequential kernel density estimation approach where variable bandwidth mean-shift was used to detect the density modes. Unlike MoG methods where the number of Gaussian is fixed, technique such as [19, 44] can adaptively estimate a variable number of modes to represent the density, therefore keeping the flexibility of a nonparametric model while achieving the efficiency of a parametric model.

Efficient implementation of KDE can be achieved through building look-up tables for the kernel function values, which facilitates real-time performance. Fast Gauss Transform has been proposed for efficient computation of KDE [10], however, the Fast Gauss Transform is only justifiable with a large number of samples required for the density estimation as well as the need for estimation at many pix-

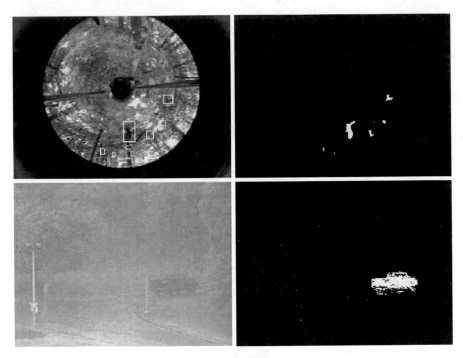

Fig. 3.3 *Top*: Detection of camouflaged targets from an omni-directional camera. *Bottom*: Detection result for a rainy day. Reproduced with permission from [11]

els in batches. For example, Fast Gauss implementation was effectively used in a layered background representation [43].

Many variations have been suggested to the basic nonparametric KDE background model. In practice, nonparametric KDE has been used at the pixel level as well as at the region level or in a domain-range representation to model a scene background. For example, in [43] a layered representation was used to model the scene background where the distribution of each layer is modeled using KDE. Such layered representation facilitates detecting the foreground under static or dynamic background and in the presence of nominal camera motion. In [49] KDE was used in a joint domain-range representation of image pixel (r, g, b, x, y), which exploits the spatial correlation between neighboring pixels. Parag et al. [42] proposed an approach for feature selection for the KDE framework where boosting based ensemble learning was used to combine different features. The approach also can be used to evaluate different kernels bandwidth choices for bandwidth selection. Recently, Sheikh et al. [50] used a KDE approach in a joint domain-range representation within a foreground/background segmentation framework from freely moving camera as will be discussed in Sect. 3.6.

In [36] a biologically inspired nonparametric background subtraction approach was proposed where a self-organizing Artificial Neural Network (ANN) model was used to model the pixel process. Each pixel is modeled with a sample arranged in a shared 2D grid of nodes where each node is represented with a weight vector with the same dimensionality as the input observation. An incoming pixel observation is mapped to the node whose weights are most similar to the input where a threshold function is used to decide background/foreground. The weights of each node are updated at each new frame using a recursive filter similar to (3.3). An interesting feature of that approach is that the shared 2D grid of nodes allows the spatial relationships between pixels to be taken into account at both the detection and update phases.

3.4 Moving Shadow Suppression

A background subtraction process on gray scale images, or on color images without carefully selecting the color space, is bound to detect the shadows of moving objects along with the objects themselves. While shadows of static objects can typically be adapted in the background process, shadows casted by moving object, i.e., dynamic shadows, constitute a sever challenge for foreground segmentation. Since the goal of background subtraction is to obtain accurate segmentation of moving foreground regions for further processing, it is highly desirable to detect such foreground regions without casted shadow attached to them. This is particularly important for human motion analysis, since shadows attached to silhouettes would cause problems in fitting body limbs and estimating body poses; consider the example shown in Fig. 3.4. Therefore, extensive researches have addressed the detection/suppression of moving (dynamic) shadows.

Avoiding the detection of shadows or suppressing the detected shadows can be achieved in color sequences by understanding how shadows affect color images. This is also useful to achieve a background model that is invariant to illumination changes. Cast shadows have a dark part (umbra) where a light source is totally occluded, and a soft transitional part (penumbra) where light is partially occluded [52]. In visual surveillance scenarios, the penumbra shadows are common since diffused and indirect light is common in indoor and outdoor scenes. Penumbra shadows can be characterized by a lower value of intensity while preserving the chromaticity of the background, i.e. achromatic shadows. Most research on detecting shadows have focused on achromatic shadows [5, 11, 23].

Let us consider the RGB color space, which is a typical output of a color camera. The brightness of a pixel is a linear combination of the RGB channels, here denoted by I

$$I = w_r R + w_g G + w_b B. \tag{3.12}$$

When an object casts a shadow on a pixel, less light reaches that pixel and the pixel seems darker. Therefore, a shadow casted on a pixel can be characterized by a change of in brightness of that pixel such that

$$\tilde{I} = \alpha I, \tag{3.13}$$

where $\tilde{I}$ is the pixel's new brightness. Similar effect happens under certain changes in illumination, e.g., turning on/off the lights. Here $\alpha < 1$ for the case of shadow, which means the pixel is darker under shadow, while $\alpha > 1$ for the case of high-lights, the pixel seems brighter. A change in the brightness of a pixel will affect all the three color channels R, G, and B. Therefore, any background model based on the RGB space, and of course gray scale imagery, is bound to detect moving shadows as foreground regions.

So, which color spaces are invariant or less sensitive to shadows and highlights? For simplicity, let us assume that the effect of the change in a pixel brightness is the same in the three channels. Therefore, the observed colors are αR, αG, αB. Any chromaticity measure of a pixel where the effect of the α factor is canceled, is in fact invariant to shadows and highlights. For example, in [11] chromaticity coordinates based on normalized RGB were used for modeling the background. Given three color variables, R, G and B, the chromaticity coordinates are defined by [35]

$$r = \frac{R}{R+G+B}, \qquad g = \frac{G}{R+G+B}, \qquad b = \frac{B}{R+G+B}. \qquad (3.14)$$

Obviously only two coordinates are enough to represent the chromaticity since $r + g + b = 1$. The above equation describes a central projection to the plane $R + G + B = 1$.[1] It can be easily seen that the chromaticity variables r, g, b are invariant to shadows and highlights (according to our assumption) since the α factor does not have an effect on them. Figure 3.4 shows the results of detection using both (R, G, B) space and (r, g) space. The figure shows that using the chromaticity coordinates allows detection of the target without detecting its shadow.

Some other color spaces also have chromaticity variable that are invariant to shadows and highlights in the same way. For example, the reader can verify that the Hue and Saturation variables in the HSV color space are invariant to the α factor and thus insensitive to shadows and highlights, while the Value variable, which represents the brightness, is variant to them. Therefore, the HSV color space has been used in some background subtraction algorithms that suppress shadows, e.g. [5]. Similarly, HSL, CIE xy spaces have the same property. On the other hand color spaces such as YUV, YIQ, YCbCr are not invariant to shadows and highlights since they are just linear transformations from the RGB space.

Although using chromaticity coordinates helps in the suppression of shadows, they have the disadvantage of losing lightness information. Lightness is related to the differences in whiteness, blackness and grayness between different objects [18]. For example, consider the case where the target wears a white shirt and walks against a gray background. In this case there is no color information. Since both white and gray have the same chromaticity coordinates, the target will not be detected using only chromaticity variables. In fact in the r, g space all the gray line (R = G = B) projects to the point $(1/3, 1/3)$ in the space, similarly for CIE xy. Therefore, there is no escape of using a brightness variable! In [11] a third "lightness" variable $s = R +$

---

[1]This is analogous to the transformation used to obtain CIE xy chromaticity space from CIE XYZ color space. The CIE XYZ color space is a linear transformation to the RGB space [1]. The chromaticity space defined by the variables r, g is therefore analogous to the CIE xy chromaticity space.

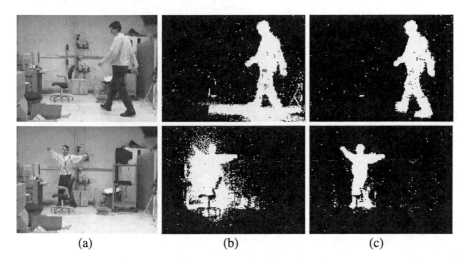

Fig. 3.4 a Original frames, **b** detection using (R, G, B) color space, **c** detection using chromaticity coordinates (r, g) and the lightness variable s. Reproduced with permission from [11]

$G + B$ was used besides r, g. While the chromaticity variables r, g are not expected to change under shadow, s is expected to change within limits which correspond to the expected shadows and highlights in the scene.

Most approaches for shadow suppression relies on the above reasoning of separating the chromaticity distortion from brightness distortion where each of these distortions are treated differently, e.g. [5, 11, 23, 25, 32]. In [23] both brightness and color distortions are defined using a chromatic cylinder model. By projecting an observed pixel color to the vector defined by that pixel's background value in the RGB color space (chromaticity line), the color distortion is defined as the orthogonal distance, while the projection defines the brightness distortion. Here a single Gaussian background model is assumed. These two measures were used to classify an observation to either background, foreground, shadows or highlights. Notice that the orthogonal distance between an observed pixel's RGB color and a chromaticity line is affected by brightness of that pixel, while the distance measured in the r–g space (or xy space) corresponds to the angles between the observed color vector and the chromaticity line, i.e., the r–g space used in [11] is a projection of a chromatic cone. In [25] a chromatic and brightness distortion model is used similar to [23, 32], however using a chromatic cone instead of a chromatic cylinder distortion model.

Another class of algorithms for shadow suppression are approaches that depend on image gradient to model the scene background. The idea is that texture information in the background will be consistent under shadow, hence using the image gradient as a feature will be invariant to cast shadows, except at the shadow boundary. These approaches utilize a background edge or gradient model besides the chromaticity model to detect shadows, e.g. [25, 26, 38, 61]. In [25] a multistage approach was proposed to detect chromatic shadows. In the first stage potential shadow region are detected by fusing color (using the invariant chromaticity cone model described above) and gradient information. In the second stage pixels in these regions are classified using different cues including spatial and temporal analysis of chrominance, brightness, and texture distortion; and a measure of diffused sky lighting denoted by "bluish effect". The approach can successfully detect chromatic shadows.

3.5 Tradeoffs in Background Maintenance

As discussed in Sect. 3.1 there are different changes that can occur in a scene background, which can be classified to: Illumination changes, Motion Changes, Structural Changes. The goal of background maintenance is to be able to cope with these changes and keep an updated version of the scene background model. In parametric background models, recursive update in the form of (3.3) (or some variant of it) is typically used for background maintenance, e.g. [30, 34, 53]. In nonparametric models, the sample of each pixel history is updated continuously to achieve adaptability [11, 40]. These recursive updates along with careful choice of the color space are typically enough to deal with both the illumination changes and motion changes previously described.

The most challenging case is where changes are introduced to the background (objects moved in or from the background) denoted here by "Structural Changes". For example, if a vehicle came and parked in the scene. A background process should detect such a car but should also adapt it to the background model in order to be able to detect other targets that might pass in front of it. Similarly if a vehicle that was already part of the scene moved out, a false detection 'hole' will appear in the scene where that vehicle was parked. There are many examples similar to these scenarios. Toyama et al. [56] denoted these situations "sleeping person" and "walking person" scenarios.

Here we point out two interwound tradeoffs that associate with maintaining any background model

Background update rate: The speed or the frequency in which a background model gets updated highly influence the performance of the process. In most parametric models, the learning rate α in (3.3) controls the speed in which the model adapts to changes. In nonparametric models, the frequency in which new samples are added to the model has the same effect. Fast model update makes the model able to rapidly adapt to scene changes such as fast illumination changes, which leads to high sensitivity in foreground/background classification. However, the model can also adapt to targets in the scene if the update is done blindly in all pixels or errors occurs in masking out foreground regions. Slow update is safer to avoid integrating any transient changes to the model. However, the classifier will lose its sensitivity in case of fast scene changes.

Selective vs. blind update: Given a new pixel observation, there are two alternative mechanisms to update a background model: 1) Selective Update: update the model only if the pixel is classified as a background sample. 2) Blind Update: just

Table 3.1 Tradeoffs in background maintenance

	Fast Update	Slow Update
Selective Update	Highest sensitivity	Less sensitivity
	Adapts to fast illumination changes	
	Bound to Deadlocks	Bound to Deadlocks
Blind Update	Adapts to targets (more False Negatives)	Slow adaptation
	No deadlocks	No deadlocks

update the model regardless of the classification outcome. Selective update is commonly used by masking out foreground-classified pixels from the update since updating the model with foreground information would lead to increased false negative, e.g., holes in the detected targets. The problem with selective update is that any incorrect detection decision will result in persistent incorrect detection later, which is a deadlock situation, as denoted by Karmann et al. [30]. For example, if a tree branch is displaced and stayed fixed in the new location for a long time, it would be continually detected. This is what leads to the 'Sleeping/Walking person' problems as noticed in [56].

Blind update does not suffer from this deadlock situations since it does not involve any update decisions; it allows intensity values that do not belong to the background to be added to the model. This might lead to more false negatives as targets erroneously become part of the model. This effect can be reduced if the update rate is slow.

The interwound effects of these two tradeoffs is shown in Table 3.1. Most background models chose a selective update approach and try to avoid the effects of detection errors by using a slow update rate. However, this is bound to deadlocks. In [11] the use of a combination of two models was proposed: a short-term model (selective and fast) and a long-term model (blind and slow). This combination tries to achieve high sensitivity and, in the same time, avoids deadlocks.

Several approaches have been proposed for dealing with specific scenarios with structural changes. The main problem is that dealing with such changes requires a higher level of reasoning about what are the objects causing such structural changes (vehicle, person, animal) and what should be done with them, which mostly depends on the application. Such high level of reasoning is typically beyond the design goal of the background process, which is mainly a low level process that knows only about pixels' appearance.

The idea of using multiple background models was further developed by Kim et al. in [33] to address scene structure changes in an elegant way. In that work, a layered background model was used where a long-term background model is used besides several multiple short-term background models that capture temporary changes in the background. An object that comes to the scene and stops is represented by a short-term background (layer). Therefore, if a second object passes in front of the stopped object, it will also be detected and represented as a layer as well. Figure 3.5 shows an overview of the approach and detection results.

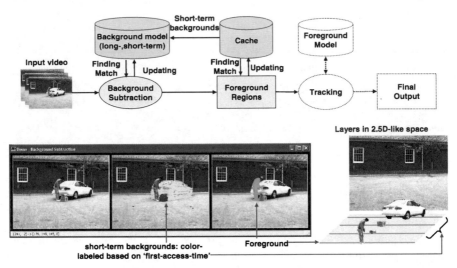

Fig. 3.5 An overview of Kim et al.'s approach [33] with short-term background layers: the foreground and the short-term backgrounds can be interpreted in a different temporal order. Reproduced with permission from [33]

3.6 Background Subtraction from a Moving Camera

A fundamental limitation for background subtraction techniques is the assumption of stationary camera. Several approaches have been suggested to alleviate this constraint and develop background subtraction techniques that can work with moving camera under some motion constraints. Rather than a pixel-level representation, a region-based representation of the scene background can help tolerate some degree of camera motion, e.g. [43]. In particular, the case of pan-tilt-zoom (PTZ) camera has been addressed because of its importance in surveillance applications. If the camera motion is a rotation with no translation (or close to zero baseline), camera motion can be modeled by a homography and image mosaicing approaches can be used to built a background model. There have been several approaches for building a background model from a panning camera based on building an image mosaic and the use of a MoG model, e.g. [39, 45, 47]. Alternatively, in [57] a representation of the scene background as a finite set of images on a virtual polyhedron is used to construct images of the scene background at any arbitrary pan-tilt-zoom setting.

Recently there have been some interests in background subtraction/foreground-background separation from freely moving cameras, e.g. [22, 29, 50]. There is a huge literature on motion segmentation [60], which exploits motion discontinuity, however, these approaches do not necessarily aim at modeling scene background and segmenting the foreground layers. Fundamentally motion segmentation by itself is not enough to separate the foreground from the background in case both of them constitutes a rigid or close to rigid motion, e.g., a car parked in the street or a person standing will have the same 3D motion w.r.t. to the camera as the rest of the scene. Similarly depth discontinuity by itself is not enough since objects of interest can be at a distance from the camera with no significant depth difference than the background.

Most notably, Sheikh et al. [50] used affine factorization to develop a framework for moving camera background subtraction. In this approach, trajectories of sparse image features are segmented using affine factorization [55]. A sparse representation of the background is maintained by estimating trajectory bases that span the background subspace. KDE was then used to model the appearance of the background and foreground from the sparse features. A Markov Random Field (MRF) was used to achieve the final labeling.

3.7   Conclusion and Further Reading

The statistical models for background subtraction that are described in this chapter are widely used within motion analysis of humans and other moving objects. The methods are often easy to implement and can operate in real time, making them ideal as a first processing step in many systems. However, as described above, the methods do have their limitations and a variety of different extensions have therefore been reported over the years and more can be expected in the future. Below we discuss some of these extensions.

In [56], linear prediction using the Wiener filter is used to predict pixel intensity given a recent history of values. The prediction coefficients are recomputed each frame from the sample covariance to achieve adaptivity. Linear prediction using the Kalman Filter was also used in [30, 31, 34].

Another approach to model a wide range of variations in the pixel intensity is to represent these variations as discrete states corresponding to modes of the environment, e.g., lights on/off, cloudy/sunny. A Hidden Markov Model (HMM) has been used for this purpose in [46, 54]. In [46], a three state HMM has been used to model the intensity of a pixel for traffic monitoring application where the three states correspond to the background, shadow, and foreground. The use of HMMs imposes a temporal continuity constraint on the pixel intensity, i.e., if the pixel is detected as a part of the foreground then it is expected to remain part of the foreground for a period of time before switching back to be part of the background. In [54], the topology of the HMM representing global image intensity is learned while learning the background. At each global intensity state the pixel intensity is modeled using a single Gaussian. It was shown that the model is able to learn simple scenarios like switching the lights on-off.

Intensity has been the most commonly used feature for modeling the background. Alternatively, edge features have also been used to model the background. The use of edge features to model the background is motivated by the desire to have a representation of the scene background that is invariant to illumination changes, as discussed in Sect. 3.4. In [59] foreground edges are detected by comparing the edges in each new frame with an edge map of the background which is called the background "primal sketch". The major drawback of using edge features to model the background is that it would only be possible to detect edges of foreground objects instead of the dense connected regions that result from pixel intensity based approaches. Fusion of intensity and edge information was used in [25, 26, 38, 61]. Among many other features studied, optical flow was used in [40] to help capture background dynamics. A general framework for feature selection based on boosting for background modeling was proposed in [42].

Besides pixel-based approaches, block-based approaches have also been used for modeling the background. Block matching has been extensively used for change detection between consecutive frames. In [24] each image block is fit to a second order bivariate polynomial and the remaining variations are assumed to be noise. A statistical likelihood test is then used to detect blocks with significant change. In [37] each block was represented with its median template over the background learning period and its block standard deviation. Subsequently, at each new frame, each block is correlated with its corresponding template and blocks with too much deviation relative to the measured standard deviation are considered to be foreground. The major drawback with block-based approaches is that the detection unit is a whole image block and therefore they are only suitable for coarse detection.

Background subtraction techniques can successfully deal with quasi moving background, e.g. scenes with dynamic textures. The nonparametric model using Kernel Density Estimation, described in Sect. 3.3.2, has very good performance in scenes with dynamic backgrounds, such as outdoor scenes with trees in the background. Several approaches were developed to address such dynamic scenes. In [51] an Auto Regressive Moving Average Model (ARMA) model was proposed for modeling dynamic textures. ARMA is a first order linear prediction model. In [62] an ARMA model was used for background modeling of scenes with dynamic texture where a robust Kalman filter was used to update the model. In [40] a combination of optical flow and appearance features was used within an adaptive kernel density estimation framework to deal with dynamic scenes.

References

1. Burger, W., Burge, M.: Digital Image Processing, an Algorithmic Introduction Using Java. Springer, New York (2008) [42]
2. Cheng, Y.: Mean shift, mode seeking, and clustering. IEEE Trans. Pattern Anal. Mach. Intell. **17**(8), 790–799 (1995) [39]
3. Comaniciu, D.: Nonparametric robust methods for computer vision. PhD thesis, Rutgers, The State University of New Jersey (January 2000) [37]
4. Comaniciu, D., Meer, P.: Mean shift analysis and applications. In: IEEE International Conference on Computer Vision (September 1999) [39]
5. Cucchiara, R., Grana, C., Piccardi, M., Prati, A.: Detecting moving objects, ghosts, and shadows in video streams. IEEE Trans. Pattern Anal. Mach. Intell. **25**, 1337–1342 (2003) [41, 42]
6. Dempster, A., Laird, N., Rubin, D.: Maximum likelihood from incomplete data via the em algorithm. J. R. Stat. Soc. B **39**, 1–38 (1977) [35]
7. Duda, R.O., Stork, D.G., Hart, P.E.: Pattern Classification. Wiley, New York (2000) [36,37]
8. Eghbali, H.J.: K-s test for detecting changes from Landsat imagery data. IEEE Trans. Syst. Man Cybern. **9**(1), 17–23 (1979) [32]

9. Elgammal, A.: Efficient kernel density estimation for realtime computer vision. PhD thesis, University of Maryland (2002) [37,38]

10. Elgammal, A., Duraiswami, R., Davis, L.S.: Efficient non-parametric adaptive color modeling using fast gauss transform. In: IEEE Conference on Computer Vision and Pattern Recognition (December 2001) [39]

11. Elgammal, A., Harwood, D., Davis, L.S.: Nonparametric background model for background subtraction. In: European Conference of Computer Vision (2000) [36,38,40-45]

12. Elgammal, A., Duraiswami, R., Harwood, D., Davis, L.S.: Background and foreground modeling using non-parametric kernel density estimation for visual surveillance. Proc. IEEE **90**(7), 1151–1163 (2002) [32]

13. Forsyth, D.A., Ponce, J.: Computer Vision a Modern Approach. Prentice Hall, New York (2002) [34]

14. Friedman, N., Russell, S.: Image segmentation in video sequences: A probabilistic approach. In: Conference on Uncertainty in Artificial Intelligence (1997) [32,35]

15. Fukunaga, K., Hostetler, L.D.: The estimation of the gradient of a density function, with application in pattern recognition. IEEE Trans. Inf. Theory **21**, 32–40 (1975) [39]

16. Gao, X., Boult, T.E.: Error analysis of background adaption. In: IEEE Conference on Computer Vision and Pattern Recognition (2000) [35,36]

17. Grimson, W.E.L., Stauffer, C., Romano, R., Lee, L.: Using adaptive tracking to classify and monitor activities in a site. In: IEEE Conference on Computer Vision and Pattern Recognition (1998) [35]

18. Hall, E.L.: Computer Image Processing and Recognition. Academic Press, San Diego (1979) [42]

19. Han, B., Comaniciu, D., Davis, L.: Sequential kernel density approximation through mode propagation: Applications to background modeling. In: Asian Conference on Computer Vision (2004) [39]

20. Haritaoglu, I., Harwood, D., Davis, L.S.: W4: who? when? where? what? a real time system for detecting and tracking people. In: International Conference on Face and Gesture Recognition (1998) [32]

21. Harville, M.: A framework for high-level feedback to adaptive, per-pixel, mixture-of-gaussian background models. In: European Conference on Computer Vision (2002) [36]

22. Hayman, E., Eklundh, J.O.: Statistical background subtraction for a mobile observer. In: International Conference on Computer Vision (2003) [46]

23. Horprasert, T., Harwood, D., Davis, L.S.: A statistical approach for real-time robust background subtraction and shadow detection. In: IEEE Frame-Rate Applications Workshop (1999) [41,43]

24. Hsu, Y.Z., Nagel, H.H., Rekers, G.: New likelihood test methods for change detection in image sequences. Comput. Vis. Graph. Image Process. **26**, 73–106 (1984) [48]

25. Huerta, I., Holte, M., Moeslund, T.B., Gonzalez, J.: Detection and removal of chromatic moving shadows in surveillance scenarios. In: International Conference on Computer Vision (2009) [43,48]

26. Jabri, S., Duric, Z., Wechsler, H., Rosenfeld, A.: Detection and location of people in video images using adaptive fusion of color and edge information. In: International Conference of Pattern Recognition (2000) [43,48]

27. Jain, R.C., Nagel, H.H.: On the analysis of accumulative difference pictures from image sequences of real world scenes. IEEE Trans. Pattern Anal. Mach. Intell. **1**(2), 206–213 (1979) [32]

28. Javed, O., Shafique, K., Shah, M.: A hierarchical approach to robust background subtraction using color and gradient information. In: IEEE Workshop on Motion and Video Computing (2002) [36]

29. Jin, Y.X., Tao, L.M., Di, H., Rao, N.I., Xu, G.Y.: Background modeling from a free-moving camera by multi-layer homography algorithm. In: International Conference on Image Processing (2008) [46]

30. Karmann, K.P., Brandt, A.V.: Moving object recognition using and adaptive background memory. In: Time-Varying Image Processing and Moving Object Recognition. Elsevier, Amsterdam (1990) [35,44,45,47]

31. Karmann, K.P., Brandt, A.V., Gerl, R.: Moving object segmentation based on adaptive reference images. In: Signal Processing V: Theories and Application. Elsevier, Amsterdam (1990) [35,47]

32. Kim, K., Chalidabhongse, T.H., Harwood, D., Davis, L.: Background modeling and subtraction by codebook construction. In: International Conference on Image Processing (2004) [43]

33. Kim, K., Harwood, D., Davis, L.S.: Background updating for visual surveillance. In: International Symposium on Visual Computing (2005) [45,46]

34. Koller, D., Weber, J., Huang, T., Malik, J., Ogasawara, G., Rao, B., Russell, S.: Towards robust automatic traffic scene analysis in real-time. In: International Conference of Pattern Recognition (1994) [35,44,47]

35. Levine, M.D.: Vision in Man and Machine. McGraw-Hill, New York (1985) [42]

36. Maddalena, L., Petrosino, A.: A self-organizing approach to background subtraction for visual surveillance applications. IEEE Trans. Image Process. 17(7), 1168–1177 (2008) [40]

37. Matsuyama, T., Ohya, T., Habe, H.: Background subtraction for nonstationary scenes. In: Asian Conference on Computer Vision (2000) [48]

38. Mckenna, S.J., Jabri, S., Duric, Z., Wechsler, H., Rosenfeld, A.: Tracking groups of people. Comput. Vis. Image Underst. 80, 42–56 (2000) [43,48]

39. Mittal, A., Huttenlocher, D.: Scene modeling for wide area surveillance and image synthesis. In: Computer Vision and Pattern Recognition (2000) [36,46]

40. Mittal, A., Paragios, N.: Motion-based background subtraction using adaptive kernel density estimation. In: Computer Vision and Pattern Recognition (2004) [38,44,48]

41. Neal, R.M., Hinton, G.E.: A new view of the em algorithm that justifies incremental and other variants. In: Learning in Graphical Models, pp. 355–368. Kluwer Academic, Dordrecht (1993) [35]

42. Parag, T., Elgammal, A., Mittal, A.: A framework for feature selection for background subtraction. In: IEEE Conference on Computer Vision and Pattern Recognition (June 2006) [38, 40,48]

43. Patwardhan, K., Sapiro, G., Morellas, V.: Robust foreground detection in video using pixel layers. IEEE Trans. Pattern Anal. Mach. Intell. 30, 746–751 (2008) [40]

44. Piccardi, M., Jan, T.: Mean-shift background image modelling. In: International Conferencing on Image Processing (2004) [39]

45. Ren, Y., Chua, C.S., Ho, Y.K.: Statistical background modeling for non-stationary camera. Pattern Recognit. Lett. 24(1–3), 183–196 (2003) [46]

46. Rittscher, J., Kato, J., Joga, S., Blake, A.: A probabilistic background model for tracking. In: European Conference on Computer Vision (2000) [47]

47. Rowe, S., Blake, A.: Statistical mosaics for tracking. Image Vis. Comput. 14(8), 549–564 (1996) [46]

48. Scott, D.W.: Multivariate Density Estimation. Wiley-Interscience, New York (1992) [36,37]

49. Sheikh, Y., Shah, M.: Bayesian modeling of dynamic scenes for object detection. IEEE Trans. Pattern Anal. Mach. Intell. 27, 1778–1792 (2005) [40]

50. Sheikh, Y., Javed, O., Kanade, T.: Background subtraction for freely moving cameras. In: International Conference on Computer Vision (2009) [40,46,47]

51. Soatto, S., Doretto, G., Wu, Y.: Dynamic textures. In: International Conference on Computer Vision (2001) [48]

52. Stauder, J., Mech, R., Ostermann, J.: Detection of moving cast shadows for object segmentation. IEEE Trans. Multimed. 1, 65–76 (1999) [41]

53. Stauffer, C., Grimson, W.E.L.: Adaptive background mixture models for real-time tracking. In: IEEE Conference on Computer Vision and Pattern Recognition (1999) [35,36,44]

54. Stenger, B., Ramesh, V., Paragios, N., Coetzee, F., Bouhman, J.: Topology free hidden Markov models: Application to background modeling. In: IEEE International Conference on Computer Vision (2001) [47]

55. Tomasi, C.: Shape and motion from image streams under orthography: A factorization method. Int. J. Comput. Vis. **9**, 137–154 (1992) [47]
56. Toyama, K., Krumm, J., Brumitt, B., Meyers, B.: Wallflower: Principles and practice of background maintenance. In: IEEE International Conference on Computer Vision (1999) [32,33, 44,45,47]
57. Wada, T., Matsuyama, T.: Appearance sphere: Background model for pan-tilt-zoom camera. In: International Conference on Pattern Recognition (1996) [46]
58. Wern, C.R., Azarbayejani, A., Darrell, T., Pentland, A.: Pfinder: Real-time tracking of human body. IEEE Trans. Pattern Anal. Mach. Intell. (1997) [32,35]
59. Yang, Y.H., Levine, M.D.: The background primal sketch: An approach for tracking moving objects. Mach. Vis. Appl. **5**, 17–34 (1992) [47]
60. Zappella, L., Lladó, X., Salvi, J.: Motion segmentation: A review. In: Conference on Artificial Intelligence Research and Development, Amsterdam, The Netherlands (2008) [46]
61. Zhang, W., Fang, X.Z., Yang, X.: Moving cast shadows detection based on ratio edge. In: International Conference on Pattern Recognition (2006) [43,48]
62. Zhong, J., Sclaroff, S.: Segmenting foreground objects from a dynamic textured background via a robust Kalman filter. In: International Conference on Computer Vision, Washington, DC, USA (2003) [48]

Chapter 4
Figure-Ground Segmentation—Object-Based

Bastian Leibe

Abstract Tracking with a moving camera is a challenging task due to the combined effects of scene activity and egomotion. As there is no longer a static image background from which moving objects can easily be distinguished, dedicated effort must be spent on detecting objects of interest in the input images and on determining their precise extent. In recent years, there has been considerable progress in the development of approaches that apply object detection and class-specific segmentation in order to facilitate tracking under such circumstances ("tracking-by-detection"). In this chapter, we will give an overview of the main concepts and techniques used in such tracking-by-detection systems. In detail, the chapter will present fundamental techniques and current state-of-the-art approaches for performing object detection, for obtaining detailed object segmentations from single images based on top–down and bottom–up cues, and for propagating this information over time.

4.1 Introduction

As described in the previous chapter, background modeling is a powerful technique to support visual tracking. However, it is only feasible when the camera is static or when it exhibits only pan/tilt/zoom motion. In many scenarios of practical interest, cameras are mounted on a moving observer. Examples for this include automotive or mobile robotics scenarios. Here, background modeling is no longer practical, and object-based approaches are required. Object-based approaches can also be helpful for static surveillance scenarios when there is a lot of background activity, e.g., in the case of a train entering the scene and filling a considerable part of the camera's field-of-view. In such a case, pure background modeling could still extract the changed image region, but this region is no longer indicative for the location of individual objects (such as pedestrians or cars moving in front of the train).

We are therefore interested in approaches that can be used to extract object information without relying on the assumption of a static background. We can approach

B. Leibe (✉)
UMIC Research Centre, RWTH Aachen University, Aachen, Germany
e-mail: leibe@umic.rwth-aachen.de

T.B. Moeslund et al. (eds.), *Visual Analysis of Humans*,
DOI 10.1007/978-0-85729-997-0_4, © Springer-Verlag London Limited 2011

this problem at different levels of detail. From the tracking side, the primary purposes of figure-ground segmentation are (a) to detect new objects, (b) to classify them into a number of categories of interest, and (c) to continue tracking them. This functionality can already be achieved if the only information available are detection bounding boxes returned by an object detector, as demonstrated by a number of successful tracking-by-detection systems [2, 17, 46, 75]. After briefly outlining the challenges of the tracking-by-detection task, we will therefore give an overview over current object detection approaches and their underlying representations, capabilities, and limitations.

In many cases, however, more detailed information about an object's appearance is required in order to disambiguate data association in difficult situations (such as after temporary occlusions). In addition, a detailed segmentation is helpful for many later processing steps, such as finer-grained body pose analysis and articulated tracking. We will therefore present approaches that can be used to obtain an object-based figure-ground segmentation as a result of the recognition process and to propagate this information over time. Finally, we will showcase several state-of-the-art tracking approaches from the literature and discuss how they make use of the concepts presented in this chapter.

4.2 Challenges and Outline

The basic idea behind tracking-by-detection approaches is to apply a detector for the target object category to each frame of an image sequence and to connect the resulting detection responses into trajectories (see Fig. 4.1).

This task brings with it the following main challenges. First, the presence of new objects of interest needs to be reliably detected, such that new tracks can be initiated. For this, we require a reliable and efficient object detector. Section 4.3 will present a choice of state-of-the-art detectors that can be used for this purpose and discuss their relative merits. Once an object or person is tracked, we need to determine whether new detections correspond to the same object and should be associated to its trajectory, or whether they show a different object. For this, we need to build up an

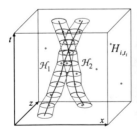

Fig. 4.1 In tracking-by-detection, an object detector is applied to each frame of an image sequence, and the resulting detection responses are grouped into trajectories. Reproduced with permission from [17, 45] ©2009/2010 IEEE

appearance model, which in turn requires figure-ground segmentation. Approaches for this are discussed in Sect. 4.4. Finally, this segmentation needs to be maintained and robustly updated over time in order to limit the amount of drift. Section 4.5 will describe several strategies that have been proposed to achieve this goal.

4.3 Object Detection Approaches

Object category detection has made immense progress in recent years [20, 22]. This holds in particular for pedestrian detection, for which a large range of approaches have been proposed [13, 25, 29, 43, 47, 67, 75]. Performance has been refined over the years through large-scale evaluations (e.g., [15]), and real-time CPU [14, 76] and GPU implementations are becoming available [56, 71]. In the following, we give an overview over the different detection approaches and their underlying representations.

4.3.1 Sliding-Window Object Detection

The simplest object detector design is the classic *sliding-window* scheme, in which a fixed-size detection window is moved over the entire image and a binary classifier is evaluated at each window location. In order to detect objects of different sizes, either the image or the detection window is rescaled and the same procedure is repeated. Thus, object detection is reduced to a set of local yes/no classification decisions, for which powerful machine learning methods can be employed. In particular, Support Vector Machines (SVMs) [68], AdaBoost [28], and Random Forest classifiers [1] have been used successfully in the past.

The large number of classification decisions associated with this scheme (depending on image size and sampling density, several 10–100 k window locations need to be evaluated for each image) places heavy constraints on the classifier's run-time and false-positive rate. For this reason, current detectors focus primarily on simple classifiers, such as linear SVMs (e.g., [13]), or make heavy use of cascading strategies [24, 69, 70]). In such a cascade, a sequence of progressively more complex classifiers is evaluated at each window location. Each cascade stage is designed to reject a high percentage of all negative examples entering this stage, while keeping all positive examples and passing them to the next stage. As a result, most window locations can be very efficiently rejected by considering only the first few cascade stages, while more effort is only spent on the most promising window locations.

Despite its simplicity, the sliding-window approach has become very popular and most current state-of-the-art detectors are based on this scheme. In the following, we will examine some of the feature representations that are used in state-of-the-art detectors with a focus on person detection.

4.3.2 Holistic Detector Representations

The simplest approach is to represent each detection window by a single feature vector encoding the entire window content. The main challenge here is to come up with a representation that is sufficiently discriminative to capture the varying appearance of the target object class and to reliably distinguish it from the background. Early representations, such as vectors of pixel intensities [54] or Haar wavelet templates [55] met only with limited success. The Histograms of Oriented Gradients (HOG) representation [13] proved more successful. Originally proposed in 2005, it is still the basis of many current detectors and has been shown to be superior to many other choices in recent large-scale evaluations [15].

The HOG representation [13] extends the idea of the popular local Scale-Invariant Feature Transform (SIFT) descriptor [49] to represent entire objects. It subdivides the detection window into a regular grid of cells (typically of size 4×4 or 8×8 pixels). For each cell, it computes a histogram of gradient orientations (typically using 9 orientation bins). Blocks of 2×2 cells are combined for contrast normalization. This representation has several advantages: (1) The use of gradients, instead of raw pixel intensities, makes the approach more robust to illumination changes. (2) The histogram representation summarizes pixel contributions over a certain region and thus adds robustness to small shifts and scale variations. (3) The subdivision into a grid of cells again adds localized information and makes the representation more discriminative than a single histogram. (4) The block normalization, finally, compensates for local contrast changes.

In order to make the feature extraction robust, it is important to limit the effects of noise and quantization as well as possible. Therefore, each pixel's contribution is weighted by its gradient magnitude and by a Gaussian centered on the entire block (so that pixels closer to the block's center get more weight). In addition, each pixel's contribution is distributed to all neighboring cells and orientation bins using trilinear interpolation. The contrast normalization is performed in two steps, as in [49], first normalizing the concatenated feature vector to unit length, then clipping each dimension to a maximum value of 0.2, and then again normalizing to unit length. This reduces the effect of overly strong gradients, which are often due to lighting effects.

Finally, all blocks in the detection window are concatenated into a single feature vector, which is again normalized to unit length. The original HOG representation for pedestrian detection uses 7×15 blocks (corresponding to 8×16 cells) and thus results in a feature vector with $7 \times 15 \times 4 \times 9 = 3780$ dimensions. The resulting feature vectors are then combined with a linear SVM classifier for efficient sliding-window classification. A learned SVM template for pedestrians is shown in Fig. 4.2a.

4.3.3 Part-Based Detectors

A drawback of holistic representations is that, since they do not explicitly model local variations in object structure (e.g., from body parts in different articulations),

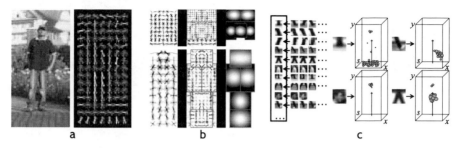

Fig. 4.2 Examples of popular detection models: **a** the window-based HOG representation by [13]; **b** the Deformable Part Model by [25, 26]; **c** the feature-based Implicit Shape Model [43]. Reproduced with permission from: (a) [13] ©2005 IEEE, (b) [26] ©2010 IEEE, (c) [43] ©2008 IEEE

they typically need a large number of training examples in order to learn the corresponding changes in global appearance. One way to model these local variations is by representing objects as an assembly of parts. Early part-based detectors [32, 51, 53, 73] use a set of manually defined appearance parts, represented by SVM or boosting classifiers, and learn a separate configuration classifier for their combination.

A more scalable solution has been proposed by Felzenszwalb et al. [25]. Their Deformable Part-based Model (DPM) has been used with wide success for a number of object categories in the PASCAL VOC Challenges [22]. The DPM consists of a global *root filter* (similar to the HOG descriptor) and a set of typically 5–6 *part filters*, extracted at a higher resolution (see Fig. 4.2b). The part locations may vary relative to the root filter location according to a Pictorial Structure [23] deformation model. This model defines the score of an object hypothesis as the sum of the individual filter scores minus the deformation cost. Given the root filter location p_0 and part filter locations $p_1, \ldots, p_n$, this score is expressed as

$$score(p_0, \ldots, p_n) = \underbrace{\sum_{i=0}^{n} \mathbf{F}_i \cdot \phi(H, p_i)}_{\text{root \& part filter scores}} - \underbrace{\sum_{i=1}^{n} \mathbf{d}_i \cdot \left[dx_i, dy_i, dx_i^2, dy_i^2 \right]^T}_{\text{deformation cost}}, \quad (4.1)$$

where the $\mathbf{F}_i$ are the learned root and part filters (see Fig. 4.2b), $\phi(H, p_i)$ is the corresponding region from the HOG-like feature pyramid H at part location p_i, $\mathbf{d}_i$ is a part-specific coefficient vector that defines the deformation cost function, and (dx_i, dy_i) denotes the displacement of the ith part relative to its anchor position.

Both the part appearances and their location distributions are learned automatically from training data. For this, [25, 26] propose a *latent SVM* formulation, which tries to optimize the part locations for each training image independently in order to arrive at a compact and discriminative model. The model and learning procedure are explained in more detail in Chap. 12. Figure 4.2b shows the models learned with this procedure for multiple aspects of pedestrians. As can be seen, the learned linear SVM templates are readily interpretable, showing the human contour and body part locations used in the corresponding detector.

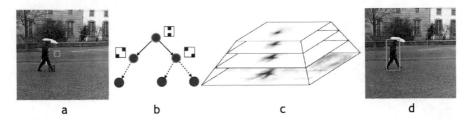

a   b   c   d

Fig. 4.3 Visualization of the Hough Forest recognition procedure from [29]. Each patch in the test image **a** is processed by a random forest classifier **b**. The activated leaves in the forest then cast probabilistic votes for the object center, which are collected in a Hough space **c**. Maxima in this Hough space correspond to object hypotheses **d**. By processing the image at several different scales, objects of different sizes can be detected. Reproduced with permission from: (a, d) [29] ©2009 IEEE, (b, c) [58]

4.3.4 Local Feature-Based Detectors

Part-based detectors are based on the assumption that the object consists of typically 5–7 semantically meaningful parts, which can be detected in each object instance. In contrast, local feature-based detectors model an object category as an assembly of potentially 1000s of local features, only a subset of which are active at any point in time. This notion has been made popular by the Implicit Shape Model (ISM) by Leibe & Schiele [43, 47], which consist of a codebook of prototypical local features ("visual words"), each of which has a stored location distribution relative to the object center (see Fig. 4.2c). For object detection, local features extracted at interest point locations are matched to the appearance codebook and then cast votes for potential object center locations in a probabilistic extension of the Generalized Hough transform. While the original ISM adopted a purely representative model based on sparsely sampled local features, several extensions have in the meantime been proposed to incorporate discriminative training [29, 50], densely sampled features [29], and improved non-maximum suppression strategies [6].

In particular the Hough Forest extension by Gall & Lempitsky [29] has been quite successful (see Fig. 4.3). This approach does not rely on interest points, but samples the image densely with a small (typically 16×16 pixel) window. At each window location, it classifies the window content into a large set of visual words using a fast Random Decision Forest classifier [1]. Each visual word, represented by a leaf node of one of the randomized trees, carries a list of stored object center locations $\mathscr{D}$ learned from training data. Whenever the leaf is activated, it casts Hough votes for possible object center locations (similar to the ISM voting procedure). Let $\mathbf{f}$ be an image patch extracted at location λ. This patch is passed through a Hough tree, ending up in leaf L (corresponding to one of the visual words used in the ISM). When leaf L is activated, it casts votes for a possible object center at positions $\mathbf{x}$ with probabilities $p(\mathbf{x}|\lambda, L)$. Those probabilities are estimated by the proportion C_L of object patches that were stored in leaf L, divided by the total number of patches $|\mathscr{D}_L|$ for this leaf. Extending the case to a forest with T trees, the voting procedure can be formally expressed as:

$$p(\mathbf{x}|\lambda, \mathbf{f}) = \sum_{t=1}^{T} p(\mathbf{x}|\lambda, \mathscr{L}_t)$$

$$= \sum_{t=1}^{T} \left[\frac{1}{|\mathscr{D}_{L_t}|} \sum_{\mathbf{d}_i \in \mathscr{D}_{L_t}} \exp \left\{ \frac{\|(\lambda - \mathbf{x}) - \mathbf{d}_i\|^2}{2\sigma^2} \right\} \right] \cdot C_{L_t}. \qquad (4.2)$$

All votes from all trees are accumulated in a Hough voting space, and local maxima from this space are extracted as object detection hypotheses. In contrast to the original ISM, Hough Forests, however, only vote for a single-object scale and consequently need to be applied to several downscaled versions of the image in sequence (Fig. 4.3c). The combination of discriminative training and dense feature sampling leads to improved detection performance, which has been shown to be on par with HOG detectors for several object categories [29, 57].

4.3.5 Use for Tracking-by-Detection

Each of the detector types discussed above can reach performance levels that are sufficient to enable tracking-by-detection applications. In particular, the part-based detector by Wu & Nevatia [73] has been demonstrated successfully for pedestrian tracking in [75]. ISM detectors have been successfully used for pedestrian and multi-view car tracking in [16, 41, 46]. Ess et al. [17] have compared ISM, HOG, and DPM detectors for street-level pedestrian tracking, where they have found HOG to perform best in cases where pedestrians occur mostly in frontal views, whereas the part-based and feature-based detectors perform better in side views, where HOG's holistic representation is no longer sufficient. In addition, recent work from our group suggests that Hough Forest detectors can reach similar performance levels as HOG on frontal views and may thus be a viable alternative [58].

4.4 Figure-Ground Segmentation

A major challenge in tracking-by-detection is to associate each new detection to the correct object track, while simultaneously discarding false positive detections. In order to perform this data association reliably, more detailed information about the tracked object needs to be extracted. In particular, color models are often used to support data association and disambiguate multiple candidate detections. However, a difficulty here is that the appearance models should only be computed over the object region, while the object detector typically just returns a bounding box containing also background structure. For reliable tracking, it is therefore advantageous to perform a further object segmentation step based on the detection results. In addition, a pixel-accurate segmentation is also useful as input for further processing steps, such as detailed body pose analysis and articulated tracking. In the following, we will therefore give an overview over different object guided segmentation approaches that can be used for this purpose.

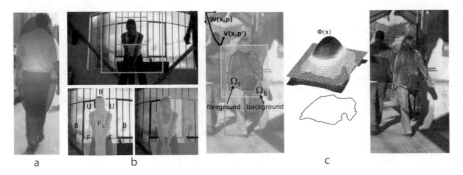

a   b   c

Fig. 4.4 Examples of figure-ground segmentation approaches that start from detection bounding boxes: **a** an elliptical prior as used in [19]; **b** the GrabCut-based segmentation refinement used in [27]; **c** the level-set segmentation used in [52]. Reproduced with permission from: (a, c) [19, 52], (b) [27] ©2008 IEEE

4.4.1 Bounding Box Priors

The simplest approach is to represent the object shape by a fixed-sized ellipse inscribed in the detection bounding box, as shown in Fig. 4.4a. Such an approach has been used successfully for pedestrian tracking in [16, 17]. In order not to include background structures between a person's legs, the ellipse used in [16, 17] focuses on the upper body, extending just slightly below the person's behinds (see Fig. 4.4a for a visualization). This placement constitutes a compromise between the desire to incorporate as much of the person's appearance as possible and the difficulty to accurately capture the shape of the articulated legs.

4.4.2 Bottom–Up Segmentation Refinement

Clearly, however, a more detailed segmentation is preferable. Starting from a detection bounding box, a set of pixels can usually be identified that clearly belong to the object (e.g., from an elliptical prior region as discussed above). Those pixels can be used to estimate the object's color distribution; other pixels that are clearly outside the object yield an estimate for the background distribution. Those two distributions can serve as input for a bottom–up segmentation procedure that tries to refine the object's contour. Such a refinement step has been proposed by [27] as an initialization for body pose estimation using the popular GrabCut segmentation approach [60]. GrabCut uses a Conditional Random Field (CRF) formulation in order to combine per-pixel appearance cues with neighborhood relations that encourage the final contour to follow color discontinuities. A fixed region inside the bounding box serves as an initialization to learn the object appearance model, while the region around the bounding box border is sampled to learn the background model. The segmentation is then performed in several iterations using graph cuts, where the appearance models are updated after each iteration (Fig. 4.4b).

A similar approach has been used in [7, 52] based on level set segmentations (see Fig. 4.4c). Here, the level set contour is initialized from a fixed-sized rectangular shape relative to the detection bounding box (using a face detector in [7] and a person detector in [52]) and it is evolved toward the object's contour for a number of iterations.

In both cases, the segmentation is performed in a bottom–up fashion. Its initialization region is given by a detection bounding box, but the subsequent segmentation process does not use any prior knowledge about the expected object shape. This makes it widely applicable to different object categories and articulations, but it also means that the segmentation process cannot take advantage of any specific knowledge of the target category. In addition, the bottom–up segmentation may get confused by object shadows, which may cause an erroneous estimate of the background pixel distribution. As a result, we run the risk of obtaining incomplete or overextended segmentations, e.g., cutting off a person's head or legs when the clothing colors are sufficiently different. In the following, we present approaches to refine this segmentation based on top–down cues (please also refer to the previous chapter for dedicated shadow removal approaches).

4.4.3 Class-Specific Top–Down Segmentation

An alternative approach is to estimate class-specific segmentation based on the detection result. This is possible using feature-based detectors such as the ISM or Hough Forests. As shown in [42, 43], the votes corresponding to a local maximum in the Hough space can be back-projected to the image in order to propagate top–down information to the patches they were originating from. This process can be used to infer local figure-ground labels [43, 44], object part annotations, or even depth maps or surface orientations from a single image [64].

In order to use this capability, the object detector needs to be provided with training examples annotated with figure-ground segmentations (or part labels, etc.). While those involve more annotation effort than simple bounding box annotations, they can in the meantime be obtained quite cheaply using, e.g., Amazon's Mechanical Turk [62].

The resulting procedure is quite easy to implement. Each vote v_j contributing to a Hough space maximum h is back-projected to its originating patch $\mathbf{f}$, augmented with a local figure-ground label $Seg(v_j)$. We can then obtain the *figure* and *ground* probabilities for each pixel $\mathbf{p}$ by averaging over all patches $\mathbf{f}_i$ containing this pixel and summing the back-projected figure-ground labels, weighted by the weight of the corresponding vote w_{v_j}.

$$
\begin{aligned}
p(\mathbf{p} = fig|h) &= \frac{1}{z} \sum_{\mathbf{f}_i \ni \mathbf{p}} \frac{1}{|\mathbf{f}_i|} \sum_{v_j \in votes(\mathbf{f}_i)} w_{v_j} Seg(v_j) \\
p(\mathbf{p} = gnd|h) &= \frac{1}{z} \sum_{\mathbf{f}_i \ni \mathbf{p}} \frac{1}{|\mathbf{f}_i|} \sum_{v_j \in votes(\mathbf{f}_i)} w_{v_j} (1 - Seg(v_j)) \\
z &= \sum_{\mathbf{f}_i \ni \mathbf{p}} \sum_{v_j \in votes(\mathbf{f}_i)} w_{v_j} .
\end{aligned}
\tag{4.3}
$$

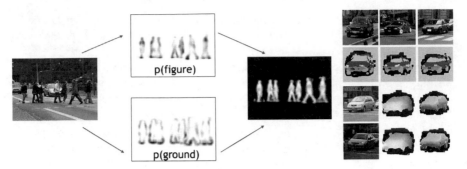

Fig. 4.5 (*Left*) Class-specific top–down segmentation procedure, as used in the ISM [43]. (*Right*) As shown by [64], this procedure can be extended in order to infer also other kinds of meta-information, including part-label annotations (*top*), depth maps, or surface orientations (*bottom*). Reproduced with permission from [58, 65]

As shown in [42, 43], this results in the correct probabilities. In practice, the top–down procedure thus boils down to a simple weighted summation of figure-ground patches, which can be implemented very efficiently on the GPU. Example results are shown in Fig. 4.5.

4.4.4 Combinations

Naturally, the advantages of top–down and bottom–up segmentation processes should be combined. Several approaches have been proposed toward this goal. Currently, MRFs and Conditional Random Fields (CRFs) seem to be the most promising direction, as they allow to easily integrate class-specific per-pixel information with region-based information and neighborhood constraints [36, 38–40, 61, 66].

In addition to applications for pure figure-ground segmentation (e.g., [36], a current trend is also to extend the segmentation to multi-class scene labeling [18, 38, 61, 72], in which every image pixel is assigned a label. This task can also be combined with object detection using hierarchical CRFs, which introduce higher-level nodes in order to group pixels belonging to the same object, while considering bottom–up cues at the pixel level [18, 38, 72]. As the hierarchical structure introduces loops in the CRF graph, inference in such models is, however, expensive. Ladicky et al. propose an improved formulation of this problem which can be optimized using graph cuts [39]. Their approach additionally refines object contours by a GrabCut segmentation, obtained as described in Sect. 4.4.2 (see Fig. 4.6).

4.5 Object Propagation

In a pure tracking-by-detection approach, information from the object detector is needed in every frame in order to follow each tracked person's movements. In practice, such strictness is, however, not necessary. Once an object has been detected and

Fig. 4.6 The approach by [39] combines top–down and bottom–up segmentation processes in a CRF framework. (*Left*) CRF structure; (*right*) improvement in segmentation quality when incorporating a GrabCut segmentation for each detected object bounding box. Reproduced with permission from [39]

segmented in one frame, its appearance is known to the system. Using the assumption that this appearance changes only slowly over time, one can employ simpler region-based trackers in order to maintain tracking over short periods. This idea can be used to stabilize tracking in cases where detection is not fully reliable, e.g., due to partial occlusions. In addition, it can be used to realize computational savings, since the frequency at which the expensive object detector is activated can be reduced [52].

4.5.1 Appearance-Based Tracking

Given an object detection bounding box as initialization, it is possible to employ low-level tracking approaches to maintain an object's appearance, e.g., using template-based [33], mean-shift [10, 11], level set [7, 12], or flow-based tracking [21]. This idea has been used in a number of person-tracking systems. Wu & Nevatia propose a tracking-by-detection approach in which a mean-shift tracker is used to bridge short gaps when no detection is available [74]. Everingham et al. [21] and Ren & Gu [59] employ a similar strategy to follow detected faces with a low-level tracker (a flow-based tracker in [21] and a correlation tracker in [59]). Bansal et al. also apply this idea for stereo-based pedestrian tracking, again in connection with a correlation tracker [5]. Mitzel et al. finally integrate pedestrian detection with level set tracking in a hybrid tracking framework, where most effort is taken over by the low-level tracker and the object detector is only activated for (re-)initialization [52]. They also evaluate the trade-off between detector activation frequency and resulting tracking quality, and they quantify the computational savings that can be achieved by such a combination.

4.5.2 Online Classification

An alternative to region-based tracking is to consider tracking as an online-classification problem [4, 31]. This notion has been made popular by the Online Boosting work by Grabner & Bischof [31]. Briefly stated, each object is represented

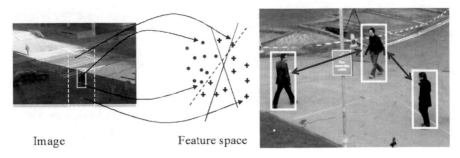

Image   Feature space

Fig. 4.7 Online classification approaches can be used to learn how to distinguish an object from the background (*left*, [4]), or to distinguish multiple tracked persons from each other (*right*, [8]). Left figure reproduced with permission from [4] ©2005 IEEE. Right figure created according to [9]

by a classifier that is trained online for the task of discriminating the object pixels from the surrounding background region (see Fig. 4.7(left)). As the object moves, both object and background appearance changes, so the classifier has to be updated after each frame. The main challenge here is to limit the amount of drift, while maintaining short update cycles for real-time processing. Combined with an object detector for automatic initialization, online-classification approaches have been successfully demonstrated for pedestrian and face tracking [4, 31].

A closely related problem is to learn online classifiers in order to reliably distinguish several tracked persons that are in close proximity (see Fig. 4.7(right)). This idea can be used in order to better separate pedestrian trajectories and avoid ID switches even under difficult viewing conditions. It has been successfully demonstrated for pedestrian tracking in [8, 37]. For both variants, the current classifiers of choice are variants of boosting [31] and randomized forests [48].

4.6 Applications

In the following, we showcase several state-of-the-art tracking approaches and discuss how they employ the concepts described in this chapter.

4.6.1 Tracking-by-Detection from a Moving Platform

Multi-person tracking from a mobile platform is an important task with many potential uses in mobile robotics and automotive applications. In such scenarios, background modeling is often not feasible and the methods described in this chapter are necessary to support tracking. A first successful mobile multi-person tracking approach has been proposed by Leibe et al. [41, 46] and later been extended by Ess et al. [17]. This approach combines tracking-by-detection with automatic ego-motion and scene geometry estimation to track multiple interacting humans in 3D world coordinates. The tracking part follows the basic idea outlined in Sect. 4.2

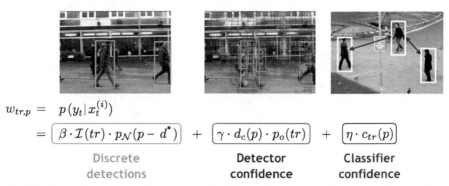

$$w_{tr,p} = p\left(y_t \mid x_t^{(i)}\right)$$

$$= \boxed{\beta \cdot \mathcal{I}(tr) \cdot p_{\mathcal{N}}(p - d^*)} + \boxed{\gamma \cdot d_c(p) \cdot p_o(tr)} + \boxed{\eta \cdot c_{tr}(p)}$$

Discrete   Detector   Classifier
detections   confidence   confidence

Fig. 4.8 The multi-person tracking approach by [8] combines discrete detections with a continuous detector confidence density and person-specific online classifiers in a particle filtering framework. Figure created according to [9]

of grouping detections into trajectory hypotheses, but supplements it by a multi-hypothesis tracking scheme based on model selection. Each trajectory is associated with a color histogram-based appearance model computed over an elliptical region inside the detection bounding boxes, as described in Sect. 4.4.1.

While originally based on the ISM detector, the tracking framework has in the meantime also been applied with the HOG and DPM detectors. All three yield good tracking performance; for street scenes with mostly frontal views of pedestrians, the HOG detector, however, seems to give the best results. Some results of the approach can be seen in Fig. 4.1(right).

4.6.2 Tracking Using the Continuous Detector Confidence

Breitenstein et al. propose an approach for tracking-by-detection from a monocular, potentially moving, uncalibrated camera [8]. Their approach is formulated in a particle filtering framework. In addition to high-confidence detections (from an ISM or HOG detector), it also uses the detector confidence, sampled densely over the entire image, as a graded observation model (see Fig. 4.8). This allows the approach to deliver stable tracking performance in situations where the detector does not yield reliable detections. In addition, the approach trains person-specific online classifiers in order to disambiguate data association and maintain person identities through occlusions. As a result of this combination, it achieves good tracking performance in a large variety of highly dynamic scenarios, including surveillance videos, webcam footage, and sports sequences.

4.6.3 Tracking-Learning-Detection

Kalal et al. [34] propose a very robust single-object tracking approach based on a combination of appearance-based low-level tracking (see Sect. 4.5.1) and tracking as online classification (see Sect. 4.5.2). The basic idea behind their approach is to derive structural constraints from confident trajectories estimated by the low-level tracker, which are then used to create hard training examples to improve an online-learned detector. Starting from an initial position, their approach first follows the object region with an adaptive Lucas–Kanade tracker and extends the trajectory as long as the normalized cross correlation (NCC) between the tracked patch and the patch selected in the first frame stays above a threshold. Based on the resulting trajectories, the approach then enforces two types of constraints: *P-constraints* require that all patches that are close to a confident trajectory should have positive labels; *N-constraints* force patches in the surrounding region to have negative labels. The current version of the classifier is then applied to the entire image and those patches are picked out that are classified in contradiction to the structural P–N constraints. The resulting patches are the ones which are hardest for the current classifier to decide and which therefore provide maximal benefit when added to the training set. Thus, novel hard training examples are iteratively added to the online-trained detector, which thus gets increasingly better at supporting the tracker in case the latter fails. In [34], Kalal et al. develop the theory of P–N learning, while [35] extends the approach by a generic (face) detector for the application of long-term face tracking in video.

4.6.4 Articulated Multi-person Tracking

Detailed human body pose estimation and tracking are very challenging tasks, especially in unconstrained outdoor scenarios, where many people overlap and partially occlude each other and where the camera itself may undergo egomotion. Articulated tracking in such scenarios has only very recently become feasible [2, 3, 30], see also Chap. 11. One of the first successful approaches was proposed by Gammeter et al. [30]. The basic idea behind this approach is to achieve the necessary degree of robustness by combining tracking components on two levels. A detection-based multi-person tracker, similar to the one described in Sect. 4.6.1, first analyzes the scene and recovers individual pedestrian trajectories, bridging sensor gaps and resolving partial occlusions. A specialized articulated tracker is then applied to each person's trajectory in parallel to estimate the person's body pose over time. The articulated tracker operates on global pedestrian silhouettes using a learned statistical model of human body dynamics. The two tracking levels are interfaced through a guided segmentation stage, which combines bottom–up cues from the image with top–down information from a human detector and the articulated tracker's shape prediction in a CRF framework, as motivated in Sect. 4.4.4 (see Fig. 4.9(left)). This combined observation model provides sufficiently precise measurements to support articulated multi-person tracking in challenging street scene scenarios (Fig. 4.9(right)).

Fig. 4.9 (*Left*) Original images and obtained class-specific segmentations that are used to enable articulated tracking from a moving platform in [30]. If no detection is available, the articulated tracker's prediction is used together with bottom–up cues in order to maintain figure-ground segmentation (red silhouettes). (*Right*) Multi-person articulated tracking results obtained by [30]. Reproduced with permission from [30]

4.7 Conclusion

This chapter has given an overview of approaches for performing figure-ground discrimination in scenarios when background modeling is not feasible. In particular, the methods presented here can be used to build tracking systems for mobile platforms or pan-tilt-zoom surveillance cameras. In addition, they are applicable for scenarios with strong background motion or unpredictable lighting changes.

The success of those methods, however, does not mean that background information should be entirely discarded. Whenever such information is available, it is a powerful cue that should be taken advantage of. Some recent approaches also explore combinations between detection-based and background modeling-based methods in order to get the best of both worlds (see, e.g., [63]). This is an interesting research direction that will be worthwhile to pursue.

Acknowledgements   Bastian Leibe's research has been funded, in parts, by the EU project EUROPA (ICT-2008-231888) and by the UMIC Cluster of Excellence (DFG EXC 89).

References

1. Amit, Y., Geman, D.: Shape quantization and recognition with randomized trees. Bull. Calcutta Math. Soc. **9**(7), 1545–1588 (1997) [55]
2. Andriluka, M., Roth, S., Schiele, B.: People tracking-by-detection and people detection-by-tracking. In: IEEE Conference on Computer Vision and Pattern Recognition (2008) [54,66]
3. Andriluka, M., Roth, S., Schiele, B.: Monocular 3D pose estimation and tracking by detection. In: IEEE Conference on Computer Vision and Pattern Recognition (2010) [66]
4. Avidan, S.: Ensemble tracking. In: IEEE Conference on Computer Vision and Pattern Recognition (2005) [63,64]
5. Bansal, M., Jung, S.-H., Matei, B., Eledath, J., Sawhney, H.: A real-time pedestrian detection system based on structure and appearance classification. In: IEEE International Conference on Robotics and Automation (2010) [63]

6. Barinova, O., Lempitsky, V., Kohli, P.: On the detection of multiple object instances using hough transforms. In: IEEE Conference on Computer Vision and Pattern Recognition (2010) [58]

7. Bibby, C., Reid, I.: Robust real-time visual tracking using pixel-wise posteriors. In: European Conference on Computer Vision (2008) [60,61,63]

8. Breitenstein, M., Reichlin, F., Leibe, B., Koller-Meier, E., Van Gool, L.: Robust tracking-by-detection using a detector confidence particle filter. In: International Conference on Computer Vision (2009) [64,65]

9. Breitenstein, M.D., Reichlin, F., Leibe, B., Meier, E.K., Van Gool, L.: Online multi-person tracking-by-detection from a single, uncalibrated camera. IEEE Trans. Pattern Anal. Mach. Intell. 33(9), 1820–1833 (2011) [64,65]

10. Collins, R.: Mean-shift blob tracking through scale space. In: IEEE Conference on Computer Vision and Pattern Recognition (2003) [63]

11. Comaniciu, D., Ramesh, V., Meer, P.: The variable bandwidth mean shift and data-driven scale selection. In: International Conference on Computer Vision (2001) [63]

12. Cremers, D., Rousson, M., Deriche, R.: A review of statistical approaches to level set segmentation integrating color, texture, motion and shape. Int. J. Comput. Vis. 72, 195–215 (2007) [63]

13. Dalal, N., Triggs, B.: Histograms of oriented gradients for human detection. In: IEEE Conference on Computer Vision and Pattern Recognition (2005) [55-57]

14. Dollar, P., Belongie, S., Perona, P.: The fastest pedestrian detector in the west. In: British Machine Vision Conference (2010) [55]

15. Dollar, P., Wojek, C., Schiele, B., Perona, P.: Pedestrian detection: A benchmark. In: IEEE Conference on Computer Vision and Pattern Recognition (2009) [55,56]

16. Ess, A., Leibe, B., Schindler, K., Van Gool, L.: A mobile vision system for robust multi-person tracking. In: IEEE Conference on Computer Vision and Pattern Recognition (2008) [59,60]

17. Ess, A., Leibe, B., Schindler, K., Van Gool, L.: Robust multi-person tracking from a mobile platform. IEEE Trans. Pattern Anal. Mach. Intell. 31(10), 1831–1846 (2009) [54,59,60,64]

18. Ess, A., Mueller, T., Grabner, H., van Gool, L.: Segmentation-based urban traffic scene understanding. In: British Machine Vision Conference (2009) [62]

19. Ess, A., Schindler, K., Leibe, B., Van Gool, L.: Object detection and tracking for autonomous navigation in dynamic environments. Int. J. Robot. Res. 29(14) (2010) [60]

20. Everingham, M., et al.: The 2005 pascal visual object class challenge. In: Machine Learning Challenges. Evaluating Predictive Uncertainty, Visual Object Classification, and Recognising Textual Entailment. LNAI, vol. 3944. Springer, Berlin (2006) [55]

21. Everingham, M., Sivic, J., Zisserman, A.: "Hello! My name is... Buffy"—Automatic naming of characters in TV video. In: British Machine Vision Conference (2006) [63]

22. Everingham, M., Van Gool, L., Williams, C.K.I., Winn, J., Zisserman, A.: The Pascal visual object classes (VOC) challenge. Int. J. Comput. Vis. 88(2), 303–338 (2010) [55]

23. Felzenszwalb, P., Huttenlocher, D.: Pictorial structures for object recognition. Int. J. Comput. Vis. 61(1) (2005) [57]

24. Felzenszwalb, P., Girshick, R., McAllester, D.: Cascade object detection with deformable part models. In: IEEE Conference on Computer Vision and Pattern Recognition (2010) [55]

25. Felzenszwalb, P., McAllester, D., Ramanan, D.: A discriminatively trained, multiscale, deformable part model. In: IEEE Conference on Computer Vision and Pattern Recognition (2008) [55,57]

26. Felzenszwalb, P., Girshick, R., McAllester, D., Ramanan, D.: Object detection with discriminatively trained part based models. IEEE Trans. Pattern Anal. Mach. Intell. 32(9) (2010) [57]

27. Ferrari, V., Marin, M., Zisserman, A.: Progressive search space reduction for human pose estimation. In: IEEE Conference on Computer Vision and Pattern Recognition (2008) [60]

28. Freund, Y., Schapire, R.E.: A decision-theoretic generalization of on-line learning and an application to boosting. In: European Conference on Computational Learning Theory, pp. 23–37 (1995) [55]

29. Gall, J., Lempitsky, V.: Class-specific hough forests for object detection. In: IEEE Conference on Computer Vision and Pattern Recognition (2009) [55,58,59]

30. Gammeter, S., Ess, A., Jaeggli, T., Schindler, K., Leibe, B., Van Gool, L.: Articulated multi-body tracking under egomotion. In: European Conference on Computer Vision (2008) [66, 67]
31. Grabner, H., Bischof, H.: On-line boosting and vision. In: IEEE Conference on Computer Vision and Pattern Recognition (2006) [63,64]
32. Heisele, B., Serre, T., Pontil, M., Poggio, T.: Component-based face detection. In: IEEE Conference on Computer Vision and Pattern Recognition, pp. 657–662 (2001) [57]
33. Jurie, F., Dhome, M.: Real time 3D template matching. In: IEEE Conference on Computer Vision and Pattern Recognition (2001) [63]
34. Kalal, Z., Matas, J., Mikolajczyk, K.: P–N learning: Bootstrapping binary classifiers by structural constraints. In: IEEE Conference on Computer Vision and Pattern Recognition (2010) [65,66]
35. Kalal, Z., Mikolajczyk, K., Matas, J.: Face-TLD: Tracking-learning-detection applied to faces. In: International Conference on Image Processing (2010) [66]
36. Kumar, M.P., Torr, P.H.S., Zisserman, A.: OBJ CUT. In: IEEE Conference on Computer Vision and Pattern Recognition (2005) [62]
37. Kuo, C.-H., Huang, C., Nevatia, R.: Multi-target tracking by on-line learned discriminative appearance models. In: IEEE Conference on Computer Vision and Pattern Recognition (2010) [64]
38. Ladický, L., Russell, C., Kohli, P., Torr, P.: Associative hierarchical crfs for object class image segmentation. In: International Conference on Computer Vision (2009) [62]
39. Ladický, L., Sturgess, P., Alahari, K., Russell, C., Torr, P.: What, where and how many? Combining object detectors and CRFs. In: European Conference on Computer Vision (2010) [62, 63]
40. Larlus, D., Verbeek, J., Jurie, F.: Category level object segmentation by combining bag-of-words models and Markov random fields. In: IEEE Conference on Computer Vision and Pattern Recognition (2008) [62]
41. Leibe, B., Cornelis, N., Cornelis, K., Van Gool, L.: Dynamic 3D scene analysis from a moving vehicle. In: IEEE Conference on Computer Vision and Pattern Recognition (2007) [59,64]
42. Leibe, B., Leonardis, A., Schiele, B.: Combined object categorization and segmentation with an implicit shape model. In: ECCV'04 Workshop on Statistical Learning in Computer Vision (2004) [61,62]
43. Leibe, B., Leonardis, A., Schiele, B.: Robust object detection with interleaved categorization and segmentation. Int. J. Comput. Vis. 77(1–3), 259–289 (2008) [55,57,58,61,62]
44. Leibe, B., Schiele, B.: Interleaved object categorization and segmentation. In: British Machine Vision Conference (2003) [61]
45. Leibe, B., Schindler, K., Cornelis, N., Van Gool, L.: Coupled object detection and tracking from static cameras and moving vehicles. IEEE Trans. Pattern Anal. Mach. Intell. 30(10) (2008) [54]
46. Leibe, B., Schindler, K., Van Gool, L.: Coupled object detection and tracking from static cameras and moving vehicles. IEEE Trans. Pattern Anal. Mach. Intell. 30(10), 1683–1698 (2008) [54,59,64]
47. Leibe, B., Seemann, E., Schiele, B.: Pedestrian detection in crowded scenes. In: IEEE Conference on Computer Vision and Pattern Recognition (2005) [55,58]
48. Leistner, C., Saffari, A., Bischof, H.: MIForests: Multiple-instance learning with randomized trees. In: European Conference on Computer Vision (2010) [64]
49. Lowe, D.: Distinctive image features from scale-invariant keypoints. Int. J. Comput. Vis. 60(2), 91–110 (2004) [56]
50. Maji, S., Malik, J.: Object detection using a max-margin hough transform. In: IEEE Conference on Computer Vision and Pattern Recognition (2009) [58]
51. Mikolajczyk, C., Schmid, C., Zisserman, A.: Human detection based on a probabilistic assembly of robust part detectors. In: European Conference on Computer Vision (2004) [57]
52. Mitzel, D., Horbert, E., Ess, A., Leibe, B.: Multi-person tracking with sparse detection and continuous segmentation. In: European Conference on Computer Vision (2010) [60,61,63]

53. Mohan, A., Papageorgiou, C., Poggio, T.: Example-based object detection in images by components. IEEE Trans. Pattern Anal. Mach. Intell. **23**(4), 349–361 (2001) [57]
54. Osuna, E., Freund, R., Girosi, F.: Training support vector machines: An application to face detection. In: IEEE Conference on Computer Vision and Pattern Recognition (1997) [56]
55. Papageorgiou, C., Poggio, T.: A trainable system for object detection. Int. J. Comput. Vis. **38**(1), 15–33 (2000) [56]
56. Prisacariu, V.A., Reid, I.D.: fastHOG—A real-time Gpu implementation of hog. Technical Report 2310/09, Dept. of Eng. Sc., Univ. of Oxford (2009) [55]
57. Razavi, N., Gall, J., Van Gool, L.: Backprojection revisited: Scalable multi-view object detection and similarity metrics for detections. In: European Conference on Computer Vision (2010) [59]
58. Rematas, K.: Efficient multi-view object detection and segmentation. Diploma Thesis, Mobile Multimedia Processing group, RWTH Aachen University (2009) [58,59,62]
59. Ren, X.: Finding people in archive films through tracking. In: IEEE Conference on Computer Vision and Pattern Recognition (2008) [63]
60. Rother, C., Kolmogorov, V., Blake, A.: Grabcut: Interactive foreground extraction using iterated graph cuts. In: ACM SIGGRAPH (2004) [60]
61. Shotton, J., Johnson, M., Cipolla, R.: TextonBoost: Joint appearance, shape and context modeling for multi-class object recognition and segmentation. In: European Conference on Computer Vision (2006) [62]
62. Sorokin, A., Forsyth, D.: Utility data annotation with Amazon Mechanical Turk. In: Workshop on Internet Vision (2008) [61]
63. Stalder, S., Grabner, H., Van Gool, L.: Cascaded confidence filter for improved tracking-by-detection. In: European Conference on Computer Vision (2010) [67]
64. Thomas, A., Ferrari, V., Leibe, B., Tuytelaars, T., Van Gool, L.: Shape-from-recognition: Recognition enables meta-data transfer. Comput. Vis. Image Underst. **113**(12), 1222–1234 (2009) [61,62]
65. Thomas, A., Ferrari, V., Leibe, B., Tuytelaars, T., Van Gool, L.: Using multi-view recognition and meta-data annotation to guide a robot's attention. Int. J. Robot. Res. **28**(8) (2009) [62]
66. Tu, Z., Chen, X., Yuille, A.L., Zhu, S.-C.: Image parsing: Unifying segmentation, detection, and recognition. In: International Conference on Computer Vision (2003) [62]
67. Tuzel, O., Porikli, F., Meer, P.: Human detection via classification on Riemannian manifolds. In: IEEE Conference on Computer Vision and Pattern Recognition (2007) [55]
68. Vapnik, V.: The Nature of Statistical Learning Theory. Springer, New York (1995) [55]
69. Vedaldi, A., Gulshan, V., Varma, M., Zisserman, A.: Multiple kernels for object detection. In: International Conference on Computer Vision (2009) [55]
70. Viola, P., Jones, M.: Robust real-time face detection. Int. J. Comput. Vis. **57**(2) (2004) [55]
71. Wojek, C., Dorko, G., Schulz, A., Schiele, B.: Sliding windows for rapid object class localization: A parallel technique. In: DAGM Annual Pattern Recognition Symposium (2008) [55]
72. Wojek, C., Schiele, B.: A dynamic conditional random field model for joint labeling of object and scene classes. In: European Conference on Computer Vision (2008) [62]
73. Wu, B., Nevatia, R.: Detection of multiple, partially occluded humans in a single image by Bayesian combination of edgelet part detectors. In: International Conference on Computer Vision (2005) [57,59]
74. Wu, B., Nevatia, R.: Tracking of multiple, partially occluded humans based on static body part detections. In: IEEE Conference on Computer Vision and Pattern Recognition (2006) [63]
75. Wu, B., Nevatia, R.: Detection and tracking of multiple, partially occluded humans by Bayesian combination of edgelet part detectors. Int. J. Comput. Vis. **75**(2), 247–266 (2007) [54,55,59]
76. Zhang, L., Nevatia, R.: Efficient scan-window based object detection using GPGPU. In: CVPR'08 CVGPU Workshop (2008) [55]

Chapter 5
Face Detection

Raghuraman Gopalan, William R. Schwartz, Rama Chellappa, and Ankur Srivastava

Abstract Face detection in still images and videos has been extensively studied over the last two decades. Attributed to the recent proliferation of cameras in consumer applications, research in face detection has gradually transformed into more unconstrained settings, with the goal of achieving performance close to humans. This presents two main challenges: (i) in addition to modeling the facial characteristics, understanding the information portrayed by the surrounding scene is important in resolving visual ambiguities, and (ii) the computational time needed for decision making should be compatible for real-time applications, since detection is primarily a front-end process on which additional knowledge extraction is built upon. This chapter begins with a review of recent work in modeling face-specific information, including appearance-based methods used by sliding window classifiers, concepts from learning and local interest-point descriptors, and then focuses on representing the contextual information shared by faces with the surrounding scene. To provide better understanding of working concepts, we discuss a method for learning the semantic context shared by the face with other human body parts that facilitates reasoning under occlusion, and then present an image representation

R. Gopalan (✉)
Department of Electrical and Computer Engineering, University of Maryland, College Park, MD 20742, USA
e-mail: raghuram@umiacs.umd.edu

W.R. Schwartz
Institute of Computing, University of Campinas, Campinas-SP 13084-971, Brazil
e-mail: wschwartz@liv.ic.unicam.br

R. Chellappa
Department of Electrical and Computer Engineering, and UMIACS, University of Maryland, College Park, MD 20742, USA
e-mail: rama@umiacs.umd.edu

A. Srivastava
Department of Electrical and Computer Engineering, and Institute for Systems Research, University of Maryland, College Park, MD 20742, USA
e-mail: ankurs@umd.edu

T.B. Moeslund et al. (eds.), *Visual Analysis of Humans*,
DOI 10.1007/978-0-85729-997-0_5, © Springer-Verlag London Limited 2011

which efficiently encodes contour information to enable fast detection of faces. We conclude the chapter by discussing some existing challenges.

5.1 Introduction

Identifying objects present in images and videos is an important problem in visual scene analysis. Faces, among different types of objects, have received considerable attention since they are one of the most common visual cues that humans use to associate themselves with other humans. Although perceived effortlessly by the human visual system, to train a machine to be adept at this task involves addressing variations in facial pose, expressions, (dis)guise, lighting conditions of the scene, and occlusions. Not surprisingly, even before the advances in computer hardware during late 1980s, there have been works that characterize facial properties using both computational and psychophysical studies [15, 16, 40]. More developments in still image-based face detection continued through the 1990s, where the primary focus was to model the facial characteristics, using both appearance and geometry, and designing robust classifiers that could separate faces from non-faces [51]. The early 2000's witnessed an increased usage of data-driven methods towards this problem, with the classic example of Viola and Jones' adaptation of boosting [48] that produced one of the first robust, real-time face detection systems which is still used in practice. Subsequently, there has been increased focus on utilizing motion information provided by videos [26], continuously adapting the classifier as new instances emerge [19], and representing contextual sources from the global scene to augment information about the presence of a face [46].

In this chapter, we provide a concise literature review of important modalities for face detection. Specifically, we start in Sect. 5.2 with a categorization of existing methods from the stand point of data representation, which includes (i) appearance-based descriptors designed for *sliding window* methods where *every* region in the image is analyzed, and (ii) using local interest-point descriptors where the analysis is performed in an *intermediate* stage containing feature responses extracted from the image. In Sect. 5.3, we consider one representative method from each of the two categories, AdaBoost [48] and bag-of-words [20, 45], respectively, and study them in detail. Section 5.4 deals with the role of context which, unlike the previous two sections, do not consider faces in isolation but rather as an *inherent part* of the global scene. Here, we present an overview of a method [9, 43] that learns relationships among different parts of a human to detect faces under occlusion. We then discuss computationally efficient methods for face detection in Sect. 5.5, which is important from a practical application perspective. After reviewing relevant work addressing this problem from the standpoint of both image description and classifier decision-making mechanism, we discuss an image representation that efficiently encodes the contour information extracted from an image to facilitate fast contour-based face localization. We then present a related topic on active learning for face detection, and discuss evaluations of current algorithms in Sect. 5.6, and then conclude the chapter with a listing of some existing challenges.

5.2 Categorization of Existing Approaches

A comprehensive survey of different approaches for face detection until the early 2000's was presented in [51], where the methods were classified into the following four main categories,

1. *knowledge-based* methods which build on human-centric perceptual observations of a face,
2. *feature invariants* that characterize properties of texture and color which are distinct to faces,
3. *template-based* methods where different realizations of faces and non-faces are correlated with test instances in a nearest-neighbor fashion, and
4. *appearance-based* methods where, rather than using separate templates, some generalization (or learning) is performed on the facial data to model their characteristics.

However, unlike most of these methods where detection was primarily performed using sliding windows,[1] recent approaches for object detection use a set of different local interest-point descriptors extracted from the entire image and then analyze their patterns to detect facial instances. A popular example is the bag-of-words approach [20]. Motivated by this, we base our classification of methods for face detection into the following two categories from a *data representation* perspective,

- **Sliding window-based:** Given a set of windows corresponding to faces and non-faces, these methods extract features such as color [13], texture [11], and contours [28], and then use statistical models such as Principal Component Analysis (PCA) [8], SVM [34], ANN [39], HMM [29] and AdaBoost [48] to learn the patterns of pixels in those windows. These models are in turn used to perform detection across windows of different image scales, by analyzing *all* regions pertaining to a test image. An illustration is shown in Fig. 5.1.
- **Local interest-point-based:** Here, the primary representation of an image (or video) is in terms of local interest-point detectors with useful invariant properties such as the Harris detector [12], Harris–Laplace [27], Hessian-Affine [27], Maximally stable extremal regions [25] among others. Feature descriptions such as SIFT [22], and Shape contexts [1] are built upon these feature detectors to form inputs for a classification engine. Hence, instead of *directly* analyzing all pixels (regions), the classifier analyzes *only* those regions with prominent feature responses. An example is given in Fig. 5.2. This is broadly referred to as the bag-of-words method, and [20] reviews all related works.

Both approaches have relative advantages; for instance, sliding window methods are computationally more expensive in general, whereas the interest-point-based methods, despite offering better resistance to minor object deformations, do not guarantee repeatability of features to the extent offered by sliding window methods. Before

---

[1] Where windows of different sizes scan the image sequentially to analyze the visual data contained in them, using one of the above four categories.

Fig. 5.1 A sample outline of detecting faces using sliding window methods. Training windows corresponding to faces and non-faces are characterized using features, from which a classifier is learnt to classify windows that are sequentially scanned from a test image

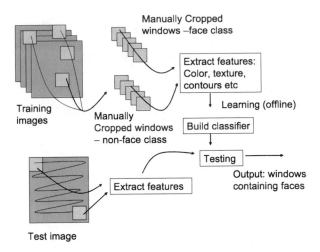

Fig. 5.2 A sample outline of detecting faces using local interest-point descriptors. Rather than analyzing the entire image using windows, relevant points (or regions) are automatically extracted from images, and their patterns are analyzed further

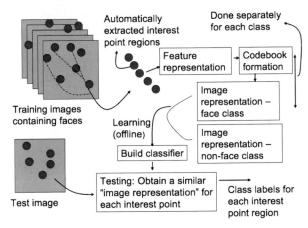

proceeding with a study on this basis, it is important to be aware of other ways of grouping methods since in addition to data *representation*, the mode of *classification* can also take one of the following two types: (i) generative methods which model the likelihood and prior, such as MRFs [4], and (ii) discriminative methods that model the posterior directly like, conditional random fields [37] and AdaBoost [48]. Further, there are different learning methods [18] in constructing the classifier such as incremental learning and batch learning, and varying representations of motion information from videos [26] and context [46].

5.3 Representative Detection Methods: AdaBoost and Bag-of-Words

We now study two fairly popular face detection methods of (i) AdaBoost [48], a sliding window method that guarantees provable detection error bounds, and (ii) bag-of-words [20] which can be used to process feature-level descriptions at interest points. We will also discuss how some facial variations such as pose and occlusions, are modeled by these methods.

5.3.1 AdaBoost

Viola and Jones [48] proposed an adaptation of boosting [7], a learning algorithm which models the *final strong* classifier using a combination of several *weak learners*, resulting in robust, real-time face detection by minimizing the upper bound on the empirical detection error. It is primarily a data-driven approach that relies heavily on the quality and balance of positive (faces) and negative (non-faces) training samples using which, different weak learners are employed to capture salient discriminative information. The algorithm is generic in recognizing different objects, as defined by the training data, and it can be used to analyze different visual properties of the object, depending on the type of weak learners used. An illustration of the working principle of AdaBoost in shown in Fig. 5.3, whose properties form the main focus of our discussion here.

We first present the basic version of boosting, the Discrete AdaBoost, proposed by Freund and Schapire [7], below.

Given: $(x_1, y_1), \ldots, (x_M, y_M)$ *where* $x_i \in X$ *are the training data patches (windows),* $y_i \in Y = \{-1, +1\}$ *their class labels (* $y_i = 1$ *for the face class, and* $y_i = -1$ *for non-faces), and a set of weak learners* h_j, $j = 1, \ldots, N_{wl}$.
Initialize the training sample weights for the first iteration, $D_1(i) = 1/M$, $\forall i = 1$ *to* M.
For iterations $t = 1, \ldots, T$, *Do:*

- *Train the base learners using the distribution* D_t.

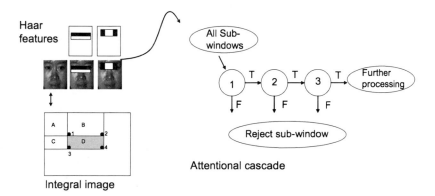

Fig. 5.3 Flow diagram of face detection using AdaBoost [48]. Integral image representation (the appearance information of region D can be computed using the value of I^* at points 1, 2, 3 and 4), information extraction using Haar filters, and attentional cascade to sort the features. Reproduced with permission from [48]

- *Get the base classifier $h_t : X \to \mathbb{R}$, which minimizes the error*

$$\varepsilon_t = \mathrm{Pr}_{i \sim D_t}\big[h_t(x_i) \neq y_i\big]. \tag{5.1}$$

- *Choose $\alpha_t \in \mathbb{R}$, which is a function of the classification accuracy.*
- *Update*:

$$D_{t+1}(i) = \frac{D_t(i)\exp(-\alpha_t\, y_i h_t(x_i))}{Z_t} \tag{5.2}$$

where Z_t is a normalization factor, chosen such that D_{t+1} will be a distribution.

Output the final classifier:

$$H(x) = \mathrm{sign}\left(\sum_{t=1}^{T} \alpha_t h_t(x)\right). \tag{5.3}$$

To detect faces using this learning algorithm, Viola and Jones [48] collected lots of examples of faces and non-faces of a fixed window size[2] to constitute X and their labels Y. The weak learners h used were Haar-filters [36], a set of rectangular filters with regions either positive or negative, using which the intensity information of the data was modeled. The positive regions, when placed on an image patch, replicate the underlying image, whereas the negative regions result in a zero output. Then, to effectively learn the strong classifier $H(x)$, the following three components were proposed.

5.3.1.1 Integral Image Representation

Since the basic input for analysis is the intensity values of the image pixels, an efficient representation of them will help reduce the computations needed for accessing those values. Viola and Jones [48] proposed Integral images, a representation which accumulates the intensity values of the pixels as one travels from the top left corner of the image to the bottom right. It can be expressed as

$$I^\star(x, y) = \sum_{x' \leq x, y' \leq y} I(x', y') \tag{5.4}$$

where $I^\star(x, y)$ is the integral image at pixel location (x, y) and $I(x, y)$ is the value of the original intensity image at that location. Hence to obtain the cumulative sum of intensities in *any* region, we require only the value of $I^\star$ in the four corners of the region, thereby resulting in considerable reduction in the amount of computations.

---

[2]To perform detection in a test image across scale, different-sized Haar features were used to analyze the image. Outputs across Haar scales were fused using non-maximal suppression [30], a post-processing stage that has a considerable impact on the final detection accuracy.

5.3.1.2 Feature Selection

The next stage is to harness the information pattern in I^* using the weak learners h. Since the number of such learners is usually very large (much more than the dimension of the data), an effective way of selecting features is needed. Hence by using Haar filters, a hierarchical ordering of the weak learners was obtained through boosting such that the first selected Haar feature would easily distinguish faces from non-faces, while the subsequent features would provide more detailed descriptions of faces.

5.3.1.3 Focus of Attention

Since the percentage of regions within an image containing faces is generally less than those with non-faces, an efficient way to utilize the above feature selection is necessary. Hence Viola and Jones [48] proposed the attentional cascade detector where each stage corresponds to a collection of weak classifiers $H(x)$, where $H_1(x)$ of stage one is the simplest among all, and it is trained to reject as many (need not be all) windows with non-faces while retaining *all* windows with faces. $H_i(x)$, $i > 1$, on the other hand, have more stringent requirement in terms of false positives (progressing gradually towards zero) and correct detection rates (being close to one always). Hence, the number of weak learners h constituting $H_i(x)$ will increase as i increases, and so does the complexity of the detector. Such a cascade results in applying the most complex detector at very few windows, since all other windows rejected by earlier (and computationally cheaper) stages will *most likely* correspond to non-faces. The generalization error bounds for this process follow from the original boosting algorithm [7], and it is dependent on the quality of training data used in determining $H_i(x)$.

5.3.1.4 Extension to Other Facial Variations

Following this method, there have been numerous other methods using boosting principles for detecting faces under variations such as pose. The modification comes in the type of boosting used such as those that avoid over-fitting of data by having real-valued confidence intervals for each classifier [6]. One such work [50] used Real AdaBoost [42] to detect faces across in-plane rotations. The main idea was to use different boosting detectors for each range of facial pose, and then use the detection probabilities of the initial stages of each detector to estimate the pose range corresponding to a test window. The detector with the highest probability is then executed *completely* to determine whether a face is present or not. Similar to this, other challenges in face detection such as occlusion, were handled through boosting by introducing exemplar occluded faces as positive training samples using which the classifier is learnt.

The methodology described here for AdaBoost can, in principle, be used to visualize the working concepts of other sliding window classifiers such as SVMs [34],

ANNs [39] etc. The main modifications appear in the cost function that is being optimized for, and in the choice of features to represent faces and non-faces such as SIFT [22] and local binary patterns[3] (LBP) [32, 33].

5.3.2 Bag-of-Words

Instead of scanning the image in terms of sequential-and-disjoint blocks, drawing inspiration from the topic models [2] prevalent in document analysis that represent document(s) using a set of keywords contained in them, bag-of-words approaches [20] represent an image or an object class using a set of low-level interest-point descriptors. It is using these descriptors, instead of features extracted from individual pixels, differentiation among objects is performed. Such an approach is also motivated by how humans perceive a scene in that, rather than looking at every window location in a sequential manner, only the 'informative' regions gather our focus-of-attention up front. We now discuss the general methodology of such methods in detecting objects.

5.3.2.1 Interest-Point Detection and Representation

This stage finds interest regions in the scene that convey relatively more 'information' than the rest. The definition of 'information' depends on the type of interest-point detector used. For instance, a contour detector will detect regions with high intensity gradients, whereas a Harris detector finds points at a fixed scale. These features are then represented using descriptors such as SIFT [22]. Given a set of training images containing faces and non-faces, without the need to crop the exact face locations, SIFT descriptors will be computed and form the primary input for the other stages of detection.

5.3.2.2 Dictionary Formation

The set of all such SIFT features, across different images containing faces and non-faces, are then analyzed to compute the codewords or dictionaries. These codewords are a reduced representation comprising of only those features, which are *most relevant* in distinguishing different classes. This is achieved through a vector quantization of SIFT descriptors by merging descriptions at different levels of classification ability.

---

[3]More references on LBP-related features can be found in the 'face analysis' section of http://www.cse.oulu.fi/MVG/LBP_Bibliography.

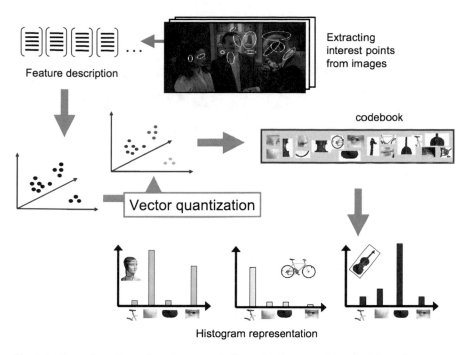

Fig. 5.4 Illustration of bag-of-words approach. Extracting interest points, obtaining a feature representation, performing quantization to obtains codebook dictionaries, and culminating with a histogram representation for different objects. Reproduced with permission from [20]

5.3.2.3 Image Representation and Classification

The class of images containing faces and non-faces is then represented using a histogram of these codewords based on which further classification is done. As before, classification can be done either through generative models such as Naive Bayes [3] and probabilistic latent semantic analysis [45], or using discriminative methods like pyramid match kernels [10]. A sample illustration of general bag-of-words approach is presented in Fig. 5.4.

An important advantage of this method is its robustness to reasonable object deformations, since the primary analysis is performed using independent interest-points portraying the object. For cases where the geometry of parts is also important, there have been extensions of this method that encode the spatial structure of feature locations [41]. A main debatable point, however, is the lack of guarantee in consistency of the underlying features. Though the features themselves have some invariant properties, most studies on this method have only empirical guarantees on the 'relevance' of a feature. This is attributed to the transition in data representation from a pixel level, as used in sliding windows, onto an intermediate feature-level that results in some 'information loss'. A formal quantification of this *loss* is important in addressing this issue.

Fig. 5.5 Information conveyed by context for object and scene perception. **a** Though the foreground objects in two images are a 90 degree rotation of each other, spatial support says the first is a car and the other is a human [46]. **b** The likelihood of regions pertaining to a car with and without top-down context [20]. Reproduced with permission from [20, 46]

5.4 Context

In contrast to the previously discussed methods that model how a facial region, in isolation, look with respect to other non-face regions, context-based methods attempts to answer some of the following questions; What information does a face share with its surroundings? Given some characteristics of the global scene, how probable is the presence of face in there? The first question is a bottom-up way of learning the object and its surroundings, whereas the second question is a top-down model of what a scene conveys about the probability of presence of an object. Hence, context can be viewed as a prior that assists the detection process.

Context, a loosely defined term in itself, comes from various sources [5] such as local pixel context that captures the statistics of a pixel with its immediate surroundings, 2D scene gist that describes global scene statistics, 3D geometry that deals with spatial support and surface orientations of object with the real world, semantic context that captures relation among objects, or between an object and activity/ event, and cultural/ illumination/ weather context, etc.

Though widely acknowledged as a useful information even in the early 1970s [31, 35], only in recent years have we witnessed substantial work in modeling contextual information. For instance, an interesting experiment performed by Torralba et al. [46] using the scene gist to determine possible regions in a scene containing the object, without running an explicit object detector, illustrated the use of context for visual inference (Fig. 5.5). This resulted in many more studies that integrated the notion of scene, object and parts into a single representation. A recent tutorial [20] provides related information on these fronts.

5.4.1 Detecting Faces Using Semantic Context

To provide a better understanding on using context to detect faces, we now describe two methods [9, 43] that model the relation shared by faces with other parts of the supporting human (inter-object semantic relationships). The contextual information was represented by learning a set of rules that capture patterns in probabilities of different detectors trained on the human parts and face, under varying degrees of visual ambiguities such as pose changes and occlusion. These rules were then used to perform inference through deterministic first-order logic [43], and with probabilistic reasoning using Markov logic networks [9]. More details are provided below.

5.4.1.1 Design of Detectors

The following set of eight detectors was used as the primary sources of information: face, full-body of the human, head (top), torso, legs, top-and-torso, torso-and-legs, and top-and-legs. The face detector was trained at a higher resolution than the other seven human part detectors.[4] The detectors belonged to the sliding window category. Given a set of training samples, with cropped windows corresponding to humans, faces and negative examples, the following features were extracted [44]; histogram of oriented gradients (HOG), and co-occurrence matrices of texture information, from each sample. The features were then vectorized and the classification was performed using partial least squares [49], a discriminative approach used for dimensionality reduction.

5.4.1.2 Inference Through First-Order Logic [43]

For each sliding window in the test image, there are a set of eight detector probabilities that describe how probable is the presence of the 'object' that is modeled by those detectors. Schwartz et al. [43] learned patterns from these probabilities by grouping them into four different cases for the human detector, and three cases for the face detector.

- Model M_1: all parts are visible
- Model M_2: top is visible, torso and legs may or may not be visible
- Model M_3: top is invisible, torso and legs are visible
- Model M_4: all body parts are invisible
- Model F_1–F_3: face is visible, partially visible, or invisible

The 'top' portion of the human detector was given more importance in models M_i since, the faces carry more discriminative information about the presence of human than the other parts. The probability intervals (upper bound u and lower bound l) of the eight detectors for these models were learnt in the training phase (Fig. 5.6). During testing, given a detection window W, the probabilities of the part-based human detectors P_j, $j = 1, \ldots, 7$ and the face detector P^f were computed. Using this information, the rank $f_W(.)$ of each model was obtained as follows,

---

[4]Since humans can be recognized at distances much farther than what is possible for detecting faces.

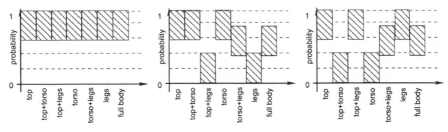

(a) M_1: all parts are visible (b) M_2: top part is visible (c) M_2: top part is visible
                                       and torso is visible   and legs are visible

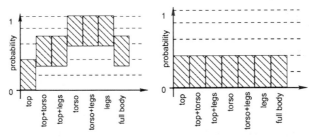

(d) M_3: top part is invisible   (e) M_4: all parts are invisible

Fig. 5.6 Detecting faces using the semantic context shared by faces with the supporting human. Probability intervals of the human detector models M_i encoding contextual rules. Reproduced with permission from [43]

$$fw(M_i) = \sum_{j=1}^{7} \begin{cases} 1 & \text{if } l_{ij} \leq P_j \leq u_{ij}, \\ 0 & \text{otherwise}, \end{cases} \tag{5.5}$$

$$fw(F_i) = \begin{cases} 1 & \text{if } l_i \leq P^f \leq u_i, \\ 0 & \text{otherwise}. \end{cases} \tag{5.6}$$

Schwartz et al. [43] then performed inference using $fw(.)$ by learning the correlation between the information conveyed by person detector models with that of the face detector. This was done through the following hypotheses.

- $H_1 : [(fw(M_1) \wedge fw(M_2)) > (fw(M_3) \wedge fw(M_4)) \mid fw(F_1)]$ – Given a high response from face detector, does the human detector response correlative positively.
- $H_2 : [(fw(M_3) \vee fw(M_4)) > (fw(M_1) \wedge fw(M_2)) \mid fw(F_1)]$ – Output of face detector is a false alarm, since the person detector has low responses for top.
- $H_3 : [fw(F_1) \mid (fw(M_1) \vee fw(M_2)) > (fw(M_3) \wedge fw(M_4))]$ – Face detector reinforces the response of human detector.
- $H_4 : [fw(F_2) \mid fw(M_3) > (fw(M_1) \wedge fw(M_2) \wedge fw(M_4))]$ – Face is occluded, but there is a human present in that window.
- $H_5 : [fw(F_3) \mid (fw(M_1) \vee fw(M_2) \vee fw(M_3)) > fw(M_4)]$ – Person detector output is a false alarm.

An analysis of the performance improvement obtained through this context modeling is presented in Fig. 5.8, where the comparison is done with the methods for detecting humans [44] and faces [28] that do not use context. However, one restriction of this method is in defining rigid probability bounds (u, l) to compute the models ranks $f_W(.)$. Hence, [9] performed a probabilistic inference of context using principles from Markov logic networks.

5.4.1.3 Probabilistic Inference Using Markov Logic Networks [9]

The second method illustrating the use of semantic context is based on Markov Logic Networks (MLN), proposed by Richardson and Domingos [38]. MLNs provide a unified framework to combine logistical and statistical aspects of artificial intelligence. Since logic handles complexity, and probability handles uncertainty, the complex and uncertain real worlds can be modeled by assigning probabilities to rules rather than enforcing hard decision bounds.

More specifically, a logical knowledge base (KB) is a set of *hard constraints* on the set of possible worlds (which describes any inference task that the user is interested in). The goal is to make them *soft constraints* since when a formula (a component of KB) is violated by the world, it becomes less probable and not impossible. Hence a MLN is a set of pairs $(\tilde{F}_i, w_i)$ where $\tilde{F}_i$ represents a formula in first-order logic and w_i its weight. Using this the probability of occurrence of a world (an event) X_W can be expressed as

$$P(X_W) \propto \exp\left(\sum_i w_i n_i(X_W)\right) \tag{5.7}$$

where n_i denotes the number of true 'groundings' (frequency of occurrence) of a formula $\tilde{F}_i$. Together with a set of constants, which specify the basic underlying relations of a problem, MLN forms a template for the Markov network using which learning and inference is performed.

To model the semantic context of faces using MLN, [9] proposed the following steps. Given the input of the eight detector probabilities $P_j, j = 1, \ldots, 7$ and P^f, do the following.

- Learn a set of rules to capture the intra-window spatial relations of the detectors (instead of the pre-specified models M_i and F_i). This includes an exhaustive combination of different detectors.
- Learn the rules explaining inter-window detector patterns, to model scene inconsistencies such as occlusions.
- Learn the confidence of these rules, $(\tilde{F}_i, w_i)$ using appropriate training exemplars and construct the MLN.
- Given a test image, perform inference by grounding the MLN templates.

The modules available in the open source Alchemy system [38] were used for these tasks. An example illustrating detection using MLN is given in Fig. 5.7, and a comparison between detection methods with and without context is given in Fig. 5.8.

Fig. 5.7 Sample detection results from the probabilistic context inference method [9] using MLN. In addition to detecting object location, information on occluding objects is obtained

Fig. 5.8 Performance comparison of methods with and without context models, on an internally collected dataset

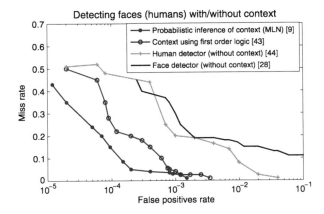

A set of 50 images with nearly 300 humans, many under occlusion, was used for this purpose. Training was done using images collected from the Internet and from standard datasets to learn the probabilities of the detectors. These results illustrate the importance of context in detecting faces, and their ability to provide more semantic information. It is interesting to study the effect of other contextual sources on the face detection accuracy, and to formally quantify the classifier's generalization ability in adapting to data instances that are very different from those seen during training stages.

5.5 Computational Efficiency

We now discuss a topic that has practical relevance in systems where the operating time for decision making is critical. This includes most of the computer vision applications, and also pertains to the problem with the integration of face detection technology in consumer cameras. The need for real-time processing is addressed in at least two aspects namely, (i) pruning the search space of the classifier, and (ii) developing image representations that facilitate efficient information access for the classifier. We provide a brief overview of these two categories.

5.5.1 Navigating the Search Space

An example of this method is the Viola and Jones detector described in Sect. 5.3.1.3 where the attentional cascade was used to reduce the number of windows that require the most expensive classifier. In a similar way, common tree- and graph-traversing methods have also been used to identify the features needed to evaluate the classifier depending on the test images. Examples include inductive decision tree pruning [23], dynamic programming [21], among others. More recently, [17] proposed a branch and bound framework for object localization using an efficient subwindow search.

5.5.2 Efficient Image Representations

Integral images discussed in Sect. 5.3.1.1 provided an efficient way to access the image intensities contained in a region. In addition to appearance, many applications rely on the shape information (primarily the contours) to localize objects. One such method is [28] that detected faces using elliptical contours. Hence in the following section, we address this issue from a computational viewpoint by proposing an image representation that provides a compact description of image contours.

5.5.2.1 Fast Contour-Based Face (Object) Localization

Analysis of contours primarily involves the computation of edge strength between a pair of arbitrary points in an image, along the path specified by the task at hand. This operation, which inherently sums up the edge values of the pixels that lie between the two interest points, scales linearly with the number of intermediate pixels. Let n', a variable, denote the range of possible number of such pixels between two arbitrary points in an image. Our main focus here is to reduce the computations involved at this stage. We put-forth a two-stage approach that has a *preprocessing* stage (5.8) of static computational complexity using which, the computational load of the *fitting* stage (5.9) is considerably reduced.

More specifically, let f^E denote the edge image corresponding to an $N_1 \times N_2$ intensity image f^I. Let $Z = N_1 \times N_2$ denote the total number of pixels in the image. Since contours can be locally well-approximated by a collection of line segments, we discretize the space of f^E into N_o different line orientations $D_i, i = 1, \ldots, N_o$. We then compute,

$$S_{D_i}(x, y) = S_{D_i}(x, y - 1) + f^E_{D_i}(x, y) \qquad (5.8)$$

where $I_l = \{S_{D_i}(x, y)\}_{i=1}^{N_o}$, $\forall (x, y) \in f^l$, the *line integral image*, contains the cumulative sum of pixels $S_{D_i}(., .)$ along different possible line orientations. Using this *preprocessing* step, we could obtain the edge strength between any pair of points, connected by a line, in $O(1)$ computations instead of the original $O(n')$ where n' can vary anywhere from 1 to $\sqrt{N_1^2 + N_2^2}$. This results in a substantial reduction in the amount of computations needed for the *fitting* stage where, to detect a contour C' comprising of M' line segments, we obtain its likelihood $L_{C'}$ in only $O(M')$ additions by the following,

$$\text{Sum}_i = \text{abs}\big(S_{D_i}(x_1, y_1) - S_{D_i}(x_2, y_2)\big), \quad \forall i = 1, \ldots, M', \qquad (5.9)$$

$$L_{C'} = \sum_{i=1}^{M'} \text{Sum}_i \qquad (5.10)$$

where $\{(x_j, y_j)\}_{j=1}^{2}$ denote one such pair of end point locations at an orientation D_i.

To provide more insight, let us now qualitatively analyze the computational complexity of contour fitting. Let P' be the set of shape primitives representing C' under different deformations such as translation, rotation, scaling and shear. To detect faces, P' would ideally comprise of ellipses with all possible parameterizations. To find the region corresponding to C' from the edge map f^E, irrespective of the matching process like correlation or the Hough transform, one needs to estimate the likelihood $L_{P_i'}$ of each of the primitives $P_i' \in P'$ at *all* possible locations in f. If N_1' denotes the total number of fitting operations, this process requires $O(N_1' n')$ computations, where n' is a variable defined previously.

To circumvent this computationally intensive process, we introduce I_l (5.8), a pre-processing stage, which has an *one-time* operational complexity of $O(Z N_o)$. Hence during fitting, we could accomplish the task of detecting *any* linearly approximated object contour in $O(N_1' M')$ operations, without the need to *separately compute* the edge strengths corresponding to *all* P_i'. The upper bound of computations needed for fitting, C_F, is therefore given by

$$C_F = O(N_1' \bar{M}_i') \qquad (5.11)$$

where $\bar{M}_i' = \max_{i \in P'} M_i'$, and M_i' is the number of line segments in the contour P_i'. This brings in computational savings since, (i) $Z N_o$ is generally several orders of magnitude less than $N_1' n'$, and (ii) C_F, in addition to being small when compared with $N_1' n'$, offers more immunity to the increase in number of contours C' when detection spans across multiple classes of objects, in addition to faces. This representation can also be extended to arbitrary curves, to better approximate the contour, however at an increased pre-processing cost. We provide an illustration of face detection using I_l, and a computational comparison of our method with a contour-based face detector without using the pre-processing I_l [28] in Fig. 5.9.

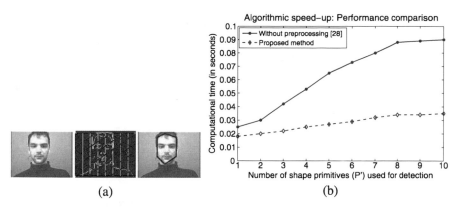

(a)   (b)

Fig. 5.9 Computationally efficient face detection using contours. **a** An overview of the proposed line integral image representation (5.8). Three line orientations were chosen ($N_o = 3$), and the facial contour was modeled as hexagons with varying side lengths. **b** Comparing the computations needed for our method with that of [28]. The image f was of size 240×320, and the computational time taken to detect faces is given as a function of the number of hexagonal contour primitives (P') used

5.6 Other Related Topics and Conclusions

Finally, we shall discuss a related topic from online learning, which improves performance of face (object) detection methods by adapting the classifier to learn from new instances, and some methods for evaluating the existing algorithms.

5.6.1 Online Learning

Humans generally adapt their inference skills by learning about the world *as they see it*. Keeping in pace with this continuous accumulation of knowledge, online learning departs from the traditional paradigm of viewing the classifier design as an *offline* stage, and establishes *feedback* with the information conveyed by new instances of visual scenes. This makes more sense because offline training assumes all prior information about the classification task is available *at that instant* when the classifier is learnt, which is this is generally not true. Therefore, learning the classifier *on-the-fly* provides a better model of prior, especially when the amount of visual data is ever-increasing.

Establishing such a feedback generally requires some form of supervision from the user in telling whether the system is making wrong decisions, either in missing to detect objects or incorrectly detecting regions that do not pertain to the specific object category. This has lead to a slew of (semi-)supervised learning techniques to adapt the previously proposed offline-classification algorithms onto this new learning paradigm. A comprehensive overview of such approaches can be found in [18]. The general form of such methods can hence be viewed as

$$Decision_t = f_2\big(f_1(Train, Test, Decision_{[0:t-1]})\big) \qquad (5.12)$$

where *Train* and *Test* refer to data pertaining to training and testing sets, and *Decision_t* denote the classifier decision at the time instant t. f_1 and f_2 are the functions corresponding to data representation, and classification. Some relevant methods using this principle for detecting faces include multiple-instance learning [24], and predicting the cost of effort (in adapting the classifier) versus reward (improvement in detection accuracy) [47].

5.6.2 Evaluations

Lastly, an important component in measuring the performance of any vision system is the availability of a good dataset on which, the receiver operating characteristics (ROC curves) are determined between correct detection rates and false accept rates. Until the early 2000's, when the face detection was still at its early stages, the CMU-MIT dataset [39] was the de facto standard for evaluations. It contains images with both frontal and profile faces. Since then, with the research on face detection focusing more on unconstrained settings, the UMASS dataset [14] offers good exemplar images to supplement the challenge. The 'characteristics' of a good dataset is, however, a debatable topic.[5]

With more than twenty years of research, contributions towards different paradigms of face detection problem have resulted in substantial strides towards matching human visual capabilities. However, as is the case with most computer vision problems, we are still short of being perfect. Some of the emerging trends that could further drive this research are as follows: (i) better *learning* strategies to *know* relevant information in the scene with minimal, and ideally zero, supervision, (ii) understanding *contextual* information in a more formal way through better computational models of the human visual process, and (iii) *computational* efficiency using concepts from graphical processing units (GPU) and cloud computing.

References

1. Belongie, S., Malik, J., Puzicha, J.: Shape matching and object recognition using shape contexts. IEEE Trans. Pattern Anal. Mach. Intell. **24**, 509–522 (2002) [73]
2. Blei, D.M., Ng, A.Y., Jordan, M.I.: Latent Dirichlet allocation. J. Mach. Learn. Res. **3**, 993–1022 (2003) [78]
3. Csurka, G., Dance, C., Fan, L., Willamowski, J., Bray, C.: Visual categorization with bags of keypoints. In: Workshop on Statistical Learning in Computer Vision, ECCV, pp. 22–32 (May 2004) [79]
4. Dass, S.C., Jain, A.K., Lu, X.: Face detection and synthesis using Markov random field models. In: International Conference on Pattern Recognition, pp. 402–405 (July 2002) [74]

---

[5]More details on these fronts are the focus of a workshop on "Face Detection: Where are we? and Where next?" held in conjunction with the European Conference on Computer Vision, 2010.

5. Divvala, S.K., Hoiem, D., Hays, J.H., Efros, A.A., Hebert, M.: An empirical study of context in object detection. In: IEEE Conference on Computer Vision and Pattern Recognition, pp. 1271–1278 (June 2009) [80]
6. Freund, Y., Schapire, R.: A short introduction to boosting. Jpn. Soc. Artif. Intell. **14**, 771–780 (1999). [77]
7. Freund, Y., Schapire, R.E.: A decision-theoretic generalization of on-line learning and an application to boosting. J. Comput. Syst. Sci. **55**, 119–139 (1997) [75,77]
8. Fukunaga, K., Koontz, W.L.G.: Application of the Karhunen–Loève expansion to feature selection and ordering. IEEE Trans. Comput. **19**, 311–318 (1970) [73]
9. Gopalan, R., Schwartz, W.: Detecting humans under partial occlusion using Markov logic networks. In: Performance Metrics for Intelligent Systems (September 2010) [72,80,81,83, 84]
10. Grauman, K., Darrell, T.: The pyramid match kernel: Discriminative classification with sets of image features. In: International Conference on Computer Vision, pp. 1458–1465 (October 2005) [79]
11. Haralick, R.M., Dinstein, I., Shanmugam, K.: Textural features for image classification. IEEE Trans. Syst. Man Cybern. **3**, 610–621 (1973) [73]
12. Harris, C., Stephens, M.: A combined corner and edge detection. In: Alvey Vision Conference, pp. 147–151 (1988) [73]
13. Hsu, R.L., Abdel-Mottaleb, M., Jain, A.K.: Face detection in color images. IEEE Trans. Pattern Anal. Mach. Intell. **24**, 696–706 (2002) [73]
14. Jain, V., Miller, E.L.: Fddb: A benchmark for face detection in unconstrained settings. Technical Report UM-CS-2010-009, University of Massachusetts, Amherst (2010) [88]
15. Kanade, T.: Picture processing system by computer complex and recognition of human faces. In: Doctoral dissertation, Kyoto University (November 1973) [72]
16. Kelly, M.D.: Visual identification of people by computer. PhD thesis, Stanford University, Stanford, CA, USA (1971) [72]
17. Lampert, C.H., Blaschko, M.B., Hofmann, T.: Efficient subwindow search: A branch and bound framework for object localization. IEEE Trans. Pattern Anal. Mach. Intell. **31**, 2129–2142 (2009) [85]
18. LeCun, Y., Huang, F.J., Bottou, L.: Learning methods for generic object recognition with invariance to pose and lighting. In: IEEE Conference on Computer Vision and Pattern Recognition, pp. 97–104 (June 2004) [74,87]
19. Lee, K.M.: Component-based online learning for face detection and verification. In: Computational Intelligence and Security, pp. 832–837 (February 2005) [72]
20. Li, F.F., Fergus, R., Torralba, A.: Recognizing and learning object categories. In: Short Course at International Conference on Computer Vision (September 2009) [72,73,75,78-80]
21. Li, X.B., Sweigart, J., Teng, J., Donohue, J., Thombs, L.: A dynamic programming based pruning method for decision trees. INFORMS J. Comput. **13**, 332–344 (2001) [85]
22. Lowe, D.G.: Distinctive image features from scale-invariant keypoints. Int. J. Comput. Vis. **60**, 91–110 (2004) [73,78]
23. Mansour, Y.: Pessimistic decision tree pruning based on tree size. In: International Conference on Machine Learning, pp. 195–201 (1997) [85]
24. Maron, O., Tomás, L.P.: A framework for multiple-instance learning. In: Neural Information Processing Systems, pp. 570–576 (December 1998) [88]
25. Matas, J., Chum, O., Urban, M., Pajdla, T.: Robust wide-baseline stereo from maximally stable extremal regions. Image Vis. Comput. **22**, 761–767 (2004) [73]
26. Mikolajczyk, K., Choudhury, R., Schmid, C.: Face detection in a video sequence—A temporal approach. In: IEEE Conference on Computer Vision and Pattern Recognition, pp. 96–103 (June 2001) [72,74]
27. Mikolajczyk, K., Schmid, C.: Scale & affine invariant interest point detectors. Int. J. Comput. Vis. **60**, 63–86 (2004) [73]
28. Moon, H., Chellappa, R., Rosenfeld, A.: Optimal edge-based shape detection. IEEE Trans. Image Process. **11**, 1209–1227 (2002) [73,83,85-87]

29. Nefian, A.V., Hayes III, M.H.: Face detection and recognition using hidden Markov models. In: International Conference on Image Processing, pp. 141–145 (October 1998) [73]

30. Neubeck, A., Gool, L.V.: Efficient non-maximum suppression. In: International Conference on Pattern Recognition, pp. 850–855 (September 2006) [76]

31. Noton, D., Stark, L.: Scanpaths in saccadic eye movements while viewing and recognizing patterns. Vis. Res. **11**, 929–932 (1971) [80]

32. Ojala, T., Pietikäinen, M., Mäenpää, T.: Multiresolution gray-scale and rotation invariant texture classification with local binary patterns. IEEE Trans. Pattern Anal. Mach. Intell. **24**, 971–987 (2002) [78]

33. Ojala, T., Pietikäinen, M., Harwood, D.: A comparative study of texture measures with classification based on featured distributions. Pattern Recognit. **29**, 51–59 (1996) [78]

34. Osuna, E., Freund, R., Girosi, F.: Training support vector machines: An application to face detection. In: IEEE Conference on Computer Vision and Pattern Recognition, pp. 130–137, IEEE Comput. Soc., Los Alamitos (1997) [73,77]

35. Palmer, S.E.: Explorations in Cognition. Freeman, New York (1975) [80]

36. Papageorgiou, C., Poggio, T.: A trainable system for object detection. Int. J. Comput. Vis. **38**, 15–33 (2000) [76]

37. Quattoni, A., Collins, M., Darrell, T.: Conditional random fields for object recognition. In: Neural Information Processing Systems, pp. 1097–1104. MIT Press, Cambridge (2004) [74]

38. Richardson, M., Domingos, P.: Markov logic networks. Mach. Learn. **62**, 107–136 (2006) [83]

39. Rowley, H., Baluja, S., Kanade, T.: Neural network-based face detection. IEEE Trans. Pattern Anal. Mach. Intell. **20**, 23–38 (1998) [73,78,88]

40. Sakai, T., Nagao, M., Fujibayashi, S.: Line extraction and pattern detection in a photograph. Pattern Recognit. **1**, 233–248 (1969) [72]

41. Savarese, S., Winn, J., Criminisi, A.: Discriminative object class models of appearance and shape by correlatons. In: IEEE Conference on Computer Vision and Pattern Recognition, pp. 2033–2040 (June 2006) [79]

42. Schapire, R.E., Singer, Y.: Improved boosting algorithms using confidence-rated predictions. Mach. Learn. **37**, 297–336 (1999) [77]

43. Schwartz, W., Gopalan, R., Chellappa, R., Davis, L.: Robust human detection under occlusion by integrating face and person detectors. In: International Conference on Biometrics, pp. 970–979 (June 2009) [72,81,82]

44. Schwartz, W.R., Kembhavi, A., Harwood, D., Davis, L.S.: Human detection using partial least squares analysis. In: Proceedings of the International Conference on Computer Vision, pp. 24–31 (September 2009) [81,83]

45. Sivic, J., Russell, B.C., Efros, A.A., Zisserman, A., Freeman, W.T.: Discovering objects and their locations in images. In: International Conference on Computer Vision, pp. 370–377 (October 2005) [72,79]

46. Torralba, A.: Contextual priming for object detection. Int. J. Comput. Vis. **53**, 169–191 (2003) [72,74,80]

47. Vijayanarasimhan, S., Grauman, K.: What's it going to cost you?: Predicting effort vs. informativeness for multi-label image annotations. In: IEEE Conference on Computer Vision and Pattern Recognition, pp. 2262–2269 (June 2009) [88]

48. Viola, P., Jones, M.J.: Robust real-time face detection. Int. J. Comput. Vis. **57**, 137–154 (2004) [72-77]

49. Wold, H.: Partial least squares. In: Encyclopedia of Statistical Sciences, vol. 6, pp. 581–591 (1985) [81]

50. Wu, B., Ai, H., Huang, C., Lao, S.: Fast rotation invariant multi-view face detection based on real AdaBoost. In: Automatic Face and Gesture Recognition, pp. 79–83(May 2004) [77]

51. Yang, M.H., Kriegman, D.J., Ahuja, N.: Detecting faces in images: A survey. IEEE Trans. Pattern Anal. Mach. Intell. **24**, 34–58 (2002) [72,73]

Chapter 6
Wide Area Tracking in Single and Multiple Views

Bi Song, Ricky J. Sethi, and Amit K. Roy-Chowdhury

Abstract Maintaining the stability of tracks on multiple targets in video over extended time periods and wide areas remains a challenging problem. Basic trackers like the Kalman filter or particle filter deteriorate in performance as the complexity of the scene increases. A few methods have recently shown encouraging results in these application domains. They rely on learning context models, the availability of training data, or modeling the inter-relationships between the tracks. In this chapter, we provide an overview of research in the area of long-term tracking in video. We review some of the methods in the literature and analyze the common sources of errors which cause trackers to fail. We also discuss the limits of performance of the trackers as multiple objects come together to form groups and crowds. On multiple real-life video sequences obtained for a single camera as well as a camera network, we compare the performance of some of the methods.

6.1 Introduction

Tracking can be defined as a problem of locating a moving object (or multiple objects) over time in the image plane. In other words, the objective of a tracker is to associate target objects in consecutive video frames so as to determine the identities and locations of objects in the video sequence. Multiple object tracking is the most fundamental task for higher level automated video content analysis for its wide application in human–computer interaction, security and surveillance, video communication and compression, augmented reality, traffic control, and video editing.

B. Song (✉) · A.K. Roy-Chowdhury
University of California, Riverside, CA 92521, USA
e-mail: bsong@ee.ucr.edu

A.K. Roy-Chowdhury
e-mail: amitrc@ee.ucr.edu

R.J. Sethi
University of California, Los Angeles, CA 90095, USA
e-mail: rickys@sethi.org

T.B. Moeslund et al. (eds.), *Visual Analysis of Humans*,
DOI 10.1007/978-0-85729-997-0_6, © Springer-Verlag London Limited 2011

Some of the most basic tracking methods include the Kalman filter, particle filter and mean-shift tracker. However, by themselves, these methods are usually not able to track over extended space–time horizons.

In addition to challenges in tracking a single object, like occlusion, appearance variation, and image noise, the critical issue in multi-target tracking is data association, i.e., the problem of linking a sequence of object observations together across image frames. Although a large number of trackers exist, their reliability falls off quickly with the length of the tracks. Stable, long-term tracking is still a challenging problem. Moreover, for multiple targets, we have to consider the interaction between the targets which may cause errors like switching between tracks, missed detections and false detections. In addition, wide area tracking over a camera network introduces certain challenges that are unique to this particular application scenario, like handoff between cameras; often, errors are caused in this handoff stage. Therefore, detection and correction of the errors in the tracks is the key to robust long-term and wide area tracking.

In this chapter, we start off with a review of current work in multi-target tracking. We briefly describe the two most basic stochastic tracking methods—the Kalman filter and particle filter, as well as two representative data association methods—Multi-Hypothesis Tracking (MHT) and Joint Probabilistic Data Association Filters (JPDAF) methods. We then analyze two common sources of errors, which allow us to identify tracklets (i.e., the short-term fragments with low probability of error). The long-term tracking problem can now be defined as developing approaches on how to associate the tracklets based on their features. Similar ideas can be applied to camera networks as tracking across non-overlapping camera networks is essentially to find the association of the targets observed in different camera views, i.e., the handoff problem. We briefly describe a recent method that provides an optimization framework and strategy for computing the associations between tracklets as a stochastic graph evolution scheme. This can be used to obtain tracks of objects that have been occluded or are difficult to disambiguate due to clutter or appearance variations. For a non-overlapping camera network, by associating the tracks from different cameras using this stochastic graph evolution framework, it will automatically lead to a solution of the handoff problem. Finally, we provide a numerical comparison of some of the approaches.

The remainder of this chapter is organized as follows: A review of tracking in single cameras is provided in Sect. 6.2. Then in Sect. 6.3, we analyze the common sources of errors in tracking. We review the issues in tracking across a camera network in Sect. 6.4. In Sect. 6.5, we briefly describe a novel tracklet association strategy using stochastic graph evolution. Section 6.6 shows how to identify groups and crowds where the tracking method may perform poorly, which will allow a tracker to automatically switch to a different strategy. We show comparison of different tracking methods and experimental results on tracking in a camera network in Sect. 6.7, and discuss possible future directions in Sect. 6.8.

6.2 Review of Multi-Target Tracking Approaches

In this section, we review the literature on multi-target tracking. We start by describing two of the most basic methods—the Kalman filter [19] and particle filter [15]. They are stochastic methods and solve tracking problems by taking the measurement and model uncertainties into account during object state estimation. They have been extensively used in the vision community for tracking, but these methods are not powerful for tracking multiple objects by themselves, e.g., the Kalman filter and particle filter assume a single measurement at each time instant. In [14], particle filters were used to track multiple objects by incorporating probabilistic MHT [31] for data association. We describe the MHT [31] and JPDAF [4] strategies for tracking multiple targets.

6.2.1 Kalman Filter Based Tracker

Consider a linear dynamical system with the following time propagation and observation models for a moving object in the scene:

$$\mathbf{x}(t+1) = \mathbf{A}\mathbf{x}(t) + \mathbf{B}\mathbf{w}(t); \quad \mathbf{x}(0), \tag{6.1}$$

$$\mathbf{z}(t) = \mathbf{F}(t)\mathbf{x}(t) + \mathbf{v}(t) \tag{6.2}$$

where $\mathbf{x}$ is the state of the target, $\mathbf{w}(t)$ and $\mathbf{v}(t)$ are zero mean white Gaussian noise ($\mathbf{w}(t) \sim \mathcal{N}(0, \mathbf{Q}^l), \mathbf{v}(t) \sim \mathcal{N}(0, \mathbf{R})$) and $\mathbf{x}(0) \sim \mathcal{N}(\mathbf{x}_0, \mathbf{P}_0)$ is the initial state of the target.

The Kalman filter is composed of two steps, prediction and correction. The prediction step uses the state model to predict the new state of the variables:

$$\bar{\mathbf{P}}(t+1) = \mathbf{A}\hat{\mathbf{P}}(t)\mathbf{A}^T + \mathbf{B}\mathbf{Q}\mathbf{B}^T,$$
$$\bar{\mathbf{x}}(t+1) = \mathbf{A}\hat{\mathbf{x}}(t). \tag{6.3}$$

The correction step uses the current observations $\mathbf{z}(t)$ to update the object's state:

$$\mathbf{K}(t+1) = \bar{\mathbf{P}}(t+1)\mathbf{F}^T\left(\mathbf{F}\bar{\mathbf{P}}(t+1)\mathbf{F}^T + \mathbf{R}\right)^{-1},$$
$$\hat{\mathbf{x}}(t+1) = \bar{\mathbf{x}}(t+1) + \mathbf{K}(t+1)\left(\mathbf{z}(t+1) - \mathbf{F}\bar{\mathbf{x}}(t+1)\right), \tag{6.4}$$
$$\hat{\mathbf{P}}(t+1) = \left(\mathbf{I} - \mathbf{K}(t+1)\mathbf{F}\right)\bar{\mathbf{P}}(t+1).$$

Extensions to this basic approach dealing with non-linear models in video applications can be found in [40].

6.2.2 Particle Filter Based Tracker

The particle filter is often used in tracking applications in video to deal with non-linear and/or non-Gaussian models [2]. The following are the main steps typically used in a particle filter based tracker with some variations.

Moving objects are often initialized using motion detection. The background modeling algorithms presented in Chap. 3 are used to learn the multimodal background through time. In addition, in many applications, by observing that most of the interested targets, like people and vehicles, are on ground plane, the rough ground plane area can be estimated [11]. Based on the ground plane information, false alarms can be removed significantly. The target regions can then be represented by rectangles with the state vector $X_t = [x, y, \dot{x}, \dot{y}, l_x, l_y]$, where (x, y) and $(\dot{x}, \dot{y})$ are the position and velocity of a target in the x and y directions, respectively, and (l_x, l_y) denote the size of the rectangle.

The observation process is defined by the likelihood distribution, $p(I_t|X_t)$, where X_t is the state vector and I_t is the image observation at t. The observation models can be generated in many ways. Here we provide an example by combining an appearance and a foreground response model, i.e.,

$$p(I_t|X_t) = p\big(I_t^a, I_t^f|X_t\big), \tag{6.5}$$

where I_t^a is the appearance information of I_t and I_t^f is the foreground response of I_t using a learned background model. I_t^f is a binary image with "1" for foreground and "0" for background. It is reasonable to assume that I_t^a and I_t^f are independent and thus (6.5) becomes

$$p(I_t|X_t) = p\big(I_t^a|X_t\big)p\big(I_t^f|X_t\big). \tag{6.6}$$

The appearance observation likelihood can for example be defined as

$$p\big(I_t^a|X_t\big) \propto \exp\big\{-B\big(ch(X_t), ch_0\big)^2\big\}, \tag{6.7}$$

where $ch(X_t)$ is the color histogram associated with the rectangle region of X_t and ch_0 is color histogram of the initialized target. $B(.)$ is the Bhattacharyya distance between two color histograms. The foreground response observation likelihood can be defined as

$$p\big(I_t^f|X_t\big) \propto \exp\left\{-\left(1 - \frac{\#F(X_t)}{\#X_t}\right)^2\right\}, \tag{6.8}$$

where $\#F(X_t)$ is the number of foreground pixels in the rectangular region of X_t and $\#X_t$ is the total number of pixels in that rectangle. $\frac{\#F(X_t)}{\#X_t}$ represents the percentage of the foreground in that rectangle. The observation likelihood would be higher if more pixels in the rectangular region of X_t belong to the foreground. The reader should note that these are representative examples only. Various models are possible, and indeed, have been used in the literature.

The particle filter is a sequential Monte Carlo method (sequential importance sampling plus resampling) which provides at each t, an N sample Monte Carlo approximation to the prediction distribution, $\pi_{t|t-1}(dx) = \Pr(X_t \in dx | I_{1:t-1})$, which is used to search for newly observed targets. These are then used to update $\pi_{t|t-1}$ to get the filtering (posterior) distribution, $\pi_{t|t}(dx) = \Pr(X_t \in dx | I_{1:t})$. A particle filter is used because the system and observation models are non-linear and the posterior can temporarily become multi-model due to background clutter.

6.2.3 Multi-Hypothesis Tracking (MHT)

This algorithm allows multiple hypotheses to be propagated in time as data are received. Multi-Hypothesis Tracking (MHT) is an iterative algorithm and is initialized with a set of current track hypotheses. Each hypothesis is a collection of disjoint tracks. For each hypothesis, the position of each object at the next time step is predicted. On receiving new data, each hypothesis is expanded into a set of new hypotheses by considering all measurement-to-track assignments for the tracks within the hypothesis. The probability of each new hypothesis is calculated. Often, for reasons of finite computer memory and computational power, the most unlikely hypotheses are deleted. The final tracks of the objects are the most likely set of associations over the time period. Note that MHT exhaustively enumerates all possible associations and is computationally exponential both in memory and time.

6.2.4 Joint Probabilistic Data Association Filters (JPDAF)

This method is specifically designed for cluttered measurement models. The idea of Joint Probabilistic Data Association Filters (JPDAF) is to compute an expected state estimate over the various possibilities of measurement-to-track associations. Assuming we have n tracks and m measurements at time t, $Z(t) = \{z_1(t), \ldots, z_m(t)\}$, the state estimation of target i is

$$\hat{x}_i(t) = E[x_i(t)|Z(t)] = \sum_{j=1}^{m} E[x_i(t)|\chi_{ij}^t, Z(t)] P(\chi_{ij}^t|Z(t))$$

where χ_{ij} denotes the event that measurement i associates to target j.

In order to overcome the large computational cost of MHT and JPDAF, various optimization algorithms such as Linear programming [17], Quadratic boolean programming [23], and Hungarian algorithm [27] are used for data association. In [44], data association was achieved through a Markov Chain Monte Carlo (MCMC) sampling based framework. In [34], a multiframe approach was proposed to preserve temporal coherency of the speed and position. They formulate the correspondence as a graph-theoretic problem to finding the best path for each point across multiple frames. They use a window of frames during point correspondence to handle occlusions whose durations are shorter than the temporal window used to perform matching.

6.3 Errors in Multi-Target Tracking

Tracking is a state estimation problem and errors are inevitable in even carefully designed strategies. Therefore, it is important to understand the sources of the errors and mitigate their effects as far as possible. There are two common errors: lost track (when the track is no longer on any target, but on the background) and track switching (when targets are close and the tracks are on the wrong target); this includes tracks merging and splitting. Identifying these situations can lead to the rules for tracklet estimation, i.e., determining short track segments where the probability of an error is low. An example is shown in Fig. 6.1. We describe these two common sources of errors.

Detection of lost track: The tracking error (TE) [4] or prediction error is the distance between the current observation and its prediction based on past observations. TE will increase when the tracker loses track and can be used to detect the unreliability of the track result. As an example, in the preceding observation model for the particle filter, TE of tracked target $\hat{X}_t$ is calculated by

$$TE(\hat{X}_t, I_t) = TE_a(\hat{X}_t, I_t) + TE_f(\hat{X}_t, I_t), \tag{6.9}$$

where $TE_a(\hat{X}_t, I_t) = B\big(ch(X_t), ch_0\big)^2$ and $TE_f(\hat{X}_t, I_t) = \left(1 - \dfrac{\#F(X_t)}{\#X_t}\right)^2.$

If a lost track is detected, it means the tracking result after this point is not reliable; in the tracking procedure, we can stop doing tracking after this point and identify a tracklet. In the case of false detection (i.e., the detected target is a part of background), or target passes through a region with similar color, or a target stops, the background modeling algorithm will adapt to treat this as a part of the background, and thus TE_f will eventually increase. Then a lost track will be detected.

Track switching: When targets are close to each other, a track switch can happen with high probability especially if the appearances of targets are similar. Thus, we can inspect the distances between targets, and break the tracks into tracklets at the points where targets are getting close, as shown in Fig. 6.1.

6.3.1 Solution Strategies

Many state-of-the-art tracking algorithms focus on how to avoid errors. In [45], the authors proposed a min-cost flow framework for global optimal data association. A tracklet association based tracking method was presented in [8], which fixed

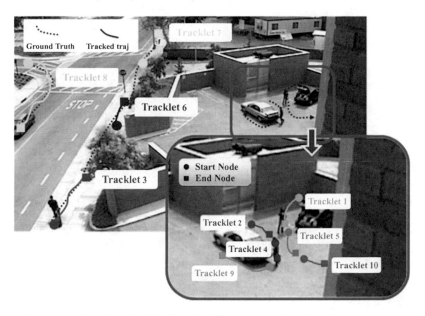

Fig. 6.1 An example of tracklet identification. The ground truth trajectories are represented by brown dotted lines. The estimated tracklets due to detection of a lost track (track of the person in lower left corner due to occlusion) and targets' close proximity (the persons moving around the cars) are clearly shown in different colors. Reproduced with permission from [35]

the affinity model heuristically and focused on searching for optimal associations. A HybridBoosted affinity model was learned in [25]. The method is built on the availability of training data under a similar environment, which may not be always feasible. The authors in [3] addressed the problem of learning an adaptive appearance model for object tracking. Context information was considered in [43] to help in tracking, by integrating a set of auxiliary objects which are learned online. It can be a powerful method in applications where it is easy to find these auxiliary objects. A joint probabilistic relation graph approach was presented in [41] to simultaneously detect and track a large number of vehicles in low frame rate aerial videos. The authors explored vehicle behavior model from road structure and generated a set of constraints to regulate both object based vertex matching and pairwise edge matching schemes. These two matching schemes were unified into a single cost minimization framework to produce a quadratic optimized association result. In [5], an inference graph was built to represent merge-split relations between the tracked blobs, so as to handle fragmentation and grouping ambiguity in tracking. In [35], an adaptive tracklet association was proposed and is explained later in Sect. 6.5.

6.3.2 Tracklet Affinity Modeling

Computing long-term associations between tracklets requires evaluating similarities between them. The estimated tracklets need to be associated based on their affinities to come up with longer tracks. The affinities between tracklets are often modeled by exploring their appearance and motion attributes. Here we provide some examples for achieving this.

Appearance model: The appearance affinity between a pair of tracklets, (T_i, T_j), can be defined based on their color histograms. Let Ch_i and Ch_j be the mean color histograms learned within T_i and T_j. Then the appearance affinity can be defined as

$$A_a(T_i, T_j) \propto \exp(-B(Ch_i, Ch_j)), \tag{6.10}$$

where $B(.)$ represents the Bhattacharyya distance between two histograms.

Motion model: As described in [42], the motion affinity can be modeled based on both the forward and backward velocities of the tracklets. The forward and backward velocities are estimated within each tracklet. Assume tracklet T_i occurs earlier in time, and tracklet T_j begins after the T_i ended, the motion affinity between T_i and T_j is defined as

$$A_m(T_i, T_j) \propto \exp\left(-\left(p_i^{\text{tail}} + v_i^F \Delta t - p_j^{\text{head}}\right)^2\right) \exp\left(-\left(p_j^{\text{head}} + v_j^B \Delta t - p_i^{\text{tail}}\right)^2\right), \tag{6.11}$$

where p_i^{tail} and p_j^{head} are the tail and head positions of T_i and T_j, v_i^F and v_j^B are their forward and backward velocities, and Δt is the time gap between T_i and T_j.

Since it is reasonable to assume that the appearance and motion are independent, the affinity of a pair of tracklets can be modeled as

$$A(T_i, T_j) = A_a(T_i, T_j) \cdot A_m(T_i, T_j). \tag{6.12}$$

6.4 Tracking in Camera Networks

Some of the existing methods on tracking in a camera network include [13, 16, 21]. The authors in [30] used location and velocity of objects moving across multiple non-overlapping cameras to estimate the calibration parameters of the cameras and the target's trajectory. In [24], a particle filter was used to switch between track prediction between non-overlapping cameras and tracking within a camera. In [20], the authors presented a method for tracking in overlapping stationary and pan-tilt-zoom cameras by maximizing a joint motion and appearance probability model. A Bayesian formulation of the problem of reconstructing the path of objects across multiple non-overlapping cameras was presented in [21] using color histograms for object appearance. A graph-theoretic framework for addressing the problem of tracking in a network of cameras was presented in [16]. An online learned discriminative appearance affinity model by adopting Multiple Instance Learning boosting algorithm was proposed in [22] for associating multi-target tracks across multiple non-overlapping cameras.

A related work that deals with tracking targets in a camera network with PTZ cameras is [29]. Here, the authors proposed a mixture between a distributed and a centralized scheme using both static and PTZ cameras in a virtual camera network environment. A framework for distributed tracking and control in camera network using Kalman-consensus filter was presented in [36, 39]. Please also see Sect. 16.3.2.

Tracking in camera networks is closely related to person re-identification in camera networks. In [10], a machine learning algorithm was used to find the best feature representation of objects, where many different kinds of simple features to be combined into a single similarity function for matching objects. In [28], the person re-identify across disjoint camera views was reformulated as a ranking problem. By learning a subspace where the potential true match is given highest ranking rather than any direct distance measure, the problem was solved using a Ensemble RankSVM. A Cross Canonical Correlation Analysis framework was formulated in [26] to detect and quantify temporal and causal relationships between regional activities within and across camera views. In [7], the authors presented an appearance-based method for person re-identification. It consists of the extraction and fusion of features that model three complementary aspects of the human appearance: the overall chromatic content, the spatial arrangement of colors into stable regions, and the presence of recurrent local motifs with high entropy. A spatiotemporal segmentation algorithm was employed in [9] to generate salient edgels and the invariant signatures were generated by combining normalized color and salient edgel histograms for establishing the correspondence across camera views. In [37, 38], it was shown that tracking in a camera network can be solved using a stochastic adaptive strategy. Adapting the feature correspondence computations by modeling the long-term dependencies between them and then obtaining the statistically optimal paths for each person differentiates this approach from existing ones. It provides a solution that is robust to errors in feature extraction, correspondence and environmental conditions.

The main new (compared to single camera tracking) challenge in the problem of tracking across non-overlapping camera networks is to find the correspondences between the targets observed in different camera views. This is often referred to as the handoff problem in camera networks. Thus, we can think of tracking over a camera network as being equivalent to finding the associations between the tracklets obtained in different single cameras. Then, the problem boils down to finding the affinities between the tracklets so as to have tracks across cameras. Depending on the applications, various features can be used like appearance, motion, calibration, travel time, 3D models, etc. As an example, we show how the travel time between entry/exit nodes of different cameras can be used in the affinity modeling. The affinity between two tracks T_i^m and T_j^n that are observed at camera C_m and C_n, respectively, can be estimated as the product of the similarity in appearance features and the travel time based similarity value, i.e.,

$$A\big(T_i^m, T_j^n\big) = A_a\big(T_i^m, T_j^n\big) A_\tau(\tau_{T_i^m, T_j^n}), \qquad (6.13)$$

where $A_a(.)$ is the appearance affinity model as in (6.10) and $A_\tau(.)$ represents the transition pattern between two camera nodes [16].

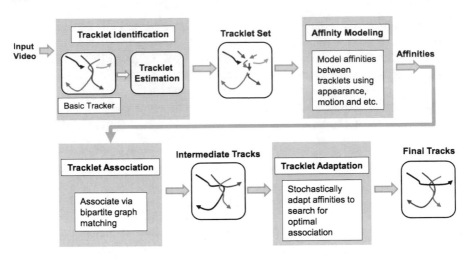

Fig. 6.2 Overview of stochastic graph evolution framework. Reproduced with permission from [35]

6.5 A Stochastic Graph Evolution Framework for Tracklet Association

In this section, we show how the affinity models between tracklets (for single or multiple cameras) can be used to find associations between them so as to obtain stable, robust long-term tracks. This is a brief review of a recent approach that is described in more detail in [35]. The method can deal with some of the most pressing challenges in multi-target tracking, e.g., occlusion within a view and handoff between cameras.

Figure 6.2 shows an overview of the scheme. The method begins by identifying tracklets, i.e., the short-term fragments with low probability of error, which are estimated from the initial tracks by evaluating the tracking performance as described in Sect. 6.3. The tracklets are then associated based on their affinities. Using the affinity model, a tracklet association graph (TAG) is created with the tracklets as nodes and affinity scores as weights. The association of the tracklets can be found by computing the optimal paths in the graph. The optimal path computation is based on the principles of dynamic programming and gives the Maximum a Posteriori Probability (MAP) estimate of tracklets' connections as the long-term tracks for each target.

The tracking problem could be solved optimally by the above tracklet association method if the affinity scores were known exactly and assumed to be independent. However, this can be a big assumption due to well-known low-level image processing challenges, like poor lighting conditions or unexpected motion of the targets. As shown in Fig. 6.3, if the similarity estimation is incorrect for one pair of tracklets, the overall inferred long track may be wrong even if all the other tracklets are connected correctly. This leads to a graph evolution scheme. The affinities (i.e., the

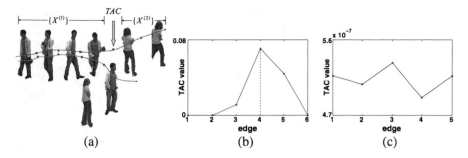

Fig. 6.3 **a** Tracklets of two targets obtained from Videoweb courtyard dataset [6]: ground truth track of the person in green T-shirt is shown with orange line, and the association results before adaptation are shown with blue line. **b–c** TAC values along the incorrect and correct association results, respectively, (note that the range of the y-axis in (c) is much smaller than (b)). It is clear that TAC has a peak at the wrong link; thus the variance of TAC along the wrongly associated tracklets is higher than the correct one. Reproduced with permission from [35]

weights on the edges of TAG) are stochastically adapted by considering the distribution of the features along possible paths in the association graph to search for the global optimum. A Tracklet Association Cost (TAC) function and an efficient optimization strategy are designed for this process. As shown in Fig. 6.3, the TAC values can be used to indicate the incorrect associations. The overall approach is able to track stably over minutes of video in challenging domains with no learning and context information.

6.6 Identifying Transitions to Groups and Crowds

When a large number of targets are in close proximity, tracking each individual target becomes very difficult and sometimes it is more desirable to treat them as a group or a crowd, which can then be tracked as a single entity. As techniques designed for non-crowded scenes usually cannot be straightforwardly extended for dealing with crowded situations, crowd analysis has attracted more and more interest in recent years. A survey on crowd analysis using computer vision techniques can be found in [18]. There are also a number of research papers on tracking in crowded scenes. In [1], an approach for people tracking in structured high-density scenarios was proposed. In their work, each frame of a video sequence is divided into cells, each cell presenting one particle. A person consists of a set of particles, and each person is affected by the layout of the scene as well as the motion of other people. The method described in [12] detects global motion patterns by constructing super tracks using flow vectors for tracking high-density crowd flows in low-resolution videos. A tracking method to deal with unstructured environments was proposed in [32], in which the motion of a crowd appears to be random with different participants moving in different directions over time (e.g., a crossway). They employ the correlated topic model, which allows each location of the scene to have various crowd behaviors.

Fig. 6.4 Physics-inspired model of transitions from individuals to groups: individuals are modeled as free particles and groups as an n-body. In these two examples, the average G_{tr} for the sequence of individuals is 23.83 while the average G_{tr} for the sequence of groups is 0.18

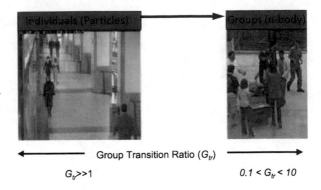

Group Transition Ratio (G_{tr})

$G_{tr} \gg 1$ $0.1 < G_{tr} < 10$

The methods on crowd analysis assume that it is known that the scene consists of a crowd. Often, we have situations where individuals merge together form a group and cannot be tracked separately any more. This detection of transitions from individuals to groups and crowds has received lesser attention. One such transitions are identified, pre-existing group/crowd analysis approaches, such as [1, 12, 32], can be employed to examine the group/crowd's dynamics.

An idea that is being currently being explored by the authors [33] involves a physics-inspired methodology to model the transition of Individuals to Groups to Crowds analogous to the transition of Individual Particles to N-Body to Fluids in fluid dynamics, as shown in Fig. 6.4, where the Group Transition Ratio (G_{tr}) categorizes the collection as individual people or groups. G_{tr} is defined based on comparing the distance between objects and their sizes. It utilizes the ideas in fluid dynamics for analysis of multi-object activities and, in a similar fashion, when $G_{tr} \ll 1$ for a collection of objects, we label them as a crowd; when $G_{tr} \gg 1$, we label them as individual objects; finally, when $G_{tr} \sim 1$ (empirically between 0.1 and 10), the objects are identified to be in a transition region and labeled as a group.

6.7 Performance Analysis

In this section, we provide comparison of some methods on multi-target tracking in single camera view and show tracking results in a camera network using the stochastic data association strategy in [37, 38].

6.7.1 Single Camera Tracking Performance

We compare the performance of several methods on the CAVIAR dataset, see next chapter for details. The CAVIAR is captured in a shopping mall corridor with heavy inter-object occlusion. To evaluate the performance quantitatively, we

Table 6.1 Evaluation metrics. Reproduced with permission from [35]

Name	Definition
GT	Num of ground truth trajectories
MT%	Mostly tracked: Percentage of GT trajectories which are covered by tracker output more than 80% in time
ML%	Mostly lost: Percentage of GT trajectories which are covered by tracker output less than 20% in time
FG	Fragments: The total Num of times that the ID of a target changed along a GT trajectory
IDS	ID switches: The total Num of times that a tracked target changes its ID with another target
RS%	Recover from short-term occlusion
RL%	Recover from long-term occlusion

Table 6.2 Tracking Results on CAVIAR dataset. Results of [25] and [45] are reported on 20 sequences; basic particle filter and [35] are reported on seven most challenging sequences of the dataset. Test data used in [35] and basic particle filter has totally 12308 frames for about 500 sec. Reproduced with permission from [35]

	GT	MT	ML	FG	IDS	RS	RL
Zhang et al. [45]	140	85.7%	3.6%	20	15	–	–
Li et al. [25]	143	84.6%	1.4%	17	11	–	–
Basic particle filter	75	53.3%	10.7%	15	19	18/42	0/8
Song et al. [35]	75	84.0%	4.0%	6	8	36/42	6/8

adopt the evaluation metrics for tracking defined in [25] and [45]. In addition, we define RS and RL to evaluate the ability of recovering from occlusion (see Table 6.1).

In CAVIAR dataset, the inter-object occlusion is high and includes long-term partial occlusion and full occlusion. Moreover, frequent interactions between targets such as multiple people talking and walking in a group make tracking more challenging. The results of [35] are shown on the relatively more challenging part of the dataset which contains 7 videos (TwoEnterShop3, TwoEnterShop2, ThreePastShop2, ThreePastShop1, TwoEnterShop1, OneShopOneWait1, OneStopMoveEnter1). Table 6.2 shows the comparison among the stochastic graph evolution framework [35], the min-cost flow approach in [45], HybridBoosted affinity modeling approach in [25] and a basic particle filter. It should also be noted that [25, 45] are built on the availability of training data under similar environments (e.g. 6 sequences in CAVIAR are used for training in [45]), while the stochastic graph evolution method [35] does not rely on any training. Some sample frames with results from [35] are shown in Fig. 6.5.

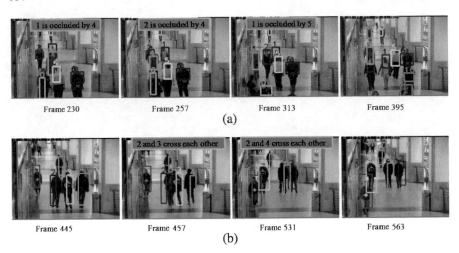

Fig. 6.5 Sample tracking results on CAVIAR dataset using [35]

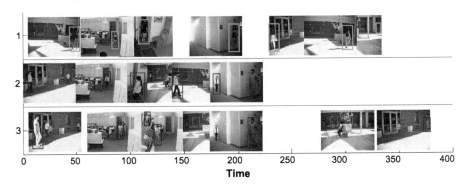

Fig. 6.6 Example of some of the images of the people in the network. The horizontal axis is the time when these images were observed, while the vertical axis is the index of the persons. The tracks of 3 of the targets are shown in different colors and clearly demonstrate the ability to deal with handoff in non-overlapping cameras

6.7.2 Camera Network Tracking

We now show some results on tracking in a camera network using the stochastic graph evolution framework as described in detail in [38]. The network consists of 7 cameras and 26 entry/exist nodes. The cameras are installed in both indoor and outdoor environments which consist of large illumination and appearance changes. We considered 9 people moving across the network for about 7 minutes. Examples of some of the images of 3 persons with tracking results are shown in Fig. 6.6. Note the significant changes of appearance. The results thus demonstrate the ability to track with handoffs. Tracking in large camera networks is still in the process of maturing and there do not exist standard datasets to compare performance of various methods. The recently released camera network dataset [6] can provide such an evaluation benchmark in the future.

6.8 Conclusions and Thoughts on Future Work

In this chapter, we reviewed existing methods in long-term tracking in single and multiple views, identified their strengths and weaknesses, analyzed the sources of errors and discussed solution strategies. We also looked at the issue of transitions between individual tracking and group tracking. Performance comparison was provided on the well-known CAVIAR dataset.

Although tracking is one of the most studied problems in computer vision, there is still some way to go before the methods are able to work in real-world situations that involve large numbers of objects in close proximity or maintain the tracks over extended space–time horizons. Technically, this requires the methods to be robust to data association errors in cluttered scenarios, when there are large variations in appearance, or when objects are not visible due to occlusions. A promising approach is to consider contextual information, i.e., not only to look at the track of each individual object but also the collection of other nearby objects. This needs to be done carefully since too much emphasis on context can be misleading. Tracking in non-overlapping camera networks has received much less attention and should be a focus area in future work. The methods should be able to scale over a large number of cameras. Standard datasets for evaluating camera network tracking need to be adopted by the tracking community. Another interesting area that has recently received interest is the development of distributed tracking frameworks, i.e., camera network tracking methods where processing is distributed over the sensor nodes [36].

Acknowledgements This work was supported in part by NSF grant IIS-0712253 and subcontract from Mayachitra Inc., through a DARPA STTR award (#W31P4Q-08-C-0464).

References

1. Ali, S., Shah, M.: Floor fields for tracking in high density crowd scenes. In: Euro. Conference on Computer Vision (2008) [101,102]
2. Arulampalam, M.S., Maskell, S., Gordon, N.: A tutorial on particle filters for online nonlinear/non-Gaussian Bayesian tracking. IEEE Trans. Signal Process. **50**, 174–188 (2002) [94]
3. Babenko, B., Yang, M., Belongie, S.: Visual tracking with online multiple instance learning. In: IEEE Conf. on Computer Vision and Pattern Recognition (2009) [97]
4. Bar-Shalom, Y., Fortmann, T.: Tracking and Data Association. Academic Press, San Diego (1988) [93,96]
5. Bose, B., Wang, X., Grimson, E.: Multi-class object tracking algorithm that handles fragmentation and grouping. In: IEEE Conf. on Computer Vision and Pattern Recognition (2007) [97]
6. Denina, G., Bhanu, B., Nguyen, H., Ding, C., Kamal, A., Ravishankar, C., Roy-Chowdhury, A., Ivers, A., Varda, B.: VideoWeb dataset for multi-camera activities and non-verbal communication. In: Bhanu, B., Ravishankar, C., Roy-Chowdhury, A., Aghajan, H., Terzopoulos, D. (eds.) Distributed Video Sensor Networks. Springer, London (2011) [101,105]

7. Farenzena, M., Bazzani, L., Perina, A., Cristani, M., Murino, V.: Person re-identification by symmetry-driven accumulation of local features. In: IEEE Conf. on Computer Vision and Pattern Recognition (2010) [99]

8. Ge, W., Collins, R.: Multi-target data association by tracklets with unsupervised parameter estimation. In: British Machine Vision Conference (2008) [96]

9. Gheissari, N., Sebastian, T., Hartley, R.: Person re-identification using spatiotemporal appearance. In: IEEE Conf. on Computer Vision and Pattern Recognition (2006) [99]

10. Gray, D., Tao, H.: Viewpoint invariant pedestrian recognition with an ensemble of localized features. In: Euro. Conference on Computer Vision (2008) [99]

11. Hoiem, D., Efros, A., Hebert, M.: Geometric context from a single image. In: IEEE Intl. Conf. on Computer Vision (2005) [94]

12. Hu, M., Ali, S., Shah, M.: Detecting global motion patterns in complex videos. In: Intl. Conf. on Pattern Recognition (2008) [101,102]

13. Huang, T., Russel, S.: Object identification in a Bayesian context. In: International Joint Conference on Artificial Intelligence (1997) [98]

14. Hue, C., Cadre, J.L., Prez, P.: Sequential Monte Carlo methods for multiple target tracking and data fusion. IEEE Trans. Signal Process. **50**(2), 309–325 (2002) [93]

15. Isard, M., Blake, A.: Condensation – conditional density propagation for visual tracking. Int. J. Comput. Vis. **29**(1), 5–28 (1998) [93]

16. Javed, O., Rasheed, Z., Shafique, K., Shah, M.: Tracking across multiple cameras with disjoint views. In: IEEE Intl. Conf. on Computer Vision (2003) [98,99]

17. Jiang, H., Fels, S., Little, J.: A linear programming approach for multiple object tracking. In: IEEE Conf. on Computer Vision and Pattern Recognition (2007) [95]

18. Junior, J.C.S.J., Musse, S.R., Jung, C.R.: Crowd analysis using computer vision techniques. IEEE Signal Process. Mag. **27**(5), 66–77 (2010) [101]

19. Kalman, R.: A new approach to linear filtering and prediction problems. Trans. ASME – J. Basic Eng. **82**, 35–45 (1990) [93]

20. Kang, J., Cohen, I., Medioni, G.: Continuous tracking within and across camera streams. In: IEEE Conf. on Computer Vision and Pattern Recognition (2004) [98]

21. Kettnaker, V., Zabih, R.: Bayesian multi-camera surveillance. In: IEEE Conf. on Computer Vision and Pattern Recognition (1999) [98]

22. Kuo, C.-H., Huang, C., Nevatia, R.: Inter-camera association of multi-target tracks by on-line learned appearance affinity models. In: Euro. Conference on Computer Vision (2010) [98]

23. Leibe, B., Schindler, K., Gool, L.V.: Coupled detection and trajectory estimation for multi-object tracking. In: IEEE Intl. Conf. on Computer Vision (2007) [95]

24. Leoputra, W., Tan, T., Lim, F.L.: Non-overlapping distributed tracking using particle filter. In: Intl. Conf. on Pattern Recognition (2006) [98]

25. Li, Y., Huang, C., Nevatia, R.: Learning to associate: HybridBoosted multi-target tracker for crowded scene. In: IEEE Conf. on Computer Vision and Pattern Recognition (2009) [97,103]

26. Loy, C., Xiang, T., Gong, S.: Multi-camera activity correlation analysis. In: IEEE Conf. on Computer Vision and Pattern Recognition (2009) [99]

27. Perera, A., Srinivas, C., Hoogs, A., Brooksby, G., Hu, W.: Multi-object tracking through simultaneous long occlusions and split-merge conditions. In: IEEE Conf. on Computer Vision and Pattern Recognition (2006) [95]

28. Prosser, B., Zheng, W., Gong, S., Xiang, T.: Person re-identification by support vector ranking. In: British Machine Vision Conference (2010) [99]

29. Qureshi, F.Z., Terzopoulos, D.: Surveillance in virtual reality: System design and multi-camera control. In: IEEE Conf. on Computer Vision and Pattern Recognition (2007) [98]

30. Rahimi, A., Darrell, T.: Simultaneous calibration and tracking with a network of non-overlapping sensors. In: IEEE Conf. on Computer Vision and Pattern Recognition (2004) [98]

31. Reid, D.: An algorithm for tracking multiple targets. IEEE Trans. Autom. Control **24**(6), 843–854 (1979) [93]

32. Rodriguez, M., Ali, S., Kanade, T.: Tracking in unstructured crowded scenes. In: IEEE Intl. Conf. on Computer Vision (2009) [101,102]

33. Sethi, R., Roy-Chowdhury, A.: Modeling and recognition of complex multi-person interactions in video. In: ACM Intl. Workshop on Multimodal Pervasive Video Analysis (2010) [102]
34. Shafique, K., Shah, M.: A non-iterative greedy algorithm for multi-frame point correspondence. IEEE Trans. Pattern Anal. Mach. Intell. **27**(1), 51–65 (2005) [95]
35. Song, B., Jeng, T., Staudt, E., Roy-Chowdhury, A.: A stochastic graph evolution framework for robust multi-target tracking. In: Euro. Conference on Computer Vision (2010) [97,100, 101,103,104]
36. Song, B., Kamal, A., Soto, C., Ding, C., Farrell, J., Roy-Chowdhury, A.: Tracking and activity recognition through consensus in distributed camera networks. IEEE Trans. Image Process. **19**(10), 2564–2579 (2010) [99,105]
37. Song, B., Roy-Chowdhury, A.: Stochastic adaptive tracking in a camera network. In: IEEE Intl. Conf. on Computer Vision (2007) [99,102]
38. Song, B., Roy-Chowdhury, A.: Robust tracking in a camera network: A multi-objective optimization framework. IEEE J. Sel. Topics Signal Process. (Special Issue on Distributed Processing in Vision Networks) **2**(4), 582–596 (2008) [99,102,104]
39. Soto, C., Song, B., Roy-Chowdhury, A.: Distributed multi-target tracking in a self-configuring camera network. In: IEEE Conf. on Computer Vision and Pattern Recognition (2009) [99]
40. Welch, G., Bishop, G.: An Introduction to the Kalman Filter. Technical report, University of North Carolina at Chapel Hill, Chapel Hill, NC, USA (1995) [93]
41. Xiao, J., Cheng, H., Sawhney, H.S., Han, F.: Vehicle detection and tracking in wide field-of-view aerial video. In: IEEE Conf. on Computer Vision and Pattern Recognition (2010) [97]
42. Xing, J., Ai, H., Lao, S.: Multi-object tracking through occlusion by local tracklets filtering and global tracklets association with detection responses. In: IEEE Conf. on Computer Vision and Pattern Recognition (2009) [98]
43. Yang, M., Wu, Y., Hua, G.: Context-aware visual tracking. IEEE Trans. Pattern Anal. Mach. Intell. **31**(7), 1195–1209 (2009) [97]
44. Yu, Q., Medioni, G., Cohen, I.: Multiple target tracking using spatio-temporal Markov chain Monte Carlo data association. In: IEEE Conf. on Computer Vision and Pattern Recognition (2007) [95]
45. Zhang, L., Li, Y., Nevatia, R.: Global data association for multi-object tracking using network flows. In: IEEE Conf. on Computer Vision and Pattern Recognition (2008) [96,103]

Chapter 7
Benchmark Datasets for Detection and Tracking

Anna-Louise Ellis and James Ferryman

Abstract There is a rising demand for the quantitative performance evaluation of automated video surveillance. To advance research in this area, it is essential that comparisons in detection and tracking approaches may be drawn and improvements in existing methods can be measured. There are a number of challenges related to the proper evaluation of motion segmentation, tracking, event recognition, and other components of a video surveillance system that are unique to the video surveillance community. These include the volume of data that must be evaluated, the difficulty in obtaining ground truth data, the definition of appropriate metrics, and achieving meaningful comparison of diverse systems. This chapter provides descriptions of useful benchmark datasets and their availability to the computer vision community. It outlines some ground truth and evaluation techniques, and provides links to useful resources. It concludes by discussing the future direction for benchmark datasets and their associated processes.

7.1 Datasets

The computer vision community lacks a standard database of videos that can be used for the evaluation of automated visual surveillance approaches. This chapter details popular benchmark datasets that may be used by researchers to assist in their investigations to provide robust solutions. Those researching the creation of automated visual surveillance systems require benchmark datasets that provide realistic settings, environmental conditions, and scenarios. In addition, it can be very time consuming to create enough scenarios to adequately test some approaches. The datasets described in this chapter address these issues. Furthermore these benchmark datasets appear in a diffuse set of published papers, and these in turn may assist current researchers in this area to contrast and compare techniques. Most provide a set of data for training a system and a separate set for testing. There are some that

A.-L. Ellis (✉) · J. Ferryman
University of Reading, Whiteknights, Reading, UK
e-mail: a.l.ellis@reading.ac.uk

J. Ferryman
e-mail: j.m.ferryman@reading.ac.uk

T.B. Moeslund et al. (eds.), *Visual Analysis of Humans*,
DOI 10.1007/978-0-85729-997-0_7, © Springer-Verlag London Limited 2011

Table 7.1 A preview of the dataset types referred to throughout this chapter

	Real World	Simulated	Multi-Camera	Single-Camera	Footage Quality
CAVIAR	shops/office	no	2	no	384 × 288, 25 fps
Daimler	traffic in vehicle	no	no	yes	640 × 480
ETISEO	metro/airport apron	no	4, 2, 1	no	mixed sensors/modality
i-LIDS	fenced area	no			
PETS 2001	street scene	no	4, 2	no	768 × 576, 25 fps[*]
PETS 2006	train station	no	4	no	768 × 576, 25 fps
PETS 2007	airport	no	4	no	768 × 576, 25 fps
PETS 2009/10	crowds	no	8	no	768 × 576 720 × 576, 25 fps
MuHAVi	human actions[**]	street lights[**]	4	no	720 × 576 704 × 576, 25 fps
ViHASi	no	avatar actions	40	no	640 × 480, 30 fps

[*]includes fixed, moving and cadiotropic lens footage

[**]contains both simulated and real world footage

require the evaluation set to remain unseen. Table 7.1 provides a preview of these datasets and their characteristics.

Both real world and simulated surveillance footage datasets are readily available to the computational vision community. They bring different strengths to an automated visual surveillance research project. Real world footage highlights the numerous challenges faced in developing robust solutions, such as rapidly shifting light levels and shadows due to ever changing cloud cover and reflective surfaces. Simulated footage offers exact control over content, can provide numerous camera angles and a means of automating time consuming ground-truthing. The datasets described in this chapter cover a variety of areas where video surveillance is common place and include typical behavior and in some, behavior of objects that may need highlighting to those requiring the surveillance.

The attempt at automated visual surveillance from the footage shot with a single camera can be affected by shortcomings such as occlusions (where one person moves in front of some other person or object), illumination differences and complex movements. Systems commonly require a multi-camera configuration approach that may be used to overcome the limitations of the single camera configurations. Occasionally the footage from a single camera is the only appropriate solution and an example is given later in the text. The multi-camera datasets use a variety of configurations, ranging from 2 to 40 separate views per scenario.

The surveillance footage may be created with a multitude of different types of resolutions, color managements, frame rates, lens types and sensors. While quality cameras may produce higher resolution images at a fast frame rate, this may not be representative of actual Closed-Circuit TeleVision (CCTV) surveillance footage. In addition, running real-time automated visual surveillance solutions using frames with increasing amounts of information, can in some cases become detrimental to

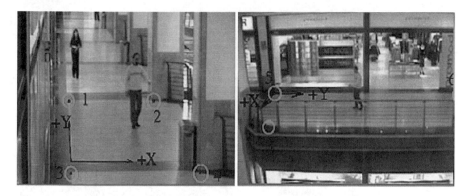

Fig. 7.1 CAVIAR (with mapping positions for ground plane homography)

the real-time performance of that solution. The resolution size, frame rate and size of the data, lens types and any other physical attributes of the datasets have been provided where known.

Finally, instructions regarding access and availability, and the Internet address for downloading each of these datasets, are available at the end of each relevant dataset description.

- CAVIAR

  The Context Aware Vision using Image-based Active Recognition (CAVIAR) [1] project datasets shown in Fig. 7.1 include two sets of video clips filmed at separate locations; the first being a building's entrance lobby and the second a city shopping center. The footage was shot to address analysis of city center surveillance, both from a view of anti-social behavior and that of potential customers in a commercial setting.

  The CAVIAR benchmark datasets collectively show people walking alone, meeting with others, window shopping, and entering and exiting shops, fighting, passing out and leaving a package in a public place. The shopping center dataset includes two separate view points that are time synchronized. For the CAVIAR project both datasets were collected using a wide angle camera lens (see Fig. 7.1) at half-resolution PAL standard (384×288 pixels, 25 frames per second) and compressed using MPEG2. The file sizes range from 6 MB to 21 MB.

  The datasets are available to download from

  http://groups.inf.ed.ac.uk/vision/CAVIAR/CAVIARDATA1/

  Please note if you publish results using the data please acknowledge the data as coming from the EC Funded CAVIAR project/IST 2001 37540 found at

  http://homepages.inf.ed.ac.uk/rbf/CAVIAR/

- ETISEO

  In a similar manner the collective datasets of Project ETISEO [12] consist of indoor and outdoor scenes, corridors, streets, building entries, a subway station and an airport apron. A snapshot of some of these scenes is displayed in Fig. 7.2

Fig. 7.2 ETISEO

The participants of Project ETISEO are composed of international industrialists and research laboratories and as such have brought a valuable broad spectrum of requirements while considering the creation of their combined footage.

For some scenarios, the researchers providing the available datasets, recognized that, in addition to multiple cameras, it is entirely possible that the use of multiple image modalities may bring further benefits toward developing robust solutions. The ETISEO project presents many of its scenes as multicamera datasets and some include additional imaging modality such as infra-red footage. These can be seen in Fig. 7.2.

The datasets are accessible from

http://www-sop.inria.fr/orion/ETISEO/download.htm

- Daimler
  Daimler's Pedestrian Detection Benchmark Data Set [6] presents an alternative automated visual surveillance task. It provides a video sequence captured from a vehicle during a 27 min drive through city traffic. The dataset consists of a specified training set containing pedestrian and non-pedestrian samples and a test set containing a sequence with more than 21,790 images with 56,492 pedestrians labeled. Examples are shown in Fig. 7.3.
  In this case using only one camera is the appropriate solution and as such this single camera benchmark datasets is of equal importance to the computer vision

Fig. 7.3 Daimler (red boxes showing "ground truth")

Fig. 7.4 MuHAVi

community. The dataset was created using a camera fitted to a moving vehicle, in an urban traffic environment, to create their pedestrian detection footage. The Daimler datasets, seen in Fig. 7.3, are at VGA resolution (640 × 480 pixels) and of 8.5 Gb in size.

The datasets are accessible from the address below, however, please take note of the license terms specified at this location for using them:

http://www.gavrila.net/Research/Pedestrian_Detection/
Daimler_Pedestrian_Benchmarks/Daimler_Pedestrian_Detection_B/
daimler_pedestrian_detection_b.html

- MuHAVi

  Addressing the need to investigate the ability to automate visual surveillance at night, the Multi-camera Human Action Video Data (MuHAVi) [14] were created as a part of the EPSRC funded REASON project. It is set in large laboratory and uses real night time street light illumination, and uneven paved surfaces which can be seen in Fig. 7.4. The video footage has sequences of actions, performed by actors, such as walk and turn back, run and stop, punch, and collapse.

Multi-camera Human Action Video Data (MuHAVi) are set in large laboratory and uses real night time street light illumination, and uneven paved surfaces as shown in Fig. 7.4.

The data may be accessed by sending an Email (subjected "MuHAVi-MAS Data") to Dr Sergio Velastin at

Sergio.Velastin@kingston.ac.uk

giving the names of the researchers who wish to use the data and their main purposes. The only requirement for using the MuHAVi-MAS data is to refer to this site in the corresponding publications. It is available to download from

http://dipersec.king.ac.uk/MuHAVi-MAS/

- ViHASi

  In contrast to the aforementioned datasets, Virtual Human Action Silhouette DataSoftware (ViHASi) [13] has emphasis on the actions performed. Software developed for animation and film industry was employed to generate videos of 20 different actions such as run, walk, punch, and collapse and was created using 9 different virtual actors which are displayed in Fig. 7.5. Each action class provides identical action motions and durations for all actors. The motion data correspond to the actions performed previously by human actors using optical or magnetic motion capture in order to produce realistic results. One of the biggest benefits of the Virtual Human Action Silhouette DataSoftware (ViHASi) datasets, which uses only "virtual" cameras, is the copious amount of viewpoints (up to 40) available for the captured actions. Virtual Human Action Silhouette DataSoftware (ViHASi) actions were captured at 30 frames per second with a 640×480 pixel resolution.

  The data may be accessed by sending an Email (subjected "ViHASi Data") to Dr Sergio Velastin at

  Sergio.Velastin@kingston.ac.uk

  giving the names of the researchers who wish to use the data and their main purposes. The only requirement for using the ViHASi data is to refer to this site in the corresponding publications. It is available to download from

  http://dipersec.king.ac.uk/VIHASI/

- PETS

  The series of international workshops on Performance Evaluation of Tracking and Surveillance (PETS) [4] endeavors to provide a platform for the objective evaluation of all participants systems on the same dataset. There are various scenarios available to download including, but not limited to, the following:
  - PETS 2001 seen in Fig. 7.6 concentrates on an outdoor car park and street setting displaying pedestrians and moving vehicles [4].
  - PETS 2006 scenarios are shot at a busy city train station and include unattended luggage of various shapes and sizes left by actors [8]. An example snapshot it seen in Fig. 7.7.

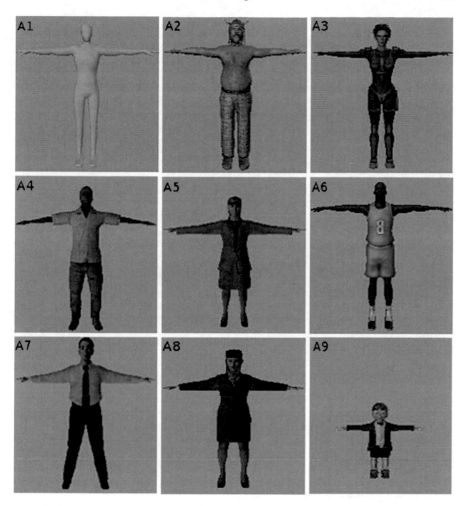

Fig. 7.5 ViHASi

- PETS 2007 datasets were created from footage taken from inside an airport's passenger departure area, shown in Fig. 7.8 and contain the following 3 scenarios, with increasing scene complexity: loitering, attended luggage removal (theft), and unattended luggage [9].
- PETS 2009/10 consider crowd scenarios (snapshots may be seen in Figs. 7.9 and 7.10) with increasing scene complexity such as walking, running, evacuation (rapid dispersion), local dispersion, crowd formation and splitting at different time instances, and were filmed in an outdoor car park setting [7].

The PETS series offers a variety of camera views. PETS 2001 is unique in that it includes the view from a catadioptric camera along side 4 independent standard views. In addition to these, an alternative scenario provides front and rear view footage from a moving vehicle. PETS 2006 and 2007 provide 4 separate views; 2

Fig. 7.6 PETS 2001

at ground level and 2 elevated shots. PETS 2009/10 have 8 camera views in total
with 4 of these positioned at ground level and 4 placed in elevated positions.

The PETS series sequences (see Figs. 7.6, 7.7, 7.8, 7.9, 7.10), other than that
of the catadioptric footage in Fig. 7.6, have resolutions of PAL standard (768 ×
576 pixels, 25 frames per second) progressive scan, and 720 × 576 pixels of de-
interlaced ffmpeg.

Please note if you publish results using these datasets please acknowledge the
relevant PETS workshop(s) and associated paper reference if applicable. The
datasets are available for download from

– PETS 2001

  http://www.cvg.cs.rdg.ac.uk/PETS2001/pets2001-dataset.html

– PETS 2006

  http://www.cvg.rdg.ac.uk/PETS2006/data.html

– PETS 2007

  http://www.cvg.rdg.ac.uk/PETS2007/data.html

– PETS 2009/2010

  http://www.cvg.rdg.ac.uk/PETS2009/a.html

Fig. 7.7   PETS 2006

- i-LIDS

  Finally the Image library for intelligent detection systems (i-LIDS) is the UK government's benchmark for Video Analytics (VA) systems developed in partnership with the Centre for the Protection of National Infrastructure. These datasets make up five scenarios which include sterile zone monitoring, amongst others. The footage includes an outside fenced area where objects of interest may appear in the detection zone [3].

  Applicants wishing to receive copies of the event detection or multiple-camera tracking datasets may find more information at:

  http://tna.europarchive.org/20100413151426/scienceandresearch.homeoffice. gov.uk/hosdb/cctv-imaging-technology/i-lids/index.html

7.2   Ground Truth

The "ground truth" refers to a process in which the means of classifying distinct details of a specific piece of footage are defined, and these classifications of that footage are produced in a data file, in order that comparisons may be made with

Fig. 7.8 PETS 2007

the output of some vision system. In many instances the ground truth is not readily available for a relevant video sequence. The reason behind this is the daunting amount of time required to generate ground truth for a particular set of videos. Researchers in the Computer Vision community are also faced with the fact that there is no single standard technique for authoring ground truth and any annotation used for classification may be too specific for general use.

7.2.1 Annotation Types

The annotation of video sequences, to create the ground truth frequently follows one of two patterns. Frame-based annotation lists all the objects that appear in each particular frame. Object-based annotation includes a list of all the frames an object appears in. The objects are commonly identified with "bounding boxes". These bounding box annotations surround the object of interest and have an identifying number and location coordinates.

The PETS 2009/2010 frame-based ground truth is available for sequence S2.L1, with the average sampling frequency being 1 frame in every 7. For the PETS 2010

Fig. 7.9 PETS 2009 Elevated Cameras

workshop each of the seven independent 2D camera views (views 1, 3, 4, 5, 6, 7, 8) were annotated using the Video Performance Evaluation Resource (ViPER) ground truth tool [11]. This provided the necessary bounding boxes and their identifying key and location for the ground truth. Ground truth data files generally exist as xml descriptions of these bounding boxes and their location. An example has been provided below:

```
<Header xsi:schemaLocation="http://www.cvg.rdg.ac.uk/
PETS2009/pets2009.xsd" Set="S2.L1" Sequence="seq1"
TimeStamp="12-34" length_frames="768">

<!-- the cameras used to obtain the results: -->
<Camera id="1"/>
<Camera id="2"/>
<Camera id="3"/>
<recording site="University Of Reading" session="1"
date="Feb 2009"/>
<software name="Gimp" version="2.6"
platform="Mac OS X"/>
```

Fig. 7.10 PETS 2009 Ground Level Cameras

```
<Frame id="frame_0190">
<!--First Detected Person -->
<Person id="1">
<BoundingBox top="216" left="212" bottom="276"
right="232">
<!-- Bounding box is defined in this view:-->
<Camera id="1"/>
</BoundingBox>
</Person>

<!--Second Detected Person -->
<Person id="2">
<BoundingBox top="236" left="228" bottom="290"
right="248">
...
</Frame>
<!-- continue for other frames similar as above.-->
</Header>
```

Fig. 7.11 CAVIAR
Annotation

The CAVIAR project includes 78 annotated sequences of between 300–2500 frames each. The sequences are connected with persistent and unique identifiers for annotated individuals and groups. Each video frame has a set of tracked objects visible in that frame. Within each frame an object is annotated with a close fitting bounding box and includes a mark up of both its location and its dominant orientation. Groups of individuals are annotated with an additional bounding box. The annotation includes semantic descriptions of current activities and situations. In essence this ground truth is frame-based and lists all the objects that appear in each particular frame. The group's xml tag lists which individuals, identifiable with a unique number, participate in each group. A pictorial example is shown in Fig. 7.11.

The CAVIAR ground truth is available to download from here:

http://groups.inf.ed.ac.uk/vision/CAVIAR/CAVIARDATA1/

The ETISEO ground truth annotation is frame-based. The data contain the object location, type and state, occlusions of these objects, if any and descriptions of events that occur between objects of interest.

Not all ground truth is xml-based. The Manually Annotated Silhouette Data (MAS) consist of the annotated footage of 5 of the action classes for MuHAVi. They include two different actors and two separate camera views. In this case the annotation consists of white silhouettesGround Truth!silhouettes of the actors performing their actions, on a black background as shown in Fig. 7.12. The silhouettes images are in PNG format and each action combination can be downloaded as a small zip file (between 1 to 3 MB).

These data are available to the researchers in computer vision community through a password protected server at the Digital Imaging Research Centre of Kingston University London. The following address provides a table of links that one can select to download the silhouette data for the corresponding action combinations:

http://dipersec.king.ac.uk/MuHAVi-MAS/

Fig. 7.12 MAS

The data may be accessed by sending an Email (subjected "MuHAVi-MAS Data") to Dr Sergio Velastin at

Sergio.Velastin@kingston.ac.uk

giving the names of the researchers who wish to use the data and their main purposes. The only requirement for using the MuHAVi-MAS data is to refer to this site in the corresponding publications.

7.2.2 Annotation Tools

ViPER-GT [11] is a Java-based tool for annotating videos with xml metadata, ranging from topics like genre and location of objects of interest to person tracking and recognition. People may be annotated using bounding boxes, ellipses, open and closed polygons, points and circles. The software allows propagation and interpolation of object values across a specified frame range.

The ViPER ground truth tool can be used to visualize existing ViPER xml ground truth data if the corresponding video sequence is available. Please note that with the ViPER ground truth annotation tool the x and y location coordinates for bounding boxes refer to the top left hand corner of the box.

Top Tip: Run your segmentation algorithm with or without tracking and reformat into ViPER (object-based) format. Remove any existing heading files and add ViPER GT tags headers. Load this xml file into ViPER GT and edit your newly created ground truth to the precision you require, THEN run evaluation metrics. (Please note the ViPER evaluation tool, described in a later section, assumes the specified coordinates of the bounding boxes to be their centroid. The ViPER ground truthing tool described here uses the top, left hand corner of the bounding boxes as their identifying location.)

ViPER-GT can be download from:

http://viper-toolkit.sourceforge.net/products/gt/

The CAVIAR project provides a JAVA-based ground truth tool which allows a user to manually annotate video sequences frame by frame. This may be downloaded from:

http://groups.inf.ed.ac.uk/vision/CAVIAR/CAVIARDATA1/xmlcaviarguibob.zip

and instructions are available at:

http://homepages.inf.ed.ac.uk/rbf/CAVIARDATA1/xmlcaviargui/manual/manual.pdf

7.2.3 Ground Truth Quality

The quality of ground truth, created by humans, will almost certainly include ambiguities in annotation labeling. Dependent on the length and complexity of the bench mark dataset, even the most dedicated of annotators may miss one or two detections. Image quality and interlacing may affect the positioning of the annotation. The process of evaluating a system, using ground truth created by humans, should include a built in level of "tolerance" for accuracy within the notation. Evaluation is described in the next section.

7.3 Evaluation

The research and development of vision systems requires the researcher to evaluate their approach using diverse benchmark datasets, if possible, and a variety of evaluation metrics. This section describes how these metrics are created, introduces some popular concepts and gives examples of some current metrics in wide use.

7.3.1 Evaluation Types and Metrics

Typically evaluation metrics are both object-based and pixel-based. Pixel-based metrics are computed from pixel counts that may be classified as true positives (TP), false positives (FP), false negatives (FN), and true negatives (TN). FP and FN refer to those that are misclassified as pixels belonging to the objects of interest (FP) or the background (FN) while TP and TN account for accurately classified pixels. These counts form the basis for metrics such as Accuracy, which is equal to the (TP + TN)/(all positives, both true and false + all negatives, both true and false).

Receiver Operating Characteristic (ROC) curves provide a standard measure of the ability of an automated surveillance system to correctly classify objects. A frequently used evaluation plots the sensitivity (true positive rate) against the specificity (1-false positive rate).

It should be noted that false positive and false negative pixels highlight the discrepancies between the detected objects of interest and the ground truth for each frame. They do not, however, assist in the assessment of the quality of the segmentation of individual objects.

Object-based metrics may refer to an individual object's segmented silhouette. Most commonly the metrics use an object's bounding box as a basis. The metrics may rely on the calculation of the amount of overlap between a detected object's bounding box and that of a ground truth bounding box. These boxes are again sometimes referred to as true positives, false negatives and false positives. The true negative measure for object-based detection is not possible in this case.

The most recent PETS workshops objectively evaluated various proposed systems [5]. The evaluation included, but was not restricted to, metrics that are formally used by the Classification of Events, Activities, and Relationships (CLEAR) consortium [2] and are described below:

Notation

- G_i^t denotes ith ground-truth object in frame t; G_i denotes the ith ground-truth object at the sequence level; N_{frames} is the number of frames in the sequence
- D_i^t denotes the ith detected object in frame t; D_i denotes the ith detected object at the sequence level
- N_G^t and N_D^t denote the number of ground-truth objects and the number of detected objects in frame t, respectively; N_G and N_D denote the number of unique ground-truth objects and the number of unique detected objects in the given sequence, respectively
- N_{frames}^i refers to the number of frames where either ground-truth object (G_i) or the detected object (D_i) existed in the sequence
- N_{mapped} refers to sequence level detected object and ground truth pairs, N_{mapped}^t refers to frame t mapped ground truth and detected object pairs
- m_t represents the missed detection count, (fp_t) is the false positive count, c_m and c_f represent, respectively, the cost functions for missed detects and false positives, and $c_s = \log_{10} \text{ID} - \text{SWITCHES}_t$

Multiple Object Detection Accuracy (MODA) is an accuracy measure that uses the number of missed detections and the number of falsely identified objects. Cost functions to allow weighting to either of these errors are included.

$$\text{MODA} = 1 - \frac{c_m(m_t) + c_f(fp_t)}{N_G^t}. \tag{7.1}$$

Multiple Object Detection Precision (MODP) gives the precision of the detection in a given frame. An overlap ratio is calculated and, in addition to a count of the number of mapped objects, the MODP is defined by

$$\text{OverLapRatio} = \sum_{i=1}^{N_{\text{mapped}}^t} \frac{|G_i^t \cap D_i^t|}{|G_i^t \cup D_i^t|}, \tag{7.2}$$

$$\text{MODP}(t) = \frac{\text{OverLapRatio}}{N_{\text{mapped}}^t}. \tag{7.3}$$

Multiple Object Tracking Accuracy (MOTA) uses the number of missed detections, the falsely identified objects, and the switches in an algorithm's output track for a given ground truth track. These switches are calculated from the number of identity mismatches in a frame, from the mapped objects in its preceding frame.

$$\text{MOTA} = 1 - \frac{\sum_{t=1}^{N_{\text{frames}}} (c_m(m_t) + c_f(f_{p_t}) + c_s)}{\sum_{t=1}^{N_{\text{frames}}} N_G^t}. \tag{7.4}$$

Multiple Object Tracking Precision (MOTP) is calculated from the spatio-temporal overlap between the ground truthed tracks and the algorithm's output tracks.

$$\text{MOTP} = \frac{\sum_{i=1}^{N_{\text{mapped}}} \sum_{t=1}^{N_{\text{frames}}^t} \left[\frac{|G_i^t \cap D_i^t|}{|G_i^t \cup D_i^t|} \right]}{\sum_{t=1}^{N_{\text{frames}}} N_{\text{mapped}}^t}. \tag{7.5}$$

ETISEO describe 22 metrics addressing five detection tasks: detection, localization, tracking, classification and event recognition. CAVIAR evaluate the performance of the detectors using the measures tracking detection rate (TRDR) and false alarm rate (FAR) and i-LIDS evaluate submitted systems using an F1 score. Details of these metrics may be found at each project's respective website.

7.3.2 Tools Available for Evaluation

Many tools are created "in-house", using a variety of xml schemas and defined metrics dependent on the particular evaluation task. There are, however, publicly available tools to download, to assist researchers in evaluating their approaches. Using a framework described by Kasturi et al. [10] it is possible to evaluate detection algorithms and the tools are available from:

http://doi.ieeecomputersociety.org/10.1109/TPAMI.2008.57

The software tool ViSEvAl (ViSualization and EvAluation), was created by the Perception Understanding Learning System Activity Recognition (PULSAR) collaboration. The results of video processing algorithms, such as detected objects of interest, and its associated ground truth data may be visualized using its GUI interface. The software has its own built in metrics to enable automated evaluation of results and provides the additional flexibility of a plugin service for user defined metrics. It is available to download from:

http://www-sop.inria.fr/teams/pulsar/EvaluationTool/ViSEvAl_Description.html

7.4 Future Direction

It is essential that researchers are able to objectively evaluate their detection and tracking algorithms with benchmark datasets. The ability to compare results, with others, whether anonymous or not, provides a realistic and encouraging research technique toward advanced, robust, real-time visual systems. This is not with out difficulty and the future direction is reliant on the further development of shared, open, performance evaluation tools, metrics and datasets. The following sections provide examples of an early indication toward this trend.

7.4.1 Web-Based Evaluation Tools

It is challenging to evaluate the benefits of individually proposed solutions even with the use of the same datasets and metrics. The results may be reported in a myriad of ways making direct comparisons between approaches problematic. During the PETS series of workshops, the concept of an online evaluation service was introduced [15]. An online system was created where the results of proposed algorithms were uploaded directly to a website, automatically evaluated and presented ranked alongside other algorithms. It is envisaged that this tool will be representative of an early example of future approaches.

7.4.2 Web-Based Evaluation Results

The Middlebury datasets, created for stereo vision research, provide a publicly available online algorithm ranking table.

http://vision.middlebury.edu/stereo/eval/

The success of the Middlebury site is due to the competitive nature of the participants in attempting to produce an evaluation result that appears at the top of the ranking system. Each evaluation result appears with a reference to an accompanying paper. This invaluable resource for stereo vision may be used as a template for a similar automated visual surveillance site.

7.4.3 Standardization of Metrics and Benchmark Datasets

A de-facto standard for metrics and an accepted set of benchmark datasets will certainly assist research toward robust visual system approaches. However, with the availability of constant evolving sensors, producing increasingly high quality, novel and informative types of imagery, the plausible applications for intelligent visual systems have expanded significantly. It is therefore increasingly difficult to find a one type fits all dataset and a generic set of evaluation metrics. Benchmark datasets and metrics must evolve in a similar fashion. The datasets of visual surveillance workshops and other such sources become popular if they are easily accessible. They in turn, become an accepted benchmark, as the literature published using these benchmarks increases. There is at present a selection of evaluation metrics that include the open source code for their operability. These details provide indicators for a future of open standards within the computer vision community.

7.4.4 Further Reading

List, T., Bins, J., Vazquez, J., Fisher, R.B.: Performance evaluating the evaluator, In: 2nd Joint IEEE International Workshop on Visual Surveillance and Performance Evaluation of Tracking and Surveillance, 2005, pp. 129–136, (15–16 Oct. 2005)

Baumann, A., Boltz, M., Ebling, J., et al.: A review and comparison of measures for automatic video surveillance systems, EURASIP Journal on Image and Video Processing, 2008, Article ID 824726 (2008)

Dee, H., Velastin, S.: How close are we to solving the problem of automated visual surveillance?, Journal on Machine Vision and Applications, Springer Berlin, **19**(5), 329–343 (2008)

Yuen, J., Russell, B., Liu, C., Torralba, A.: LabelMe video: Building a video database with human annotations, In: 12th International Conference on Computer Vision (2009)

Velastin, S.A., Remagnino, P.: Intelligent distributed surveillance systems, The Institution of Electrical Engineers (IEE), ISBN/ISSN 0-86341-504-0 (2005)

References

1. Caviar – Context Aware Vision Using Image-based Active Recognition. http://homepages. inf.ed.ac.uk/rbf/CAVIAR/ [111]
2. CLEAR: Classification of Events, Activities and Relationships – Evaluation Campaign and Workshop. http://www.clear-evaluation.org/ [124]
3. i-LIDS. The Image Library for Intelligent Detection Systems. http://tna.europarchive.org/ 20100413151426/scienceandresearch.homeoffice.gov.uk/hosdb/cctv-imaging-technology/ i-lids/index.html [117]
4. IEEE International Workshops on Performance Evaluation of Tracking and Surveillance (PETS), 2000–2005. http://www.visualsurveillance.org [114]
5. Ellis, A., Shahrokni, A., Ferryman, J.M.: Pets2009 and winter-pets 2009 results: A combined evaluation. In: IEEE International Workshop on Performance Evaluation of Tracking and Surveillance (PETS-Winter) (Dec. 2009) [124]
6. Enzweiler, M., Gavrila, D.M.: Monocular pedestrian detection: Survey and experiments. IEEE Trans. Pattern Anal. Mach. Intell. **31**(12), 2179–2195 (2009) [112]
7. Ferryman, J., Shahrokni, A.: Pets2009: Dataset and challenge. In: IEEE International Workshop on Performance Evaluation of Tracking and Surveillance (PETS-Winter) (Dec. 2009) [115]

8. Ferryman, J., Thirde, D.: An overview of the pets2006 dataset. In: IEEE International Work-shop on Performance Evaluation of Tracking and Surveillance (PETS) (Jun. 2006) [114]
9. Ferryman, J., Tweed, D.: An overview of the pets2007 dataset. In: IEEE International Work-shop on Performance Evaluation of Tracking and Surveillance (PETS) (Oct. 2007) [115]
10. Kasturi, R., Goldgof, D., Soundararajan, P., Manohar, V., Garofolo, J., Bowers, R., Boonstra, M., Korzhova, V., Zhang, J.: Framework for performance evaluation of face, text, and vehicle detection and tracking in video: Data, metrics, and protocol. IEEE Trans. Pattern Anal. Mach. Intell. **31**(2), 319–336 (2009) [125]
11. The Language and Media Processing Laboratory (LAMP): Viper: The video performance evaluation resource. http://viper-toolkit.sourceforge.net/ [119,122]
12. Nghiem, A.T., Bremond, F., Thonnat, M., Valentin, V.: Etiseo, performance evaluation for video surveillance systems. In: IEEE Conference on Advanced Video and Signal Based Surveillance (2007) [111]
13. Ragheb, H., Velastin, S., Remagnino, P., Ellis, T.: ViHASi: Virtual human action silhouette data for the performance evaluation of silhouette-based action recognition methods. In: Work-shop on Vision Networks for Behavior Analysis,(2008) [114]
14. Singh, S., Velastin, S., Hossein, R.: MuHAVi: A multicamera human action video dataset for the evaluation of action recognition methods. In: IEEE Conference on Advanced Video and Signal Based Surveillance (Sep. 2010) [113]
15. Young, D.P., Ferryman, J.M.: Pets metrics: On-line performance evaluation service. In: IEEE International Workshop on Visual Surveillance and Performance Evaluation of Tracking and Surveillance (Oct. 2005) [126]

Part II
Pose Estimation

Chapter 8
Articulated Pose Estimation and Tracking: Introduction

Leonid Sigal

8.1 Introduction

Part I addresses the problems of detecting, localizing and tracking of people in images at a coarse scale. Inference of location in space, or in the image, maybe sufficient for high level reasoning required in surveillance (e.g., see Chap. 23) or autonomous vehicle navigation [10]. However, for many applications a finer level of understanding of human movement is necessary. Action and activity recognition, scene interpretation and many other higher level understanding and reasoning tasks can be facilitated by the knowledge of the configuration of the body over time. One of the most compelling applications, however, is Motion Capture (MoCap). Motion capture is used routinely in the entertainment industry for character animation (e.g., James Cameron's Avatar) but is also useful for clinical analysis of pathologies and sport training. Motion capture is also slowly making its way into consumer applications such as gaming (Xbox Kinect).

Most current motion-capture systems (e.g., from Vicon) are based on active or retro-reflective markers that are placed on the body of an actor at key anatomic locations. The 3D positions of these markers are recovered through triangulation. The skeleton motion is estimated by fitting the human kinematic structure to the marker motion. This technology, while very accurate, is both intrusive and costly. As a consequence there is a large interest in vision-based marker-less MoCap technologies.

This part of the book focuses on the challenging problem of recovering configurations (poses) of people from images and/or image sequences. In computer vision, this is often termed *articulated pose estimation* and *articulated tracking*. Pose estimation approaches, such us those discussed in Chaps. 11 and 12 focus on the recovery of body configuration from individual images. Tracking approaches, on the other

L. Sigal (✉)
Disney Research, Pittsburgh, PA, USA
e-mail: lsigal@disneyresearch.com

T.B. Moeslund et al. (eds.), *Visual Analysis of Humans*,
DOI 10.1007/978-0-85729-997-0_8, © Springer-Verlag London Limited 2011

hand, focus on evolution of the configuration over time based on an image sequence (see Chaps. 9 and 10). Pose estimation is in a sense more general, as tracking can be cast as the problem of pose estimation at every frame. That said, pose estimation is substantially more challenging, and, in practice, both of these classes of methods have their place. Traditionally these problems have been treated separately, but the line between tracking and pose estimation is starting to blur with recent research [2].

Most of the chapters in the book take a probabilistic approach to addressing these problems, as this provides a sound framework to account for uncertainty and ambiguities that naturally exist in this domain. That said, Chap. 9 discusses some deterministic alternatives (which can, in turn, be interpreted as particular forms of inference in probabilistic models (see Sect. 9.3.1.4)).

8.2 Challenges

Despite many years of research, articulated pose estimation and tracking remain very challenging and largely unsolved problems. Among the most significant challenges that make these problems difficult are: (1) variability of human visual appearance in images, (2) variability in lighting conditions, (3) variability in human physique, (4) partial occlusions due to self articulation and layering of objects in the scene, (5) complexity of human skeletal structure, (6) high dimensionality of the pose, and (7) the loss of 3D information that is intrinsic in image formation. To date there is no approach that can produce satisfactory results in general unconstrained settings, while dealing with all aforementioned challenges.

All of the above challenges are significant; however, (7) is of particular importance. Most of the ambiguities, in practice, come from inability to observe the 3D structure of the scene and of the subject directly. Having observations from multiple cameras often resolves such ambiguities and leads to solutions that are accurate for practical use. Recovery from the monocular observations is substantially more challenging, and consequently is the focus of current research.

8.3 Models and Inference

Nearly all methods, that address the aforementioned problems of pose estimation and tracking, can be categorized into four major classes: generative model based approaches, discriminative model based approaches, part-based model approaches and geometric approaches. The chapters in this part of the book focus on the first three categories as those tend to correspond to the most prominent research directions. Geometric approaches are briefly covered in Sect. 8.3.4. While theoretically interesting, geometric approaches, often require unrealistic assumptions that make them hard to use in realistic imaging conditions. For example, they often assume knowledge of correspondences across time or camera views. Because of the limitations these methods are rarely used by themselves, but rather in combination with other generative or discriminative models (e.g., [26]).

8.3.1 Generative Methods

Generative model approaches attempt to model all the intricacies of the process that generates an image of a moving person. An ideal generative model would take into account both the complexity of the motion and appearance, and would be able to generate fair photo-realistic samples of images of moving people in realistic scenes (akin to those observed in the world).[1] Formulating such a rich model or doing inference[2] in it, is, however, impractical. Many simplifying assumptions must be made in practice. This often includes simplifying assumptions (in the form of statistical independence) on human appearance, imaging process, human motion, lighting, etc. Such assumptions are severely violated in practice, which, in turn, leads to weak generative models that are unable to capture statistical subtleties. Samples from such models are hardly indicative of images we can observe in the world. Despite this, such models are still very useful for inference of pose. The common ingredients for building a generative model for pose inference are described in Chap. 9 and Chap. 10.

The major benefit of the Bayesian generative paradigm is that posterior distribution of interest, that encodes the distribution over pose given the image, can be expressed as a product of the image likelihood and a prior. The likelihood intuitively measures the consistency of a given pose with the image observations, and the prior—the probability of a person assuming a given pose or a sequence of poses. Different likelihood functions and inference methods are discussed in Chap. 9. While many generative methods exist that perform favorably in multi-view settings, inference of pose in a monocular video remains a challenge. A good pose or motion prior is required to bootstrap the inference and bias results toward more acceptable solutions. Chapter 10 introduces and discusses a large variety of prior models currently present in the literature.

Most prior models, to date, have focused on characterizing a set of plausible poses, or motions, using statistical models obtained from MoCap data (see Chap. 10). Such models are effective, but are also limited in their ability to generalize across the environments (e.g., to different slope of the ground plane, or coefficient of friction) that can significantly change the nuances of a motion. In recent years there have been a few attempts at building more generic prior models that rely mainly on the dynamic physical interactions between the subject and environment to characterize plausible motions (e.g., [5, 12]). Physics-based models are appealing, as priors, due to their inherent abilities to generalize and produce realistic physically-plausible motions. This class of models is relatively novel for vision and requires further exploration. More detailed discussion of physics-based priors is given in Chap. 10, Sect. 10.5.

---

[1] A realistic generative model for a human hand was introduced in [6]. The model includes shape, appearance, and lighting parameters, and is capable of generating realistic samples.

[2] Inference involves figuring out a set of parameters for this model that makes a given observed image, or sequence, very likely.

8.3.2 Discriminative Methods

Discriminative model approaches forego modeling the prior and the likelihood separately and instead try to learn the posterior distribution directly. Resulting models
take the form of probabilistic, and often multi-modal, regression. A number of popular alternatives in this class of methods are discussed in Chap. 12. Unlike generative
model methods, discriminative approaches tend to be faster and are also easier to implement. When the distribution of test and training images are similar they tend to
perform very well, even in a challenging monocular setting. However, generalization
to instances unobserved during training is often a challenge. In addition, discriminative models require one to define the input image features and the form of output
poses a priori, making it difficult to deal with missing or incomplete observations.

8.3.3 Part-Based Methods

Part-based models in various incarnations have been used in object detection [8] and
activity recognition [24]. The appeal of such models for pose estimation arises from
their ability to allow inference in very complex natural scenes from just a single
image. This ability stems from the flexible formulation that models a body as a
collection of body parts connected by statistical *constraints* imposed by the body.
In this formulation the inference over high dimensional pose of the skeleton is cast
as a number of low-dimensional inference problems, each of which can be solved
efficiently (as opposed to the traditional generative and discriminative approaches
that often require inference or learning in a high dimensional space).

The efficiency in inference often comes at a cost of simplifying assumptions.
Mathematically convenient form for distributions over configuration of, and/or interaction between, parts are typically assumed [7, 9, 15]. As a result, most of the
part-based models are limited to reasoning about the pose in 2D and are incapable
of recovering 3D pose from monocular images. That said, few part-based models for
reasoning about 3D pose from *multi-view* observations do exist [18]. In a monocular
setting, part-based models are often combined with generative models for inference
of 3D pose in hierarchical frameworks [2, 19].

Most part-based models used for pose estimation are generative in nature (e.g.,
[11]), but often contain discriminatively trained likelihood models for individual
parts [11]. Discriminative variants are also gaining popularity, e.g., [28]. Chapter 11
gives a systematic and unified account of part-based models in the literature, covering everything from the early models like Pictorial Structures [7] to the state-of-the-
art methods that use Mixtures of Parts [28] for robust inference.

8.3.4 Geometric Methods

Methods discussed so far are statistical in nature and rely on prior models to resolve
ambiguities that arise in recovering 3D pose from images; geometric approaches

rely on projective geometry instead. Geometric models can further be categorized into two sub-classes: reconstruction-based and factorization-based.

Reconstruction-based: Reconstruction-based methods typically assume availability or annotation of joint locations in an image and rely on known skeletal size and/or strong anthropometry prior to reduce the ambiguity in 3D pose reconstruction. A prime example is the approach by Taylor [20], where a known skeletal size was assumed and an analytical solution to recover 3D orientation of the bone segments up to an undetermined weak perspective camera scale is presented. Barron and Kakadiaris [3] extended this idea by also estimating anthropometric parameters from a single image. They formulate the problem as one of non-linear optimization with a multivariate Gaussian prior on bone lengths learned from a representative population. In both cases, manual correspondences for joints were given along with a manually specified relative depth layering of joints in the image. The latter was needed to address the depth ambiguities in order to obtain a unique solution.

An approach for obtaining automatic correspondences was proposed by Mori et al. in [13]. More recently Wei et al. [25] proposed an extension that allows simultaneous reconstruction of skeletal proportions, pose, and camera parameters from multiple images of the same subject. The use of multiple images allows one to eliminate many of the ambiguities. A thorough analysis shows that a minimum of 5 frames are necessary to obtain a well-behaved optimization problem. The approach is further extended in [26] by proposing a system for recovering 3D pose based on a number of sparse image annotations and intermediate tracking.

Reconstruction based approaches are viable alternatives in applications where manual interaction or intervention is possible. Currently, however, there are no reliable automatic methods for recovering the joint locations required for these methods to work well.

Factorization-based: Factorization-based methods are rooted in the classic computer vision problem of Structure-from-Motion (SfM) [21]. In essence, they are extensions of SfM to a case of non-rigid articulated objects [4]. For example, Tresadern et al. [23] developed a factorization method to recover segment lengths as well as joint angles using a large number of feature trajectories obtained from a monocular sequence. Yan et al. [27] used rank constraints to segment feature trajectories and then built the kinematic chain as a minimum spanning tree of a graph constructed from the segmented motion subspaces. Impressive results were also obtained by Akhter et al. [1] and Torresani et al. [22]. Factorization-based approaches tend to work very well when clean feature trajectories are present. They are able to deal with some amounts of noise in correspondences, but the ability to obtain correspondences automatically in everyday image sequences remains a major challenge.

It is worth mentioning that an interesting approach that utilizes augmented SfM paradigm for marker-less motion capture was recently introduced by Shiratori et al. in [16]. In [16] a system for capturing human motion using a set of small cameras mounted on the body is presented. In contrast to most prior vision-based methods (that assume cameras in the world and recover a subjects' motion by observing how he or she moves in the image) the proposed system recovers motion of the skeleton indirectly, by observing how the world moves with respect to the set of cameras strapped to the body.

8.4 Alternative Sensors

While the chapters in this part of the book focus on obtaining pose(s) from images and/or video, it is important to mention that other sensor technologies may be useful in simplifying the problem. Xbox Kinect [17], for example, uses structured light sensor to recover 3D pose. The technology is truly impressive, but comes with it's own limitations. For example, one cannot use the camera outside as the near infrared structured light patterns are affected by bright sunlight. The range of the device is also limited, though this limitation is likely to be resolved with more expensive and higher resolution sensors. The depth observations that come from a depth sensor certainly simplify the problem of pose estimation, but do not solve it completely as self-occlusions can confuse the algorithm [17]. Despite all of these limitations, the performance that Kinect delivers is impressive.

Along similar lines, several groups have started to look at combining vision-based technology with other sensors. For example, in [14] information form regular video cameras is combined with accelerometer data obtained using Inertial Measurement Units (IMUs) attached to the extremities. This significantly improves the performance of the system, as visually hard-to-observe degrees of freedom can now be more easily resolved.

Alternative sensor systems, like the one proposed in [14] or developed by the Xbox team, achieve impressive performance and have many practical consumer applications. However, the boost in performance often comes at an expense of instrumenting the environment or the person. The general problem of inferring the 3D pose of a person from monocular stock camera footage or a photograph is still a challenging and largely unsolved problem.

References

1. Akhter, I., Sheikh, Y., Khan, S., Kanade, T.: Nonrigid structure from motion in trajectory space. In: Advances in Neural Information Processing Systems (2008) [135]
2. Andriluka, M., Roth, S., Schiele, B.: Monocular 3d pose estimation and tracking by detection. In: IEEE Computer Society Conference on Computer Vision and Pattern Recognition (2010) [132,134]
3. Barron, C., Kakadiaris, I.A.: Estimating anthropometry and pose from single image. In: IEEE Computer Society Conference on Computer Vision and Pattern Recognition, pp. 669–676 (2000) [135]
4. Bregler, C., Hertzmann, A., Biermann, H.: Recovering non-rigid 3d shape from image streams. In: IEEE Computer Society Conference on Computer Vision and Pattern Recognition, vol. 2, pp. 690–696 (2000) [135]
5. Brubaker, M.A., Fleet, D.J.: The kneed walker for human pose tracking. In: IEEE Computer Society Conference on Computer Vision and Pattern Recognition (2008) [133]

6. de La Gorce, M., Fleet, D.J., Paragios, N.: Model-based 3d hand pose estimation from monocular video. IEEE Trans. Pattern Anal. Mach. Intell. **33**(9), 1793–1805 (2011) [133]
7. Felzenszwalb, P., Huttenlocher, D.: Pictorial structures for object recognition. Int. J. Comput. Vis. **61** (2005) [134]
8. Felzenszwalb, P., McAllester, D., Ramanan, D.: A discriminatively trained, multiscale, deformable part model. In: IEEE Computer Society Conference on Computer Vision and Pattern Recognition (2008) [134]
9. Ferrari, V., Marin-Jimenez, M., Zisserman, A.: Progressive search space reduction for human pose estimation. In: IEEE Computer Society Conference on Computer Vision and Pattern Recognition (2008) [134]
10. Gavrila, D.M., Munder, D.: Multi-cue pedestrian detection and tracking from a moving vehicle. Int. J. Comput. Vis. **73**(1), 41–59 (2007) [131]
11. Schiele, B., Andriluka, M., Roth, S.: Pictorial structures revisited: People detection and articulated pose estimation. In: IEEE Computer Society Conference on Computer Vision and Pattern Recognition (2009) [134]
12. Sigal, L., Vondrak, M., Jenkins, O.C.: Physical simulation for probabilistic motion tracking. In: IEEE Computer Society Conference on Computer Vision and Pattern Recognition (2008) [133]
13. Mori, G., Malik, J.: Estimating human body configurations using shape context matching. In: European Conference on Computer Vision, pp. 666–680 (2002) [135]
14. Pons-Moll, G., Baak, A., Helten, T., Muller, M., Seidel, H.-P., Rosenhahn, B.: Multisensorfusion for 3d full-body human motion capture. In: IEEE Computer Society Conference on Computer Vision and Pattern Recognition (2010) [136]
15. Ramanan, D.: Learning to parse images of articulated objects. In: Advances in Neural Information Processing Systems (2006) [134]
16. Shiratori, T., Park, H.S., Sigal, L., Sheikh, Y., Hodgins, J.: Motion capture from body-mounted cameras. ACM Trans. Graph. (2011) [135]
17. Shotton, J., Fitzgibbon, A., Cook, M., Blake, A.: Real-time human pose reconstruction in parts from single depth images. In: IEEE Computer Society Conference on Computer Vision and Pattern Recognition (2011) [136]
18. Sigal, L., Bhatia, S., Roth, S., Black, M.J., Isard, M.: Tracking loose-limbed people. In: IEEE Computer Society Conference on Computer Vision and Pattern Recognition (2004) [134]
19. Sigal, L., Black, M.J.: Predicting 3d people from 2d pictures. In: IV Conference on Articulated Motion and Deformable Objects (2006) [134]
20. Taylor, C.J.: Reconstruction of articulated objects from point correspondences in a single uncalibrated image. Comput. Vis. Image Underst. **80**(3), 349–363 (2000) [135]
21. Tomasi, C., Kanade, T.: Shape and motion from image streams under orthography. Int. J. Comput. Vis. **9**(2), 137–154 (1992) [135]
22. Torresani, L., Hertzmann, A., Bregler, C.: Nonrigid structure-from motion: Estimating shape and motion with hierarchical priors. IEEE Trans. Pattern Anal. Mach. Intell. **30**(5), 878–892 (2008) [135]
23. Tresadern, P., Reid, I.: Articulated structure from motion by factorization. In: IEEE Computer Society Conference on Computer Vision and Pattern Recognition, vol. 2, pp. 1110–1115 (2005) [135]
24. Wang, Y., Mori, G.: Learning a discriminative hidden part model for human action recognition. In: Advances in Neural Information Processing Systems (2008) [134]
25. Wei, X., Chai, J.: Modeling 3d human poses from uncalibrated monocular images. In: IEEE International Conference on Computer Vision (2009) [135]
26. Wei, X., Chai, J.: Videomocap: Modeling physically realistic human motion from monocular video sequences. ACM Trans. Graph. **29**(4) (2010) [132,135]
27. Yan, J., Pollefeys, M.: Automatic kinematic chain building from feature trajectories of articulated objects. In: IEEE Computer Society Conference on Computer Vision and Pattern Recognition, vol. 1, pp. 712–719 (2006) [135]
28. Yang, Y., Ramanan, D.: Articulated pose estimation using flexible mixtures of parts. In: IEEE Computer Society Conference on Computer Vision and Pattern Recognition (2011) [134]

Chapter 9
Model-Based Pose Estimation

Gerard Pons-Moll and Bodo Rosenhahn

Abstract Model-based pose estimation algorithms aim at recovering human motion from one or more camera views and a 3D model representation of the human body. The model pose is usually parameterized with a kinematic chain and thereby the pose is represented by a vector of joint angles. The majority of algorithms are based on minimizing an error function that measures how well the 3D model fits the image. This category of algorithms usually has two main stages, namely defining the model and fitting the model to image observations. In the first section, the reader is introduced to the different kinematic parametrization of human motion. In the second section, the most commonly used representations of the human shape are described. The third section is dedicated to the description of different error functions proposed in the literature and to common optimization techniques used for human pose estimation. Specifically, local optimization and particle-based optimization and filtering are discussed and compared. The chapter concludes with a discussion of the state-of-the-art in model-based pose estimation, current limitations and future directions.

9.1 Kinematic Parametrization

In this chapter our main concern will be on estimating the human pose from images. Human motion is mostly articulated, i.e., it can be accurately modeled by a set of connected rigid segments. A *segment* is a set of points that move rigidly together. To determine the pose, we must first find an appropriate parametrization of the human motion. For the task of estimating human motion a *good* parametrization must have the following attributes.

G. Pons-Moll (✉) · B. Rosenhahn
Leibniz University, Hanover, Germany
e-mail: pons@tnt.uni-hannover.de

B. Rosenhahn
e-mail: rosenhahn@tnt.uni-hannover.de

T.B. Moeslund et al. (eds.), *Visual Analysis of Humans*,
DOI 10.1007/978-0-85729-997-0_9, © Springer-Verlag London Limited 2011

Attributes of a good parametrization for human motion:

- Pose configurations are represented with the minimum number of parameters.
- Human motion constraints, such as articulated motion, are naturally described.
- Singularities can be avoided during optimization.
- Easy computation of derivatives of segment positions and orientations w.r.t. the parameters.
- Simple rules for concatenating motions.

A commonly used parametrization that meets most of the above requirements is a kinematic chain, which encodes the motion of a body segment as the motion of the previous segment in the chain and an angular motion about a body joint. For example, the motion of the lower arm is parametrized as the motion of the upper arm and a rotation about the elbow. The motion of a body segment relative to the previous one is parametrized by a rotation. Parameterizing rotations can be tricky since it is a non-Euclidean group, which means that if we travel any integer number of loops around an axis in space we will end up in the same point. We now briefly review the different parametrization of rotations that have been used for human tracking.

9.1.1 Rotation Matrices

A rotation matrix $\mathbf{R}_{3\times3}$ is an element of $SO(3)$. Elements of $\mathbf{R} \in SO(3)$ are the group of 3×3 orthonormal matrices with $\det(\mathbf{R}) = 1$ that represent rotations [34]. A rotation matrix encodes the orientation of a frame B that we call *body frame* relative to a second one S that we call *spatial frame*. Given a point $\mathbf{p}$ with body coordinates, $\mathbf{p}_b = (\lambda_x, \lambda_y, \lambda_z)^T$, we might write the point $\mathbf{p}$ in spatial coordinates as

$$\mathbf{p}_s = \lambda_x \mathbf{x}_s^B + \lambda_y \mathbf{y}_s^B + \lambda_z \mathbf{z}_s^B, \tag{9.1}$$

where $\mathbf{x}_s^B$, $\mathbf{y}_s^B$, $\mathbf{z}_s^B$ are the principal axis of the body frame B written in spatial coordinates. We may also write the relationship between the spatial and body frame coordinates in matrix form as $\mathbf{p}_s = \mathbf{R}_{sb}\mathbf{p}_b$. From this it follows that the rotation matrix is given by

$$\mathbf{R}_{sb} = \begin{bmatrix} \mathbf{x}_s^B & \mathbf{y}_s^B & \mathbf{z}_s^B \end{bmatrix}. \tag{9.2}$$

Now consider a frame B whose origin is translated w.r.t. frame S by $\mathbf{t}_s$ (the translation vector written in spatial coordinates). In this case, the coordinates of frames S and B are related by a rotation and a translation, $\mathbf{p}_s = \mathbf{R}_{sb}\mathbf{p}_b + \mathbf{t}_s$. Hence, a pair $(\mathbf{R} \in SO(3), \mathbf{t} \in \mathbb{R}^3)$ determines the configuration of a frame B relative to another S and is the product space of $\mathbb{R}^3$ with $SO(3)$ denoted as $SE(3) =$

Fig. 9.1 *Left*: rigid body motion seen as a coordinate transformation. *Right*: rigid body motion seen as a relative motion in time

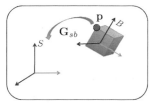 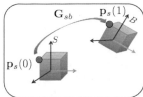

$\mathbb{R}^3 \times SO(3)$. Elements of $SE(3)$ are $\mathbf{g} = \{\mathbf{R}, \mathbf{t}\}$. Equivalently, writing the point in homogeneous coordinates $\bar{\mathbf{p}}_b = \begin{bmatrix} \mathbf{p}_b \\ 1 \end{bmatrix}$ allows us to use the more compact notation

$$\bar{\mathbf{p}}_s = \mathbf{G}_{sb}\bar{\mathbf{p}}_b, \quad \text{where} \quad \mathbf{G}_{sb} = \begin{bmatrix} \mathbf{R}_{sb[3\times3]} & \mathbf{t}_{s[3\times1]} \\ \mathbf{0}_{[1\times3]} & 1 \end{bmatrix}. \tag{9.3}$$

The rigid body motion is then completely represented by the matrix $\mathbf{G}_{sb}$ which is the homogeneous representation of $\mathbf{g}_{sb}$. The reader unfamiliar with rotation matrices might be surprised because the definitions given here for rotation and rigid motion do not represent motion of points in a fixed frame but rather transformations between coordinate systems. This does not correspond to our informal understanding of rotations. Consequently, *do rotations and rigid body motion represent coordinate transformations or motion?* The answer is: both. To see this, consider a point $\mathbf{p}$ in a rigid body, see Fig. 9.1, and imagine that the body and spatial frames coincide at $t = 0$ see Fig. 9.1 right, consequently $\mathbf{p}_s(0) = \mathbf{p}_b$. At this time we apply the rigid body motion to the point such that the point now moves to a new position $\mathbf{p}_s(1)$. We can write it as

$$\bar{\mathbf{p}}_s(1) = \mathbf{G}_{sb}\bar{\mathbf{p}}_s(0), \tag{9.4}$$

where the coordinates of $\mathbf{p}_s(1)$ and $\mathbf{p}_s(0)$ are both relative to the spatial frame. This new interpretation of rigid motion will be very useful when we talk about human motion in the next section. Both interpretations of rigid motion are correct and depending on the context one is preferable over the other, (e.g., to think about world-to-camera mapping it is better to interpret it as a coordinate transformation but when we think of human motion it is most of the times more intuitive to think of rigid motion as the relative motion between temporal instants). Rotations can be combined by simple matrix multiplication. However, representing rotations with rotation matrices is suboptimal for optimization problems. This is because from the nine numbers composing the matrix, six additional constraints must be imposed during optimization in order to ensure that the matrix is orthonormal. Therefore, representing angular motions with rotation matrices is problematic for motion tracking because we need more parameters than strictly needed.

9.1.2 Euler Angles

One method for describing the orientation of a frame B relative to another frame S is as follows: start with frame B coincident with frame S, rotate B α degrees about the x-axis of frame S, then rotate β degrees about the y-axis of frame S and finally rotate γ degrees about the z-axis (of frame S again). This corresponds to the x, y, z Euler angles defined in frame S. There are several conventions on the order in which these rotations are carried out; for example, it is also possible to perform the rotation in the order z, y, z. Therefore, when we talk about Euler angles the order of the rotations must be specified. It is very important to note with respect to which frame the rotations are defined, they can be defined on the fixed reference frame S or alternatively on the moving frame B. Therefore, a rotation matrix can always be written as the composition of three rotations around the x, y, z axes (9.5). Note that had we chosen the rotations to be defined in the moving frame B, the order would be inverted.

$$\mathbf{R} = \begin{bmatrix} \cos(\gamma) & -\sin(\gamma) & 0 \\ \sin(\gamma) & \cos(\gamma) & 0 \\ 0 & 0 & 1 \end{bmatrix} \begin{bmatrix} \cos(\beta) & 0 & -\sin(\beta)) \\ 0 & 1 & 0 \\ \sin(\beta) & 0 & \cos(\beta) \end{bmatrix} \begin{bmatrix} 1 & 0 & 0 \\ 0 & \cos(\alpha) & -\sin(\alpha) \\ 0 & \sin(\alpha) & \cos(\alpha) \end{bmatrix}.$$

$$(9.5)$$

In this manner, a rotation is completely defined by a triplet of Euler angles (α, β, γ). The derivatives of a rotation with respect to the Euler angles are easy to compute. Additionally, differential equation integration in parameter space is straightforward, for example to update one of the three angles: $\alpha_t = \alpha_{t-1} + \dot{\alpha}$. Unfortunately, Euler angles have a well known problem: when two of the rotation axis align one of the rotations is lost. This well known singularity of Euler parametrization is called gimbal lock.

9.1.3 Quaternions

Quaternions generalize complex numbers and can be used to represent 3D rotations the same way as complex numbers can be used to represent planar rotations. Formally, a quaternion is a vector quantity of the form $\mathbf{q} = q_w + q_x \cdot \mathbf{i} + q_y \cdot \mathbf{j} + q_z \cdot \mathbf{k}$ with $\mathbf{i}^2 = \mathbf{j}^2 = \mathbf{k}^2 = \mathbf{i} \cdot \mathbf{j} \cdot \mathbf{k} = -1$. Unit length quaternions form a set called S^3 which can be used to carry out rotations. They can also be interpreted as a scalar q_w plus a 3-vector $(q_w, \mathbf{v})$. One nice property about quaternions is that rotations can be carried out in parameter space via quaternion product. Given two quaternions $\mathbf{q}_1 = (q_{w,1}, \mathbf{v}_1)$ and $\mathbf{q}_2 = (q_{w,2}, \mathbf{v}_2)$ the quaternion product denoted by $(\circ)$ is defined as

$$\mathbf{q}_1 \circ \mathbf{q}_2 = (q_{w,1}q_{w,2} - \mathbf{v}_1 \cdot \mathbf{v}_2, \; q_{w,1}\mathbf{v}_2 + q_{w,2}\mathbf{v}_1 + \mathbf{v}_1 \times \mathbf{v}_2). \qquad (9.6)$$

If we want to rotate a vector $\mathbf{a}$ we can simply use the quaternion product. Thereby, a rotation by an angle θ about an axis ω is represented by the quaternion:

$$\mathbf{q} = [q_w, q_x, q_y, q_z]^T = \left(\cos\left(\frac{\theta}{2}\right), \omega \sin\left(\frac{\theta}{2}\right) \right) \qquad (9.7)$$

and the vector **a** is rotated with

$$\mathbf{a}' = Rotate(\mathbf{a}) = \mathbf{q} \circ \tilde{\mathbf{a}} \circ \bar{\mathbf{q}}, \tag{9.8}$$

where $\circ$ denotes quaternion product, $\tilde{\mathbf{a}} = [0, \mathbf{a}]$ is a zero scalar component appended with the original vector **a** and $\bar{\mathbf{q}} = (q_w, -\mathbf{v})$ is the complex conjugate of **q**. Additionally, there exist simple formulas for computing the rotation matrix from a quaternion and vice versa. Furthermore, the four partial derivatives $\frac{\partial \mathbf{R}}{\partial q_w}, \frac{\partial \mathbf{R}}{\partial q_x}, \frac{\partial \mathbf{R}}{\partial q_y}, \frac{\partial \mathbf{R}}{\partial q_z}$ exist and are linearly independent in S^3 which means there are no singularities. Probably this last property is the most interesting but this comes at the expense of using 4 numbers instead of just 3. This means that during optimization we must impose a quadratic constraint so that the quaternion keeps unit length. Integrating ODEs can also be problematic since the quaternion velocity $\dot{\mathbf{q}}$ generally lies in the tangent space of S^3 and any movement in the tangent plane will push the quaternion *off* S^3. Nonetheless, there exist solutions to these limitations [25, 41]. Since unit quaternions directly represent the space of rotations and are free of singularities they provide an efficient representation of rotations. Particularly, quaternions have proven to be very useful for the interpolation of key-frame poses because they respect $SO(3)$ geometry.

9.1.4 Axis–Angle

To model human joint motion it is often needed to specify the axis of rotation of the joint. For example we might want to specify the motion of the knee joint as a rotation about an axis perpendicular to the leg and parallel to the hips. Therefore, for our purpose the axis–angle representation is optimal because rotations are described as an angle θ and an axis in space $\omega \in \mathbb{R}^3$ where θ determines the amount of rotation about ω. Unlike quaternions the axis–angle, requires only three parameters $\theta\omega$ to describe a rotation. It does not suffer from gimbal lock and their singularities occur in a region of parameter space that can be easily avoided. Since it will be our parametrization of choice to model human joint motion we will give a brief introduction to the formulation of twists and exponential maps. For a more detailed description we refer the reader to [34].

9.1.4.1 The Exponential Formula

Every rotation **R** can be written in exponential form in terms of the axis of rotation $\omega \in \mathbb{R}^3$ and the angle of rotation θ as

$$\mathbf{R} = \exp(\theta\widehat{\omega}), \tag{9.9}$$

where $\widehat{\omega} \in so(3)$ is the skew symmetric matrix constructed from ω. The elements of $so(3)$ are skew symmetric matrices i.e., matrices that verify $\{\mathbf{A} \in \mathbb{R}^{3\times3} | \mathbf{A} = -\mathbf{A}^T\}$.

Given the vector $\theta(\omega_1, \omega_2, \omega_3)$ the skew symmetric matrix is constructed with the wedge operator $\wedge$ as follows:

$$\theta\widehat{\omega} = \theta \begin{bmatrix} 0 & -\omega_3 & \omega_2 \\ \omega_3 & 0 & -\omega_1 \\ -\omega_2 & \omega_1 & 0 \end{bmatrix}. \tag{9.10}$$

By definition, the multiplication of the matrix $\widehat{\omega}$ with a point $\mathbf{p}$ is equivalent to the cross product of the vector ω with the point.

To derive the exponential formula in (9.9) consider a 3D point $\mathbf{p}$ rotating about an axis ω intersecting the origin at a unit constant angular velocity. Recall from elementary physics that the tangential velocity of the point may be written as

$$\dot{\mathbf{p}}(t) = \omega \times \mathbf{p}(t) = \widehat{\omega}\mathbf{p}(t) \tag{9.11}$$

which is a differential equation that we can integrate to obtain

$$\mathbf{p}(t) = \exp(\widehat{\omega}t)\mathbf{p}(0). \tag{9.12}$$

It follows that if we rotate θ units of time the net rotation is given by

$$\mathbf{R}(\theta, \omega) = \exp(\theta\widehat{\omega}). \tag{9.13}$$

The exponential map of a matrix $\mathbf{A} \in \mathbb{R}^{n \times m}$ is analogous to the exponential used for real numbers $a \in \mathbb{R}$. In particular the Taylor expansion of the exponential has the same form:

$$\exp(\theta\widehat{\omega}) = e^{(\theta\widehat{\omega})} = I + \theta\widehat{\omega} + \frac{\theta^2}{2!}\widehat{\omega}^2 + \frac{\theta^3}{3!}\widehat{\omega}^3 + \cdots. \tag{9.14}$$

Exploiting the fact that $(\theta\widehat{\omega})$ is screw symmetric, we can easily compute the exponential of the matrix $\widehat{\omega}$ in closed form using the *Rodriguez formula*:

$$\exp(\theta\widehat{\omega}) = I + \widehat{\omega}\sin(\theta) + \widehat{\omega}^2(1 - \cos(\theta)), \tag{9.15}$$

where only the square of the matrix $\widehat{\omega}$ and sine and cosine of real numbers have to be computed. Note that this formula allows us to reconstruct the rotation matrix from the angle θ and the axis of rotation ω by simple operations and this is probably the main justification of using the axis–angle representation at all.

9.1.4.2 Exponential Maps for Rigid Body Motions

The exponential map formulation can be extended to represent rigid body motions, namely any motion composed by a rotation $\mathbf{R}$ and a translation $\mathbf{t}$. This is done by extending the parameters $\theta\omega$ with $\theta v \in \mathbb{R}^3$ which is related to the translation along the axis of rotation and the location of the axis. These six parameters form the *twist coordinates* $\theta\xi = \theta(v_1, v_2, v_3, \omega_1, \omega_2, \omega_3)$ of a twist. Analogous to (9.9), any rigid motion $\mathbf{G} \in \mathbb{R}^{4\times 4}$ can be written in exponential form as

$$\mathbf{G}(\theta, \omega) = \begin{bmatrix} \mathbf{R}_{3\times 3} & \mathbf{t}_{3\times 1} \\ \mathbf{0}_{1\times 3} & 1 \end{bmatrix} = \exp(\theta\widehat{\xi}), \qquad (9.16)$$

where the 4×4 matrix $\theta\widehat{\xi} \in se(3)$ is the *twist action* and is a generalization of the screw symmetric matrix $\theta\widehat{\omega}$ of (9.10). The twist action is constructed from the twist coordinates $\theta\xi \in \mathbb{R}^6$ using the wedge operator $^\wedge$

$$[\theta\xi]^\wedge = \theta\widehat{\xi} = \theta \begin{bmatrix} 0 & -\omega_3 & \omega_2 & v_1 \\ \omega_3 & 0 & -\omega_1 & v_2 \\ -\omega_2 & \omega_1 & 0 & v_3 \\ 0 & 0 & 0 & 0 \end{bmatrix} \qquad (9.17)$$

and its exponential can be computed using the formula

$$\exp(\theta\widehat{\xi}) = \begin{bmatrix} \exp(\theta\widehat{\omega}) & (I - \exp(\theta\widehat{\omega}))(\omega \times v + \omega\omega^T v\theta) \\ \mathbf{0}_{1\times 3} & 1 \end{bmatrix} \qquad (9.18)$$

with $\exp(\theta\widehat{\omega})$ computed by using the Rodriguez formula (9.15) as explained before.

9.1.4.3 The Logarithm

For human tracking it is sometimes needed to obtain the twist parameters given a transformation matrix $\mathbf{G}$. In particular if we want to obtain the resulting twist of two consecutive twists this operation is needed. In [34], a constructive way is given to compute the twist which generates a given transformation matrix $\mathbf{G}$. For the case $\mathbf{R} = \mathbf{I}$, the twist is given by

$$\theta\xi = \theta\left(0, 0, 0, \frac{\mathbf{t}}{\|\mathbf{t}\|}\right), \qquad \theta = \|\mathbf{t}\|. \qquad (9.19)$$

For the other cases, the motion velocity θ and the rotation axis ω are given by

$$\theta = \cos^{-1}\left[\frac{tr(\mathbf{R}) - 1}{2}\right], \qquad \omega = \frac{1}{2\sin(\theta)} \begin{bmatrix} \mathbf{R}_{32} - \mathbf{R}_{23} \\ \mathbf{R}_{13} - \mathbf{R}_{31} \\ \mathbf{R}_{21} - \mathbf{R}_{12} \end{bmatrix}. \qquad (9.20)$$

From (9.18) it follows that to obtain v, the matrix

$$\mathbf{A} = \left(I - \exp(\theta\widehat{\omega})\right)\widehat{\omega} + \omega\omega^T\theta \qquad (9.21)$$

needs to be inverted and multiplied with the translation vector $\mathbf{t}$,

$$v = \mathbf{A}^{-1}\mathbf{t}. \qquad (9.22)$$

We call this transformation from a rigid motion $\mathbf{G} \in SE(3)$ to a twist $\theta\xi \in \mathbb{R}^6$ the logarithm, $\theta\xi = \log(\mathbf{G})$.

Fig. 9.2 Screw motion, *left*:
the cross product of the
scaled axis $\theta\omega$ and the vector
$(\mathbf{p}_s - \mathbf{q})$ results in the
tangential velocity of the
point $\dot{\mathbf{p}}_s = \theta\omega \times (\mathbf{p}_s - \mathbf{q})$.
Equivalently, the tangential
velocity may be written using
the twist $\dot{\mathbf{p}}_s = \widehat{\xi}\mathbf{p}_s$. *Right*:
generalized screw motion
with rotation and translation
along the axis

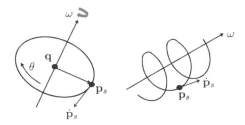

9.1.4.4 Adjoint Transformation

Given a twist $\xi_b = (v_b, \omega_b) \in \mathbb{R}^6$ with coordinates in the body frame B, we can find
the coordinates of the twist in the spatial frame S. Given that the configuration of B
relative to frame S is the rigid motion $\mathbf{g} = (\mathbf{R}, \mathbf{t}) \in SE(3)$, the twist coordinates in
the spatial frame are given by

$$\xi_s = \mathrm{Ad}_\mathbf{g}\,\xi_b, \quad \mathrm{Ad}_\mathbf{g} = \begin{bmatrix} \mathbf{R} & \mathbf{t}^\wedge \mathbf{R} \\ \mathbf{0}_{3\times 3} & \mathbf{R} \end{bmatrix}, \tag{9.23}$$

where Ad_g is the *adjoint transformation* associated with $\mathbf{g}$, see [34]. To see this, note
that the angular components are related by the rotation $\omega_s = \mathbf{R}\omega_b$ (the same way we
rotate points we can rotate the axes). From this it follows that $v_s = \mathbf{R}v_b + \mathbf{t}^\wedge \mathbf{R}\omega_b$.
Equivalently, the action $\widehat{\xi}_s$ of a twist with twist coordinates ξ_s is related to the action
$\widehat{\xi}_b$ with twist coordinates ξ_b by

$$\widehat{\xi}_s = \mathbf{G}\,\widehat{\xi}_b\,\mathbf{G}^{-1}. \tag{9.24}$$

Recall that the product of a twist $\widehat{\xi}$ by a point results in the velocity of the point
$\mathbf{v_p}$, see Fig. 9.2. Furthermore, *a twist with twist coordinates ξ_a in a given frame A,
applies on points $\mathbf{p}_a$ defined in the same frame A and this results in the velocity of
the point relative to frame A $\mathbf{v}_{\mathbf{p}_a}$.* Thus, we can interpret (9.24) the following way:
the velocity in spatial coordinates of a point $\mathbf{p}_s$ is obtained by first transforming
the point to body coordinates $\mathbf{p}_s \mapsto \mathbf{p}_b$ with $\mathbf{G}^{-1}$, then finding the velocity of the
point in body coordinates $\mathbf{v}_{\mathbf{p}_b}$ using the twist action $\widehat{\xi}_b$ and finally transforming
the velocity back to spatial coordinates $\mathbf{v}_{\mathbf{p}_s}$ with $\mathbf{G}$. One can prove that indeed this
results in the spatial velocity

$$\bar{\mathbf{v}}_{\mathbf{p}_s} = \left(\mathbf{G}\,\widehat{\xi}_b\,\mathbf{G}^{-1}\right)\bar{\mathbf{p}}_s = \left(\mathbf{G}\,\widehat{\xi}_b\,\mathbf{G}^{-1}\right)\mathbf{G}\,\bar{\mathbf{p}}_b = \mathbf{G}\,\widehat{\xi}_b\,\bar{\mathbf{p}}_b = \mathbf{G}\,\bar{\mathbf{v}}_{\mathbf{p}_b}, \tag{9.25}$$

where $\bar{\mathbf{v}}_{\mathbf{p}_s} = [\mathbf{v}_{\mathbf{p}_s}\,0]$ are the homogeneous coordinates of the vector $\mathbf{v}_{\mathbf{p}_s}$. An interesting property that stems from (9.24) and (9.25) is that $\mathbf{G}$ can be shifted inside the
exponential

$$\exp\left(\widehat{\xi}_s\right) = \mathbf{G}\exp\left(\widehat{\xi}_b\right)\mathbf{G}^{-1} = \exp\left(\mathbf{G}\,\widehat{\xi}_b\,\mathbf{G}^{-1}\right) \tag{9.26}$$

Fig. 9.3 Kinematic chain: the motion is given by the concatenation of joint angular motions. Note how the twists ξ are transformed to ξ' when parent articulations move

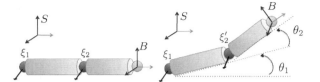

which means that to express a rigid body motion $\exp(\xi)$ in another coordinate system we can simply transform the corresponding twist action with $\mathbf{G}$. The same way we can interpret a rigid motion applied to a point as a coordinate transformation or as a relative motion, we can interpret the adjoint transform applied to twists as a transformation that brings a twist from their initial coordinates ξ to their coordinates ξ' (defined in the same frame) after the rigid motion $\mathbf{g}$ is applied, see Fig. 9.3. Indeed, we will make frequent use of this interpretation in the next sections when we have to keep track of human joints locations and orientations during tracking.

9.1.5 Kinematic Chains

Human motion is articulated and we want to model the motion taking all the joints into account at the same time. For example, consider the motion of the hand, this motion will be the concatenation of motions of their parent joints, wrist, elbow, shoulder and root. To formulate this we now define two coordinate frames, the spatial frame S, which is usually fixed and the body frame B, which is the coordinate system attached to the segment of interest. Note that the body frame moves along with the segment and therefore a control point in the segment in body coordinates $\mathbf{p}_b$ is always constant. Consider the arm in Fig. 9.3 with two segments and only two degrees of freedom. To obtain the coordinates of a control point in the hand in spatial coordinates $\mathbf{p}_s$ from their body coordinates $\mathbf{p}_b$ we can concatenate the rigid motions along the chain:

$$\bar{\mathbf{p}}_s = \mathbf{G}_{sb}\bar{\mathbf{p}}_b = \mathbf{G}_1\mathbf{G}_2\mathbf{G}_{sb}(\mathbf{0})\bar{\mathbf{p}}_b, \tag{9.27}$$

where $\mathbf{G}_1$, $\mathbf{G}_2$ are the rigid motion matrices of the upper and lower arm, respectively, and $\mathbf{G}_{sb}(\mathbf{0})$ is the transformation between B and S at the zero pose. By using the fact that the motion of each individual joint is generated by a twist associated with a joint axis (see Fig. 9.3) we can write the spatial coordinates of a point in the body as a function of the joint angles in the chain:

$$\bar{\mathbf{p}}_s = \mathbf{G}_{sb}(\theta_1, \theta_2) = e^{\hat{\xi}_1\theta_1}e^{\hat{\xi}_2\theta_2}\mathbf{G}_{sb}(\mathbf{0})\bar{\mathbf{p}}_b. \tag{9.28}$$

Any new articulation joint will represent an additional twist in the chain, Fig. 9.3. If we generalize this procedure for any limb of the human body we can define what is known in the robotics literature as the forward kinematics map. The forward kinematics is then defined as the mapping between the vector of joint angles

$\Theta = (\theta_1, \theta_2, \ldots, \theta_n)^T$ to the transformation matrix between the spatial and body frames $\mathbf{G}_{sb}$. If we define Q as the space of joint angle vectors, then the forward kinematics $\mathbf{G}_{sb} : Q \to SE(3)$ is given by

$$\mathbf{G}_{sb}(\Theta) = e^{\widehat{\xi}_1 \theta_1} e^{\widehat{\xi}_2 \theta_2} \cdots e^{\widehat{\xi}_n \theta_n} \mathbf{G}_{sb}(\mathbf{0}), \qquad (9.29)$$

where ξ are constant twists in the reference configuration, i.e., the starting *zero pose*. For human tracking it is usual to take $\mathbf{G}_{sb}(\mathbf{0})$ to be the identity, i.e., the body and spatial frame are coincident at the beginning for every single limb on the human body.

9.1.5.1 The Articulated Jacobian

The articulated Jacobian[1] is a matrix $\mathbf{J}_\Theta \in \mathbb{R}^{6 \times n}$ that maps joint velocities to a rigid body motion velocity represented by a twist and it may be written as

$$\mathbf{J}_\Theta = \begin{bmatrix} \xi_1 & \xi_2' & \cdots & \xi_n' \end{bmatrix}, \qquad (9.30)$$

where $\xi_i' = \mathrm{Ad}_{(e^{\widehat{\xi}_1 \theta_1} \ldots e^{\widehat{\xi}_{i-1} \theta_{i-1}})} \xi_i$ is the ith joint twist transformed to the current pose, Fig. 9.3. To obtain ξ_i' an option is to update at every time step the twists with the accumulated motion of parent joints in the chain. Note that the form of the Jacobian is different for every limb in the body since different body parts are influenced by different joints. Now given a pose determined by Θ and point in the body in spatial coordinates $\mathbf{p}_s$ we can obtain the increment $\Delta \mathbf{p}_s$ in position as a function of the increment in parameter space $\Delta \Theta$ as

$$\Delta \bar{\mathbf{p}}_s = [\mathbf{J}_\Theta \cdot \Delta \Theta]^\wedge \bar{\mathbf{p}}_s = \begin{bmatrix} \xi_1 \Delta \theta_1 + \xi_2' \Delta \theta_2 + \cdots + \xi_n' \Delta \theta_n \end{bmatrix}^\wedge \bar{\mathbf{p}}_s, \qquad (9.31)$$

where $^\wedge$ is the wedge operator defined in (9.17) and we drop the homogeneous component after the multiplication of $[\mathbf{J}_\Theta \cdot \Delta \Theta]^\wedge \bar{\mathbf{p}}_s$. We can interpret the formula as follows: the total displacement of the point $\mathbf{p}_s$ is the sum of individual displacements generated by the angle increments $\Delta \theta_i$ in upper joints keeping the others fixed. It is very important to note that the result of $[\mathbf{J}_\Theta \cdot \Delta \Theta]$ are the twist coordinates ξ_s of the rotational ω and "linear velocity" v of the body expressed in the spatial frame. Note that the product $\widehat{\xi}_s \bar{\mathbf{p}}_s$ results in the point increment in homogeneous coordinates $\Delta \bar{\mathbf{p}}_s = [\Delta \mathbf{p}_s \ 0]$. Since we are not interested in the last homogeneous component, in the following we will confuse $\Delta \bar{\mathbf{p}}_s$ with $\Delta \mathbf{p}_s$ by dropping the homogeneous component after the multiplication $\widehat{\xi}_s \mathbf{p}_s$.

---

[1] We call it articulated Jacobian and not *manipulator Jacobian* as in Murray et al. [34] because we find it more appropriate in this context.

Table 9.1 Table of existing joints to model human motion

Joint	DoF	Unknown parameter	Example
Root	6	$\xi = \theta[v\ \omega]^T$	All body
Ball	3	$\theta\omega$	Hips
Saddle	2	θ_1, θ_2	Wrist
Revolute	1	θ	Knee

9.1.6 Human Pose Parametrization

Now we have the necessary mathematical tools to model all the joints in the human model. We identify three kinds of joints in the human body according the *DoF*, see Table 9.1. The *root joint* that determines the overall orientation and position of the body has 6 *DoF* and can be modeled as a twist $\theta\xi$ with the six components as free parameters. *Ball joints* capable of any rotation with no translation can be efficiently modeled as twist with known joint location $\mathbf{q}$ and unknown axis of rotation $\theta\omega$ [38]. Finally, simple *revolute joints* are only capable of rotations about a fixed known axis. For revolute joints the twist is constant and is given by

$$\xi = \begin{bmatrix} -\omega \times \mathbf{q} \\ \omega \end{bmatrix} \tag{9.32}$$

and the only unknown is the rotation angle θ, see Fig. 9.2 for a geometrical interpretation. This last category is very convenient to constrain the motion of 1 *DoF* joints (e.g., the knee).

In the literature the common choice is to model the root joint with six free parameters and to model all the other joints with the concatenation of revolute joints. Thereby, a ball joint is modeled by three consecutive revolute joints, i.e., three consecutive rotations about three fixed axes. The free parameters are then the angles about each of the three axes $\theta_1, \theta_2, \theta_3$. This parametrization is very similar to the Euler angles and has the same limitations in terms of singularities, i.e., it is not free of gimbal lock. However, to keep the notation simple, in the following we assume that we parametrize ball joints as three consecutive revolute joints. For a description of the parametrization of ball joints using a single free axis of rotation we refer the reader to [38].

Therefore, the pose configuration of the human is usually encoded with a scaled twist ξ for the root joint and a vector of n joint angles for the rest of the joints. Let us denote the state vector of pose parameters at time t, as

$$\mathbf{x}_t := (\xi, \Theta), \quad \Theta := (\theta_1 \theta_2 \ldots \theta_n). \tag{9.33}$$

Thereby, a human pose is totally determined by a D-dimensional state vector $\mathbf{x}_t \in \mathbb{R}^D$, with $D = 6 + n$.

9.1.6.1 The Pose Jacobian

For local optimization it is necessary to know the relationship between increments in the pose parameters and increments in the position of a point in a body segment. This relationship is given by the pose Jacobian $\mathbf{J_x}(\mathbf{p}_s) = \frac{\Delta \mathbf{p}_s}{\Delta \mathbf{x}}$. In this paragraph, we derive the analytical expression for the pose Jacobian. We start our derivation from the expression of the point increment of (9.31). Let us denote with $\Delta \xi = [\Delta v_1 \ \Delta v_2 \ \Delta v_3 \ \Delta \omega_1 \ \Delta \omega_2 \ \Delta \omega_3]$ the relative twist corresponding to the root joint. The six coordinates of the scaled relative twist $\Delta \xi$ are now free parameters we will want to estimate. By using the identity $[u + w]^\wedge = \widehat{u} + \widehat{w}$ we can rewrite (9.31) as increments in pose parameter space

$$
\begin{aligned}
\Delta \mathbf{p}_s &= \left[\Delta \xi + \xi_1' \Delta \theta_1 + \cdots + \xi_n' \Delta \theta_n \right]^\wedge \bar{\mathbf{p}}_s \\
&= \widehat{\Delta \xi} \bar{\mathbf{p}}_s + \widehat{\xi_1'} \bar{\mathbf{p}}_s \Delta \theta_1 + \cdots + \widehat{\xi_n'} \bar{\mathbf{p}}_s \Delta \theta_n,
\end{aligned}
\tag{9.34}
$$

where we can isolate the parameters of the root joint $\Delta \xi$ rewriting $\widehat{\Delta \xi} \bar{\mathbf{p}}_s$

$$
\widehat{\Delta \xi} \bar{\mathbf{p}}_s = \Delta v + \Delta \omega \times \mathbf{p}_s = \Delta v - \mathbf{p}_s^\wedge \Delta \omega = \left[\mathbf{I}_{[3 \times 3]} \mid -\mathbf{p}_s^\wedge \right] \Delta \xi
\tag{9.35}
$$

and substituting this expression in (9.34) again

$$
\begin{aligned}
\Delta \mathbf{p}_s &= \left[\mathbf{I}_{[3 \times 3]} \mid -\mathbf{p}_s^\wedge \right] \Delta \xi + \widehat{\xi_2'} \bar{\mathbf{p}}_s \Delta \theta_2 + \cdots + \widehat{\xi_n'} \bar{\mathbf{p}}_s \Delta \theta_n \\
&= \mathbf{J_x}(\mathbf{p}_s) \Delta \mathbf{x},
\end{aligned}
\tag{9.36}
$$

where $\Delta \mathbf{x} = [\Delta \xi \ \Delta \Theta]$ is the differential vector of pose parameters and

$$
\mathbf{J_x}(\mathbf{p}_s) = \left[\mathbf{I}_{[3 \times 3]} \quad -\mathbf{p}_s^\wedge \quad \widehat{\xi_1'} \bar{\mathbf{p}}_s \quad \widehat{\xi_2'} \bar{\mathbf{p}}_s \quad \cdots \quad \widehat{\xi_n'} \bar{\mathbf{p}}_s \right]
\tag{9.37}
$$

is the positional Jacobian $\mathbf{J_x}(\mathbf{p}_s) \in \mathbb{R}^{3 \times D}$ of a point $\mathbf{p}_s$ with respect to the pose parameters which we denote as *pose Jacobian*. For a given point in the body $\mathbf{p}_s$ in a configuration $\mathbf{x}$, $\mathbf{J_x}(\mathbf{p}_s) : \mathbb{R}^D \mapsto \mathbb{R}^3$ maps an increment of the pose parameters $\Delta \mathbf{x}$ to a positional increment of the point $\Delta \mathbf{p}_s$. We identify two main blocks in the pose Jacobian: the first six columns that correspond to the non constant relative twist $\Delta \xi$ of the root joint, and the rest of the columns (*joint columns*) that correspond to the point velocity contribution of each joint angle. Consequently, the column entries of joints that are not parents of the point are simply zero $\mathbf{0}_{3 \times 1}$. The analytical pose Jacobian derived here is general and will appear in every local optimization method using the parametrization described in (9.33).

9.2 Model Creation

A very important step in the pose estimation pipeline is the 3D model creation. This involves the initialization of the 3D surface mesh and the skeletal kinematic structure. We can roughly classify the approaches for shape initialization according to the level of detail. We find three main classes, methods that approximate the human body using *geometric primitives*, methods that use a subject specific *body scan* to build a 3D mesh model and finally methods that estimate *detailed shape from images* without a body scan of the subject.

9.2.1 Geometric Primitives

A wide variety of geometric primitives have been used to approximate the body shape. Early works used a simplified body model-based on a collection of articulated planar rectangles [28]. More sophisticated models have used cylinders [42], truncated cones, ellipsoids [45] or Gaussian blobs [36]. These geometric primitives can then be parametrized using very few numbers e.g., the shape of the cylinders is encoded as the height and radius. Thereby, if not initialized manually, the vector of shape parameters ϕ is estimated from images in a calibration step. The parameters include internal proportions, limb lengths and volumes.

9.2.2 Detailed Body Scans

Whole-body 3D scans provide a very accurate measurement of the surface shape. However, the model creation from a 3D scan is more involved than using simple geometric primitives. The output from a 3D scans is usually a dense 3D point cloud and a triangulated mesh. However, the triangulated mesh contains holes due to self occlusions. To initialize the model for tracking three main pre-processing steps are needed, (i) fit a template mesh to the 3D point cloud of the scanner, (ii) create a skeleton and (iii) bind skin to the skeleton bones. The last is known as skinning and the whole process is known as rigging.

- *Template mesh registration*: Since the triangulated mesh from the laser scan contains holes, a template mesh has to be morphed to fit the point cloud. This can be done with standard non-rigid registration techniques [1, 49]. Current non-rigid registration techniques require a set corresponding control points between the template mesh and the scan. The correspondences can be obtained, for example, with *Correlated Correspondence* technique which matches similar looking surface regions while minimizing the deformation [4]. Given the correspondences non-rigid registration is used to fit the template to the scan.
- *Skeleton fitting*: The skeleton determines the motion of the model. For the creation of the skeleton we must choose the number of joint articulations and the

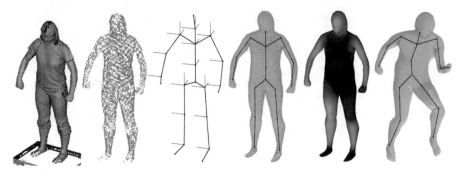

Fig. 9.4 Processing pipeline for model rigging from a body scan; from *left to right*: body scan surface, down-sampled 3D point cloud, skeleton with the twist axis orientations in black, registered template mesh, skinned model and animated model

degrees of freedom for every joint. Rough human models use only 15 degrees of freedom while models used for movie production contain over 60. For human pose estimation from images many researchers use 20–30 *DoF*, which gives a good compromise between degree of realism and robustness. For every joint we must determine two things: the location and the orientation of the axis of rotation ω, see Fig. 9.4. The skeleton is usually edited manually before tracking.

- *Skinning*: Given the registered template mesh and the skeleton we have to determine for every vertex in the surface to which body part it belongs, i.e. we must assign a joint index to every vertex. For realistic animations, however, the representation of human motion as rigid parts is too simplistic, specially for regions close to the articulations. To obtain a smooth deformation an option is to use *linear blend skinning* [32], which approximates the motion of points close to a joint by a weighted linear combination of neighboring joints. For example the motion of the shoulder vertices would be given by a combination of the torso and arm motions. The motion of a point $\mathbf{p}_s(0)$ in the reference pose is then given by

$$\bar{\mathbf{p}}_s = \sum_{i \in \mathcal{N}} w_i \mathbf{G}_{sb}^i(\mathbf{x}_t)\bar{\mathbf{p}}_s(0), \tag{9.38}$$

where $i \in \mathcal{N}$ are the indices of their neighboring joints, and w_i are the weights. A simple rule to set the weights is to make them inversely proportional to the distance to neighboring joint locations $w_i = 1/d_i$. However, this produces severe artifacts. Several algorithms from the graphics community attempt to solve the skinning problem. As a matter of fact, open source software is available to compute the weights given a mesh and a skeleton [6]. Nevertheless, to keep notation simple, throughout this chapter we assume each point is assigned a single joint with weight equal one. We want to emphasize, however, that linear blend skinning *does not change* the formulation on kinematic chains described in the previous section since it is based on linear combinations of rigid motions.

The whole pipeline for mesh registration and rigging is shown in Fig. 9.4.

9.2.3 Detailed Shape from Images

Body scan models are limited by the availability of range scanners. To overcome this limitation a recent research direction has focused on the estimation of detailed shape from images [5, 26]. This is achieved by finding parametrization learned from a database of human scans that encodes human shape and pose variation across individuals [2, 3]. All subjects in the database are scanned in different poses to account for both shape and pose deformation. The pose is usually encoded by a combination of rigid and non-rigid deformations, and the shape variation is modeled with a set of PCA coefficients learned from the database.

As a final comment, there exist approaches that use neither a skeleton nor shape knowledge from a database [12, 18]. In contrast, such approaches directly deform the mesh geometry by non-rigid deformation to fit a set of multiview silhouettes. While impressive results are achieved with such methods, high quality silhouettes are needed and at least eight cameras are used.

9.3 Optimization

Now that we have the mathematical tools to generate the 3D models and to represent human motion, our aim is to recover this motion form one or multiview images. Model-based algorithms are classified as generative model approaches because independently of the optimization scheme used, they all model the likelihood of the observations for a given configuration of pose parameters. The pose that best explains the observations is typically found by minimizing an error function that measures how well the model fits the image data. Even using multiple cameras and relatively simple background settings this poses a hard optimization problem. Difficulties arise from model-image matching ambiguities, depth ambiguities and the high dimensionality of the state space. An additional difficulty is that the space of plausible poses only represents a small region of the full parameter space $\mathbb{R}^D$. The ability to obtain better results by constraining search to a sub-space of plausible poses will be discussed at length in Chap. 10. The key components for successful tracking, which we will describe here, are the design of the cost function and the optimization strategy. In this section we describe the different optimization strategies for human pose estimation and the type of error functions used.

9.3.1 Local Optimization

Given an initial estimate, local optimization methods are based on iteratively linearizing the error function to find a descent direction. Usually, these methods converge to a local optimum and consequently their performance strongly depends on the initialization. During tracking, the knowledge of the estimates in previous frames can simplify the task: in the simplest case the initial estimate is given by the pose obtained in the previous frame, or alternatively motion models can be used to make good predictions closer to the true pose. We distinguish three main families of local optimization methods for human pose estimation: methods based on *correspondences*, *optical flow* and *regions*.

9.3.1.1 Correspondence-Based

Almost all early approaches for 3D human pose estimation were *correspondence-based* and still it remains one of the most popular strategies. A reason for that is that these approaches are computationally efficient while providing very accurate results in many situations. The key idea is to collect a set of correspondences between 3D points $\mathbf{p}_i$ of the model and the *image observations* $\mathbf{r}_i$. Then, the distance between the projection of the 3D model points $\tilde{\mathbf{r}}_i$ (*predictions*) and the image observations is minimized with respect to the pose parameters $\mathbf{x}_t$, see Fig. 9.5.

> Hence, *correspondence-based* algorithms consist of three main stages
>
> 1. *Feature extraction*: extract image observations (e.g., silhouettes, edges, SIFT features)
> 2. *Model image association*: match the model 3D points with the image observations and collect this correspondences
> 3. *Descent strategy*: find the pose parameters that bring the model points into correspondence with the image observations

Feature extraction: Different features like image silhouettes, image edges, and SIFT have been used and combined for human pose estimation. Edge and silhouettes where used in very early works and continue to be dominant for human pose estimation because they are relatively easy to extract and are stable to illumination changes. Therefore, we will explain in detail a motion capture system based on silhouettes and then the integration of additional features like SIFT will become obvious. In the context of human tracking a silhouette is a binary image with white pixels indicating the foreground i.e., the region of the subject we want to track. In indoor environments, silhouettes can be obtained with great accuracy via background subtraction techniques [35]. In outdoor environments, it is considerably more challenging but also possible if background images are available. Once the silhouettes are obtained, the image contour is obtained with an edge detector.

Model image association: For the correspondences, since we want to predict the image contour, only points belonging to the *occluding contour* are considered. A point belongs to the occluding contour $\mathbf{p}_i \in \mathcal{O}$ if its surface normal $\hat{\mathbf{n}}$ is perpendicular to the line $\mathbf{L}$ connecting the camera center $\mathbf{O}$ and the point. In other words,

Fig. 9.5 From *left to right*: original image, silhouette from background subtraction, rendering of the projected mesh at the current pose, correspondences by contour matching, animated model seen from a virtual view

the occluding contour is the set of points in the mesh that project to the silhouette contour of the projected mesh.

To find the points of the occluding contour there are two main strategies, the first and the simplest one is to test for every point in the mesh if the surface normal is perpendicular to the projection ray:

$$\mathbf{p} \in \mathscr{O} \quad \text{if } \hat{\mathbf{n}} \cdot (\mathbf{p} - \mathbf{C}) < \varepsilon, \tag{9.39}$$

where ε is a small positive threshold. In practice, however, this approach is problematic since the accuracy of $\hat{\mathbf{n}}$ strongly depends on the mesh resolution (number of vertices of the mesh). One solution is to look for sign changes of the angle between the triangle normal and the projection ray. The second strategy is to first render a binary silhouette projection on the image, project all the vertices of the mesh and retain only those on the silhouette boundary. To render the silhouette image, all the visible surface triangles are projected to the image and filled using typical graphics raster-scan algorithms. Alternatively, the rendering can be very efficiently performed on the GPU using OpenGL. At this point we have two sets of points, the 3D points in the occluding contour $\mathbf{p}_i \in \mathscr{O}$ and the 2D points from the image contour $\mathbf{r}_i \in \mathscr{I}$. The correspondences can be found by finding for every point projection $\tilde{\mathbf{r}}_i = \text{Pr}_c(\mathbf{p}_i)$ the k-nearest neighbors in the image contour. This will result in a set of 3D–2D correspondences $(\mathbf{p}_i, \mathbf{r}_i)$ or 2D–2D correspondences $(\tilde{\mathbf{r}}_i, \mathbf{r}_i)$. We note that finding correct correspondences is a hard problem with probably many local minima. To leverage this, additional terms based on overlap between the model and image silhouette can be included into the matching cost [44].

Descent strategies: Collecting many of these correspondences $(\tilde{\mathbf{r}}_i, \mathbf{r}_i)$ the error function $e : \mathbb{R}^D \mapsto \mathbb{R}$ may be defined as the sum of squared re-projection errors in the image

$$e(\mathbf{x}_t) = \sum_i^N \mathbf{e}_i^2(\mathbf{x}_t) = \sum_i^N \left\| \tilde{\mathbf{r}}_i(\mathbf{x}_t) - \mathbf{r}_i \right\|^2 \tag{9.40}$$

which we want to minimize with respect to the pose parameters $\mathbf{x}_t$. Note that in the case of 2D–2D correspondences the individual residual errors $\mathbf{e}_i \in \mathbb{R}^2$ are 2D error vectors $\mathbf{e}_i = (\Delta r_{i,x}, \Delta r_{i,y})$. Equation (9.40) is a classical non-linear least squares that can be re-written in vector form as

$$e(\mathbf{x}_t) = \mathbf{e}^T \mathbf{e}, \tag{9.41}$$

where $\mathbf{e} \in \mathbb{R}^{2N}$ is the total residual error $\mathbf{e} = (\mathbf{e}_1^T, \mathbf{e}_2^T, \dots, \mathbf{e}_N^T)$. Equation (9.41) can be efficiently minimized using a *Gauss–Newton* style minimization. The trick is to iteratively linearize the vector function $\mathbf{e} \in \mathbb{R}^{2N}$ around the solution with the Jacobian matrix $\mathbf{J}_t$ to find a descent step. In the literature, the expression for the Jacobian matrix is often omitted due to space limitations. Therefore, we reproduce here how to derive the analytical expression of the Jacobian matrix $\mathbf{J}_t \in \mathbb{R}^{2N \times D}$ of the residual error $\mathbf{e}$. We start by deriving the expression for the Jacobian of the error of a single correspondence $\mathbf{J}_{t,i} = \frac{\Delta \mathbf{e}_i}{\Delta \mathbf{x}}$. It is straightforward to see that the individual error Jacobian equals the prediction Jacobian $\mathbf{J}_{t,i} = \frac{\Delta \mathbf{e}_i}{\Delta \mathbf{x}} = \frac{\Delta \tilde{\mathbf{r}}_i}{\Delta \mathbf{x}}$ because only the prediction $\tilde{\mathbf{r}}_i$ depends on the pose parameters. Recall that the matrix $\mathbf{J}_{t,i} \in \mathbb{R}^{2 \times D}$ maps increments in the pose parameters $\Delta \mathbf{x}$ to increments in the predictions $\Delta \tilde{\mathbf{r}}_i$. To compute the Jacobian it is useful to identify the set of transformations applied to a point $\mathbf{p}_s(0)$ in the reference pose to the final projection in the image $\tilde{\mathbf{r}}$. We can visualize this with the diagram

$$\mathbf{p}_s(0) \xrightarrow{\ \mathbf{G}_{sb}(\mathbf{x}_t)\ } \mathbf{p}_s \xrightarrow{\ g_c := \mathbf{M}_{ext}\ } \mathbf{p}_c \xrightarrow{\ g_p := f(\frac{X}{Z}+o_x, \frac{X}{Z}+o_y)\ } \tilde{\mathbf{r}},$$

where $\mathbf{G}_{sb}(\mathbf{x}_t)$ is the concatenation of rigid motions in the kinematic chain given by the pose parameters $\mathbf{x}_t$, $g_c(\mathbf{p}) \mapsto \mathbf{M}_{ext}\mathbf{p}$ is the extrinsic camera matrix that transforms a point from spatial coordinates $\mathbf{p}_s$ to camera coordinates $\mathbf{p}_c$ and $g_p(X, Y, Z) \mapsto (f\frac{X}{Z} + o_x, f\frac{X}{Z} + o_y)$ is the perspective projection of 3D point in camera coordinates onto the image plane (with f denoting the focal length, (o_x, o_y) the principal point and we assume the skew coefficient is one). Now we can compute the Jacobians $\mathbf{J}_c \in \mathbb{R}^{3 \times 3}$, $\mathbf{J}_p \in \mathbb{R}^{2 \times 3}$ of the functions g_c, g_p separately as

$$g_c : \mathbb{R}^3 \to \mathbb{R}^3, \quad \mathbf{p}_c^i = \mathbf{M}_{ext}\bar{\mathbf{p}}_s^i = \mathbf{R}_{cs}\mathbf{p}_s^i + \mathbf{t}_{cs} = \begin{bmatrix} X \\ Y \\ Z \end{bmatrix}, \quad \mathbf{J}_c = \mathbf{R}_{cs},$$

$$g_p : \mathbb{R}^3 \to \mathbb{R}^2, \quad \tilde{\mathbf{r}}_i = g_p(\mathbf{p}_c^i) = \left(f\frac{X}{Z} + o_x, f\frac{Y}{Z} + o_y \right), \quad \mathbf{J}_p = f \begin{bmatrix} \frac{1}{Z} & 0 & -\frac{X}{Z^2} \\ 0 & \frac{1}{Z} & -\frac{Y}{Z^2} \end{bmatrix},$$

where the Jacobian of g_c is directly the rotational component of the extrinsics, $\mathbf{R}_{cs}$ because it is a linear map and the Jacobian of g_p is computed by direct application of the definition of the Jacobian matrix. By applying the chain rule, the Jacobian of the composed mapping $\mathbf{J}_{t,i}$ might be written as

$$\mathbf{J}_{t,i} = \frac{\Delta \tilde{\mathbf{r}}_i}{\Delta \mathbf{x}_t} = \frac{\Delta \tilde{\mathbf{r}}_i}{\Delta \mathbf{p}_c} \cdot \frac{\Delta \mathbf{p}_c}{\Delta \mathbf{p}_s} \cdot \frac{\Delta \mathbf{p}_s}{\Delta \mathbf{x}_t} = \mathbf{J}_p \mathbf{R}_{cs} \mathbf{J}_{\mathbf{x}}(\mathbf{p}_s^i), \tag{9.42}$$

where $\mathbf{J_x}(\mathbf{p}_s^i)$ is the pose Jacobian derived earlier in (9.37). It is straightforward to see that the Jacobian of total residual error $\mathbf{J}_t \in \mathbb{R}^{2N \times D}$ may be written by stacking the individual point Jacobians $\mathbf{J}_{t,i} \in \mathbb{R}^{2 \times D}$

$$\mathbf{J}_t = \frac{\Delta \mathbf{e}}{\Delta X_t} = \begin{bmatrix} \mathbf{J}_{t,1} \\ \mathbf{J}_{t,2} \\ \vdots \\ \mathbf{J}_{t,N} \end{bmatrix}. \tag{9.43}$$

With the analytical expression of the residual Jacobian the Gauss–Newton method calculates the descent step as follows:

$$\begin{aligned}
\Delta \mathbf{x} &= \arg\min_{\Delta \mathbf{x}} \frac{1}{2} \mathbf{e}^T (\mathbf{x}_t + \Delta \mathbf{x}) \mathbf{e} (\mathbf{x}_t + \Delta \mathbf{x}) \\
&= \arg\min_{\Delta \mathbf{x}} \frac{1}{2} (\mathbf{e} + \mathbf{J}_t \Delta \mathbf{x})^T (\mathbf{e} + \mathbf{J}_t \Delta \mathbf{x}) \\
&= \arg\min_{\Delta \mathbf{x}} \frac{1}{2} \mathbf{e}^T \mathbf{e} + \Delta \mathbf{x}^T \mathbf{J}_t^T \mathbf{e} + \frac{1}{2} \Delta \mathbf{x}^T \mathbf{J}_t^T \mathbf{J}_t \Delta \mathbf{x},
\end{aligned} \tag{9.44}$$

where $\mathbf{e} = \mathbf{e}(\mathbf{x}_t)^T$ and $\mathbf{J}_t = \mathbf{J}_t(\mathbf{x}_t)$ are evaluated at the current estimation $\mathbf{x}_t$. Finally, derivating with respect to $\Delta \mathbf{x}$ and equating to zero we find that the descent step is

$$\Delta \mathbf{x} = -\left(\mathbf{J}_t^T \mathbf{J}_t\right)^{-1} \mathbf{J}_t^T \mathbf{e}. \tag{9.45}$$

At every iteration of the Gauss–Newton algorithm the step is computed using (9.45) and the pose parameters are updated $\mathbf{x}_{t+1} = \mathbf{x}_t + \Delta \mathbf{x}$. This procedure is repeated until the algorithm converges. The step $\Delta \mathbf{x}$ always decreases the error function $e(\mathbf{x}_t)$ as long as the Jacobian matrix $\mathbf{J}_t$ has full rank. In the *Levenberg–Marquadt* algorithm, the Gauss–Newton step is modified

$$\Delta \mathbf{x} = -\left(\mathbf{J}_t^T \mathbf{J}_t + \mu \mathbf{I}\right)^{-1} \mathbf{J}_t^T \mathbf{e} \tag{9.46}$$

by introducing an additional dynamically chosen parameter $\mu \mathbf{I}$ that improves the performance. If the step decreases the error, the step is accepted and the value of μ is reduced. If the step increases the error, μ is increased and a new step is computed. When μ is large the method performs like standard gradient descent, slow but guaranteed to converge. When μ is small it performs like Gauss–Newton. Once the algorithm has converged the obtained pose estimate is used as initialization for the next frame, new correspondences are found in the new image and the process is repeated. For large motions one often needs to re-project the model to the image several times to obtain refined correspondences, similar to the standard Iterative Closest Point (ICP) registration method [7, 52].

Different error functions: Different error functions have been proposed in the literature. For example, Rosenhahn et al. [39] directly minimize the sum of squared

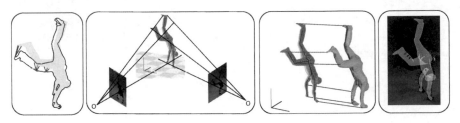

Fig. 9.6 Different error functions, from *left to right*: minimization of re-projection error (2D–2D correspondences), point to line distance error minimization (2D–3D correspondences), point to point distance error minimization (3D–3D correspondences) and region-based tracker

distances between 3D model points $\mathbf{p}_s^i$ and the projection rays L_i casted by the corresponding 2D image observations $\mathbf{r}_i$. Writing the projection line in Plücker co-ordinates $L_i = (\mathbf{m}_i, \mathbf{n}_i)$ the error may be written as

$$e(\mathbf{x}_t) = \sum_i^N \mathbf{e}_i^2(\mathbf{x}_t) = \sum_i^N \left\| \mathbf{p}_s^i(\mathbf{x}_t) \times \mathbf{n}_i - \mathbf{m}_i \right\|^2, \tag{9.47}$$

where the residuals are 3D distance error vectors $\mathbf{e}_i \in \mathbb{R}^3$. In this case it is straight-forward to show that the Jacobian of the error of one correspondence pair is given by $\mathbf{J}_{t,i} = \mathbf{n}_i^{\wedge} \mathbf{J_x}(\mathbf{p}_s^i) \in \mathbb{R}^{3 \times D}$.

Another alternative used by several authors [14, 16] is to first reconstruct the visual hull [30] from the multiview images obtaining a rough volume of the human shape. Then the matching is done between the model points and the points from the visual hull resulting in a set of 3D–3D correspondences $(\mathbf{p}_s^i, \mathbf{q}_s^i)$. The error function is then simply the distance between 3D points

$$e(\mathbf{x}_t) = \sum_i^N \mathbf{e}_i^2(\mathbf{x}_t) = \sum_i^N \left\| \mathbf{p}_s^i(\mathbf{x}_t) - \mathbf{q}_s^i \right\|^2 \tag{9.48}$$

with $\mathbf{e}_i \in \mathbb{R}^3$ where in this case the Jacobian is directly $\mathbf{J}_{t,i} = \mathbf{J_x}(\mathbf{p}_s^i)$.

In Fig. 9.6 an illustration of common error functions is shown.

Combining features: Other kind of features like SIFT or optical flow can be integrated as additional correspondences into this framework as long as they can be predicted given a pose estimate. The combination of features should robustify the tracker [11].

9.3.1.2 Optical Flow-Based

Optical flow is the apparent motion in the image projection of 3D object in the world. The displacement $[u \; v]$ of every pixel $[x \; y]$ from one frame to the next one is computed assuming that the intensity remains constant. This is known as the *brightness constancy* assumption and it may be written as $I(x, y, t - 1) = I(x + u, y + v, t)$. The first-order Taylor expansion of the right hand side of the equation leads to the remarkable normal optical flow constraint equation [33],

$$\begin{bmatrix} I_x & I_y \end{bmatrix} \cdot \begin{bmatrix} u \\ v \end{bmatrix} - I_t = 0, \tag{9.49}$$

where I_x, I_y and I_t are the spatial and temporal derivatives of the image. Generally, neighboring pixels are assumed to move together according to a given motion model. Bregler et al. [9, 10] used a human motion model to parameterize the motion flow $[u\ v]$. Specifically, he finds for every pixel in the image the corresponding 3D point in the human model $\mathbf{p}_s$. Then the motion $[u\ v]$ is simply given by the projection of the 3D point displacement $\Delta\mathbf{p}_s$ onto the image plane. This can be written as

$$\begin{bmatrix} I_x & I_y \end{bmatrix} \cdot \mathrm{Pr}_c(\Delta\mathbf{p}_s) - I_t = 0, \tag{9.50}$$

where we recall that Pr_c denotes projection on the image plane (in [9, 10] an orthographic camera projection is assumed), and the point displacement is given by $\Delta\mathbf{p}_s = \mathbf{J_x}\Delta\mathbf{x}_t$ (9.36). Note the strong correlation with correspondence-based algorithms by interpreting (9.50) as the linearization of the error function $\mathbf{e}_i(\mathbf{x}_t) = I(x + u, y + v, t) - I(x, y)$ for one correspondence. Here only $[u\ v]$ depend on the pose parameters. The total error function $e(\mathbf{x}_t)$ can be interpreted then as the sum of squared pixel intensity differences. Unfortunately, approaches relying exclusively on optical flow have two main drawbacks. First, when the motion is large, the Taylor expansion in (9.49) produces large estimate errors. Second, while image features like edges and silhouettes provide an absolute measurement, relying on optical flow causes error accumulation which results in drift and tracking failure [31]. Nevertheless, [10] was the first work in human pose estimation to use the elegant twists and exponential maps formulation from the robotics community.

9.3.1.3 Region-Based

Region-based methods are based on separating the foreground figure (the human silhouette) from the background by maximizing the dissimilarity between region density functions (usually the density functions are approximated by simple histograms of pixel intensities and colors). Popular approaches to achieve this are level sets or graph-cuts [8, 13]. This process can be coupled with human pose estimation in an EM scheme. An initial human pose estimate defines two regions in the image, namely the interior of the projected silhouette and the exterior. This initial boundary is then used as a shape prior for a level-set segmentation. Thereafter, correspondences between the segmentation and the projected silhouette are obtained and the pose is estimated using a correspondence-based method. This process of pose estimation and segmentation is iterated until convergence. Some works have coupled the feature extraction and the descent strategy. The work by [17, 40] skips the segmentation step and directly shifts the points belonging to the occluding contour

$\tilde{\mathbf{r}} \in \mathcal{O}$ inwards or outwards (orthogonal to the contour line) according to the posterior probability densities. If the foreground posterior is bigger than the background posterior the point is shifted outwards, otherwise the point is shifted inwards, see Fig. 9.6. This implicitly generates correspondence pairs between points and shifted points which feed a correspondence-based tracker.

9.3.1.4 Probabilistic Interpretation

We have seen that local optimization methods, either correspondence-based, optical flow or region-based are based on defining an error function and linearizing the residual error vector via its Jacobian to find a descent step. As a final comment, we note that one can give a probabilistic interpretation to the error functions defined above. Gathering image observations at time t in a random vector $\mathbf{y}_t$, (observations can be 2D point locations, lines, 3D points, feature descriptors, appearance, . . .) the MAP estimate is given by

$$\mathbf{x}_{t,\mathrm{MAP}} = \arg\max_{\mathbf{x}_t} p(\mathbf{x}_t | \mathbf{y}_t) = \arg\max_{\mathbf{x}_t} p(\mathbf{y}_t | \mathbf{x}_t) p(\mathbf{x}_t), \qquad (9.51)$$

where $p(\mathbf{y}_t | \mathbf{x}_t)$ is the likelihood of the observations for a given pose $\mathbf{x}_t$ and $p(\mathbf{x}_t)$ is the prior knowledge we have about human motion (which will be discussed in the next chapter). If the errors associated with the observations are independent and have a Gaussian distribution, the likelihood takes the form

$$p(\mathbf{x}_t | \mathbf{y}_t) = p(\mathbf{y}_t | \mathbf{x}_t) p(\mathbf{x}_t) \propto \exp\left(-\sum_i^N \mathbf{e}_i^2(\mathbf{y}_t^i | \mathbf{x}_t)\right) p(\mathbf{x}_t), \qquad (9.52)$$

where $\mathbf{e}_i^2(\mathbf{y}_t^i | \mathbf{x}_t)$ is the individual error for a given image observation. Equivalently to (9.51), the MAP estimate can be obtained by the minimization of the negative log-likelihood and an additional prior term $e_p(\mathbf{x}_t)$

$$\mathbf{x}_{\mathrm{MAP}} = \arg\min_{\mathbf{x}_t} -\log\big(p(\mathbf{y}_t | \mathbf{x}_t)\big) - \log\big(p(\mathbf{x}_t)\big) = \arg\min_{\mathbf{x}_t} e(\mathbf{x}_t) + e_p(\mathbf{x}_t). \quad (9.53)$$

Therefore, the minimization of the sum of squared error functions $e(\mathbf{x})$ defined in the previous subsections (e.g. (9.40), (9.47) and (9.48)) are equivalent to a MAP estimator if the observation errors are independent and Gaussian (without prior it is actually equivalent to a maximum likelihood (ML) estimator). Consequently, the error function should be designed to model the cost density associated with the observations [45]. This interpretation will be particularly useful when we see optimization methods based on stochastic search. Probabilistic formulation of the pose tracking problem is more thoroughly discussed in Sect. 10.1.1 of Chap. 10.

9.3.2 Particle-Based Optimization and Filtering

A well known problem of local optimization methods is that since they are based on propagating a single pose hypothesis, when there is a tracking error the system can in general not recover from it. To overcome this limitation, stochastic search techniques have been introduced for human pose estimation. This group of methods are based on approximating the likelihood of the image given the pose parameters by propagating a set of particles from one time step to the next one.

9.3.2.1 Particle Filter

Problems in human pose estimation arise from kinematic singularities, depth and orientation ambiguities and occlusions. For all these reasons the posterior density $p(\mathbf{x}_t|\mathbf{y}_{1:t})$ and the observation process $p(\mathbf{y}_t|\mathbf{x}_t)$ are highly peaked and highly multi-modal. The image likelihood $p(\mathbf{y}_t|\mathbf{x}_t)$ is the probability of observing certain image features given a pose $\mathbf{x}_t$, and $p(\mathbf{x}_t|\mathbf{y}_{1:t})$ is the probability of the pose parameters considering the history of all observations from previous images $1:t$. To see this multimodality, note that many configurations in pose parameter space $\mathbf{x}$ explain well the observations $\mathbf{y}_{1:t}$ (for example any rotation by an angle α about the axis of a limb will project to almost the same image location). It is well known that in this case a Kalman filter will fail. In these cases the posterior can be approximated by a particle filter.[2] A particle filter approximates the posterior $p(\mathbf{x}_t|\mathbf{y}_{1:t})$ by a set of particles $\{\pi_t^{(i)}, \mathbf{x}_t^{(i)}\}_{i=1}^N$ where the weights are normalized so that $\sum_N \pi_t^{(i)} = 1$. Each particle $\mathbf{x}_t^{(i)}$ corresponds to one configuration of pose parameters (9.33), and the weights are chosen to be proportional to the likelihood $\pi^{(i)} \propto p(\mathbf{y}_t|\mathbf{x}_t = \mathbf{x}_t^{(i)})$. At each time step the pose parameters can be estimated by the mean of the weighted particles,

$$\mathbf{x}_t^* = \mathbb{E}_\mathbf{x}[\mathbf{x}_t] \simeq \sum_N \pi_t^{(i)} \mathbf{x}_t^{(i)} \tag{9.54}$$

or by the mode of the particle set $\mathbf{x}_t^* = \mathbb{M}_\mathbf{x}[\mathbf{x}_t] = \mathbf{x}_t^{(i)}$ with $\pi_t^{(i)} = \max(\pi_t^{(n)})$.

Assuming a first-order Markov process $(p(\mathbf{x}_t|\mathbf{x}_{1:t-1}) = p(\mathbf{x}_t|\mathbf{x}_{t-1}))$ the posterior distribution can be updated recursively:

$$p(\mathbf{x}_t|\mathbf{y}_{1:t}) \propto p(\mathbf{y}_t|\mathbf{x}_t)p(\mathbf{x}_t) \int p(\mathbf{x}_t|\mathbf{x}_{t-1})p(\mathbf{x}_{t-1}|\mathbf{y}_{1:t-1})\,d\mathbf{x}_{t-1}, \tag{9.55}$$

where the integral computes the pose prediction from the previous time step posterior $p(\mathbf{x}_{t-1}|\mathbf{y}_{1:t-1})$ propagated with the dynamical model $p(\mathbf{x}_t|\mathbf{x}_{t-1})$. The prediction is then weighted by the likelihood function $p(\mathbf{y}_t|\mathbf{x}_t)$ times the prior $p(\mathbf{x}_t)$ if available. In a particle filter setting, (9.55) is approximated by *importance sampling*.

---

[2]See also Chap. I, Sect. 6.2.2.

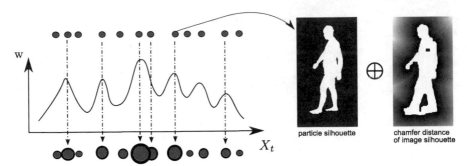

Fig. 9.7 *Particle Filter*: on the *left* the weighting function is shown as a function of the pose parameters. The function is multimodal and it is difficult to tell where the maximum is from the particle distribution. On the *right*: the weighting function is evaluated for every particle $\mathbf{x}_t^{(i)}$. The weighting function should be fast to evaluate, in this example, it consists of a simple overlap measure between the particle silhouette and the chamfer distance transformed image silhouette

Given a set of weighted particles approximating the posterior in the previous frame $\mathscr{P}_{t-1}^+ := \{\pi_{t-1}^{(i)}, \mathbf{x}_{t-1}^{(i)}\}_{i=1}^N$, N particles are drawn from $\mathscr{P}_{t-1}$ with replacement and probability proportional to their weights obtaining a new set of unweighted particles $\{\tilde{\mathbf{x}}_{t-1}^{(i)}\}_{i=1}^N$. Thereafter, the particles are propagated to the next frame by sampling from the dynamical model $p(\mathbf{x}_t | \tilde{\mathbf{x}}_{t-1}^{(i)})$ producing a new unweighted set of predictions $\mathscr{P}_t^- := \{\mathbf{x}_t^{(i)}\}_{i=1}^N$. Finally, every particle in $\mathscr{P}_t^-$ is weighted according to the likelihood in the new frame $\pi_t^{(i)} = p(\mathbf{y}_t | \mathbf{x}_t^{(i)})$ obtaining the final weighted set $\mathscr{P}_t^+ := \{\pi_t^{(i)}, \mathbf{x}_t^{(i)}\}_{i=1}^N$ that approximates the updated posterior $p(\mathbf{x}_t | \mathbf{y}_{1:t})$.

Likelihood functions: Ideally, to model the observation process $p(\mathbf{y}_t | \mathbf{x}_t)$ the complicated image formation process has to be synthesized, i.e., illumination, human appearance rendering on the image, clothing, occlusions, shadows, etc. Since $p(\mathbf{y}_t | \mathbf{x}_t)$ has to be evaluated for every particle in the set $p(\mathbf{y}_t | \mathbf{x}_t = \mathbf{x}_t^{(i)})$, this is obviously computationally infeasible. In practice, to make the problem tractable an intuitive function $w(\mathbf{y}_t, \mathbf{x}_t = \mathbf{x}_t^{(i)})$ is constructed that approximates the probability $p(\mathbf{y}_t | \mathbf{x} = \mathbf{x}_k^{(i)})$. This function takes into account only image observations $\mathbf{y}_t$ that can be modeled easy and efficiently (e.g., edges, coarse foreground appearance or silhouettes). Actually, the error functions $e(\mathbf{x}_t)$ described for local optimization might be used to set the weights w as

$$w(\mathbf{y}_t, \mathbf{x}_t = \mathbf{x}_t^{(i)}) = \exp(-e(\mathbf{x}_t^{(i)})), \tag{9.56}$$

where, as explained in Sect. 9.3.1.4, we interpret the error as the cost density associated with the observations. To gain in efficiency, a chamfer distance can be pre-computed in the original image silhouette or edge map, see Fig. 9.7. Then, simple overlap measures between the synthesized particle silhouette and the chamfer distance image are computed [19, 23, 51]. Another commonly used feature in the weighting function is appearance, whose associated cost can be evaluated with histogram comparison [23, 42]. For a comparative study of the influence of different likelihood/weighting functions we refer the reader to [43]. Nonetheless, the computation of $w(\mathbf{y}_t, \mathbf{x}_t = \mathbf{x}_t^{(i)})$ is a very expensive operation if it has to be evaluated for many particles. In addition, the number of particles required to approximate $p(\mathbf{x}_t | \mathbf{y}_{1:t})$ grows exponentially with the dimensionality of $\mathbf{x}$, which makes the particle filter intractable for realistic human models with more than 30 DoF. Furthermore, even using a large number of particles the search can be misdirected if many local modes are present in $w(\mathbf{y}_t, \mathbf{x}_t = \mathbf{x}_t^{(i)})$; see Fig. 9.7.

9.3.2.2 Annealed Particle Filter

The annealed particle filter (APF) is a modification of the particle filter and it was introduced for human pose estimation by Deutscher et al. [19]. The goal here is to modify the particle filter such that the number of needed particles is drastically reduced and the particles do not congregate around local maxima. The APF is motivated from simulated annealing methods designed for global optimization of multimodal functions [29]. The key idea is to gradually introduce the influence of narrow peaks in the weighting function $w(\mathbf{y}_t, \mathbf{x}_t)$. This is achieved by starting a search run in successive layers gradually changing the weighting function as

$$w_m(\mathbf{y}_t, \mathbf{x}_t) = w(\mathbf{y}_t, \mathbf{x}_t)^{\beta m}, \qquad (9.57)$$

for $\beta_0 > \beta_1 > \cdots > \beta_M$. The run is started at layer M, where w_M is broad and reflects the overall trend of w without the influence of so many local maxima. As we move to the next layer, β increases and therefore the local peaks become more accentuated. For initialization, an initial set of samples is drawn from a proposal distribution q_{M+1}. During tracking we might choose this distribution to be the set of particles from the previous frame or the propagated particles if we use a motion model. For initialization in the first frame the distribution should be spread with a high variance, see for example [22]. Once the algorithm is initialized the optimization consists of the following steps executed at every layer: *weighting*, *resampling* and *diffusion*, see Fig. 9.8 and the pseudo code in Algorithm 1.

- *Weighting*: The surviving particles of the previous layer are assigned new weights $w_{t,m}(\mathbf{y}_t, \mathbf{x}_{t,m}^{(i)})^{\beta m}$ with the new annealing scheme βm. At this point a new proposal distribution has been formed $q_m = \{\pi_{t,m}^{(i)}, \mathbf{x}_{t,m}^{(i)}\}_{i=1}^N$.
- *Resampling*: N new samples are drawn from the distribution q_m with probability equal to the weights, this can be efficiently done with multinomial sampling. Note that particles with high weight (low error) will be selected with higher probability and therefore a higher number of particles concentrate around the maximum of the weighting function. Gall et al. [21, 23] proposes a generalization of the resampling strategy that improves the performance of the APF. In this modification, particles with high weight are with high probability retained in the set without replacement.

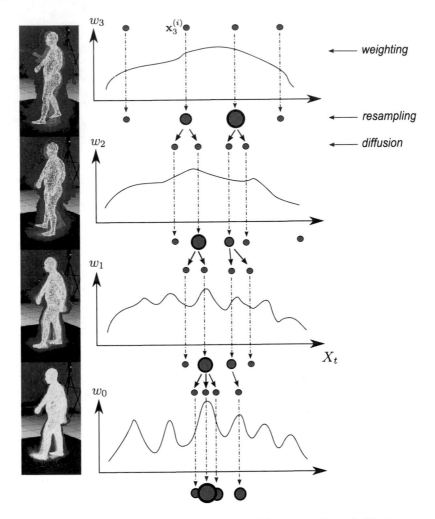

Fig. 9.8 *Annealed particle filter*: At each layer the weighting, resampling and diffusion steps are performed. The influence of the peaks is gradually introduced into the weighting function w_m. Consequently, the particles converge at the global maximum in the last layer w_0 and do not get trapped in local maxima peaks as opposed to the standard particle filter. Additionally, on the left column, the distribution of the particles projected to the image is shown, where particles with higher weights are brighter (left column images are courtesy of Gall et al. [23])

- *Diffusion*: In order to explore the search space the particles are diffused by some function. A common choice is to shift every particle by adding a sample from a multivariate Gaussian with covariance Σ_m. The covariance Σ_m can be chosen to be proportional to the particle set variance since this provides a measure of uncertainty (The more uncertainty, the farther away we have to explore the search space.) The run in the layer terminates with the diffusion step and the particles are used to initialize the weighting step of the next layer.

Algorithm 1 Annealed particle filter

Require: number of layers M, number of samples N, initial distribution q_{M+1},
   Initialize: Draw N initial samples from $q \rightarrow \mathbf{x}_{t,m}^{(i)}$
   for layer $m = M$ to 0 **do**
      1. *WEIGHTING*
      start from the set of unweighted particles of the previous layer
      for $i = 1$ to N **do**
         compute $w_{t,m}(\mathbf{y}_t, \mathbf{x}_{t,m}^{(i)})^{\beta m}$
         set $\pi_{t,m}^{(i)} \propto w_{t,m}(\mathbf{y}_t, \mathbf{x}_{t,m}^{(i)})^{\beta m}$
      end for
      set $q_m = \{\pi_{t,m}^{(i)}, \mathbf{x}_{t,m}^{(i)}\}_{i=1}^N$
      2. *RESAMPLING*
      draw N samples from $q_{t,m} \rightarrow \mathbf{x}_{t,m}^{(i)}$ {Can be done with multinomial sampling}
      3. *DIFFUSION*
      $\mathbf{x}_{t,m-1}^{(i)} = \mathbf{x}_{t,m}^{(i)} + \mathbf{B}_{t,m}$ {$\mathbf{B}_{t,m}$ is a sample from a multivariate Gaussian with $\mathcal{N}(0, \Sigma)$}
   end for

Once the algorithm has finished the last annealing run, the pose estimate is obtained by the mean of the final set of particles of the last layer, $\mathbf{x}_t^* = \mathbb{E}_{\mathbf{x}_t}[q_0] = \sum_i \pi_{t,0}^{(i)} \mathbf{x}_{t,0}^{(i)}$. Although the APF can be used recursively as the standard PF in (9.55) using some heuristics, it can be considered a single frame global optimization algorithm. While the APF is computationally more efficient in locating global minima in the likelihood function $p(\mathbf{y}_t|\mathbf{x}_t)$ than the particle filter, the main disadvantage is not being able to work within a robust Bayesian framework [19]. The reason for that is that the set of particles of q_0 congregate *only* around one maximum of the observation process $p(\mathbf{y}_t|\mathbf{x}_t)$ at the current frame t. Therefore, the particles are not well distributed for the next frame and usually a heuristic has to be used to spread them to search in the next frame. By contrast, in the PF (which needs much more samples) the final particle set represents the total posterior $p(\mathbf{x}_t|\mathbf{y}_{1:t})$ which might contain multiple maxima. Therefore the PF can represent inherent ambiguities by maintaining multiple modes at the expense of a significant loss in accuracy.

9.3.2.3 Tailored Optimization Methods

Although an exhaustive survey of the proposed sampling methods and likelihood functions used in the literature for human tracking is out of the scope of this chapter, it is worth to highlight some optimization procedures tailored for the problem of human pose estimation. Choo and Fleet [15] use a Markov Chain similar to (9.55) but use every particle as initialization for local optimization on the likelihood function. Similarly, Sminchisescu and Triggs [45] also combine particle-based sampling with local optimization, but additionally sample along the most uncertain directions calculated from the local likelihood Hessian matrix at the fitted optima. Along this lines, importance samplers have been proposed that focus samples on regions likely to contain transitions states leading to nearby minima [46, 47]. Another way to locate multiple optima in monocular images is to exploit the geometry of the problem to deterministically enumerate the set of poses that result in the same projection [48, 50]. To make the sampling tractable in the high-dimensional space, state partitions have also been used [20, 24]. These partitions are either specified manually by sequentially tracking different kinematic branches (e.g. torso, limbs and head) [24] or selected automatically from the parameter variances in the particle set [20]. Every optimization scheme has its own advantages/disadvantages but a common key component in all of them for successful tracking is a good background subtraction.

9.4 Discussion

The basic mathematical tools necessary for anyone who wants to implement a human pose estimation system have been introduced, namely kinematic structure representation and model creation. A unified formulation has been presented for the most common model-based pose estimation algorithms seen in the literature. We have seen that the model image association problem for pose estimation is usually formulated as the minimization/maximization of an error/likelihood function. The two main strategies have been described, namely local and particle-based optimization. Local optimization methods are faster and more accurate but in practice, if there are visual ambiguities, or really fast motions, the tracker might fail catastrophically. To achieve more robustness, particle filters can be used because they can represent uncertainty through a rigorous Bayesian paradigm. The problem here is that the number of particles needed to achieve reasonable results grows exponentially with the dimensionality of the pose parameter space which makes them unpractical for human models with more than 20 DoF. To reduce the number of needed particles, the annealed particle filter can be used at the expense of not being able to work in a fully Bayesian framework. A further problem of global optimization methods is that while robust, they do not provide a single temporally consistent motion but rather a jittery motion which must be post-processed to obtain visually acceptable results. Combinations of global and local optimization have also been proposed to compensate for the drawbacks of each strategy [15, 23, 45]. Nonetheless, current approaches do not capture detailed movement such as hand orientation or axial arm rotation. This stems from depth and orientation ambiguities inherent in the images (i.e., any rotation about a limb axis projects to the same image). To overcome this limitations Pons-Moll et al. [37] proposes a hybrid tracker that combines correspondence-based local optimization with five inertial sensors placed at body extremities to obtain a much accurate and detailed human tracker, see Fig. 9.9. The key idea is to fuse both sensor types in a joint optimization to exploit the advantages of each sensor type (accurate position from images and accurate orientation from inertial sensors).

Although over the last decade significant progress has been made in model-based human pose estimation, there remain a number of open problems and challenges.

First, while tracking of walking motions in semi-controlled settings is more or less reliable, robust tracking of arbitrary and highly dynamic motions is still challenging even in controlled setups. Second, monocular tracking is a highly ambiguous and difficult problem which is still far from being solved. Although monocular

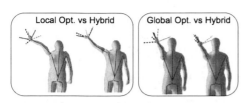

Fig. 9.9 *Left*: current approaches, either local or global optimization cannot capture axial rotation accurately; the combination of a video-based tracker with inertial sensors (hybrid tracker) allows to capture detailed motion. *Right*: motion capture in uncontrolled scenarios is one of the principal future challenges (outdoor images on the right are courtesy of Hasler et al. [27])

tracking has attracted a lot of attention because of the complexity of the problem, most solutions rely on restrictive setups with very simple motions. Monocular tracking is particularly interesting because in many practical settings only a single view sequence is available as in video footage archives such as YouTube. Third, tracking arbitrary motions in outdoor settings has been mostly unaddressed [27] Fig. 9.9, and remains one of the open problems in computer vision. Indeed, this must be one of the final goals since in these scenarios standard commercial motion capture systems based on optical markers cannot be used. Outdoor human tracking would allow to capture sport motions in their real competitive setup. Fourth, tracking people in the office or in the streets interacting with the environment is still an extremely challenging problem to be solved. In this chapter we have covered the mathematical tools for generative model-based pose estimation. Another active research area to increase robustness and accuracy is the modeling of priors for human motion; this involves using temporal context, building motion and physical models which will be described in the next chapter.

References

1. Allen, B., Curless, B., Popović, Z.: Articulated body deformation from range scan data. In: ACM Transactions on Graphics, pp. 612–619. ACM, New York (2002) [151]
2. Allen, B., Curless, B., Popović, Z.: The space of human body shapes: Reconstruction and parameterization from range scans. In: ACM Transactions on Graphics, pp. 587–594. ACM, New York (2003) [153]
3. Anguelov, D., Srinivasan, P., Koller, D., Thrun, S., Rodgers, J., Davis, J.: Scape: shape completion and animation of people. ACM Trans. Graph. **24**, 408–416 (2005) [153]
4. Anguelov, D., Srinivasan, P., Pang, H.C., Koller, D., Thrun, S., Davis, J.: The correlated correspondence algorithm for unsupervised registration of nonrigid surfaces. In: Advances in Neural Information Processing Systems, p. 33. MIT Press, Cambridge (2005) [151]
5. Balan, A.O., Sigal, L., Black, M.J., Davis, J.E., Haussecker, H.W.: Detailed human shape and pose from images. In: IEEE Computer Society Conference on Computer Vision and Pattern Recognition (2007) [153]
6. Baran, I., Popović, J.: Automatic rigging and animation of 3d characters. In: ACM Transactions on Graphics, p. 72. ACM, New York (2007) [152]
7. Besl, P., McKay, N.: A method for registration of 3d shapes. IEEE Trans. Pattern Anal. Mach. Intell. **12**, 239–256 (1992) [157]

8. Boykov, Y., Veksler, O., Zabih, R.: Fast approximate energy minimization via graph cuts. IEEE Trans. Pattern Anal. Mach. Intell. **23**(11), 1222–1239 (2001) [159]

9. Bregler, C., Malik, J.: Tracking people with twists and exponential maps. In: IEEE Computer Society Conference on Computer Vision and Pattern Recognition, pp. 8–15 (1998) [159]

10. Bregler, C., Malik, J., Pullen, K.: Twist based acquisition and tracking of animal and human kinematics. Int. J. Comput. Vis. **56**, 179–194 (2004) [159]

11. Brox, T., Rosenhahn, B., Gall, J., Cremers, D.: Combined region and motion-based 3d tracking of rigid and articulated objects. IEEE Trans. Pattern Anal. Mach. Intell. **32**(3), 402–415 (2010) [158]

12. Cagniart, C., Boyer, E., Ilic, S.: Free-form mesh tracking: A patch-based approach. In: IEEE Computer Society Conference on Computer Vision and Pattern Recognition, pp. 1339–1346 (2010) [153]

13. Chan, T.F., Vese, L.A.: Active contours without edges. IEEE Trans. Image Process. **10**(2), 266–277 (2001) [159]

14. Cheung, K.M.G., Baker, S., Kanade, T.: Shape-from-silhouette of articulated objects and its use for human body kinematics estimation and motion capture. In: IEEE Computer Society Conference on Computer Vision and Pattern Recognition, vol. 1 (2003) [158]

15. Choo, K., Fleet, D.J.: People tracking using hybrid Monte Carlo filtering. In: IEEE International Conference on Computer Vision, vol. 2, pp. 321–328 (2001) [165,166]

16. Corazza, S., Mündermann, L., Gambaretto, E., Ferrigno, G., Andriacchi, T.P.: Markerless motion capture through visual hull, articulated icp and subject specific model generation. Int. J. Comput. Vis. **87**(1), 156–169 (2010) [158]

17. Dambreville, S., Sandhu, R., Yezzi, A., Tannenbaum, A.: Robust 3d pose estimation and efficient 2d region-based segmentation from a 3d shape prior. In: Forsyth, D., Torr, P., Zisserman, A. (eds.) European Conference on Computer Vision. Lecture Notes in Computer Science, vol. 5303, pp. 169–182. Springer, Berlin (2008) [159]

18. de Aguiar, E., Stoll, C., Theobalt, C., Ahmed, N., Seidel, H.-P., Thrun, S.: Performance capture from sparse multi-view video. In: ACM Transactions on Graphics, pp. 1–10. ACM, New York (2008) [153]

19. Deutscher, J., Blake, A., Reid, I.: Articulated body motion capture by annealed particle filtering. In: IEEE Computer Society Conference on Computer Vision and Pattern Recognition, vol. 2, pp. 126–133 (2000) [162,163,165]

20. Deutscher, J., Davison, A., Reid, I.: Automatic partitioning of high dimensional search spaces associated with articulated body motion capture. In: IEEE Computer Society Conference on Computer Vision and Pattern Recognition, vol. 2 (2001) [166]

21. Gall, J., Potthoff, J., Schnorr, C., Rosenhahn, B., Seidel, H.: Interacting and annealing particle filters: Mathematics and a recipe for applications. J. Math. Imaging Vis. **28**, 1–18 (2007) [163]

22. Gall, J., Rosenhahn, B., Seidel, H.: Clustered stochastic optimization for object recognition and pose estimation. In: DAGM. Lecture Notes in Computer Science, vol. 4713, pp. 32–41. Springer, Berlin (2007) [163]

23. Gall, J., Rosenhahn, B., Brox, T., Seidel, H.: Optimization and filtering for human motion capture. Int. J. Comput. Vis. **87**, 75–92 (2010) [162-164,166]

24. Gavrila, D., Davis, L.: 3D model based tracking of humans in action: A multiview approach. In: IEEE Computer Society Conference on Computer Vision and Pattern Recognition (1996) [166]

25. Grassia, S.: Practical parameterization of rotations using the exponential map. J. Graph. Tools **3**, 29–48 (1998) [143]

26. Hasler, N., Ackermann, H., Rosenhahn, B., Thormaehlen, T., Seidel, H.: Multilinear pose and body shape estimation of dressed subjects from image sets. In: IEEE Computer Society Conference on Computer Vision and Pattern Recognition, pp. 1823–1830 (2010) [153]

27. Hasler, N., Rosenhahn, B., Thormaehlen, T., Wand, M., Gall, J., Seidel, H.-P.: Markerless motion capture with unsynchronized moving cameras. In: IEEE Computer Society Conference on Computer Vision and Pattern Recognition, pp. 224–231 (2009) [167]

28. Ju, S.X., Black, M.J., Yacoob, Y.: Cardboard people: A parameterized model of articulated image motion. In: International Workshop on Automatic Face and Gesture Recognition, pp. 38–44 (1996) [151]

29. Kirkpatrick, S., Gelatt Jr., C.D., Vecchi, M.P.: Optimization by simulated annealing. Science 220(4598), 671–680 (1983) [163]

30. Laurentini, A.: The visual hull concept for silhouette-based image understanding. IEEE Trans. Pattern Anal. Mach. Intell. 16(2), 150–162 (1994) [158]

31. Lepetit, V., Fua, P.: Monocular model-based 3d tracking of rigid objects: A survey. Found. Trends Comput. Graph. Vis. 1(1), 1–89 (2005) [159]

32. Lewis, J.P., Cordner, M., Fong, N.: Pose space deformation: a unified approach to shape interpolation and skeleton-driven deformation. In: ACM Transactions on Graphics, pp. 165–172. ACM, New York (2000) [152]

33. Lucas, B.D., Kanade, T.: An iterative image registration technique with an application to stereo vision. In: International Joint Conference on Artificial Intelligence, vol. 3, pp. 674–679 (1981) [159]

34. Murray, R.M., Li, Z., Sastry, S.S.: Mathematical Introduction to Robotic Manipulation. CRC Press, Baton Rouge (1994) [140,143,145,146,148]

35. Piccardi, M.: Background subtraction techniques: A review. In: Proc. IEEE Int Systems, Man and Cybernetics Conf., vol. 4, pp. 3099–3104 (2004) [154]

36. Plankers, R., Fua, P.: Articulated soft objects for video-based body modeling. In: IEEE International Conference on Computer Vision, vol. 1, pp. 394–401 (2001) [151]

37. Pons-Moll, G., Baak, A., Helten, T., Mueller, M., Seidel, H.-P., Rosenhahn, B.: Multisensor-fusion for 3d full-body human motion capture. In: IEEE Computer Society Conference on Computer Vision and Pattern Recognition, pp. 663–670 (2010) [166]

38. Pons-Moll, G., Rosenhahn, B.: Ball joints for marker-less human motion capture. In: Proc. IEEE Workshop Applications of Computer Vision (WACV) (2009) [149]

39. Rosenhahn, B., Brox, T.: Scaled motion dynamics for markerless motion capture. In: IEEE Computer Society Conference on Computer Vision and Pattern Recognition (2007) [157]

40. Schmaltz, C., Rosenhahn, B., Brox, T., Cremers, D., Weickert, J., Wietzke, L., Sommer, G.: Region-based pose tracking. In: Proc. 3rd Iberian Conference on Pattern Recognition and Image Analysis, vol. 4478, pp. 56–63 (2007) [159]

41. Shoemake, K.: Animating rotation with quaternion curves. ACM SIGGRAPH Computer Graphics 19, 245–254 (1985) [143]

42. Sidenbladh, H., Black, M., Fleet, D.: Stochastic tracking of 3d human figures using 2d image motion. In: Vernon, D. (ed.) European Conference on Computer Vision. Lecture Notes in Computer Science, vol. 1843, pp. 702–718. Springer, Berlin (2000) [151,163]

43. Sigal, L., Balan, A.O., Black, M.J.: Humaneva: Synchronized video and motion capture dataset and baseline algorithm for evaluation of articulated human motion. Int. J. Comput. Vis. 87(1), 4–27 (2010) [163]

44. Sminchisescu, C.: Consistency and coupling in human model likelihoods. In: International Workshop on Automatic Face and Gesture Recognition (2002) [155]

45. Sminchisescu, C., Triggs, B.: Covariance scaled sampling for monocular 3d body tracking. In: IEEE Computer Society Conference on Computer Vision and Pattern Recognition, vol. 1 (2001) [151,160,165]

46. Sminchisescu, C., Triggs, B.: Building roadmaps of local minima of visual models. In: European Conference on Computer Vision, pp. 566–582 (2002) [165]

47. Sminchisescu, C., Triggs, B.: Hyperdynamics importance sampling. In: European Conference on Computer Vision, pp. 769–783 (2002) [165]

48. Sminchisescu, C., Triggs, B.: Kinematic jump processes for monocular 3d human tracking. In: IEEE Computer Society Conference on Computer Vision and Pattern Recognition (2003) [166]

49. Sumner, R.W., Popović, J.: Deformation transfer for triangle meshes. In: ACM Transactions on Graphics, pp. 399–405. ACM, New York (2004) [151]

50. Taylor, C.J.: Reconstruction of articulated objects from point correspondences in a single un-calibrated image. In: IEEE Computer Society Conference on Computer Vision and Pattern Recognition, vol. 1, pp. 677–684 (2000) [166]
51. Vondrak, M., Sigal, L., Jenkins, O.C.: Physical simulation for probabilistic motion tracking. In: IEEE Computer Society Conference on Computer Vision and Pattern Recognition (2008) [162]
52. Zhang, Z.: Iterative points matching for registration of free form curves and surfaces. Int. J. Comput. Vis. 13(2), 119–152 (1994) [157]

Chapter 10
Motion Models for People Tracking

David J. Fleet

Abstract This chapter provides an introduction to models of human pose and motion for use in 3D human pose tracking. We concentrate on probabilistic latent variable models of kinematics, most of which are learned from motion capture data, and on recent physics-based models. We briefly discuss important open problems and future research challenges.

10.1 Introduction

Prior information about human pose and motion has been essential for resolving ambiguities in video-based pose estimation and tracking. Motion estimation may be relatively straightforward if one is given several cameras and a constrained setting with minimal occlusion (e.g., [8, 18, 30]), but the general monocular problem remains difficult without prior information. A prior model biases pose estimation toward plausible poses when pose might otherwise be under-constrained, or when measurements might be noisy, or missing due to occlusion. A good prior model should be sufficiently general to admit all (or most) plausible motions of the human body, but also strong enough to resolve ambiguities and alleviate the inherent challenges imposed by the high-dimensional estimation task. Finding the right balance between these competing goals is difficult. Most successful recent techniques for monocular pose tracking have focused on the use of strong, *activity-specific* prior models learned from human motion capture data.

This chapter provides a tutorial introduction to models of human pose and motion for video-based people tracking. We adopt a probabilistic framework, as it is perhaps the most straightforward and well-understood calculus for coping with uncertainty and fusing noisy sources of information. We first outline the basic probabilistic formulation, and then introduce the principal types of motion models.

D.J. Fleet (✉)
Department of Computer Science, University of Toronto, Toronto, Canada
e-mail: fleet@cs.toronto.edu

T.B. Moeslund et al. (eds.), *Visual Analysis of Humans*,
DOI 10.1007/978-0-85729-997-0_10, © Springer-Verlag London Limited 2011

10.1.1 Human Pose Tracking

From a single camera it is hard to escape depth-scale ambiguities, missing observations of body parts due to occlusion, and reflection ambiguities where different 3D poses produce similar images. Because of these sources of uncertainty, it has become common to formulate human pose tracking as a *Bayesian filtering* problem. As such, the goal is to approximate the posterior probability distribution over human poses or motions, given the image measurements (or observations).

Formally, let $\mathbf{x}_t$ denote the state of the body at time t. It represents the unknown parameters of the model we wish to estimate. In our case, the state typically comprises the joint angles of the body along with the position and orientation of the body in world coordinates. Different parameterizations of the joint angles are discussed in Chap. 9, Sect. 9.1. Tracking is formulated in terms of the posterior probability distribution over state sequences, $\mathbf{x}_{1:t} \equiv (\mathbf{x}_1, \ldots, \mathbf{x}_t)$, given the observation history, $\mathbf{z}_{1:t} \equiv (\mathbf{z}_1, \ldots, \mathbf{z}_t)$; i.e.,

$$p(\mathbf{x}_{1:t}|\mathbf{z}_{1:t}) = \frac{p(\mathbf{z}_{1:t}|\mathbf{x}_{1:t})p(\mathbf{x}_{1:t})}{p(\mathbf{z}_{1:t})}. \tag{10.1}$$

Here, the two key factors are $p(\mathbf{x}_{1:t})$, the prior motion model, and $p(\mathbf{z}_{1:t}|\mathbf{x}_{1:t})$, the likelihood model. The likelihood is the probability of observing the image measurements given a state sequence. In effect the likelihood provides a measure of the consistency between a hypothetical motion and the given image observations. The observations might simply be the image at time t, or they might be a collection of image measurements at time t (e.g., image edge locations or optical flow). The denominator in (10.1), $p(\mathbf{z}_{1:t})$, does not depend on the state sequence, and can therefore be treated as an unknown constant for the purposes of this chapter.

Inference is the process of computing (or approximating) the posterior distribution (10.1), or estimating the most probable motion (i.e., the MAP estimate). This is intractable for most pose tracking problems of interest. Even approximating $p(\mathbf{x}_{1:t}|\mathbf{z}_{1:t})$ is difficult because of the high dimensionality of the motion $\mathbf{x}_{1:t}$, and the observations $\mathbf{z}_{1:t}$. For these reasons it is common to simplify the model, and therefore the computations required for inference.

One way to simplify inference is to assume that the observations are independent given the states. In other words, one assumes that the joint likelihood can be written as a product of simpler likelihoods, one for each time step:

$$p(\mathbf{z}_{1:t}|\mathbf{x}_{1:t}) = \prod_{i=1}^{t} p(\mathbf{z}_i|\mathbf{x}_i). \tag{10.2}$$

For good generative models, which account for observations up to additive white noise, this is a reasonable assumption. But in many cases it is more a matter of convenience because it allows for more efficient inference, and the specification of the likelihood is typically more straightforward. Common measurement models and likelihood functions are discussed in Chap. 9.

Given the conditional independence of the observations, we can express the posterior distribution at time t in terms of the likelihood at time t, the motion model, and the posterior at time $t - 1$:

$$p(\mathbf{x}_{1:t}|\mathbf{z}_{1:t}) \propto p(\mathbf{z}_t|\mathbf{x}_t)p(\mathbf{x}_t|\mathbf{x}_{1:t-1})p(\mathbf{x}_{1:t-1}|\mathbf{z}_{1:t-1}). \tag{10.3}$$

One can further simplify (10.3) by modeling motion as a first-order Markov process:

$$p(\mathbf{x}_t|\mathbf{x}_{1:t-1}) = p(\mathbf{x}_t|\mathbf{x}_{t-1}). \tag{10.4}$$

While this is not strictly necessary, it greatly simplifies the formulation of motion models and inference process. In particular, it means that the posterior can be expressed recursively, where all past history of any significance is represented entirely within the posterior distribution at the previous time step.

Nevertheless, the number of unknowns in $\mathbf{x}_{1:t}$ grows linearly with the number of time steps, so for long sequences the posterior in (10.3) is difficult to compute. The size of the covariance matrix, for example, is quadratic in the dimension of $\mathbf{x}_{1:t}$. Another way to simplify inference is to focus solely on the state at the current time. This *marginal* posterior distribution, called the filtering distribution, is given by:

$$p(\mathbf{x}_t|\mathbf{z}_{1:t}) = \int_{\mathbf{x}_{1:t-1}} p(\mathbf{x}_{1:t}|\mathbf{z}_{1:t})$$

$$\propto p(\mathbf{z}_t|\mathbf{x}_t) \int_{\mathbf{x}_{t-1}} p(\mathbf{x}_t|\mathbf{x}_{t-1})p(\mathbf{x}_{t-1}|\mathbf{z}_{1:t-1}). \tag{10.5}$$

Two main factors comprise the filtering distribution, namely, the likelihood, $p(\mathbf{z}_t|\mathbf{x}_t)$, and the prediction distribution, $p(\mathbf{x}_t|\mathbf{z}_{1:t-1})$, given by the integral in (10.5). The recursive form of the filtering distribution leads to well-known, online inference methods. The simplest such method, suitable for linear-Gaussian observation and motion models, is the well-known Kalman filter (e.g., [43, 74, 80]). Unfortunately the Kalman Filter is not suitable for human pose tracking where the dynamics are usually nonlinear and likelihood functions are usually non-Gaussian and multimodal.

A natural alternative for inference with non-Gaussian, multi-modal posterior distributions is the particle filter (a.k.a. sequential Monte Carlo methods [13, 19, 31]). Such methods approximate the filtering distribution with a weighted set of state samples, and then use sample statistics to approximate expectation under the posterior or filtering distribution. They were first applied broadly to visual tracking with the CONDENSATION algorithm [29]. They have since been used extensively for monocular tracking of 3D human pose with various likelihood functions and prior motion models (e.g., [6, 11, 26, 27, 38, 40, 50, 57, 60, 61, 64]). For a more detailed discussion of sequential Monte Carlo methods, see the review article by Doucet et al. [13].

Finally, tracking typically requires a good initial guess for the pose in the first frame to initialize inference. Initial guesses are also useful to facilitate recovery from tracking failures. Methods for detecting people (see Chap. 11), and discriminative methods for single-frame 3D pose estimation (see Chap. 12) provide natural mechanisms to address these problems.

10.2 Kinematic Joint Limits and Smooth Motion

The kinematic structure of the human body permits a limited range of motion in each joint. Knees and elbows, for example, should not be hyper-extended under normal circumstances, and the torso cannot tilt or twist arbitrarily. One central role of a prior model is to ensure that the poses estimated from an image or image sequence will satisfy such biomechanical limits. While joint limits are often enforced using thresholds, imposed independently on each rotational DOF, the true nature of joint limits in the human body is more complex. In particular, joint limits are dynamic and dependent on the state of other joints [22]. Fortunately, depending on the joint parameterization, many joint constraints can be specified as linear inequalities. This is sometimes useful since, when combined with linear or quadratic objective criteria, one obtains a linear or quadratic programming problem (e.g., see [10]).

While further research on joints limits is needed to understand general limits and individual variability, it appears clear that joint limits by themselves do not encode sufficient prior knowledge to facilitate tractable and robust inference of pose from monocular video (e.g., [57]). Rather, we require some form of density model that captures the *plausibility* of feasible poses and motions under typical circumstances.

Perhaps the simplest prior model of human motion is a smooth, low-order Markov process (e.g., [21, 48, 57, 74]). A common first-order model specifies that the pose $\mathbf{y}$ at time $t + 1$ is equal to the pose at time t, up to additive noise:

$$\mathbf{y}_{t+1} = \mathbf{y}_t + \eta. \tag{10.6}$$

The *process noise* η is usually assumed to be mean-zero Gaussian, with covariance Λ, i.e., $\eta \sim \mathcal{N}(0, \Lambda)$. It follows that the conditional density of $\mathbf{y}_{t+1}$ is $\mathbf{y}_{t+1} | \mathbf{y}_t \sim \mathcal{N}(\mathbf{y}_t, \Lambda)$. Equivalently, it follows that $p(\mathbf{y}_{t+1} | \mathbf{y}_t) = G(\mathbf{y}_{t+1}; \mathbf{y}_t, \Sigma)$ where $G(\mathbf{y}; \mu, \Lambda)$ is a Gaussian function, parameterized by its mean μ and covariance Λ, evaluated at $\mathbf{y}$. Second-order models exploit velocity for future predictions. That is, one can express $\mathbf{y}_{t+1}$ in terms of $\mathbf{y}_t$ and $\mathbf{y}_{t-1}$, often with a damping constant $0 < \kappa < 1$; e.g.,

$$\mathbf{y}_{t+1} = \mathbf{y}_t + \kappa(\mathbf{y}_t - \mathbf{y}_{t-1}) + \eta. \tag{10.7}$$

Damping helps control divergence when predictions occur over multiple time steps.

Equations (10.6) and (10.7) are linear models, the general form of which, i.e.,

$$\mathbf{y}_{t+1} = \sum_{\tau=1}^{L} \mathbf{A}_\tau \mathbf{y}_{t-\tau+1} + \eta, \tag{10.8}$$

is an Lth-order linear-Gaussian dynamical system (or Linear Dynamic System (LDS)). In most cases, the parameters of the transition model are set manually. For instance, one can set the matrices $\mathbf{A}_\tau$ to be diagonal, as in (10.6) and (10.7), and then assume a diagonal covariance matrix, Λ, that is fixed or increases in proportion to $\|\mathbf{y}_t - \mathbf{y}_{t-1}\|^2$ [11].

One can also learn dynamical models from motion capture data (e.g., [44]). In this way one can capture some of the coupling between different joints. But LDS learning often suffers from over-fitting with high-dimensional state spaces. This is because the number of parameters in the transition matrices $\mathbf{A}_n$ is quadratic in the state dimension. Large data sets are usually necessary.

The main attraction with smooth LDS priors is their generality. They can be applied to a wide diversity of motions, which is useful when the activity is not known a priori. Nevertheless, LDS models are sometimes problematic since they are often too weak to adequately constrain people tracking. This is especially problematic with monocular videos where the image evidence is often weak. In constrained settings, where observations from three or more cameras are available, and occlusions are limited, such models have been shown to achieve satisfactory performance [11].

10.3 Linear Kinematic Models

When one knows or has inferred the type of motion being tracked (e.g., see Part III on activity recognition), or the identity of the person performing the motion, one can apply prior models that are specific to the activity and/or the subject. The common approach is to learn models off-line (prior to tracking) from motion capture data. Typically one wants a low-dimensional *latent* parameterization of the pose, and a dynamical model that captures typical pose sequences (i.e., motions).

To introduce the idea, consider a dataset $\mathscr{D} = \{\mathbf{y}^{(i)}\}_{i=1,\dots,N}$ comprising N poses $\mathbf{y}^{(i)} \in \mathbb{R}^D$, e.g., from a motion capture acquisition system. Each training pose comprises the angles of each joint degree of freedom, and relevant aspects of global orientation and position with respect to the world coordinate frame.[1] Many activities of interest, like walking, exhibit strong regularities when repeated by one or several people. As a result, one can posit that the data lie on or near a low-dimensional manifold in the (high-dimensional) pose space.

PCA can be used to approximate poses in a low-dimensional subspace, using the sum of a mean pose, $\mu_{\mathscr{D}} = \frac{1}{N} \sum_{i=1}^{N} \mathbf{y}^{(i)}$, and a linear combination of basis vectors. For a data matrix $\mathbf{A}$, the ith column of which is $\mathbf{y}^{(i)} - \mu_{\mathscr{D}}$, the Singular Value Decomposition (SVD) factorizes $\mathbf{A}$ into orthogonal matrices $\mathbf{U}$ and $\mathbf{V}$, with $\mathbf{U} \equiv [\mathbf{u}_1, \dots, \mathbf{u}_D]$, and a diagonal matrix $\mathbf{S}$ containing singular values arranged in non-increasing order, such that $\mathbf{A} = \mathbf{U}\mathbf{S}\mathbf{V}^T$. Choosing the first B singular vectors $\{\mathbf{u}_j\}_{j=1,\dots,B}$ (a.k.a., the *eigen-poses*), a pose is approximated by

$$\mathbf{y} \approx \mu_{\mathscr{D}} + \sum_{j=1}^{B} x_j \mathbf{u}_j, \tag{10.9}$$

where x_j are scalar coefficients and $B \ll D$ controls the fraction of the variance in $\mathbf{A}$ accounted for by the subspace approximation. As such, the estimation of the pose

---

[1] Global position and orientation with respect to the world coordinate frame are somewhat arbitrary, and often excluded. Global orientation with respect to gravity, height above the ground, and the change in position with respect to the body-centric coordinate frame should be included.

can be replaced by the estimation of the coefficients $\mathbf{x} \equiv [x_1, \ldots, x_B]$. Since B is typically much smaller than the dimensionality of the pose space D, pose estimation is greatly simplified.

In addition to the subspace pose model we need a dynamical model to capture the temporal evolution of pose. Perhaps the simplest such model is a LDS, like those in Sect. 10.2, but applied to the subspace parameters $\mathbf{x}$ rather than directly to the pose. The combination of a linear subspace projection (PCA) and a subspace LDS has been widely studied (e.g., see [71]); in computer vision it is often referred to as a *Dynamic Texture* [12]. Most such models assume a first-order LDS, but higher-order models are sometimes useful [28]. The key advantage of the subspace dynamical model over the LDS model in (10.8) is the fact that the number of parameters in the transition matrices is quadratic in the dimension of the subspace rather than the dimension of the pose observations. Unfortunately, subspace LDS models do not capture nonlinearities that are common in human motion.

10.3.1 Motion PCA: Evolving Pose Subspace

Although modeling pose trajectories within a latent pose space can be difficult, modeling the motion directly is sometimes effective. That is, one can learn a linear, activity-specific kinematic model of the entire pose trajectory directly, rather than as a sequence of poses within a pose space. Originally formulated by Sidenbladh et al. [57], this approach has been used successfully in several ways [59, 66, 69].

As above, assume that each *pose* vector, $\mathbf{y} \in \mathbb{R}^D$, comprises joint angles and global DOFs. Writing the pose at time t as $\mathbf{y}_t$, we can express a *motion* as a vector comprising all joint angles throughout the entire sequence of M poses; i.e.,

$$\mathbf{m} = \left(\mathbf{y}_1^T, \ldots, \mathbf{y}_M^T\right)^T. \tag{10.10}$$

A training corpus typically involves multiple people performing the same activity multiple times. Because training motions occur at different speeds, or might be sampled at different rates, the first step of learning a model is to align and resample the training motions. For periodic sequences (e.g., walking) one can use the fundamental frequency to determine the period (the duration of one cycle), and the phase needed for alignment. For non-periodic motions one can also manually segment and align the motions, or use some form of *dynamic time warping* (e.g., see [46, 69]).[2] The canonical motion is then represented as a sequence of M (interpolated) poses, indexed by phase, $\phi_n \in (0, 1]$, where $\phi_n = \frac{n}{M}$ and $0 \le n < M$. Each training motion is a real-valued vector of length $D \times M$.

---

[2]Because the data are joint angles, interpolation is normally accomplished using *quaternion spherical interpolation* [56]. Naturally, the temporal sampling rate must be sufficiently high that one can interpolate the pose signal with reasonable accuracy.

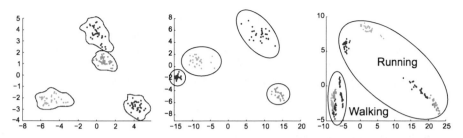

Fig. 10.1 Projections of training data onto the first two principal directions for a walk model (*left*), a run model (*middle*), and a model learned from walking and running data (*right*). Walking data comprised 4 mocap samples for each of 4 subjects (color coded) walking at 9 speeds varying from 3 to 7 km/h. Running data were from the same subjects at 7 speeds ranging from 6 to 12 km/h. Solid curves separating clusters are drawn for purposes of visualization. (Adapted from [69])

Given a collection of training motions, $\mathscr{D} = \{\mathbf{m}^{(i)}\}_{i=1}^{N}$, one can use PCA to form a subspace model. In this way a motion is expressed as a linear combination of a mean motion μ and a set of *eigen-motions* $\{\mathbf{b}_j\}_{j=1}^{B}$:

$$\mathbf{m} \approx \mu + \sum_{j=1}^{B} x_j \mathbf{b}_j. \tag{10.11}$$

The scalar coefficients, $\mathbf{x} = (x_1, \ldots, x_B)^T$, characterize a particular motion. One typically chooses B so that a significant fraction (e.g., 90%) of the empirical data variance is captured by the subspace projection. A pose is then defined to be a function of $\mathbf{x}$, the subspace coefficients, and the phase, ϕ; i.e.,

$$\mathbf{y}(\mathbf{c}, \phi) \approx \mu(\phi) + \sum_{j=1}^{B} x_j \mathbf{b}_j(\phi). \tag{10.12}$$

Here, $\mathbf{b}_j$ denotes an eigen-motion, and $\mathbf{b}_j(\phi)$ is an *eigen-pose* at phase ϕ. Similarly, $\mu(\phi)$ is the mean pose at phase ϕ. In effect, the motion subspace yields a pose subspace that evolves as a function of ϕ. Nonlinearities in the evolution of the pose subspace are encoded implicitly in the eigen-motions.

With this model Sidenbladh et al. [57] formulated tracking as the estimation of global position, the speed of motion, the phase ϕ, and the subspace coefficients $\mathbf{x}$ at each frame. A particle filter was used for inference, to cope with transient pose ambiguities. Urtasun et al. [69] showed that motion-based PCA provides a convex model for many motions of interest such as walking and jogging (see Fig. 10.1). That is, random draws from the underlying Gaussian model over the subspace coefficients produces plausible poses and motions. They also found that walks of different speeds for the same subject were tightly clustered in the subspace. This enabled motion-based recognition [69]. Troje [66] showed that this representation of walking facilitates the inference of other meaningful attributes, including gender and aspects of mental state. Sigal et al. [59] has since extended this to the inference of human attributes from video-based 3D pose data. But it is not clear how this representation can be extended to deal with different activities. Indeed, Urtasun et al. [69] showed that random samples drawn from a simple model learned from running and walking motions are not always plausible motions; i.e., a Gaussian density function is not an adequate prior over multiple activities within a single subspace.

10.4 Nonlinear Kinematic Models

A periodic motion like walking follows a 1D cyclic trajectory in the high-dimensional pose space. Thus, while (linear) subspace models often require many dimensions to adequately span the empirical pose data, the underlying dimensionality of the motions may actually be significantly lower. One could, for example, parameterize position along a periodic pose trajectory with a 1D model. Allowing for variability, from cycle to cycle, or from person to person, one might posit that the poses lie on or near a low-dimensional, *nonlinear* manifold. The goal of a low-dimensional latent model is to parameterize the structure of the manifold. With nonlinear models one might be able to find more effective low-dimensional parameterizations than one might find with linear models.

The earliest nonlinear models used embedding methods for nonlinear dimensionality reduction (e.g., [54]). Such methods provide low-dimensional latent positions for each training pose, but they do not provide a closed-form function that maps new poses to latent positions (often called out-of-sample extensions). Accordingly, methods based on nonlinear dimensionality reduction augment the embedding with learned mappings between the latent space and the observation (pose) space, along with a density model over the latent positions of the training poses (e.g., [14, 60]). More recent methods, like the Gaussian Process Latent Variable Model (GPLVM), formulate and optimize a coherent model that incorporates the mappings, the embedding, and the density model.

10.4.1 Gaussian Process Latent Variable Model

The Gaussian Process Latent Variable Model (GPLVM)[3] is a nonlinear generalization of probabilistic PCA [33]. It is a generative latent variable model that comprises a low-dimensional latent space, and a stochastic, nonlinear mapping from the latent space to the original observation space. Conceptually, one hopes that the latent model captures the underlying *causes* for the high-dimensional training data. The GPLVM is useful for visualizing high-dimensional data [33], and it has been shown to generalize well even with small or moderate amounts of training data [68].

---

[3]http://staffwww.dcs.shef.ac.uk/people/N.Lawrence/gpsoftware.html is a comprehensive GPLVM code base. GPLVM code is also in the Matlab toolbox for dimensionality reduction available at http://homepage.tudelft.nl/19j49/.

To explain the basic GPLVM it is easiest to first examine Gaussian Process (GP) regression[51]. To that end, consider a mapping from a vector-valued input, $\mathbf{x}$, to a scalar output, y. Let the mapping be expressed in parametric form as

$$y = g(\mathbf{x}) + \eta, \tag{10.13}$$

where η is mean-zero Gaussian, with variance β, and g has a generalized linear form. That is, let g be a weighted sum of nonlinear basis functions $\phi_j(\mathbf{x})$:

$$g(\mathbf{x}) = \sum_{j=1}^{J} w_j \phi_j(\mathbf{x}) = \mathbf{w}^T \Phi(\mathbf{x}), \tag{10.14}$$

where $\mathbf{w} \equiv (w_1, \ldots, w_J)^T$, and the vector $\Phi(\mathbf{x}) = (\phi_1(\mathbf{x}), \ldots, \phi_J(\mathbf{x}))^T$ comprises the basis functions evaluated at $\mathbf{x}$. To complete the model, we assume a mean-zero Gaussian prior for $\mathbf{w}$ with unit covariance, $\mathbf{w} \sim \mathcal{N}(0; \mathbf{I})$, and we let the *noise* η be independent of $\mathbf{w}$.

Because y in (10.13) is a linear function of Gaussian random variables, it is also Gaussian, and therefore characterized by its mean and covariance. Because $\mathbf{w}$ and η are both mean-zero, it follows that y is mean-zero:

$$\mu(\mathbf{x}) \equiv E[y] = E[\mathbf{w}^T \Phi(\mathbf{x}) + \eta] = 0. \tag{10.15}$$

One can also show that, given two inputs, $\mathbf{x}$ and $\mathbf{x}'$, the covariance of their outputs, y and y', satisfies

$$k(\mathbf{x}, \mathbf{x}') \equiv E[yy'] = E\left[\left(\mathbf{w}^T \Phi(\mathbf{x}) + \eta\right)\left(\mathbf{w}^T \Phi(\mathbf{x}') + \eta'\right)\right]$$
$$= \Phi(\mathbf{x})^T \Phi(\mathbf{x}') + \beta \delta(\mathbf{x}, \mathbf{x}'), \tag{10.16}$$

where δ is 1 when $\mathbf{x}$ and $\mathbf{x}'$ are the same inputs, and 0 otherwise. One can derive (10.16) using the model assumptions, $E[\mathbf{w}] = 0$, $E[\mathbf{w}\mathbf{w}^T] = \mathbf{I}$, $E[w_j \eta] = 0$, and $E[\eta^2] = \beta$. The functions $\mu(\mathbf{x})$ and $k(\mathbf{x}, \mathbf{x}')$ are referred to as the mean function and the kernel (or covariance) function, respectively.

The mapping from $\mathbf{x}$ to y in (10.13) is a Gaussian Process (GP). It is a continuous stochastic process that is fully specified by its mean and covariance functions. For instance, with the appropriate choice of Gaussian basis functions [51], we obtain the well-known RBF kernel, combined with the variance of the additive noise:

$$k(\mathbf{x}, \mathbf{x}') = \alpha \exp\left(-\frac{\gamma}{2} \|\mathbf{x} - \mathbf{x}'\|^2\right) + \beta \delta(\mathbf{x}, \mathbf{x}'), \tag{10.17}$$

where the α, β and γ are the *hyperparameters* of the kernel; i.e., α determines the magnitude of the covariance, γ determines the effective correlation length in the latent space, and β determines the variance of the additive noise. Alternative assumptions about the form of $\{\phi_j(\mathbf{x})\}$ in (10.14) lead to different kernel functions.

The GP model has several appealing properties. One stems from the formulation of $p(y|\mathbf{x})$ as the marginalization of $p(y, \mathbf{w}|\mathbf{x})$. By marginalizing over $\mathbf{w}$, e.g., instead of estimating **w** using maximum likelihood, the GP mitigates over-fitting problems that commonly occur when one has only small or moderate amounts of training data. The GP also provides a measure of uncertainty in y (i.e., the variance) which is useful in many applications. Finally, with the GP one does not have to specify the basis functions (i.e., the features) directly. Rather, one only needs to specify the form of the kernel function [41, 51].

Suppose one is given IID training pairs, $\mathscr{D} = \{(\mathbf{x}^{(i)}, y^{(i)})\}_{i=1,...,N}$, with mean-zero outputs $y^{(i)}$. To learn a GP model one does not have to estimate **w**, but one does have to estimate the kernel hyperparameters. This is usually done by maximizing the empirical data likelihood, i.e. the density over $\mathbf{z} \equiv (y^{(1)}, \dots, y^{(N)})^T$ conditioned on $\{\mathbf{x}^{(i)}\}$. It follows from the GP model that the data likelihood is mean-zero Gaussian with a covariance (kernel) matrix **K** having elements $\mathbf{K}_{ij} = k(\mathbf{x}^{(i)}, \mathbf{x}^{(j)})$:

$$p\big(\mathbf{z} \,|\, \{\mathbf{x}^{(i)}\}, \theta\big) = \frac{1}{\sqrt{(2\pi)^N |\mathbf{K}|}} \exp\left(-\frac{1}{2}\mathbf{z}^T \mathbf{K}^{-1} \mathbf{z}\right), \qquad (10.18)$$

where θ is the vector of hyperparameters upon which $k(\cdot, \cdot)$ depends. Differentiating the log likelihood with respect to θ can be done in closed form, and hence can be used for optimization (e.g., with *scaled conjugate gradient*).

For pose data, the GP outputs must be vector-valued, i.e., $\mathbf{y}^{(i)} \in \mathbb{R}^D$. The training pairs are then given by $\mathscr{D} = \{(\mathbf{x}^{(i)}, \mathbf{y}^{(i)})\}_{i=1,...,N}$. If one uses the same kernel function for all output dimensions, then the joint likelihood function is the product of the likelihood for each output dimension. More specifically, let $\mathbf{Y} = [\mathbf{y}^{(1)}, \dots, \mathbf{y}^{(N)}]^T$, and let $\mathbf{y}_d$ be the dth column of $\mathbf{Y}$; i.e., $\mathbf{y}_d$ comprises the dth element of each of the N training outputs. Then, one can write the joint GP data likelihood as the product of likelihoods for each dimension $\mathbf{y}_d$:

$$p\big(\mathbf{Y} \,|\, \{\mathbf{x}^{(i)}\}, \theta\big) = \prod_{d=1}^{D} \frac{1}{\sqrt{(2\pi)^N |\mathbf{K}|}} \exp\left(-\frac{1}{2}\mathbf{y}_d^T \mathbf{K}^{-1} \mathbf{y}_d\right), \qquad (10.19)$$

where θ is the vector of kernel hyperparameters. By using the same kernel matrix for each observation dimension we greatly reduce the number of hyperparameters. Further, a common kernel naturally captures correlations among the different output dimensions that depend directly on the corresponding latent positions. That is, although the conditional distribution is the product of 1D densities, the different observation dimensions are not independent. Rather, they depend on the common kernel matrix. That said, when modeling pose data, different dimensions (e.g., joint angles) have significantly different variances. In this case, it is useful to discard the common scale parameter (α in (10.17)), and instead use a separate scale parameter for each observation dimension (e.g., see [20, 68]).

GP regression is a *supervised* model, where training data include both **x** and **y**. The GPLVM is an *unsupervised* model, where **Y** is the only available training data [33]. Learning a GPLVM therefore entails the estimation of a latent representative (position) for each training sample, in addition to the hyperparameters θ. Lawrence [33] showed that for linear features, i.e., $\Phi(\mathbf{x}) = \mathbf{x}$, the GPLVM is equivalent to probabilistic PCA. In this sense the GPLVM is a generalization of probabilistic PCA to nonlinear mappings.

GPLVM learning entails numerical optimization to maximize the joint posterior $p(\mathbf{Y}|\{\mathbf{x}^{(i)}\}, \theta)p(\{\mathbf{x}^{(i)}\})p(\theta)$ with respect to $\{\mathbf{x}^{(i)}\}$ and θ. The prior over the latent representatives is typically a broad Gaussian density. The prior over the hyperparameters is typically uninformative, unless domain-specific knowledge is available. A good initial guess for the optimization is often critical; one can use PCA or some other form of nonlinear dimensionality reduction method like Locally Linear Embedding (LLE) [54]. Usually the dimension of the latent space is chosen manually.

A key property of the GPLVM is its predictive distribution. Given a new latent position, $\mathbf{x}$, the distribution over the observation space is Gaussian, with a simple closed-form expression for its mean and covariance:

$$\mathbf{y}|\mathbf{x}, \mathbf{Y}, \{\mathbf{x}^{(i)}\} \sim \mathcal{N}\left(\mathbf{m}(\mathbf{x}); \sigma^2(\mathbf{x})\right), \tag{10.20}$$

$$\text{where} \qquad \mathbf{m}(\mathbf{x}) = \mathbf{Y}^T \mathbf{K}^{-1} \mathbf{k}(\mathbf{x}), \tag{10.21}$$

$$\sigma^2(\mathbf{x}) = k(\mathbf{x}, \mathbf{x}) - \mathbf{k}(\mathbf{x})^T \mathbf{K}^{-1} \mathbf{k}(\mathbf{x}), \tag{10.22}$$

$$\mathbf{k}(\mathbf{x}) = \left(k\left(\mathbf{x}, \mathbf{x}^{(1)}\right), \dots, k\left(\mathbf{x}, \mathbf{x}^{(N)}\right)\right)^T. \tag{10.23}$$

The predictive distribution is central to inferring a new pose. Effectively, these equations show that, given a latent position $\mathbf{x}$, the mean prediction for $\mathbf{y}$ in (10.21) is just a weighted sum of training poses; the weights are a function of the kernel distances between $\mathbf{x}$ and the latent training representatives, along with the pre-computed, inverse kernel matrix $\mathbf{K}^{-1}$. One can also use this predictive distribution to find the latent position $\mathbf{x}$ that is maximally consistent with a given pose $\mathbf{y}$.[4]

Another useful expression is the likelihood of a new pair $(\mathbf{x}, \mathbf{y})$, since during tracking we often need to estimate both quantities. In particular, up to an additive constant, the negative log probability of a pair $(\mathbf{x}, \mathbf{y})$, given $\mathbf{Y}$ and $\{\mathbf{x}^{(i)}\}$, is

$$L(\mathbf{x}, \mathbf{y}) = \frac{\|(\mathbf{y} - \mathbf{m}(\mathbf{x}))\|^2}{2\sigma^2(\mathbf{x})} + \frac{D}{2}\ln\sigma^2(\mathbf{x}) + \frac{1}{2}\|\mathbf{x}\|^2. \tag{10.24}$$

Minimizing $L(\mathbf{x}, \mathbf{y})$ therefore aims to minimize reconstruction errors (i.e., to keep $\mathbf{y}$ close to the mean $\mathbf{m}(\mathbf{x})$), while keeping latent positions close to the training data (i.e., to keep $\sigma^2(\mathbf{x})$ small). The third term in (10.24) is the prior over latent positions that usually has relatively little influence on the optimized latent positions. Figure 10.2 depicts this log likelihood for GPLVMs learned from a walk and a golf swing.

For visual tracking one can combine a suitable log likelihood term for the image data, with the log prior over new points, $L(\mathbf{x}, \mathbf{y})$, in order to formulate an objective

---

[4]The GPLVM has a closed-form mapping from $\mathbf{x}$ to $\mathbf{y}$, but there is no closed-form inverse mapping. As a consequence, optimization is required to find the optimal $\mathbf{x}$ for a given $\mathbf{y}$.

Fig. 10.2 GPLVM latent spaces learned from mocap data: (*left*) one walk cycle and (*right*) a golf swing. Red crosses are optimized latent points $\mathbf{x}^{(i)} \in \mathbb{R}^2$. Grayscale depicts $-D \ln \sigma^2(\mathbf{x}) - \mathbf{x}^T \mathbf{x}$; lighter points imply a lower variance (10.22) and hence more likely poses. (Adapted from [68])

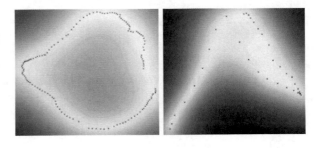

function. Because $L(\mathbf{x}, \mathbf{y})$ is easily differentiated one can use continuous optimization to find MAP estimates [68], or one can use a sequential Monte Carlo method for inference [50]. During tracking one usually estimates both $\mathbf{x}$ and $\mathbf{y}$ at each frame. In some cases one may wish to search only over $\mathbf{x}$, using the deterministic mapping from $\mathbf{x}$ to $\mathbf{y}$ given by the mean, $\mathbf{m}(\mathbf{x})$ [67]. This has the advantage that one searches a much smaller state space, but it comes with the disadvantage that one is explicitly limited to a linear combination of the training poses with no additional stylistic variability.

10.4.2 Gaussian Process Dynamical Model

The GPLVM is formulated for IID training data, drawn fairly from the true pose density over the observation space. By ignoring the obvious temporal coherence in the sequences of poses that is significant in human motion, the GPLVM often produces models in which consecutive poses do not always correspond to nearby points in the latent space. Conversely, one might expect a good model to map smooth pose trajectories to smooth latent trajectories, thereby facilitating temporal prediction and effective tracking. The Gaussian Process Dynamical Model (GPDM)[5], as the name suggests, is an extension of the GPLVM to incorporate temporal structure for times-series data, thereby promoting smoothness in the latent representation of motion.

The GPDM replaces the IID prior over inputs $\{\mathbf{x}^{(i)}\}$ with a GP prior over latent trajectories. For example, let latent positions at time t be predicted by a first-order model, defined by a matrix $\mathbf{A}$, a feature vector $\Psi(\mathbf{x})$, and Gaussian noise, $\eta \sim \mathcal{N}(\mathbf{0}, \xi \mathbf{I})$:

$$\mathbf{x}_t = \mathbf{A}\Psi(\mathbf{x}_{t-1}) + \eta. \tag{10.25}$$

For linear features, $\Psi(\mathbf{x}_t) = \mathbf{x}_t$, this model (10.25) reduces to an auto-regressive model (cf., (10.8)). But like the GPLVM, one can incorporate nonlinear features and analytically marginalize out the weights $\mathbf{A}$ (assuming a Gaussian prior over the columns of $\mathbf{A}$). This provides a GP prior over the latent sequences that correspond to training motions. (See [67, 77] for the mathematical details.)

---

[5]GPDM Code: http://www.dgp.toronto.edu/~jmwang/gpdm/.

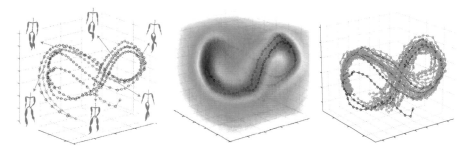

Fig. 10.3 A 3D GPDM is learned from 3 walk cycles. (*Left*) The latent positions of training poses are shown as blue circles. (*Middle*) The pose variance as a function of latent position is color coded, with red (blue) points having small (large) variance. (*Right*) Each green trajectory is a random sample from the latent dynamical model; the mean motion of which is the red trajectory in the left plot. (Adapted from [77])

Fig. 10.4 Monocular tracking results with a GPDM learned from walking data. The 3D person is tracked despite the almost total occlusion by the bush on the *left* side of the image, where only the head is visible by the end of the sequence. (Adapted from [67])

The GPDM combines a nonlinear mapping from latent points to observations, with nonlinear dynamical predictions. Marginalizing over the weight matrices of both mappings helps reduce potential over-fitting problems. Learning entails the estimation of a latent position for each training pose, with the hyperparameters for the latent mapping and the dynamical model. Figure 10.3 depicts a GPDM learned from three gait cycles of walking. Color in Fig. 10.3(middle) is analogous to the greylevel in Fig. 10.2. Warmer colors (red) indicate small variances, hence more likely poses. Cooler colors (blue) indicate larger variances and hence unlikely poses. Like the GPLVM, GPDM predictions are analytical and straightforwardly combined with an image likelihood for pose tracking [67]. Figure 10.4 depicts the monocular estimation of walking, despite significant occlusion by the bushes on the left side of the image.

10.4.3 Constrained Latent Spaces and Other Variants

The GPLVM does not work well with large datasets because learning and inference are, respectively, cubic and quadratic in the number of training poses. Approxima-

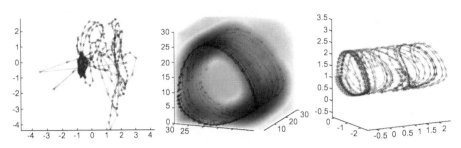

Fig. 10.5 (*Left*) A GPDM is learned from mocap data of people walking and running. The latent trajectories are not smooth, and trajectories drawn from the dynamical model are not realistic motions. (*Middle*) This GPDM is constrained to lie on a cylindrical topology, with an LLE prior that encourages nearby poses to remain close in the latent space. (*Right*) Random trajectories simulated by the model (in red and green) produce plausible motions. (Adapted from [70])

tions to the covariance matrix can be used to improve efficiency (e.g., [49]), but their use requires care, since local minima often fail to produce useful models. Similar approximations to the GPDM have not been formulated.

A second issue concerns the sensitivity of the GPLVM and GPDM optimizations to the initial guess, and the fact that many local minima do not represent useful models [77] (e.g., see Fig. 10.5(left)). Such local minima are especially problematic when there is significant stylistic variability in the training data. Given the number of unknowns in the learning problem, and the lack of structure imposed on the latent representation, this problem is not particularly surprising.

To address these issues, several interesting GPLVM variants have appeared in recent years. They demonstrate some of the ways in which one can impose more structure on the latent representation in order to produce more useful models.

10.4.3.1 Back-Constraints and Topological Constraints

The GPLVM ensures that nearby latent positions map to similar poses. The converse is not true; similar poses do not necessarily get mapped to nearby latent positions. Despite the use of a dynamical prior, even the GPDM does not always produce smooth models with useful temporal predictions. To ensure smooth latent models, Lawrence and Quiñonero-Candela [35] introduced *back-constraints*. They suggested that one might parameterize latent position in terms of a smooth function of the observation space. For example, one might write the jth coordinate of the ith latent position as $x_{ij} = h_j(\mathbf{y}^{(i)}; \mathbf{a}_j)$, where $\{\mathbf{a}_j\}_{j=1,...,d}$ denotes the parameters of the mapping, and d is the dimension of the latent space. For instance, h might be expressed as a form of kernel-based regression, so nearby poses in the observation space map to similar latent positions. Rather than directly estimating the latent positions, learning a back-constrained GPLVM entails the estimation of the mapping parameters $\{\mathbf{a}_j\}$, by maximizing the empirical data likelihood.

Back-constraints can be used to model temporal dependence, thereby ensuring that time-series data will be mapped to smooth latent trajectories. They can also be used to specify latent topological structure. For instance, Urtasun et al. [70] used back-constraints to parameterize a cylindrical latent topology when modeling cyclic gaits, like walking and running. They also incorporated local, *soft back-constraints* to encourage nearby poses to map to nearby latent positions. This is done in much the same way that LLE optimizes low-dimensional positions to maintain distances to nearby points in the observation space.

The combination of the cylindrical topology and the preservation of local neighborhoods produces the latent representation depicted in Fig. 10.5(middle). This model captures running and walking performed by multiple subjects. Random samples from the model appear natural, including transitions between walking and running (e.g., Fig. 10.5(right)). By comparison, the GPDM has difficulty coping with such stylistic diversity; GPDMs like that in Fig. 10.5(left) are typical for these training data, and do not produce plausible gaits.

10.4.3.2 Multi-factor GPLVM

One way to capture significant stylistic diversity is to blend models that capture individual styles. For example, motivated by linear style interpolation and multilinear models (e.g., [53, 65, 72]), one might consider a weighted sum of GPs, $\{g_i(\mathbf{x})\}$:

$$y = \sum_i s_i g_i(\mathbf{x}) + \eta = \sum_i s_i \mathbf{w}_i^T \Phi(\mathbf{x}) + \eta = \sum_i \sum_j s_i w_{ij}^T \phi_j(\mathbf{x}) + \eta. \qquad (10.26)$$

This is a generative model for y with latent variables $\mathbf{z} = (\mathbf{x}, \mathbf{s})$. The latent space is composed of two subspaces, one for the blending weights $\mathbf{s} = (\ldots, s_i, \ldots)$, representing style, and one for $\mathbf{x}$ which captures the phase dependence of the pose.

If we assume Gaussian weight vectors, $\mathbf{w}_i \sim \mathcal{N}(\mathbf{0}, \mathbf{I})$, and Gaussian process noise, $\eta \sim \mathcal{N}(0, \beta)$, then it follows that y is a mean-zero GP with covariance function

$$k(\mathbf{z}, \mathbf{z}') = \mathbf{s}^T \mathbf{s}' \Phi(\mathbf{x})^T \Phi(\mathbf{x}') + \beta \delta(\mathbf{z}, \mathbf{z}'), \qquad (10.27)$$

where δ is 1 when $\mathbf{z}$ and $\mathbf{z}'$ correspond to the same measurements, and 0 otherwise. The covariance function in (10.27) has two key factors, namely, the linear kernel on $\mathbf{s}$, and the nonlinear kernel on $\mathbf{x}$. This two-factor, scalar GP model is readily generalized to three or more factors, and to vector-valued outputs [76]. Each factor is associated with an individual latent subspace, and the covariance function (10.27) involves the product of one kernel for each factor.

Such multi-factor GPLVMs are particularly useful for mocap data where *side information* is often available. That is, for each mocap sample one typically knows the type of gait (e.g. run, walk, jog), as well as the subject's identity, age, weight, etc., all of which contribute to the motion style. In a multi-factor GPLVM, each type of side information would be represented as a separate latent factor. As an example, Wang et al. [76] learned a three-factor model, using the subject's *identity*, the *gait* type (walk, stride or jog), and the *phase* of the gait cycle. All motions of one individual, independent of gait and phase, are constrained to share the same latent position in the identity subspace. All walking motions, independent of the subject and phase, share the same position in the gait subspace. And so on. With side information used in this way, the multi-factor GPLVM imposes structure on the latent space; structure that the GPDM would be unlikely to discover. As a result, multi-factor models tends to converge more readily to useful kinematic models, for different datasets and initial conditions.

Interestingly, one can view the multi-factor GPLVM as a Bayesian generalization of multilinear models (e.g., [65, 72]). The two models are very similar when one uses linear features (e.g., $\Phi(\mathbf{x}) = \mathbf{x}$ in (10.26)). One key difference is that the GPLVM marginalizes over the weights (i.e., the multilinear core tensor), which reduces the number of the unknowns that must be estimated and mitigates potential over-fitting problems. The second difference is that the multi-factor GPLVM generalizes naturally to nonlinear features (cf., [15]). When designed properly it is also possible to express the kernel matrix as product of much smaller kernels [75], greatly reducing the complexity of learning and inference.

10.4.3.3 Hierarchical GPLVM

Lawrence and Moore [34] proposed a hierarchy of GPLVMs in which latent positions at one level are specified by the output of a GP at the next level. This is another way to impose structure on a latent representation. One use of the Hierarchical GPLVM (hGPLVM) is to capture temporal coherence [34]. An initial GP maps time, or the gait phase, to a Gaussian density over positions in a latent pose space. A second GP then maps position in the latent pose space to a Gaussian density over pose in the original observation space. A temporal model like this has been used successfully for tracking in [1].

The hGPLVM could be used to model coordination between interacting people. The pose (or motion) of each person might be modeled by two separate GPLVMs. To coordinate their motions, a third GP simultaneously specifies Gaussian densities over the latent positions in the two person-specific GPLVM latent spaces.

One could also use the hGPLVM to model the coordination of different parts of the body, like that depicted in Fig. 10.6 [34]. This model has six GPLVMs at the lowest level of the hierarchy (leaves of the tree). Each is responsible for one part of the body, mapping a latent position to a Gaussian density over pose (of its corresponding part). At the next level there are latent models that specify the coordination of the legs and of the upper body. The *lower body* model outputs Gaussian densities over latent positions within the left and right leg models to control leg swing. The hierarchy also includes multiple activities. In Fig. 10.6(right) the two activities are waving while the legs are standing still, and walking with no appreciable arm swing. Notice that the intermediate nodes of the hierarchy capture the latent structure of body parts for both activities. This hierarchical model of human motion was used successfully in [9] for tracking a person walking while waving an arm, thereby composing a new motion from elements of the two training motions.

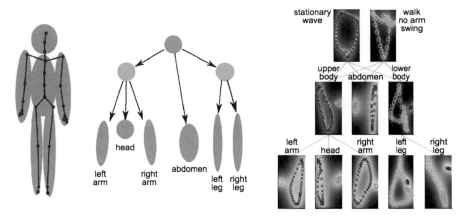

Fig. 10.6 In a hierarchical GPLVM, a latent position at one node provides Gaussian densities over its descendants. Here it is used to coordinate different body parts, for two activities, waving while standing still, and walking no arm swing. Red and green points, respectively, depict the latent positions at each node that correspond to poses from these two activities. (Adapted from [9])

10.4.4 Switching Linear Dynamical Systems

One way to model data in the vicinity of a smooth, low-dimensional manifold, is to use local linear models, much as one might approximate a smooth curve with a piecewise linear function. One such model for time-series data, like human motion, is the *switching linear dynamical system* (e.g. [16, 44, 45, 47]). A Switching Linear Dynamical System (SLDS) comprises a set of LDS models and a discrete switching variable that specifies which LDS is active at each time. Each LDS captures the evolution of pose within a local region of the pose space, and can be viewed as an atomic *moveme*. During tracking one maintains a probability distribution over the switching variable, and a Gaussian density over pose for each LDS. If one marginalizes out the switching variable, one obtains a Gaussian mixture model over pose.

SLDS models are attractive for their intuitive simplicity, but they require large datasets and can be hard to learn. For each LDS (see (10.8)) one requires a transition matrix and a covariance matrix for the process noise. For a D-dimensional pose vector there are $O(D^2)$ parameters for each transition matrix and for each covariance matrix. An SLDS with N components also requires $O(N^2)$ parameters to specify the temporal transition matrix for the switching variable. Hence, the number of unknowns to be optimized is large. One also faces a difficult model selection problem as one needs to decide how many LDS components to use in the model. Over-fitting and local minima are significant problems when learning SLDS models.

Li et al. advocate a model that addresses some of these shortcomings [36–38]. First, they express each linear component as a (latent) subspace LDS. Each components has a low-dimensional subspace that is learned with factor analysis (or PCA), and a LDS that models the evolution of the subspace coordinates. Second, the different local subspace models are configured to form a consistent global model using

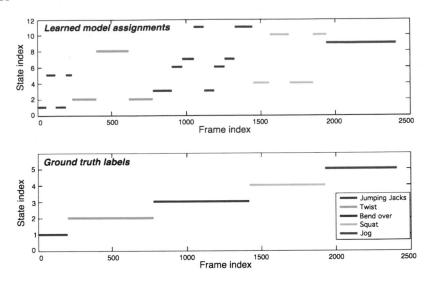

Fig. 10.7 (*Bottom*) Ground truth activity labels for a 2405 frame mocap sequence comprising five distinct activities. (*Top*) The most probable state of the switching variable for an 11-component SLDS model learned using Li's variational Bayes formulation. (Reproduced with permission from [36])

the Coordinated Mixture of Factor Analyzers[6] [55, 73]. Learning is formulated using variational Bayes, which also enables the automatic determination of the number of linear components and their dimensions. Li et al. demonstrated the effectiveness of this model for monocular tracking in [37, 38].

One interesting property of this class of models is its potential to model diverse styles and activities. For example, Fig. 10.7 depicts a model learned from a 2405 frame training sequence of 56D human mocap data. The sequences comprising 5 activities, namely jumping jacks, twisting, bending, squats and jogging. Figure 10.7(bottom) depicts the activity labels throughout the sequence. The learning algorithm automatically selected 11 subspace-LDS components, each with 7 dimensions. Figure 10.7(top) depicts the most likely assignment of pose to each of the 11 components. Notice how the 11 components decompose the data into coherent atomic motions, each of which appears to be specific to a single activity. The last segment was captured by a single component since the jogging was done in place with minimal limb movement [36]. Such multi-activity models have not yet been used for video-based tracking with complex motion sequences.

---

[6]Code for the coordinated mixture of factor analyzers is included in the Matlab toolbox for dimensionality reduction available at http://homepage.tudelft.nl/19j49/.

10.4.5 Conditional Restricted Boltzmann Machines

A third promising class of latent variable models has recently emerged based on the Restricted Boltzmann Machine (RBM) (e.g., [23, 25]). An RBM is a probabilistic graphical model. It comprises a bipartite graph over the observation (visible) variables and the latent variables. As a result, conditioned on the state of the latent variables, the observation variables are independent of one another, and *vice versa*. In the usual RBM all variables are binary-valued, but it can be extended to real-valued observations, and is therefore applicable to modeling human pose. With its bipartite structure, RBM learning and inference are efficient. Learning is linear in the number of training exemplars with an algorithm known as *contrastive divergence* [23].

The Conditional Restricted Boltzmann Machines (CRBM) is an extension of the RBM to model time-series data[7] [63]. This is accomplished by conditioning the latent and observation variables at time t on the observations at the previous N time steps (for an Nth-order model). The *implicit mixture of CRBMs* (imCRBM) [62, 64] is an extension of the CRBM to include latent style variables. These style variables, much like those in the multi-factor GPLVM, modulate the weights (interaction potentials) of the CRBM in order to achieve distinct motion styles. If one marginalizes over these style variables one obtains a mixture of CRBMs (i.e., an imCRBM).

Like the coordinated mixture of factor analyzers above, imCRBM learning can be supervised or unsupervised. When supervised, the style or activity labels are provided. In the unsupervised case the model discovers atomic motion primitives from the training data. An impressive diversity of styles can be learned and used for synthesis [62]. A variation of the model was used for monocular tracking in [64].

Figure 10.8 depicts the behavior of a CRBM and an imCRBM in combination with a basic particle filter for monocular pose tracking. The input video (HUMANEVA S3, combo [58]) begins with walking and then transitions to jogging around frame 400. All models were trained on walking and jogging data from the same subject (S3), but with no transitions. Figure 10.8(top-left) depicts RMSE for 3D joint position as at each frame for four trackers: 1) an annealed particle filter for baseline comparison; 2) a plain CRMB; 3) a supervised imCRBM (i.e., imCRBM-2L) trained *with* walk and jog activity labels; and 4) an unsupervised imCRBM with 10 latent activity labels (i.e., imCRBM-10U). CRBM-based models perform better than baseline. The two imCRBMs with activity-specific components are more reliable than the basic CRBM in tracking the motion through the transition from walking to running.

Figure 10.8(top-right) depicts the approximate posterior distribution over activity labels for the supervised model (imCRBM-2U) and the unsupervised model (imCRBM-10U). Uncertainty is evident in the vicinity of the walk-jog transition. Also notice that the unsupervised model appears to have discovered activity labels that correspond to coherent atomic movements. Interestingly they appear to be specific to the activity and the phase of the gait cycle. The bottom rows of Fig. 10.8 depict MAP estimates of a particle filter with the imCRBM-2U motion prior.

---

[7]Code: http://www.cs.nyu.edu/~gwtaylor/code/.

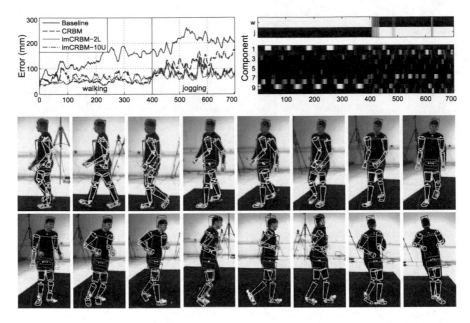

Fig. 10.8 (*Top-left*) RMSE for monocular pose tracking based on CRBM and imCRBM for a HumanEva sequence with walking and jogging. (*Top-right*) Posterior distribution over activity labels for a supervised imCRBM with two labels (walk/jog), and for an unsupervised imCRBM with 10 latent activities. The unsupervised model learns coherent motion primitives. (*Bottom 2 rows*) Output of the particle filter with the supervised imCRBM prior motion model. (Adapted from [64])

While learning is challenging with sophisticated models like the CRBM and the imCRBM [24], this is an interesting class of models. Like the SLDS, RBM models are parametric, and thus do not suffer from having to store all the training data (as does the non-parametric GPLVM for instance). Furthermore, inference is very fast, and learning is linear in the number of training samples. As a consequence the CRBM and imCRBM can be trained on very large mocap corpora.

10.4.6 Heterogeneity, Compositionality, and Exogenous Factors

Most state-of-the-art approaches to tracking human motion rely on learned kinematic models. This is true of generative models and of discriminative model techniques (see Chap. 12). With the development of new models and learning algorithms, recent methods for people tracking have produced very encouraging results. Nevertheless, important issues remain. Existing models only work well with a handful of activities, and modest stylistic diversity. They remain unable to model human motion over extended sequences in which people seamlessly transition from activity to activity. Generalization to a wide range of motion styles is similarly lacking.

The lack of *compositionality* in current models is one of the key barriers to improved generalization. For example, because limbs move with some degree of independence, there are myriad ways one might compose leg and arm movements. People usually walk with a counter-phase oscillation of the arms and legs. Sometimes they walk with relatively little arm swing, e.g., if carrying a heavy object. And sometimes they walk with a hand raised, waving to a friend. A compositional model would model the elementary parts of the body, along with the ways they might be composed to form the whole. This would avoid the combinatorial explosion in the size of training datasets that one would otherwise have to collect to model human motion holistically. Other than the hierarchical GPLVM model, all of the models described above are holistic, not compositional (cf., [9]).

Another issue concerns generalization with respect to exogenous factors. Not surprisingly, human motion is often more variable in natural environments than in the laboratory. People do not walk the same way on a slippery ice rink as they would on the underlying concrete pad once the ice is removed. They lean while carrying heavy objects or walking up a steep hill. The motion of one person may also depend greatly on other nearby people, or on external objects like the ball that one attempts to drive with the swing of a baseball bat. Current kinematic motion models do not generalize naturally when such factors are in play. They do not maintain balance, adapt to ground slope or surface roughness for example. As a consequence, the 3D motions estimated with kinematic models are sometimes overtly implausible. Visible artifacts in tracking walking people include jerky motions, pose estimates for which the feet float above or penetrate the ground plane, foot-skate (where feet slide along the ground), and out-of-plane rotations that violate balance.

One way to build richer kinematic models is to gather much more mocap data, e.g., with varying ground slope, compliance, friction, roughness, loads or scene constraints, etc. But it remains unclear whether one would be able to collect such a voluminous amount of training data. And if one could do so, it is unclear how learning algorithms would be able to cope with the shear size of the resulting training corpus.

10.5 Newtonian (Physics-Based) Models

One way to mitigate some of the shortcomings of kinematic models is to incorporate constraints on motion and multi-body interactions based on Newtonian principles. For an articulated body with pose $\mathbf{y}$, the *equations of motion* from classical mechanics comprise a system of ordinary differential equations that relate accelerations, denoted $\ddot{\mathbf{y}}$, to forces:

$$\mathbf{M}\ddot{\mathbf{y}} = \mathbf{f}_{\text{joints}} + \mathbf{f}_{\text{gravity}} + \mathbf{f}_{\text{contact}} + \mathbf{a}. \qquad (10.28)$$

The mass matrix $\mathbf{M}$ depends on the mass, inertial properties and pose of the body. The right side of (10.28) includes internal joint forces (or torques), due mainly muscle activations. The external forces acting on the body include forces due to gravity $\mathbf{f}_{\text{gravity}}$ and external contact. Contact forces in turn depend on surface geometry and the dynamics of the contact interface between two bodies, like stiffness and friction for example. Finally, **a** denotes generalized Coriolis and centrifugal forces that occur with rotation and angular momentum. The equations of motion are somewhat tedious to derive properly, but articulated bodies typically permit textbook formulations. Importantly, many of these forces can be derived from first principles, and they provide important constraints on motion and interactions.

When combined with a suitable control mechanism, physics-based models offer several advantages over kinematic models. First, physics-based models should ensure that estimated motions are physically plausible, mitigating problems associated with foot placement and balance for example. Second, physics-based models should generalize in ways that are difficult for purely kinematic models. For example the change in body orientation that occurs as one carries a heavy load or walks down a steep hill should occur naturally to maintain balance. Third, the use of Newtonian and biomechanical principles of human locomotion may greatly reduce the current reliance on large corpora of human motion capture data. Indeed, many important characteristics of human locomotion can be attributed to optimality principles that produce stable, efficient gaits (e.g., [7, 32]). Last, but not least, interactions and environmental factors are central to physics-based models, so one should be able to exploit such models to simultaneously infer both human motion and the properties of the world with which the subject interacts.

Despite their potential, there is relatively little work on physics-based models for people tracking.[8] One barrier stems from the complexity of full-body dynamics and contact (e.g., [5]). Sensitivity to initial conditions, integration noise, and motion discontinuities at collisions mean that full-body simulation and control entail significant computational challenges. This remains true of modern humanoid robotics, biomechanics (e.g., [52]), and character animation (e.g., [39]).

10.5.1 Planar Models of Locomotion

Fortunately, there are reasons to believe that there exist low-dimensional abstractions of human locomotion which might be suitable for people tracking. Research in biomechanics and robotics has shown that the dynamics of bipedal walking is well described by relatively simple, planar, *passive-dynamic walking* models. Early models, such as those introduced by McGeer [42], were entirely passive and could walk downhill solely under the force of gravity; stable, bipedal walking is the natural limit cycle of their dynamics. Powered extensions of such models have since been built and studied to explore the biomechanical principles of human locomotion [7, 17, 32, 42]. They walk stably on level-ground, exhibiting human-like gaits and energy-efficiency, and they can be used to model the preferred relationship between speed and step-length in human walking [32].

---

[8]Several papers have used elastic solid models with depth inputs and a Kalman filter (e.g., [43, 80]); but these domains involve relatively simple dynamics with smooth, contact-free motions.

Inspired by these abstractions, Brubaker et al. [2, 3] developed two models of human walking, the *Anthropomorphic Walker* and the *Kneed Walker* (see Fig. 10.9). These models exhibit essential physical properties, namely balance and ground contact, while walking and running with human-like gaits and efficiency. The Kneed Walker comprises a torso, two legs with knees, and a rounded foot that rolls along the ground to simulate the effects of ankle articulation. The model's kinematic, mass and inertial parameters are drawn from the biomechanics literature [42, 52]. Model forces are parameterized as linear torsional springs (i.e., joint-based PD controllers).

One fascinating property of such models is that a good prior model can be found through controller optimization, rather than fitting mocap data. Brubaker et al. [2] were able to optimize many controllers for different operating points (e.g., ground slopes, locomotion speeds and step-lengths), thereby defining an effective manifold of control settings. Their probabilistic model was defined in the vicinity of this manifold by adding Gaussian noise to the optimal control parameters. A random gait could then be produced by randomly drawing the control parameters and simulating the model using the equations of motion. This dynamics model is low-dimensional and exhibits stable human-like gaits with realistic ground contact, all in the 2D sagittal plane. The 3D kinematic model is then constrained to be consistent with the planar dynamics, and to move smoothly in its remaining degrees of freedom (DOF).

Tracking was performed using physical simulation within a particle filter (see Fig. 10.9). The tracker handled occlusion, varying gait styles, and turning, producing realistic 3D reconstructions. With lower-body occlusions, it still produced realistic reconstructions and estimate the time and location of ground contact. When applied to the benchmark HUMANEVA dataset, monocular tracking errors in joint position are in the 65 mm–100 mm range [3]. Importantly, the prior model for this tracker does not rely on mocap training data from the same subjects performing the same motions like most other techniques that have been tested on HUMANEVA.

10.5.2 Discussion: 3D Full-Body Models

Recent research has begun to consider physics-based models for full-body 3D control, motivated in part by the success of optimal planar models [2, 3] and the state-space SIMBICON controller [81]. In particular, Wang et al. [78, 79] have shown that human-like bipedal motion can be obtained by optimizing joint-space controllers with a collection of objective criteria motivated by empirical findings in biomechanics. The resulting motions appear reasonably natural, and adapt readily to different body morphologies (e.g., tall or short), different environmental constraints (e.g., walking on ice, or a narrow beam), and to various forms of uncertainty in either environmental conditions (e.g., wind or surface roughness) or internal noise (e.g., neural motor noise). While fascinating, such controllers are difficult to learn with over a hundred degrees of freedom, and they have not yet exhibited the degree of stylistic variation that one might need to track arbitrary people.

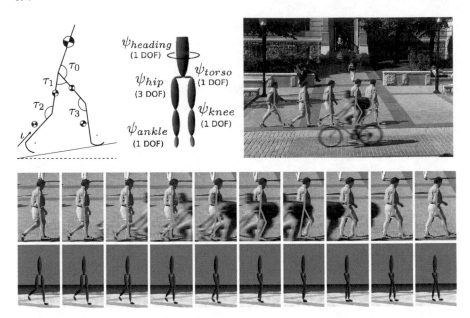

Fig. 10.9 (*Top row*) Composite of image sequence showing a walking subject and an occluding cyclist. The green stick figure in the right composite depicts on the MAP estimate of the pose on selected frames. (*Bottom two rows*) Cropped frames around occlusion. The green skeleton and blue 3D rendering depict the recovered MAP trajectory. (Adapted from [2])

Another largely untapped research direction concerns the inference of human interactions with the environment. Brubaker et al. [4] have recently proposed a generic framework for estimating external forces due to gravity and surface contact from human motion. They define a generic measure of physical realism for human motion, and optimize various exogenous factors (e.g., gravity, ground plane position and orientation) that are necessary to maximize realism. Initial results on motion capture data are very good, and results on video-based motion information are encouraging. With general 3D formulations like this we might hope to build models of human motion that readily cope with ambiguity and noise without resorting to activity-specific latent variable models that are commonly used today.

10.6 Discussion

Progress in modeling human motion has been significant over the last decade, but many research directions remain unexplored. As discussed above, kinematic models have to move beyond activity-specific motions to much more complex sequences of multiple activities and natural transitions between them. Compositionality is largely unexplored, as is the related issue concerning a suitable computational definition of atomic motion primitives, in terms of which complex motions can be decomposed.

The use of dynamics is in its infancy. Open questions include the use of full-body 3D control mechanisms, and the ability to use physical principles to help detect and infer human interactions. Finding good control mechanisms appears essential for modeling human motion with effective, low-dimensional parameterizations. Physics-based models should also apply to biological motion in general, since the basic principles of locomotion appear common to bipeds and quadrupeds. Finally, there are many potential ways in which physics might be augmented with kinematic properties learned from motion capture data.

Acknowledgements   Many thanks to research colleagues with whom I have worked on modeling human motion: Michael Black, Marcus Brubaker, Aaron Hertzmann, Geoff Hinton, Hedvig Kjellström, Neil Lawrence, Roland Memisevic, Leonid Sigal, Graham Taylor, Niko Troje, Raquel Urtasun, and Jack Wang. We gratefully acknowledge generous financial support from NSERC Canada and the Canadian Institute for Advanced Research (CIfAR).

References

1. Andriluka, M., Roth, S., Schiele, B.: Monocular 3d pose estimation and tracking by detection. In: IEEE Computer Society Conference on Computer Vision and Pattern Recognition (2010) [186]
2. Brubaker, M.A., Fleet, D.J.: The kneed walker for human pose tracking. In: IEEE Computer Society Conference on Computer Vision and Pattern Recognition (2008) [193,194]
3. Brubaker, M.A., Fleet, D.J., Hertzmann, A.: Physics-based person tracking using the anthropomorphic walker. Int. J. Comput. Vis. **87**(1–2), 140–155 (2010) [193]
4. Brubaker, M.A., Sigal, L., Fleet, D.J.: Estimating contact dynamics. In: IEEE International Conference on Computer Vision, pp. 2389–2396 (2009) [194]
5. Brubaker, M.A., Sigal, L., Fleet, D.J.: Physics-based human motion modeling for people tracking: A short tutotial. In: Notes from IEEE ICCV Tutorial (2009). (Available from http://www.cs.toronto.edu/~ls/iccv2009tutorial/) [192]
6. Choo, K., Fleet, D.J.: People tracking using hybrid Monte Carlo filtering. In: IEEE International Conference on Computer Vision, vol. II, pp. 321–328 (2001) [173]
7. Collins, S.H., Ruina, A.: A bipedal walking robot with efficient and human-like gait. In: International Conference on Robotics and Automation (2005) [192]
8. Corazza, S., Muendermann, L., Chaudhari, A., Demattio, T., Cobelli, C., Andriacchi, T.: A markerless motion capture system to study musculoskeletal biomechanics: Visual hull and simulated annealing approach. Ann. Biomed. Eng. **34**(6), 1019–1029 (2006) [171]
9. Darby, J., Li, B., Costens, N., Fleet, D.J., Lawrence, N.D.: Backing off: Hierarchical decomposition of activity for 3d novel pose recovery. In: British Machine Vision Conference (2009) [186,187,191]
10. de La Gorce, M., Fleet, D.J., Paragios, N.: Model-based 3d hand pose estimation from monocular video. IEEE Trans. Pattern Anal. Mach. Intell. **33**(9), 1793–1805 (2011) [174]
11. Deutscher, J., Reid, I.: Articulated body motion capture by stochastic search. Int. J. Comput. Vis. **61**(2), 185–205 (2005) [173-175]
12. Doretto, G., Chiuso, A., Wu, Y.N., Soatto, S.: Dynamic textures. Int. J. Comput. Vis. **51**(2), 91–109 (2003) [176]
13. Doucet, A., Godsill, S., Andrieu, C.: On sequential Monte Carlo sampling methods for Bayesian filtering. Stat. Comput. **10**(3), 197–208 (2000) [173]
14. Elgammal, A.M., Lee, C.-S.: Inferring 3d body pose from silhouettes using activity manifold learning. In: IEEE Computer Society Conference on Computer Vision and Pattern Recognition, vol. 2, pp. 681–688 (2004) [178]

15. Elgammal, A.M., Lee, C.-S.: Separating style and content on a nonlinear manifold. In: IEEE Computer Society Conference on Computer Vision and Pattern Recognition, vol. 1, pp. 478–485 (2004) [186]

16. Fox, E.B., Sudderth, E.B., Jordan, M.I., Willsky, A.S.: Nonparametric Bayesian learning of switching linear dynamical systems. In: Advances in Neural Information Processing Systems, pp. 457–464 (2008) [187]

17. Full, R.J., Koditschek, D.E.: Templates and anchors: Neuromechanical hypotheses of legged locomotion on land. J. Exp. Biol. **202**, 3325–3332 (1999) [192]

18. Gall, J., Rosenhahn, B., Brox, T., Seidel, H.-P.: Optimization and filtering for human motion capture. Int. J. Comput. Vis. **87**(1–2), 75–92 (2010) [171]

19. Gordon, N.J., Salmond, D.J., Smith, A.F.M.: Novel approach to nonlinear/non-Gaussian Bayesian state estimation. IEE Proc., F, Radar Signal Process. **140**, 107–113 (1993) [173]

20. Grochow, K., Martin, S.L., Hertzmann, A., Popovic, Z.: Style-based inverse kinematics. ACM Trans. Graph. **23**(3), 522–531 (2004) [180]

21. Hauberg, S., Sommer, S., Pedersen, K.S.: Gaussian-like spatial priors for articulated tracking. In: European Conference on Computer Vision, vol. 1, pp. 425–437 (2010) [174]

22. Herda, L., Urtasun, R., Fua, P.: Hierarchical implicit surface joint limits for human body tracking. Comput. Vis. Image Underst. **99**(2), 189–209 (2005) [174]

23. Hinton, G.E.: Training products of experts by minimizing contrastive divergence. Neural Comput. **14**(8), 1771–1800 (2002) [189]

24. Hinton, G.E.: A practical guide to training restricted Boltzmann machines. Technical Report UTML TR 2010-003, Department of Computer Science, University of Toronto (2010) [190]

25. Hinton, G.E., Osindero, S., Teh, Y.W.: A fast learning algorithm for deep belief nets. Neural Comput. **18**(7), 1527–1554 (2006) [189]

26. Hou, S., Galata, A., Caillette, F., Thacker, N.A., Bromiley, P.A.: Real-time body tracking using a Gaussian process latent variable model. In: IEEE International Conference on Computer Vision (2007) [173]

27. Howe, N.R., Leventon, M.E., Freeman, W.T.: Bayesian reconstruction of 3d human motion from single-camera video. In: Advances in Neural Information Processing Systems, pp. 820–826 (1999) [173]

28. Hyndman, M., Jepson, A.D., Fleet, D.J.: Higher-order autoregressive models for dynamic textures. In: British Machine Vision Conference (2007) [176]

29. Isard, M., Blake, A.: CONDENSATION – Conditional density propagation for visual tracking. Int. J. Comput. Vis. **29**(1), 5–28 (1998) [173]

30. Kakadiaris, L., Metaxas, D.: Model-based estimation of 3D human motion. IEEE Trans. Pattern Anal. Mach. Intell. **22**(12), 1453–1459 (2000) [171]

31. Kong, A., Liu, J.S., Wong, W.H.: Sequential imputations and Bayesian missing data problems. J. Am. Stat. Assoc. **89**(425), 278–288 (1994) [173]

32. Kuo, A.D.: A simple model of bipedal walking predicts the preferred speed–step length relationship. J. Biomech. Eng. **123**(3), 264–269 (2001) [192]

33. Lawrence, N.D.: Probabilistic non-linear principal component analysis with Gaussian process latent variable models. J. Mach. Learn. Res. **6**, 1783–1816 (2005) [178,180]

34. Lawrence, N.D., Moore, A.J.: Hierarchical Gaussian process latent variable models. In: International Conference on Machine Learning, pp. 481–488 (2007) [186]

35. Lawrence, N.D., Quiñonero-Candela, J.: Local distance preservation in the gp-lvm through back constraints. In: International Conference on Machine Learning, pp. 513–520 (2006) [184]

36. Li, R.: Simultaneous learning of non-linear manifold and dynamical models for high-dimensional time series. PhD thesis, Boston University (2009) [187,188]

37. Li, R., Tian, T.-P., Sclaroff, S., Yang, M.-H.: 3d human motion tracking with a coordinated mixture of factor analyzers. Int. J. Comput. Vis. **87**(1–2), 170–190 (2010) [187,188]

38. Li, R., Yang, M.-H., Sclaroff, S., Tian, T.-P.: Monocular tracking of 3d human motion with a coordinated mixture of factor analyzers. In: European Conference on Computer Vision, vol. 2, pp. 137–150 (2006) [173,187,188]

39. Liu, C.K., Hertzmann, A., Popović, Z.: Learning physics-based motion style with nonlinear inverse optimization. ACM Trans. Graph. **24**(3), 1071–1081 (2005) [192]
40. Lu, Z., Carreira-Perpiñán, M.Á., Sminchisescu, C.: People tracking with the Laplacian eigenmaps latent variable model. In: Advances in Neural Information Processing Systems, pp. 1705–1712 (2007) [173]
41. MacKay, D.J.C.: Information Theory, Inference, and Learning Algorithms. Cambridge University Press, Cambridge (2003) [180]
42. McGeer, T.: Dynamics and control of bipedal locomotion. J. Theor. Biol. **163**, 277–314 (1993) [192,193]
43. Metaxas, D., Terzopoulos, D.: Shape and nonrigid motion estimation through physics-based synthesis. IEEE Trans. Pattern Anal. Mach. Intell. **15**(6), 580–591 (1993) [173]
44. North, B., Blake, A., Isard, M., Rittscher, J.: Learning and classification of complex dynamics. IEEE Trans. Pattern Anal. Mach. Intell. **22**(9), 1016–1034 (2000) [174,187]
45. Oh, S.M., Rehg, J.M., Balch, T.R., Dellaert, F.: Learning and inferring motion patterns using parametric segmental switching linear dynamic systems. Int. J. Comput. Vis. **77**(1–3), 103–124 (2008) [187]
46. Pan, W., Torresani, L.: Unsupervised hierarchical modeling of locomotion styles. In: International Conference on Machine Learning, p. 99 (2009) [176]
47. Pavlovic, V., Rehg, J.M., MacCormick, J.: Learning switching linear models of human motion. In: Advances in Neural Information Processing Systems, pp. 981–987 (2000) [187]
48. Poon, E., Fleet, D.J.: Hybrid Monte Carlo filtering: Edge-based people tracking. In: Workshop on Motion and Video Computing, pp. 151–158 (2002) [174]
49. Quiñonero-Candela, J., Rasmussen, C.E.: A unifying view of sparse approximate Gaussian process regression. J. Mach. Learn. Res. **6**, 1939–1959 (2005) [184]
50. Raskin, L.M., Rivlin, E., Rudzsky, M.: Using Gaussian process annealing particle filter for 3d human tracking. EURASIP J. Adv. Sig. Proc. (2008) [173]
51. Rasmussen, C.E., Williams, C.K.I.: Gaussian Processes for Machine Learning. MIT Press, Cambridge (2006) [179,180]
52. Robertson, D.G.E., Caldwell, G.E., Hamill, J., Kamen, G., Whittlesey, S.N.: Research Methods in Biomechanics. Human Kinetics, Champaign (2004) [192,193]
53. Rose, C., Cohen, M.F., Bodenheimer, B.: Verbs and adverbs: Multidimensional motion interpolation. IEEE Comput. Graph. Appl. **18**(5), 32–40 (1998) [185]
54. Roweis, S.T., Saul, L.K.: Nonlinear dimensionality reduction by locally linear embedding. Science **290**(550), 2323–2326 (2000) [178,181]
55. Roweis, S.T., Saul, L.K., Hinton, G.E.: Global coordination of local linear models. In: Advances in Neural Information Processing Systems, pp. 889–896 (2001) [188]
56. Shoemake, K.: Animating rotation with quaternion curves. In: ACM Transactions on Graphics, pp. 245–254 (1985) [176]
57. Sidenbladh, H., Black, M.J., Fleet, D.J.: Stochastic tracking of 3d human figures using 2d image motion. In: European Conference on Computer Vision, vol. 2, pp. 702–718 (2000) [173,174,176,177]
58. Sigal, L., Balan, A.O., Black, M.J.: Humaneva: Synchronized video and motion capture dataset and baseline algorithm for evaluation of articulated human motion. Int. J. Comput. Vis. **87**(1–2), 4–27 (2010) [189]
59. Sigal, L., Fleet, D.J., Troje, N., Livne, M.: Human attributes from 3d pose tracking. In: European Conference on Computer Vision (2010) [176,177]
60. Sminchisescu, C., Jepson, A.: Generative modeling for continuous non-linearly embedded visual inference. In: International Conference on Machine Learning, pp. 759–766 (2004) [173,178]
61. Sminchisescu, C., Triggs, B.: Kinematic jump processes for monocular 3D human tracking. In: IEEE Computer Society Conference on Computer Vision and Pattern Recognition, vol. 1, pp. 69–76, Madison (2003) [173]
62. Taylor, G.W., Hinton, G.E.: Factored conditional restricted Boltzmann machines for modeling motion style. In: International Conference on Machine Learning (2009) [189]

63. Taylor, G.W., Hinton, G.E., Roweis, S.T.: Modeling human motion using binary latent variables. In: Advances in Neural Information Processing Systems, pp. 1345–1352 (2006) [189]
64. Taylor, G.W., Sigal, L., Fleet, D.J., Hinton, G.E.: Dynamical binary latent variable models for 3d human pose tracking. In: IEEE Computer Society Conference on Computer Vision and Pattern Recognition, pp. 631–638 (2010) [173,189,190]
65. Tenenbaum, J.B., Freeman, W.T.: Separating style and content with bilinear models. Neural Comput. **12**(6), 1247–1283 (2000) [185,186]
66. Troje, N.: Decomposing biological motion: A framework for analysis and synthesis of human gait patterns. J. Vis. **2**(5), 371–387 (2002) [176]
67. Urtasun, R., Fleet, D.J., Fua, P.: 3D people tracking with Gaussian process dynamical models. In: IEEE Computer Society Conference on Computer Vision and Pattern Recognition, vol. 1, pp. 238–245 (2006) [182,183]
68. Urtasun, R., Fleet, D.J., Hertzmann, A., Fua, P.: Priors for people tracking from small training sets. In: IEEE International Conference on Computer Vision, vol. 1, pp. 403–410 (2005) [178, 180,182]
69. Urtasun, R., Fleet, D.J., Fua, P.: Motion models for 3D people tracking. Comput. Vis. Image Underst. **104**(2–3), 157–177 (2006) [176-178]
70. Urtasun, R., Fleet, D.J., Geiger, A., Popovic, J., Darrell, T., Lawrence, N.D.: Topologically-constrained latent variable models. In: International Conference on Machine Learning, pp. 1080–1087 (2008) [184,185]
71. Van Overschee, P., De Moor, B.: N4SID: Subspace algorithms for the identification of combined deterministic-stochastic systems. Automatica **30**(1), 75–93 (1994) [176]
72. Vasilescu, M.A.O.: Human motion signatures: Analysis, synthesis, recognition. In: International Conference on Pattern Recognition, vol. III, pp. 456–460 (2002) [185,186]
73. Verbeek, J.J.: Learning nonlinear image manifolds by global alignment of local linear models. IEEE Trans. Pattern Anal. Mach. Intell. **28**(8), 1236–1250 (2006) [188]
74. Wachter, S., Nagel, H.H.: Tracking persons in monocular image sequences. Comput. Vis. Image Underst. **74**(3), 174–192 (1999) [173]
75. Wang, J.M.: Locomotion synthesis methods for humanoid characters. PhD thesis, University of Toronto (2010) [186]
76. Wang, J.M., Fleet, D.J., Hertzmann, A.: Multifactor Gaussian process models for style-content separation. In: International Conference on Machine Learning, pp. 975–982 (2007) [185]
77. Wang, J.M., Fleet, D.J., Hertzmann, A.: Gaussian process dynamical models for human motion. IEEE Trans. Pattern Anal. Mach. Intell. **30**(2), 283–298 (2008) [182-184]
78. Wang, J.M., Fleet, D.J., Hertzmann, A.: Optimizing walking controllers. ACM Trans. Graph. **28**(5) (2009) [193]
79. Wang, J.M., Fleet, D.J., Hertzmann, A.: Optimizing walking controllers for uncertain inputs and environments. ACM Trans. Graph. **29**(4) (2010) [193]
80. Wren, C.R., Pentland, A.: Dynamic models of human motion. In: International Conference on Automatic Face and Gesture Recognition, pp. 22–27 (1998) [173,192]
81. Yin, K., Loken, K., van de Panne, M.: Simbicon: Simple biped locomotion control. ACM Trans. Graph. **26**(3) (2007) [193]

Chapter 11
Part-Based Models for Finding People and Estimating Their Pose

Deva Ramanan

Abstract This chapter will survey approaches to person detection and pose estimation with the use of part-based models. After a brief introduction/motivation for the need for parts, the bulk of the chapter will be split into three core sections on Representation, Inference, and Learning. We begin by describing various gradient-based and color descriptors for parts. We next focus on representations for encoding structural relations between parts, describing extensions of classic pictorial structures models to capture occlusion and appearance relations. We will use the formalism of probabilistic models to unify such representations and introduce the issues of inference and learning. We describe various efficient algorithms designed for tree-structured models, as well as focusing on discriminative formalisms for learning model parameters. We finally end with applications of pedestrian detection, human pose estimation, and people tracking.

11.1 Introduction

Part models date back to the generalized cylinder models of Binford [3] and Marr and Nishihara [40] and the pictorial structures of Fischler and Elschlager [24] and Felzenszwalb and Huttenlocher [18]. The basic premise is that objects can be modeled as a collection of local templates that deform and articulate with respect to one another (Fig. 11.1).

Contemporary work: Part-based models have appeared in recent history under various formalisms. Felzenszwalb and Huttenlocher [18] directly use the pictorial structure moniker, but also notably develop efficient inference algorithms for matching them to images. Constellation models [7, 20, 64] take the same approach, but use a sparse set of parts defined at keypoint locations. Body plans [25] are another representation that encodes particular geometric rules for defining valid deformations of local templates.

D. Ramanan (✉)
Department of Computer Science, University of California, Irvine, USA
e-mail: dramanan@ics.uci.edu

T.B. Moeslund et al. (eds.), *Visual Analysis of Humans*,
DOI 10.1007/978-0-85729-997-0_11, © Springer-Verlag London Limited 2011

Star models: A particularly common form of geometric constraint is known as a "star model", which states that part placements are independent within some root coordinate frame. Visually speaking, one can think of springs connecting each part to some root bounding box. This geometric model can be implicitly encoded in an implicit shape model [38]. One advantage of the implicit encoding is that one can typically deal with a large vocabulary of parts, sometimes known as a codebook of visual words [57]. Oftentimes such codebooks are generated by clustering candidate patches typically found in images of people. Poselets [4] are recent successful extension of such a model, where part models are trained discriminatively using fully supervised data, eliminating the need for codebook generation through clustering. K-fan models generalize star models [9] by modeling part placements as independent given the location of K reference parts.

Tree models: Tree models are a generalization of star model that still allow for efficient inference techniques [18, 28, 45, 51]. Here, the independence assumptions correspond to child parts being independently placed in a coordinate system defined by their parent. One common limitation of such models is the so-called "double-counting" phenomena, where two estimated limbs cover the same image region because their positions are estimated independently. We will discuss various improvements designed to compensate for this limitation.

Related approaches: Active appearance models [8, 41] are a similar object representation that also decomposes an object into local appearance models, together with geometric constraints on their deformation. Notably, they are defined over continuous domains rather than a discretized state space, and so rely on continuous optimization algorithms for matching. Alternatively, part-based representations have also been used for video analysis by requiring similar optical flow for pixels on the same limb [5, 32].

11.2 Part Models

In this section, we will overview techniques for building localized part models. Given an image I and a pixel location $\mathbf{l}_i = (x_i, y_i)$, we write $\phi(I, \mathbf{l}_i)$ for the local descriptor for part i extracted from a fixed size image patch centered at $\mathbf{l}_i$. It is helpful to think of part models as fixed-size templates that will be used to generate part detections by scanning over the image and finding high-scoring patches. We will discuss linearly parameterized models where the local score for part i is computed with a dot product $\mathbf{w}_i \cdot \phi(I, \mathbf{l}_i)$. This allows one to use efficient convolution routines to generate scores at all locations in an image. To generate detections at multiple scales, one can search over an image pyramid. We will discuss more detailed parameterizations that include orientation and foreshortening effects in Sect. 11.3.2.

11.2.1 Color Models

The simplest part model is one directly based on pixel color. A head part should, for example, contain many skin pixels. This suggests that augmenting a head part template with a skin detector will be beneficial. In general, such color-based models will not work well for limbs because of intra-class variation; people can appear in a variety of clothes with various colors and textures. Indeed, this is one of the reasons why human pose estimation and detection is challenging. In some scenarios, one may know the appearance of clothing a priori; for example, consider processing sports footage with known team uniforms. We show in Sects. 11.4.2 and 11.6.3 that one can learn such color models automatically from a single image or a video sequence. Color models can be encoded non-parametrically with a histogram (e.g., 8 bins per RGB axis resulting in a $8^3 = 512$ descriptor), or a parametric model which is typically either a Gaussian or a mixture of Gaussians. In the case of a simple Gaussian, the corresponding color descriptor $\phi_{RGB}(I, \mathbf{l}_i)$ encodes standard sufficient statistics computed over a local patch; the mean ($\mu \in \mathbb{R}^3$) and covariance ($\Sigma \in \mathbb{R}^{3 \times 3}$) of the color distribution. We show an example of a part-specific color model in Fig. 11.2.

11.2.2 Oriented Gradient Descriptors

Most recognition approaches do not work directly with pixel data, but rather some feature representation designed to be more invariant to small changes in illumination, viewpoint, local deformation, etc. One of the most successful recent developments in object recognition is the development of engineered, invariant descriptors, such as the SIFT [39] and the HOG descriptor [10]. The basic approach is to work with normalized gradient orientation histograms rather than pixel values. We will go over HOG, as that is a particularly common representation. Image gradients are computed at each pixel by finite differencing. Gradients are then binned into one of (typically) 9 orientations over local neighborhoods of 8 × 8 pixel. A particularly simple implementation of this is obtained by computing histograms over non-overlapping neighborhoods. Finally, these orientation histograms are normalized by aggregating orientation statistics from a local window of 16 × 16 pixels (Fig. 11.3). Notably, in the original definition of [10], each orientation histogram is normalized with respect to multiple (4, to be exact) local windows, resulting in vector of 36 numbers to encode the local orientation statistics of a 8 × 8 neighborhood "cell". Felzenszwalb et al. [17] demonstrate that one can reduce the dimensionality of this descriptor to 13 numbers by looking at marginal statistics. The final histogram descriptor for a patch of $n_x \times n_y$ neighborhood cells is $\phi(I, \mathbf{l}_i) \in \mathbb{R}^{13 n_x n_y}$.

11.3 Structural Constraints

In this section, we describe approaches for composing the part models defined in the previous section into full body models.

Fig. 11.1 One the *left*, we
show a pictorial structure
model [18, 24] which models
objects using a collection of
local part templates together
with geometric constraints,
often visualized as springs.
On the *right*, we show a
pictorial structure for
capturing an articulated
human "puppet" of
rectangular limbs, where
springs have been drawn in
red for clarity. (Reproduced
with permission from [24])

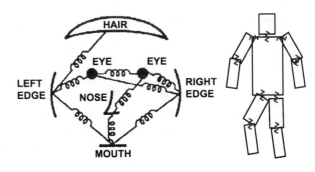

11.3.1 Linearly Parameterized Spring Models

Assume we have a K-part model, and let us write the location of the kth part as $\mathbf{l}_k$.
Let us write $\mathbf{x} = \{\mathbf{l}_1, \ldots, \mathbf{l}_K\}$ for a particular *configuration* of all K parts. Given an
image I, we wish to score each possible configuration $\mathbf{x}$:

$$S(I, \mathbf{x}) = \sum_{i=1}^{K} \mathbf{w}_i \cdot \phi(I, \mathbf{l}_i) + \sum_{i,j \in E} \mathbf{w}_{ij} \cdot \psi(I, \mathbf{l}_i, \mathbf{l}_j). \tag{11.1}$$

We would like to maximize the above equation over $\mathbf{x}$, so that for a given image,
our model can report the best-scoring configuration of parts.

Appearance term: We write $\phi(I, \mathbf{l}_i)$ for the image descriptor extracted from
location $\mathbf{l}_i$ in image I, and $\mathbf{w}_i$ for the HOG filter for part i. This local score is akin
to the linear template classifier described in the previous section.

Deformation term: Writing $dx = x_j - x_i$ and $dy = y_j - y_i$, we can now define

$$\psi(I, \mathbf{l}_i, \mathbf{l}_j) = \begin{bmatrix} dx & dx^2 & dy & dy^2 \end{bmatrix}^T \tag{11.2}$$

which can be interpreted as the negative spring energy associated with pulling part j
from a canonical relative location with respect to part i. The parameters $\mathbf{w}_{ij}$ specify
the rest location of the spring and its rigidity; some parts may be easier to shift
horizontally versus vertically. In Sect. 11.3.3, we derive these linear parameters from
a Gaussian assumption on relative location, where the rest position of the spring is
the mean of the Gaussian, and rigidity is specified by the covariance of the Gaussian.
    We define E to be the (undirected) edge set for a K-vertex relational graph
$G = (V, E)$ that denotes which parts are constrained to have particular relative locations. Intuitively, one can think of G as the graph obtained from Fig. 11.1 by replacing parts with vertices and springs with edges. Felzenszwalb and Huttenlocher [18]

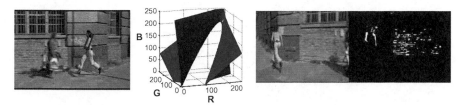

Fig. 11.2 On the *left*, pixels used to train a color-based model for an arm. Pixels inside the red rectangle are treated as positive examples, while pixels outside are treated as negatives. On the *left center*, we show the discriminant boundary learned by a classifier (specifically, logistic regression defined on quadratic RGB features). On the *right* two images, we show a test image and arm-pixel classification results using the given discriminant boundary. (Reproduced with permission from [48] ©2005 IEEE)

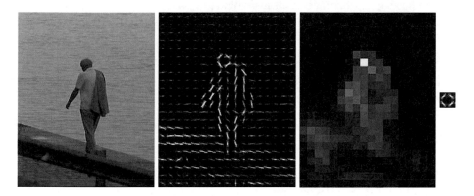

Fig. 11.3 On the *left*, we show an image. On the *center left*, we show its representation under a HOG descriptor [10]. A common visualization technique is to render an oriented edge with intensity equal to its histogram count, where the histogram is computed over a 8×8 pixel neighborhood. We can use the same technique to visualize linearly parameterized part models; we show a "head" part model on the *right*, and its associated response map for all candidate head location on the *center right*. We see a high response for the true head location. Such invariant representations are useful for defining part models when part colors are not known a priori or not discriminative

show that this deformation model admits particularly efficient inference algorithms when G is a tree (as is the case for the body model in the right of Fig. 11.1).

For greater flexibility, one could also make the deformation term depend on the image I. For example, one might desire consistency in appearance between left and right body parts, and so one could augment $\psi(I, \mathbf{l}_i, \mathbf{l}_j)$ with squared difference between color histograms extracted at locations $\mathbf{l}_i$ and $\mathbf{l}_j$ [62]. Finally, we note that the score can be written as a function of the part appearance and spatial parameters:

$$S(I, \mathbf{x}) = \mathbf{w} \cdot \Phi(I, \mathbf{x}),$$

where $\mathbf{w}$ is a concatenated vector of part templates $\mathbf{w}_i$ and pairwise springs $\mathbf{w}_{ij}$, while $\Phi(I, \mathbf{x})$ is a concatenated vector of HOG descriptors $\phi(I, \mathbf{l}_i)$ and relative offsets $\psi(I, \mathbf{l}_i, \mathbf{l}_j)$.

11.3.2 Articulation

The classic approach to modeling articulated parts is to augment part location $\mathbf{l}_i$ with pixel position, orientation, and foreshortening

$$\mathbf{l}_i = (x_i, y_i, \theta_i, s_i).$$

This requires augmenting the spatial relational model (11.2) with model of relative orientation and relative foreshortening, as well as relative location. Notably, this enhanced parameterization increases the computational burden of scoring the local model, since one must convolve an image with a family of rotated and foreshortened part templates.

While [18] advocates explicitly modeling foreshortening, recent work [1, 45, 49, 50] appears to obtain good results without it, relying on the ability of the local detectors to be invariant to small changes in foreshortening. [49] also demonstrates that by formulating the above scoring function in probabilistic terms and extracting the *uncertainty* in estimates of body pose (done by computing marginals), one can estimate foreshortening. In general, parts may also differ in appearance due to other factors such as out-of-plane rotations (e.g., frontal versus profile faces) and semantic part states (e.g., an open versus a closed hand).

In recent work, [65] foregoes an explicit modeling of articulation, and instead model oriented limbs with mixtures of non-articulated part models—see Sect. 11.6.2. This has the computational advantage of sharing computation between articulations (typically resulting in orders of magnitude speedups), while allowing mixture models to capture other appearance phenomena such as out-of-plane orientation, semantic part states, etc.

11.3.3 Gaussian Tree Models

In this section, we will develop a probabilistic graphical model over part locations and image features. We will show that the log posterior of part locations given image features can be written in the form of (11.1). This provides an explicit probabilistic motivation for our scoring function, and also allows for the direct application of various probabilistic inference algorithms (such as sampling or belief propagation). We will also make the simplifying assumption that the relational graph $G = (V, E)$ is a directed tree rooted at part/vertex $i = 1$. This will allow for tractable inference algorithms and will also simplify our exposition.

Spatial prior: Let us first define a prior over a configuration of parts $\mathbf{x}$. We assume this prior factors into a product of local terms:

$$p(\mathbf{x}) = p(\mathbf{l}_1) \prod_{ij \in E} p(\mathbf{l}_j | \mathbf{l}_i). \tag{11.3}$$

The first term is a prior over locations of the root part, which is typically the torso. To maintain a translation invariant model, we will set $p(\mathbf{l}_1)$ is to be uninformative.

The next terms specify spatial priors over the location of a part given its parent in the directed graph G. We model them as diagonal-covariance Gaussian density defined the relative location of part i and j:

$$p(\mathbf{l}_j|\mathbf{l}_i) = \mathcal{N}(\mathbf{l}_j - \mathbf{l}_i; \mu_j, \Sigma_j) \quad \text{where} \quad \Sigma_j = \begin{bmatrix} \sigma_{j,x} & 0 \\ 0 & \sigma_{j,y} \end{bmatrix}. \tag{11.4}$$

The ideal rest position of part j with respect to its parent is given by μ_j. If part j is more likely to deform horizontally rather an vertically, one would expect $\sigma_{j,x} > \sigma_{j,y}$.

Feature likelihood: We would like a probabilistic model that explains all features observed at all locations in an image, including those generated by parts and those generated by a background model. We write L for the set of all possible locations in an image. We denote the full set of observed features as

$$\{\phi(I, \mathbf{l}') \,|\, \mathbf{l}' \in L\}.$$

If we imagine a pre-processing step that first finds a set of candidate part detections (e.g., candidate torsos, heads, etc.), we can intuitively think of L as the set of locations associated with all candidates. Image features at a subset of locations $\mathbf{l}_i \in L$ are generated from an appearance model for part i, while all other locations from L (not in $\mathbf{x}$) generate features from a background model:

$$p(I|\mathbf{x}) = \prod_i p_i\big(\phi(I, \mathbf{l}_i)\big) \prod_{\mathbf{l}' \in L \backslash \mathbf{x}} p_{bg}\big(\phi(I, \mathbf{l}')\big)$$

$$= Z \prod_i r\big(\phi(I, \mathbf{l}_i)\big),$$

$$\text{where} \quad r\big(\phi(I, \mathbf{l}_i)\big) = \frac{p_i(\phi(I, \mathbf{l}_i))}{p_{bg}(\phi(I, \mathbf{l}_i))} \quad \text{and} \quad Z = \prod_{\mathbf{l}' \in L} p_{bg}\big(\phi(I, \mathbf{l}')\big). \tag{11.5}$$

We write $p_i(\phi(I, \mathbf{l}_i))$ for the image likelihood of observing feature $\phi(I, \mathbf{l}_i)$ given an appearance model for part i. We write $p_{bg}(\phi(I, \mathbf{l}'))$ for the likelihood of observing feature $\phi(I, \mathbf{l}')$ given a background appearance model. The overall likelihood is, up to a constant, only dependent on features observed at part locations. Specifically, it depends on the *likelihood ratio* of observing the features given a part model versus a background model. Let us assume the image feature likelihood in (11.5) are Gaussian densities with a part or background-specific mean α and a single covariance Σ:

$$p_i\big(\phi(I, \mathbf{l}_i)\big) = \mathcal{N}\big(\phi(I, \mathbf{l}_i); \alpha_i, \Sigma\big) \quad \text{and} \quad p_{bg}\big(\phi(I, \mathbf{l}_i)\big) = \mathcal{N}\big(\phi(I, \mathbf{l}_i); \alpha_{bg}, \Sigma\big). \tag{11.6}$$

Log-linear posterior: The relevant quantity for inference, the posterior, can now be written as a log-linear model:

$$p(\mathbf{x}|I) \propto p(I|\mathbf{x}) P(\mathbf{x}) \tag{11.7}$$

$$\propto \exp^{\mathbf{w} \cdot \Phi(I, \mathbf{x})}, \tag{11.8}$$

where w and $\Phi(I, \mathbf{x})$ are equivalent to their definitions in Sect. 11.3.1. Specifically, one can map Gaussian mean and variances to linear parameters as below, providing a probabilistic motivation for the scoring function from (11.1).

$$\mathbf{w}_i = \Sigma^{-1}(\alpha_i - \alpha_{bg}), \qquad \mathbf{w}_{ij} = -\left[\frac{\mu_{j,x}}{\sigma_{j,x}^2} \quad \frac{1}{2\sigma_{j,x}^2} \quad \frac{\mu_{j,y}}{\sigma_{j,y}^2} \quad \frac{1}{2\sigma_{j,y}^2} \right]^T. \tag{11.9}$$

Note that one can relax the diagonal-covariance assumption in (11.4) and part-independent covariance assumption in (11.6) and still obtain a log-linear posterior, but this requires augmenting $\Phi(I, \mathbf{x})$ to include quadratic terms.

11.3.4 Inference

MAP estimation: Inference corresponds to maximizing $S(I, \mathbf{x})$ from (11.1) over $\mathbf{x}$. When the relational graph $G = (V, E)$ is a tree, this can be done efficiently with Dynamic Programming (DP). Let kids(j) be the set of children of j in E. We compute the message part j passes to its parent i by

$$\text{score}_j(\mathbf{l}_j) = \mathbf{w}_j \cdot \phi(I, \mathbf{l}_j) + \sum_{k \in \text{kids}(j)} m_k(\mathbf{l}_j), \tag{11.10}$$

$$m_j(\mathbf{l}_i) = \max_{\mathbf{l}_j} \text{score}_j(\mathbf{l}_j) + \mathbf{w}_{ij} \cdot \psi(I, \mathbf{l}_i, \mathbf{l}_j). \tag{11.11}$$

Equation (11.10) computes the local score of part j, at all pixel locations $\mathbf{l}_j$, by collecting messages from the children of j. Equation (11.11) computes for every location of part i, the best scoring location of its child part j. Once messages are passed to the root part ($j = 1$), score$_1(\mathbf{l}_1)$ represents the best scoring configuration for each root position. One can use these root scores to generate multiple detections in image I by thresholding them and applying non-maximum suppression (NMS). By keeping track of the argmax indices, one can backtrack to find the location and type of each part in each maximal configuration.

Computation: The computationally taxing portion of DP is (11.11). Assume that there are $|L|$ possible discrete pixel locations in an image. One has to loop over $|L|$ possible parent locations, and compute a max over $|L|$ possible child locations and types, making the computation $O(|L|^2)$ for each part. When $\psi(I, \mathbf{l}_i, \mathbf{l}_j)$ is a quadratic function of relative part locations ($\mathbf{l}_j - \mathbf{l}_i$) and L is a set of locations on a pixel grid (as is the case for us), the inner maximization in (11.11) can be efficiently computed in $O(|L|)$ with a max-convolution or distance transform [18], making the overall maximization $O(|L|K)$ for a K-part model.

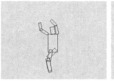

Fig. 11.4 Felzenszwalb and Huttenlocher [18] describe efficient dynamic programming algorithms for computing the MAP body configuration, as well as efficient algorithms for sampling from the posterior over body configurations. Given the image and foreground silhouette (used to construct part models) on the *left*, we show two sampled body configurations on the *right* two images. (Reproduced with permission from [18])

Sampling: Felzenszwalb and Huttenlocher [18] also point out that tree models allow for efficient sampling (Fig. 11.4). As opposed to traditional approaches to sampling, such as Gibbs sampling or MCMC methods, sampling from a tree-structured model requires *zero burn-in time*. This is because one can directly compute the root marginal $p(\mathbf{l}_1|I)$ and pairwise conditional marginals $p(\mathbf{l}_j|\mathbf{l}_i, I)$ for all edges $i, j \in E$ with the sum-product algorithm (analogous to the forward-backward algorithm for inference on discrete Hidden Markov Models). The forward pass corresponds to "upstream" messages, passed from part j to its parent i:

$$p(\mathbf{l}_j|\mathbf{l}_i, I) \propto p(\mathbf{l}_j|\mathbf{l}_i)a_j(\mathbf{l}_j), \tag{11.12}$$

$$a_j(\mathbf{l}_j) \propto \exp^{\mathbf{w}_j \cdot \phi(I,\mathbf{l}_j)} \prod_{k \in \text{kids}(j)} \sum_{\mathbf{l}_k} p(\mathbf{l}_k|\mathbf{l}_j, I). \tag{11.13}$$

When part location $\mathbf{l}_i$ is parameterized by an (x, y) pixel position, one can represent the above terms as 2D images. The image a_j is obtained by multiplying together response images from the children of part j and from the local template $\mathbf{w}_j$. When $p(\mathbf{l}_j|\mathbf{l}_i) = f(\mathbf{l}_j - \mathbf{l}_i)$, the summation in (11.13) can be computed by convolving image a_k with filter f. When using a Gaussian spatial model (11.4), the filter is a standard Gaussian smoothing filter, for which many efficient implementations exist. At the root, the image $a_1(\mathbf{l}_1)$ is the true conditional marginal $p(\mathbf{l}_1|I)$. Given cached tables of $p(\mathbf{l}_1|I)$ and $p(\mathbf{l}_j|\mathbf{l}_i, I)$, one can efficiently generate samples by the following: Generate a sample from the root $\mathbf{l}_1' \sim p(\mathbf{l}_1|I)$, and then generate a sample from the next ordered part given its sampled parent: $\mathbf{l}_j' \sim p(\mathbf{l}_j|\mathbf{l}_i', I)$. Each involves a table lookup, making the overall sampling process very fast.

Marginals: It will also be convenient to directly compute singleton and pairwise marginals $p(\mathbf{l}_i|I)$ and $p(\mathbf{l}_j, \mathbf{l}_i|I)$ for parts and part-parent pairs. These marginals can be directly visualized to capture the uncertainty in pose (Fig. 11.5). This can be done by first computing the upstream messages in (11.13), where the root marginal is given by $p(\mathbf{l}_1|I) = a_1(\mathbf{l}_1)$. and then computing downstream messages from part i to its child part j:

$$p(\mathbf{l}_j, \mathbf{l}_i | I) = p(\mathbf{l}_j | \mathbf{l}_i, I) p(\mathbf{l}_i | I),$$
$$p(\mathbf{l}_j | I) = \sum_{\mathbf{l}_i} p(\mathbf{l}_j, \mathbf{l}_i | I). \tag{11.14}$$

11.4 Non-tree Models

In this section, we describe constraints and associated inference algorithms for non-tree relational models.

11.4.1 Occlusion Constraints

Tree-based models imply that left and right body limbs are localized independently given a root torso. Since left and right limb templates look similar, they may be attracted to the same image region. This often produces pose estimates whose left and right arms (or legs) overlap, or the so-called "double-counting" phenomena. Though such configurations are physically plausible, we would like to assign them a lower score than a configuration that explains more of the image. One can do this by introducing a constraint that an image region an only be claimed by a single part. There has been a body of work [33, 55, 59] developing layered occlusion models for part-based representations. Most do so by adding an additional visibility flag $v_i \in \{0, 1\}$ for part i:

$$p(I | \mathbf{x}, \mathbf{v}) = \prod_i p_i\big(\phi(I, \mathbf{l}_i)\big)^{v_i} \prod_{\mathbf{l}' \in L \backslash \mathbf{x}} p_{bg}\big(\phi(I, \mathbf{l}')\big), \tag{11.15}$$

$$p(\mathbf{v} | \mathbf{x}) \propto \prod_C \text{vis}(\mathbf{v}_C, \mathbf{l}_C), \tag{11.16}$$

where C is a clique of potentially overlapping parts, and vis is a binary visibility function that assigns 1 to valid configurations and visibility states (and 0 otherwise). One common approach is to only consider pairwise cliques of potentially overlapping parts (e.g., left/right limbs). In this case vis would assign 0 to configurations of left and right limbs that are overlapping and both labeled as visible. Such occlusion-aware models have been shown to reduce or eliminate the double-counting phenomena (Fig. 11.6). Other extensions include modeling visibility at the pixel level rather than the part level, allowing for parts to be partially visible [55]. During inference, one may marginalize out the visibility state $\mathbf{v}$ and simply estimate part locations $\mathbf{x}$, or simultaneously estimate both. In either case, probabilistic dependencies between left and right limbs violate classic tree independence assumptions—e.g., left and right limbs are no longer independently localized for a fixed root torso.

11.4.2 Appearance Constraints

People, and objects in general, tend to be consistent in appearance. For example, left and right limbs often look similar in appearance because clothes tend to be mirror symmetric [42, 46]. Upper and lower limbs often look similar in appearance, depending on the particular types of clothing worn (shorts versus pants, long sleeves versus short sleeves) [62]. Constraints can even be long-scale, as the hands and face of a person tend to have similar skin tones. Finally, an additional cue is that of *background* consistency; consider an image of a person standing on a green field. By enforcing the constraint that body parts are not green, one can essentially subtract out the background [21, 45].

Pairwise consistency: One approach to enforcing appearance constraints is to break them down into pairwise constraints on pairs of parts. One can do this by defining an augmented pairwise potential

$$\psi(I, \mathbf{l}_i, \mathbf{l}_j) = \left\| \phi_{\mathrm{RBG}}(I, \mathbf{l}_i) - \phi_{\mathrm{RGB}}(I, \mathbf{l}_j) v \right\|^2, \qquad (11.17)$$

where $\phi_{\mathrm{RBG}}(I, \mathbf{l}_i)$ are color models extracted from a window centered at location $\mathbf{l}_i$. One would need to augment the relational graph G with connections between pairs of parts with potential appearance constraints. The associated linear parameters would learn to what degree certain parts look consistent. Tran and Forsyth show such cues are useful [62]. Ideally, this consistency should depend on additional latent factors; if the person is wearing pants, both the upper, lower, left, and right leg should look consistent in appearance. We see such encodings as a worthwhile avenue of future research. Additionally, one can augment the above potentials with image-specific cues. For example, the lack of a strong intervening contour between a putative upper and lower arm location may be further evidence of a correct localization. Sapp et al. explore such cues in [52, 53].

Global consistency: Some appearance constraints, such as a background model, are non-local. To capture them, we can augment the entire model with latent appearance variables a.

$$\phi(I, \mathbf{l}_i, a) = \begin{bmatrix} \phi(I, \mathbf{l}_i) \\ f(\phi_{\mathrm{RGB}}(I, \mathbf{l}_i), a_i, a_{bg}) \end{bmatrix}, \qquad (11.18)$$

where we define a_i to be appearance of part i and a_{BG} is the appearance of the background. Ramanan [45] treats these variables as latent variables that are estimated simultaneously with part locations $\mathbf{l}_i$. This is done with an iterative inference algorithm whose steps are visualized in Fig. 11.5. Ferrari et al. [21] learn such variables by applying a foreground–background segmentation engine on the output of a upright person detector.

11.4.3 Inference with Non-tree Models

As we have seen, tree models allow for a number of efficient inference procedures. But we have also argued that there are many cues that do not decompose into tree constraints. We briefly discuss a number of extensions for non-tree models. Many of them originated in the tracking literature, in which (even tree-structured) part-

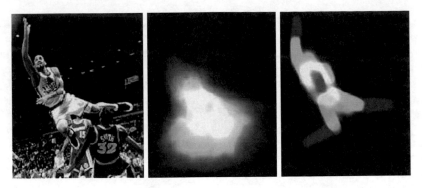

Fig. 11.5 One can compute part marginals using the sum-product algorithm [45]. Given part marginals, one can render a weighted rectangular mask at all image locations, where weights are given by the marginal probability. Lower limbs are rendered in blue, upper limbs and the head are rendered in green, and the torso is rendered in red. Regions of strong color correspond to pixels that likely to belong to a body part, according to the model. In the *center*, part models are defined using edge-based templates. On the *right*, part models are defined using color models. (Reproduced with permission from [45])

Fig. 11.6 Sigal and Black [55] demonstrate that the "double-counting" in tree models (*top row*) can be eliminated with an occlusion-aware likelihood model (*bottom row*). (Reproduced with permission from [55] ©2006 IEEE)

based models necessarily contain loops once one imposes a motion constraint on each part—e.g., an arm must not only lie near its parent torso, but must also lie near the arm position in the previous frame.

Mixtures of trees: One straightforward manner of introducing complexity into a tree model is to add a global, latent variable, making a mixture model $\mathbf{x} = \{l_1, \ldots, l_K, z_{\text{global}}\}$. For example, the latent variable could specify the viewpoint of the person; one may expect different spatial locations of parts given this latent variable. Given this latent variable, the overall model reduces to a tree. This suggests the following inference procedure:

$$\max_{\mathbf{x}} S(I, \mathbf{x}) = \max_{z_{\text{global}}} \max_{\{l_1,...,l_K\}} S(I, \mathbf{x}), \qquad (11.19)$$

where the inner maximization can exploit standard tree-based DP inference algorithms. Alternatively, one can compute a posterior by averaging the marginals produced by inference on each tree. Ioffe and Forsyth use such models to capture occlusion constraints [27]. Lan and Huttenlocher use mixture models to capture phases of a walking cycle [36], while Wang and Mori [63] use additive mixtures, trained discriminatively in a boosted framework, to model occlusion constraints between left/right limbs. Tian and Sclaroff point out that, if spring covariances are shared across different mixture components, one can reuse distance transform computations across mixtures [61]. Johnson and Everingham [31] demonstrate that part appearances may also depend on the mixture component (e.g., faces may appear frontally or in profile), and define a resulting mixture tree-model that is state-of-the-art.

Generating tree-based configurations: One approach is to use tree-models as a mechanism for generating candidate body configurations, and scoring the configurations using more complex non-tree constraints. Such an approach is similar to N-best lists common in speech decoding. However, in our case, the N-best configurations would tend to be near-duplicates—e.g., one-pixel shifts of the best-scoring pose estimate. Felzenszwalb and Huttenlocher [18] advocate the use of sampling to generate multiple configurations. These samples can be re-scored to obtain an estimate of the posterior over the full model, an inference technique known as importance sampling. Buehler et al. [6] argues that one obtains better samples by sampling from max-marginals. One promising area of research is the use of branch-and-bound algorithms for optimal matching. Tian and Sclaroff [60] point out that one can use tree structures to generate lower bounds which can be used to guide search over the space of part configurations.

Loopy belief propagation: A successful strategy for dealing with "loopy" models is to apply standard tree-based belief propagation (for computing probabilistic or max-marginals) in an iterative fashion. Such a procedure is not guaranteed to converge, but often does. In such situations it can be shown to minimize a variational approximation to the original probabilistic model. One can reconstruct full joint configurations from the max-marginals, even in loopy models [66].

Continuous state-spaces: There has also been a family of techniques that directly operate on a continuous state space of l_i rather than discretizing to the pixel grid. It is difficult to define probabilistic models on continuous state spaces. Because posteriors are multi-model, simple Gaussian parameterizations will not suffice. In the tracking literature, one common approach to adaptively discretize the search space using a set of samples or particles. Particle filters have the capability to capture non-Gaussian, multi-modal distributions. Sudderth et al. [58], Isard [29], and Sigal et al. [56] develop extensions for general graphical models, demonstrating results for the task of tracking articulated models in videos. In such approaches, samples for a part are obtained by a combination of sampling from the spatial prior $p(\mathbf{l}_j | \mathbf{l}_i)$ and the likelihood $p_i(\phi(I, \mathbf{l}_i))$. Techniques which focus on the latter are known as data-driven sampling techniques [26, 37].

11.5 Learning

The scoring functions and probabilistic models defined previously contain parameters specifying the appearance of each part $\mathbf{w}_i$ and parameters specifying the contextual relationships between parts $\mathbf{w}_{ij}$. We would like to set these parameters so that they reflect the statistics of the visual world. To do so, we assume training data given with images and annotated part locations $\{I^{(n)}, \mathbf{x}^{(n)}\}$. We also assume that the edge structure E is fixed and known (e.g., as shown in Fig. 11.1). We will describe a variety of methods for learning parameters given these data.

11.5.1 Generative Models

The simplest method for learning is to learn parameters that maximize the joint likelihood of the data:

$$\mathbf{w}_{ML} = \operatorname*{argmax}_{\mathbf{w}} \prod_n p\left(I^{(n)}, \mathbf{x}^{(n)} \mathbf{w}\right) \tag{11.20}$$

$$= \operatorname*{argmax}_{\mathbf{w}} \prod_n \prod_i p\left(I^{(n)} | \mathbf{l}_i^{(n)}, \mathbf{w}_i\right) \prod_{i,j \in E} p\left(\mathbf{l}_j^{(n)} | \mathbf{l}_i^{(n)}, \mathbf{w}_{ij}\right). \tag{11.21}$$

Recall that the weights $\mathbf{w}$ are a function of Gaussian parameters $\{\mu, \sigma, \alpha, \Sigma\}$ as in (11.9). We can learn each parameter by standard Gaussian maximum likelihood (ML) estimation, which requires computing sample estimates of means and variances. For example, the rest position for part i is given by the average relative location of part i with respect to its parent from the labeled data. The appearance template for part i is given by computing its average appearance, computing the average appearance of the background, and taking the difference weighted by a sample covariance.

11.5.2 Conditional Random Fields

One of the limitations of a probabilistic generative approach is that assumptions of independence and Gaussian parameterizations (typically made to ensure tractability) are not likely to be true. Another difficulty with generative models is that they are not tied directly to a pose estimation task. While generative models allow us to sample and generate images and configuration, we want a model that produces accurate pose estimates when used for *inference*.

Discriminative models are an attempt to accomplish the latter. One approach to doing this, advocated by [50], is to estimate parameters that maximize the posterior probability $p(\mathbf{x}^{(n)}|I^{(n)})$ over the training set:

$$\underset{\mathbf{w}}{\operatorname{argmax}} \prod_n p\left(\mathbf{x}^{(n)}|I^{(n)},\mathbf{w}\right). \tag{11.22}$$

This in turn can be written as

$$\underset{\mathbf{w}}{\operatorname{argmin}} L_{\mathrm{CRF}}(\mathbf{w}) \quad \text{where} \quad L_{\mathrm{CRF}}(\mathbf{w}) = \lambda\frac{1}{2}\|\mathbf{w}\|^2 + \sum_n Z_w\left(I^{(n)}\right) - \mathbf{w}\cdot\Phi\left(I^{(n)},\mathbf{x}^{(n)}\right)$$

$$\text{and} \quad Z_w\left(I^{(n)}\right) = \sum_{\mathbf{x}'} \exp^{\mathbf{w}\cdot\Phi(I^{(n)},\mathbf{x}')}, \tag{11.23}$$

where we have taken logs to simplify the expression (while preserving the argmax) and added an optional but common regularization term (to reduce the tendency to overfit parameters to training data). The second derivative of $L_{\mathrm{CRF}}(\mathbf{w})$ is non-negative, meaning that it is a convex function whose optimum can be found with simple gradient descent: $\mathbf{w} := \mathbf{w} + \text{stepsize}\frac{\partial L_{\mathrm{CRF}}(\mathbf{w})}{\partial \mathbf{w}}$. Ramanan and Sminchisescu [50] point out that such a model is an instance of a CRF [35], and show that the gradient is obtained by computing expected sufficient statistics, requiring access to posterior marginals $p(\mathbf{l}_i|I^{(n)},\mathbf{w})$ and $p(\mathbf{l}_i,\mathbf{l}_j|I^{(n)},\mathbf{w})$. This means that each iteration of gradient descent will require the two-pass "sum-product" inference algorithm (11.14) to compute the gradient for each training image.

11.5.3 Structured Max-margin Models

One can generalize the objective function from (11.23) to other types of losses. Assume that in addition to training images of people with annotated poses $\{I^{(n)},\mathbf{x}^{(n)}\}$, we are also given a negative set of images of backgrounds. One can use this training data to define a structured prediction objective function, similar to those proposed in [19, 34]. To do so, we note that, because the scoring function $S(I,\mathbf{x})$ is linear in model parameters w, it can be written as $S(I,\mathbf{x}) = \mathbf{w}\cdot\Phi(I,\mathbf{x})$.

$$\underset{\mathbf{w},\xi_n\geq 0}{\arg\min} \quad \lambda\frac{1}{2}\|\mathbf{w}\|^2 + \sum_n \xi_n$$

$$\text{s.t.} \quad \forall n \in \text{pos} \quad \mathbf{w}\cdot\Phi(I^{(n)},\mathbf{x}^{(n)}) \geq 1 - \xi_n$$

$$\forall n \in \text{neg}, \forall\mathbf{x} \quad \mathbf{w}\cdot\Phi(I^{(n)},\mathbf{x}) \leq -1 + \xi_n. \tag{11.24}$$

The above constraint states that positive examples should score better than 1 (the margin), while negative examples, for all configurations of parts, should score less than -1. The objective function penalizes violations of these constraints using slack variables ξ_n. Traditional structured prediction tasks do not require an explicit negative training set, and instead generate negative constraints from positive examples with mis-estimated labels $\mathbf{x}$. This corresponds to training a model that tends to score a ground-truth pose highly and alternate poses poorly. While this translates directly to a pose estimation task, the above formulation also includes a "detection" component: it trains a model that scores highly on ground-truth poses, but generates low scores on images without people. Recent work has shown the above to work well for *both* pose estimation and person detection [34, 65].

The above optimization is a Quadratic Programming (QP) with an exponential number of constraints, since the space of $\mathbf{x}$ is $|L|^K$. Fortunately, only a small minority of the constraints will be active on typical problems (e.g., the support vectors), making them solvable in practice. This form of learning problem is known as a structural SVM, and there exists many well-tuned solvers such as the cutting plane solver of SVMStruct [23] and the Stochastic Gradient Descent (SGD) solver in [17], and the dual decomposition method of [34].

11.5.4 Latent-Variable Structural Models

In many cases, it maybe difficult to obtain "reliable" estimates of part labels. Instead, assume every positive example comes with a domain X_n of possible latent values. For example, limb parts are often occluded by each other or the torso, making their precise location unknown. Because part models are defined in 2D rather than 3D, it is difficult for them to represent out-of-plane rotations of the body. Because of this, left/right limb assignments are defined with respect to the image, and not the coordinate system of the body (which maybe more natural when obtaining annotated data). For this reason, it also may be advantageous to encode left/right limb labels as latent.

Coordinate descent: In such cases, there is a natural algorithm to learn structured models with latent part locations. One begins with a guess for the part locations on positive examples. Given this guess, one can learn a w that minimizes (11.24) by solving a QP using a structured SVM solver. Given the learned model w, one can re-estimate the labels on the positive examples by running the current model: $\mathrm{argmax}_{\mathbf{x} \in X_n} \mathbf{w} \cdot \Phi(I^{(n)}, \mathbf{x}^{(n)})$. Felzenszwalb et al. [19] show that both these steps can be seen as coordinate descent on an auxiliary loss function that depends on both $\mathbf{w}$ and the latent values on positive examples $X_{\mathrm{pos}} = \{\mathbf{x}^{(n)} : n \in \mathrm{pos}\}$.

$$L_{\mathrm{SVM}}(\mathbf{w}, X_{\mathrm{pos}}) = \lambda \frac{1}{2} \|\mathbf{w}\|^2 + \sum_{n \in \mathrm{pos}} \max\left(0, 1 - \mathbf{w} \cdot \Phi\left(I^{(n)}, \mathbf{x}^{(n)}\right)\right)$$

$$+ \sum_{n \in \mathrm{neg}} \max_{\mathbf{x}}\left(0, 1 + \mathbf{w} \cdot \Phi\left(I^{(n)}, \mathbf{x}\right)\right). \quad (11.25)$$

We show examples of learned models in Fig. 11.7.

11.6 Applications

In this section, we briefly describe the application of part-based models for pedestrian detection, human pose estimation, and tracking. Please also see Chap. 4 for relevant discussion.

11.6.1 Pedestrian Detection

One important consideration with part-based representations is that object instances must be large enough to resolve and distinguish parts—it is, for example, hard to discern individual body parts on a 10 pixel-tall person. [43] describe an extension of part-based models that allow them to behave as rigid templates when evaluated on small instances (Fig. 11.8).

11.6.2 Pose Estimation

Popular benchmarks for pose estimation in unconstrained images include the parse dataset of [45] and the Buffy stickman dataset [21]. The dominant approach in the community is to use articulated models, where part locations $l_i = (x_i, y_i, \theta_i)$ include both pixel position and orientation. State-of-the-art methods with such an approach include [31, 52]. The latter uses a large set of heterogeneous image features, while the former uses the HOG descriptor described here.

Appearance constraints: Part templates by construction must be invariant to clothing appearance. But ideally, one would like to use templates tuned for a particular person in a given image, and furthermore, tuned to discriminate that person from the particular background. [45] describe an iterative approach that begins with invariant edge-based detectors and sequentially learns color-based part models tuned to the particular image. Specifically, one can compute posterior marginals $p(l_i|I, w)$ given clothing-invariant templates w. These posteriors provide weights for image windows as to how likely they belong to particular body parts. One can update templates w to include color information by taking a weighted average of features computed from these image windows, and repeat the procedure. Ferrari et al. [22] describe an alternate approach to learning color models by performing foreground/background segmentations on windows found by upper-body detectors (Fig. 11.9).

Mixtures of parts: [65] point out that one can model small rotations and foreshortenings of a limb template with a "local" part-based model parameterized solely by pixel position. To model large rotations, one can use a mixture of such part models. Combining such models for different limbs, one can obtain

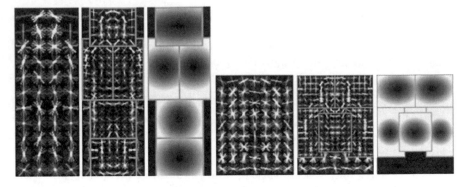

Fig. 11.7 We show the discriminative part models of Felzenszwalb et al. [17] trained to find people. The authors augment their latent model to include part locations and a discrete mixture component that, in this case, finds full (*left*) versus upper-body people (*right*). On benchmark datasets with occluded people, such as the well-known PASCAL Visual Object Challenge [15], such occlusion-aware models are crucial for obtaining good performance. Notably, these models are trained using weakly supervised benchmark training data that consist of bounding boxes encompassing the entire object. The part representation is learned automatically using the coordinate descent algorithm described in Sect. 11.5.4. (Reproduced with permission from [17] ©2010 IEEE)

Fig. 11.8 On the *left*, we show the discriminative part model of [17] (shown in Fig. 11.7) applied to the Caltech Pedestrian Benchmark [11]. The model performs well for instances with sufficient resolution to discern parts (roughly 80 pixels or higher), but does not detect small pedestrians accurately. We show the multiresolution part model of [43] (*right*) which behaves as a part-model for large instances and a rigid template for small instances. By tailoring models to specific resolutions, one can tune part templates for larger base resolutions, allowing for superior performance in finding both large and small people. (Reproduced with permission from [43])

a final part model where each part appearance can be represented with a mixture of templates. Importantly, the pairwise relational spring model must be extended to now model a collection of springs for each mixture combination, together with a co-occurrence constraint on particular mixture combinations. For example, two parts on the same limb should be constrained to always have consistent mixtures, while parts across different limbs may have different mixtures be-

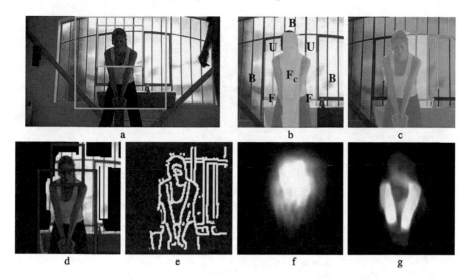

Fig. 11.9 The pose estimation algorithm of [22] begins by detecting upper bodies (using the discriminative part-model shown in Fig. 11.7), performing a local foreground/background segmentation, and using the learned foreground/background appearance models to produce the final posterior marginal over poses shown in (**g**). (Reproduced with permission from [22] ©2009 IEEE)

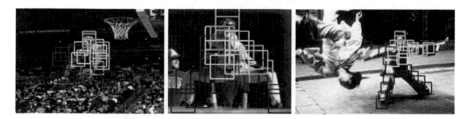

Fig. 11.10 We show pose estimation results from the flexible mixtures-of-part models from [65]. Rather than modeling parts as articulated rectangles, the authors use local mixtures of non-oriented part models to capture rotations and foreshortening effects. (Reproduced with permission from [65] ©2011 IEEE)

cause limbs can flex. Inference now corresponds to estimating both part locations l_i and mixture labels c_i. Inference on such models is fast, typically taking a second per image on standard benchmarks, while surpassing the performance of past work (Fig. 11.10).

11.6.3 Tracking

To obtain a model for tracking, one can replicate a K-part model for T frames, yielding a spatiotemporal part model with KT parts. However, the relational model E must be augmented to encode dynamic as well as kinematic constraints—an arm

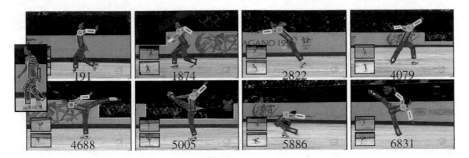

Fig. 11.11 We show tracking results from the appearance-model-building tracker of [49]. The styled pose detection (using edge-based part models invariant to clothing) is shown on the *left inset*. From this detection, the algorithm learns color appearance models for individual body parts. These models are used in a tracking-by-detection framework that tends to be robust and track for long sequences (as evidenced by the overlaid frame numbers). (Reproduced with permission from [49] ©2007 IEEE)

part must lie near its parent torso part *and* must lie near the arm part estimated in the previous frame. One can arrive at such a model by assuming a first-order Markovian model of object state:

$$p(\mathbf{x}_{1:T}, I_{1:T}) = \prod_t p(\mathbf{x}_t | \mathbf{x}_{t-1}) p(I_t | \mathbf{x}_t). \qquad (11.26)$$

By introducing high-order dependencies, the motion model $p(\mathbf{x}_t | \mathbf{x}_{t-1})$ can be augmented to incorporate physical dynamics (e.g., minimizing acceleration). If we restrict ourselves to first-order models and redefine $I = I_{1:T}$, we can use the same scoring function as (11.1):

$$S(I, \mathbf{x}_{1:T}) = \sum_{i=1}^{KT} \mathbf{w}_i \cdot \phi(I, \mathbf{l}_i) + \sum_{i,j \in E} \mathbf{w}_{ij} \cdot \psi(I, \mathbf{l}_i, \mathbf{l}_j), \qquad (11.27)$$

where the relational graph $G = (V, E)$ consists of KT vertices with edges capturing both spatial and temporal constraints. Temporal constraints add loops to the model, making global inference difficult (e.g., an estimated arm must lie near its parent torso and the estimated arm in the previous frame).

A popular approach to inference in such tracking models is the use of particle filters [12, 30, 54]. Here, the distribution over the state of the object $\mathbf{x}_t$ is represented by a set of particles. These particles are propagated through the dynamic model, and are then re-weighted by evaluating the likelihood. However, the likelihood can be highly multi-model in cluttered scenes. For example, there maybe many image regions that locally look like a limb, which can result in drifting particles latching onto the wrong mode. A similar, but related difficulty is that such trackers need to be hand-initialized in the first frame. Note that drifting and the requirement for hand initialization seem to be related, as one way to build a robust tracker is to continually re-initialize it. Nevertheless, particle filters have proved effective for scenarios in which manually initialization is possible, there exist strong likelihood models (e.g., background-subtracted image features), or one can assume strong dynamic models (e.g., known motion such as walking). Consequently a more thorough introduction to particle filtering is given in Chap. 9 and to dynamic models in Chap. 10.

Tracking by detection: One surprisingly effective strategy for inference is to remove the temporal links from (11.27), in which case inference reduces to an *independent* pose estimation task for each frame. Though computationally demanding, such "tracking by detection" approaches tend to be robust because an implicit tracker is re-initialized every frame. The resulting pose estimates will necessarily by temporally noisy, but one can apply low-pass filtering algorithms as a post-processing step to remove such noise [49].

Tracking by model-building: Model-based tracking should be easier with a better model. Ramanan and Forsyth [47] argue that this observation links together tracking and object detection; namely one should be able to track with a more accurate detector. This can be accomplished with a latent variable tracking model where object location *and* appearance are treated as unknown variables to be estimated. This is analogous to the appearance constraints described in Sect. 11.4.2, where an gradient-based part model was augmented with the latent RGB appearance.

One can apply this observation to tracking people: given an arbitrary video, part appearance models must initially be clothing-invariant. But when using part model in a tracking-as-detection framework, one ideally would like part models tuned to the appearance of particular people in the video. Furthermore, if there exist multiple people interacting with each other, one can use such appearance-specific models to disambiguate different people. One approach to doing this is to first detect people with a rough, but usable part model built on invariant edge-based part templates $\mathbf{w}_i$. By averaging together the appearance of detected body parts, one can learn instance specific appearance models $\mathbf{w}_i'$. One can exploit the fact that the initial part detection can operate at high precision and low recall; one can learn appearance from a sparse set of high-scoring detections, and then later use the known appearance to produce a dense track. This initial high-precision detection can be done *opportunistically* by tuning the detector for stylized poses such as lateral walking poses, where legs occupy a distinctive scissor profile [48] (Fig. 11.11).

11.7 Discussion and Open Questions

We have discussed part-based models for the task of detecting people, estimating their pose, and tracking them in video sequences. Part-based models have a rich history in vision, and currently produce state-of-the-art methods for general object recognition (as evidenced by the popular annual PASCAL Visual Object challenge [15]). A large part of their success is due to engineered feature representations (such as [10]) and structured, discriminative algorithms for tuning parameters. Various open-source codebases for part-based models include [14, 16, 44].

While detection and pose-estimation are most naturally cast as classification (does this window contain a person or not?) and regression (predict a vector of part locations), one would ideally like recognition systems to generate much more complex reports. Complexity may arise from more detailed description of the person's state, as well as contextual summaries that describe the relationship of a person to their surroundings. For example, one may wish to understand the visual attributes of people, including body shape [2], as well as the colors and articles of clothing being worn [37]. One may also wish to understand interactions with nearby objects and/or nearby people [13, 67].

Such reports are also desirable because they allow us to reason about non-local appearance constraints, which may in turn lead to better pose estimates and detection rates. For example, it is still difficult to estimate the articulation of lower arms in unconstrained images. Given the attribute that a person of interest is wearing a full-hand shirt, one can learn a clothing appearance model from the torso to help aid in localizing arms. Likewise, it is easier to parse an image of two people hugging when one reasons jointly about the body pose of both people.

Such reasoning may require new representations. Perhaps part models provide one framework, but to capture the rich space of such visual phenomena, one will need a vocabulary of hundreds or even thousands of local part templates. This poses new difficulties in learning and inference. Relational models must also be extended beyond simple springs to include combinatorial constraints between visual attributes (one should not instance both a tie and skirt part) and flexible relations between people and their surroundings. To better understand clothing and body pose, inference may require the use of bottom–up grouping constraints to estimate the spatial layout of body parts, as well as novel appearance models for capturing material properties beyond pixel color.

Acknowledgements   This work has been supported by NSF Grant 0954083 and ONR-MURI Grant N00014-10-1-0933.

References

1. Andriluka, M., Roth, S., Schiele, B.: Pictorial structures revisited: People detection and articulated pose estimation. In: IEEE Computer Society Conference on Computer Vision and Pattern Recognition, pp. 1014–1021 (2009) [204]
2. Balan, A., Black, M.J.: The naked truth: Estimating body shape under clothing. In: European Conference on Computer Vision, pp. 15–29 (2008) [220]
3. Binford, T.O.: Visual perception by computer. In: IEEE Conference on Systems and Control, vol. 313 (1971) [199]
4. Bourdev, L., Malik, J.: Poselets: Body part detectors trained using 3d human pose annotations. In: IEEE Computer Society Conference on Computer Vision and Pattern Recognition, pp. 1365–1372 (2010) [200]
5. Bregler, C., Malik, J.: Tracking people with twists and exponential maps. In: IEEE Computer Society Conference on Computer Vision and Pattern Recognition, pp. 8–15 (1997) [200]
6. Buehler, P., Everingham, M., Huttenlocher, D.P., Zisserman, A.: Long term arm and hand tracking for continuous sign language TV broadcasts. In: British Machine Vision Conference (2008) [211]

7. Burl, M., Weber, M., Perona, P.: A probabilistic approach to object recognition using local photometry and global geometry. In: European Conference on Computer Vision, pp. 628–641 (1998) [199]

8. Cootes, T.F., Edwards, G.J., Taylor, C.J.: Active appearance models. In: European Conference on Computer Vision, vol. 2, pp. 484–498 (1998) [200]

9. Crandall, D., Felzenszwalb, P.F., Huttenlocher, D.P.: Spatial priors for part-based recognition using statistical models. In: IEEE Computer Society Conference on Computer Vision and Pattern Recognition, vol. 1, pp. 10–17 (2005) [200]

10. Dalal, N., Triggs, B.: Histograms of oriented gradients for human detection. In: IEEE Computer Society Conference on Computer Vision and Pattern Recognition, vol. 1, pp. 886–893 (2005) [201,203,219]

11. Dollar, P., Wojek, C., Schiele, B., Perona, P.: Pedestrian detection: A benchmark. In: IEEE Computer Society Conference on Computer Vision and Pattern Recognition, pp. 304–311 (2009) [216]

12. Duetscher, J., Blake, A., Reid, I.: Articulated body motion capture by annealed particle filtering. In: IEEE Computer Society Conference on Computer Vision and Pattern Recognition, vol. 2, pp. 126–133 (2000) [218]

13. Eichner, M., Ferrari, V.: We are family: joint pose estimation of multiple persons. In: European Conference on Computer Vision, pp. 228–242 (2010) [220]

14. Eichner, M., Marin-Jimenez, M., Zisserman, A., Ferrari, V.: 2d articulated human pose estimation software. http://www.vision.ee.ethz.ch/~calvin/articulated_human_pose_estimation_code/ [219]

15. Everingham, M., Van Gool, L., Williams, C.K.I., Winn, J., Zisserman, A.: The pascal visual object classes (voc) challenge. Int. J. Comput. Vis. 88(2), 303–338 (2010) [216,219]

16. Felzenszwalb, P.F., Girshick, R.B., McAllester, D., Ramanan, D.: Discriminatively trained deformable part models. http://people.cs.uchicago.edu/~pff/latent/ [219]

17. Felzenszwalb, P.F., Girshick, R.B., McAllester, D., Ramanan, D.: Object detection with discriminatively trained part based models. IEEE Trans. Pattern Anal. Mach. Intell. 32(9), 1627–1645 (2010) [201,214,216]

18. Felzenszwalb, P.F., Huttenlocher, D.P.: Pictorial structures for object recognition. Int. J. Comput. Vis. 61(1), 55–79 (2005) [199,200,202,204,206,207,211]

19. Felzenszwalb, P.F., McAllester, D., Ramanan, D.: A discriminatively trained, multiscale, deformable part model. In: IEEE Computer Society Conference on Computer Vision and Pattern Recognition, pp. 1–8 (2008) [213]

20. Fergus, R., Perona, P., Zisserman, A.: et al. Object class recognition by unsupervised scale-invariant learning. In: IEEE Computer Society Conference on Computer Vision and Pattern Recognition, vol. 2, pp. 264–271 (2003) [199]

21. Ferrari, V., Marin-Jimenez, M., Zisserman, A.: Progressive search space reduction for human pose estimation. In: IEEE Computer Society Conference on Computer Vision and Pattern Recognition, pp. 1–8 (2008) [209,215]

22. Ferrari, V., Marin-Jimenez, M., Zisserman, A.: Pose search: Retrieving people using their pose. In: IEEE Computer Society Conference on Computer Vision and Pattern Recognition, pp. 1–8 (2009) [215,217]

23. Finley, T., Joachims, T.: Training structural svms when exact inference is intractable. In: International Conference on Machine Learning, pp. 304–311 (2008) [214]

24. Fischler, M.A., Elschlager, R.A.: The representation and matching of pictorial structures. IEEE Trans. Comput. C-22(1), 67–92 (1973) [199,202]

25. Forsyth, D.A., Fleck, M.M.: Body plans. In: IEEE Computer Society Conference on Computer Vision and Pattern Recognition, pp. 678–683 (2002) [199]

26. Hua, G., Yang, M.H., Wu, Y.: Learning to estimate human pose with data driven belief propagation. In: IEEE Computer Society Conference on Computer Vision and Pattern Recognition, vol. 2, pp. 747–754 (2005) [212]

27. Ioffe, S., Forsyth, D.: Human tracking with mixtures of trees. In: IEEE International Conference on Computer Vision, vol. 1, pp. 690–695 (2002) [211]

28. Ioffe, S., Forsyth, D.A.: Probabilistic methods for finding people. Int. J. Comput. Vis. **43**(1), 45–68 (2001) [200]
29. Isard, M.: Pampas: Real-valued graphical models for computer vision. In: IEEE Computer Society Conference on Computer Vision and Pattern Recognition, vol. 1, pp. 613–620 (2003) [212]
30. Isard, M., Blake, A.: Condensation – conditional density propagation for visual tracking. Int. J. Comput. Vis. **29**(1), 5–28 (1998) [218]
31. Johnson, S., Everingham, M.: Clustered pose and nonlinear appearance models for human pose estimation. In: British Machine Vision Conference (2010) [211,215]
32. Ju, S.X., Black, M.J., Yacoob, Y.: Cardboard people: A parameterized model of articulated image motion. In: International Conference on Automatic Face and Gesture Recognition (1996) [200]
33. Kumar, M.P., Torr, P.H.S., Zisserman, A.: Learning layered pictorial structures from video. In: Indian Conference on Computer Vision, Graphics and Image Processing (2004) [208]
34. Kumar, M.P., Zisserman, A., Torr, P.H.S.: Efficient discriminative learning of parts-based models. In: IEEE Computer Society Conference on Computer Vision and Pattern Recognition, pp. 552–559 (2010) [213,214]
35. Lafferty, J., McCallum, A., Pereira, F.: Conditional random fields: Probabilistic models for segmenting and labeling sequence data. In: International Conference on Machine Learning, pp. 282–289 (2001) [213]
36. Lan, X., Huttenlocher, D.P.: Beyond trees: Common-factor models for 2d human pose recovery. In: IEEE Computer Society Conference on Computer Vision and Pattern Recognition, vol. 1, pp. 470–477 (2005) [211]
37. Lee, M.W., Cohen, I.: Proposal maps driven mcmc for estimating human body pose in static images. In: IEEE Computer Society Conference on Computer Vision and Pattern Recognition, vol. 2, pp. 334–341 (2004) [212,220]
38. Leibe, B., Leonardis, A., Schiele, B.: An implicit shape model for combined object categorization and segmentation. In: Toward Category-Level Object Recognition, pp. 508–524 (2006) [200]
39. Lowe, D.G.: Distinctive image features from scale-invariant keypoints. Int. J. Comput. Vis. **60**(2), 91–110 (2004) [201]
40. Marr, D., Nishihara, H.K.: Representation and recognition of the spatial organization of three-dimensional shapes. Proc. R. Soc. Lond. B, Biol. Sci. **200**(1140), 269–294 (1978) [199]
41. Matthews, I., Baker, S.: Active appearance models revisited. Int. J. Comput. Vis. **60**(2), 135–164 (2004) [200]
42. Mori, G., Ren, X., Efros, A.A., Malik, J.: Recovering human body configurations: Combining segmentation and recognition. In: IEEE Computer Society Conference on Computer Vision and Pattern Recognition (2004) [209]
43. Park, D., Ramanan, D., Fowlkes, C.: Multiresolution models for object detection. In: European Conference on Computer Vision, pp. 241–254 (2010) [215,216]
44. Ramanan, D.: Learning to parse images of articulated bodies. http://www.ics.uci.edu/~dramanan/papers/parse/index.html [219]
45. Ramanan, D.: Learning to parse images of articulated bodies. Adv. Neural Inf. Process. Syst. **19**, 1129–1136 (2007) [200,204,209,210,215]
46. Ramanan, D., Forsyth, D.A.: Finding and tracking people from the bottom up. In: IEEE Computer Society Conference on Computer Vision and Pattern Recognition, vol. 2, pp. 467–474 (2003) [209]
47. Ramanan, D., Forsyth, D.A.: Using temporal coherence to build models of animals. In: IEEE International Conference on Computer Vision, vol. 1, pp. 338–345 (2003) [219]
48. Ramanan, D., Forsyth, D.A., Zisserman, A.: Strike a pose: Tracking people by finding stylized poses. In: IEEE Computer Society Conference on Computer Vision and Pattern Recognition, vol. 1, pp. 271–278 (2005) [203,219]
49. Ramanan, D., Forsyth, D.A., Zisserman, A.: Tracking people by learning their appearance. IEEE Trans. Pattern Anal. Mach. Intell. **29**(1), 65–81 (2007) [204,218,219]

50. Ramanan, D., Sminchisescu, C.: Training deformable models for localization. In: IEEE Computer Society Conference on Computer Vision and Pattern Recognition, vol. 1, pp. 206–213 (2006) [204,213]
51. Ronfard, R., Schmid, C., Triggs, B.: Learning to parse pictures of people. In: European Conference on Computer Vision, pp. 700–714 (2002) [200]
52. Sapp, B., Jordan, C., Taskar, B.: Adaptive pose priors for pictorial structures. In: IEEE Computer Society Conference on Computer Vision and Pattern Recognition, pp. 422–429 (2010) [209,215]
53. Sapp, B., Toshev, A., Taskar, B.: Cascaded models for articulated pose estimation. In: European Conference on Computer Vision, pp. 406–420 (2010) [209]
54. Sidenbladh, H., Black, M., Sigal, L.: Implicit probabilistic models of human motion for synthesis and tracking. In: European Conference on Computer Vision, pp. 784–800 (2002) [218]
55. Sigal, L., Black, M.J.: Measure locally, reason globally: Occlusion-sensitive articulated pose estimation. In: IEEE Computer Society Conference on Computer Vision and Pattern Recognition, vol. 2, pp. 2041–2048 (2006) [208,210]
56. Sigal, L., Isard, M., Sigelman, B.H., Black, M.J.: Attractive people: Assembling loose-limbed models using non-parametric belief propagation. In: Advances in Neural Information Processing Systems, vol. 16 (2004) [212]
57. Sivic, J., Zisserman, A.: Video google: Efficient visual search of videos. In: Toward Category-Level Object Recognition, pp. 127–144 (2006) [200]
58. Sudderth, E., Ihler, A., Isard, M., Freeman, W., Willsky, A.: Nonparametric belief propagation. Commun. ACM 53(10), 95–103 (2010) [212]
59. Sudderth, E., Mandel, M., Freeman, W., Willsky, A.: Distributed occlusion reasoning for tracking with nonparametric belief propagation. In: Advances in Neural Information Processing Systems, vol. 17, pp. 1369–1376 (2004) [208]
60. Tian, T.P., Sclaroff, S.: Fast globally optimal 2D human detection with loopy graph models. In: CVPR, pp. 81–88 (2010) [211]
61. Tian, T.P., Sclaroff, S.: Fast multi-aspect 2d human detection. In: European Conference on Computer Vision, pp. 453–466 (2010) [211]
62. Tran, D., Forsyth, D.: Improved human parsing with a full relational model. In: European Conference on Computer Vision, pp. 227–240 (2010) [203,209]
63. Wang, Y., Mori, G.: Multiple tree models for occlusion and spatial constraints in human pose estimation. In: European Conference on Computer Vision, pp. 710–724 (2008) [211]
64. Weber, M., Welling, M., Perona, P.: Unsupervised learning of models for recognition. In: European Conference on Computer Vision, pp. 18–32 (2000) [199]
65. Yang, Y., Ramanan, D.: Articulated pose estimation with flexible mixtures of parts. In: IEEE Computer Society Conference on Computer Vision and Pattern Recognition (2011) [204,214, 215,217]
66. Yanover, C., Weiss, Y.: Finding the M most probable configurations using loopy belief propagation. In: Advances in Neural Information Processing Systems (2004) [211]
67. Yao, B., Fei-Fei, L.: Modeling mutual context of object and human pose in human-object interaction activities. In: IEEE Computer Society Conference on Computer Vision and Pattern Recognition, pp. 17–24 (2010) [220]

Chapter 12
Feature-Based Pose Estimation

Cristian Sminchisescu, Liefeng Bo, Catalin Ionescu, and Atul Kanaujia

Abstract In this chapter we review challenges and methodology for feature-based predictive three-dimensional human pose reconstruction, based on image and video data. We argue that reliable 3D human pose prediction can be achieved through an alliance between image descriptors that encode multiple levels of selectivity and invariance and models that are capable to represent multiple structured solutions. For monocular systems, key to reliability is the capacity to leverage prior knowledge in order to bias solutions not only to kinematically feasible sets, but also toward typical configurations that humans are likely to assume in everyday surroundings. In this context, we discuss several predictive methods including large-scale mixture of experts, supervised spectral latent variable models and structural support vector machines, asses the impact of the various choices of image descriptors, review open problems, and give pointers to datasets and code available online.

C. Sminchisescu (✉)
Institute for Numerical Simulation (INS), Faculty of Mathematics and Natural Science,
University of Bonn, Bonn, Germany
e-mail: cristian.sminchisescu@ins.uni-bonn.de
Institute for Mathematics of the Romanian Academy (IMAR), Bucharest, Romania
url: www.imar.ro/clvp

L. Bo
University of Washington, Seattle, USA
e-mail: lfb@cs.washington.edu

C. Ionescu
INS, University of Bonn, Bonn, Germany
e-mail: catalin.ionescu@ins.uni-bonn.de

A. Kanaujia
ObjectVideo, Reston, VA, USA
e-mail: atul.kanaujia@objectvideo.com

T.B. Moeslund et al. (eds.), *Visual Analysis of Humans*,
DOI 10.1007/978-0-85729-997-0_12, © Springer-Verlag London Limited 2011

12.1 Introduction

In this paper, we focus on the three-dimensional reconstruction of human poses, represented as vectors of joint angles or 3D joint positions, based on information extracted using video cameras. We will primarily be interested in methods that are applicable to *monocular images*, although the methodology generalizes to multi-camera settings. Inference from monocular images has practical applicability and cognitive relevance. In many practical settings, only a single image sequence is available as in the case of archival movie footage, or when consumer devices are used as interface tools for gesture or activity recognition. Even when several cameras are available, fully exploiting the information in multiple views to limit uncertainty may not lead to intrinsically simpler optimization problems, as the subjects of interest may be occluded by other people or by scene elements. A robust human motion analysis system needs to handle incomplete, ambiguous or noisy observation sources that are typical of many real scenes.

From a cognitive viewpoint, *paradoxical monocular stereoscopy* [32] is the apparently seamless human ability to reconstruct the 3D structure of a scene qualitatively, using only one eye or given only a single photograph of a visual scene. As this type of monocular inference is geometrically under constrained, the mechanism that makes it possible has to do with the ability to use strong priors that link familiar scene structures and their image projection statistics. In the long run, a well-trained computer vision system should be able to leverage such priors, in order to come close to the performance of the human visual system.

The inference of human or animal motion based on images has been already studied extensively. On one hand, there exist commercial motion capture systems that represent the standard for the special effects industry, virtual and augmented reality, or medical applications and video games. These systems are very accurate but they need several calibrated and synchronized cameras, controlled illumination, and special clothing with passive markers for simplifying the image correspondence problem. On the other hand, and it is the path we pursue, there exist approaches that work with increasingly more natural images, obtained with uncalibrated, unsynchronized cameras, in natural uninstrumented environments, and filming subjects wearing their own clothing and no markers.

General difficulties: Reconstructing the three-dimensional human pose and motion of people at the office, on the street, or outdoors based on images acquired with a single (or even multiple) video camera(s) is one of the open problems in computer vision. Some of the common challenges were already discussed in previous chapters, most notably in Chap. 8. The difficulties compound: people have many degrees of freedom, deform and articulate, and their appearance spans a significant range due to different body proportions and clothing. When analyzing people in realistic imaging conditions, the backgrounds cannot be controlled. Recently there is a trend to move toward operation in complex environments where people are viewed against more complex backgrounds and in a more diverse set of poses. Handling such environments would be in principle possible by means of integrated systems that combine person detection (or localization) and 3D reconstruction [4, 13, 25, 55, 60]. However, each subproblem remains difficult to solve: human detectors alone [22] cannot always handle general human poses, and even if they did, the bounding box of a person viewed against a non-uniform background still leaves a complex figure-ground search space to explore before the 3D pose can be predicted reliably (it is generally well understood that predictors based on silhouettes generalize relatively well if the input quality is good and the predictor was trained using a distribution sufficiently well sampled from the set of human poses typical of the problem domain [3, 61]). Another approach would be to use more sophisticated 2d human models for localization, for example, akin to those discussed in Chap. 11, with parts that mirror the true human body limbs [4, 21, 23, 44, 46]. A difficulty to overcome is the localization of people under strong perspective effects and the relatively high false positive rates. Overall, approaches based on integrated human detection and pose reconstruction remain promising, and it remains to be seen how the modeling and inference components will evolve.

Monocular ambiguities: A major difficulty for 3D human pose inference from monocular images is the quasi-unobservability of kinematic degrees of freedom that generate motion in depth. For unknown limb (link) lengths this leads to continuous nonrigid 'affine folding' ambiguities, but once lengths are known these reduce to twofold 'forwards/backwards flipping' ambiguities for each link. Under no additional pose constraints, the full model thus has $O(2^{\#links})$ formal inverse kinematics solutions. Reconstructing articulated 3D pose from monocular model-image point correspondences in an unconstrained human pose class is well understood to be ambiguous, according to the geometric [39, 41, 64] (see Chap. 8, Sect. 8.3.4) and computational studies [15, 18, 45, 50, 61–63] of the problem.

For real image features, the problem is more difficult to analyze geometrically (see the computational studies in [18, 45, 49, 61, 62, 65]), but poses that correspond to reflective placements of limbs w.r.t. the camera rays of sight often produce only marginally different projections, with comparable likelihoods, even under similarity measures based on quite elaborate image features [19, 51, 62]. Subtle differences indeed exist between configurations that are 'close-in-depth' and those that are 'far-in-depth', but these usually give the perceived ground truth pose a relative margin only for very accurate subject models and for image observations collected under no data association errors (it remains unclear under what circumstances this is possible). In principle, shadows offer supplementary cues [5], but the key relevant regions remain difficult to identify in scenes with complex lighting and for unknown people wearing deformable clothing, and different solutions become practically indistinguishable for objects placed further away in depth from the camera.

In a sufficiently general model complexity class, monocular ambiguities can persist in video, when dynamic constraints are considered [58], and can also persist for models biased using prior knowledge [45, 57, 61] (for illustrations of both static and dynamic ambiguities, see videos at http://sminchisescu.ins.uni-bonn.de/talks/).

In the long run, a combination of low-complexity models and appropriate context management may produce solutions—effectively 'controlled hallucinations'—that are unambiguous *in their class* rather than in general. This may turn out to be more effective than a 'hardliner' approach where models capable of representing all kinematically possible human poses are made unambiguous by fusing all 'cues'. In fact, the hypothesis that stable visual perceptions can be formed despite extensive sets of ambiguities (e.g., bas-relief, pictorial depth, structure-from-motion) is not foreign to researchers in both computer vision and psychophysics [6, 32, 33].

Generative and discriminative methods: In this chapter we will primarily describe 3D human pose reconstruction methods based on discriminative models [3, 45, 48, 61], which can be trained to predict pose distributions given image descriptor inputs. This strategy contrasts with the one used in generative model algorithms [18, 54, 64], discussed in Chaps. 9 and 10, that search the pose space for configurations with good image likelihood (alignment). Each class of methods provides complementary advantages. Generative models are flexible at representing large classes of poses and are useful for training and hypothesis verification, but inference is expensive and good observation models are difficult to construct without simplifying assumptions. Discriminative predictors offer the promise of speed, automation and complete flexibility in selecting the image descriptor (overcomplete bases or overlapping features of the observation can be designed without simplifying independence assumptions), but have to model multi-valued image-to-3D relations and their reliance on a training set makes generalization to very different poses, body proportions, or scenes where people are filmed against background clutter, problematic. N.b. clearly, these remain hard problems for any method, be it generative or discriminative.

Degree of training data realism: The design of multi-valued pose predictors and the temporal density propagation in conditional chains is, at present, well understood [45, 53, 59, 61], but the trade offs inherent in the acquisition of a sufficiently representative training set or the design of image descriptors with good resistance to clutter and intra-class variations was explored less. The construction of realistic *pose labeled* human databases (images of humans and their 3D poses) is inherently difficult because no existing system can provide accurate 3D ground truth for humans in real-world, non-instrumented scenes. Current solutions rely either on motion acquisition systems like Vicon, but these operate in engineered environments, where subjects wear special costumes and markers and the background is simplified, or on quasi-synthetic databases, generated by CG characters, animated using motion capture, and placed on real image backgrounds [2, 60]. In both cases, there is a risk that models learned using these training sets may not generalize well when confronted with the diversity of real-world scenes. In the long run, the development of more sophisticate rendering and mixed reality frameworks, or the design of sophisticated capture sensors is likely to improve the quality of existing training sets significantly (some progress has been reported in designing systems along these lines [72]). For more detailed discussion of the currently available datasets for both training and benchmark testing see Chap. 13.

12.1.1 The Need for Structure Modeling

We will formulate human pose reconstruction as a structured learning problem, where we predict a multivariate output from a multivariate input and a joint training set (this methodology will apply to any continuous structured prediction problem in computer vision). Here, the input is the image or its descriptor (e.g., a 'bag of words' histogram model that quantizes the occurrence of a feature over the image, for instance a local edge distribution) and the output is a scene representation, an object shape or a three-dimensional human pose. Both the inputs and the outputs are high-dimensional and strongly correlated. At basic level, image features are spatially coherent (nearby pixels more often have similar color, contrast or edge orientation than not), whereas outputs are structured due to physical constraints in the world. For example, three-dimensional human poses are constrained at scene level by the ground plane and the location of typical objects, at physical level by gravity, balance and joint/body limits, and at functional level by the strong body part correlations in motions like walking, running, jumping that have regular or periodic structure, hence, at least locally, low intrinsic dimensionality (see Fig. 12.1). Given the recent availability of training data [1, 52], there has been increasing interest in example-intensive, discriminative approaches to 3D human pose reconstruction, either based on nearest-neighbor schemes [43, 48], parametric predictors [3, 45, 60], trained using images of people and their corresponding 3D ground truth pose. A shortcoming of existing methods is their inability to model interdependencies between outputs.

Structured data can be modeled either by including sophisticated constraints into regression methods (linear or non-linear manifold assumptions [16, 17, 31, 60]), or by designing new cost functions. There is a choice of modeling correlations as part of the loss function, or as a form of regularization. One possibility is to endow manifolds with probabilistic formulations that allow mapping between data and intrinsic

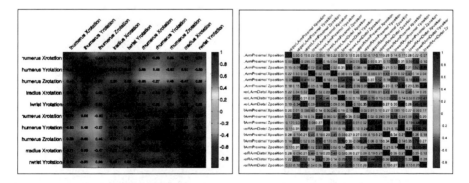

Fig. 12.1 Joint angle correlation statistics from human motion capture data. *Left* plot shows the correlations present in walking motions, whereas the *right* plot shows correlations for more diverse motions, including humans walking, jogging, involved in conversations or boxing. Notice not only the strong correlations in the single activity regime, but also their persistence in the more diverse motion set

spaces, or computing probabilities for new datapoints [36, 57]. Additionally, graph-based geometric constraints inspired by spectral non-linear embeddings have also been integrated in a latent variable model in an *unsupervised* setting initially by [57], more recently by [29, 40] and subsequently, in a GPLVM formulation [70]. Latent variable models of this type have become popular in vision [4, 29, 36, 40, 56, 57, 69, 70, 74] predominantly as unsupervised intermediate representations, sep-arately linked with images and used for visual inference in conjunction with par-ticle filters [40, 57, 69] or image-based manifold predictors [29]. This turned out to be effective but is potentially suboptimal: the manifold discovered using unsu-pervised learning is not necessarily ideal for prediction or inference. For instance, the variance of the two distributions is by no means calibrated: the noise model of the image-to-manifold predictor could be way different than the input variance of the manifold-to-output model, negatively impacting the output estimate. Addressing such consistent end-to-end model training considerations, we will explore structured prediction methods based on manifold formulations in Sect. 12.3.

Another approach to structured prediction relies on max-margin formulations in conjunction with kernels defined over multivariate input and output spaces. Struc-tural support vector machines, initially introduced for discrete state spaces [68], can be generalized to continuous outputs by learning a scoring function so that the pair corresponding to the given input–output training example ranks higher than a pair formed by the given input and any other output [38, 75]. The methods we will present can be viewed as a generalization of [68, 75] to integrated localization and state estimation problems with continuous structured inputs and outputs. A method-ology adapted for simultaneous person localization and continuous pose estimation will be described in Sect. 12.4.

12.1.2 The Need for Selectivity and Invariance in Image Descriptors

A difficulty in the creation of reliable feature-based pose prediction systems is the design of image descriptors that are distinctive enough to differentiate among differ-ent poses, yet invariant to *within the same pose class differences*—people in similar stances, but differently proportioned, or photographed on different backgrounds.

Exiting methods have successfully demonstrated that bag of features or regular-grid based representations of local descriptors (e.g., bag of shape context features, block of SIFT features [2, 60]) can be effective at predicting 3D human poses, but the representations tend to be too inflexible for reconstruction in general scenes. It is more appropriate to view them as two useful extremes of a multilevel, hierarchical representation of images—a family of descriptors that progressively relaxes block-wise, rigid local spatial image encodings to increasingly weaker spatial models of position/geometry accumulated over increasingly larger image regions. Selecting the most competitive representation for an application—a typical set of people, mo-tions, backgrounds or scales—reduces to either directly or implicitly learning a met-ric in the space of image descriptors, so that both good invariance and distinctiveness is achieved, e.g., for 3D reconstruction, suppress noise by maximizing correlation within the desired pose invariance class, yet keep different classes separated, and turn off components that are close to being statistically random for the task of prediction, disregarding the class.

Multilevel, hierarchical encodings are necessary in order to obtain image descriptors with good resistance to deformations, clutter or misalignments in the dataset. But they do not entirely eliminate the need for problem-dependent similarity measures for descriptor comparison, as their components may still be perturbed by clutter or may not be relevant for the task. We will thus favor hierarchical, coarse to fine image descriptors that combine multilevel image encodings and metric learning algorithms based on Canonical Correlation Analysis (CCA) and Relevant Component Analysis (RCA). These refine and further align the image descriptors within individual pose invariance classes in order to better tolerate deformation, misalignment and clutter in the training and test sets. Below, we will review several descriptors that have been shown to be effective for human pose prediction (see [28, 60] for details):

Multilevel Spatial Blocks (MSB)   is an encoding derived by Kanaujia et al. [28] and consists of a set of layers, each a regular grid of overlapping image blocks, with increasingly large (SIFT) descriptor cell size. Descriptors within each layer and across layers are concatenated, orderly, in order to obtain encodings of an entire image or sub-window. This is a multiscale generalization of the encoding proposed by Sminchisescu et al. [60] for pose prediction in the context of learning joint generative–discriminative methods.

HMAX   [47] is a hierarchical, multilayer model inspired by the anatomy of the visual cortex. It alternates layers of template matching (simple cell) and max pooling (complex cell) operations in order to build representations that are increasingly invariant to scale and translation. Simple layers use convolution with local filters (template matching against a set of prototypes), in order to compute higher-order (hyper) features, whereas complex layers pool their afferent units over limited ranges, using a MAX operation, in order to increase invariance. Rather than learning the bottom layer, the model uses a bank of Gabor filter simple cells, computed at multiple positions, orientations and scales. Higher layers use simple cell prototypes, obtained by randomly sampling descriptors in the equivalent layer of a training set (k-means clustering can also be used), hence the construction of the hierarchical model has to be done stage-wise, bottom–up, as layers become available.

Hyperfeatures   [3] is a hierarchical, multilevel, multi-scale encoding similar in organization with HMAX, but more homogeneous in the way it repeatedly accumulates/averages template matches to prototypes (local histograms) across layers, instead of winner-takes-all MAX operations followed by template matching to prototypes.

Spatial pyramid [37] is a hierarchical model based on encodings of spatially localized histograms, over increasingly large image regions. The bottom layer contains the finest grid, with higher layers containing coarser grids with bag of feature (SIFT) encodings computed within each one. Originally, the descriptor was used to build a pyramid kernel as a linear combination of layered, histogram intersections kernels, but it can also be used stand-alone, in conjunction with linear predictors. It aligns well with the design of our 3D predictors, which can be either linear or kernel-based.

Vocabulary tree [42] builds a coarse-to-fine, multilevel encoding using hierarchical k-means clustering. The model is learned divisively—the training set is clustered at top level, then recursively split, with a constant branching factor, and retrained within each subgroup. Nistér and Stévenius collect measurements on a sparse grid (given by MSER interest points) and encode any path to a leaf by a single integer. This is compact and gives good results for object retrieval, but is usually not sufficiently smooth for continuous pose prediction problem, where it collapses qualitatively different poses to identical encodings. To adapt for the task, Kanaujia et al. [28] learn the same vocabulary tree, but construct stage-wise encodings by concatenating all levels. At each level they store the continuous distances to prototypes and recursively descend in the closest sub-tree. Entries in unvisited sub-trees are set to zero. For each image, the tree-based encodings of patches are accumulated on a regular grid and normalized.

The quantitative performance of different image features and metric learning methods for a monocular human pose estimation task, in conjunction with mixture of expert predictors (described in detailed in Sect. 12.2), is illustrated in Fig. 12.2.

12.2 Modeling Complex Image to Pose Relations

Monocular ambiguities and the invariance demands on the image descriptors make the modeling of image to pose relations difficult. One possibility is to train a standard function approximator (e.g., a kernel regressor) to map from image feature inputs to the continuous 3D human pose variable [3]. However, in ambiguous input regions, the accuracy of the regression model will be low. Empirical studies show that for sufficiently diverse datasets, the relations are strongly multi-valued and require explicit forms of modeling the different solutions. One very powerful approach is the conditional mixture of experts models (cMoE) [59, 61].[1] The versatility of cMoE relies on a balanced combination of several attractive properties: (i) *conditioning on input* eliminates the need for simplifying naive Bayes assumptions, common

---

[1]Standard kernel regression models can be viewed as a special case of a conditional mixture with a single expert ($M = 1$). We will thus not include separate derivations for kernel regression, the restriction to $M = 1$ in (12.1) being straightforward.

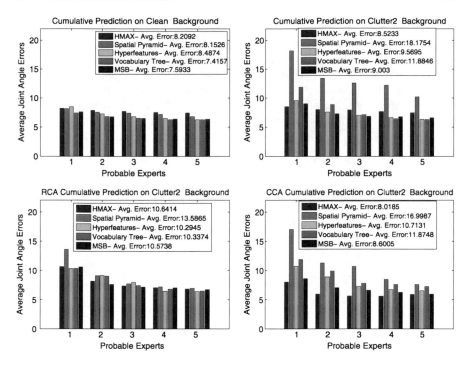

Fig. 12.2 Quantitative prediction errors cumulated for 5 different motions and 5 image encodings: HMAX, Hyperfeatures, Spatial Pyramid, Vocabulary Tree, Multilevel Spatial Blocks (MSB), and 2 metric learning and correlation analysis methods (RCA, CCA). A single activity-independent model (a conditional Bayesian mixture of experts) was trained on the entire dataset. Each plot shows the error in the best-k experts, for $k = 1, \ldots, 5$, the total number of experts used. The kth bar was computed by selecting the value closest to ground truth among the ones predicted by the most probable k experts. (Reproduced with permission from [28] ©2007 IEEE)

with generative models, and allows for diverse, potentially non-independent feature functions of the input (in this case, the image) to be encoded in its descriptor. This makes it possible to model non-trivial image correlations and enhances the predictive power of the input representation. (ii) *multi-valued nature of outputs* allows for multiple plausible hypotheses—as opposed to a single one—to be faithfully represented; (iii) *contextual predictions* offer versatility by means of ranking (gating) functions that are paired with the experts, and adaptively score their competence in providing solutions, for each input. This allows for nuanced, finely tuned responses; (iv) *probabilistic consistency* enforces data modeling according to its density via formal, conditional likelihood parameter training procedures; (v) *Bayesian formulations and automatic relevance determination mechanisms* favor sparse models with good generalization capabilities. All these features make the cMoE model suitable for fast, automatic feedforward 3D prediction, either as a stand-alone, indexing system, or as an initialization method, in conjunction with complementary visual search and feedback mechanisms [55, 60].

A significant downside of existing mixture of experts algorithms [7, 20, 27, 28, 61] is their scalability. The algorithms require an expensive double loop algorithm (an iteration within another iteration) based on Newton optimization, to compute the gate functions, a factor that makes models with more than 10,000 datapoints and large input dimension impractical to train. In this section we review computationally efficient cMoE algorithms that combine forward feature selection based on marginal likelihood and functional gradient boosting with techniques from bound optimization, in order to train models that are one order of magnitude larger (100,000 examples and up), in time that is more than one order of magnitude faster than previous methods.

Conditional mixture of experts: We work with a probabilistic conditional model:

$$P(x|\mathbf{r}) = \sum_{j=1}^{M} g_j(\mathbf{r}) p_j(x) \tag{12.1}$$

with:

$$g_j(\mathbf{r}) \equiv g(\mathbf{r}|\boldsymbol{\lambda}_j) = \frac{e^{\boldsymbol{\lambda}_j^{\top}\mathbf{r}}}{\sum_k e^{\boldsymbol{\lambda}_k^{\top}\mathbf{r}}}, \tag{12.2}$$

$$p_j(x) \equiv p_j\left(x|\mathbf{r}, \mathbf{w}_j, \sigma_j^2\right) = \mathcal{N}\left(x|\mathbf{w}_j^{\top}\mathbf{r}, \sigma_j^2\mathbf{I}\right), \tag{12.3}$$

where $\mathbf{r}$ are predictor variables, x are outputs or responses, g are *input-dependent* positive gates. g are normalized to sum to 1 for consistency, by construction, for any given input $\mathbf{r}$. In the model, p are Gaussian distributions (12.3) with variance $\sigma^2\mathbf{I}$, centered at linear regression predictions given by models with weights $\mathbf{w}$. Whenever possible, we drop the index of the experts (*but not the one of the gates*). The weights of experts have Gaussian priors, controlled by hyperparameters $\boldsymbol{\alpha}$:

$$p(\mathbf{w}|\boldsymbol{\alpha}) = (2\pi)^{-D/2} \prod_{d=1}^{D} \alpha_d^{1/2} \exp\left\{-\frac{\alpha_d w_d^2}{2}\right\} \tag{12.4}$$

with $\dim(\mathbf{w}) = D$. The parameters of the model, including experts and gates are collectively stored in $\boldsymbol{\theta} = \{(\mathbf{w}_i, \boldsymbol{\alpha}_i, \sigma_i, \boldsymbol{\lambda}_i) \mid i = 1, \ldots, M\}$. To learn the model, we design iterative, approximate Bayesian EM algorithms. In the E-step we estimate the posterior:

$$h_j \equiv h_j(x, \mathbf{r}|\mathbf{w}_j, \sigma_j, \boldsymbol{\lambda}_j) = \frac{g_j(\mathbf{r}) p_j(x)}{\sum_{k=1}^{M} g_k(\mathbf{r}) p_k(x)} \tag{12.5}$$

and let $h_j^{(i)} = h_j(x^{(i)}, \mathbf{r}^{(i)})$ be the probability that the expert j has generated datapoint i. Parenthesized superscripts index datapoints. In the M-step we solve two optimization problems, one for each expert and another for the corresponding gate. The first learns the expert parameters, based on training data weighted according to the current membership estimates h. The second optimization trains the gates g to predict h. The complete log-likelihood (Q-function) for the conditional mixture of Bayesian experts can be derived as [27]:

$$Q = \sum_{i=1}^{N} \log P\left(x^{(i)}|\mathbf{r}^{(i)}\right) = \sum_{i=1}^{N} \sum_{j=1}^{M} h_j^{(i)}\left(\log g_j^{(i)} + \log p_j^{(i)}\right) = L_g + L_p. \quad (12.6)$$

The likelihood decomposes into two factors, one for the gates and the other for the experts. The experts can be fitted independently using sparse Bayesian learning, under the change of variables $\mathbf{r}^{(t)} \leftarrow \sqrt{h^{(t)}}\mathbf{r}^{(t)}$ and $x^{(t)} \leftarrow \sqrt{h^{(t)}}x^{(t)}$. The equations for the gates are coupled and require iteration *during each* M-step. Although the problem is convex, it is computationally expensive to solve because the cost is not quadratic and the inputs are high-dimensional. A classical iteratively reweighted least squares (IRLS), or a naive Newton implementation, requires $O(N(MD)^2 + (MD)^3)$ computation, multiple times during each step which is prohibitive for large problems (e.g., for 15 experts and 10,000 training samples with 1,000 input dimension, the computational cost becomes untenable even on today's most powerful desktops). Note that the cost of computing the Hessian (the first complexity term above) becomes higher than the one of inverting it (the second term) when the number of training samples is very large.

Training the experts: For Bayesian learning with Gaussian priors and observation likelihoods, the expert posterior and predictive uncertainty (marked with '*') are computable in closed form:

$$\boldsymbol{\mu} = \sigma^2 \boldsymbol{\Sigma} \mathbf{R} \mathbf{X}, \quad (12.7)$$

$$\boldsymbol{\Sigma} = \left(\sigma^{-2}\mathbf{R}\mathbf{R}^{\top} + \mathbf{A}\right)^{-1}, \quad (12.8)$$

$$x^* = \boldsymbol{\mu}^{\top}\mathbf{r}, \qquad \left(\sigma^2\right)^* = \mathbf{r}^{\top}\boldsymbol{\Sigma}\mathbf{r}, \quad (12.9)$$

where $\mathbf{A} = \text{diag}[\alpha_1, \ldots, \alpha_D]$, $\mathbf{R}$ stores the training set inputs columnwise and $\mathbf{X}$ their corresponding vector of x-outputs (see Fig. 12.3 for illustration). The marginal likelihood of the experts is:

$$L_p(\boldsymbol{\alpha}) = \sum_{i=1}^{N} \log p\left(x^{(i)} \mid \mathbf{r}^{(i)}, \boldsymbol{\alpha}, \sigma^2\right) = \sum_{i=1}^{N} \log \int p\left(x^{(i)} \mid \mathbf{r}^{(i)}, \mathbf{w}, \sigma^2\right) p(\mathbf{w}|\boldsymbol{\alpha}) d\mathbf{w}$$

$$(12.10)$$

$$= -\frac{1}{2}\left\{N \log 2\pi + \log |\mathbf{K}| + \mathbf{X}^{\top}\mathbf{K}^{-1}\mathbf{X}\right\}, \quad (12.11)$$

where $\mathbf{K} = \sigma^2\mathbf{I} + \mathbf{R}^{\top}\mathbf{A}^{-1}\mathbf{R}$. It can be shown that the marginal likelihood decomposes as [67]:

$$L_p(\boldsymbol{\alpha}) = L_p(\boldsymbol{\alpha}_{\backslash i}) + l(\alpha_i) \quad (12.12)$$

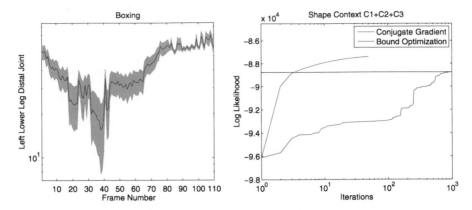

Fig. 12.3 (*Left*) Mean prediction and errorbars for one variable of our Bayesian model, cf. (12.7). (*Right*) Comparative convergence behavior of our Bound Optimization (BO) and the Conjugate Gradient (CG) method when fitting the gates on a training set of 35,000 datapoints. Notice the rapid convergence of BO and that after significantly more iterations CG has not yet converged to the maximum of the log-likelihood. (Reproduced with permission from [11] ©2008 IEEE)

with

$$l(\alpha_i) = \frac{1}{2}\left\{\log\alpha_i - \log(\alpha_i + s_i) + \frac{q_i^2}{\alpha_i + s_i}\right\}, \tag{12.13}$$

where $s_i = \mathbf{C}_i^\top \mathbf{K}_{\backslash i}^{-1} \mathbf{C}_i$ and $q_i = \mathbf{C}_i^\top \mathbf{K}_{\backslash i}^{-1} \mathbf{X}$, $\mathbf{C}_i$ collects the ith column from the matrix $\mathbf{R}^\top$, $\mathbf{K}_{\backslash i}$, $\alpha_{\backslash i}$ are the matrix and vector obtained with the corresponding entry of the input vector removed, and $L_p(\boldsymbol{\alpha}_{\backslash i})$ is the log-likelihood.

Training the gates: The log-likelihood component that corresponds to the gates decomposes as ($\boldsymbol{\lambda}$ is the $D \times M$-dimensional vector of all gate parameters $\boldsymbol{\lambda}_i$):

$$L_g(\boldsymbol{\lambda}) = \sum_{i=1}^{N}\sum_{j=1}^{M} h_j^{(i)} \log g_j^{(i)} = \sum_{i=1}^{N}\sum_{j=1}^{M}\left\{h_j^{(i)}\boldsymbol{\lambda}_j^\top\mathbf{r}_i - \log\sum_{j=1}^{M}\exp(\boldsymbol{\lambda}_j^\top\mathbf{r}_i)\right\}. \tag{12.14}$$

For efficiency, we use bound optimization [34, 35] and maximize a surrogate function $\mathscr{F}$ with $\boldsymbol{\lambda}^{(t+1)} \leftarrow \arg\max_{\boldsymbol{\lambda}} \mathscr{F}(\boldsymbol{\lambda}|\boldsymbol{\lambda}^{(t)})$ (the upper parameter superscript is index for the iteration number in this case). This is guaranteed to monotonically increase the objective, provided that $L_g(\boldsymbol{\lambda}) - \mathscr{F}(\boldsymbol{\lambda}|\boldsymbol{\lambda}^{(t)})$ reaches its minimum at $\boldsymbol{\lambda} = \boldsymbol{\lambda}^{(t)}$. A natural surrogate is the second-order Taylor expansion of the objective around $\boldsymbol{\lambda}^{(t)}$, with a bound $\mathbf{H}_b$ on its second derivative (Hessian) matrix $\mathbf{H}$, so that $\mathbf{H}(\boldsymbol{\lambda}) \succeq \mathbf{H}_b$, $\forall\boldsymbol{\lambda}$:

$$\mathscr{F}(\boldsymbol{\lambda}|\boldsymbol{\lambda}^{(t)}) = \frac{1}{2}\boldsymbol{\lambda}^\top\mathbf{H}_b\boldsymbol{\lambda} + \boldsymbol{\lambda}^\top(\mathbf{g}(\boldsymbol{\lambda}^{(t)}) - \mathbf{H}_b\boldsymbol{\lambda}^{(t)}). \tag{12.15}$$

The gradient and Hessian of L_g can be computed analytically:

$$\mathbf{g}(\boldsymbol{\lambda}) = \sum_{i=1}^{N}(\mathbf{U}_i - \mathbf{v}_i(\boldsymbol{\lambda})) \otimes \mathbf{r}_i \tag{12.16}$$

with $\mathbf{U}_i = [h_1^{(i)}, \ldots, h_M^{(i)}]^\top$, $\otimes$ the Kronecker product, and $\mathbf{v}_i(\boldsymbol{\lambda}) = [g_1(\mathbf{r}_i), \ldots, g_M(\mathbf{r}_i)]^\top$. The Hessian matrix of L_g is:

$$\mathbf{H}(\boldsymbol{\lambda}) = -\sum_{i=1}^{N}\left(\mathbf{V}_i(\boldsymbol{\lambda}) - \mathbf{v}_i(\boldsymbol{\lambda})\mathbf{v}_i(\boldsymbol{\lambda})^\top\right) \otimes \left(\mathbf{r}_i\mathbf{r}_i^\top\right), \tag{12.17}$$

where $\mathbf{V}_i(\boldsymbol{\lambda}) = \mathrm{diag}[g_1(\mathbf{r}_i), \ldots, g_M(\mathbf{r}_i)]$ (the dimensionality of the Hessian is $D \times M$). The Hessian is lower bounded by a negative definite matrix which depends on the input, but *remarkably*, is independent of $\boldsymbol{\lambda}$ [12]:

$$\mathbf{H}(\boldsymbol{\lambda}) \succeq \mathbf{H}_b \equiv -\frac{1}{2}\left[\mathbf{I} - \frac{\mathbf{1}\mathbf{1}^\top}{M}\right] \otimes \sum_{i=1}^{N}\mathbf{r}_i\mathbf{r}_i^\top, \tag{12.18}$$

where $\mathbf{1} = [1, 1, \ldots, 1]^\top$. The parameter update is based on the standard Newton step:

$$\boldsymbol{\lambda}^{(t+1)} \leftarrow \boldsymbol{\lambda}^{(t)} - \mathbf{H}_b^{-1}\mathbf{g}(\boldsymbol{\lambda}^{(t)}). \tag{12.19}$$

To fit the gates we use a forward greedy algorithm that combines gradient boosting and bound optimization. It selects the variables according to functional gradient boosting [24] and optimizes the resulting sub-problems using bound optimization, as described above. To compute the functional gradient, we rewrite the objective in terms of functions $F_j(\mathbf{r}^{(i)})$. This method is applicable to any differentiable log-likelihood:

$$L_g = \sum_{i=1}^{N}\sum_{j=1}^{M}\left\{h_j^{(i)}F_j(\mathbf{r}^{(i)}) - \log\sum_{j=1}^{M}\exp(F_j(\mathbf{r}^{(i)}))\right\}. \tag{12.20}$$

The functional gradient corresponding to one component of F_j is:

$$d_j^{(i)} = \frac{\partial L_g(F_j(\mathbf{r}^{(i)}))}{\partial F_j(\mathbf{r}^{(i)})} = h_j^{(i)} - \frac{\exp(F_j(\mathbf{r}^{(i)}))}{\sum_{j=1}^{M}\exp(F_j(\mathbf{r}^{(i)}))} \tag{12.21}$$

with the full gradient of the jth gate assembled as $\nabla\mathbf{f}_j = [d_j^{(1)}, \ldots, d_j^{(N)}]^\top$—the steepest descent direction in function space. For feature selection, we choose the row vector $\mathbf{v}$ of $\mathbf{R}$ with weight index not already in the active set S, and most correlated (collinear) with the gradient [24]:

$$i = \underset{k \notin S, j=1,\ldots,M}{\arg\max}\left|\mathbf{v}_k^\top\nabla\mathbf{f}_j\right|. \tag{12.22}$$

We initialize $\lambda = 0$ and select the ith variable, incrementally, based on the gate parameter estimates at the previous round of selection. Once the ith variable is selected, we optimize (12.14) with respect to all pre-selected i variables using bound optimization. We use the solution of the previous iteration to quick-start the current optimization problem (this is convex but a good initialization saves iterations). The advantage of bound optimization in a greedy forward selection context is that we can efficiently update the Hessian bound using the Woodbury inversion identity. Thus, the cost of each iteration is $O(cNMD)$ where c is a small constant, and the total cost of selecting the k variables is $O(kNMD)$. When the specified number of variables is reached, we terminate. Unlike gradient boosting where the only current selected variable is optimized, we also perform back-fitting [71], i.e. optimize all selected variables in each round. To speed-up computation, it is possible to optimize the weights of the gating networks sequentially—fix the weights of other gating networks than the one currently optimized—the problem in (12.21). This requires the solution to a sequence of k-dimensional problems (usually $k \ll D$) and can be significantly cheaper than updating all gate parameters simultaneously, especially when denser (less sparse) models are desired. To sparsify the gating network, one can consider forward selection ideas based on maximizing the marginal likelihood, along the same lines as used for experts. However, the computational cost of this approach is high even for fast Bayesian approximations to multinomial classification. Differently from Bayesian regression, there is no analytical expression for the marginal likelihood, hence we have to resort on Laplace approximation. But this only works around the maximized posterior point, so we have to recompute the most probable weight and the corresponding Hessian matrix after adding or deleting an input entry (or basis function). For large problems this operation is computationally prohibitive.

12.3 Manifolds: Supervised Spectral Latent Variable Models

A variety of computer vision and machine learning tasks require the analysis of high-dimensional ambient signals, e.g. 2d images, 3D range scans or data obtained from human motion capture systems. The goal is to learn compact, perceptual (latent) models of the data generation process and use them to interpret new measurements. For example, the variability in an image sequence filming a rotating teapot is non-linearly produced by latent factors like rotation variables and the lighting direction. Our subjective, *perceived* dimensionality partly mirrors the latent factors, being significantly smaller than the one directly *measured*—the high-dimensional sequence of image pixel vectors. Similarly, filming a human running or walking requires megabytes of wildly varying images, yet in a representation that properly correlates the human joint angles, the intrinsic dimensionality is effectively 1—the phase of the walking cycle. The argument can go on, but underlines the intuitive idea that the space of all images is much larger than the set of physically possible ones, which, in turn is larger than the one typically observed in most every day's scenes. If this is true, perceptual inference cannot proceed without an appropriate, arguably probabilistic model of correlation, a natural way to link perceptual and measured inferences. This implies a non-linear subset, or a manifold assumption, at least in the large-sample regime: the low-dimensional perceptual structure lives in the high-dimensional space of direct observations. To unfold it, we need faithful, topographic representations of the observed data—effectively forms of continuity and locality: nearby observations should map to nearby percepts and faraway observations should map faraway. Given this, we want to be able to consistently answer the following questions: How to represent a percept or an image? What is the probability of an observed image? What is the probability of a given percept? What is the conditional probability of a percept given an image and vice versa?

In this section we introduce probabilistic models with geometric properties in order to marry spectral embeddings, parametric latent variable models, and structured image predictors. We refer to these conditional probabilistic constructs, defined on top of an irregular grid (or unfolding) obtained from a spectral embedding as Supervised Spectral Latent Variable Models (SSLVM).

We will work with a training set $(\mathbf{r}_i, \mathbf{y}_i)$, $i = 1, \ldots, N$ with inputs $\mathbf{r}$ and outputs $\mathbf{y}$, both multivariate. We construct a latent variable model with intermediate (hidden) representation $\mathbf{x}$ with distribution that preserves geometric constraints among outputs $\mathbf{y}$, and at the same time offers good predictive power when regressed against the inputs $\mathbf{r}$.

12.3.1 Conditional Latent Variable Model

The joint distribution over latent and output variables, conditioned on inputs is:

$$p(\mathbf{y}, \mathbf{x}|\mathbf{r}, \boldsymbol{\theta}, \boldsymbol{\delta}) = p(\mathbf{y}|\mathbf{x}, \boldsymbol{\theta})p(\mathbf{x}|\mathbf{r}, \boldsymbol{\delta}) \qquad (12.23)$$

with $(\boldsymbol{\theta}, \boldsymbol{\delta})$ parameters of the two distributions (in the sequel dropped whenever not essential for readability). The conditional response is calculated by integrating the latent space:

$$p(\mathbf{y}|\mathbf{r}) = \int p(\mathbf{y}|\mathbf{x})p(\mathbf{x}|\mathbf{r}) \, d\mathbf{x} \approx \frac{1}{S}\sum_{s=1}^{S} p\left(\mathbf{y}|\mathbf{x}^{(s)}\right). \qquad (12.24)$$

Since we work with non-linear conditional models $p(\mathbf{x}|\mathbf{r})$ and $p(\mathbf{y}|\mathbf{x})$ the integral in (12.24) cannot be computed analytically. Hence, we approximate using a MCMC estimate based on S samples drawn from the conditional $p(\mathbf{x}|\mathbf{r})$ [66].[2] This is tractable and efficient because the latent conditional is usually low-dimensional and has, for our choice of models, a convenient parametric form—either Gaussian for regression or Gaussian mixture in the case of conditional mixtures of experts models. Specifically, we use:

$$p(\mathbf{y}|\mathbf{x}) = p\left(\mathbf{y}|\mathbf{x}, \boldsymbol{\theta} = (\mathbf{W}, \boldsymbol{\Sigma})\right) = \mathcal{N}\left(\mathbf{W}\boldsymbol{\Phi}(\mathbf{x}), \boldsymbol{\Sigma}\right) \qquad (12.25)$$

---

[2]Sampled configurations have parenthesized superscripts; subscripts index training datapoints.

and $p(\mathbf{x}|\mathbf{r})$ given by a mixture of expert model described in Sect. 12.2. The latent space conditional is obtained using Bayes' rule:

$$p(\mathbf{x}|\mathbf{y},\mathbf{r}) = \frac{p(\mathbf{y}|\mathbf{x})p(\mathbf{x}|\mathbf{r})}{p(\mathbf{y}|\mathbf{r})} = \frac{p(\mathbf{y}|\mathbf{x})p(\mathbf{x}|\mathbf{r})}{\frac{1}{S}\sum_{s=1}^{S}p(\mathbf{y}|\mathbf{x}^{(s)})}. \qquad (12.26)$$

For pairs of training data i and MC latent samples s, we abbreviate $p_{(s,i)} = p(\mathbf{x}^{(s)}|\mathbf{y}_i,\mathbf{r}_i)$. Notice how the choice of latent conditional $p(\mathbf{x}|\mathbf{r})$ influences the membership probabilities in (12.26). We can compute either the conditional mean or the mode (better for multimodal distributions) in latent space, using the same MC integration method used for (12.24):

$$\mathrm{E}\{\mathbf{x}|\mathbf{y}_n,\mathbf{r}_n\} = \int p(\mathbf{x}|\mathbf{y}_n,\mathbf{r}_n)\mathbf{x}\,d\mathbf{x} = \sum_{s=1}^{S}p_{(s,n)}\mathbf{x}_s, \qquad (12.27)$$

$$s_{\max} = \arg\max_{s} p_{(s,n)}. \qquad (12.28)$$

The model has the components for consistent calculations in both the latent and output spaces: $p(\mathbf{x}|\mathbf{r})$ gives the latent space distribution, (12.24) the output marginal, (12.25) provides the conditional (or mapping) from latent to output, and (12.27) and (12.28) give the mean or mode of the mapping from output to latent space. More accurate but also more expensive mode-finding approximations can be obtained by direct gradient ascent on (12.26). Latent conditionals given partially observed $\mathbf{y}$ vectors are easy to compute, using (12.26). The distribution on $\mathbf{y}$ is Gaussian and unobserved components can be integrated analytically—this effectively removes them from the mean and the corresponding lines and columns of the covariance. Computations like these are useful as often outputs can have missing entries, e.g., marker drop-outs in a motion capture system during training, 'pattern completion' or restoration of an image under the latent model during testing, see, e.g., Fig. 12.4, right.

Implicit latent geometric constraints: Assume that distances between outputs $\mathbf{y}$ are stored in a vector $\mathbf{D}$ of size N^2, with entries $d(\mathbf{y}_i,\mathbf{y}_j)$ where d is an arbitrary similarity function that can be the Euclidean distance, a Gaussian centered at the first argument, or a geodesic distance in the data graph (these will be used to model distance preserving constraints like the ones encountered in PCA/MDS, Laplacian Eigenmaps or isometric feature mapping (Isomap), respectively). Consider a similar vector $\mathbf{L}$ of corresponding latent space distances $d(\mathrm{E}(\mathbf{x}|\mathbf{y}_i),\mathrm{E}(\mathbf{x}|\mathbf{y}_j))$, where $\mathrm{E}(\mathbf{x}|\mathbf{y})$ is the conditional expectation of latent variable $\mathbf{x}$ given $\mathbf{y}$, cf. (12.27). We use vectors of pairwise distances among outputs and their corresponding latent conditional expectations in order to construct an implicit geometric constraint (or penalty) in latent space:

$$C = (\mathbf{D}-\mathbf{L})(\mathbf{D}-\mathbf{L})^{\top} \qquad (12.29)$$

which is 0 if output distances are preserved in latent space and large otherwise. Notice that $d(\mathbf{x}_i,\mathbf{x}_j)$ gives the distance between the ith and jth point in data or

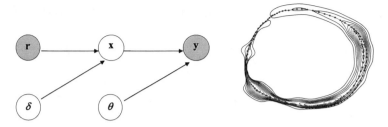

Fig. 12.4 (*Left*) Graphical Model of SSLVM. Shaded nodes indicate observed random variables (**y** being observed only in training). We jointly learn two conditional distributions $p(\mathbf{x}|\mathbf{r}) = p(\mathbf{x}|\mathbf{r}, \boldsymbol{\delta})$ and $p(\mathbf{y}|\mathbf{x}) = p(\mathbf{y}|\mathbf{x}, \boldsymbol{\theta})$ with a constraint that the geometry of the outputs, as encoded in distances between datapoints $d(\mathbf{y}_i, \mathbf{y}_j)$ is implicitly preserved among their corresponding latent pre-image expectations $d(\mathrm{E}(\mathbf{x}|\mathbf{y}_i), \mathrm{E}(\mathbf{x}|\mathbf{y}_j))$. (*Right*) shows the conditional latent space distribution $p(\mathbf{x}|\mathbf{y})$ for a walking model given only the left arm variables are observed (shoulder and elbow, here 5 out of 41 variables); the latent coordinate corresponding to the complete vector of 'ground truth' joint angles is shown with a circle. Notice that 3 modes that arise due to uncertainty from missing data. (Reproduced with permission from [29] ©2007 IEEE)

latent space, rather than the relative spatial positions of points in data and latent space. Clearly $d(\mathbf{x}, \mathbf{x}) = 0$. However, our method does not explicitly require distance properties. We can work, in principle, with any similarity measure such as the inner product. Notice also the dependence of the penalty on $\mathrm{E}(\mathbf{x}|\mathbf{y}) = \mathrm{E}(\mathbf{x}|\mathbf{y}, \boldsymbol{\theta})$, which is a function of the current parameters $\boldsymbol{\theta}$ of the latent to output model $p_{\boldsymbol{\theta}}(\mathbf{y}|\mathbf{x})$, cf. (12.25), (12.26) and (12.27). The penalty ensures that under the latent space posterior, the implicit latent space distances $\mathrm{E}(\mathbf{x}|\mathbf{y}_i)$ among configurations $\mathbf{x}$ that correspond to datapoints $\mathbf{y}_i$ under the current model $\boldsymbol{\theta}$, are preserved (distances $d(\mathbf{y}_i, \mathbf{y}_j)$). Notice that no matter the spectral constraint used, the resulting model is highly non-linear: latent variables depend non-linearly on inputs and outputs depend non-linearly on latent the variables.

The *implicit geometric constraint regularizer* in (12.29) requires the calculation of conditional expectations for the latent variables given output data, which may at first appear to be more complex. Notice that the regularizer does not depend explicitly on latent variables, hence we do not optimize latent variables explicitly—this would be underconstrained, prone to overfitting, and computationally prohibitive for models with more than a few latent dimensions. Furthermore, the proposed expression can be approximated efficiently by considering the inner product as a form distance function:

$$d\big(\mathrm{E}(\mathbf{x}|\mathbf{y}_i), \mathrm{E}(\mathbf{x}|\mathbf{y}_j)\big) = \sum_{s=1}^{S} \sum_{t=1}^{S} p_{(s,i)} p_{(t,j)} \mathbf{x}_s^{\top} \mathbf{x}_t. \qquad (12.30)$$

Typically, most $p_{(s,i)}$ will be close to zero. Removing those does not reduce the evaluation of distance functions but offers large speedups when computing its derivative, since $\mathbf{x}_s^{\top} \mathbf{x}_t$ can be stored ahead of time.

Learning algorithm: We learn the conditional model in (12.23) by optimizing a penalized image likelihood criterion that consists of the marginal likelihood (12.24) averaged over a dataset and the geometric penalty on the latent space (12.29):

$$\mathscr{L}(\boldsymbol{\theta}, \boldsymbol{\delta}) = \log \prod_{i=1}^{N} p(\mathbf{y}_i | \mathbf{r}_i) - \lambda C = \sum_{i=1}^{N} \log p(\mathbf{y}_i | \mathbf{r}_i) - \lambda C \qquad (12.31)$$

$$= \sum_{i=1}^{N} \log \sum_{s=1}^{S} p\big(\mathbf{y}_i | \mathbf{x}^{(s)}, \mathbf{r}_i\big) - \lambda C \qquad (12.32)$$

and λ is the regularizing (trade-off) parameter. In practice we will optimize a cost $\mathscr{F}$ that is the penalized expectation of the complete data log-likelihood $\mathscr{L}_c$:

$$\mathscr{F} = \big\langle \mathscr{L}_c(\boldsymbol{\theta}, \boldsymbol{\delta}) \big\rangle - \lambda C = \sum_{i=1}^{N} \sum_{s=1}^{S} p_{(s,i)} \log p\big(\mathbf{y}_i | \mathbf{x}^{(s)}\big) - \lambda C. \qquad (12.33)$$

We train the model by estimating $p(\mathbf{x}|\mathbf{r})$ and $p(\mathbf{y}|\mathbf{x})$ in alternation. We initialize the latent coordinates $\mathbf{x}_i$ corresponding to the given output data $\mathbf{y}_i$ using dimensionality reduction, based on the type of geometric constraint we wish to impose, e.g., PCA, Isomap or Laplacian Eigenmaps, and we use their corresponding distances between datapoints $d(\mathbf{y}_i, \mathbf{y}_j)$ in the penalty term C, see (12.29). Then, we first train $p(\mathbf{x}|\mathbf{r})$ based on $(\mathbf{r}_i, \mathbf{x}_i)$ data, and $p(\mathbf{y}, \mathbf{x})$ by sampling from the learned model $p(\mathbf{x}|\mathbf{r})$ with target data $\mathbf{y}_i$ and the constraint C. Then, we alternate between generating data $(E(\mathbf{x}|\mathbf{y}_i), \mathbf{r}_i)$ for training the input model $p(\mathbf{x}|\mathbf{r})$, and training the output model $p(\mathbf{y}|\mathbf{x})$ using EM: in the *E-step* we estimate the membership probabilities cf. (12.26), and in the *M-step* we solve a penalized weighted regression problem as in (12.33), with weights given by (12.26) and penalty given by C (12.29). Notice that C changes since $E(\mathbf{x}|\mathbf{y})$ is a function of the current $\boldsymbol{\theta} = (\mathbf{W}, \boldsymbol{\Sigma})$ parameters of $p(\mathbf{y}|\mathbf{x})$, cf. (12.27) and (12.25).

12.4 Structural SVM: Joint Localization and State Estimation

In the previous sections we have described predictive methods that are accurate, scalable, and can handle the ambiguity in the image to pose relationships by explicitly representing multiple solutions using mixture of experts models. We have also shown how this methodology can be constrained and made even faster by imposing low-dimensional manifold constraints. One of the remaining problems is to integrate person detection and pose estimation. One option is to combine the mixture of experts prediction with a front-end person detector or localizer. This approach has been pursued in [60] and [55], respectively.

In this section, we consider an alternative approach where we learn a structured scoring function in the joint space of image bounding box coordinates of a person and his or her continuous 3D pose. We consider a learning setting, where we are given a set of the input–output pairs $\{\mathbf{r}_i, \mathbf{z}_i\}_{i=1}^{N}$, with N is the size of training set and $\mathbf{z} \in Z$ are interdependent outputs. We aim to learn a function that best represents the relationship between inputs and outputs. In structured learning, the discriminative function is a linear combination of joint features

$$g(\mathbf{r}) = \arg\min_{\mathbf{z}} f_{\mathbf{w}}(\mathbf{r}, \mathbf{z}) = \mathbf{w}^\top \Psi(\mathbf{r}, \mathbf{z}), \tag{12.34}$$

where $\mathbf{w}$ is a parameter vector and $\Psi(\mathbf{r}, \mathbf{z})$ is a feature vector induced by a joint kernel $K(\mathbf{r}, \mathbf{z}, \mathbf{r}', \mathbf{z}') = \Psi(\mathbf{r}, \mathbf{z})^\top \Psi(\mathbf{r}', \mathbf{z}')$. The specific form of joint features $\Psi(\mathbf{r}, \mathbf{z})$ is problem-dependent, an aspect that will be discussed in the sequel. The scoring function $f_{\mathbf{w}}(\mathbf{r}, \mathbf{z})$ can be interpreted as a compatibility that measures how well the output $\mathbf{z}$ matches the input $\mathbf{r}$.

To learn the discriminative function, $f_{\mathbf{w}}(\mathbf{r}, \mathbf{z})$, the structural SVM (structSVM) maximizes the generalized maximum margin loss:

$$\min_{\mathbf{w}, \xi} \frac{1}{2} \mathbf{w}^\top \mathbf{w} + C\xi$$

$$\text{s.t.} \quad \forall (\bar{\mathbf{z}}_1, \dots, \bar{\mathbf{z}}_N) \in Z^N$$

$$\frac{1}{N} \mathbf{w}^\top \sum_{j=1}^{N} \left[\Psi(\mathbf{r}_j, \mathbf{z}_j) - \Psi(\mathbf{r}_j, \bar{\mathbf{z}}_j) \right] \geq \frac{1}{N} \sum_{j=1}^{N} \Delta(\mathbf{z}_j, \bar{\mathbf{z}}_j) - \xi, \tag{12.35}$$

where $\Delta(\mathbf{z}_j, \bar{\mathbf{z}}_j)$ is a loss function that should decrease as the output $\bar{\mathbf{z}}_j$ approaches the ground truth $\mathbf{z}_j$. We use the so-called '1-slack formulation', which is equivalent to the 'n-slack' analog, but is more efficient in conjunction with cutting plane algorithms (we use) due to a significantly smaller dual problem [26].

Under infinitely many constraints, standard duality does not apply. However, for any small δ we can assume a finite δ-cover of our data domain, where the constraints are locally uniform. This allows to recast the problem into one with finite (yet large) number of constraints. In this case, the primal/dual theory implies that the parameter $\mathbf{w}$ has the form:

$$\mathbf{w} = \frac{1}{N} \sum_{\bar{\mathbf{Z}} \in Z^N} \alpha_{\bar{\mathbf{Z}}} \sum_{j=1}^{N} \left[\Phi(\mathbf{r}_j, \mathbf{z}_j) - \Phi(\mathbf{r}_j, \bar{\mathbf{z}}_j) \right], \tag{12.36}$$

where $\bar{\mathbf{Z}} = (\bar{\mathbf{z}}_1, \dots, \bar{\mathbf{z}}_N)$.

Joint kernel for location and state estimation: For joint localization and state (pose) estimation, the input is an image, $\mathbf{r}$, and the output is the bounding box of the object *together* with its corresponding continuous state (e.g., 2d or 3D pose): $\mathbf{z} = (\mathbf{y}, \mathbf{x})$. We use $\mathbf{r}|\mathbf{y}$ to denote the feature vector of image regions restricted within the bounding box instantiated by $\mathbf{y}$. Here, we consider a joint kernel where the combined feature vector can be written as a tensor product over the two corresponding subspaces

$$\Psi(\mathbf{r}, \mathbf{z}) = \phi(\mathbf{r}|\mathbf{y}) \otimes \varphi(\mathbf{x}), \tag{12.37}$$

where $\otimes$ denotes the tensor product, $\phi(\mathbf{r}|\mathbf{y})$ is the feature induced by the kernel $K_{r|y}(\mathbf{r}|\mathbf{y}, \mathbf{r}'|\mathbf{y}')$ defined over the image region and $\varphi(\mathbf{x})$ is the feature vector induced by the state/pose kernel $K_x(\mathbf{x}, \mathbf{x}')$. For the tensor product feature vector, the joint location and state kernel is chosen to have the following form [68]:

$$K(\mathbf{r}, \mathbf{z}, \mathbf{r}', \mathbf{z}') = \Psi(\mathbf{r}, \mathbf{z})^\top \Psi(\mathbf{r}', \mathbf{z}') = K_{r|y}(\mathbf{r}|\mathbf{y}, \mathbf{r}'|\mathbf{y}') K_x(\mathbf{x}, \mathbf{x}'). \qquad (12.38)$$

Equation (12.38) implies that the joint kernel is a product of components computed over image regions within the bounding box and the corresponding state, respectively. This tensor product feature is rather general and can handle many types of structured outputs, including multiclass and sequential constraints. In vision, kernels are used to compare statistics or image features, e.g., as inner products of histograms defined over regions. This includes for example, bag-of-feature models, regular grids like HOG, as well as spatial pyramids based on weighted combinations of histogram intersection kernels computed at multiple levels of image encoding. An attractive feature of histogram kernels is that partially overlapping image regions share underlying statistics.

On the other hand, since we work with continuous states, $\varphi(\mathbf{x})$ is a feature vector induced by the kernels defined over continuous variables. Concurrently, we wish the kernel function to be normalized to prevent the slack variable ξ from diverging to infinity for some outputs. One possible (but by no means the only) choice satisfying these desiderata is the Gaussian kernel. This is defined over continuous variables and its 2-norm $\|\varphi(\mathbf{x})\|_2 = \sqrt{K_x(\mathbf{x}, \mathbf{x})} = 1$. Thus, for most of our experiments, the state/pose kernel has the form: $K_x(\mathbf{x}, \mathbf{x}') = \exp(-\gamma_x \|\mathbf{x} - \mathbf{x}'\|^2)$.

When designing a similarity measure between two different input–output features, intuitively, we wish: 1) input–output pairs with distant inputs should be dissimilar; and 2) input–output pairs whose inputs are nearby but outputs are distant should also be dissimilar; otherwise stated *only* the input–output pairs with both similar inputs *and* similar outputs should be similar. The joint kernel we use satisfies the above conditions because it is the product of two kernels defined over inputs and outputs, respectively; hence its value is small if any one of the two kernel component values is small (dissimilar). In this respect, the joint kernel is more expressive than a classical kernel, only defined over inputs, where the input–output pairs with similar inputs but dissimilar outputs have negative impact and can pull the estimate in contradictory directions. For localization and state estimation, the advantage of a joint kernel over separable ones is that given a test image, the training data with dissimilar states/poses from the test input will have reduced impact on the bounding box search and estimate. This may explain why continuous structSVM achieves better performance than support vector regression (SVR) and other unstructured methods in our experience [25]. In addition, the model also includes search/ranking in the space of possible object locations in the image, described next.

Output loss function: The output loss $\Delta(\mathbf{z}, \mathbf{z}')$ should reflect how well $\mathbf{z}$ approaches the ground truth output $\mathbf{z}'$. Within our joint tensor product kernel formulation, the loss function definition should be compatible with both the image and the state/pose kernels. For the image kernel, we adapt the score used in the PASCAL visual object challenge [8]:

$$\Delta_y(\mathbf{y}, \mathbf{y}') = 1 - \frac{\text{Area}(\mathbf{y} \cap \mathbf{y}')}{\text{Area}(\mathbf{y} \cup \mathbf{y}')}, \tag{12.39}$$

where the quality of object localization is based on the amount of area overlap, where $\text{Area}(\mathbf{y} \cap \mathbf{y}')$ is the intersection of the two bounding boxes $\mathbf{y}$ and $\mathbf{y}'$, and $\text{Area}(\mathbf{y} \cup \mathbf{y}')$ is their union. For state/pose estimation, it is natural to consider the loss function as a square distance in the reproducing kernel Hilbert space induced by the kernel function $K_x(\mathbf{x}, \mathbf{x}')$:

$$\Delta_x(\mathbf{x}, \mathbf{x}') = \left\| \varphi(\mathbf{x}) - \varphi(\mathbf{x}') \right\|^2 = K_x(\mathbf{x}, \mathbf{x}) + K_x(\mathbf{x}', \mathbf{x}') - 2K_x(\mathbf{x}, \mathbf{x}'). \tag{12.40}$$

This implies that if a state is far from the ground truth, it has high loss, otherwise small loss. We define the joint output loss as the weighted sum of losses for object localization and state estimation:

$$\Delta(\mathbf{z}, \mathbf{z}') = \gamma \Delta_y(\mathbf{y}, \mathbf{y}') + (1 - \gamma)\Delta_x(\mathbf{x}, \mathbf{x}'), \tag{12.41}$$

with $0 \leq \gamma \leq 1$ balancing the two terms.

Cutting plane algorithm: When training the model with continuous outputs, the number of constraints is infinite, and it is infeasible to solve the optimization (12.35) for all the constraints. Fortunately, the maximum margin loss has a sparsity-promoting effect, with most constraints inactive in the final solution. The cutting plane algorithm creates a nested sequence of successively tighter relaxations of the original optimization problem and finds a small set of active constraints that ensures a sufficiently accurate solution—a practical training method (see our Fig. 12.5a). The algorithm starts with an empty working set $S = \varnothing$ of constraints. At each iteration, it finds the most violated constraint for the ith training input If the amount of violation exceeds the current value of the slack variable ξ by more than ε, the potential support vector $\overline{\mathbf{Z}} = (\overline{\mathbf{z}}_1, \ldots, \overline{\mathbf{z}}_N)$ is added to the working set $S = S \cup \overline{\mathbf{Z}}$. After the working set is updated, the optimization (12.35) is solved in the dual with constraints $\overline{Z} \in S$ and The algorithm stops when no violation is larger than the desired precision ε. Notice that at the first iteration, the set of constraints S is empty—in this case finding the most violated constraint simplifies to maximizing the loss $\Delta(\mathbf{z}_i, \mathbf{z})$ with respect to the output $\mathbf{z}$. Unlike the n-slack formulation, the dual problem for the I-slack usually remains compact, as only a single constraint is added per iteration. Sample detection and 3d human pose reconstruction results obtained using this methodology are shown in Fig. 12.6.

12.4.1 Software

Discriminative pose prediction code, including multi-valued predictors based on mixture of experts [11], structured predictors based on twin Gaussian Pro-

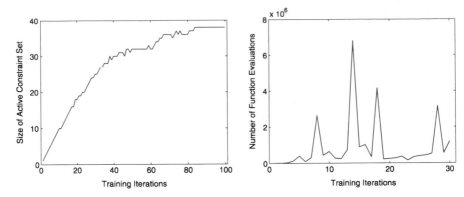

Fig. 12.5 (*Left*) Size of the active constraint set (i.e., the number of support vectors) as function of iteration. The number of support vectors saturates at about 80 iterations, indicating convergence of the cutting plane algorithm. Notice that support vectors (points with non-zero dual variables) in the *1*-slack formulation are linear combinations of multiple examples and no longer correspond to a single training data point. (*Right*) Number of function evaluations for the branch-and-bound algorithm in the training stage of a joint structural SVM, based on bag-of-words SIFT (image size 640 × 480). Notice that the number of function evaluations is significantly higher during some of the iterations compared to the others, confirming that the hardness of search is closely linked to the structural SVM parameters, **w**. (Reproduced with permission from [25] ©2009 IEEE)

cesses [10], and spectral latent variable models [9, 29] can be found on our website, at: http://sminchisescu.ins.uni-bonn.de/code.

12.5 Challenges and Open Problems

Over the past 15 years, there has been significant progress in 3D human pose recovery, both conceptually—understanding the limitations of existing likelihood or search algorithms, and deriving improved procedures and conceptually new models and image features to overcome them—and practically, by building systems that can reconstruct shape and perform fine body measurements from images [53], model complex physical properties [14, 73], recover 3D human motion from multiple views [18, 30] or reconstruct human pose from complex monocular video footage like dancing or movies [28, 64].

For real-world applications, one of the main challenges is to automatically understand people in-vivo, and in an integrated fashion. Typical computations are to find the people, infer their poses, recognize their activities, the objects and the interactions.

Many of the existing human motion analysis systems are still complex to construct, computationally expensive, and cannot seamlessly deal with significant structural variability, multiple interacting people and severe occlusion or lighting changes. A convincing transition between the laboratory and the real world remains to be realized. A shortcoming of existing systems is their inability to provide a satisfactory solution to the problem of model selection and the management of the

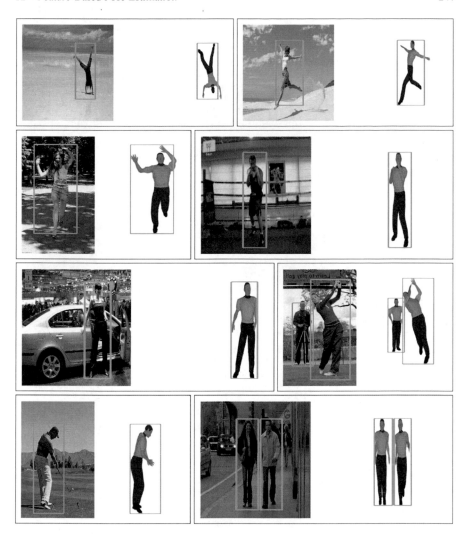

Fig. 12.6 Localization and 3D human pose reconstructions in real-world images, for structSVM models trained on a dataset of quasi-real images. The framework allows the localization and reconstruction of multiple people. (Reproduced with permission from [25] ©2009 IEEE)

level of detail. Anyone who watches movies, TV or other sources of video can easily notice to what limited extent the people are visible in close-up full-body views. The subjects are frequently occluded by other people, by scene elements, or simply clipped to obtain partial views for artistic or practical reasons—the camera operator tends to focus on the relevant aspects of the gesture and pose rather than the entire body, and so should, perhaps, the computer vision algorithms. This suggests that monolithic models may have to be replaced with a set of models that can flexibly represent partial views and multiple level of detail. Level of detail, albeit considered in the different sense of 2D, vs. 2.5D vs. 3D may need to be modeled and inferred automatically. The extent of 2D to 3D 'lifting', ranging from none, partial to full, should ideally be calibrated to the task and correlated with the degree of scene observability, or with the image resolution. Working with multiple models raises inference questions of deciding what model is appropriate, switching between different models in a tractable manner, or managing the trade-off between run-time inference and indexing based on prior knowledge. The interaction between human pose reconstruction and activity recognition will probably emerge as a natural solution within the broader scope of coherent scene understanding.

Acknowledgements   This work has been supported in part by the European Commission under MCEXT-025481 and by CNCSIS-UEFISCU under project PN II-RU-RC-2/2009. This chapter reviews research presented in [9, 11, 25, 28].

References

1. CMU Human Motion Capture Database. Available online at http://mocap.cs.cmu.edu/search.html (2003) [229]
2. Agarwal, A., Triggs, B.: Hyperfeatures – multilevel local coding for visual recognition. In: European Conference on Computer Vision (2006) [228]
3. Agarwal, A., Triggs, B.: A local basis representation for estimating human pose from cluttered images. In: Asian Conference on Computer Vision (2006) [227-229,231,232]
4. Andriluka, M., Roth, S., Schiele, B.: People tracking-by-detection and people-detection-by-tracking. In: IEEE Computer Society Conference on Computer Vision and Pattern Recognition (2008) [227,230]
5. Balan, A., Black, M., Haussecker, H., Sigal, L.: Shining a light on human pose: On shadows, shading and the estimation of pose and shape. In: IEEE International Conference on Computer Vision (2007) [227]
6. Battu, B., Krappers, A., Koenderink, J.: Ambiguity in pictorial depth. Perception **36**, 1290–1304 (2007) [228]
7. Bishop, C., Svensen, M.: Bayesian mixtures of experts. In: Conference on Uncertainty in Artificial Intelligence (2003) [234]
8. Blaschko, M.B., Lampert, C.H.: Learning to localize objects with structured output regression. In: European Conference on Computer Vision, pp. 2–15 (2008) [245]
9. Bo, L., Sminchisescu, C.: Supervised spectral latent variable models. In: International Conference on Artificial Intelligence and Statistics (2009) [246,248]
10. Bo, L., Sminchisescu, C.: Twin Gaussian processes for structured prediction. Int. J. Comput. Vis. **87** (2010) [246]
11. Bo, L., Sminchisescu, C., Kanaujia, A., Metaxas, D.: Fast algorithms for large scale conditional 3D prediction. In: IEEE Computer Society Conference on Computer Vision and Pattern Recognition (2008) [236,245,248]
12. Böhning, D.: Multinomial logistic regression algorithm. Ann. Inst. Stat. Math. **44**, 197–200 (2001) [237]
13. Bourdev, L., Malik, J.: Poselets: Body part detectors trained using 3d human pose annotations. In: IEEE International Conference on Computer Vision (2009) [227]
14. Brubaker, M., Fleet, D.: The Kneed Walker for human pose tracking. In: IEEE Computer Society Conference on Computer Vision and Pattern Recognition (2008) [246]
15. Choo, K., Fleet, D.: People tracking using hybrid Monte Carlo filtering. In: IEEE International Conference on Computer Vision (2001) [227]
16. Cook, R.D.: Regression Graphics. Wiley-Interscience, New York (1988) [229]

17. Cortes, C., Mohri, M., Weston, J.: A general regression technique for learning transductions. In: International Conference on Machine Learning, pp. 153–160 (2005) [229]
18. Deutscher, J., Blake, A., Reid, I.: Articulated body motion capture by annealed particle filtering. In: IEEE Computer Society Conference on Computer Vision and Pattern Recognition (2000) [227,228,246]
19. Deutscher, J., Davidson, A., Reid, I.: Articulated partitioning of high dimensional search spaces associated with articulated body motion capture. In: IEEE Computer Society Conference on Computer Vision and Pattern Recognition (2001) [227]
20. Edwards, D., Lauritzen, S.: The TM algorithm for maximising a conditional likelihood function. Biometrika **88**(4), 961–972 (2001) [234]
21. Eichner, M., Ferrari, V.: We are family: Joint pose estimation of multiple persons. In: European Conference on Computer Vision (2010) [227]
22. Felzenszwalb, P., Girshick, R., McAllester, D., Ramanan, D.: Object detection with discriminatively trained part-based models. IEEE Trans. Pattern Anal. Mach. Intell. **32**, 1627–1645 (2010) [227]
23. Felzenszwalb, P., Huttenlocher, D.: Pictorial structures for object recognition. Int. J. Comput. Vis. **61**(1) (2005) [227]
24. Friedman, J.: Greedy function approximation: A gradient boosting machine. Ann. Stat. **29**(5), 1189–1232 (2001) [237]
25. Ionescu, C., Bo, L., Sminchisescu, C.: Structural SVM for visual localization and continuous state estimation. In: IEEE International Conference on Computer Vision (2009) [227,244, 246-248]
26. Joachims, T., Finley, T., Yu, C.: Cutting-plane training of structural SVMs. Mach. Learn. **77**, 27–59 (2009) [243]
27. Jordan, M., Jacobs, R.: Hierarchical mixtures of experts and the EM algorithm. Neural Comput. **6**, 181–214 (1994) [234,235]
28. Kanaujia, A., Sminchisescu, C., Metaxas, D.: Semi-supervised hierarchical models for 3D human pose reconstruction. In: IEEE Computer Society Conference on Computer Vision and Pattern Recognition (2006) [231-234,246,248]
29. Kanaujia, A., Sminchisescu, C., Metaxas, D.: Spectral latent variable models for perceptual inference. In: IEEE International Conference on Computer Vision, vol. 1 (2007) [230,241, 246]
30. Kehl, R., Bray, M., Gool, L.V.: Full body tracking from multiple views using stochastic sampling. In: IEEE Computer Society Conference on Computer Vision and Pattern Recognition (2005) [246]
31. Kim, M., Pavlovic, V.: Dimensionality reduction using covariance operator inverse regression. In: IEEE Computer Society Conference on Computer Vision and Pattern Recognition (2008) [229]
32. Koenderink, J.: Pictorial relief. Philos. Trans. R. Soc., Math. Phys. Eng. Sci. **356**(1740), 1071–1086 (1998) [226,228]
33. Koenderink, J., van Doorn, A.: The internal representation of solid shape with respect to vision. Biol. Cybern. **32**(3), 211–216 (1979) [228]
34. Krishnapuram, B., Carin, L., Figueiredo, M.T., Hartemink, A.J.: Sparse multinomial logistic regression: Fast algorithms and generalization bounds. IEEE Trans. Pattern Anal. Mach. Intell. **27**(6), 957–968 (2005) [236]
35. Lange, K., Hunter, D., Yang, I.: Optimization transfer using surrogate objective functions. J. Comput. Graph. Stat. **9**, 1–59 (2001) [236]
36. Lawrence, N.: Probabilistic non-linear component analysis with Gaussian process latent variable models. J. Mach. Learn. Res. **6**, 1783–1816 (2005) [230]
37. Lazebnik, S., Schmid, C., Ponce, J.: Beyond bags of features: Spatial pyramid matching for recognizing natural scene categories. In: IEEE Computer Society Conference on Computer Vision and Pattern Recognition (2006) [232]
38. LeCun, Y., Chopra, S., Hadsell, R., Ranzato, R.M., Huang, F.: A tutorial on energy-based learning. In: Predicting Structured Data. MIT Press, Cambridge (2006) [230]

39. Lee, H.J., Chen, Z.: Determination of 3D human body postures from a single view. Comput. Vis. Graph. Image Process. **30**, 148–168 (1985) [227]
40. Lu, Z., Perpinan, M.C., Sminchisescu, C.: People tracking with the Laplacian eigenmaps latent variable model. In: Advances in Neural Information Processing Systems (2007) [230]
41. Morris, D., Rehg, J.: Singularity analysis for articulated object tracking. In: IEEE Computer Society Conference on Computer Vision and Pattern Recognition, pp. 289–296 (1998) [227]
42. Nistér, D., Stévenius, H.: Scalable recognition with a vocabulary tree. In: IEEE Computer Society Conference on Computer Vision and Pattern Recognition (2006) [232]
43. Poppe, R.: Evaluating example-based human pose estimation: Experiments on HumanEva sets. In: HumanEva Workshop CVPR (2007) [229]
44. Ramanan, D., Sminchisescu, C.: Training deformable models for localization. In: IEEE Computer Society Conference on Computer Vision and Pattern Recognition (2006) [227]
45. Rosales, R., Sclaroff, S.: Learning body pose via specialized maps. In: Advances in Neural Information Processing Systems (2002) [227-229]
46. Sapp, B., Toshev, A., Taskar, B.: Cascaded models for articulated pose estimation. In: European Conference on Computer Vision (2010) [227]
47. Serre, T., Wolf, L., Poggio, T.: Object recognition with features inspired by visual cortex. In: IEEE Computer Society Conference on Computer Vision and Pattern Recognition, pp. 994–1000 (2005) [231]
48. Shakhnarovich, G., Viola, P., Darrell, T.: Fast pose estimation with parameter sensitive hashing. In: IEEE International Conference on Computer Vision (2003) [228,229]
49. Sidenbladh, H., Black, M.: Learning image statistics for Bayesian tracking. In: IEEE International Conference on Computer Vision (2001) [227]
50. Sidenbladh, H., Black, M., Fleet, D.: Stochastic tracking of 3D human figures using 2D image motion. In: European Conference on Computer Vision (2000) [227]
51. Sidenbladh, H., Black, M., Sigal, L.: Implicit probabilistic models of human motion for synthesis and tracking. In: European Conference on Computer Vision (2002) [227]
52. Sigal, L., Balan, A., Black, M.: HumanEva: Synchronized video and motion capture dataset and baseline algorithm for evaluation of articulated human motion. Int. J. Comput. Vis. **87**, 4–27 (2006) [229]
53. Sigal, L., Balan, A., Black, M.J.: Combined discriminative and generative articulated pose and non-rigid shape estimation. In: Advances in Neural Information Processing Systems (2007) [228,246]
54. Sigal, L., Bhatia, S., Roth, S., Black, M., Isard, M.: Tracking loose-limbed people. In: IEEE Computer Society Conference on Computer Vision and Pattern Recognition (2004) [228]
55. Sigal, L., Black, M.: Predicting 3d people from 2d pictures. In: International Workshop on Articulated Motion and Deformable Objects (2006) [227,233,242]
56. Sigal, L., Memisevic, R., Fleet, D.: Shared kernel information embedding for discriminative inference. In: IEEE Computer Society Conference on Computer Vision and Pattern Recognition (2009) [230]
57. Sminchisescu, C., Jepson, A.: Generative modeling for continuous non-linearly embedded visual inference. In: International Conference on Machine Learning, pp. 759–766 (2004) [227, 230]
58. Sminchisescu, C., Jepson, A.: Variational mixture smoothing for non-linear dynamical systems. In: IEEE Computer Society Conference on Computer Vision and Pattern Recognition, vol. 2, pp. 608–615 (2004) [227]
59. Sminchisescu, C., Kanaujia, A., Li, Z., Metaxas, D.: Discriminative density propagation for 3D human motion estimation. In: IEEE Computer Society Conference on Computer Vision and Pattern Recognition, vol. 1, pp. 390–397 (2005) [228,232]
60. Sminchisescu, C., Kanaujia, A., Metaxas, D.: Learning joint top–down and bottom–up processes for 3D visual inference. In: IEEE Computer Society Conference on Computer Vision and Pattern Recognition (2006) [227-231,233,242]
61. Sminchisescu, C., Kanaujia, A., Metaxas, D.: BM^3E: Discriminative density propagation for visual tracking. IEEE Trans. Pattern Anal. Mach. Intell. (2007) [227,228,232,234]

62. Sminchisescu, C., Triggs, B.: Building roadmaps of local minima of visual models. In: European Conference on Computer Vision, vol. 1, pp. 566–582 (2002) [227]
63. Sminchisescu, C., Triggs, B.: Hyperdynamics importance sampling. In: European Conference on Computer Vision, vol. 1, pp. 769–783 (2002) [227]
64. Sminchisescu, C., Triggs, B.: Kinematic jump processes for monocular 3D human tracking. In: IEEE Computer Society Conference on Computer Vision and Pattern Recognition, vol. 1, pp. 69–76 (2003) [227,228,246]
65. Sminchisescu, C., Triggs, B.: Mapping minima and transitions in visual models. Int. J. Comput. Vis. **61**(1) (2005) [227]
66. Sminchisescu, C., Welling, M.: Generalized darting Monte-Carlo. In: International Conference on Artificial Intelligence and Statistics, vol. 1 (2007) [239]
67. Tipping, M., Faul, A.: Fast marginal likelihood maximisation for sparse Bayesian models. In: International Conference on Artificial Intelligence and Statistics (2003) [235]
68. Tsochantaridis, I., Joachims, T., Hofmann, T., Altun, Y.: Large margin methods for structured and interdependent output variables. J. Mach. Learn. Res. **6**, 1453–1484 (2005) [230,244]
69. Urtasun, R., Fleet, D., Hertzmann, A., Fua, P.: Priors for people tracking in small training sets. In: IEEE International Conference on Computer Vision (2005) [230]
70. Urtasun, R., Fleet, D., Geiger, A., Popovic, J., Darrell, T., Lawrence, N.: Topologically-constrained latent variable models. In: International Conference on Machine Learning (2008) [230]
71. Vincent, P., Bengio, Y.: Kernel matching pursuit. Mach. Learn. **48**, 165–187 (2002) [238]
72. Vlasic, D., Adelsberger, R., Vannucci, G., Barwell, J., Gross, M., Matusik, W., Popovic, J.: Practical motion capture in everyday surroundings. ACM Trans. Graph. (2007) [228]
73. Vondrak, M., Sigal, L., Jenkins, O.C.: Physical simulation for probabilistic motion tracking. In: IEEE Computer Society Conference on Computer Vision and Pattern Recognition (2008) [246]
74. Wang, J., Fleet, D.J., Hertzmann, A.: Gaussian process dynamical models. In: IEEE Trans. Pattern Anal. Mach. Intell. (2008) [230]
75. Weston, J., Schölkopf, B., Bousquet, O., Mann, T., Noble, W.: Joint kernel maps. In: International Work-Conference on Artificial Neural Networks, pp. 176–191 (2005) [230]

Chapter 13
Benchmark Datasets for Pose Estimation and Tracking

Mykhaylo Andriluka, Leonid Sigal, and Michael J. Black

Abstract This chapter discusses the needs for standard datasets in the articulated pose estimation and tracking communities. It describes the datasets that are currently available and the performance of state-of-the-art methods on them. We discuss issues of ground-truth collection and quality, complexity of appearance and poses, evaluation metrics and partitioning of data. We also discusses limitations of current datasets and possible directions in developing new datasets for future use.

13.1 Introduction

The ultimate goal of research in the area of the articulated human pose estimation is to develop an approach capable of inferring a 3D configuration of the human body given an image or a sequence of images taken in an uncontrolled environment such as an outdoor street scene or a sporting event.

In order to gradually approach this complex problem the research has been focusing on a number of special cases, each with its own set of simplifying assumptions. As a result, there exist a number of distinctive performance evaluation scenarios that significantly differ from one another in terms of what is available as an input to the pose estimation algorithm and what precision in pose estimation is expected as an output. Such specialization of the human pose estimation algorithms is also directly reflected by the benchmarks and performance metrics established in the

M. Andriluka (✉)
Max Planck Institute for Computer Science, Saarbrücken, Germany
e-mail: andriluka@mpi inf.mpg.de

L. Sigal
Disney Research, Pittsburgh, USA
e-mail: lsigal@disneyresearch.com

M.J. Black
Max Planck Institute for Intelligent Systems, Tübingen, Germany
e-mail: black@tuebingen.mpg.de
Department of Computer Science, Brown University, Providence, USA
e-mail: black@cs.brown.edu

T.B. Moeslund et al. (eds.), *Visual Analysis of Humans*,
DOI 10.1007/978-0-85729-997-0_13, © Springer-Verlag London Limited 2011

Table 13.1 Overview of the publicly available datasets for 2D and 3D human pose estimation

	Dataset	Data Format	Annotation	Error Metric	# of frames	Clutter	Pose Complex
Monocular 2D	Agarwal/Triggs [1]	POSER Images	3D MoCap	AJA	Train: 1,927 Test: 418	No	Simple
	Buffy Stickmen [16]	Images	2D Up-Body Pose	PCP	748	Lots	Everyday
	ETHZ PASCAL Stickmen [12]	Images	2D Up-Body Pose Bounding Box	PCP	549	Lots	Everyday
	UIUC Stickmen [51]	Images	2D Up-Body Pose	PCP	Train: 346 Test: 247	Little	Complex
	People [41]	Images	2D Full-Body Pose	Perplexity PCP	Train: 100 Test: 205	Lots	Complex
	Leeds Sports Poses Dataset [29]	Images	2D Full-Body Pose	PCP	Train: 1,000 Test: 1,000	Lots	Complex
	Human–Object Interaction Dataset [56]	Images	2D Full-Body Pose 2D Sport Equip	PCP	Train: 180 Test: 120	Little	Complex
	H3D (Poselet) [8]	Images	2D Full/Partial Pose 3D Full/Partial Pose Region Segmentation	N/A N/A N/A	Train: 750 Test: 250	Lots	Complex
Multi-view 3D	HUMANEVA [45]	Multi-view Videos	3D MoCap	AJP	56 seq. ≈ 80,000	Little Lab	Everyday
	MPI08 [40]	Multi-view Videos	Inertial Sensors 3D Laser Scans	AJA	54 seq. ≈ 24,000	No Chromakey	Everyday + Complex
	Stanford ToF [22]	ToF Depth	3D MoCap 3D Laser Scans	AMP	27 seq.	Some	Everyday + Complex

computer vision community. The goal of this chapter is to present an overview of these benchmarks and to highlight the differences between various special cases of the articulated human pose estimation problem.

In Table 13.1 we present a concise summary of the publicly available datasets for the evaluation of the 2D and 3D human pose estimation algorithms. Observe that the available datasets vary significantly with respect to complexity of human poses, amount of background clutter and type of ground-truth annotations. In some of the datasets, in addition to the images, the pose estimation algorithms are provided with auxiliary information such as segmentation of the person (e.g., Agarwal/Triggs [1] or HUMANEVA [45]) and/or the person bounding box (e.g., Buffy Stickmen [16]).

Such variety among the datasets reflects the diversity of the settings in which human pose estimation has been considered in the computer vision literature. On one end of the spectrum are approaches, like [1, 28], that consider this problem in the controlled environments and assume that the person is largely segmented in the image. These approaches demonstrate impressive performance and are able to estimate 3D human poses from monocular images [1]; they are also able to deal with complex and unusual body configurations [28]. On the other end of the spectrum are approaches that aim at pose estimation in uncontrolled conditions such as outdoor street scenes [4, 18, 21], but are often only capable of estimating poses of people performing simple motions such as walking or running.

The two most popular settings considered in the recent literature are (1) monocular 2D pose estimation from single images captured in the uncontrolled environments (see Chap. 11) and (2) 3D pose estimation from image *sequences* captured under laboratory conditions (see Chaps. 9 and 10). In both of these settings it is possible to acquire high-quality ground-truth poses of people which are obtained by manual annotation of the body joints for (1) and using the marker-based motion capture technology for (2). Several attempts have been made to push the state-of-the-art beyond these settings. For example, [24] propose an approach for 3D human pose estimation in outdoor environments and are able to estimate poses of people performing variety of motions such as running, jumping and climbing. However, their pose estimation algorithm requires images obtained from multiple viewpoints with a relatively large baseline and relies on audio to synchronize the video streams.

We will devote the rest of this chapter to the analysis of the currently available performance evaluation benchmarks for monocular and multi-view 2D and 3D human pose estimation.

13.2 Datasets for Monocular 2D Human Pose Estimation

Monocular human pose estimation is an important and long-standing problem in computer vision with early work dating back several decades [25]. Over the years the focus of research in this area has shifted from pose estimation in controlled laboratory conditions toward more realistic scenarios. In Fig. 13.1 we present an overview of the publicly available datasets for monocular human pose estimation; we have included both well established and recently introduced datasets which are likely to have influence on the future work. In Fig. 13.1 we have attempted to order the datasets from left to right according to their *complexity*. While such an ordering is clearly subjective, we have tried to base it on objective factors such as the amount of the background clutter and variability in the scale and poses of people.

Early work on human pose estimation has been focused on the recovery of poses from silhouettes and often assumed that figure/ground segmentation is available. While impressive results have been obtained in this setting [2, 52], it is not clear how well these approaches generalize to more complex settings with cluttered backgrounds and multiple overlapping human subjects. Initial attempts to estimate poses in such complex conditions often demonstrated only qualitative results [42], have been evaluated using limited number of images [35] or even employed manual steps in order to generate the final pose estimates [57]. More recently, however, a relatively large number of benchmark datasets, for both full and partial body pose estimation, became available.

[Agarwal&Triggs,
PAMI'06]

"ETHZ PASCAL Stickmen"
[Eichner et al., BMVC'09]

"People"
[Ramanan, NIPS'06]

"Buffy Stickmen"
[Ferrari et al., CVPR'08]

"UIUC Stickmen"
[Tran&Forsyth, ECCV'10]

"Leeds Sports Poses" (LSP)
[Johnson&Everingham, BMVC'10]

"H3D Dataset"
[Bourdev&Malik, ICCV'09]

Human-Object Interaction (HOI)
[Yao&Fei-Fei, CVPR'10]

PASCAL Layout Challenge
[Everingham et al., IJCV'10]

Fig. 13.1 Publicly available datasets in the area of monocular human pose estimation ordered according to their complexity

Full-body human pose estimation: One of the first attempts to assemble a representative dataset for 2D human pose estimation has been made in [41]. Ramanan in [41] introduced the "People" dataset[1] consisting of 305 annotated images of fully visible people performing a large variety of activities such as walking, standing, sports, dancing and martial arts. For each image the dataset contains manual annotations of the endpoints of the 10 body parts. The annotated parts are head, torso, upper and lower arms and upper and lower legs.

A representative sample of the images from the "People" dataset is shown in Fig. 13.2 and example of annotations in Fig. 13.5. Notice that both poses and ap-

---

[1] Note that in some publications this dataset is also referred to as the "Iterative Image Parsing" (IIP) dataset.

Fig. 13.2 Several example images from the "People" dataset [41]

pearance of people vary greatly across the images and that images often contain very cluttered backgrounds (e.g., (g) and (h)). Also note that in some images body parts are significantly foreshortened (e.g., legs in images (i) and (j)) or occluded (e.g., right leg in image (g) or upper arm in image (f)). Notice that, with a few exceptions, images are tightly cropped around the person and that all images are rescaled so that humans appear at roughly the same scale. Despite these simplifications the "People" dataset presents significant challenges and is actively used for benchmarking in the recent literature [3, 29, 30, 47, 50]. Although state-of-the-art algorithms are able to robustly localize body parts such as the torso and head, the recognition rates for more difficult body parts such as the forearms are much lower with the best methods being able to find only around 45% of these parts correctly according to Percentage of Correctly estimated body Parts (PCP) metric (see Sect. 13.4) [30].

While playing an important role in the recent progress of the 2D human pose estimation algorithms, the "People" dataset has a number of drawbacks. In particular, the annotations of the body parts lack occlusion labels and do not distinguish between the left and right body limbs. The images are rescaled so that people have the same image height, but this rescaling is only approximate and introduces additional noise during training. Finally, the training portion of the "People" dataset contains only 100 images, which makes it difficult to train complex statistical models that typically require larger training sets.

In the last couple of years several datasets have been introduced to address these limitations. The "Leeds Sports Poses" (LSP) dataset proposed in [29] contains 2,000 images of people performing various sports activities such as football, baseball, tennis, acrobatics and parkour. The dataset is evenly split into 1,000 training and test images. Similarly to the "People" dataset in the LSP dataset the images are tightly cropped around the persons bounding box and rescaled so that people appear at a fixed scale. Effectively, this provides the pose estimation algorithm with an estimate of the position and scale of the person in the image and makes the pose estimation problem significantly easier. The knowledge of position and scale is a reasonable simplifying assumption, since one can expect that in the future these quantities can be estimated reliably from the image context or by a person detector [16, 26]. Compared with the "People" dataset, the LSP dataset contains a significantly larger number of training images and more detailed annotations of the body limbs that include occlusion labels and differentiate between the left and right body limbs (see Fig. 13.5). Recently, the authors of the LSP dataset have introduced a new training set that contains 10,000 images of people in a large variety of body poses [30]. Since manual annotation of such a large number of images is problematic, the annotations were obtained using Amazon's mechanical turk and are noisier than the LSP and "People" datasets.

An interesting recent addition to the collection of 2D pose estimation benchmarks is the Human–Object Interaction (HOI) dataset proposed in [23] and augmented with pose and object annotations in [56]. The HOI dataset is more structured in terms of human poses compared to "People" and LSP datasets. It contains images of people performing 6 well-defined activities: cricket batting, cricket bowling, tennis forehand, tennis serve, croquet shot and volleyball smash. For each activity the dataset contains 50 images that are split into 30 images for training and 20 images for testing. Unlike the "People" and LSP datasets, in the HOI dataset people appear at different scales and are sometimes only partially visible. However, in contrast to the "People" dataset, the background in the images is mostly simple and contains little clutter. The important property of the HOI dataset is that each image contains additional supervisory information in the form of activity labels and also includes annotations of the objects that are in contact with the person. The annotated objects are cricket bat, croquet mallet, tennis racket and volleyball. These additional annotations allow one to learn joint activity-specific models for objects and human poses that show significantly better performance compared to models that do not take human–object interaction into account [56]. The main drawback of the HOI dataset is the limited number of activities and limited number of images for each activity, which makes it difficult to exploit the full potential of statistical learning techniques and might lead to overfitting.

Upper-body human pose estimation: The "People" and LSP datasets are generic in the sense that they contain images of people across a wide range of poses and viewpoints. Recently, several datasets were introduced that address a more specific setting of frontal upper-body pose estimation. In this setting the people are much easier to detect [16], which allows one to estimate poses of people in the real-world images without requiring additional information such as image position and scale. This setting also appears to be very useful in practice since in many cases people do appear in the images in the near-frontal view as for example in the TV shows [16] or when posing for family photographs [13].

The two commonly used datasets for 2D upper-body estimation are the "Buffy Stickmen" (Buffy) dataset [16] and "ETHZ PASCAL Stickmen" (ETHZ) dataset

Fig. 13.3 Several example images from the "Buffy Stickmen" dataset [16]

[12]. The Buffy dataset in its most recent release[2] includes 748 images from 5 episodes of the TV show "Buffy the Vampire Slayer" (see Fig. 13.3 for several examples). The results in the literature are typically reported for the test set of 276 images from 3 episodes. The training set is not strictly defined and different publications use different data for training (e.g., "People" dataset in [3] and cross-validation on the "Buffy" dataset in [43]). The ETHZ dataset contains 549 images of people selected from the PASCAL VOC dataset [14]. Both the Buffy and ETHZ datasets contain people at different scales in front of cluttered backgrounds. In this sense these datasets are more realistic compared with the "People" [41] or LSP datasets [29] in which images are rescaled and cropped around the person bounding box. The key difference between Buffy and ETHZ datasets is that the images in the Buffy dataset come from the TV show and are filmed with high-end equipment under studio illumination conditions. The images in the ETHZ dataset are a collection of amateur photographs and are consequently of lower quality. Another difference is that people in the Buffy dataset are limited to a handful of characters from the show. In particular, many images depict the lead character Buffy and a couple of her friends. In contrast, in the ETHZ, with a very few exceptions, every image corresponds to a different person. Given these factors the ETHZ dataset appears to be more diverse with respect to imaging conditions and appearance of people, and is therefore less likely to be prone to overfitting.

Being a representative sample of images from the TV shows and community photo collections the "Buffy" and ETHZ datasets do have some bias toward typical everyday human poses with both hands down along the torso. This has been

---

[2]The dataset underwent modification since the publication of [16], see the documentation provided with the dataset for details.

Fig. 13.4 Several example images from the "PASCAL VOC Person Layout" dataset [14]

criticized in the recent work [51] where a new "UIUC Stickmen" (UIUC) dataset is proposed that features lager pose variability. The UIUC dataset includes 582 images which are split into 236 images for testing and 346 images for training. The scale of people varies across the dataset, but the majority of the images are cropped around the person. Most of the images in the UIUC dataset depict people playing badminton or frisbee and consequently have simple backgrounds without much clutter. Therefore, the UIUC and "Buffy"/ETHZ datasets appear to be complementary in the sense that the former includes more diverse and complex poses while the latter include more complex appearance of people and more cluttered backgrounds.

We conclude our review with a discussion of the "Humans in 3D" (H3D) [8] and "PASCAL VOC Person Layout" (PASCAL Layout) [14] datasets. Both datasets consist of the images obtained from the Flickr[3] community photo collection website and are among the most challenging datasets for human pose estimation that exist today. The complexity comes from a combination of different factors such as cluttered backgrounds, rare poses, body part occlusions and large variability in scale and viewing direction. While these factors are present in the other pose estimation datasets as well, they typically appear in isolation. For example, the "People" dataset includes people in complex poses, but most of the images contain fully visible people and scale of the people is fixed. In the HOI dataset people are at times partially occluded by the image boundaries and appear in complex poses, but the backgrounds in this dataset are rather simple. In Fig. 13.4 we show several example images from the PASCAL Layout dataset. Note the atypical poses, viewpoint variation and part occlusions present in most of the images. Notice that in contrast to other datasets people are often occluded by scene objects (e.g., by the cart in the fourth image in the first row, or the stove in the second image in the first row).

Although remarkable progress has been made in human pose estimation in the recent years it appears that both H3D and PASCAL Layout datasets are at the moment beyond the state of the art. In particular, despite the availability of high-quality

---

[3] www.flickr.com

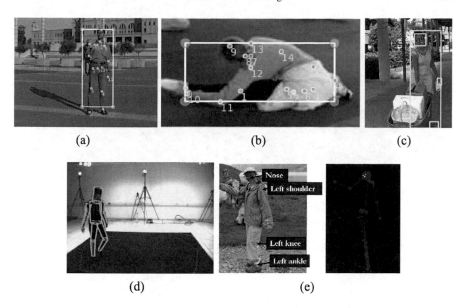

Fig. 13.5 Examples of the pose annotations on the "People" (**a**), "LSP" (**b**), "PASCAL VOC Person Layout" (**c**), "HumanEva" (**d**) and H3D (**e**) datasets. Note that in contrast to "People" dataset in the "LSP" dataset joints are additionally labeled as visible (yellow) or occluded (green)

3D annotations of the body parts, the H3D dataset has so far been used for the evaluation of human detection only. There has also been little activity in the PASCAL VOC Challenge related to the Person Layout dataset and only a handful of results are available on this dataset to date. In the case of the PASCAL Layout dataset this could be, in part, due to a very strict evaluation criteria that require precise localization of the body parts and only takes head, hands and feet parts into account [14]. The evaluation criteria for the PASCAL Layout dataset have been recently relaxed, so one might expect more attention drawn to this dataset in the near future.

13.3   Datasets for 3D Human Pose Estimation and Tracking

Much of the research in 3D human pose estimation has been focused on performing this task in controlled laboratory environments [7, 10, 20, 45]; see Fig. 13.6 for typical images from publicly available datasets. This is motivated on one hand by the additional complexity involved in inferring 3D poses from monocular images, and on the other by the lack of tools to accurately obtain ground-truth 3D pose data in realistic outdoor environments. The latter is further discussed in Sects. 13.4.1 and 13.4.2.

The most established benchmarks in this area are perhaps the HUMANEVA and HUMANEVA-II datasets [45] illustrated in Fig. 13.6(left). At the time of this book's publication over 380 individuals and groups around the world had registered to obtain access to the dataset, with results on included sequences appearing in dozens

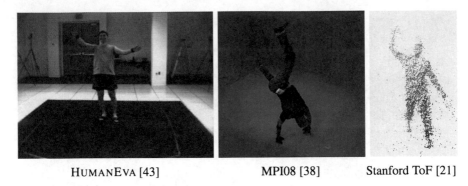

HUMANEVA [43]   MPI08 [38]   Stanford ToF [21]

Fig. 13.6 Publicly available datasets in the area of multi-view articulated pose tracking

of publications. These datasets provide synchronized[4] ground-truth and multi-view video (from seven and four cameras, respectively) for a number of subjects performing a diverse set of predefined motions such as walking, running, throwing a ball and boxing. The images in these datasets are obtained with a set of static calibrated cameras and the people are captured in front of relatively simple laboratory backgrounds. As a consequence, for these datasets, both person detection and body segmentation problems can be to a large extent solved by performing background subtraction (though the silhouettes are still noisy). This fact coupled with the availability of images from multiple viewpoints allows impressive pose estimation performance as described in Sect. 13.6.

One alternative to the HUMANEVA datasets, is the MPI08 [40] dataset (Fig. 13.6 (middle)) that uses inertial sensors to obtain ground-truth orientation of extremities. The benefit of the setup is that, at least in principle, it allows us to capture ground-truth poses in more realistic outdoor settings. That said, all the data in the dataset, so far, were captured indoors and with green screen backgrounds, hence having even less background clutter when compared with the HUMANEVA datasets.

The renewed interest in using depth information, which came from recent sensor technologies such as time-of-flight cameras and structured light sensors (Xbox Kinect), prompted introduction of Stanford ToF [22] dataset (Fig. 13.6(right)). The dataset is unique in that it provides depth image sequences obtained using a time-of-flight camera along with 3D poses obtained using a synchronized motion capture system.

The difference between the datasets discussed here and those in the previous sections is the quality of the results that are expected. The 3D datasets like HUMANEVA or MPI08 focus on the problem of marker-less MoCap. Consequently the error metrics and the simplified imaging conditions are in support of this task. The 2D datasets, discussed in the previous section, on the other hand, focus on coarser inference of pose but in less constrained settings.

---

[4]In HUMANEVA synchronization was obtained through off-line optimization, and in HUMANEVA-II the video frames were synchronized in hardware.

13.4 Attributes and Properties of Datasets

One way to characterize the different datasets is to look at the significant dimensions along which they differ. Here we outline a number of attributes that affect the complexity of the dataset and the performance of methods in it.

13.4.1 Real versus Simulated Images

Datasets for evaluation come in variety of forms. Because obtaining real datasets with known 3D poses is typically hard and time consuming, some researchers have relied on synthetic datasets in the past. With computer graphics packages such as POSER (e frontier, Scotts Valley, CA) [1, 44] or MAYA (Autodesk, San Rafael, CA) [48, 49], semi-realistic images of humans can be rendered and used for evaluation. Early examples include datasets by Agarwal and Triggs in [1], Shakhnarovich et al. in [44][5] and Sminchisescu in [48]. In all cases the datasets consist of synthetically generated images, with simplified appearance, and corresponding poses coming from marker-based MoCap sequences.

Simulated datasets such as these are easy to create; all that is needed is MoCap data, and large copra of MoCap sequences readily exists on the web, e.g., the CMU MoCap Database[6]. The key benefit of using a synthetic data is the ability to have *exact* ground-truth 3D poses for evaluation. The shortcoming is that such datasets often do not exhibit the same distribution of image features that exist in real images (e.g., variations in clothing (type and texture), complex and noisy backgrounds, noise in imaging process, and lighting are all contributing factors). As a result, performance on the simulated images is often too optimistic and is not necessarily indicative of performance on real images under typical conditions.

To alleviate some of these problems, semi-realistic datasets were introduced, where real backgrounds were used with simulated characters [49]. These resolve some, but not all, of the issues. The general consensus is that both training and testing using real image data are better. With real images, however, obtaining ground truth is trickier. In laboratory environments motion capture data can be collected simultaneously with video and used as ground truth (e.g., HUMANEVA dataset [45], Stanford ToF dataset [22]); in non-laboratory environments images can be annotated by hand (e.g., Buffy Stickmen [16], ETHZ PASCAL Stickmen [12], People dataset [41]). Annotating 3D poses by hand is a complex and time consuming task and to our knowledge only one dataset with such data exists to date: the H3D Poselet Dataset [8]. That said, it is unclear to what extent 3D pose annotations obtained in this way are truly indicative of the poses of the subjects in images, as several assumptions must be made to lift the annotations from 2D to 3D.

---

[5]Neither of the datasets in [44] or [48] is currently publicly available.

[6]http://mocap.cs.cmu.edu/

13.4.2 Sources of Ground Truth

As is alluded to in the previous section, ground truth for comparison can be obtained in a variety of ways. The most *accurate* estimates of the pose for comparison are obtained using hardware synchronized optical motion capture data (e.g., HUMANEVA-II [45]). However, this restricts collection of data to indoors laboratory environments and also restricts the appearance of people to mostly tight fitting clothing.[7]

In MPI08 [40] dataset, Pons-Moll et al. proposed the use inertial measurement unit (IMU) sensors for collection of 3D pose data in order to alleviate the need for indoor collection. Collection of ground truth with an IMU-based system is appealing, but all such systems, to date, exhibit significant drift and are unable to recover the 3D position of the body in the world. As a result only short sequences can be collected reliably. Experimental systems that combine IMUs with other sensors (e.g., [53]) show promise but are not readily available in the consumer market. Such systems may ultimately provide means of capturing datasets in outdoor environments (without obscuring parts of the body in terms of appearance).

Meanwhile, those interested in testing algorithms on natural images obtained in unconstrained environments, mainly resort to hand annotation of images. This process typically involves annotation of visible (and sometimes not fully visible) joints of the body (e.g., "People" [41] and Stickmen Datasets [12, 16, 51]). A 2D skeleton can then be generated by connecting the annotated joints with limb segments. This process carries a certain unquantifiable error, since it involves human intervention. However, it does allow ground-truth annotations for arbitrary complex scenes. Manual annotation of 3D pose, similarly takes the form of 2D joint annotation, but augmented with geometric solvers and optimization to reconstruct 3D pose (e.g., H3D Dataset [8]). Consequently the annotation tool used for creating the H3D Dataset is publicly available [8]. To date this is the only tool available for manually annotating 3D poses in single images.

13.4.3 Evaluation Measure

Beyond the data and ground-truth annotation, the key to establishing the performance on any given dataset is the error metric. There are many metrics that were introduced over the years, some quantitative, some qualitative. Here we focus on the most popular quantitative metrics in the literature.

13.4.3.1 Average Joint Position Error

Given an arbitrarily parameterized skeleton (e.g., common parameterizations are discussed in Chap. 9, Sect. 9.1), the pose of the body can easily be converted to joint

---

[7]Optical motion capture systems are unable to deal with loose clothing that does not drape tightly over the limbs of the body.

locations (or other prominent marker locations rigidly attached to the skeleton). In the case of a kinematic chain parametrization, for example, this conversion takes the form of simple forward kinematics. Because of this property, which makes this measure parametrization independent, average joint position (AJP) error is often the error measure of preference; examples of the datasets that advocate this measure include [22, 45, 54]. AJP error measure is also consistent with measures that are used to validate traditional marker-based motion capture systems (e.g., Vicon[8]). Given a pose, $\mathbf{x}$, the AJP metric is defined as follows:

$$\mathbf{E}_{\text{AJP}}(\mathbf{x}, \hat{\mathbf{x}}) = \frac{1}{N} \sum_{i=1}^{N} \| \mathscr{J}_i(\mathbf{x}) - \mathscr{J}_i(\hat{\mathbf{x}}) \|, \qquad (13.1)$$

where $\mathscr{J}_i(\mathbf{x})$ are a set of functions that map[9] the pose of the body, $\mathbf{x}$, to the location of ith joint either in the world or in the image (depending on whether the error is defined in 2D or 3D); $\mathbf{x}$ is the ground truth and $\hat{\mathbf{x}}$ is the estimated pose, and N is the total number of joints in the body. Similarly, one can define an error measure based on an arbitrary set of predefined *markers* rigidly attached to the body segments; this we call average marker position (AMP) error. One can additionally average over the number of frames to obtain an error over a sequence, e.g. for tracking.

Despite the obvious benefits, $\mathbf{E}_{\text{AJP}}$ has also an obvious fault in that it assumes that the skeletal proportions are known or can be estimated well from the image. In other words, even if the pose is recovered perfectly, miss-estimation of the skeleton structure or morphology would likely lead to significant systematic errors.

13.4.3.2 Average Joint Angle Error

A way to factor out the skeletal proportions from the error metric, is through the use of the average joint angle (AJA) error instead. Since joint angles are independent of limb lengths or skeleton position in space, this makes another natural choice for the error metric; consequently, this error metric was explored in [1, 40]. The error measure can be defined as follows:

$$\mathbf{E}_{\text{AJA}}(\mathbf{x}, \hat{\mathbf{x}}) = \frac{1}{N} \sum_{i=1}^{N} \left| [\theta_i(\mathbf{x}) - \theta_i(\hat{\mathbf{x}})] \bmod \pm 180° \right|, \qquad (13.2)$$

where N is the number of joints in the body, θ_i is the true and $\hat{\theta}_i$ is the estimated joint angles for the ith joint. Since $\mathbf{x}$ is often encoded using joint angles, $\theta_i(\mathbf{x})$ is typically a selector function that simply selects an element of $\mathbf{x}$. If $\mathbf{x}$ is encoded using positions, inverse kinematics can be used to obtain the corresponding joint

---

[8]http://www.vicon.com

[9]Note that $\mathscr{J}_i(\mathbf{x}) \equiv \mathbf{G}_{si}(\mathbf{x})$ according to the formulation in Chap. 9, Sect. 9.1.5.

angle representation. Because angles wrap around, special care must be taken to ensure proper treatment of joint angles, hence mod ± 180°.

The key issue with this metric is the fact that it is highly dependent on the parametrization of the joints in the body. In other words, it is hard to compare results obtained with different parameterizations of the skeletal structure.

13.4.3.3 Pixel Overlap

Another alternative advocated in prior work (e.g., [54]) is the pixel overlap (PO) error measure. This error measures the consistency of estimated and true pose by looking at the overlap of estimated and true pose in the image plane. This can be formulated as follows:

$$E_{PO}(\mathbf{x}, \hat{\mathbf{x}}) = \frac{\sum_{(x,y)} \mathrm{Proj}(\mathbf{x}, (x, y)) \cdot \mathrm{Proj}(\hat{\mathbf{x}}, (x, y))}{\sum_{(x,y)} \mathrm{Proj}(\mathbf{x}, (x, y))}, \qquad (13.3)$$

where $\mathrm{Proj}(\mathbf{x}, (x, y))$ is a binary function that is 1 if the projection of the body under the pose $\mathbf{x}$ covers pixel (x, y) and is 0 otherwise. Note that for a 2D pose the projection is simply an identity function.

While this metric is easy to compute, it also has a number of disadvantages. First, it is biased toward measuring the correct location of major parts of the body, e.g., torso, since they occupy larger portions of the image. Second, this measure is sensitive to the model of the outer surface of the body, not just the pose. Lastly, similar to average joint position, this measure is sensitive to the morphology of the body.

13.4.3.4 Percentage of Correctly Estimated Body Parts

PCP is perhaps the most popular measure in the community today for 2D pose estimation. The PCP measure was initially proposed by Ferrari et al. [16] for evaluation of pose estimation on the Buffy [16] dataset. According to PCP criterion a body part returned by the algorithm is considered *correct* if its (proximal and distal) segment endpoints lie within X% of the length of the ground-truth segment from their annotated location; typically, X is taken to be 50%. One can almost think of this error measure as the *binary* version of joint position error.

The PCP measure is popular due to the simplicity of its interpretation, which can be thought of as the fraction of body parts that are localized with acceptable accuracy. The plaguing issue is the fact that the measure is limited by the threshold on X that is typically set to be rather loose at 50%. Current pose estimation approaches are getting closer to obtaining 100% performance on the Buffy Stickmen dataset with this measure (e.g., [55] obtains 89.1 PCP). Recently it has been proposed to plot PCP as a function of X [12]; this produces what is called a PCP curve and addresses the reliance on an arbitrarily chosen threshold. Note, that several recent methods for pose estimation [19] also estimate body shape, and for these methods the evaluation of pixel overlap is more appropriate than PCP.

13.4.3.5 Perplexity

Yet another measure of performance in the literature is based on the notion of *perplexity* [41]; a measure coming from the information theory community. The perplexity measure is defined by

$$\mathbf{E}_{\text{Perplexity}}(\mathbf{x}_{1:T}) = -\frac{1}{T} \sum_t \log p(\mathbf{x}_t | I_t), \qquad (13.4)$$

where once again $\mathbf{x}_t$ is the ground-truth pose for image I_t and T is the total number of images in the test dataset. Note that the perplexity measure is not a function of estimated pose, rather it measures the average probability of the true pose under the learned model. This measure is appealing computationally, since it also measures the ambiguity of the model. That said, this measure is extremely hard to interpret and hence it gained relatively little support from the community after the original introduction by Ramanan in [41].

13.4.4 Complexity of Motion and Appearance

One of the less tangible, but critical, aspects of the benchmark dataset is the complexity of appearance and motion that test images or sequences in the dataset contain. We have already discussed the complexity of appearance and motion to a considerable extent in Sects. 13.2 and 13.3. The only discussion point we would like to bring up here is that *perceived* complexity of the data is not necessarily the same as the *actual* complexity that the algorithm may encounter. For example, a gymnast on a pommel horse may appear in a variety of complex perceived poses, however, if the arms and legs are well separated they are likely to be correctly detected by current algorithms (see, e.g., [3, 12, 16]). On the other hand, in cluttered street scenes the appearance of people and their poses are less extreme, but current approaches may have a harder time estimating pose in those instances properly.

13.5 Case Study: Monocular 2D Human Pose Estimation

To understand how benchmark datasets have helped to shape the current landscape of monocular 2D pose estimation, we focus on the "People" and "Buffy Stickmen" datasets described in Sec. 13.2 since they are the two most widely used 2D pose estimation datasets today.

Much of the recent work related to the "People" and "Buffy" datasets is based on the pictorial structures framework [15, 17]. In this framework the model of the person is defined in terms of rigid parts that are related to each other via spatial and appearance constraints. The detailed description of this class of models is given in Chap. 11. The majority of recent approaches to single-frame 2D pose estimation is hence best characterized as model-based and bottom–up [3, 29, 41, 43, 47, 50, 55]. This is in contrast to model-free feed-forward approaches, discussed in Chap. 12, that are largely successful in recovering human poses from silhouettes and segmented images [1, 52]. In principle, integrated top–down approaches should be applicable to real-world images as well and there exist some interesting results in this direction [27, 32]. However this work has either not been evaluated on the benchmarks such as "People" or "Buffy" [27] or has not demonstrated significant improvements compared to bottom–up methods [32].

Several methods from the literature combine bottom–up and top–down approaches at different stages of the inference. For example, in [15] the initial stage is bottom–up and allows to compute the posterior distributions of the positions of the body parts. In the top–down stage these posteriors are used to sample full-body configurations which are then evaluated using the global scoring function. In [43] the top–down approach is used in the first stage in order to adapt the prior distribution to the pose of the person. This stage is then followed by bottom–up inference where the adapted prior distribution is used to identify the locations of the body parts. The approach of [43] appears to be particularly effective on the frontal upper-body pose estimation datasets such as "Buffy" where the set of poses is constrained enough so that the initial top–down stage has a high chance of identifying a suitable prior distribution.

Within the pictorial structures framework the recent approaches differ in how they represent the appearance of body parts, which part relationships are taken into account and how these relationships are encoded in the model. Despite the overall complexity of the problem, some observations regarding effectiveness of various design choices can be drawn based on the considered benchmarks.

Appearance representation: The most successful approaches to date rely on appearance representations based on the local image features and discriminative classifiers. The most commonly used features are perhaps Shape Context (SC) [5] and HOG [11]. The best published result to date on the "Buffy" dataset is obtained by [55] who report 89.1 PCP while relying on HOG features. The particular appearance features do not seem to be crucial, for example the approach of [3] achieves 83.1 PCP while relying on Shape Context features and also a significantly simpler model. On the other hand it seems to be important to use robust local features in contrast to pixel-wise appearance templates previously used in the literature [15, 41]. For example, on the "People" dataset the approach of [3] achieves 55.2 PCP using Shape Context and only 37.5 PCP using the appearance templates from [41].

In addition to gradient-based appearance features such as HOG and SC several approaches have attempted to integrate other types of appearance information. For example, it has been proposed to use color features in order to define similarity constraints between left and right body limbs [50, 51] or as an additional cue for separating foreground and background [12, 41]. The use of additional features, however, often results in only moderate improvements. For example on the "Buffy" dataset Tran and Forsyth [51] are able to improve from 59.6 to 62.8 PCP by using color and geometric features. Similarly, on the "People" dataset Tian and Sclaroff [50] improve from 55.6 to 56.4 PCP using color features.

Part relationships and inference: The basic pictorial structures model proposed in [15] has a tree-structure with part relationships modeling kinematic constraints between body parts. The kinematic constraints are typically assumed to be represented with Gaussian distributions which allows efficient inference with dynamic programming or convolution. While being computationally efficient this model has difficulties in capturing the full range of possible body poses. The limitation comes from the single Gaussian distribution that is employed to model the overall spatial arrangement of the body parts.

Much of the recent work has been focused on models that are able to better represent the space of possible body poses and the corresponding appearance of body parts while at the same time allowing efficient inference. To this end several authors have proposed to rely on mixtures of pictorial structures models. Early work in this direction is due to [33] who propose the *common factor model* (CFM) that extends the basic pictorial structure model with an additional variable that encodes non-tree dependencies between parts. Conditioned on the value of the factor the model becomes a tree, which allows efficient inference.

Until recently the best performance on the "People" dataset has been achieved by the approach of Johnson and Everingham [30] in which they rely on a mixture of pictorial structure models obtained by clustering the poses in the training data. The improvement due to the mixture model is substantial. On the LSP dataset the approach of [29] achieves 44.7 PCP using the basic PS model and 55.1 PCP using a mixture model with 4 components. The best result on the LSP dataset is 62.7 PCP, achieved by the model of Johnson and Everingham [30], which is similar to the one in [29] but uses a 16 component mixture model and is trained on the larger training set. On the "People" dataset the model of [30] achieves 67.4 PCP, which compares favorably to the approaches of [3, 47], which rely on simpler one-component body models.

One of the best performing approaches on the "Buffy" dataset is due to Sapp et al. [43] who parametrize the spatial prior distribution based on the observed image features. This approach is related to the CFM approach of [33], but employs image data to determine the particular pictorial structures model that will be used for the inference, whereas the CFM marginalizes over the discrete set of pictorial structure models corresponding to different values of the common factor.

Recently, both Johnson and Everingham [30] and Sapp et al. [43] were outperformed by the mixture-of-parts (MP) model of Yang and Ramanan [55]. MP achieves 74.9 PCP on the "People" dataset, which is a significant improvement over 67.4 PCP achieved by [30]. On the "Buffy" dataset MP achieves 89.1 PCP, which is again a reasonable improvement compared to the best previous result of 85.9 PCP achieved by [43]. The MP approach introduces a number of improvements over previously proposed approaches. In contrast to previous works, such as [29], that were building on the mixtures of the full-body models, the MP model employs mixture models on the level of pairwise relationships between model parts. The MP model uses a larger number of model parts which allows it to model foreshortening of limbs and makes it flexible with respect to body dimensions. The parameters of the appearance and spatial components of the MP model are learned in a unified framework which allows one to automatically determine their relative importance. Jointly these improvements lead to significantly better results. However, it remains for the future work to determine the influence of each of these factors on the overall performance of the model.

13.6 Case Study: 3D Human Pose Estimation

Similar to the way the "People" [41] and "Buffy" [16] datasets advanced 2D pose estimation, HUMANEVA [45] has led to many advances in 3D pose estimation and tracking over the course of the last five to six years since its release in 2007. The success and acceptability of HUMANEVA dataset in the community steamed from: (i) its ability to provide ground-truth 3D poses, (ii) availability of multi-view synchronized video data and (iii) to a large extent independence of the dataset and evaluation metrics from the specific vision task (e.g., while not designed for action recognition, it has been used for this task by Ning et al. in [38]). The flexibility and the generality of the dataset, while making it popular, also made it challenging to compare and benchmark the methods directly.

Despite these challenges the dataset did serve as a catalyst for advancing state-of-the-art and provided some fundamental insights into current approaches to 3D pose estimation and tracking. The HUMANEVA datasets are particularly popular with model-based top–down approaches, such as those discussed in Chaps. 9 and 10, and discriminative feed-forward methods discussed in Chap. 12. A number of observations can be made based on the reported performance on the dataset.[10]

Based on the performance on HUMANEVA datasets we argue that pose tracking is mostly a solved problem when it comes to a single subject in a static laboratory environment with a large number of calibrated views, controlled lighting and clothing. Performance of video-based methods in such scenarios, assuming large number of cameras, can rival marker-based systems [10] with error of under 15 mm per joint on average. In particular, commercial vision-based motion capture systems are now becoming available on the market (e.g. by Organic Motion, Inc.). It can also be observed that generative models that use back-projection for likelihood evaluation appear to be more tolerant to observations coming from fewer camera views as opposed to voxel-based methods (not explicitly covered in this book). For example, [20] obtain 32–45 mm error as opposed to [10] with $\approx$ 80 mm error with four camera views.

We note that performance of generative methods is highly effected by the design of the likelihood, the choice and implementation of the inference algorithm. The

---

[10]Those observations are abridged from the editorial written by Leonid Sigal and Michael J. Black [46].

effects of these choices can be seen in the results of several methods using different implementations of the Annealed Particle Filter; for example, [39] report performance of 106.9 mm on average; [45] 68 mm; [20] 29.9 mm with a richer likelihood. Generative methods also require strong, often motion-specific and subject-specific, priors to be competitive for monocular pose estimation and tracking as is shown by [34, 36] and [9].

Discriminative models (e.g., [7]) tend to be more accurate than other 3D monocular tracking methods, achieving errors in the range of 33.9–85 mm with most around 40–50 mm. Interestingly, performance seems to depend less critically on the choice of features and the exact form of inference than it does for generative methods (see [7]).

Little can be said about the expected performance of part-based models as few approaches in this category have been applied to HUMANEVA dataset; exceptions include [6] and [4]. Most part-based models focus on the datasets described in the previous sections.

Note that the observations we make here also resonate in the preceding chapters. While we quote some specific instances of algorithms here that we feel are representative of the classes of approaches considered and observations we can make, we want to note that many other competitive approaches are in existence and are being developed. Despite being extremely popular and instrumental in driving the state-of-the-art within the field in the last few years, there is a concern that the HUMANEVA dataset is becoming somewhat obsolete as new approaches are able to deal with greater variation and imaging complexities then those exhibited in the data.

13.7 Datasets for the Future

In Sects. 13.2 and 13.3 of this chapter we have reviewed several popular datasets for 2D and 3D human pose estimation and tracking. While the more established datasets such as "People" [41] or "Buffy Stickmen" [16] do have limitations such as the small number of training images, missing occlusion labels or limited variation in human poses, these limitations have been largely addressed in the more recent datasets such as "Leeds Sports Poses" [29] and "Humans in 3D" (H3D) [8]. For example, the dataset recently proposed in [30] includes 10,000 images of people in a large variety of body poses, albeit containing somewhat noisy annotations obtained with Amazon's mechanical turk. There is no doubt that this or similar image collections will eventually become more properly annotated and will play an important role in further pushing the state of the art in human pose estimation.

The current de-facto standard for the evaluation of performance of the 2D human pose estimation is the PCP measure which we described in Sect. 13.4. This measure is focused on estimation of the image locations of the body parts while neglecting important attributes of the 2D pose such as body part occlusions, torso and head orientation, and body shape. These attributes in turn might be crucial for higher level tasks such as action recognition and 3D pose estimation. We believe that extensions of the current performance metrics that incorporate additional pose attributes and more detailed 2D pose and shape annotations are important for making further progress in 2D human pose estimation. Furthermore, all current performance metrics in 2D and 3D, are developed based on convenience and simplicity. It is well known that they are not highly correlated with human perception. Research on metrics that are perceptually motivated is important for practical applications such as marker-less motion capture. We postulate that such research is forthcoming.

The datasets from [29, 30] contain images of thousands of individuals performing a large variety of activities, but include only static images with 2D ground-truth annotations. The datasets that contain image sequences and include 3D annotations are significantly more scarce. In part this is because 3D ground-truth poses are much harder to obtain and in part because only recently has it become possible to process and store the large volumes of data required to work with image sequences. For example, the HUMANEVA datasets [45] include image sequences of only a handful of human subjects performing a small number of predefined activities. The dataset introduced in [40] contains people performing complex activities such as cartwheels and karate kicks, but again includes images of only a few human subjects captured in front of simple backgrounds. There is a need for datasets that include images and image sequences with 3D ground truth that are captured in realistic conditions and include more variability in backgrounds and human motions. In order to make such datasets useful for evaluation of a broader range of techniques they should also include observations from a range sensor such as time-of-flight camera and provide ground-truth measurements of the body shape of the subjects. While traditional marker-based motion capture systems are difficult to use in non-laboratory environments, recent developments in motion capture based on inertial sensors [53] and marker-less motion capture [40] should enable reliable ground-truth measurements offering potential for a broader range of imaging conditions and human motions. Datasets that contain multiple interacting people are also likely to take front stage in near future as algorithms that can handle such scenarios are starting to emerge [37].

As we discussed in Sects. 13.5 and 13.6, there exist significant conceptual differences between approaches that demonstrate state-of-the-art performance on monocular 2D pose estimation datasets introduced in Sect. 13.2 and on multi-view 3D pose estimation datasets introduced in Sect. 13.3. Given that, it appears that one of the important objectives for future work is to merge these two currently disjoint lines of research with the goal of achieving robust 3D pose estimates of people captured in everyday surroundings. This is an ambitious goal that is likely to require more tight integration between pose estimation, human detection, object detection and overall scene interpretation. Recent results suggest that modeling human–object interactions can significantly improve the performance of both 2D and 3D pose estimation algorithms [31, 56]. While being important, these results were obtained on the datasets with a limited number of images that had little diversity with respect to type of objects and human actions. We believe that creation of the datasets that combine annotations of scene types, human activities, human poses and human–object interactions would further advance the state of the art in multiple areas such as action recognition and human pose estimation.

References

1. Agarwal, A., Triggs, B.: 3d human pose from silhouettes by relevance vector regression. In: IEEE Computer Society Conference on Computer Vision and Pattern Recognition, vol. 2, pp. 882–888 (2004) [254,255,263,265,268]
2. Agarwal, A., Triggs, B.: Recovering 3d human pose from monocular images. IEEE Trans. Pattern Anal. Mach. Intell. **28**, 44–58 (2006) [255]
3. Andriluka, M., Roth, S., Schiele, B.: Pictorial structures revisited: People detection and articulated pose estimation. In: IEEE Computer Society Conference on Computer Vision and Pattern Recognition (2009) [257,259,268]
4. Andriluka, M., Roth, S., Schiele, B.: Monocular 3d pose estimation and tracking by detection. In: IEEE Computer Society Conference on Computer Vision and Pattern Recognition (2010) [255,271]
5. Belongie, S., Malik, J., Puzicha, J.: Shape context: A new descriptor for shape matching and object recognition. In: Advances in Neural Information Processing Systems (2000) [268]
6. Bergtholdt, M., Kappes, J.H., Schmidt, S., Schnörr, C.: A study of parts-based object class detection using complete graphs. Int. J. Comput. Vis. **87**(1–2), 93–117 (2010) [271]
7. Bo, L., Sminchisescu, C.: Twin Gaussian processes for structured prediction. Int. J. Comput. Vis. **87**(1–2), 28–52 (2010) [261,271]
8. Bourdev, L., Malik, J.: Poselets: Body part detectors trained using 3d human pose annotations. In: IEEE International Conference on Computer Vision (2009). http://www.eecs.berkeley.edu/~lbourdev/h3d/ [254,260,263,264,271]
9. Brubaker, M., Fleet, D., Hertzmann, A.: Physics-based person tracking using the anthropomorphic walker. Int. J. Comput. Vis. **87**(1–2), 140–155 (2010) [271]
10. Corazza, S., Mündermann, L., Gambaretto, E., Ferrigno, G., Andriacchi, T.: Markerless motion capture through visual hull, articulated ICP and subject specific model generation. Int. J. Comput. Vis. **87**(1–2), 156–169 (2010) [261,270]
11. Dalal, N., Triggs, B.: Histograms of oriented gradients for human detection. In: IEEE Computer Society Conference on Computer Vision and Pattern Recognition (2005) [268]
12. Eichner, M., Ferrari, V.: Better appearance models for pictorial structures. In: British Machine Vision Conference (2009). http://www.vision.ee.ethz.ch/~calvin/ethz_pascal_stickmen/index.html [254,259,263,264,266-268]
13. Eichner, M., Ferrari, V.: We are family: Joint pose estimation of multiple persons. In: European Conference on Computer Vision (2010) [258]
14. Everingham, M., Van Gool, L., Williams, C.K.I., Winn, J., Zisserman, A.: The pascal visual object classes (voc) challenge. Int. J. Comput. Vis. **88**(2), 303–338 (2010). http://pascallin.ecs.soton.ac.uk/challenges/VOC/ [259-261]
15. Felzenszwalb, P.F., Huttenlocher, D.P.: Pictorial structures for object recognition. Int. J. Comput. Vis. **61**(1), 55–79 (2005) [267,269]
16. Ferrari, V., Marin-Jimenez, M., Zisserman, A.: Progressive search space reduction for human pose estimation. In: IEEE Computer Society Conference on Computer Vision and Pattern Recognition (2008). http://www.robots.ox.ac.uk/~vgg/data/stickmen/index.html [254, 258,259,263,264,266,267,270,271]
17. Fischler, M.A., Elschlager, R.A.: The representation and matching of pictorial structures. IEEE Trans. Comput. **C-22**(1), 67–92 (1973) [267]
18. Fossati, A., Dimitrijevic, M., Lepetit, V., Fua, P.: Bridging the gap between detection and tracking for 3D monocular video-based motion capture. In: IEEE Computer Society Conference on Computer Vision and Pattern Recognition (2007) [255]
19. Freifeld, O., Weiss, A., Zuff, S., Black, M.J.: Contour people: A parameterized model of 2D articulated human shape. In: Computer Vision and Pattern Recognition (2010) [266]
20. Gall, J., Rosenhahn, B., Brox, T., Seidel, H. P.: Optimization and filtering for human motion capture. Int. J. Comput. Vis. **87**(1–2), 75–92 (2010) [261,270,271]
21. Gammeter, S., Ess, A., Jaeggli, T., Schindler, K., Leibe, B., Van Gool, L.: Articulated multibody tracking under egomotion. In: European Conference on Computer Vision (2008) [255]

22. Ganapathi, V., Plagemann, C., Koller, D., Thrun, S.: Real time motion capture using a single time-of-flight camera. In: IEEE Computer Society Conference on Computer Vision and Pattern Recognition (2010). http://ai.stanford.edu/~varung/cvpr10/ [254,262,263,265]

23. Gupta, A., Kembhavi, A., Davis, L.S.: Observing human–object interactions: Using spatial and functional compatibility for recognition. IEEE Trans. Pattern Anal. Mach. Intell. 31(10), 1775–1789 (2009) [258]

24. Hasler, N., Rosenhahn, B., Thormahlen, T., Wand, M., Gall, J., Seidel, H.-P.: Markerless motion capture with unsynchronized moving cameras. In: IEEE Computer Society Conference on Computer Vision and Pattern Recognition (2009) [255]

25. Hogg, D.: Model-based vision: a program to see a walking person. Image Vis. Comput. 1(1), 5–20 (1983) [255]

26. Hoiem, D., Efros, A., Hebert, M.: Putting objects in perspective. In: IEEE Computer Society Conference on Computer Vision and Pattern Recognition (2006) [258]

27. Ionescu, C., Bo, L., Sminchisescu, C.: Structural SVM for visual localization and continuous state estimation. In: IEEE International Conference on Computer Vision (2009) [268]

28. Jiang, H.: Human pose estimation using consistent max-covering. In: IEEE International Conference on Computer Vision (2009) [254,255]

29. Johnson, S., Everingham, M.: Clustered pose and nonlinear appearance models for human pose estimation. In: British Machine Vision Conference (2010) [254,257,259,268,269,271, 272]

30. Johnson, S., Everingham, M.: Learning effective human pose estimation from inaccurate annotation. In: IEEE Computer Society Conference on Computer Vision and Pattern Recognition (2011) [257,258,269,271,272]

31. Kjellström, H., Kragić, D., Black, M.J.: Tracking people interacting with objects. In: IEEE Computer Society Conference on Computer Vision and Pattern Recognition (2010) [272]

32. Kumar, M.P., Zisserman, A., Torr, P.H.S.: Efficient discriminative learning of parts-based models. In: IEEE International Conference on Computer Vision (2009) [268]

33. Lan, X., Huttenlocher, D.P.: Beyond trees: Common-factor models for 2d human pose recovery. In: IEEE International Conference on Computer Vision (2005) [269]

34. Lee, C.-S., Elgammal, A.: Coupled visual and kinematic manifold models for tracking. Int. J. Comput. Vis. 87(1–2), 118–139 (2010) [271]

35. Lee, M.W., Cohen, I.: Proposal maps driven MCMC for estimating human body pose in static images. In: IEEE Computer Society Conference on Computer Vision and Pattern Recognition (2004) [255]

36. Li, R., Tian, T.-P., Sclaroff, S., Yang, M.-H.: 3d human motion tracking with a coordinated mixture of factor analyzers. Int. J. Comput. Vis. 87(1–2), 170–190 (2010) [271]

37. Liu, Y., Stoll, C., Gall, J., Scidel, H.P., Theobalt, C.: Markerless motion capture of interacting characters using multi-view image segmentation. In: Computer Vision and Pattern Recognition (2011) [272]

38. Ning, H., Xu, W., Gong, Y., Huang, T.: Latent pose estimator for continuous action recognition. In: European Conference on Computer Vision, pp. 419–433 (2008) [270]

39. Peursum, P., Venkatesh, S., West, G.: A study on smoothing for particle filtered 3d human body tracking. Int. J. Comput. Vis. 87(1–2), 53–74 (2010) [271]

40. Pons-Moll, G., Baak, A., Helten, T., Müller, M., Seidel, H.-P., Rosenhahn, B.: Multisensor-fusion for 3d full-body human motion capture. In: IEEE Computer Society Conference on Computer Vision and Pattern Recognition (2010). http://www.tnt. uni-hannover.de/project/MPI08_Database/ [254,262,264,265,272]

41. Ramanan, D.: Learning to parse images of articulated bodies. In: Advances in Neural Information Processing Systems (2006). http://www.ics.uci.edu/~dramanan/papers/parse/people.zip [254,256,257,259,263,264,267,268,270,271]

42. Ren, X., Berg, A.C., Malik, J.: Recovering human body configurations using pairwise constraints between parts. In: IEEE International Conference on Computer Vision (2005) [255]

43. Sapp, B., Jordan, C., Taskar, B.: Adaptive pose priors for pictorial structures. In: IEEE Computer Society Conference on Computer Vision and Pattern Recognition (2010) [259,268,269]

44. Shakhnarovich, G., Viola, P., Darrell, T.: Fast pose estimation with parameter-sensitive hashing. In: IEEE International Conference on Computer Vision, vol. 2, pp. 750–759 (2003) [263]
45. Sigal, L., Balan, A.O., Black, M.J.: Humaneva: Synchronized video and motion capture dataset and baseline algorithm for evaluation of articulated human motion. Int. J. Comput. Vis. **87**(1–2), 4–27 (2010). http://vision.cs.brown.edu/humaneva/index.html [254,261,264, 265,270-272]
46. Sigal, L., Black, M.J.: Guest editorial: State of the art in image- and video-based human pose and motion estimation. Int. J. Comput. Vis. **87**(1–2), 1–3 (2010) [270]
47. Singh, V., Nevatia, R., Huang, C.: Efficient inference with multiple heterogeneous part detectors for human pose estimation. In: European Conference on Computer Vision (2010) [257, 268,269]
48. Sminchisescu, C., Kanaujia, A., Li, Z., Metaxas, D.: Conditional visual tracking in kernel space. In: Advances in Neural Information Processing Systems (2005) [263]
49. Sminchisescu, C., Kanaujia, A., Metaxas, D.: Learning joint top–down and bottom–up processes for 3d visual inference. In: IEEE Computer Society Conference on Computer Vision and Pattern Recognition (2006) [263]
50. Tian, T.-P., Sclaroff, S.: Fast globally optimal 2d human detection with loopy graph models. In: IEEE Computer Society Conference on Computer Vision and Pattern Recognition (2010) [257,268,269]
51. Tran, D., Forsyth, D.: Improved human parsing with a full relational model. In: European Conference on Computer Vision (2010) [254,260,264]
52. Urtasun, R., Darrell, T.: Local probabilistic regression for activity-independent human pose inference. In: IEEE International Conference on Computer Vision (2009) [255,268]
53. Vlasic, D., Adelsberger, R., Vannucci, G., Barnwell, J., Gross, M., Matusik, W., Popović, J.: Practical motion capture in everyday surroundings. ACM Trans. Graph. **26**(3), 35 (2007) [264,272]
54. Wang, P., Rehg, J.M.: A modular approach to the analysis and evaluation of particle filters for figure tracking. In: IEEE Computer Society Conference on Computer Vision and Pattern Recognition, vol. 1, pp. 790–797 (2006). http://www.cc.gatech.edu/~pingwang/ Project/FigureTracking.html [265,266]
55. Yang, Y., Ramanan, D.: Articulated pose estimation with flexible mixtures-of-parts. In: IEEE Computer Society Conference on Computer Vision and Pattern Recognition (2011) [266,268]
56. Yao, B., Fei-Fei, L.: Modeling mutual context of object and human pose in human–object interaction activities. In: IEEE Computer Society Conference on Computer Vision and Pattern Recognition (2010). http://ai.stanford.edu/~bangpeng/resource/mutual_ context_annotation.rar [254,258,272]
57. Zhang, J., Luo, J., Collins, R., Liu, Y.: Body localization in still images using hierarchical models and hybrid search. In: IEEE Computer Society Conference on Computer Vision and Pattern Recognition (2006) [255]

Part III
Recognition

Chapter 14
On Human Action

Aaron Bobick and Volker Krüger

14.1 The Problem

The recognition of action—or behavior or activity—has become a key focus of research not only in computer vision but also in robotics. Numerous application domains including surveillance, smart-homes, rehabilitation, entertainment, animation and human–robot interaction are all predicated upon understanding human activity. All these applications have in common that they all use sensory input, all need to capture the movements of an acting agent and based on this they almost always ask the same principle question: Given a human being in the field of sensory input, *what is the person doing*?

This topic, however, represents a fundamentally different type of computation than has been described in previous chapters. Until this point, the chapters in this book have focused on either image quantities such as segmenting the pixels of a person from the background, or on three dimensional properties that can be said to have an objectively correct answer, e.g. recover the three dimensional pose of a person. But when considering the overall task of action recognition the notion of objective correctness becomes problematic.

Consider, for example, the simple scenario of someone washing dishes. There is still the problem of pose estimation: the hand moves in the direction of the dish and then moves back (perhaps affixing itself to the dish in the process). But one could also say that the person is Reaching for the Dish, Lifting the

A. Bobick (✉)
Georgia Institute of Technology, Atlanta, GA, USA
e-mail: afb@cc.gatech.edu

V. Krüger
Aalborg University Copenhagen, Ballerup, Denmark
e-mail: vok@cvmi.aau.dk

T.B. Moeslund et al. (eds.), *Visual Analysis of Humans*,
DOI 10.1007/978-0-85729-997-0_14, © Springer-Verlag London Limited 2011

Dish, and Bringing the Dish to the Body. Together these three movements support the assertion Washing the dish. And, of course, the person is in the process of Washing Dishes. Which label is correct?

Unfortunately, there is no unique answer to this question. Focusing on human actions and following the arguments from neuroscience [41, 42] and physiology [36] that human movements are built from motor primitives or *action units*, analogous to speech being a composition of phonemes, it is clear that actions can be described at different levels of abstraction. These descriptions consider movement at different levels of complexity, e.g., in terms of primitives (phonemes), actions (words), activities (sentence) and context (language) [5], or in terms of *change, event, verb, episode* and *history* [35]. Therefore, one is able to find labels at different abstraction levels, and all of the above suggested answers are correct, depending upon which abstraction level is of interest to the observer.

In addition, the label most relevant to the goals of the observed agent depends upon the overall task established by the domain. A system that is observing a stroke patient over time to assess mobility would need to be able to recover precisely pose and limb trajectories. A robot learning what it means to wash dishes might need to understand that it needs to grasp the dish and then place it under water, etc. And a system that is assisting an elderly person by monitoring their behavior in their home might need to determine that the kitchen is being appropriately cared for and no intervention is needed [23].

Regardless of the label sought, the ability to find a label for an observed action requires first and foremost the ability to recognize the action at some level of description. This, however, is a non-trivial task for several reasons: our dish-washing action can be observed from radically different viewing directions; the action itself can be performed by different people in their own "style"; the dish-washing action consists not only of arm movements but also requires a considerable amount of interaction with various and partially specific objects, and the relative state of those objects is key; and, finally, the amount of training data is limited.

However, one can also evaluate the action on a task level by asking what *effect* the human action has on the state of the environment. By defining a task as the anticipated change of the environment, the task level description is concerned with how a scene state changes upon a human action. The task of washing the dishes then becomes the task of changing the state of the dishes from dirty to clean. Like an embodied action, the task-level description of an action can have different abstraction levels, and, intuitively, the abstraction levels of the task-level description and of the physical human actions correlate. By comparing the two descriptions, it becomes evident that an action can be described by two dual pieces of information: the task-level, which is defined on the scene state space, and the embodied human actions that are required to manipulate the scene state space in order to cause the anticipated change. While the task can have a unique description, different physical actions are likely to lead to the same effect on the scene. In that sense, the task-level description seems to provide the semantic description of a physical action.

It is this consideration of task that, perhaps, sets activity recognition in a robotics context apart from such activity as is often studied in computer vision [8, 47]. In the latter case the fundamental task is the appropriate labeling of a given video sequence with respect to some predefined activity vocabulary. In this context, a discriminatively trained, machine learning paradigm can often be exploited. A database of training examples of a variety of labeled activities is provided, some element of processing is done, typically to extract relevant moving or contextual components, features of these elements are computed over time, and then some classification mechanism is trained to determine the appropriate label for test sequences. This approach has become one of the dominant paradigms in computer vision in the last decade.

In the context of robotics, there are situations in which determining the appropriate label for an action or even action primitive is sufficient. An example might be gesture-based control (see also Chaps. 17, 25 and 27)—a specific action by a human conveys meaning to a robot by assigning a specific label: *"turn right"* or *"stop"*. Indeed a potent communication system can be formed by recognizing parametrized gesture [27, 49] where gesture and primitives are recognized categorically (*"move"*) but the pose is extracted to determine the appropriate control parameter, e.g. the intended direction.

14.2 Action Learning and Imitation

For general robotics scenarios a labeling driven approach as outlined above is usually not adequate. Continuing in our theme of domestic service, consider a robot that is to be instructed on what it means to set-the-dinner-table. A current focus in human–robot interaction (HRI) research is to teach the robot simply by *showing* robot what to do. This paradigm is referred to as *teaching (or learning) by demonstration* [3, 7, 14, 24, 29, 33, 39, 40, 43]: the robot is provided with one or more demonstrations of the table-setting action so that it becomes able to do two things: First, it needs to be able to *recognize* the action when performed again by a different agent. Second, it needs to store information about this action so that it is able to perform the action itself. An important aspect is that the setting of the environment is likely to change and look different over different performances. Furthermore, a robot that has to set a dinner table may have to plan the order of handling plates, silverware and glasses in a manner different from previously demonstrated. This means that it is usually not sufficient to just memorize and replicate the previously seen human movements. Instead, the robot must be able to identify the sub-tasks based on which it is able to build a model of that action and then use that model either to recognize or to plan new executions of that action in different environment settings.

In this learning context several questions arise that are vital both for recognition and for planning the execution of an action:

1. Up to what level should a known example movement equal a new performance? For example, are finger motions modeled as individual joint trajectories or as a unified "grasp". This is a question of imitation vs. emulation [53] on different abstraction levels of the action. The answer depends on the domain: In a rehabilitation context, precise movements matter while in a dish cleaning scenario the

precise movements are likely irrelevant because it is the end-result of the action that matters.

2. How should the dynamic scene be modeled including both the objects and the changes that can be done to them? For example, we need to model that the saucers are usually placed under the cups. Furthermore, this requires the notion of object *affordances* [15, 16] that describe the set of actions an actor can apply to an object. For example a door affords (or *suggests*) to be opened or closed, depending on its state. The affordances can be considered as constraining the actions that are likely to be performed give the set of objects on which the agent is acting.

3. How should we model that the temporal order of some sub-tasks might or might not be significant? For example, the temporal order of placing the silverware and the dishes on the table is irrelevant except with respect to those dishes that are to be stacked.

4. The entire scene may change during task execution so that the robot will have to re-plan in order to achieve a given goal. For action recognition, re-planning is a considerable complication [10, 25].

In general, imitation is not the same as learning to perform: the former implies a literal copy whereas the latter reflects the ability to execute under a variety of conditions. Likewise, for robotics, action recognition implies understanding the elements that are relevant to the successful performance of the task associated with the action.

14.3 Framing the Problem

Here we present a variety of general approaches to the action recognition problem, each reflecting a rather distinct notion of what the fundamental problem is. And each of these directions is represented by at least one chapter in this part of the book.

14.3.1 Action Recognition as a Specific Labeling

The last decade has seen an proliferation of activity recognition datasets in the computer vision community. These range in complexity from a relatively controlled environment of people doing simple actions in front of a fixed background viewed by a static camera [19, 45] to scenes taken from commercially produced movies—for example the aptly named Hollywood dataset [31, 34]. Indeed, Chap. 15 gives an overview over some of the key methodologies presently used in the computer vision community, while Chap. 20 at the end of this part of the book presents more than a dozen such datasets and discusses the performance of various algorithms on the labeling task.

Inherent in the task defined by these datasets is typically the notion of discriminatively trained recognition methods [45]. The fundamental differences between the approaches taken in attacking the recognition problem is what features are extracted from the video, what additional information is available, what the structure of the underlying representation of the action possibilities is, and then how the information is integrated to achieve a probabilistic labeling of the action. Specific actions defined by human motion—such the Weizman dataset examples of `walking` or `two-hands-waving`—are typically addressed by considering the signal as a space–time volume [4, 19], where much more semantically defined actions such as `driving a car` integrate a variety of interest points having specific spatial-temporal relationships (see for example [18]). But fundamentally there is a classification problem defined over a fixed set of labels whose definition is derived— learned— from training data.

One specific application of the action recognition labeling paradigm is that of *gesture recognition*. Gesture has received significant attention in the computer vision community during the past two decades—for some early references see [22]. The dominant approach to this problem is a specific set of image or body features whose position in a body centered coordinate frame vary in time and whose evolution in time is probabilistically modeled based upon training data. The inference problem in this domain is typically easier than the more general datasets described above because of controlled viewing conditions and a much reduced variability in the action that may occur. However, gesture provides an intriguing control modality for Human Machine Interaction (HMI) and thus the automated understanding of such actions is of importance to the robotics field.

14.3.2 Action Recognition as Primitive Sequence Decomposition

"Merely" being able to label an action scene provides no information as to *how* that same task is accomplished. This, however, is likely to be necessary in scenarios that are highly variable such as our kitchen scenario which is indeed being explored by work such as [2] and examples of which are contained the "kitchen dataset" [9]. Robotics research in activity recognition has often embraced action primitives and "generative models" to represent them (see Chap. 17). But note that here, generative models means something more than in the computer vision and machine learning communities where generative models explicitly encode the probability of each class of action producing a particular perceptual signal. In robotics, generative implies an explicit modeling of each of the categories of action: the notion of generative models often embraces representations that not only support the recognition of an action but also permit the robot to synthesize such an action itself [6, 11, 43, 44]. Generative models have the appealing property that adding new action categories does not impact previously learned descriptions of other actions. Unlike "discriminative" models that represent the boundaries between actions, generative models represent the actions themselves, allowing greater flexibility in their use, though sometimes providing a reduced classification performance [37]. Additionally, generative models allow the vision system to identify novel and previously unseen actions if none of the available models are able to explain the new observation sufficiently well.

One general approach to such a generative model is the notion of *action primitives*. This idea can be motivated by the finding of so-called *mirror-neurons* [17, 41, 42], and neuro-biological evidence suggesting that the representation of visually perceived, learned and recognized actions is the same as the one used to drive the motor control of the body. In this model, the action recognition process is characterized as the decomposition of continuous human behavior into a sequence of action primitives such as *reaching*, *picking up*, and *putting down*. Recognition requires being able to hypothesize which sequence of primitives would be most likely to have generated the observed data. Indeed, quite early Arbib [1] proposed the idea of movement primitives, which can be viewed as sequences of actions that accomplish a complete goal-directed behavior. Conceptually, the idea of movement primitives is important from a computation point of view and because it allows us to abstract complex motions as symbols, thus providing the basis for higher level cognitive processes, such as planning.

And in even earlier psychophysics, Newtson et al. [36] reports behavioral experiments where human observers are shown to be able to segment ongoing activity into temporal parts named *action units*. It has further been shown [36] that the resulting segmentation is reliable and systematically related to relevant features of the action.

The idea to model actions on different abstraction levels seems natural. However, there are a number of open questions concerning action primitives. First, there is no consensus in the literature about how to encode the movement primitives. Proposals include generative (in terms of execution) models as indicated above, but also non-linear attractor systems and even discriminative models. Furthermore, there is no consensus how to identify the "right" set of primitives and if there actually is such a unique set. Many authors define the set of primitives by hand while others employ statistical learning schemes [27, 28]. In Computer Vision, topic models are often used to identify some kind of action primitives, e.g., in surveillance applications [48] (see Chap. 16). However, a complication for learning action primitives for human body movements is that the primitives are typically parameterized with discrete and/or continuous control or task parameters. For example the primitive *reaching for an object* is necessarily conditioned by the location of the object; likewise a *pointing* primitive is conditioned by the intended direction. Thus the observed human movements for a particular primitive can appear vastly different for different parameters implying that a simplistic clustering based on the visual appearance will fail to determine such a primitive exists. Consequently, how to identify automatically a set of action primitives from a set of observations is an open problem. A detailed discussion about action primitives can be found in the Chaps. 16 and 17.

14.3.3 Action, Objects and Context

In addition to a generative model for human movements, a task-level description is required that allows the system to model also the interaction with objects. One of the links between the generative models for the action primitives and the task-level description are the objects in the scenario to which the action primitives are applied. Objects can constrain the actions in several ways: The arm movement within a reaching movement is constrained by the location of the object and the hand movement (grasp) is constrained by the size of the object, its weight and possibly its surface. The term *object affordances* was used by Gibson [16] to refer to the set of *action possibilities* that a specific object *affords* to a given agent. A further constraint on actions is the context in which they are applied. Considering the domestic scenario above, we grasp a cup differently when cleaning than when we want to drink from it. Considering these relations between objects, actions and context, an action recognition task can be greatly simplified if it is conditioned on the involved object and the context. Conversely, an object recognition task is simplified if we can see a human applying an action on the object. A number of recent publications in computer vision [20, 26, 46, 51, 52] were based on this observation. This view that objects, action and context are intertwined is the basis of the concept of object-action complexes (OACs) [50]. To formalize the notion and use of objects, actions and context, Chap. 18 provides a detailed introduction to these terms and demonstrates how object recognition and action recognition can be approached as a joint problem using a graphical model, and where the recognition problem is treated as an inference problem of missing data.

14.3.4 Action Recognition in Computer Vision

Finally, there are approaches to action recognition that are highly relevant for video surveillance applications. In this paradigm, a large set of data of different behavior executions is available. Certain low level features are defined to describe the activity locally in time and space, and then the entire corpus is represented using this vocabulary. Examples of such an approach include using extremely low level space–time descriptors [12, 30] or some event primitives (e.g. *door opens*) designed for the specific scene [21]. Details of relevant space–time features and various recognition strategies relevant not only for surveillance applications are discussed in detail in Chap. 15.

Once so characterized, the data corpus is analyzed with two specific goals in mind. The first is basically a clustering of experiences such that they share specific attributes. The mechanics of achieving this structuring can be achieved by explicit analysis of the similarities between local frames [21] or by a more holistic approach that attempts to recover a compact description based upon co-occurrence of the lower level properties [32, 38, 48]. Indeed, Chap. 16 presents one instance of this latter approach motivated by topic analysis of documents and applied to trajectories of tracked objects. The analogy is that trajectories correspond to documents, locations along the trajectories to words, and semantically meaningful regions of a scene to topics.

The second potential goal, and one that perhaps is currently highly relevant to surveillance applications, is that of complex activities involving multiple interacting objects such as humans, cars, suitcases, etc. A detailed discussion is provided in Chap. 15.

14.4 Facial Expressions for the Analysis of Human Behavior

Another aspect of the analysis of human action and behavior is the analysis of facial expressions. Facial expression analysis is vital for a large number of applications, including recognition of emotions and intentions, recognition of the level of alertness, social computing as well as perceptual user interfaces, human-machine interaction, marketing and animations and many more. Key features for describing facial expressions are the facial action units [13] which mark 44 different and specific locations on the human face. Based on these features, various recognition approaches can be employed for recognition. Many of the approaches used for human action recognition are also commonly applied in face gesture modeling, such as HMMs, Dynamic Bayesian networks (DBNs) or CRFs. Chapter 19 provides an excellent overview of the different methodologies.

References

1. Arbib, M.A.: Perceptual structures and distributed motor control. In: Brooks, V.B. (ed.) Handbook of Physiology, Section 2: The Nervous System (Vol. II, Motor Control, Part 1), pp. 1449–1480. Am. Physiol. Soc., Bethesda (1981) [284]
2. Beetz, M., Jain, D., Mösenlechner, L., Tenorth, M.: Towards performing everyday manipulation activities. Robot. Auton. Syst. **58**(9), 1085–1095 (2010) [283]
3. Billard, A.: Imitation: A review. In: Arbib, M. (ed.) Handbook of Brain Theory and Neural Network, pp. 566–569. MIT Press, Cambridge (2002) [281]
4. Bobick, A., Davis, J.: The representation and recognition of action using temporal templates. IEEE Trans. Pattern Anal. Mach. Intell. **23**(3), 257–267 (2001) [283]
5. Bobick, A.F.: Movements, activity, and action: The role of knowledge in the perception of motion. In: Royal Society Workshop on Knowledge-based Vision in Man and Machine, London, England, p. 70 (February 1997) [280]
6. Breazeal, C., Scassellati, B.: Robots that imitate humans. Trends Cogn. Sci. **6**(11), 481–487 (2002) [283]
7. Calinon, S., Guenter, F., Billard, A.: Goal-directed imitation in a humanoid robot. In: International Conference on Robotics and Automation, Barcelona, Spain, pp. 299–304 (April 18–22, 2005) [281]
8. Cedras, C., Shah, M.: Motion-based recognition: A survey. Image Vis. Comput. **13**(2), 129–155 (1995) [280]
9. De la Torre, F., Hodgins, J., Montano, J., Valcarcel, S., Forcada, R., Macey, J.: Guide to the Carnegie Mellon university multimodal activity (cmu-mmac) database. Technical Report CMU-RI-TR-08-22, Robotics Institute, Carnegie Mellon University (July 2009) [283]
10. Demiris, Y., Johnson, M.: Distributed, predictive perception of actions: a biologically inspired robotics architecture for imitation and learning. Connect. Sci. J. **15**(4), 231–243 (2003) [282]
11. Dillmann, R.: Teaching and learning of robot tasks via observation of human performance. Robot. Auton. Syst. **47**, 109–116 (2004) [283]
12. Dollar, P., Rabaud, V., Cottrellm, G., Belongie, S.: Behavior recognition via sparse spatio-temporal features. In: IEEE International Workshop on Performance Evaluation of Tracking and Surveillance (PETS) (2005) [285]

13. Ekman, P., Friesen, W.: Facial Action Coding System: A Technique for the Measurement of Facial Movement. Consulting Psychologists Press, Palo Alto (1978) [286]
14. Ekvall, S., Kragic, D.: Grasp recognition for programming by demonstration tasks. In: IEEE International Conference on Robotics and Automation, ICRA'05, Barcelona, Spain, April 18–22, pp. 748–753 (2005) [281]
15. Gibson, J.J.: The Theory of Affordances. In: Shaw, R., Bransford, J. (eds.) Perceiving, Acting, and Knowing. Lawrence Erlbaum, Mahwah (1977) [282]
16. Gibson, J.J.: The Ecological Approach to Visual Perception. Psychology Press, London (1997) [282,285]
17. Giese, M., Poggio, T.: Neural mechanisms for the recognition of biological movements. Nat. Rev., Neurosci. **4**, 179–192 (2003) [284]
18. Gilbert, A., Illingworth, J., Bowden, R.: Action recognition using mined hierarchical compound features. IEEE Trans. Pattern Anal. Mach. Intell. **33**(5), 883–897 (2011) [283]
19. Gorelick, L., Blank, M., Shechtman, E., Irani, M., Basri, R.: Actions as space–time shapes. In: IEEE International Conference on Computer Vision (ICCV) (2005) [282,283]
20. Gupta, A., Kembhavi, A., Davis, L.S.: Observing human–object interactions: Using spatial and functional compatibility for recognition. IEEE Trans. Pattern Anal. Mach. Intell. **31**(10), 1775–1789 (2009) [285]
21. Hamid, R., Maddi, S., Johnson, A., Bobick, A., Essa, I., Isbell, C.L.: A novel sequence representation for unsupervised analysis of human activities. Artif. Intell. **173**(14), 1221–1244 (2009) [285]
22. Huang, Y.W.T.: Vision-based gesture recognition: A review. In: Proceedings of the International Gesture Workshop on Gesture-Based Communication in Human–Computer Interaction. GW '99, pp. 103–115. Springer, London (1999) [283]
23. Jain, A., Kemp, C.: El-e: An assistive mobile manipulator that autonomously fetches objects from flat surfaces. Auton. Robots **28**, 45–64 (2010) [280]
24. Jenkins, O.C., Mataric, M.J.: Performance-derived behavior vocabularies: Data-driven acquisition of skills from motion. Int. J. Humanoid Robot. **1**(2), 237–288 (2004) [281]
25. Johnson, M., Demiris, Y.: Hierarchies of coupled inverse and forward models for abstraction in robot action planning, recognition and imitation. In: Proceedings of the AISB 2005 Symposium on Imitation in Animals and Artifacts, Newcastle upon Tyne, UK, pp. 69–76 (2005) [282]
26. Kjellström, H., Kragić, D., Black, M.J.: Tracking people interacting with objects. In: Computer Vision and Pattern Recognition (2010) [285]
27. Krueger, V., Baby, S., Herzog, D., Ude, A., Kragic, D.: Learning actions from observations. IEEE Robot. Autom. Mag. **17**(2), 30–43 (2010) [281,284]
28. Kulić, D., Takano, W., Nakamura, Y.: Incremental learning, clustering and hierarchy formation of whole body motion patterns using adaptive hidden Markov chains. Int. J. Robot. Res. **27**(7), 761–784 (2008) [284]
29. Kuniyoshi, Y., Inaba, M., Inoue, H.: Learning by watching, extracting reusable task knowledge from visual observation of human performance. IEEE Trans. Robot. Autom. **10**(6), 799–822 (1994) [281]
30. Laptev, I., Lindeberg, T.: Space–time interest points. In: IEEE International Conference on Computer Vision (2003) [285]
31. Laptev, I., Marszałek, I., Schmid, C., Rozenfeld, B.: Learning realistic human actions from movies. In: Computer Vision and Pattern Recognition (2008) [282]
32. Liu, H., Feris, R., Krüger, V., Sun, M.-T.: Unsupervised action classification using space–time link analysis. EURASIP Journal on Image and Video Processing **2010**, 10 (2010). Article ID 626324 [285]
33. Lopes, M.C., Victor, J.S.: Visual transformations in gesture imitation: What you see is what you do. In: IEEE International Conference on Robotics and Automation, ICRA03, Taipei, Taiwan, September 14–19, pp. 2375–2381 (2003) [281]
34. Marszałek, M., Laptev, I., Schmid, C.: Actions in context. In: Computer Vision and Pattern Recognition (2009) [282]

35. Nagel, H.-H.: From image sequences towards conceptual descriptions. Image Vis. Comput. **6**(2), 59–74 (1988) [280]
36. Newtson, D., Engquist, D., Bois, J.: The objective basis of behavior units. J. Pers. Soc. Psychol. **35**(12), 847–862 (1977) [280,284]
37. Ng, A.Y., Jordan, M.I.: On discriminative vs. generative classifiers: A comparison of logistic regression and naive bayes. In: Int. Conf. Neural Information Processing Systems: Natural and Synthetic, Vancouver, British Columbia, Canada (December 3–8, 2001) [283]
38. Niebles, J.C., Wang, H., Fei-Fei, L.: Unsupervised learning of human action categories using spatial-temporal words. Int. J. Comput. Vis. **79**(3), 299–318 (2008) [285]
39. Ogawara, K., Iba, S., Kimura, H., Ikeuchi, K.: Recognition of human task by attention point analysis. In: IEEE International Conference on Intelligent Robot and Systems IROS'00, Takamatsu, Japan, pp. 2121–2126 (2000) [281]
40. Ogawara, K., Iba, S., Kimura, H., Ikeuchi, K.: Acquiring hand-action models by attention point analysis. In: IEEE International Conference on Robotics and Automation (ICRA01), Seoul, Korea, May 21–26, pp. 465–470 (2001) [281]
41. Rizzolatti, G., Fogassi, L., Gallese, V.: Parietal cortex: From sight to action. Curr. Opin. Neurobiol. **7**, 562–567 (1997) [280,284]
42. Rizzolatti, G., Fogassi, L., Gallese, V.: Neurophysiological mechanisms underlying the understanding and imitation of action. Nature Reviews **2**, 661–670 (2001) [280,284]
43. Schaal, S.: Is imitation learning the route to humanoid robots? Trends Cogn. Sci. **3**(6), 233–242 (1999) [281,283]
44. Schaal, S., Ijspeert, A.J., Billard, A.: Computational approaches to motor learning by imitation. Philos. Trans. R. Soc. Lond. B, Biol. Sci. **358**(1431), 537–547 (2003) [283]
45. Schuldt, C., Laptev, I., Caputo, B.: Recognizing human actions: A local SVM approach. In: International Conference on Pattern Recognition (ICPR), pp. 32–36 (2004) [282]
46. Torralba, A.: Contextual priming for object detection. Int. J. Comput. Vis. **53**(2), 169–191 (2003) [285]
47. Turaga, P., Chellappa, R., Subrahmanian, V.S., Udrea, O.: Machine recognition of human activities: A survey. IEEE Trans. Circuits Syst. Video Technol. **18**(11), 1473–1488 (2008) [280]
48. Wang, X., Ma, X., Grimson, E.: Unsupervised activity perception in crowded and complicated scenes using hierarchical Bayesian models. IEEE Trans. Pattern Anal. Mach. Intell. **31**, 539–555 (2009) [284]
49. Wilson, A., Bobick, A.: Parametric hidden Markov models for gesture recognition. IEEE Trans. Pattern Anal. Mach. Intell. **21**, 884–900 (1999) [281]
50. Wörgötter, F., Agostini, A., Krüger, N., Shylo, N., Porr, B.: Cognitive agents – a procedural perspective relying on the predictability of object-action-complexes (OACs). Robot. Auton. Syst. **57**(4), 420–432 (2009) [285]
51. Yao, B., Fei-Fei, L.: Grouplet: A structured image representation for recognizing human and object interactions. In: IEEE Conference on Computer Vision and Pattern Recognition (2010) [285]
52. Yao, B., Fei-Fei, L.: Modeling mutual context of object and human pose in human–object interaction activities. In: IEEE Conference on Computer Vision and Pattern Recognition (2010) [285]
53. Zentall, T.R.: Imitation: Definitions, evidence, and mechanisms. Animal Cognition **9**, 335–353 (2006) [281]

Chapter 15
Modeling and Recognition of Complex Human Activities

Nandita M. Nayak, Ricky J. Sethi, Bi Song, and Amit K. Roy-Chowdhury

Abstract Activity recognition is a field of computer vision which has shown great progress in the past decade. Starting from simple single person activities, research in activity recognition is moving toward more complex scenes involving multiple objects and natural environments. The main challenges in the task include being able to localize and recognize events in a video and deal with the large amount of variation in viewpoint, speed of movement and scale. This chapter gives the reader an overview of the work that has taken place in activity recognition, especially in the domain of complex activities involving multiple interacting objects. We begin with a description of the challenges in activity recognition and give a broad overview of the different approaches. We go into the details of some of the feature descriptors and classification strategies commonly recognized as being the state of the art in this field. We then move to more complex recognition systems, discussing the challenges in complex activity recognition and some of the work which has taken place in this respect. Finally, we provide some examples of recent work in complex activity recognition. The ability to recognize complex behaviors involving multiple interacting objects is a very challenging problem and future work needs to study its various aspects of features, recognition strategies, models, robustness issues, and context, to name a few.

N.M. Nayak (✉) · B. Song · A.K. Roy-Chowdhury
University of California, Riverside, 900 University Ave. Riverside, CA 92521, USA
e-mail: nandita.nayak@email.ucr.edu

B. Song
e-mail: bsong@ee.ucr.edu

A.K. Roy-Chowdhury
e-mail: amitrc@ee.ucr.edu

R.J. Sethi
University of California, Los Angeles, 4532 Boelter Hall, CA 90095-1596, USA
e-mail: rickys@sethi.org
Information Sciences Institute, University of Southern California, 4676 Admiralty Way, Marina del Rey, CA 90292, USA

T.B. Moeslund et al. (eds.), *Visual Analysis of Humans*,
DOI 10.1007/978-0-85729-997-0_15, © Springer-Verlag London Limited 2011

15.1 Introduction

Activity recognition is the task of interpretation of the activities of objects in video over a period of time. The goal of an activity recognition system is to extract information on the movements of objects and/or their surroundings from the video data so as to conclude on the events and context in the video in an automated manner. In a simple scenario where the video is segmented to contain only one execution of a human activity, the objective of the system is to correctly classify the activity into its category, whereas in a more complex scenario of a long video sequence containing multiple activities, it may also involve the detection of the starting and ending points of all occurring activities in the video [1].

Activity recognition has been a core area of study in computer vision due to its usefulness in diverse fields such as surveillance, sports analysis, patient monitoring and human computer interaction systems. These diverse applications in turn lead to several kinds of activity recognition systems. For example, in a surveillance system, the interest could be in being able to identify an abnormal activity—such as abandoning of a baggage, unusual grouping of people, unusual movements in a public place, etc. A patient monitoring system might require the system to be familiar with the movements of a patient. A sports analysis system would aim at the detection of certain known events, such as a goal detection or kick detection in a soccer game or the statistical learning of the semantics of the play. A traffic monitoring system would require a detection of events such as congestion, accidents or violation of rules. A gesture based human computer interface such as in video games would require posture and gesture recognition.

Although there is no formal classification of activities into different categories, for the sake of understanding, we will divide activities into simple and complex activities based on the complexity of the recognition task. An activity which involves a single person and lasts only a few seconds can be termed as a simple activity. Such video sequences consist of a single action to be categorized. Some examples of simple activities are running, walking, waving, etc. and do not contain much extraneous noise or variations. Although it is uncommon to find such data in the real world, these video sequences are useful in the learning and testing of new models for activity recognition. Popular examples of such activities are found in the Weizmann [6] and KTH [53] datasets.

The task of understanding the behaviors of multiple interacting objects (for e.g. people grouping, entering and exiting facilities, group sports) by visual analysis will be termed as complex activity recognition in this chapter. Recognition of complex behaviors makes the analysis of high-level events possible. For example, complex activity recognition can help to build automated recognition systems for suspicious multi-person behaviors such as group formations and dispersal. Some examples of complex activity datasets are the UT-Interaction dataset [50] and the UCR videoweb dataset [12].

In this chapter, we will look at some techniques of activity recognition. We will start with an overview of the description and classification techniques in activity recognition and take a brief glimpse at abnormal activity recognition. Next, we will show some examples of features used in activity recognition followed by some common recognition strategies. We will then discuss what complex activities are and look at some of the challenges in complex activity recognition. Finally, we will discuss some examples of recent approaches used in the modeling of complex activities.

15.1.1 Overview of Activity Recognition Methods

The basic steps involved in an activity recognition system are the extraction of features from the video frames and inference of activities from features. A popular approach to activity recognition has been the use of local interest points. Each interest point has a local descriptor to describe the characteristics of the point. Motion analysis is thus brought about by the analysis of feature vectors. Some researchers used spatial interest points to describe a scene [16, 19, 31]. Such approaches are termed as local approaches [8]. Over time, researchers described other robust spatio-temporal feature vectors. SIFT (scale invariant feature transform) [34] and STIP (space time interest points) [28] are commonly used local descriptors in videos. A more recent approach is to combine multiple features in a multiple instance learning (MIL) framework to improve accuracy [9].

Another approach to action recognition is global analysis of the video [8]. This involves a study of the overall motion characteristics of the video. Many of these methods use optical flow to represent motion in a video frame. One example of this method is in [3]. These approaches often involve modeling of the flow statistics over time. Optical flow histograms have commonly been used to compute and model flow statistics like in [15] which demonstrates the use of optical flow histograms in the analysis of soccer matches. In some other cases, human activities have been represented by 3-D space–time shapes where classification is performed by comparing geometric properties of these shapes against training data [6, 60].

Methods which have been used for modeling activities can be classified as non-parametric, volumetric and parametric time-series approaches [57]. Non-parametric approaches typically extract a set of features from each frame of the video. Non-parametric approaches could involve generation of 2D templates from image features [7, 44], 3D object models using shape descriptors or object contours [6] or manifold learning by dimensionality reduction methods such as PCA, LLE [45] and Laplacian eigenmaps [4]. Parametric methods involve learning the parameters of a model for the action using training data. These could involve HMM [33] and linear [11] and non-linear dynamical systems [41]. Volumetric methods of action recognition perform sub volume matching or use filter banks for spatio-temporal filtering [61]. Some researchers have used multiple 2D videos to arrive at a 3D model which is then used for view invariant action recognition [40].

15.1.2 Abnormal Activity Recognition

One of the important applications of activity recognition is the detection of suspicious or anomalous activities. This is the task of being able to detect anything "out of ordinary" in an automated manner. Abnormal activity recognition is about separating events which contain large deviations from the expected. The main challenge in the task is to define normalcy or anomaly. Since it is not always easy to define anomaly, a practical approach to abnormal activity detection is to detect normal events and treat the rest as anomaly [22].

When training data are available, a common approach is to model the normal activities using the training data. Graphical models have popularly been used in such cases. For example, HMMs have been used in a weakly supervised learning framework in [59] for anomaly detection in industrial processes. Here, the whole frame is taken as a feature vector and reduced to a lower dimension before modeling using HMMs. The authors in [58] use HMMs to model the configuration of multiple point objects in a scene. Abnormal activities are identified as a change in this model. Anomalies are detected by modeling the co-occurrence of pixels during an action using MRFs in [5].

When training data are not available, attempts have been made to detect anomalous activities by an unsupervised clustering of the data in a given video [35]. Dense clusters are classified as normal whereas rare ones could be anomalous. Anomalous activities have been detected using spatio-temporal context or the surrounding motion in [22]. Crowd anomalies have been detected by crowd motion modeling using Helmholtz decomposition of flow in [38].

15.2 Feature Descriptors

The first step in an activity recognition system is to extract a set of features which constitute the description of motion in the video. These features are the input to the recognition system. Researchers have used several feature descriptors in activity recognition. These can be broadly categorized into two kinds—local descriptors which represent small spatio-temporal regions of the video and global descriptors which are used to represent motion in an entire segment of the video [8]. In this section, we will briefly look into some of the popular image descriptors.

15.2.1 Local Features

We will begin with some examples of local features. The idea behind these features is that they represent points or regions of high interest in the video. It is believed that there is similarity between the local features extracted for similar actions. Thereafter, activity matching is achieved by a comparison of the feature set of the given videos. Examples of local features for different activities are seen in Fig. 15.1.

Fig. 15.1 This figure shows the cuboidal features marked for actions boxing, hand clapping and hand waving. These are typical examples of simple activities. The figure is taken from [32]

15.2.1.1 Spatio-temporal Interest Points

Spatio-temporal interest points [28] are points of high gradient in the space–time volume of a video. These are inspired from the SIFT points [34] which are popularly used by the object recognition community. It was found that these points are fairly invariant to scale, rotation and change in illumination. Given a video sequence, the spatio-temporal interest points are extracted by first computing a scale-space representation $\mathbf{L}$ by convolution with a spatio-temporal Gaussian kernel $g(x, y, t; \sigma, \tau) = 1/(2\pi\sigma^2\sqrt{2\pi\tau})\exp(-(x^2 + y^2)/2\sigma^2 - t^2/2\tau^2)$ with spatial and temporal scale parameters σ and τ. At any point $p(x, y, t)$ in the video, a second moment matrix μ is defined as

$$\mu(\mathbf{p}) = \int_{q\in\mathbb{R}^3} (\nabla\mathbf{L}(\mathbf{q}))(\nabla\mathbf{L}(\mathbf{q}))^T g(p - q; \sigma_i, \tau_i)\, dq, \tag{15.1}$$

where $\nabla\mathbf{L} = (L_x, L_y, L_z)^T$ denotes the spatio-temporal gradient vector and ($\sigma_i = \gamma\sigma$, $\tau_i = \gamma\tau$) are spatial and temporal integration scales with $\gamma = \sqrt{2}$. In other words, μ denotes the gradient of point p in its neighborhood. The interest points are detected as the spatio-temporal corners which are given by significant variations of image value both over space and time. These would correspond to the points where the eigenvalues of μ attain a maxima. The interest points are found by computing the maxima of the interest point operator

$$\mathbf{H} = \det(\mu) - k(\text{trace}(\mu))^2$$
$$= \lambda_1\lambda_2\lambda_3 - k(\lambda_1 + \lambda_2 + \lambda_3)^3 \tag{15.2}$$

over (x, y, t) subject to $\mathbf{H} \geq 0$ with $k \approx 0.005$. Here, λ_1, λ_2 and λ_3 are the eigenvalues of μ. Next, a feature descriptor is defined for each spatio-temporal interest point. The authors of [28] have shown the use of several kinds of descriptors, some of which are give below:

1. Output of a combination of space–time derivative filters or Gaussian derivatives up to order 4 evaluated at the interest point. These are scale normalized derivatives.

2. Histograms of either spatio-temporal gradients or optical flow computed over a windowed neighborhood or several smaller neighborhoods at different scales for each interest point. These are termed as position dependent histograms since the coordinates are measured relative to the interest point and used together with local image measurements.
3. A lower dimensional representation of either optical flow or spatio-temporal gradient vectors (L_x, L_y, L_z) computed over the spatio-temporal neighborhood of the interest point obtained using PCA.

There are also other descriptors defined such as position independent histograms and global histograms. The reader is recommended to look into [28] for details of these descriptors and a detailed description of the method.

Recognition is performed by examining the feature descriptors of each action. A classifier is trained on these descriptors to obtain the set of features which represent each activity. This method has been used in the recognition of simple actions like walk, run, wave, etc. The use of these features has also been extended to the recognition of multi-person activities [49].

15.2.1.2 Cuboidal Features

Spatio-temporal interest points are direct 3D counterparts to 2D interest points such as SIFT [34] which look at corners. They are sparse in nature and may not identify all interesting regions of the video. An alternative would be to use cuboidal features [14] which are more dense and represent any strong changes in the video. Here, we look at a response function defined over the image intensities directly. For a stack of images denoted by $I(x, y, t)$, the response function is given by

$$R = (I * g * h_{ev})^2 + (I * g * h_{od})^2, \qquad (15.3)$$

where $g(x, y; \sigma)$ is the 2D Gaussian smoothing kernel applied along the spatial dimensions, and h_{ev} and h_{od} are a quadrature pair [18] of 1D Gabor filters applied temporally. These are given by $h_{ev}(t; \tau, w) = -\cos(2\pi t w) \exp(-t^2/\tau^2)$ and $h_{ov}(t; \tau, w) = -\sin(2\pi t w) \exp(-t^2/\tau^2)$, where ω is taken to be $4/\tau$. The two parameters σ and τ correspond to the spatial and temporal scale of the detector. A stationary camera is assumed.

The interest points are detected as the local maxima of this response function. Any region with spatially distinguishing characteristics undergoing a complex motion is found to induce a strong response of the function. Therefore, in addition to spatio-temporal corners, the detector picks points which exhibit periodicity in image intensities and other kinds of non-linear motion like rotations.

A spatio-temporal cuboid is extracted at each interest point, the size of which is chosen such that it contains most of the data which contributed to the response function. A normalization is applied to the cuboids to make them invariant to small changes in appearance, motion or translation. Three methods have been suggested to extract feature vectors, which are:

1. the normalized pixel values,
2. the brightness gradient calculated at each spatio-temporal location (x, y, t) giving rise to three channels (G_x, G_y, G_t) and
3. windowed optical flow.

In each method, various kinds of descriptors were explored such as flattened vectors, 1-D histograms and N-D histograms. It was found that the flattened vectors gave the best performance.

   This method has been used in behavior recognition of animals such as mice, detection of facial expression and also in the recognition of human activities. Examples of cuboidal features detected for single person activities are seen in Fig. 15.1.

15.2.1.3 Volumetric Features

The volumetric features [25] are cuboidal volumes in the 3D spatio-temporal domain which represent regions of interest in the video. These features are capable of recognizing actions that may not generate sufficient interest points, such as smooth motion. Volumetric features are found to be robust to changes in scale, viewpoint and speed of action.

   Volumetric features are computed on the optical flow of a video. The optical flow is separated into its horizontal and vertical components and volumetric features are computed on each component. For a stack of n frames, the horizontal and vertical components are computed as $v_x(x, y, t)$ and $v_y(x, y, t)$ at pixel locations (x, y) and time t. Two kinds of volumetric features are extracted, "one box features" which are the cumulative sum of the optical flow component and "two box features", which are the differences between cumulative sums over combinations of two boxes calculated over the stack of frames. These features are computed over a chosen number of combinations of windows placed over the volume. The size of the window is varied to extract features at different scales in space and time. The reduced set of volumetric features for each action is identified by a training procedure on these features. These have been effective in the recognition of activities which involve uniform motion, such as drinking coffee, picking an object, etc.

15.2.2 Global Features

The idea behind global features is to represent the motion in an entire frame or a set of frames by a global descriptor. Activities are modeled as a sequence of these global features. Such features are also called sequential features [1]. Here, we will look at some examples of global features.

15.2.2.1 Motion Descriptors

Motion descriptors [15] are a set of descriptors used for the recognition of actions in low resolution sports videos where the bounding box of each person is available.

Motion of the object in each frame is represented by a single motion descriptor. Actions are identified by matching the sequence of motion descriptors, which are based on optical flow.

First, a figure centric spatio-temporal volume is computed for each person. This is done by tracking the human figure and constructing a window at each frame centered at the figure. Optical flow is computed at each frame on the window. The optical flow vector field $\mathbf{V}$ is split into horizontal $\mathbf{V_x}$ and vertical $\mathbf{V_y}$ components, each of which is rectified into four non-negative channels $\mathbf{V_x^+}$, $\mathbf{V_x^-}$, $\mathbf{V_y^+}$ and $\mathbf{V_y^-}$. These are normalized and smoothed with a Gaussian to obtained blurred versions $\widehat{\mathbf{Vb}}_x^+$, $\widehat{\mathbf{Vb}}_x^-$, $\widehat{\mathbf{Vb}}_y^+$ and $\widehat{\mathbf{Vb}}_y^-$. The concatenation of these four vectors gives the motion descriptor of each frame.

Matching is performed by comparing the motion descriptor of each frame of one video with each frame of another video using normalized correlation to generate a frame-to-frame similarity matrix $\mathbf{S}$. The final motion–motion similarity is obtained by a weighted sum of the frame-to-frame similarities over a temporal window $\mathbf{T}$, assigning higher weights to near diagonal elements since a match would result in a stronger response close to the diagonal.

15.2.2.2 Histogram of Oriented Optical Flow (HOOF)

We have seen that optical flow has been used as a reliable representation of motion information in much of the work described above. It has been shown in [8] that histograms of optical flow can also be used as motion descriptors of each frame. An activity is modeled as a non-linear dynamic system of the time series of these features. This method has been used in the analysis of single person activities.

When a person moves through a scene, it induces a very characteristic optical flow profile. This profile is captured in the histogram of optical flow which can be considered as a distribution of the direction of flow. Optical flow is binned according to its primary angle after a normalization of magnitude which ensures scale invariance. This histogram is known as the histogram of oriented optical flow. Histograms of different videos can be compared using various metrics like geodesic kernels, χ^2 distance and Euclidean distance. The time series of these distances is then evaluated using Binet–Cauchy kernels.

15.2.2.3 Space–Time Shapes

Actions can be considered as three-dimensional shapes induced by silhouettes in the space–time volume. The authors in [60] have computed space–time shapes by extracting various shape properties using the Poisson's equation and used for representation and classification.

Silhouettes are extracted by background subtraction of the input frames. The concatenation of these silhouettes formes the space–time shape S of each video. A

Poisson equation is formed by assigning each space–time point within this shape the mean time required to reach the boundary. This is done through the equation

$$\nabla^2 \mathbf{F}(\mathbf{x}, \mathbf{y}, \mathbf{t}) = -1, \qquad (15.4)$$

with $(x, y, t) \in S$ and the Laplacian of $\mathbf{F}$ being $F_{xx} + F_{yy} + F_{tt}$ subject to Dirichlet boundary conditions. $\mathbf{F}$ is obtained by solving the Poisson equation. A 3×3 Hessian matrix $\mathbf{H}$ is computed at each point of $\mathbf{F}$. It is shown that the different eigenvalues of $\mathbf{H}$ are proportional to different properties of the space–time shape such as plateness (uniformity of depth), stickness (uniformity of height and width) and ballness (curvature of the surface). These properties put together form the global descriptor of the action. The Euclidean distance between these measures is taken to be the distance between two actions.

15.3 Recognition Strategies

In the previous section, we described a few examples of local and global features used in activity recognition systems. The recognition strategy in most of these approaches was either a distance measure computed over the feature descriptors or a shape matching strategy. These methods of recognition are known as non-parametric methods [57]. This section discusses some recognition strategies which attempt to design parametric models or reasoning based models for activities. We will look at a few examples which will describe the state of the art in model based recognition strategies.

15.3.1 Hidden Markov Models

Hidden Markov models (HMMs) are one of the most popular state space models used in activity recognition [57]. These models are effective in modeling temporal evolution of dynamical systems. In the activity recognition scenario, each activity is considered to be composed of a finite set of states. The features which are extracted from a video are considered as the observed variables, whereas the states themselves are hidden. Given the observations, the temporal evolution of a video is modeled as a sequence of probabilistic changes from one state to another. Classification of activities is performed by a comparison of these models.

An example of the use of HMMs is found in [24] where it has been used for identification of persons using gait. The features used here are the outer contour of the binarized silhouette or the silhouette themselves. The features are fed to a Hidden Markov Model as the observations over a period of time and the transition across these features as the hidden variables. The modeling of gait of each person involves computation of the initial probability vector (π), the state transition probability matrix ($\mathbf{A}$) and the output probability distribution ($\mathbf{B}$). These parameters are estimated using the Baum–Welch algorithm.

15.3.2 Stochastic Context-Free Grammars

The use of grammars in activity recognition is one of the more recent approaches. These methods are suitable in the modeling of complex interactions between objects or in modeling the relations between sub-activities. These methods express the structure of a process using a set of production rules [57]. Context-Free Grammars (CFGs) are a formalism similar to language grammars which looks at activities as being constructed from words (action primitives). Stochastic CFGs are a probabilistic extension of this concept. Here, the structural relation between primitives is learnt from training sequences.

A typical example of stochastic CFGs can be found in [23]. Here, stochastic CFGs are used for recognizing patterns in normal events so as to detect abnormal events in a parking lot scene. An attribute grammar (AG) is defined as

$$AG = (G, SD, AD, R, C), \tag{15.5}$$

where G is the underlying CFG given by $G = (V_N, V_T, P, S)$ with V_N and V_T are the non-terminal and terminal nodes, P are the set of productions and S are the symbols; SD is the semantic domain consisting of coordinates and functions operating on the coordinates, AD are the attributes of each type associated with each symbol occurring in the productions in P, R is the set of attribute evaluation rules associated with each production $p \in P$ and C is the set of semantic conditions associated with P. The production rules here could be certain sub-events or features of the video. The attributes are the characteristics associated with each production, for example the location of the objects associated with the production.

The attribute grammar of an event is obtained by studying the relationships between the different attributes associated with the event. Any new event is parsed and the attributes are evaluated with the known attribute grammar. Any event which does not satisfy this grammar is termed an abnormal event.

15.4 Complex Activity Recognition

There are four characteristics which can be used to define activities. These are: kinesics (movement of people or objects), proxemics (the proximity of people with each other or objects), haptics (people–object contact) and chronemics (change with time) [2]. Simple activities are those which consist of one or few periodic atomic actions. They typically span a short duration of time, not more than a few seconds. Some examples of simple activities are walking, running, jumping, bending, etc. Most work on simple activity recognition [49] has focused on the analysis of kinesics and chronemics. Although there is no formal definition of a complex activity, in this chapter we will describe a complex activity as one which could involve one or more persons interacting with each other or with some objects. Typical examples of complex activities are a soccer goal, people grouping together and two person activities such as handshake or punching. We see that these activities also involve proxemics and possibly haptics in addition to kinesics and chronemics.

In the field of activity recognition, focus has slowly been shifting from the analysis of simple activities to complex activities. This is because in a real world scenario, we often find that an atomic action does not occur by itself but occurs as an interaction between people and objects. We will now briefly discuss some of the work which has taken place in complex activity recognition.

As compared to a simple activity recognition system, the inherent structure and semantics of complex activities require higher-level representation and reasoning methods [57]. There have been different approaches used to analyze complex activities. One common approach has been the use of graphical models. Graphical models encode the dependencies between random variables which in many cases are the features which represent the activity. These dependencies are studied with the help of training sequences. Some examples of graphical models commonly used are Bayesian networks (BNs), HMMs and Petri nets. BNs and DBNs are graphical models that encode complex conditional dependencies between a set of random variables which are encoded as local conditional probability densities. These have been used to model two person interactions like kicking, punching, etc. by estimating the pose using BNs and the temporal evolution using DBNs [43, 62]. A grid based belief propagation method was used for human pose estimation in [29]. Graphical models often model activities as a sequential set of atomic actions. A statistical model is created for each activity. The likelihood of each activity is given by the probability of the model generating the obtained observations [48].

A popular approach for modeling complex activities has been the use of stochastic and CFGs. It is often noticed that a complex large-scale activity often can be considered as a combination of several simple sub-activities that have explicit semantic meanings [63]. Constructing grammars can provide useful insights in such cases. These methods try to learn the rules describing the dynamics of the system. These often involve hierarchical approaches which parallel language grammars in terms of construction of sentences from words and alphabets. A typical example is when the activity recognition task is split into two steps. First, bottom–up statistical method can be used to detect simple sub-activities. Then the prior structure knowledge is used to construct a composite activity model [20]. In another instance, CFGs in [47] followed a hierarchical approach where the lower-levels are composed of HMMs and Bayesian Networks, whereas the higher level interactions are modeled by CFGs [57]. More complex models like Dependent Dirichlet Process–Hidden Markov Models (DDP–HMMs) have the ability to jointly learn co-occurring activities and their time dependencies [27].

Knowledge and logic based approaches have also been used in complex activity recognition [57]. Logic based approaches construct logical rules to describe the presence of an activity. For instance, a hierarchical structure could be used by defining descriptors of actions extracted from low-level features through several mid-level layers. Next, a rule based method is used to approximate the probability of occurrence of a specific activity by matching the properties of the agent with the expected distributions for a particular action [37]. Recently, the use of visual cues to detect relations among persons have been explored in a social network model [13].

Description based methods try to identify relationships between different actions such as "before", "after", "along with", etc. The algorithm described in [49] is one such method which uses spatio-temporal feature descriptors. The Bag of Words approach [21] disregards order and tries to model complex activities based on the occurrence probabilities of different features. Attempts have been made to improve on this idea by identifying neighborhoods which can help in recognition [26] and by accommodating pairwise relationships in the feature vector to consider local ordering of features [36]. Hierarchical methods have also been proposed which build complex models by starting from simpler ones and finding relationships between them [42].

Many of these approaches require either tracking body parts, or contextual object detection, or atomic action/primitive event recognition. Sometimes tracks and precise primitive action recognition may not be easily obtained for complex/interactive activities since such scenes frequently contain occlusions and clutter. Spatio-temporal feature based approaches, like [14], hold promise since no tracking is assumed. The statistics of these features are then used in recognition schemes [21]. Recently, spatial and long-term temporal correlations of these local features were considered and promising results shown. The work in [8] models the video as a time-series of frame-wide feature histograms and brings the temporal aspect into picture. A matching kernel using "correlograms" was presented in [52], which looked at the spatial relationships. A recent work [48] proposes a match function to compare spatio-temporal relationships in the feature by using temporal and spatial predicates, which we will describe in detail later.

Often, there are not enough training videos available for learning complex human activities; thus, recognizing activities based on just a single video example is of high interest. An approach of creating a large number of semi-artificial training videos from an original activity video was presented in [46]. A self-similarity descriptor that correlates local patches was proposed in [56]. A generalization of [56] was presented in [54], where space–time local steering kernels were used.

15.4.1 Challenges in Complex Motion Analysis

Activity recognition is a challenging task for several reasons. Any activity recognition system is efficient only if it can deal with changes in pose, lighting, viewpoint and scale. These variations increase the dimensionality of the problem. These problems are prevalent to a greater degree when it comes to complex activity analysis. There is a large amount of structural variation in a complex activity, therefore the dimension of the feature space is high. The feature space also becomes sparser with the dimension, thus requiring a larger number of samples to build efficient class-conditional models thus bringing in the Curse of Dimensionality [57]. Issues of scale, viewpoint and lighting also get harder to deal with for this reason.

Most of the simple activity recognition systems in the past had been tested on sequences recorded in a noise free controlled environment. Although these systems might work reasonably well in such an environment, they may not work in a real world environment which contains noise and background clutter. This problem is more prominent in a complex recognition system since there are multiple motions in the scene and they can easily be confused with the clutter.

Another challenge in complex motion analysis is the presence of multiple activities occurring simultaneously. Although many approaches can deal with noise with sufficient training data, there are difficulties in recognizing hierarchical activities with complex temporal structures, such as an activity composed of concurrent sub-events. Therefore many methods are more suited for modeling sequential activities rather than concurrent ones [48]. In addition, as stated in [48], as an activity gets more complex, many existing approaches need a greater amount of training data, preventing them from being applied to highly complex activities.

15.5 Some Recent Approaches in Complex Activity Recognition

As discussed in the previous section, there are several approaches which have been adopted to extend activity recognition to more complex scenarios. In this section, we will look into a few examples of activity recognition which involve activities of single or multiple objects in a natural setting.

15.5.1 Spatio-temporal Relationship Match

The use of spatio-temporal features have been extended to the recognition of multi-person activities like handshake, push, kick and punch by the analysis of spatio-temporal relationships in [49]. Spatio-temporal interest points are often used in a Bag-of-Features framework where the combinations of interest points are learnt for classification by discarding its temporal ordering. Although this works fairly well in recognition of simple activities, ordering plays a key role in recognition of more complex activities involving multiple tasks. Here, in addition to looking at the combination of interest points, we also need to study the spatio-temporal relationships between these interest points.

The method in [49] aims to compare the structure of interest points between two videos to determine their similarity. After computing the spatio-temporal interest points over the video and the time duration for which each point is detected (start time and end time), the spatial and temporal relationship between these points is calculated. The spatial relationships are quantified using predicates *near*, *far*, *xnear* (x-coordinate is near) and *ynear* (y-coordinate is near). These predicates are set based on a threshold. Similarly, some of the temporal predicates are *equals* (complete time overlap and equal durations), *before* (one completes before the other starts), *meets* (one starts as the other ends), *overlaps* (partial time overlap), *during* (complete time overlap but unequal durations), *starts* (both start together) and *finishes* (both end together). A 3D histogram whose dimensions are *featuretype* × *featuretype* ×

relationship is formed for each video. Two videos are compared by computing the similarity between the bins of their corresponding histograms using a bin counting mechanism termed as a *spatio-temporal relationship match kernel*. This method has been shown to be effective in activity classification using a training database and in localization of events in a scene containing multiple unrelated activities using a partial matching of bins.

15.5.2 String of Feature Graphs

String of Feature Graphs are a generalization of the method in [49]. Here, a string representation which matches the spatio-temporal ordering is proposed as the feature model of a video. Each string consists of a set of feature graphs, each of which contains the spatio-temporal relationship between feature points in a certain time interval. Similarities between activities are identified using a graph matching framework on these strings. This method has also been used to recognize activities involving multiple persons in the presence of other irrelevant persons [17].

Given a video, the first step is to extract the spatio-temporal interest points. The video is divided into time intervals of length t_I. A graph is constructed using the features in each time interval, the nodes of the graph being the feature points and edge weights being the pairwise spatio-temporal distance between them. The construction of a feature graph is illustrated in Fig. 15.2a. The similarity between two such feature graphs can be calculated by finding the correspondence between these graphs. This can be done using the spectral technique given in [30].

The comparison of two video sequences can be performed by the comparison of their corresponding feature graphs. Since there could be a difference in speeds of actions even between two similar activities, the time series of feature graphs have to be normalized for comparison. A technique called dynamic time warping [51] uses a dynamic programming technique to match two time series in a flexible manner. This method is used here to compute the overall distance between two activities as illustrated in Fig. 15.2b.

String of Feature Graphs can be used in a query based retrieval of activities with a single or very few example videos.

15.5.3 Stochastic Integration of Motion and Image Features for Hierarchical Video Search

The problem of matching activity videos in a large database containing videos of several complex activities is a challenging problem due to the extremely large search space. The authors in [55] suggest a way of performing a search in such scenarios in an efficient manner. This method is a typical example of the application of stochastic search algorithms in activity recognition.

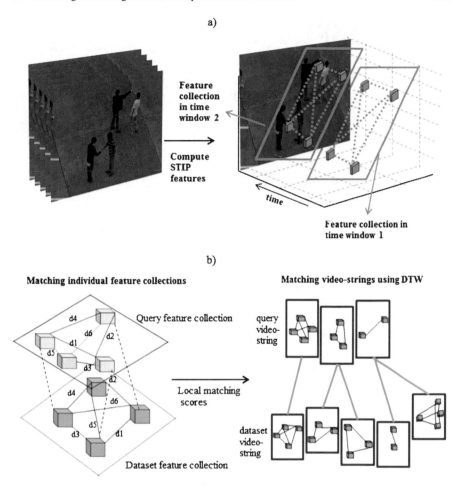

Fig. 15.2 The construction and comparison of strings of feature graphs. **a** shows the construction of a graph using spatio-temporal relations between STIP features in a time window. **b** illustrates matching of two videos using dynamic time warping

An activity is composed of two kinds of data—spatial data in the form of pixel values and motion data in the form of flow. The search algorithm proceeds in a acceptance-rejection manner alternating between the pixel and motion information. The search is based on the Hamiltonian Monte Carlo, which is an improvised version of the traditional MCMC technique. The Hamiltonian Monte Carlo search consists of the following basic steps.

1. Generate a random sample from the data distribution
2. Dynamic Transition Step—Perturbation via Hamiltonian dynamics, also known as the Leapfrog step
3. Metropolis-Hastings Step: acceptance/rejection of the proposed random sample

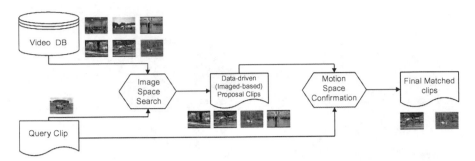

Fig. 15.3 This figure shows the overall algorithm for a hierarchical video search using stochastic integration of motion and image features

Given a video database, for each video, the image and motion features are computed. The image features used are shape of the silhouette or shape of the trajectory of an object. The motion features are the trajectory or spatio-temporal interest points. After computing these features on the entire database, a probability distribution is defined over both these features for each activity. The search for a particular activity would require finding the maxima of the joint distribution of both these features for that activity. To do this, the authors employ the Data Driven Hamiltonian Monte Carlo mechanism. The motion space is sampled randomly. The sample is then accepted or rejected based on the Metropolis-Hastings algorithm. The next sample is chosen after the dynamic transition step. The procedure repeats till the maxima is reached. The overall algorithm is illustrated in Fig. 15.3.

The method is found to be effective in search of natural videos, for example, videos from the YouTube database.

15.5.4 Dynamic Modeling of Streaklines for Motion Pattern Analysis

Natural videos consist of multiple objects interacting with each other in complex ways. The underlying patterns of motion contain valuable information about the activities and optical flow can be used to extract these patterns. A streakline can be defined as locations of all particles in a vector field at a given time that passed through a particular point. Streaklines have been used in the analysis of crowded videos in [38]. This concept can be extended to the task of activity recognition. The streaklines representation can be combined with dynamical systems modeling approaches in order to analyze the motion patterns in a wide range of natural videos. This combination provides a powerful tool to identify similar segments in a video that exhibit similar motion patterns.

Given a video, we can compute streaklines over time windows of a particular size. These streaklines capture the motion information over the entire time window. Since similar motions result in similar streaklines, we can cluster the streaklines

Fig. 15.4 The utility of streaklines in activity recognition. **a** and **b** show the segmentation of streaklines for two videos of a car turning left. **c** plots the streaklines in the two cases

based on their similarity to identify segments of the video with similar motion. In a multi-object video, this segmentation helps to separate out different object motions. Next, these clusters are modeled as a linear dynamical system (e.g. an ARMA). Here, the actual motion of the underlying pixel is taken to be the input to the model and the observed streaklines form the output. The distance between any two models representing motion patterns can be computed using the subspace angles as defined in [10]. Figure 15.4a and b show two videos containing cars turning left. The streakline cluster is overlaid on the image. We notice that the segmentation has extracted this motion and similar motions result in similar segmentation. Figure 15.4b shows the segmented streaklines for the two videos. It can be seen that they look very similar.

This method is suitable to analyze videos which have multiple objects moving in the scene and exhibiting different motions. Since we are separately modeling each motion pattern, this allows for a partial matching of videos and also in the grouping of similar videos in an unsupervised manner.

15.6 Conclusion

In this chapter, we discussed a few techniques in activity recognition. An activity recognition system generally requires a set of features to represent the activity and a recognition strategy for classification. Features can either be local (describing a small region of the scene) or global (describing the entire scene). We have discussed different local features with different levels of sparsity. For example, spatio-temporal features are usually corners, cuboidal features are more dense and represent regions of strong changing motion, and volumetric features are capable of identifying regions of uniform motion. Global features represent the entire scene of a certain level of detail. For example, HOOF features represent an entire frame with the histogram of its flow field while space time shapes are a collection of silhouettes.

We have looked at a variety of recognition strategies. In some cases, a classifier is learnt on the set of features. In some other applications, activities are modeled using these features as observations. Graphical models and stochastic grammars can model co-occurrences of features. Logic based approaches classify based on relationships between these features. We have also defined what complex activities are, the challenges involved and the common recognition strategies used. We discussed some recent work in complex activity recognition which looked at different applications like modeling multi-person interactions, localizing motion patterns and searching methods for complex activities. Abnormal activity recognition is an application where activities in a scene are modeled so as to identify anomalies.

The main challenge for future work in this area will be to develop descriptors and recognition strategies that can work in natural videos under a wide variety of environmental conditions.

15.6.1 Further Reading

This chapter presents an overview the state of the art in activity recognition and briefly describes a few methods of activity recognition. The description in Sect. 15.1.1 is based on the survey presented in [57]. We recommend the reader to go through this reference for a comprehensive survey of work which has taken place in activity recognition. We also recommend the reader to [1] for an overview in sequential and hierarchical methods of complex activity recognition. There are several feature descriptors used in this field, a few of which we described. We also recommend the reader to the work in [39] for a comparison of the different local descriptors.

Acknowledgements This work has been partially supported by the DARPA VIRAT program and NSF award IIS-0905671.

References

1. Aggarwal, J.K., Cai, Q.: Human motion analysis: A review. Comput. Vis. Image Underst. **73**(3), 428–440 (1999) [290,295,306]
2. Anderson, P.A.: Nonverbal Communication: Forms and Functions, 2nd edn. Waveland Press, Long Grove (2008) [298]
3. Barron, J.L., Fleet, D.J., Beauchemin, S.S.: Performance of optical flow techniques. Int. J. Comput. Vis. **12**, 43–77 (1994) [291]
4. Belkin, M., Niyogi, P.: Laplacian eigenmaps and spectral techniques for embedding and clustering. In: Advances in Neural Information Processing Systems, pp. 585–591 (2001) [291]
5. Benezeth, Y., Jodoin, P.M., Saligrama, V., Rosenberger, C.: Abnormal events detection based on spatio-temporal co-occurrences. In: Computer Vision and Pattern Recognition, pp. 2458–2465 (2009) [292]
6. Blank, M., Gorelick, L., Shechtman, E., Irani, M., Basri, R.: Actions as space–time shapes. In: International Conference on Computer Vision, Washington, DC, USA, pp. 1395–1402 (2005) [290,291]
7. Bobick, A.F., Davis, J.W.: The recognition of human movement using temporal templates. IEEE Trans. Pattern Anal. Mach. Intell. **23**(3), 257–267 (2001) [291]
8. Chaudhary, R., Ravichandran, A., Hager, G.D., Vidal, R.: Histograms of oriented optical flow and Binet–Cauchy kernels on nonlinear dynamical systems for the recognition of human actions. In: Computer Vision and Pattern Recognition, pp. 1932–1939 (2009) [291,292,296]

9. Cinbis, N.I., Sclaroff, S.: Object, scene and actions: Combining multiple features for human action recognition. In: European Conference on Computer Vision, pp. 494–507 (2010) [291]
10. Cock, K.D., Moor, B.D.: Subspace angles and distances between ARMA models. Syst. Control Lett. **46**(4), 265–270 (2002) [305]
11. Cuntoor, N.P., Chellappa, R.: Epitomic representation of human activities. In: Computer Vision and Pattern Recognition, pp. 1–8 (2007) [291]
12. Denina, G., Bhanu, B., Nguyen, H., Ding, C., Kamal, A., Ravishanka, C., Roy-Chowdhury, A., Ivers, A., Varda, B.: Videoweb dataset for multi-camera activities and non-verbal communication. In: Distributed Video Sensor Networks. Springer, London (2010) [290]
13. Ding, L., Yilmaz, A.: Learning relations among movie characters: A social network perspective. In: European Conference on Computer Vision, pp. 410–423 (2010) [299]
14. Dollar, P., Rabaud, V., Cottrell, G., Belongie, S.: Behavior recognition via sparse spatio-temporal features. In: Visual Surveillance and Performance Evaluation of Tracking and Surveillance, pp. 65–72 (2005) [294,300]
15. Efros, A.A., Berg, A.C., Mori, G., Malik, J.: Recognizing action at a distance. In: International Conference of Computer Vision, pp. 726–733 (2003) [291,295]
16. Forstner, W., Gulch, E.: A fast operator for detection and precise location of distinct points, corners and centres of circular features. In: ISPRS Intercommission Conference on Fast Processing of Photogrammetric Data, pp. 281–305 (1987) [291]
17. Gaur, U.: Complex activity recognition using string of feature graphs. Master's thesis, University of California, Riverside, CA, USA (2010) [302]
18. Granlund, G.H., Knutsson, H.: Signal Processing for Computer Vision. Kluwer, Dordrecht (1995) [294]
19. Harris, C., Stephens, M.: A combined corner and edge detector. In: Fourth Alvey Vision Conference, pp. 147–151 (1988) [291]
20. Ivanov, Y.A., Bobick, A.F.: Recognition of visual activities and interactions by stochastic parsing. IEEE Trans. Pattern Anal. Mach. Intell. **22**(8), 852–872 (2000) [299]
21. Wang, H., Niebles, J.C., Fei-Fei, L.: Unsupervised learning of human action categories using spatial-temporal words. In: British Machine Vision Conference (2006) [300]
22. Jiang, F., Yuan, J., Tsaftaris, S.A., Katsaggelos, A.K.: Anomalous video event detection using spatiotemporal context. Comput. Vis. Image Underst. **115**, 323–333 (2011) [292]
23. Joo, S.W., Chellappa, R.: Attribute grammar-based event recognition and anomaly detection. In: Computer Vision and Pattern Recognition Workshop, p. 107 (2006) [298]
24. Kale, A., Sundaresan, A., Rajagopalan, A.N., Cuntoor, N.P., Roy-Chowdhury, A.K., Krueger, V., Chellappa, R.: Identification of humans using gait. IEEE Trans. Image Process. **13**, 1163–1173 (2004) [297]
25. Ke, Y., Sukthankar, R., Hebert, M.: Efficient visual event detection using volumetric features. In: International Conference on Computer Vision, vol. 1, pp. 166–173 (2005) [295]
26. Kovashka, A., Grauman, K.: Learning a hierarchy of discriminative space–time neighborhood features for human action recognition. In: Computer Vision and Pattern Recognition, pp. 2046–2053 (2010) [300]
27. Kuettel, D., Breitenstein, M.D., Gool, L.J.V., Ferrari, V.: What's going on? discovering spatio-temporal dependencies in dynamic scenes. In: Computer Vision and Pattern Recognition, pp. 1951–1958 (2010) [299]
28. Laptev, I., Lindeberg, T.: Local descriptors for spatio-temporal recognition. In: First International Workshop on Spatial Coherence for Visual Motion Analysis (2004) [291,293,294]
29. Lee, M.W., Nevatia, R.: Human pose tracking in monocular sequence using multilevel structured models. IEEE Trans. Pattern Anal. Mach. Intell. **31**(1), 27–38 (2009) [299]
30. Leordeanu, M., Hebert, M.: A spectral technique for correspondence problems using pairwise constraints. In: International Conference of Computer Vision, vol. 2, pp. 1482–1489 (October 2005) [302]
31. Lindeberg, T.: Feature detection with automatic scale selection. Int. J. Comput. Vis. **30**, 79–116 (1998) [291]
32. Liu, H., Feris, R.S., Krueger, V., Sun, M.T.: Unsupervised action classification using space–time link analysis. EURASIP J. Image Video Process. **2010**, Article ID 626324 (2010) [293]

33. Liu, Z., Sarkar, S.: Improved gait recognition by gait dynamics normalization. IEEE Trans. Pattern Anal. Mach. Intell. **28**, 2006 (2006) [291]
34. Lowe, D.G.: Object recognition from local scale-invariant features. In: International Conference on Computer Vision, Washington, DC, USA, pp. 1150–1157 (1999) [291,293,294]
35. Makris, D., Ellis, T.: Learning semantic scene models from observing activity in visual surveillance. IEEE Trans. Syst. Man Cybern. **35**(3), 397–408 (2005) [292]
36. Matikainen, P., Hebert, M., Sukthankar, R.: Representing pairwise spatial and temporal relations for action recognition. In: European Conference on Computer Vision (September 2010) [300]
37. Medioni, G., Nevatia, R., Cohen, I.: Event detection and analysis from video streams. IEEE Trans. Pattern Anal. Mach. Intell. **23**, 873–889 (1998) [299]
38. Mehran, R., Moore, B.E., Shah, M.: A streakline representation of flow in crowded scenes. In: European Conference on Computer Vision, pp. 439–452 (2010) [292,304]
39. Mikolajczyk, K., Schmid, C.: A performance evaluation of local descriptors. IEEE Trans. Pattern Anal. Mach. Intell. **27**, 1615–1630 (2005) [306]
40. Natarajan, P., Singh, V.K., Nevatia, R.: Learning 3d action models from a few 2d videos for view invariant action recognition. In: Computer Vision and Pattern Recognition, pp. 2006–2013 (2010) [291]
41. North, B., Blake, A., Isard, M., Rittscher, J.: Learning and classification of complex dynamics. IEEE Trans. Pattern Anal. Mach. Intell. **22**, 1016–1034 (2000) [291]
42. Park, S.: A hierarchical Bayesian network for event recognition of human actions and interactions. Assoc. Comput. Mach. Multimedia Syst. J. **10**, 164–179 (2004) [300]
43. Park, S., Aggarwal, J.K.: Recognition of two-person interactions using a hierarchical Bayesian network. In: ACM SIGMM International Workshop on Video Surveillance, New York, NY, USA, pp. 65–76 (2003) [299]
44. Polana, R., Nelson, R.C.: Detection and recognition of periodic, nonrigid motion. Int. J. Comput. Vis. **23**(3), 261–282 (1997) [291]
45. Roweis, S.T., Saul, L.K.: Nonlinear dimensionality reduction by locally linear embedding. Science **290**, 2323–2326 (2000) [291]
46. Ryoo, M.S., Yu, W.: One video is sufficient? human activity recognition using active video composition. In: IEEE Workshop on Motion and Video Computing (2011) [300]
47. Ryoo, M.S., Aggarwal, J.K.: Recognition of composite human activities through context-free grammar based representation. In: Computer Vision and Pattern Recognition, pp. 1709–1718 (2006) [299]
48. Ryoo, M.S., Aggarwal, J.K.: Semantic representation and recognition of continued and recursive human activities. Int. J. Comput. Vis. **82**(1), 1–24 (2009) [299-301]
49. Ryoo, M.S., Aggarwal, J.K.: Spatio-temporal relationship match: Video structure comparison for recognition of complex human activities. In: International Conference on Computer Vision, pp. 1593–1600 (2009) [294,298,300-302]
50. Ryoo, M.S., Chen, C., Aggarwal, J.K., Roy-Chowdhury, A.: An overview of contest on semantic description of human activities (SDHA) 2010. In: International Conference on Pattern Recognition, Berlin, Heidelberg, pp. 270–285 (2010) [290]
51. Sakoe, H., Chiba, S.: Dynamic programming algorithm optimization for spoken word recognition. IEEE Trans. Acoust. Speech Signal Process. **26**(1), 43–49 (1978) [302]
52. Savarese, S., DelPozo, A., Niebles, J.C., Fei-Fei, L.: Spatial-temporal correlations for unsupervised action classification. In: IEEE Workshop on Motion and Video Computing (2008) [300]
53. Schuldt, C., Laptev, I., Caputo, B.: Recognizing human actions: A local SVM approach. In: International Conference on Pattern Recognition (2004) [290]
54. Seo, H.J., Milanfar, P.: Detection of human actions from a single example. In: International Conference on Computer Vision (2009) [300]
55. Sethi, R.J., Roy-Chowdhury, A.K., Ali, S.: Activity recognition by integrating the physics of motion with a neuromorphic model of perception. In: IEEE Workshop on Motion and Video Computing (2009) [302]

56. Shechtman, E., Irani, M.: Matching local self-similarities across images and videos. In: Computer Vision and Pattern Recognition (2007) [300]
57. Turaga, P.K., Chellappa, R., Subrahmanian, V.S., Udrea, O.: Machine recognition of human activities: A survey. IEEE Trans. Circuits Syst. Video Technol. **18**(11), 1473–1488 (2008) [291,297-300,306]
58. Vaswani, N., Roy-Chowdhury, A., Chellappa, R.: "Shape activity": A continuous state HMM for moving/deforming shapes with application to abnormal activity detection. IEEE Trans. Image Process. **14**, 1603–1616 (2005) [292]
59. Wersborg, I.S., Bautze, T., Born, F., Diepold, K.: A cognitive approach for a robotic welding system that can learn how to weld from acoustic data. In: Computational Intelligence in Robotics and Automation, Piscataway, NJ, USA, pp. 108–113 (2009) [292]
60. Yilmaz, A., Shah, M.: Actions sketch: A novel action representation. In: Computer Vision and Pattern Recognition, vol. 1, pp. 984–989 (2005) [291,296]
61. Young, R.A., Lesperance, R.M.: The Gaussian derivative model for spatial-temporal vision. Spat. Vis. **2001**, 3–4 (2001) [291]
62. Zeng, Z., Qiang, J.: Knowledge based activity recognition with dynamic Bayesian network. In: European Conference in Computer Vision, Crete, Greece (2010) [299]
63. Zhang, Z., Huang, K.Q., Tan, T.N.: Complex activity representation and recognition by extended stochastic grammar. In: Asian Conference on Computer Vision, pp. 150–159 (2006) [299]

Chapter 16
Action Recognition Using Topic Models

Xiaogang Wang

Abstract In this book chapter, we will introduce approaches of using topic models for action recognition. Topic models were originally developed in language processing. In recent years, they were applied to action recognition and other computer vision problems, and achieved great success. Topic models are unsupervised. The models of actions are learned through exploring the co-occurrence of visual features without manually labeled training examples. This is important when there are a large number of actions to be recognized in a large variety of scenes. Most topic models are hierarchical Bayesian models and they jointly model simple actions and complicated actions at different hierarchical levels. Knowledge and contextual information can be well integrated into topic models as priors. We will explain how topic models can be used in different ways for action recognition in different scenarios. For examples, the scenes may be sparse or crowded. There may be a single camera view or multiple camera views. The camera settings may be near-field or far-field. In different scenarios, different features, such as trajectories, local motions and spatial-temporal interest points, are used for action recognition.

16.1 Introduction

Action recognition from video sequences has a wide variety of applications in both public and private environments, such as homeland security [4, 67], crime prevention [2, 12, 14], traffic control [31, 32, 57], accident prediction and detection [1], and monitoring patients, elderly and children at home [36]. These applications include a large variety of scenes such as airports, train stations, highways, parking lots, stores, shopping malls and offices. Due to the fast growing of cheap sensors and video data and also a growing need for security and efficient information retrieval, there are increasing demands on automatic action recognition. Over the past decade, significant work has been reported on this topic. Literature reviews can be found in [26, 39].

Some existing approaches [24, 28, 30] required manually labeling examples to train classifiers or discriminative models for action recognition. Some of them re-

X. Wang (✉)
Department of Electronic Engineering, Chinese University of Hong Kong, Hong Kong, China
e-mail: xgwang@ee.cuhk.edu.hk

T.B. Moeslund et al. (eds.), *Visual Analysis of Humans*,
DOI 10.1007/978-0-85729-997-0_16, © Springer-Verlag London Limited 2011

quired training different classifiers or models for different scenes. Because of the large number of different action categories to be recognized and the large variety of different scenes, people prefer algorithms [60, 69, 70] which automatically learn the models of the actions in the target scenes without supervision.

Many approaches [13, 51, 60, 67, 69, 70] directly used motion feature vectors to describe video clips without tracking objects. For example, Zelnik-Manor and Irani [69] modeled and clustered video clips using multi-resolution histograms. Zhong et al. [70] also computed global motion histograms and did word-document analysis on videos. Their words were frames instead of moving pixels. They clustered video clips through the partition of a bipartite graph. Without object detection and tracking, a particular activity cannot be separated from other activities simultaneously occurring in the same clip, as is common in crowded scenes. These approaches treated a video clip as an integral entity and tagged the whole clip as normal or abnormal. They were often applied to simple data sets where there was only one kind of activity in a video clip.

In some approaches, objects (or their parts) were first detected, tracked and classified into different classes. Their tracks were used as features to model activities [43, 53, 64]. These approaches fail when object detection, tracking, and/or recognition do not work well, especially in crowded scenes. Some systems model primitive events, such as "move, stop, enter-area, turn-left", and use these primitives as components to model complicated activities and interactions [19, 24]. These primitive events are learned from labeled training examples, or their parameters are manually specified. When switching to a new scene, new training samples must be labeled and parameters must be tuned or re-learned.

In recent years, inspired by the great success of topics models, such as probabilistic Latent Semantic Analysis (pLSA) [23] and Latent Dirichlet Allocation (LDA) [8], in the applications of language processing, they have been also applied to action recognition. Significant progress has been made. Topic models recognize actions through exploring the co-occurrence of features at different hierarchical levels. Compared with other approaches, topic models have some attractive features. Firstly, they are unsupervised and learn the models of actions without requiring manually labeling training examples. They can also separate co-occurring actions without human intervention. Secondly, topic models allow the models of different action classes to share features and training data. Therefore the models of action classes can be learned more robustly avoiding the overfitting problem. Thirdly, most topic models are hierarchical Bayesian models, which allows one to jointly model simple and complicated actions at different levels. Knowledge and various constraints can be nicely added into Bayesian frameworks as priors. Thus they can better solve problems which are difficult for nonBayesian approaches such as jointly modeling actions in multiple views and dynamically updating the models of actions. Lastly, they can be well integrated with non-parametric Bayesian models, which use Dirichlet Processes (DP) [17] as priors to automatically learn the number of action classes from data without being manually specified.

In this chapter, we will introduce three types of approaches of using topic models for action recognition in different scenarios based on different types of features.

The approaches introduced in Sect. 16.3 assume that cameras are stationary and scenes are parse. The trajectories of objects are available by tracking objects and are used as features for action recognition. The approaches in Sect. 16.4 assume that the cameras are stationary, scenes are crowded and there different types of actions simultaneously happening. It is very difficult to detect and track objects in crowded scenes because of frequent occlusions (see also Chap. 6). Local motions (such as moving pixels) as computed, e.g., in Chaps. 3 and 4 are used as features to model actions without tracking objects. Topic models are able to separate co-occurring actions and jointly model simple actions and complicated global behaviors of the videos. In both Sects. 16.3 and 16.4, topic models can recognize actions in single camera views or multiple camera views. In Sect. 16.5, cameras are not necessary to be stationary and interest points are used as features to recognition human actions in near fields.

16.2 Topic Models

Under topic models in language processing, words, such as "professor" and "university", often co-existing in the same documents are clustered into the same topic, such as "education". A document is modeled as a mixture of topics and each word is generate from a single topic. PLSA [23] and LDA [8] are two popular topic models. Their graphical models are shown in Fig. 16.1. Suppose there are M documents in the data set. Each document j has N_j words. Each word w_{ji} is assigned one of the K topics according to its topic label z_{ji}. Under pLSA the joint probability $P(\{w_{ji}\}, \{d_j\}, \{z_{ji}\})$ has the form of the graphical model shown in Fig. 16.1a. The conditional probability $P(w_{ji}|d_j)$ marginalizing over topics z_{ji} is given by

$$P(w_{ji}|d_j) = \sum_{k=1}^{K} P(z_{ji} = k|d_j)P(w_{ji}|z_{ji} = k). \tag{16.1}$$

$P(z_{ji} = k|d_j)$ is the probability of topic k occurring in document d_j. $P(w_{ji}|z_{ji} = k)$ is the probability of word w_{ji} occurring in topic k and is the model of topic k. Fitting the pLSA model involves determining $P(w_{ji}|z_{ji})$ and $P(z_{ji} = k|d_j)$ by maximizing the following objective function using the expectation-maximization (EM) algorithm:

$$L = \prod_{j=1}^{M} \prod_{i=1}^{N_j} P(w_{ji}|d_j). \tag{16.2}$$

pLSA is a generative model only for training documents but not for new documents. PLSA does not provide probabilistic model at the level of documents. Each model is represented by a list of numbers $p(z|d_j)$, but these numbers are not generated from a probabilistic model. This shortcoming has been addressed by LDA, whose graphical model is shown in Fig. 16.1b. The generative process of LDA is described as following.

Fig. 16.1 Graphical models
of pLSA and LDA

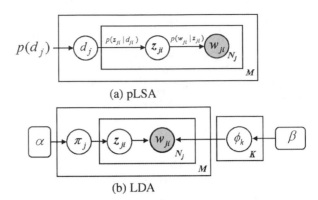

(a) pLSA

(b) LDA

1. $\{\phi_k\}$ are models of topics and are discrete distributions over the codebook of words. They are generated from a Dirichlet prior $Dir(\phi_k; \beta)$ given by β.
2. Each document j has a multinomial distribution π_j over K topics and it is generated from a Dirichlet prior $Dir(\pi_j; \alpha)$ given by α.
3. Each word i in document j is assigned to one of the K topics and its label z_{ji} is sampled from a discrete distribution $Discrete(z_{ji}; \pi_j)$ given by π_j.
4. The observed word w_{ji} is sampled from the model of its topic: $Discrete(w_{ji}|\phi_{z_{ji}})$.

α and β are hyperparameters. ϕ_k, π_j and z_{ji} are hidden variables to be inferred. The joint distributions of the LDA model is

$$p\big(\{w_{ji}\}, \{z_{ji}\}, \{\phi_k\}, \{\pi_j\}|\alpha, \beta\big)$$

$$= \prod_{k=1}^{K} p(\phi_k|\beta) \prod_{j=1}^{M} p(\pi_j|\alpha) \prod_{i=1}^{N_j} p(z_{ji}|\pi_j) p(w_{ji}|\phi_{z_{ji}}). \quad (16.3)$$

Under LDA, if two words often co-occur in the same documents, one of the topic models will have large distributions on both of them.

Both pLSA and LDA require the number of object classes to be known in advance. As an extension of LDA, Hierarchical Dirichlet Process (HDP) proposed by Teh et al. [55] could automatically learn the number of topics from data using Dirichlet Processes [17] as priors.

When topic models are applied to action recognition, words, documents and topics will be mapped to some specific concepts in the context of action recognition. Under topic models, visual features are quantized into visual words. Topic models will explore the co-occurrence of visual words to learn the models of action classes. Although the co-occurrence of visual words is commonly observed in actions and can be used to learn the models of action classes, the "bag-of-words" assumption loses the spatial and temporal relationship among visual words, which is also very important for action recognition. Therefore, when topic models are applied to action recognition, they are modified to incorporate such information. Topic models also have been widely applied other computer vision problems such as object segmentation [59] and scene categorization [16]. One of the major advantages of topic models is their unsupervised nature. This is very important for discovering classes of actions from large amounts of video surveillance data and videos collected from the web. Topic models are hierarchical Bayesian models, under which topics are middle-level representations. Through sharing topics among documents, training data are shared, which avoids the overfitting problem to some extent. Topic models are hierarchical Bayesian models, which can flexibly include spatial and temporal information as priors.

16.2.1 Inference on Topic Models

Doing inference on the hidden variables of topic models is a big challenge. For example, in LDA the posteriors of hidden variables need to be computed,

$$p(\{\pi_j\}, \{\phi_k\}, \{z_{ji}\}|\{w_{ji}\}, \alpha, \beta) = \frac{p(\{\pi_j\}, \{\phi_k\}, \{z_{ji}\}, \{w_{ji}\}|\alpha, \beta)}{p(\{w_{ji}\}|\alpha, \beta)}. \tag{16.4}$$

However, this posterior distribution is intractable to compute. A variety of approximate inference algorithms were proposed. Blei et al. [8] proposed a variational inference algorithm on LDA. It considers a family of lower bounds, indexed by a set of variational parameters. The target posterior distribution is approximated by found the tightest lower bound by an optimization procedure. Variational inference methods for Dirichlet processes are also proposed [5, 6]. A drawback of variational inference is that it is not clear how big the gap is between the found lower bound and the target distribution.

Another type of inference methods are based on MCMC [29]. Griffiths et al. [21] proposed a collapsed Gibbs sampling algorithm for the inference on LDA. It generates a sequence of samples from the distribution (16.4) in iterative steps. At each step, a hidden variable is sampled given other variables sampled from previous steps. The hidden variables π_j and ϕ_k can be analytically marginalized without being sampled and the sampling efficiency can be improved. Only z_{ji} needs to be sampled from the distribution,

$$p(z_{ji}|\{z_{j'i'}\}^{-ji}, \alpha, \beta) \propto \frac{m_{k,w_{ji}}^{-ji} + \beta}{m_{k\cdot}^{-ji} + W \cdot \beta} \cdot \frac{n_{jk}^{-ji} + \alpha}{K \cdot \alpha + n_{j\cdot}^{-ji}}, \tag{16.5}$$

where W is the size of the dictionary, m_{kw} is the number of words assigned to topic k with value w, $m_{k\cdot}$ is the number of words assigned to topic k, n_{jk} is the number of words assigned to topic k in document j, $n_{j\cdot}$ is the total number of words in document j. $m_{kw_{ji}}^{-ji}$, $m_{k\cdot}^{-ji}$, n_{jk}^{-ji} and $n_{j\cdot}^{-ji}$ are the same statistics as m_{kw}, $m_{k\cdot}$, n_{jk} and $n_{j\cdot}$ except that they have excluded the word i in document j. ϕ_k and π_j can be estimated from $\{z_{ji}\}$,

$$\hat{\phi}_k = \frac{m_{kw} + \beta}{m_{k\cdot} + W \cdot \beta}, \tag{16.6}$$

$$\hat{\pi}_j = \frac{n_{jk} + \alpha}{K \cdot \alpha + n_j}. \tag{16.7}$$

Teh et al. [55] used collapsed Gibbs sampling to do inference on HDP. One of the drawbacks of MCMC is its low efficiency. Also there is hard to get the theoretical justification on the convergence of a MCMC sampling algorithm. In order to improve the efficiency of inference, distributed inference for topic models are proposed [40].

16.3 Far-Field Action Recognition Based on Trajectories of Objects

16.3.1 Single Camera View

In far-field video surveillance, if there is only one camera view and the scene is sparse, objects can be detected and tracked. In far-field settings, the captured videos are of low resolution and poor quality, and therefore it is difficult to compute more complicated visual features. Usually only positions of objects are recorded along the tracks, which are called trajectories. The majority of visible actions of objects are distinguished by the patterns of objects moving from one location to another and trajectories are used as features for action recognition. Many approaches were proposed to cluster trajectories into different action classes and detect abnormal trajectories. New trajectories were classified into one of the existing clusters. Most of the existing approaches [27, 39, 64] first defined the pairwise similarities between trajectories and the computed similarity matrix was input to some standard clustering algorithms.

An approach of clustering trajectories using topic models was proposed in [63]. In this approach, trajectories are treated as documents, observations (points) on trajectories are treated as words, and semantic regions are treated as topics. Observations are quantized into words according to a feature codebook based on their locations and moving directions. To build the feature codebook, the 2D space of the scene in uniformly divided into small cells and the moving direction is quantized into four. In the physical world, objects move along some paths. We refer to the subsets[1] of paths commonly taken by objects as semantic regions, i.e. two paths may share one semantic region as shown in Fig. 16.2. Semantic regions are modeled as discrete distributions over the quantized space of the scene and moving directions. Their models are learned from the co-occurrence of features. When we track objects, identity co-occurrence of feature values can be observed. Identity co-occurrence means that two feature values are observed on the same trajectory

---

[1]If a path is viewed as a set of quantized spatial locations and moving directions, semantic regions are subsets of paths and they can obtained through the operations of intersection and set difference between paths.

Fig. 16.2 Example to explain the modeling of semantic regions and actions. There are three semantic regions (indicated by different colors) which form two paths. Both trajectories A and C pass through regions 1 and 2, so they are clustered into the same action class. Trajectory B passes through regions 1 and 3, so it is clustered into a different action class. Figure reproduced with permission from [63]. © 2008 IEEE

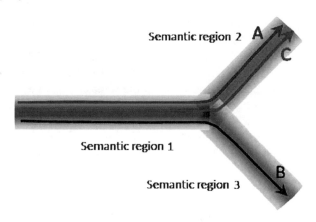

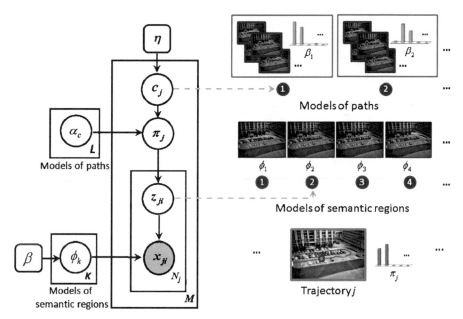

Fig. 16.3 Graphical model of the LDA mixture model for action recognition based on trajectories

and they are related to the same object. If two locations are on the same semantic regions, they are connected by many trajectories and both of them will have large weights on one of the models of semantic regions learned by the topic model. On the other hand, if two trajectories pass through the same combination of semantic regions, they are on the same path and thus they belong to the same action class. A Dual Hierarchical Dirichlet Processes (Dual-HDP) model was proposed in [63] to jointly learns the models of semantic regions and cluster trajectories into different paths (action classes). Dual-HDP is a non-parametric extension of the LDA mixture model, whose graphical model is shown in Fig. 16.3. To simplify the description, we only explain the LDA mixture model below. The advantage of Dual-HDP is to automatically learn the number of semantic regions and the number of paths from data using Dirichlet processes as priors.

The LDA model in Fig. 16.1b does not model clusters of trajectories (documents). All the trajectories share the same Dirichlet prior α. In action recognition, we assume that trajectories of the same action class are on the same path and pass through the same set of semantic regions (topics). So they would be grouped into the same clusters and share the same Dirichlet prior over semantic regions. In the LDA mixture model shown in Fig. 16.3, the M trajectories are grouped into L clusters. Each cluster c has its own Dirichlet prior α_c. For a trajectory j, its cluster label c_j is first drawn from a discrete distribution η. The joint distribution of hidden variables c_j, π_j, z_{ji} and observed words x_{ji} is given by

$$
p\big(\{x_{ji}\}, \{z_{ji}\}, \{\pi_j\}, \{c_j\}, \{\phi_k\}|\{\alpha_c\}, \beta, \eta\big)
$$

$$
= \prod_{k=1}^{K} p(\phi_k|\beta) \prod_{j=1}^{M} p(c_j|\eta) p(\pi_j|\alpha_{c_j}) \prod_{i=1}^{N_j} p(z_{ji}|\pi_j) p(x_{ji}|z_{ji}, \phi_{z_{ji}}). \qquad (16.8)
$$

z_{ji}, π_j, c_j, ϕ_k and α_c can be learned using variational methods [61] or collapsed Gibbs sampling [63]. Once the models ($\{\phi_k\}$) of semantic regions and the models $\{\alpha_c\}$ of paths are learned and fixed, they can be used to classify a new trajectory into one of the unsupervisedly learned paths (action classes). They also be used to detect abnormal trajectories which do not fit any of the existing path models.

In [63], experiments were conducted on a large-scale trajectory data set including more than 40,000 trajectories collected from a parking lot scene. Some results are shown in Fig. 16.4. These semantic regions and trajectory clusters represent some typical activities happening in this scene. For example, the first cluster in Fig. 16.4 explains vehicles entering and leaving the parking lot. The last cluster explains pedestrians entering the parking lot and crossing the grass field. Some abnormal trajectories are detected. Many of them are pedestrian walking along the grass field. Some are pedestrian crossing the parking lot and turning back in the middle. These activities are uncommonly seen in this scene. They do not fit topic models, have low likelihoods and therefore are detected as abnormalities.

16.3.2 Multiple Camera Views

The approach proposed in [63] was only applicable to a single camera view. In [65, 66], this topic model was extended to jointly model actions in multiple camera views. Many existing approaches [33, 56] (see also Part I, Sect. 6.4) of action recognition in multiple camera views required inference on the topology of a camera network and a solution to the correspondence problem, i.e. tracking objects across camera views. Some had constraints on the topology of camera views (e.g. camera views must have significant overlaps) and required a lot of human effort. The approach proposed in [66] recognized actions in multiple camera views without doing

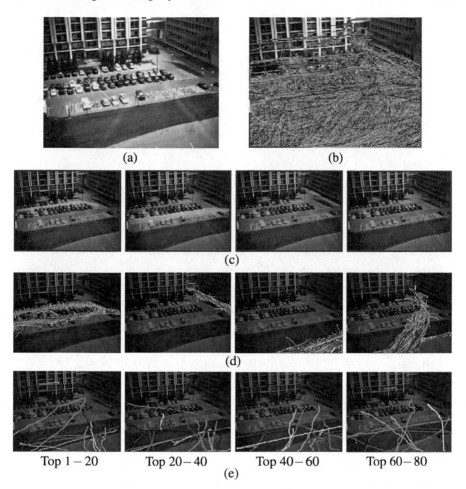

Top 1 − 20   Top 20 − 40   Top 40 − 60   Top 60 − 80
(e)

Fig. 16.4 Experimental results of the approach in [63] on more than 40,000 trajectories collected from a parking lot scene. **a** The background image of the parking lot scene. **b** Trajectories collected from the parking lot scene within one week. **c** Learned models of semantic regions. Colors represent different moving directions: → (red), ← (cyan), ↑ (magenta), and ↓ (blue). **d** Clusters of trajectories. They represent different classes of actions. **e** Detected top 80 abnormal trajectories. Figure partially reproduced with permission from [63]. © 2008 IEEE

inference on the topology of camera views and without solving the correspondence problem. It assumed that the topology of camera views was unknown and arbitrary, and the cameras were not calibrated. The camera views might be disjoint. Objects were first tracked in each camera view independently without being tracked across camera views. The goal was to learn the model of an action with distributions in all the camera views and cluster trajectories across camera views without supervision. As an extension of [63, 66] assumed that if two trajectories were observed in two camera views around the same time, they were more likely to be the same object and thus should have a higher probability to be in the same action class under the

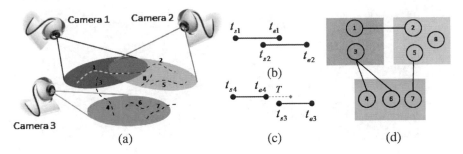

Fig. 16.5 Example of building a network connecting trajectories in multiple camera views. **a** Trajectories in three camera views. **b** The temporal extents of trajectories 1 and 2. **c** The temporal extents of trajectories 3 and 4. **d** The network connecting trajectories. See text for details. Figure reproduced from [66]. © 2008 IEEE

model to be learned. A smoothness constraint, which required that two trajectories with strong temporal correlation should have the same action label to avoid penalty, was added as prior in the hierarchical Bayesian model to cluster trajectories across camera views.

A network is built connecting trajectories observed in multiple camera views based on their temporal extents. Each trajectory is a node on the network. Let t_{si} and t_{ei} be the starting and ending time of trajectory i. T is a positive temporal threshold. It is roughly the maximum transition time of objects moving between adjacent camera views. If trajectories a and b are observed in different camera views and their temporal extents are close,

$$(t_{sa} \leq t_{sb} \leq t_{ea} + T) \vee (t_{sb} \leq t_{sa} \leq t_{eb} + T), \tag{16.9}$$

then a and b will be connected by an edge on the network. This means that a and b may be the same object since they are observed by cameras around the same time. There is no edge between two trajectories observed in the same camera view. An example can be found in Fig. 16.5. As shown in (a), the views of cameras 1 and 2 overlap and are disjoint with the view of camera 3. Trajectories 1 and 2 observed by cameras 1 and 2 correspond to the same object moving across camera views. Their temporal extents overlap, as shown in (b), so they are connected by an edge on the network as shown in (d). Trajectories 3 and 4 observed by cameras 1 and 3 correspond to an object crossing disjoint views. Their temporal extents have no overlap, but the gap is smaller than T as shown in (c), so they are also connected. Trajectories 3 and 6, 5 and 7 do not correspond to the same objects, but their temporal extents are close, so they are also connected on the network. A single trajectory 3 can be connected to two trajectories (4 and 6) in other camera views. An edge on the network indicates a possible correspondence candidate only based on the temporal information of trajectories. But we do not really solve the correspondence problem when building the trajectory network, since many edges are actually false correspondences. The network simply keeps all of the possible candidates.

In Fig. 16.6, we use an example to describe the high-level picture of this approach. Trajectories a and b are observed in different camera views and connected

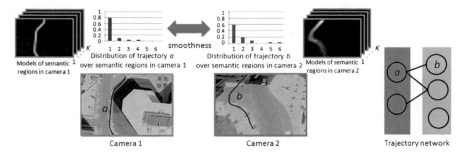

Fig. 16.6 Example to describe the high-level picture of our model. See detail in the text. Figure reproduced with permission from [66]. © 2009 IEEE

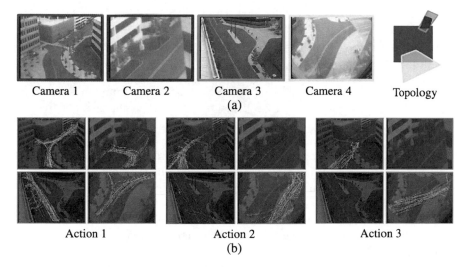

Fig. 16.7 Experimental results of the approach in [66] on a street scene. **a** Camera views and their topology in a street scene. When the topology of camera views is plotted, the fields of camera views are represented by different colors: blue (camera 1), red (camera 2), green (camera 3), yellow (camera 4). However, the approach in [66] does not require knowledge of the topology of the cameras in advance. **b** Examples of trajectory clusters which correspond to different action classes in the street scene. Figure partially reproduced with permission from [66]. © 2009 IEEE

by an edge on the trajectory network. Points on trajectories are assigned to semantic regions by fitting models of semantic regions. The model of a semantic region has joint distributions in all the camera views. Both a and b have distributions over semantic regions. The smoothness constraint requires that their distributions over semantic regions are similar in order to have small penalty. In this example, both trajectory a and b have a larger distribution on semantic region 1, so the models of semantic region 1 in two different camera views can be related to the same action class.

Examples of trajectory clusters obtained by the approach in [66] on a street scene with four cameras are shown in Fig. 16.7. Action 1 captures vehicles moving on the road. It is observed by all of the four cameras. Vehicles first move from the top-right corner to the bottom-left corner in the view of camera 4. Then they enter the bottom region in the view of camera 1 and move upward. Some vehicles disappear at the exit points observed in the views of cameras 2 and 3, and some move further beyond the view of camera 3. In action 2, pedestrians first walk along the sidewalk in the view of camera 1, and then cross the street as observed by camera 4.

16.4 Far-Field Action Recognition Based on Local Motions

The approaches introduced in Sect. 16.3 do not work well in crowded scenes where it is difficult to detect and track objects because of frequent occlusions. In [61, 62], an approach was proposed to jointly detect single-agent actions and global behaviors of video clips in crowded scenes using Dual-HDP. In crowded scenes, different types of single-agent actions often happen simultaneously and it is difficult to separate them without detecting and tracking objects. Global behaviors are characterized by the combinations of different types of single-agent actions co-occurring in the video clips. Although some approaches [69, 70] used motion feature vectors of video clips to model global behaviors of whole video clips without tracking objects, they had difficulty of separating co-occurring activities. The approach in [62] used moving pixels to drive the representation of actions and global behaviors without tracking objects. It assumed that motion features related to the same action class had temporal correlation because an action typically generates continuous motions in time. It leaned action models over motion features by exploring temporal co-occurrence information of features and separated co-occurring actions without human labeling effort using topic models. These action models were used as components to model more complicated global behaviors of video clips. This approach is introduced below.

It computes local motions as low-level features. Moving pixels are detected in each frame as follows: it computes the intensity difference between two successive frames, on a pixel basis. If the difference at a pixel is above a threshold, that pixel is detected as a moving pixel. The motion direction at each moving pixel is obtained by computing optical flow [37]. The moving pixels are quantized according to a codebook, as follows. Each moving pixel has two features: position and direction of motion. To quantize position, the scene is uniformly divided into cells. The motion of a moving pixel is quantized into four directions. Thus each detected moving pixel is assigned a word from the codebook based on rough position and motion direction. The whole video sequence is uniformly divided into nonoverlapping short clips, e.g. each video clip lasts 10 seconds. In this approach, video clips are treated as documents, moving pixels are treated as words, and actions are treated as topics.

The LDA mixture model was used in [61] and it was extended to Dual-HDP in [62]. The LDA mixture model is shown in Fig. 16.8 and will be explained. Suppose that a long video sequence is divided into M short video clips. Video clip j has N_j moving pixels. x_{ji} is the observed feature value of moving pixel i in video clip j. All the moving pixels are clustered into K actions. Actions are shared by

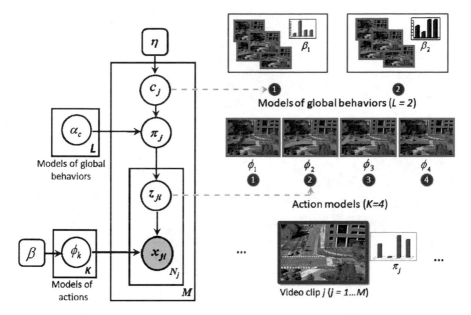

Fig. 16.8 Graphical model of the LDA mixture model for activity analysis based on moving pixels

all the video clips. ϕ_k is the discrete distribution of an action class over locations and moving directions. In the example shown in Fig. 16.8, there are four action classes. Action classes 1 and 3 are vehicles crossing the street intersection. Action class 2 is vehicle turning left and action class 4 is vehicles turning right. All the video clips are clustered into L global behaviors. Each global behavior c has a different prior distribution α_c over action classes. In this example, there are two global behaviors. Global behavior one has a larger weight on action class three than other action classes. Global behavior 2 has larger weights on action classes 1, 3 and 4. Each video clip j choose one of the global behaviors from a distribution η. c_j is the global behavior indicator. Video clip j samples a distribution π_j over action classes from the prior given by its global behavior. Each moving pixel i in video clips j chooses an action class from distribution π_j and sample its feature values x_{ji} from the distribution given by its action class. z_{ji} is the action class indicator. Under this model, if two motion features often co-occur in the same video clips, they have strong temporal correlation and will be grouped into the same action model. Video clips belong to the same global behavior have similar sets of co-occurring actions. This model can be used for action detection (since moving pixels are labeled as different action classes) and temporal segmentation of video sequences (since video clips are labeled as different global behaviors). If video clips and moving pixels do not fit the learned LDA mixture model, they are detected as abnormalities.

In [62], the approach was tested on a 90 minutes long video sequence taken from a traffic scene. 29 models of action classes of vehicles and pedestrians were learned. Examples of the models of action classes are shown in Fig. 16.9. They represent the actions of vehicles crossing the intersection, vehicles turning left, vehicles turn-

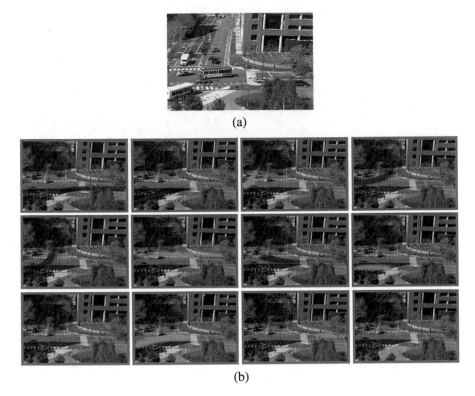

(a)

(b)

Fig. 16.9 Examples of models of action classes learned by the approach proposed in [62] in a crowded traffic scene. **a** Background image of the traffic scene. **b** Models of action classes. Colors represent different moving directions. Their meanings are the same as in Fig. 16.4. Figure partially reproduced with permission from [62]. © 2009 IEEE

ing right and pedestrians walking on crosswalks. Five types of global behaviors are learned in this scene. They correspond to different types of traffic modes. Their distributions over action classes are shown in Fig. 16.10. Figure 16.11 shows the confusion matrix of assigning short video clips to different five different global behaviors compared with manually labeled ground truth. Figure 16.12 shows the top five detected abnormal video clips. The red color highlights the regions with abnormal motions in the video clips. The detected abnormal actions are pedestrians and bicycles crossing the road abnormally.

Besides [62], some other approaches of action recognition using topic models based on local motions were also proposed in recent years. Li et al. [34] first segmented the scene into different spatial regions, called semantic regions, by the spatial distribution of atomic video events in the scene. Within each semantic region, video events were clustered to extract visual words. These visual words represented how object behave locally in each region. The behavior correlations within and across the segmented semantic regions were modeled by a proposed hierarchical pLSA model. At the first stage, local behavior correlations within each region

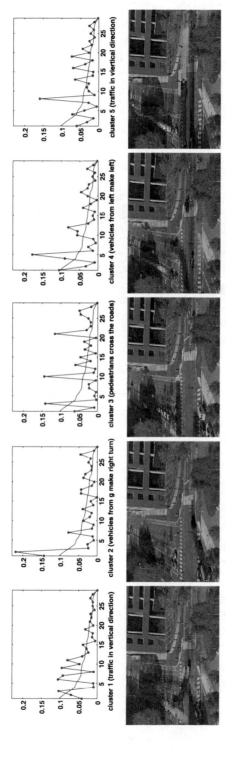

Fig. 16.10 The short video clips are grouped into five global behaviors. *In the first row*, we the mixtures plot $\{\pi_c\}$ over 29 action classes as prior of each global behaviors represented by red curves. For comparison, the blue curve in each plot is the average topic mixture over the whole data set. The x-axis is the index of action classes. The y-axis is the mixture over action classes. *In the second row*, we show a video clip as an example for each type of global behaviors and mark the motions of the five largest actions in that video clip. Notice that colors distinguish different action classes in the same video (the same color may correspond to different topics in different video clips) instead of representing motion directions as in Fig. 16.9. Figure reproduced with permission from [62]. © 2009 IEEE

Fig. 16.11 The confusion
matrix of assigning short
video clips into different
global behaviors. Figure
reproduced with permission
from [62]. © 2009 IEEE

cluster by HDP model

149	0	2	0	0
8	74	4	2	11
10	3	60	1	2
4	0	2	88	11
4	2	6	5	92

Manually label

Fig. 16.12 Results of abnormality detection using the approach in [62]. The top five video clips with the highest abnormality (lowest likelihood) are shown. In each video clip, the regions with motions of high abnormality are highlighted. Figure reproduced with permission from [62]. © 2009 IEEE

were modeled. Then the local behavior patterns were used as the input of the second stage for global behavior inference and abnormality detection. The models discussed above do not model the temporal dependency between video clips. A Markov clustering topic model was proposed in [25] to model the temporal dependency. It integrated the DBN and LDA. Visual events were clustered into activities, these activities were clustered into global behaviors, and behaviors were correlated over time. In [35], a Temporal Order Sensitive LDA (TOS-LDA) model was proposed to discover behavior global correlations over a distributed camera network. TOS-LDA encoded temporal orders among visual words and could represent both long-scale behavior co-occurrences and short-scale temporal order dynamics in a single model. [68] also treated local motions and video clips as words and documents, and cluster local motions based on their co-occurrence in video clips. However, instead of using topic models, diffusion maps embedding were used based on the measure of conditional entropy. Motion patterns were detected as different spatial and temporal scales. All these models are unsupervised and applicable to crowded scenes.

Most of the approaches discussed in this section model actions through exploring the co-occurrence of motion features. They worked well for scenes, such as traffic scenes, where at different time different subsets of activities were observed. However, they may fail in scenes where all types of actions happen simultaneously most of time with significant temporal overlaps. In this type of scenes, without tracking objects, the temporal co-occurrence information alone is not discriminative enough and the models of different action classes may not be well separated. The semantic regions learned from local motions also tend to be in short range compared with those learned from trajectories. These are the limitations of this type of approaches to be addressed in the future work.

16.5 Near-Field Action Recognition Based on Interest Points

Topic models have also been used to recognize human actions in near-field settings. Niebles et al. [42] proposed an approach of extracting spatial-temporal words from space–time interest points and using pLSA to capture the co-occurrence of spatial-temporal words. A video sequence is a collection of spatial-temporal words and is treated as a document. Topic models corresponded to human action classes. This approach is applicable to moving cameras.

Space–time interest points are detected using the approach proposed in [15]. Let I be a video sequence. Gaussian filters and Gabor filters are applied to the video sequence to obtain the responses R as following,

$$R = (I * g * h_{ev})^2 + (I * g * h_{od})^2,$$

$$h_{ev}(t; \tau, \omega) = -\cos(2\pi t \omega)e^{-\frac{t^2}{\tau^2}},$$

$$h_{od}(t; \tau, \omega) = -\sin(2\pi t \omega)e^{-\frac{t^2}{\tau^2}}.$$

$g(x, y; \sigma)$ is a Gaussian smoothing kernel with the standard deviation σ. It is applied to the spatial dimensions x and y. h_{ev} and h_{od} are 1D Gabor filters and are applied to the time dimension t. ω is chosen as $4/\tau$. With these filters, regions undergoing complex motions induces large responses. Therefore, space–time interest points are extracted at the local maxima of the responses. Examples of detected interest points are shown in Fig. 16.13. Around each interest point, a visual descriptor is calculated by concatenating the gradients into a vector. These descriptors are projected to a lower dimensional space using PCA and quantized into spatial-temporal words by k-means clustering. The model of an action class is a discrete distribution over the codebook and is learn as a topic model under pLSA.

Let $P(w|z)$ be the distribution of topic z over the codebook and its is learned from the training set. A new video sequence d_{test} is projected on the simplex spanned by the learned $P(w|z)$. The mixing coefficients $P(z|d_{\text{test}})$ is estimated by minimizing the KL divergence between the measured empirical distribution $\tilde{P}(w|d_{\text{test}})$ and

Fig. 16.13 Human action recognition using the approach proposed in [42]. Rectangles indicate detected interest points. Different colors represent different topics (action classes). Red: walking; blue: jogging; green: running; and yellow: hand waving. The figure is reproduced from [42]

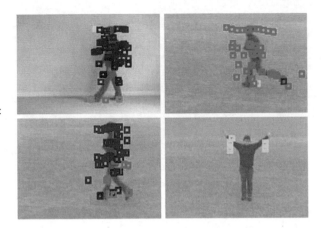

$P(w|d_{\text{test}}) = \sum_{k=1}^{K} P(z = k|d_{\text{test}})P(w|z_k)$. The optimization problem is solved by the EM algorithm. In order to localize multiple actions in a single video sequence, each interest point with word value w is assigned to one the action classes k by finding the maximum posterior,

$$P(z = k|w, d_{\text{test}}) = \frac{P(w|z = k)P(z = k|d_{\text{test}})}{\sum_{l=1}^{K} P(w|z = l)P(z = l|d_{\text{test}})}.$$

In [42], this approach was tested on the KTH human motion data set [49], which includes 598 video sequences of 6 action classes. Some examples of recognized actions are shown in Fig. 16.13. Recognition accuracies of different methods on this data set are reported in Table 20.1 in Chap. 20. The topic model proposed in [42] outperforms other methods. Moreover, the method in [42] is unsupervised without requiring manually labeling training data, while other methods in comparison are supervised. The method in [42] assumes that there are multiple actions in a video sequence, while other methods assume that there is only one action in a video sequence.

The method in [42] completely ignored the geometric relationship among spatial-temporal words with the "bag-of-words" assumption. This limits its discriminative power. In [41], an approach was proposed to combine the constellation model, which captured the geometric relationship of different parts of objects, and the "bag-of-words" model. The proposed approach model human actions at different hierarchical levels. At the higher level, the human action is model as a constellation of P parts. At the lower layer, each part is associated to a bag of spatial-temporal features.

16.6 Conclusion and Discussion

In this chapter, we introduce different types of approaches using topic models to recognize actions in different scenarios. In these approaches, words, documents and topics are mapped into different concepts under different contexts of action recognition. When the scene is sparse and objects can be well tracked, trajectories of objects are treated as documents, observations on trajectories are treated as words, and semantic regions are treated as topics. In crowded scenes, where objects are untrackable, short video clips are treated as documents, moving pixels are treated as words and action classes are treated as topics. In near-field action recognition, video sequences are treated as documents, spatial-temporal interest points are treated as words and action classes are treated as topics. Topic models can be extended from a single camera views to multiple camera views. The models of action classes are unsupervisedly learned through exploring the identity co-occurrence or temporal co-occurrence of visual features. Topic models can also be well integrated non-parametric Bayesian models to automatically learn to the number of action classes.

As a direction of the future work, topic models need to better capture the spatial and temporal relationship of words and documents. In far-field action recognition, both trajectories and local motions used as low-level features have their limitations. It worth to explore topic models based on tracklets (fragments of trajectories) when the scenes are crowded and all types of actions happen simultaneously with significant temporal overlap. Topic models have been applied to recognize actions over a small camera network (with fewer than ten cameras). However, some video surveillance applications (such as monitoring the traffic flows in large cities) require action recognition over a very large camera network with hundreds or even thousands of cameras. How to apply topic models in these scenarios is another research direction to be explored.

16.6.1 Further Reading

In computer vision, besides action recognition, topic models have also been applied to scene categorization [16], object recognition [50, 54] and image semantic segmentation [11, 48, 59] and image search [3]. The original topic models developed in language processing have been extended to incorporate spatial and temporal information to better solve computer vision problems [44, 54, 58, 59]. In recent years, many other topic models, such as dynamic topic models [9], author-topic model [47], HMM-LDA [22], polylingual topic models [38], correlated topic models [10], and supervised topic model [7] were proposed. It would be also interesting to see how these models can be applied to solve computer vision problems. Topic models are hierarchical Bayesian models, which have some nice properties of jointly modeling simple and complicated actions at different hierarchical levels and effectively addressing the overfitting problem through modeling the dependency among parameters. To better understand hierarchical Bayesian models, [18] is recommended. Topic models can be well integrated with non-parametric Bayesian models, which use Dirichlet processes as priors to automatically learn the number of clusters driven by data. Both LDA and the LDA mixture model have their non-parametric versions, HDP [55] and Dual-HDP [62]. More advanced models based on HDP can be found in [20, 45, 46, 52].

References

1. Atev, S., Arumugam, H., Masaoud, O., Janardan, R., Papanikolopoulos, N.P.: A vision-based approach to collision prediction at traffic intersections. IEEE Trans. Intell. Transp. Syst. **6**, 416–423 (2005) [311]
2. Ayers, D., Shah, M.: Monitoring human behavior from video taken in an office environment. Image Vis. Comput. **19**, 833–846 (2001) [311]
3. Barnard, K., Duygulu, P., Forsyth, D., Freitas, N., Blei, D.M., Jordan, M.J.: Matching words and pictures. J. Mach. Learn. Res. **3**, 1107–1135 (2003) [329]
4. Bird, N.D., Masoud, O., Papanikolopoulos, N.P., Isaacs, A.: Detection of loitering individuals in public transportation area. IEEE Trans. Intell. Transp. Syst. **6**, 167–177 (2005) [311]
5. Blei, D.M., Jordan, M.I.: Variational methods for the Dirichlet process. In: Proc. Int'l Conf. Machine Learning (2004) [315]
6. Blei, D.M., Jordan, M.I.: Variational inference for Dirichlet process mixtures. Journal of Bayesian Analysis **1**, 121–144 (2005) [315]
7. Blei, D.M., McAuliffe, J.D.: Supervised topic models. In: Proc. Neural Information Processing Systems Conf. (2007) [329]
8. Blei, D.M., Ng, A.Y., Jordan, M.I.: Latent Dirichlet allocation. J. Mach. Learn. Res. **3**, 993–1022 (2003) [312,313,315]
9. Blei, D.M., Lafferty, J.D.: Dynamic topic models. In: Proc. Int'l Conf. Machine Learning (2006) [329]
10. Blei, D.M., Lafferty, J.D.: A correlated topic model of science. Annals of Applied Statistics **1**, 17–35 (2007) [329]
11. Cao, L., Fei-Fei, L.: Spatially coherent latent topic model for concurrent object segmentation and classification. In: Proc. Int'l Conf. Computer Vision (2007) [329]
12. Datta, A., Shah, M., Da, N., Lobo, V.: Person-on-person violence detection in video data. In: Proc. Int'l Conf. Pattern Recognition (2002) [311]
13. Davis, J.W., Bobick, A.F.: The representation and recognition of action using temporal templates. In: Proc. IEEE Int'l Conf. Computer Vision and Pattern Recognition (1997) [312]
14. Dever, J., Lobo, N.V., Shah, M.: Automatic visual recognition of armed robbery. In: Proc. Int'l Conf. Pattern Recognition (2002) [311]
15. Dollar, P., Rabaud, V., Cottrell, G., Belongie, S.: Behavior recognition via sparse spatio-temporal features. In: Proc. IEEE International Workshop on Visual Surveillance and Performance Evaluation of Tracking and Surveillance (2005) [327]
16. Fei-Fei, L., Perona, P.: A Bayesian hierarchical model for learning natural scene categories. In: Proc. IEEE Int'l Conf. Computer Vision and Pattern Recognition (2005) [314,329]
17. Ferguson, T.S.: A Bayesian analysis of some nonparametric problems. Ann. Stat. **1**, 209–230 (1973) [312,314]
18. Gelman, A., Carlin, J.B., Stern, H.S., Rubin, D.B.: Bayesian Data Analysis. Chapman & Hall, London (2004) [329]
19. Ghanem, N., Dementhon, D., Doermann, D., Davis, L.: Representation and recognition of events in surveillance video using petri net. In: CVPR Workshop (2004) [312]
20. Griffin, J.E., Steel, M.F.J.: Order-based dependent Dirichlet processes. J. Am. Stat. Assoc. **101**, 179–194 (2006) [329]
21. Griffiths, T.L., Steyvers, M.: Finding scientific topics. In: Proc. of the National Academy of Sciences of the United States of America (2004) [315]
22. Griffths, T.L., Steyvers, M., Blei, D.M., Tenenbaum, J.B.: Integrating topics and syntax. In: Proc. Neural Information Processing Systems Conf. (2004) [329]
23. Hofmann, T.: Probabilistic latent semantic analysis. In: Proc. of Uncertainty in Artificial Intelligence (1999) [312,313]
24. Honggeng, S., Nevatia, R.: Multi-agent event recognition. In: Proc. Int'l Conf. Computer Vision (2001) [311,312]
25. Hospedales, T., Gong, S., Xiang, T.: A Markov clustering topic model for mining behaviour in video. In: Proc. Int'l Conf. Computer Vision (2009) [326]

26. Hu, W., Tan, T., Wang, L., Maybank, S.: A survey on visual surveillance of object motion and behaviors. IEEE Trans. Syst. Man Cybern., Part C, Appl. Rev. **34**, 334–352 (2004) [311]
27. Hu, W., Xiao, X., Fu, Z., Xie, D., Tan, T., Maybank, S.: A system for learning statistical motion patterns. IEEE Trans. Pattern Anal. Mach. Intell. **28**, 1450–1464 (2006) [316]
28. Intille, S.S., Bobick, A.F.: A framework for recognizing multi-agent action from visual evidence. In: Proc. National Conf. Artificial Intelligence (1999) [311]
29. Jordan, M.: Learning in Graphical Models. MIT Press, Cambridge (1999) [315]
30. Ke, Y., Suckthanlar, R., Hebert, M.: Event detection in crowded videos. In: Proc. Int'l Conf. Computer Vision (2007) [311]
31. Khoshabeh, R., Gandhi, T., Trivedi, M.M.: Multi-camera based traffic flow characterization and classification. In: Proc. IEEE Conf. Intelligent Transportation Systems (2007) [311]
32. Kumar, P., Ranganath, S., Hu, W., Sengupta, K.: Framework for real-time behavior interpretation from traffic video. IEEE Trans. Intell. Transp. Syst. **6**, 43–53 (2005) [311]
33. Lee, L., Romano, R., Stein, G.: Monitoring activities from multiple video streams: Establishing a common coordinate frame. IEEE Trans. Pattern Anal. Mach. Intell. **22**, 758–768 (2000) [318]
34. Li, J., Gong, S., Xiang, T.: Scene segmentation for behaviour correlation. In: Proc. European Conf. Computer Vision (2008) [324]
35. Li, J., Gong, S., Xiang, T.: Discovering multi-camera behaviour correlations for on-the-fly global activity prediction and anomaly detection. In: Proc. of IEEE Int'l Workshop on Visual Surveillance (2009) [326]
36. Lin, C., Ling, Z.: Automatic fall incident detection in compressed video for intelligent homecare. In: Proc. IEEE Int'l Conf. Computer Communications and Networks (2007) [311]
37. Lucas, B.D., Kanade, T.: An iterative image registration technique with an application to stereo vision. In: Proc. Int'l Joint Conf. Artificial Intelligence, pp. 674–680 (1981) [322]
38. Mimno, D., Wallach, H.M., Naradowsky, J., Smith, D.A., MaCallum, A.: Polylingual topic models. In: Proc. of Conference on Empirical Methods in Natural Language Processing (2009) [329]
39. Morris, B.T., Trivedi, M.M.: A survey of vision-based trajectory learning and analysis for surveillance. IEEE Trans. Circuits Syst. Video Technol. **18**, 1114–1127 (2008) [311,316]
40. Newman, D., Asuncion, A., Smyth, P., Welling, M.: Distributed inference for latent Dirichlet allocation. In: Proc. Neural Information Processing Systems Conf. (2007) [316]
41. Niebles, J.C., Fei-Fei, L.: A hierarchical model of shape and appearance for human action classification. In: Proc. IEEE Int'l Conf. Computer Vision and Pattern Recognition (2007) [328]
42. Niebles, J.C., Wang, H., Li, F.: Unsupervised learning of human action categories using spatial-temporal words. In: Proc. British Machine Vision Conference (2006) [327,328]
43. Oliver, N., Rosario, B., Pentland, A.: A Bayesian computer vision system for modeling human interactions. IEEE Trans. Pattern Anal. Mach. Intell. **22**, 831–843 (2000) [312]
44. Passino, G., Patras, I., Izquierdo, E.: Latent semantics local distribution for CRF-based image semantic segmentation. In: Proc. British Machine Vision Conference (2009) [329]
45. Ren, L., Dunson, D.B., Carin, L.: The dynamic hierarchical Dirichlet process. In: Proc. Int'l Conf. Machine Learning (2008) [329]
46. Rodriguez, A., Dunson, D.B., Gelfand, A.E.: The nested Dirichlet process. Technical report, Working Paper 2006-19, Duke Institute of Statistics and Decision Sciences (2006) [329]
47. Rosen-Zvi, M., Griffths, T., Steyvers, M., Smyth, P.: Probabilistic author-topic models for information discovery. In: Proc. of ACM Special Interest Group on Knowledge Discovery and Data Mining (2004) [329]
48. Russell, B.C., Efros, A.A., Sivic, J., Freeman, W.T., Zisserman, A.: Using multiple segmentations to discover objects and their extent in image collections. In: Proc. IEEE Int'l Conf. Computer Vision and Pattern Recognition (2006) [329]
49. Schuldt, C., Laptev, I., Caputo, B.: Recognizing human actions: A local SVM approach. In: Proc. Int'l Conf. Pattern Recognition (2004) [328]
50. Sivic, J., Russell, B.C., Efros, A.A., Zisserman, A., Freeman, W.T.: Discovering object categories in image collections. In: Proc. Int'l Conf. Computer Vision (2005) [329]

51. Smith, P., Lobo, N.V., Shah, M.: Temporal boost for event recognition. In: Proc. Int'l Conf. Computer Vision (2005) [312]
52. Srebro, N., Roweis, S.: Time-varying topic models using dependent Dirichlet processes. Technical report, Department of Computer Science, University of Toronto (2005) [329]
53. Stauffer, C., Grimson, E.: Learning patterns of activity using real-time tracking. IEEE Trans. Pattern Anal. Mach. Intell. **22**, 747–757 (2000) [312]
54. Sudderth, E.B., Torralba, A., Freeman, W.T., Willsky, A.S.: Describing visual scenes using transformed objects and parts. Int. J. Comput. Vis. **77**, 291–330 (2007) [329]
55. Teh, Y.W., Jordan, M.I., Beal, M.J., Blei, D.M.: Hierarchical Dirichlet process. J. Am. Stat. Assoc. **101**, 1566–1581 (2006) [314,316,329]
56. Thirde, D., Borg, M., Ferryman, J., Aguilera, J., Kampel, M.: Distributed multi-camera surveillance for aircraft servicing operations. In: Proc. IEEE Int'l Conf. Computer Vision and Pattern Recognition (2005) [318]
57. Veeraraghavan, H., Maoud, O., Papanikolopoulos, N.: Computer vision algorithms for intersection monitoring. IEEE Trans. Intell. Transp. Syst. **4**, 78–89 (2003) [311]
58. Verbeek, J., Triggs, B.: Region classification with Markov field aspect models. In: Proc. IEEE Int'l Conf. Computer Vision and Pattern Recognition (2007) [329]
59. Wang, X., Grimson, E.: Spatial latent Dirichlet allocation. In: Proc. Neural Information Processing Systems Conf. (2007) [314,329]
60. Wang, Y., Jiang, T., Drew, M.S., Li, Z., Mori, G.: Unsupervised discovery of action classes. In: Proc. IEEE Int'l Conf. Computer Vision and Pattern Recognition (2006) [312]
61. Wang, X., Ma, X., Grimson, E.: Unsupervised activity perception by hierarchical Bayesian models. In: Proc. IEEE Int'l Conf. Computer Vision and Pattern Recognition (2007) [318, 322]
62. Wang, X., Ma, X., Grimson, E.: Unsupervised activity perception in crowded and complicated scenes using hierarchical Bayesian models. IEEE Trans. Pattern Anal. Mach. Intell. **31**, 539–555 (2009) [322-326,329]
63. Wang, X., Ma, K.T., Ng, G., Grimson, E.: Trajectory analysis and semantic region modeling using a nonparametric Bayesian model. In: Proc. IEEE Int'l Conf. Computer Vision and Pattern Recognition (2008) [316-319]
64. Wang, X., Tieu, K., Grimson, E.: Learning semantic scene models by trajectory analysis. In: Proc. European Conf. Computer Vision (2006) [312,316]
65. Wang, X., Tieu, K., Grimson, E.: Correspondence-free multi-camera activity analysis and scene modeling. In: Proc. IEEE Int'l Conf. Computer Vision and Pattern Recognition (2008) [318]
66. Wang, X., Tieu, K., Grimson, E.: Correspondence-free activity analysis and scene modeling in multiple camera views. IEEE Trans. Pattern Anal. Mach. Intell. (2009) [318,320,321]
67. Xiang, T., Gong, S.: Beyond tracking: Modelling activity and understanding behaviour. Int. J. Comput. Vis. **67**, 21–51 (2006) [311,312]
68. Yang, Y., Liu, J., Shah, M.: Video scene understanding using multi-scale analysis. In: Proc. Int'l Conf. Computer Vision (2009) [326]
69. Zelnik-Manor, L., Irani, M.: Event-based analysis of video. In: Proc. IEEE Int'l Conf. Computer Vision and Pattern Recognition (2001) [312,322]
70. Zhong, H., Shi, J., Visontai, M.: Detecting unusual activity in video. In: Proc. IEEE Int'l Conf. Computer Vision and Pattern Recognition (2004) [312,322]

Chapter 17
Learning Action Primitives

Dana Kulić, Danica Kragic, and Volker Krüger

Abstract The use of action primitives plays an important role in modeling actions. Action primitives are motivated not only by neurobiological findings, they also allow an efficient and effective action modeling from an information-theoretic viewpoint. Different approaches for modeling action primitives have been proposed. This chapter overviews the recent approaches for learning and modeling action primitives for human and robot action and describes common approaches such as stochastic methods and dynamical systems approaches. Active research questions in the field are introduced, including temporal segmentation, dimensionality reduction, and the integration of action primitives into complex behaviors.

17.1 Introduction

Research on human motion and other biological movement postulates that movement behavior is composed of *action primitives*: simple, atomic movements that can be combined and sequenced to form complex behavior [88]. Action primitives allow for complex actions to be decomposed into an alphabet of primitives, and for grammar-like descriptions to be constructed to govern their order of use. A similar strategy of using primitives can be found in linguistics where utterances of words are broken down into phonemes. Action primitives enable a "symbolic" description of complex action instances as words over the alphabet of action primitives, which subsequently enables the use of techniques from AI and automata theory for pars-

D. Kulić (✉)
University of Waterloo, Waterloo, Canada
e-mail: dkulic@ece.uwaterloo.ca

D. Kragic
Centre for Autonomous Systems, Royal Institute of Technology – KTH, Stockholm, Sweden
e-mail: dani@kth.se

V. Krüger
Aalborg University Copenhagen, Ballerup, Denmark
e-mail: vok@cvmi.aau.dk

T.B. Moeslund et al. (eds.), *Visual Analysis of Humans*,
DOI 10.1007/978-0-85729-997-0_17, © Springer-Verlag London Limited 2011

ing and planning. This chapter complements the discussions on motion learning in Chap. 16.

The recognition and learning of these primitives has received a lot of attention in the research literature, in the AI, vision and robotics communities. From the vision perspective, formulating the recognition problem in terms of action primitives rather than continuous movement significantly reduces the search space, facilitating movement recognition. From the robotics and AI perspective, using action primitives to generate movement improves computational efficiency, both in motion planning and control. Motion planning becomes simplified because it can be carried out over the space of action primitives, rather than over the much larger muscle/joint space. Similarly, the control problem becomes simplified because controllers can be designed locally (within a single action primitive), rather than having to operate over the entire movement space.

Most approaches used for learning and modeling of action primitives are of a generative type, even though discriminative approaches exist. One reason is that generative models allow in principle to generate and recognize actions at the same time. A further reason is that generative models are able to identify previously unseen primitives if the available action primitive models are not able to explain the new observation sufficiently well. Discriminative models, on the other hand, have to choose among the known models, which means that they implicitly assume that the set of known primitives is exhaustive.

17.1.1 Connections to Biological Models of Movement Primitives

Research on action primitives has been motivated by evidence from biology and neuroscience for the presence of action primitives at several different hierarchy levels in the animal and human brain. Studies of frogs and birds reveal evidence of muscle synergies, coordinated, synchronized movements of multiple muscle units such as swim kicks and wing movements which are generated by the firing of a single neuron in the spinal cord [70]. Recent research on primates and humans has uncovered the mirror neuron system, thought to encode a sensorimotor representation of action primitives [82, 83]. The mirror neuron system is believed to be a neural mechanism which links action observation and execution.

A key question in biology and cognitive science is the model of learning, i.e.: how do the mirror neurons acquire their mirror-like properties? Heyes and Ray [33, 34] propose the Associative Sequence Learning (ASL) theory of imitation. Learning proceeds via two sets of associative processes, forming sequence associations between sensory representations and associations between the sensory and motor representations. Meltzoff [66, 67] proposes the *Active Intermodal Mapping* theory, which postulates that infants possess an innate ability to map from perception to motor acts, and that initially captured motions get progressively refined through repeated practice. These theories imply that the development of the imitation mechanism is highly experience-dependent, consisting of correlation links between sensory and motor data which are formed over time. However, some researchers [9] postulate that many of the animal behaviors classified as imitation can more accurately be explained by priming mechanisms, such as stimulus enhancement, emulation and response facilitation. They argue that the main imitation mechanism used by primates and humans is not at the action level, but rather at the program level, i.e., primates learn to imitate the efficient organization of the actions, while the individual actions comprising the complex behavior are learned by other means, such as trial and error. Similarly, Wolhschlager et al. [104] propose the *goal-directed imitation* (GOADI) theory, which suggests that imitation is guided by cognitively specified goals. According to the theory, the imitator does not imitate the exact movements produced by the demonstrator, but instead extracts from the demonstrator a hierarchy of goals and subgoals present in the task. These goals and subgoals are then accomplished by motor programs already in the imitator's repertoire which are most strongly associated with the achievement of the given goal.

These neurobiological findings have been used as models for implementing artificial action primitive recognition and learning systems, most commonly by modeling the mirror neuron system [12, 39] and hypothesizing that implementing algorithms which learn from observation and by imitation of action primitives will facilitate robot learning and provide an intuitive and human-like programming interface [8, 88].

17.2 Representations and Learning of Movement Primitives

A key question in learning action primitives is the mathematical representation of the primitive. Two broad representation classes are most commonly used: stochastic models and dynamical systems models. These methods are outlined in Fig. 17.1. Other techniques for modeling movement primitives, such as B-splines [99], B-spline wavelets [98] or polynomial functions [73], have also been proposed, but are not covered here due to space constraints.

17.2.1 Stochastic Approaches

Stochastic models represent each action primitive as a stochastic dynamical system, where the evolution of the system state is governed by a stochastic process, and observation of the system is impeded by noise. Two types of stochastic models can be used: generative or discriminative. Generative models are the ones used most commonly as they can be used to both recognize the action primitive and also generate a prototype, for example on a robot or in an animation, analogous to the idea of the mirror neurons (see Sect. 17.1.1). On the other hand, discriminative models can only be used to classify actions; a further short-coming is their inability to detected unknown actions. The choice of model type is strongly influenced by the target application, most activity recognition systems focus on discriminative models, where only recognition capability is required. On the other hand, in situations

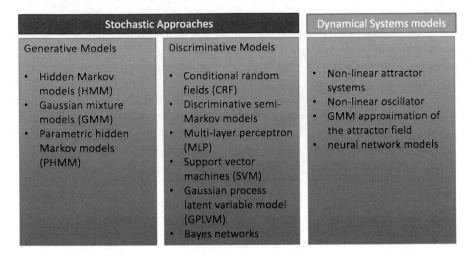

Fig. 17.1 This figure summarizes the different approaches used to model action primitives

where reproduction of the demonstrated actions is required (robotics, animation, etc.), generative models are typically used.

17.2.1.1 Generative Models

The most commonly used generative stochastic models are HMMs [79] and Gaussian Mixture Models (GMMs) [80]. HMMs have been a popular technique for human motion modeling, and have been used in a variety of applications, including skill transfer [19, 105], robot assisted surgery [41, 52, 81], sign language and gesture modeling [4, 36, 92] and motion prediction [3, 35]. Developing from the earlier work on *Teaching by Showing* [59], a common paradigm in robotics research is Programming by Demonstration (PbD) [4, 6, 18, 19, 46].

An HMM models the trajectory dynamics of the motion by the evolution of a hidden variable through a finite set of states. The hidden state variable evolves according to a stochastic state transition model $A[N, N]$, where N is the number of states in the model. The probability of a state being the initial state is given by the initial state distribution $\pi[N]$. The hidden state cannot be observed directly, only a vector of output variables is observable, from which the hidden state needs to be inferred. The output variables and each hidden state are related through the output distribution model $B[N, K]$, where K is the dimension of the output vector. For continuous output variables, the output distribution model typically used is a Gaussian or mixture of Gaussians.

When modeling action primitives, the output variables typically describe joint angles, Cartesian coordinates of key body points, or object positions. An HMM is used to represent each action primitive. Training the model consists of learning the model parameters A, B, π to find the parameters that maximize the likelihood that the trained model generated the exemplar data. The Baum–Welch algorithm, a type of Expectation Maximization (EM), is typically used to perform the training [79]. Once the models are trained, recognition of novel observations is implemented by computing the likelihood that each of the known models produced the novel observation, and selecting the highest likelihood model as the recognized model.

Since the HMM represents a stochastic model of the action, there is not a unique trajectory which can be used for action reproduction. A representative trajectory can be generated by first sampling from the state transition model to generate a state sequence, and then sampling from each state output distribution to generate an output sequence. However, this can result in a noisy trajectory which does not respect continuity constraints. To generate an appropriate trajectory, several techniques have been proposed: One approach is to repeat the sampling many times and average over the generated trajectory [39]. As the number of samples approaches infinity, the generated trajectory will approach the most likely trajectory. However, this procedure is time consuming as many trajectories must be generated. A second approach is to use a deterministic generation approach, by selecting first the most likely state sequence, and then the mean from each output distribution in the case of a Gaussian output function, or the weighted sum of means in the case of the mixture of Gaussians model [57]. This approach is fast, but discards the information about allowable trajectory variations from the mean. Both of these generation approaches typically require a post-processing smoothing step to ensure a smooth trajectory. A final approach is to include both position and velocity information in the output variables, and use the velocity information to aid with smoothing [93, 94].

A second type of stochastic model which can be used to encode action primitives is the GMM [80]. In this approach, the time-series data of an action primitive is modeled as a mixture of multivariate Gaussian distributions.

The model parameters are learned using the EM algorithm. Unlike the HMM model, where the temporal evolution of the trajectory is encoded through the evolution of the hidden state, the GMM does not contain any explicit timing information. The GMM is encoding the spatial variance, but not the timing of the advancement along the trajectory. To encode timing information, two approaches are possible: adding time as an additional variable in the observation vector [14], or encoding both the position and velocity in the observation vector, rather than modeling time explicitly [29]. With the first approach, simply adding time to the observation vector is typically not sufficient, as it does not account for temporal variability across demonstrations. To address this issue, a pre-processing step is added to temporally align the exemplar data sets using dynamic time warping.

With the second approach, no pre-processing is required, but the size of the output vector is doubled to include both the position and velocity of each variable of interest. Once the model structure is selected and the model is trained for each primitive, Gaussian mixture regression can be used to generate a trajectory.

The strengths of stochastic models in general include their ability to capture both the spatial and temporal variability in the movement, and in particular to capture the change in variance along the movement. For example, in a goal reaching movement, the human demonstrator will typically exhibit high variance at the start of the movement, as there is significant variability in the starting location, but very low variance at the goal location. HMMs and GMMs can explicitly capture this feature of the action primitive by encoding both the mean location and the variance around that location for key points along the trajectory. Another advantage of stochastic modeling is the ability to handle data noise and missing data.

Stochastic generative models are also convenient for movement recognition and comparison. Due to the stochastic representation, both a likelihood and a distance measure comparing movements are easily computed, allowing movement differences and similarities to be analyzed [54, 57].

On the other hand, a weakness of basic HMMs and GMMs is the lack of parametrization. For example, if a reaching movement is learned for a specific reach target, it is not intuitive how to adapt the learned model to a new reach target. Parametric Hidden Markov Models (PHMMs) have been proposed to address this issue [54, 103]. The PHMM extends basic HMMs by adding a latent parameter modeling the systematic variation within a class.

A related issue of stochastic generative models is the lack of generalization away from the trained trajectories, and the lack of appropriate trajectory when the system is disturbed. Recent work has addressed this issue by adding a control command pushing the system toward the learned trajectory [13].

Another issue with stochastic models is the requirement for multiple examples of a motion, in order to determine valid statistics. This has traditionally meant that training data must be collected off-line, and limited potential for on-line and continuous learning. Recent research [11, 57, 58] has proposed algorithms for incremental, on-line learning of stochastic models to overcome this limitation.

A final issue with stochastic models concerns the parameter selection problem, i.e., how to select the appropriate number of states (in an HMM), or the number of mixtures (in a GMM). With simple learning systems with few action primitives, it may be possible for the designer to specify the parameters manually, however, this technique is not appropriate when the potential number of motion primitives is large and not known ahead of time. Several techniques have been proposed, including iterative addition and merging of states [20], using SVMs as a pre-processing step to determine the appropriate number of states [23], the Bayesian information criterion [5], the Akaike information criterion [56], or the use of a variable structure HMM which can be incrementally adapted [54, 57].

17.2.1.2 Discriminative Models

Discriminative models formulate the action primitive learning problem as a *classification* problem. With this formulation, the key issues are how to find the most discriminant features, and how to find the cluster boundaries, via supervised learning. The questions of feature selection and classifier training are common topics in machine learning research, where many general algorithms have been proposed. A recent example is the work of Han et al. [32], who use a hierarchical Gaussian Process Latent Variable Model (GPLVM) to find a reduced dimensionality subspace over the motion features. A conditional random field (CRF) model is

then applied to estimate each motion pattern in the corresponding manifold subspace, and a support vector machine classifier is used to distinguish between the
motions. In another exemplar implementation [89], features based on boundary and
content characteristics are manually selected by the designers, and then a discriminative semi-Markov model is used to simultaneously distinguish between motions
and identify segment points between motions. Loesch et al. [63] evaluate several
general machine learning methods for feature selection and classification of human
activity, focusing on motions representing typical at home activities. For the feature
selection algorithms, the Evaluation of Information Gain from Attribute (EIGA)
and the Correlation-based Feature Subset Selection (CbFSS) methods are compared.
The EIGA method measures the utility of a feature based on the information gain
with respect to the activity class. The CbFSS method evaluates the utility of a subset
of features by considering the predictive ability of each feature relative to the degree of redundancy between the subset of features. For the classification algorithms,
Naive Bayesian Network (NBN), BN, Multilayer Perceptron (MLP), Radial Basis
Function Network (RBF) and SVM are compared. The results show that CbFSS is
usually slightly better than EIGA at selecting features, regardless of the classifier
used. The classifier results show that NBN and RBF have poor results, while BN,
MLP and SVM have good performance, which for the case of MLP and SVM increases with the number of features used. Since multiple classification algorithms
give similar performance, it can be concluded that the selected data features have
intrinsic high information value, so that the classifier selection is not very important.
Thus, feature selection plays a significant role in classification performance.

A strong assumption commonly made in case of generative models such as
HMM or its variants is that the observations are conditionally independent in order to insure computational tractability. To accommodate for long-range dependencies among observations or multiple overlapping features of observations at multiple time steps stochastic grammars and parsing would have to be used subsequently [22].

CRFs [60] elegantly avoid the independence assumption of HMMs and are able
to incorporate both overlapping features and long-term dependencies into the model.
Although CRFs have been extensively used in the area of computer vision and machine learning, there are almost no examples of their use in the robotics community.
An example of their use in an integrated object/action recognition work is presented
in [47] (see also Chap. 18: *Contextual Action Recognition*), where a method for classifying manipulation actions in the context of the objects manipulated and classifying objects in the context of the actions used to manipulate them has been presented.

17.2.2 Dynamical Systems Approaches

Dynamical systems approaches model an action primitive as an evolution of state
variables in a dynamic system. Typically, a differential equation is used to describe
the state evolution [37, 71, 86], but ANN based models have also been proposed

[40, 72]. With differential equation based approaches, a distinction must be made between goal oriented motion (for example, reaching, tennis swinging, etc.), and cyclic motion, such as walking, swimming, etc. For goal oriented motions, the evolution of the trajectory is modeled as a non-linear attractor, while for cyclic motions, a non-linear oscillator is used. The trajectory dynamics are typically described in state-space form, with an additional phase dynamics to allow for non uniform rate of advancement along the trajectory [37]:

$$\dot{v} = \alpha_v \big(\beta_v (g - x) - v \big), \qquad \dot{x} = \alpha_x v, \tag{17.1}$$

$$\dot{z} = \alpha_z \big(\beta_z (g - y) - z \big), \qquad \dot{y} = \alpha_y \big(f(x, v) + z \big). \tag{17.2}$$

Here, z is the state variable, g is a known goal state, α_z, β_z, α_v, β_v are time constants, and $f(x, v) = \sum b_i \varphi(x, v)$ is a non-linear function model. The state variable z is a vector of the motion variables of interest, typically joint angles or body or object Cartesian positions. (x, v) is a linear 2nd order dynamical system representing the evolution of the temporal variable, allowing time evolution along the trajectory to be modified. By choosing α_v, β_v such that the system is critically damped, the system has guaranteed monotonic global convergence to the goal. An action primitive is learned by learning the non-linear function $f(x, v)$ which best approximates the demonstrated action. A common approach is to use a locally linear approximation for the non-linear function

$$f(x, v) = \frac{\sum_{i=1}^{k} w_i b_i v}{\sum_{i=1}^{k} w_i}, \quad w_i = \exp\left(-\frac{1}{2} d_i (\bar{x} - c_i)^2\right), \quad \bar{x} = \frac{x - x_0}{g - x_0}, \tag{17.3}$$

where b_i are the weights to be learned, and d_i is the region of validity for each locally linear model. The weights can now be learned from demonstration data by a regression algorithm [87], such as locally weighted projection regression [101]. Dynamical model approaches have been used successfully to learn and reproduce fast and accurate motions [77], such as tennis swinging [86], ball hitting [76] and catching [48], and pick and place actions [75].

For cyclic motions, instead of using a point goal attractor, a limit cycle attractor is used [71]:

$$\dot{r} = \alpha_r (A - r), \qquad \dot{\varphi} = \omega. \tag{17.4}$$

Here, r is the oscillator amplitude, A is the desired amplitude, and φ is the phase. The cyclic motion state equation is then:

$$\dot{z} = \alpha_z \big(\beta_z (g - y) - z \big), \qquad \dot{y} = \alpha_y \big(f_i(r, \varphi) + z \big), \tag{17.5}$$

where g becomes the setpoint about which the oscillation takes place, and the non-linear function to be learned is $f(r, \varphi)$. To coordinate multiple degrees of freedom (DoF), a single oscillator, described by (17.4), is coupled to a unique non-linear function associated with each DoF.

This approach has been demonstrated for gait with humanoid robots [71], where the parameters of the dynamical system are learned from human motion data.

A strength of dynamical systems approaches is their ability to represent complex trajectory shapes, including complex phase relationships and movement reversals. Dynamical systems also offer good mechanisms for parametrization and generalization. For example, for a reaching motion, the location of the target can be easily modified by changing the value of the goal in the state equation. Recently, techniques for automatically learning the required goal location when a new environment is encountered have also been proposed [100]. The system behavior is defined for the entire state space, not only near the observed demonstration trajectory. This allows the system to respond appropriately when disturbances during execution push the system away from the trained trajectory. This can also be beneficial for robot systems needing to generate a trajectory for a novel instantiation of a task. However, the generation of trajectories far away from the demonstrated one can be questionable from the point of view of action recognition, as there is no guarantee that the motion generated by the equation away from the demonstrated trajectory will be similar to human motion. Another weakness of dynamical systems approaches is that data noise and missing data cannot be easily handled by this type of model.

Recent work has also proposed combining dynamical systems approaches with stochastic methods, by combining an HMM trajectory with a learned attractor field [31], or by approximating the dynamic equation with a GMM [29].

17.2.3 Measurement Systems

For the purpose of generating training data, different sensory modalities have been used. A popular approach to generate the training data is through kinesthetic training where the teacher manually guides the robot through the desired motion [5, 14, 23, 40]. The work of [38] incorporates the use of a laser range finder to learn assembly tasks.

Data gloves have been used for both learning of assembly tasks [16] and human grasping strategies [19]. Magnetic sensors in different configurations have been used both for generating arm [10] and hand [4, 24, 25] trajectories.

Finally, there are examples of different vision based approaches. A common approach is to use motion capture systems [39, 54, 57] that require special equipment and markers on the humans to be tracked. The most user-friendly approach is to develop techniques for generating the training data from humans based solely on observation from video camera without any fiducial markers. A detailed discussion of related methods can be found in Part II of this book in a number of different chapters.

There have also been systems that perform one part of the training using various simulated environments [1, 18]. Recent work presented in [91] uses a simulator to generate training data for symbolic task learning. Finally, approaches that integrate several sensory modalities such as visual and verbal cues have been presented in [74].

17.3 Dimensionality Reduction

An important problem to solve when learning action primitives is the curse of dimensionality. The representation of full body motion such as walking, dancing or running requires a kinematic model with high DoF (typically 15–20), with higher order models required for better accuracy [55]. When the actions to be learned also include interaction with the environment, additional data may need to be included in the action primitive representation, including Cartesian data about the body location, and the location of pertinent objects in the environment, such as the object to be lifted, the location of obstacles, etc. However, not all the data may be important for each action primitive (for example, leg data may not be important for reaching), and it may also be possible that, while the observed data may be high-dimensional, there may be a latent variable actuating the motion which is of lower dimensionality. For example, in a cyclic motion such as walking, the movement of the joints is synchronized and not independent, and could be described with a lower dimensionality latent variable.

Dimensionality reduction techniques can be classified either by the type of algorithm used to find the reduced dimensionality subspace, or based on the processing stage at which the reduction takes place. One approach is to apply dimensionality reduction at the input stage, i.e., attempt to either remove spurious input variables, or find input variable features which reduce the dimensionality of the input vector [5, 43]. A second approach is to introduce dimensionality reduction during model learning for each action primitive. This technique is commonly used with locally weighted projection regression (LWPR) learning [101]. A final approach is to search for a low dimensional relationship describing the space of models [95].

The basic idea of the dimensionality reduction techniques is to model the relationship between some low dimensional representation $\mathbf{X} = \{\mathbf{x}_1, \ldots, \mathbf{x}_N\}$ with $\mathbf{x}_i \in \Re^D$ and observations $\mathbf{Y}$ through a mapping f.

$$\mathbf{y}_i = f(\mathbf{x}_i). \tag{17.6}$$

We can generalize roughly the methods for dimensionality reduction to *spectral* and *generative* methods.

17.3.1 Spectral Dimensionality Reduction

The most known spectral methods for linear dimensionality reduction are PCA [45] and metric multidimensional scaling (MDS) [15]. Metric MDS computes the low dimensional representation of a high-dimensional data set based on preserving the inner products between the input data. PCA on the other hand preserves its covariance structure up to a rotation.

More specifically, the goal of MDS is to find a geometrical configuration of data points which respects a specific proximity relationship, [15]. The proximity relationship is represented using the square matrix $\mathbf{D}$ with elements d_{ij} representing the pairwise distances between entity i and j. The objective in MDS is to find a set of points $\mathbf{X}$ which under the Euclidean distance metric approximates the proximity measure defined by $\mathbf{D}$ leading to the following objective:

$$\text{argmin}_{\mathbf{X}} = \sum_i^N \sum_j^N d_{ij} - \|\mathbf{x}_i - \mathbf{x}_j\|_{\text{L2}}, \tag{17.7}$$

which can be solved in closed form as an eigenvalue-problem.

Possibly the most well-known algorithm for dimensionality reduction is PCA [45]. The objective in PCA is to find a rotation of the current axes such that each consecutive basis-vector maximizes the variance of the data. This is done by diagonalizing the co-variance matrix $\mathbf{C} = \mathbf{Y}^T\mathbf{Y}$ and projecting the data on the dimensions representing the dominant portion of the variance in the data. PCA is an instance of MDS and leads to the same solution (up to scale) when using Euclidean distance as the proximity relation when constructing $\mathbf{D}$.

Even though PCA has been successfully applied in many scenarios it is built on the assumption that the intrinsic representation is simply a linear subspace of the original data. Since this is commonly not the case, it has lead to a large body of work in extending MDS to be able to handle non-linear embeddings.

In Isomap [96] the proximity matrix is computed by finding the shortest path through the proximity graph whereas in Maximum Variance Unfolding (MVU) [102] the minimum proximity allowed without violating the proximity graph are used. Further algorithms such as Locally Linear Embeddings (LLE) [84] and Laplacian Eigenmaps [2] are also based on proximity graphs aiming to extend a truncated distance measure to a global one.

Methods based on MDS are attractive as they are associated with convex objectives. However, PCA assumes a linear subspace and the non-linear extensions suffer significantly when there is noise in the data, as the local distance measure is very sensitive. Further, even though assumed to exist, none of the algorithms does model the inverse to the generative mapping. This means that having found the intrinsic representation of the data, mapping previously unseen points onto this representation is non-trivial.

17.3.2 Generative Dimensionality Reduction

Here, it is assumed that the observed data $\mathbf{Y}$ have been generated from $\mathbf{X}$, often referred to as the *latent* representation of the data, through a mapping parameterized by $\mathbf{W}$. The models are often referred to as *latent variable models for dimensionality reduction*. By assuming the observed data $\mathbf{Y}$ to be independent and identically distributed and corrupted by Gaussian noise leads to the likelihood of the data,

$$p\left(\mathbf{Y}|\mathbf{X}, \mathbf{W}, \beta^{-1}\right) = \prod_{i=1}^N \mathcal{N}\left(\mathbf{y}_i | f(\mathbf{x}_i, \mathbf{W}), \beta^{-1}\right), \tag{17.8}$$

where β^{-1} is the noise variance.

In the Bayesian formalism both the parameters of the mapping **W** and the latent location **X** are nuisance variables. Seeking the manifold representation of the observed data we want to formulate the posterior distribution over the parameters given the data, $p(\mathbf{X}, \mathbf{W}|\mathbf{Y})$. This means inverting the generative mapping through Bayes' Theorem which implies marginalization over both the latent locations **X** and the mapping **W**. Reaching the posterior means we need to formulate prior distributions over **X** and **W**. However, this is severely ill-posed as there is an infinite number of combinations of latent locations and mappings that could have generated the data. To proceed assumptions about the relationship need to be made.

In Probabilistic PCA (PPCA) [97] the generative mapping is assumed to be linear which together with placing a spherical Gaussian prior over **X** means that the parameters of the mapping **W** can be found through maximum likelihood.

In order to cope with problems related to applying mixture models in high-dimensional spaces, GPLVM [61] was suggested. Rather than marginalizing over the latent locations and finding the maximum likelihood solution of the mapping the GPLVM takes the opposite approach. A prior over the mapping f is specified through the use of GP. One advantage of the GPLVM is that it is straight forward to specify additional prior distributions over the latent locations. Examples of employing GPLVM in robotics applications have been presented in [7].

17.3.3 Approaches Specific to Action Primitives

When using dynamic movement primitives, dimensionality reduction can be incorporated into the training process by using Partial Least Squares during the regression [101]. In this approach, orthogonal projections of the input data are recursively computed, and single variable regression is performed along these projections on the residuals of the previous iteration step. If the number of degrees of freedom of the data is significantly lower than the input space, fewer projections will be needed to get accurate fitting. The method also automatically excludes irrelevant input dimensions. This approach takes advantage of the fact that the models used are local, and on the assumption that movement data are locally low dimensional, so that local models can be significantly lower dimensioned than the full state space.

Jenkins and Matarić [44] describe an algorithm for dimensionality reduction for spatio-temporal data, based on the Isomap algorithm [96]. In the extended algorithm, neighborhoods are defined both spatially and temporally, and then distances between temporally adjacent points are reduced prior to generating the global distance matrix. Two versions of the algorithm are presented, one when the data are continuous, and one when the data have been pre-segmented. The algorithm is applied to robot and human motion data, and is able to extract lower-dimensional manifolds capturing looping behavior (for example, multiple executions of the same motion) much better than PCA or the original Isomap algorithm.

17.4 Segmentation

Many of the algorithms proposed for learning action primitives through observation consider the case where the number of actions to be learned are specified by the designer, the demonstrated actions are observed and segmented a priori, and the learning is a one shot, off-line process. In this case, there is no need to autonomously segment or cluster the motion data, as this task is performed off-line by the designer. However, during natural human movement, action primitives appear as combinations and sequences, and are observed by the learning system as a single continuous stream of time-series data. In order to perform on-line learning from continuous observation, the action primitives must be identified in the continuous stream of observation, this is the problem of *autonomous segmentation*. Existing data segmentation algorithms can be divided into two broad categories: algorithms which take advantage of known motion primitives to perform the segmentation, and unsupervised algorithms which require no a priori knowledge of the motions.

17.4.1 Movement Primitives Known a priori

The first class of segmentation algorithms perform segmentation, given a known set of motion primitives. In other words, given an alphabet of motion primitives P, for any observation $O = a_1 a_2 a_3 \cdots a_T$ that consists of the movement primitives a_i, our goal is to recover these primitives and their precise order.

The recovery of the motion primitives is a non-trivial problem. HMMs have been used commonly to segment and label sequences. Applications can be found in biology where HMMs have been used on biological sequences [22] or in computational linguistics where HMMs are applied to a variety of problems including text and speech processing, detection of phonemes, etc. [65, 79]. Let $\mathbf{X}_t$ be the random variable over the observation sequences and $\mathbf{Y}_t$ be the random variable over the sequences of possible movement primitives (or labels), then an HMM is able to provide us with a joint distribution $p(\mathbf{X}_t, \mathbf{Y}_t)$. However, when using HMMs for modeling p, one important assumption is that the $\mathbf{Y}_t$ are all pairwise independent, as we had pointed out already earlier in Sect. 17.2.1.2. This is because an HMM is not able to model long-range statistical dependencies between the primitives. In order to model statistical dependencies, stochastic context-free grammars are often used [22].

As an alternative to generative models, discriminative models such as CRFs [60] can be used. Like HMMs, CRFs are finite state models, however contrary to HMMs, CRFs generalize to analogs of stochastic CFG [60] and are able to assign a well-defined probability distribution over possible labelings of the entire sequence of labels, given the entire observation sequence. To be precise, CRFs are undirected graphical models over the observed variables $\mathbf{X}_t$ and the state variables $\mathbf{Y}_t$ and the graph $\mathcal{G}$ modeling the distribution of $\mathbf{Y}_t$ given the observations $\mathbf{X}_t$. The graph $\mathcal{G}$ is unconstrained as long as it represents the conditional independencies in the label sequences being modeled. The likelihood of a sequence $\mathbf{y}_t$ of motion primitives, given an observation $\mathbf{x}_t$, is given as

$$P(\mathbf{y}_t | \mathbf{x}_t, \boldsymbol{\theta}) = \frac{1}{Z} \prod_{c \in C} \Theta(\mathbf{y}_t, \mathbf{x}_t; \boldsymbol{\theta}), \qquad (17.9)$$

where C is the set of cliques in $\mathscr{G}$ and Θ a potential function over the set of cliques given as

$$\Theta(\mathbf{y}_t, \mathbf{x}_t; \boldsymbol{\theta}) = \exp\left(\sum_k \theta_{c,k} f_k(\mathbf{y}_c, \mathbf{x}_c)\right). \qquad (17.10)$$

Here, $\{f_k\}$ are called *feature functions*. The parameter Z is a normalizing factor. During training, the parameters $\boldsymbol{\theta}$ are found, and belief propagation is used to compute (17.9). A CRF computes the most probable label for each time step which provides us with the required segmentation.

17.4.2 Assumption About Segment Point Indicators

A second class of algorithms attempts to isolate action primitives and identify segmentation points without any a priori knowledge about the action primitives being observed. In this case, some assumption must be made about the underlying structure of the data at a segmentation point. For example, several algorithms have been developed for segmenting motions based on the velocity properties of the observation vector [27, 62, 78]. In Pomplun and Matarić [78], a segment is recognized when the root mean square (RMS) value of the joint velocities falls below a certain threshold. In this case, the assumption is that there will be a pause in the motion between motion primitives. While this assumption allows for easy identification of segment points, it is fairly restrictive and not representative of natural, fluid human motion. In Fod et al. [27], it is assumed that there is a change in the direction of movement accompanying a change between motion primitives. Therefore, a segmentation point is recognized when a Zero Velocity Crossing (ZVC) is detected in the joint angle data, in a sufficient number of dimensions. Lieberman and Breazeal [62] improve upon this approach by automating the threshold selection and adding heuristic rules for creating segments when there is contact with the environment. This approach works well when the number of DoF of the observation vector is fairly small, but it becomes more difficult to tune the algorithm as the number of joints increases. For example, it becomes more difficult to select a single threshold for the RMS value of the joint velocities which will accurately differentiate between segments at rest and segments in motion when the dimension space is large and different types of motions (arm vs. full body motions) are considered.

Koenig and Matarić [49] develop a segmentation algorithm based on the variance of the feature data. The algorithm searches for a set of segment points which minimize a cost function of the data variance. In a related approach, Kohlmorgen and Lemm [50] describe a system for automatic on-line segmentation of time-series data, based on the assumption that data from the same motion primitive will belong to the same underlying distribution. The incoming data are described as a series of probability density functions, which are formulated as the states of a HMM, and a minimum cost path is found among the states using an accelerated version of the Viterbi algorithm. This algorithm has been successfully applied to human motion capture data with high DoF [42, 55]. In [53] Bayes propagation over time in combination with a particle filtering approach is used for on-line segmentation of the time-series data. Here, the primitives are also modeled as HMMs, but the approach estimates the MAP of each primitive, given the data, directly [53]. It is also possible to improve the segmentation result by including information about any known motion primitives [58] of by including knowledge about an object on which the action is applied [54].

17.5 Connections to Learning at Higher Levels of Abstraction

The use of action primitives is closely connected to the use of higher-level models such as grammars that govern how these primitives are interlinked with each other. Furthermore, primitives are often meant to cause a very specific effect on the environment, such as *remove an object*, *push an object* or *insert object A into object B*. To formalize the possible effect on the environment, grammatical production rules for action primitives, objects, object states and object affordances are often used [17, 26]. Affordances were first introduced by J.J. Gibson [28] and refer to action possibilities that an object or an environment offers to the acting agent. E.g., a door can be {*open* or *closed*}, and the affordance is {*close door*, *open door*}. The observation that objects and actions are intertwined is not new to robotics researchers [21, 26, 30, 51, 64, 69, 90].

Objects and production rules can be specified a priori by an expert and the scene state is often considered to be independent from the presence of the agent itself. For surveillance applications, simple predefined grammars are used to describe actions such as "leaving a bag" or "taking a bag". However, for robotics, it must also be taken into account that a robot might physically not be able to execute a particular action because it might be, e.g., in a wrong location or it might be too weak. The research on *motion planning* takes this into account, while in most cases it is assumed that the environment does not change while the agent performs the planning movements. However, unless the programmer has a precise model of the physical robot body as well as for the scene objects, the affordances need to be learned by the robot itself through exploration. In order to learn how valid and appropriate an action is, the robot eventually needs to try to execute them [21, 26, 30, 90]. This could be interpreted as "playing" or "discovering". Similarly to humans, the learning process can in some cases be biased through imitation learning. In [26] a robot learns affordances of objects on a table by poking, pulling and pushing them. In [21, 85] the authors formalize the relationship between action, affordances and effect,

$$\big(\textit{effect}\,(\textit{state}, \textit{action})\big), \tag{17.11}$$

that describes a certain *effect* if an *action* is applied on a scene while being in a certain *state*. In robotics, a developmental approach [68] can be used, by first letting the robot apply a predefined set of actions randomly on its environment and record what effects each action has on the environment. In [21] this is called a *relation instance*. Here, *state* is the scene state as perceived by the robot before the action, and *effect* marks the changes of the environment due to the action, again, as perceived by the robot. After quantizing the principally continuous set of effects into a small set of discrete *effect-id*s, a SVM or similar can be used to model and predict the effects vs. scene state and action relationships in (17.11). This way, one becomes able to generate and recognize goal-directed actions and behaviors, where a goal is defined to be a desired or final effect in a given scene state. To perform scene understanding in a surveillance scenario the systematic application of the relationships in (17.11) can be used to predict the possible outcomes of the actions observed thus far, and for goal-directed robot control one has to generate the desired effect by a systematic application of its available set of actions given the relationships in (17.11).

17.6 Conclusions and Open Questions

Learning action primitives from observation of human motion is an active research area with many potential applications, including activity and behavior recognition, robot learning, and sports training and rehabilitation. Two dominant approaches have emerged for representing action primitives: stochastic models and dynamical systems models. Other active research areas include dimensionality reduction, extracting action primitives from continuous time-series data via segmentation, and incorporating action primitives into higher order models of behavior. While significant advances have been made, many open questions remain before a fully autonomous action primitive learning system can be realized. Many of the current systems are semi-autonomous, where data are collected off-line, manually sorted and pre-processed and algorithm parameters selected and tuned by the designers. In these systems, typically the number and type of action primitive to be learned must be specified a priori, limiting the generality and re-useability of such systems. A second issue is the choice of representation for the input data, such as the choice of joint angle or Cartesian representation of the motion, or the choice of representation frame when describing object motion. In current systems, this choice is typically made by the designer, which is simple when the action is straightforward and known a priori, but becomes more difficult when the action incorporates both self-motion and interaction with the environment. A third open research goal is a fully autonomous segmentation system capable of segmenting full body motion composed of arbitrary action primitives, where there may be a significant overlap among the primitives. Tied to this goal is the fundamental question of primitive ambiguity and how a primitive is defined: should this be done by the autonomous system, or by the human demonstrator. Another open issue when applying learned action primitives to movement generation by a robot is how the primitive should be adapted to the robot's own morphology and sensorimotor loop (i.e., combining learning from observation and practice).

References

1. Aleotti, J., Caselli, S., Reggiani, M.: Leveraging on a virtual environment for robot programming by demonstration. Robot. Auton. Syst. **47**(2–3), 153–161 (2004) [341]
2. Belkin, M., Niyogi, P.: Laplacian eigenmaps and spectral techniques for embedding and clustering. Adv. Neural Inf. Process. Syst. **14**, 585–591 (2002) [343]
3. Bennewitz, M., Burgard, W., Cielniak, G., Thrun, S.: Learning motion patterns of people for compliant robot motion. Int. J. Robot. Res. **24**(1), 31–48 (2005) [336]
4. Bernardin, K., Ogawara, K., Ikeuchi, K., Dillmann, R.: A sensor fusion approach for recognizing continuous human grasping sequences using hidden Markov models. IEEE Trans. Robot. **21**(1), 47–57 (2005) [336,341]
5. Billard, A., Calinon, S., Guenter, F.: Discriminative and adaptive imitation in uni-manual and bi-manual tasks. Robot. Auton. Syst. **54**, 370–384 (2006) [338,341,342]
6. Billard, A., Calinon, S., Dillmann, R., Schaal, S.: Robot programming by demonstration. In: Siciliano, B., Khatib, O. (eds.) Handbook of Robotics, pp. 1371–1394. Springer, Berlin (2008) [336]
7. Bitzer, S., Vijayakumar, S.: Latent spaces for dynamic movement primitives. In: IEEE Int. Conf. on Humanoid Robots, pp. 574–581 (2009) [344]
8. Breazeal, C., Scassellati, B.: Robots that imitate humans. Trends Cogn. Sci. **6**(11), 481–487 (2002) [335]
9. Byrne, R.W., Russon, A.E.: Learning by imitation: A hierarchical approach. Behav. Brain Sci. **21**, 667–721 (1998) [334]
10. Calinon, S., Billard, A.: Active teaching in robot programming by demonstration. In: IEEE Int. Conf. on Robot and Human Interactive Communication, pp. 702–707 (2007) [341]
11. Calinon, S., Billard, A.: Incremental learning of gestures by imitation in a humanoid robot. In: ACM/IEEE Int. Conf. on Human–Robot Interaction, pp. 255–262 (2007) [338]
12. Calinon, S., Billard, A.: Learning of gestures by imitation in a humanoid robot. In: Nehaniv, C.L., Dautenhahn, K. (eds.) Imitation and Social Learning in Robots, Humans and Animals, pp. 153–177. Cambridge University Press, Cambridge (2007) [335]
13. Calinon, S., D'halluin, F., Sauser, E.L., Caldwell, D.G., Billard, A.G.: Learning and reproduction of gestures by imitation. IEEE Robot. Autom. Mag. **17**(2), 44–54 (2010) [338]
14. Calinon, S., Guenter, F., Billard, A.: On learning, representing and generalizing a task in a humanoid robot. IEEE Trans. Syst. Man Cybern., Part B, Cybern. **37**(2), 286–298 (2007) [337,341]
15. Cox, T.F., Cox, M.A.A.: Multidimensional Scaling. Chapman & Hall, London (2001) [342]
16. Tung, C.P., Kak, A.C.: Automatic learning of assembly task using DataGlove system. In: IEEE Int. Conf. on Intelligent Robots and Systems, vol. 1, pp. 1–8 (1995) [341]
17. Demiris, Y., Johnson, M.: Distributed, predictive perception of actions: A biologically inspired robotics architecture for imitation and learning. Connect. Sci. **15**(4), 231–243 (2003) [347]
18. Dillmann, R.: Teaching and learning of robot tasks via observation of human performance. Robot. Auton. Syst. **47**, 109–116 (2004) [336,341]
19. Dillmann, R., Rogalla, O., Ehrenmann, M., Zollner, R., Bordegoni, M.: Learning robot behaviour and skills based on human demonstration and advice: The machine learning paradigm. In: Int. Symp. on Robotics Research, pp. 229–238 (1999) [336,341]
20. Dixon, K.R., Dolan, J.M., Khosla, P.K.: Predictive robot programming: Theoretical and experimental analysis. Int. J. Robot. Res. **23**(9), 955–973 (2004) [338]
21. Dogar, M.R., Cakmak, M., Ugur, E., Sahin, E.: From primitive behaviors to goal-directed behavior using affordances. In: IEEE Int. Conf. on Intelligent Robots and Systems, pp. 729–734 (2007) [347,348]
22. Durbin, R., Eddy, S., Krogh, A., Mitchison, G.: Biological sequence analysis: Probabilistic models of proteins and nucleic acids. Cambridge University Press, Cambridge (1998) [339, 345]

23. Ekvall, S., Aarno, D., Kragic, D.: Online task recognition and real-time adaptive assistance for computer-aided machine control. IEEE Trans. Robot. **22**(5), 1029–1033 (2006) [338, 341]
24. Ekvall, S., Kragic, D.: Interactive grasp learning based on human demonstration. In: IEEE Int. Conf. on Robotics and Automation, vol. 4, pp. 3519–3524 (2004) [341]
25. Ekvall, S., Kragic, D.: Grasp recognition for programming by demonstration tasks. In: IEEE Int. Conf. on Robotics and Automation, pp. 748–753 (2005) [341]
26. Fitzpatrick, P., Metta, G., Natale, L., Rao, S., Sandini, G.: Learning about objects through action - initial steps towards artificial cognition. In: IEEE Int. Conf. on Robotics and Automation, vol. 3, pp. 3140–3145 (2003) [347]
27. Fod, A., Matarić, M.J., Jenkins, O.C.: Automated derivation of primitives for movement classification. Auton. Robots **12**(1), 39–54 (2002) [346]
28. Gibson, J.J.: The theory of affordances. In: Shaw, R., Bransford, J. (eds.) Perceiving, Acting and Knowing: Toward an Ecological Psychology, pp. 67–82. Lawrence Erlbaum Associates Publishers, New York (1977) [347]
29. Gribovskaya, E., Khansari-Zadeh, S.M., Billard, A.: Learning non-linear multivariate dynamics of motion in robotic manipulators. Int. J. Robot. Res. (2010, in press) [337,341]
30. Griffith, S., Sinapov, J., Miller, M., Stoytchev, A.: Toward interactive learning of object categories by a robot: A case study with container and non-container objects. In: IEEE Int. Conf. on Development and Learning, pp. 1–6 (2009) [347]
31. Guenter, F., Billard, A.G.: Using reinforcement learning to adapt an imitation task. In: IEEE Int. Conf. on Intelligent Robots and Systems, pp. 1022–1027 (2007) [341]
32. Han, L., Wu, X., Liang, W., Hou, G., Jia, Y.: Discriminative human action recognition in the learned hierarchical manifold space. Image Vis. Comput. **28**, 836–849 (2010) [338]
33. Heyes, C.: Causes and consequences of imitation. Trends Cogn. Sci. **5**(6), 253–261 (2001) [334]
34. Heyes, C., Ray, E.: What is the significance of imitation in animals? Adv. Study Behav. **29**, 215–245 (2000) [334]
35. Ho, M.A.T., Yamada, Y., Umetani, Y.: An adaptive visual attentive tracker for human communicational behaviors using HMM-based TD learning with new state distinction capability. IEEE Trans. Robot. **21**(3), 497–504 (2005) [336]
36. Iba, S., Paredis, C.J.J., Khosla, P.K.: Interactive multi-modal robot programming. Int. J. Robot. Res. **24**(1), 83–104 (2005) [336]
37. Ijspeert, A.J., Nakanishi, J., Schaal, S.: Movement imitation with nonlinear dynamical systems in humanoid robots. In: IEEE Int. Conf. on Robotics and Automation, pp. 1398–1403 (2002) [339,340]
38. Ikeuchi, K., Suchiro, T.: Towards an assembly plan from observation, part i: Assembly task recognition using face-contact relations (polyhedral objects). In: IEEE Int. Conf. on Robotics and Automation, vol. 3, pp. 2171–2177 (1992) [341]
39. Inamura, T., Toshima, I., Tanie, H., Nakamura, Y.: Embodied symbol emergence based on mimesis theory. Int. J. Robot. Res. **23**(4–5), 363–377 (2004) [335,337,341]
40. Ito, M., Tani, J.: On-line imitative interaction with a humanoid robot using a dynamic neural network model of a mirror system. Adapt. Behav. **12**(2), 93–115 (2004) [340,341]
41. Jacob, R., Richards, C., Hannaford, B., Sinanan, M.N.: Hidden Markov models of minimally invasive surgery. Stud. Health Technol. Inform. **70**, 279–285 (2000) [336]
42. Janus, B., Nakamura, Y.: Unsupervised probabilistic segmentation of motion data for mimesis modeling. In: IEEE Int. Conf. on Advanced Robotics, pp. 411–417 (2005) [347]
43. Jenkins, O.C., Matarić, M.: Performance-derived behavior vocabularies: Data-driven acquisition of skills from motion. Int. J. Humanoid Robot. **1**(2), 237–288 (2004) [342]
44. Jenkins, O.C., Matarić, M.: A spatio-temporal extension to isomap nonlinear dimension reduction. In: Int. Conf. on Machine Learning, pp. 441–448 (2004) [344]
45. Jolliffe, I.T.: Principal Component Analysis. Springer, New York (2002) [342,343]
46. Kang, S.B., Ikeuchi, K.: Toward automatic robot instruction from perception – temporal segmentation of tasks from human hand motion. IEEE Trans. Robot. Autom. **11**, 432–443 (1993) [336]

47. Kjellstrom, H., Romero, J., Kragic, D.: Visual object-action recognition: Inferring object affordances from human demonstration. Comput. Vis. Image Underst. **115**, 81–90 (2011) [339]
48. Kober, J., Mohler, B., Peters, J.: Learning perceptual coupling for motor primitives. In: IEEE Int. Conf. on Intelligent Robots and Systems (2008) [340]
49. Koenig, N., Matarić, M.J.: Behavior-based segmentation of demonstrated tasks. In: Int. Conf. on Development and Learning (2006) [346]
50. Kohlmorgen, J., Lemm, S.: A dynamic HMM for on-line segmentation of sequential data. In: Neural Information Processing Systems, pp. 793–800 (2001) [347]
51. Kozima, H., Nakagawa, C., Yano, H.: Emergence of imitation mediated by objects. In: Int. Workshop on Epigenetic Robotics, pp. 59–61 (2002) [347]
52. Kragic, D., Marayong, P., Li, M., Okamura, A.M., Hager, G.D.: Human–machine collaborative systems for microsurgical applications. Int. J. Robot. Res. **24**(9), 731–742 (2005) [336]
53. Krueger, V., Grest, D.: Using hidden Markov models for recognizing action primitives in complex actions. In: Scandinavian Conf. on Image Analysis, pp. 203–212 (2007) [347]
54. Krüger, V., Herzog, D., Baby, S., Ude, A., Kragic, D.: Learning actions from observations. IEEE Robot. Autom. Mag. **17**(2), 30–43 (2010). [338,341,347]
55. Kulić, D., Nakamura, Y.: On-line segmentation of whole body human motion data for large kinematic models. In: IEEE Int. Conf. on Intelligent Robots and Systems, pp. 4300–4305 (2009) [342,347]
56. Kulić, D., Takano, W., Nakamura, Y.: Incremental on-line hierarchical clustering of whole body motion patterns. In: IEEE Int. Symp. on Robot and Human Interactive Communication, pp. 1016–1021 (2007) [338]
57. Kulić, D., Takano, W., Nakamura, Y.: Incremental learning, clustering and hierarchy formation of whole body motion patterns using adaptive hidden Markov chains. Int. J. Robot. Res. **27**(7), 761–784 (2008) [337,338,341]
58. Kulić, D., Takano, W., Nakamura, Y.: On-line segmentation and clustering from continuous observation of whole body motions. IEEE Trans. Robot. **25**(5), 1158–1166 (2009) [338]
59. Kuniyoshi, Y., Inaba, M., Inoue, H.: Teaching by showing: Generating robot programs by visual observation of human performance. In: Int. Symp. on Industrial Robots, pp. 119–126 (1989) [336]
60. Lafferty, J., McCallum, A., Pereira, F.: Conditional random fields: Probabilistic models for segmenting and labeling sequence data. In: Int. Conf. on Machine Learning, pp. 282–289 (2001) [339,345]
61. Lawrence, N.D.: Probabilistic non-linear principal component analysis with Gaussian process latent variable models. J. Mach. Learn. Res. **6**, 1783–1816 (2005) [344]
62. Lieberman, J., Breazeal, C.: Improvements on action parsing and action interpolation for learning through demonstration. In: IEEE Int. Conf. on Humanoid Robots, pp. 342–365 (2004) [346]
63. Loesch, M., Schmidt-Rohr, S., Knoop, S., Vacek, S., Dillmann, R.: Feature set selection and optimal classifier for human activity recognition. In: IEEE Int. Conf. on Robot and Human Interactive Communication, pp. 1022–1027 (2007) [339]
64. Lopes, M.C., Victor, J.S.: Visual learning by imitation with motor representations. IEEE Trans. Syst. Man Cybern., Part B, Cybern. **35**(3), 438–449 (2005) [347]
65. Manning, C., Schuetze, H.: Foundations of Statistical Natural Language Processing. MIT Press, Cambridge (1999) [345]
66. Meltzoff, A.N.: Imitation as a mechanism of social cognition: Origins of empathy, theory of mind, and the representation of action. In: Goswami, U. (ed.) Blackwell Handbook of Childhood Cognitive Development, pp. 6–25. Blackwell Sci., Oxford (2002) [334]
67. Meltzoff, A.N.: Imitation and other minds: The 'like me' hypothesis. In: Hurley, S., Chater, N. (eds.) Perspectives on Imitation: From Neuroscience to Social Science, vol. 2, pp. 55–77. MIT Press, Cambridge (2005) [334]
68. Metta, G., Sandini, G., Natale, L., Manzotti, R., Panerai, F.: Development in artificial systems. In: EDEC Symp. at the Int. Conf. on Cognitive Science, Beijing, China (2001) [348]

69. Montesano, L., Lopes, M., Bernardino, A., Santos-Victor, J.: Learning object affordances: From sensory motor coordination to imitation. IEEE Trans. Robot. **24**(1), 15–26 (2008) [347]
70. Mussa-Ivaldi, F.A., Bizzi, E.: Motor learning through the combination of primitives. Philos. Trans. R. Soc. Lond. B, Biol. Sci. **355**, 1755–1769 (2000) [334]
71. Nakanishi, J., Morimoto, J., Endo, G., Cheng, G., Schaal, S., Kawato, M.: Learning from demonstration and adaptation of biped locomotion. Robot. Auton. Syst. **47**, 79–91 (2004) [339,340]
72. Ogata, T., Sugano, S., Tani, J.: Open-end human–robot interaction from the dynamical systems perspective: mutual adaptation and incremental learning. Adv. Robot. **19**, 651–670 (2005) [340]
73. Okada, M., Tatani, K., Nakamura, Y.: Polynomial design of the nonlinear dynamics for the brain-like information processing of whole body motion. In: IEEE Int. Conf. on Robotics and Automation, pp. 1410–1415 (2002) [335]
74. Paradowitz, M., Zoellner, R., Knoop, S., Dillmann, R.: Incremental learning of tasks from user demonstrations, pas experiences and vocal comments. IEEE Trans. Syst. Man Cybern., Part B, Cybern. **37**(2), 322–332 (2007) [341]
75. Pastor, P., Hoffmann, H., Asfour, T., Schaal, S.: Learning and generalization of motor skills by learning from demonstration. In: IEEE Int. Conf. on Robotics and Automation, pp. 763–768 (2009) [340]
76. Peters, J., Schaal, S.: Applying the episodic natural actor-critic architecture to motor primitive learning. In: European Symposium on Artificial Neural Networks (2007) [340]
77. Peters, J., Schaal, S.: Reinforcement learning for operational space control. In: IEEE Int. Conf. on Robotics and Automation, pp. 2111–2116 (2007) [340]
78. Pomplun, M., Matarić, M.J.: Evaluation metrics and results of human arm movement imitation. In: IEEE Int. Conf. on Humanoid Robotics (2000) [346]
79. Rabiner, L.R.: A tutorial on hidden Markov models and selected applications in speech recognition. Proc. IEEE **77**(2), 257–286 (1989) [336,337,345]
80. Redner, R.A., Walker, H.F.: Mixture densities, maximum likelihood and the em algorithm. SIAM Rev. **26**(2), 195–239 (1984) [336,337]
81. Reiley, C.E., Plaku, E., Hager, G.D.: Motion generation of robotic surgical tasks: Learning from expert demonstrations. In: Int. Conf. of the IEEE Engineering in Medicine and Biology Society (2010) [336]
82. Rizzolatti, G., Craighero, L.: The mirror-neuron system. Annu. Rev. Neurosci. **27**, 169–192 (2004) [334]
83. Rizzolatti, G., Fogassi, L., Gallese, V.: Neurophysical mechanisms underlying the understanding and imitation of action. Nat. Rev., Neurosci. **2**, 661–670 (2001) [334]
84. Roweis, S.T., Saul, L.K.: Nonlinear dimensionality reduction by locally linear embedding. Science **290**(5500), 2323–2326 (2000) [343]
85. Sahin, E., Cakmak, M., Dogar, M.R., Ugur, E., Uecoluk, G.: To afford or not to afford: A new formalization of affordances toward affordance-based robot control. Adapt. Behav. **15**(4), 447–472 (2007) [347]
86. Schaal, S.: Dynamic movement primitives – a framework for motor control in humans and humanoid robotics. In: Kimura, H., Tsuchiya, K., Ishiguro, A., Witte, H. (eds.) Adaptive Motion of Animals and Machines, pp. 261–280. Springer, Tokyo (2006) [339,340]
87. Schaal, S., Atkeson, C.G., Vijayakumar, S.: Scalable techniques from nonparametric statistics for real time robot learning. Appl. Intell. **17**, 49–60 (2002) [340]
88. Schaal, S., Ijspeert, A., Billard, A.: Computational approaches to motor learning by imitation. Philos. Trans. R. Soc. Lond. B, Biol. Sci. **358**, 537–547 (2003) [333,335]
89. Shi, Q., Wang, L., Cheng, L., Smola, A.: Human action segmentation and recognition using discriminative semi-Markov models. Int. J. Comput. Vis. 1–11 (2010) [339]
90. Sinapov, J., Stoytchev, A.: Detecting the functional similarities between tools using a hierarchical representation of outcomes. In: IEEE Int. Conf. on Development and Learning, pp. 91–96 (2008) [347]

91. Song, D., Huebner, K., Kyrki, V., Kragic, D.: Learning task constraints for robot grasping using graphical models. In: IEEE Int. Conf. on Intelligent Robots and Systems, pp. 1579–1585 (2010) [341]
92. Startner, T., Pentland, A.: Visual recognition of American sign language using hidden Markov models. In: Int. Conf. on Automatic Face and Gesture Recognition, pp. 189–194 (1995) [336]
93. Sugiura, K., Iwahashi, N.: Learning object-manipulation verbs for human–robot communication. In: Workshop on Multi-Modal Interfaces in Semantic Interaction, pp. 32–38 (2007) [337]
94. Sugiura, K., Iwahashi, N.: Motion recognition and generation by combining reference-point-dependent probabilistic models. In: IEEE Int. Conf. on Intelligent Robots and Systems, pp. 852–857 (2008) [337]
95. Takano, W., Yamane, K., Sugihara, T., Yamamoto, K., Nakamura, Y.: Primitive communication based on motion recognition and generation with hierarchical mimesis model. In: IEEE Int. Conf. on Robotics and Automation, pp. 3602–3608 (2006) [342]
96. Tenenbaum, J.B., de Silva, V., Langford, J.C.: A global geometric framework for nonlinear dimensionality reduction. Science **290**, 2319–2323 (2000) [343,344]
97. Tipping, M.E., Bishop, C.M.: Probabilistic principal component analysis. J. R. Stat. Soc., Ser. B, Stat. Methodol. **61**(3), 611–622 (1999) [344]
98. Ude, A., Atkeson, C.G., Riley, M.: Programming full-body movements for humanoid robots by observation. Robot. Auton. Syst. **47**(2–3), 93–108 (2004) [335]
99. Ude, A., Riley, M., Nemec, B., Kos, A., Asfour, T., Cheng, G.: Synthesizing goal-directed actions from a library of example movements. In: IEEE Int. Conf. on Humanoid Robots, pp. 115–121 (2007) [335]
100. Ude, A., Gams, A., Asfour, T., Morimoto, J.: Task-specific generalization of discrete and periodic dynamic movement primitives. IEEE Trans. Robot. **26**(5), 800–815 (2010) [341]
101. Vijayakumar, S., D'Souza, A., Schaal, S.: Incremental online learning in high dimensions. Neural Comput. **17**, 2602–2634 (2005) [340,342,344]
102. Weinberger, K.Q., Sha, F., Saul, L.K.: Learning a kernel matrix for nonlinear dimensionality reduction. In: Int. Conf. Machine Learning, pp. 106–111 (2004) [343]
103. Wilson, A.D., Bobick, A.F.: Parametric hidden Markov models for gesture recognition. IEEE Trans. Pattern Anal. Mach. Intell. **21**(9), 884–900 (1999) [338]
104. Wohlschlaeger, A., Gattis, M., Bekkering, H.: Action generation and action perception in imitation: An instance of the ideomotor principle. Philos. Trans. R. Soc. Lond. B, Biol. Sci. **358**, 501–515 (2003) [335]
105. Yang, J., Xu, Y., Chen, C.S.: Human action learning via hidden Markov model. IEEE Trans. Syst. Man Cybern., Part A, Syst. Hum. **27**(1), 34–44 (1997) [336]

Chapter 18
Contextual Action Recognition

Hedvig Kjellström (Sidenbladh)

Abstract The scope of this chapter is contextual information in analysis of human actions. We first discuss the definition of context in visual action recognition. Context in action recognition is here divided into four categories, *object context*, *scene context*, *semantic context*, and *photogrammetric context*. The value of all these types of context is twofold: First, *context improves action recognition*, provided that it offers information that is complementary to the human pose data on which the action recognition is based. Second, *context makes semi-supervised learning easier*, since it provides more views of the action, to some degree independent of the human pose view. A number of different methods for contextual action recognition are then reviewed, followed by a method-level description of a contextual object–action recognition method. We finally discuss future directions for the field of contextual action recognition.

18.1 Introduction

An overwhelming majority of human actions are interactive in the sense that they relate to the world around the human. During action, the human interacts both with other humans and with objects in the scene, moving them about and changing their states. The action in itself is also contextually grounded in—that is, partly defined by—the type of scene in which it takes place, and in other actions taking place at the same time, before or afterwards.

H. Kjellström (Sidenbladh) (✉)
CSC/CVAP, KTH, SE-100 44 Stockholm, Sweden
e-mail: hedvig@kth.se

T.B. Moeslund et al. (eds.), *Visual Analysis of Humans*,
DOI 10.1007/978-0-85729-997-0_18, © Springer-Verlag London Limited 2011

Example (Having breakfast)
The activity of having-breakfast is composed of several different actions at different time scales, some taking place concurrently, like making-coffee and pouring-water-into-coffee-pot, some taking place in sequence, like making-coffee and drinking-coffee.
Furthermore, having-breakfast involves interaction with the scene and objects in the scene. During a drinking-coffee action, the cup is in the human hand, being moved about; the position and velocity of the cup change. The filling state of the cup also changes from full to empty during the course of the action.
Last, the activity of having-breakfast is much more likely to take place in a kitchen than in, say, a public-library.
These are examples of semantic context, object context and scene context that can be used in visual recognition of the actions in the activity of having-breakfast.

In the example, as well as in the rest of the chapter, a single/atomic human action, like reaching, is, somewhat heuristically, denoted *action*, while a composite human action, like playing-soccer is denoted *activity*.

In earlier chapters of this volume, the concept of human action was introduced, and different alternatives for representing human action were described. This chapter will focus on how contextual information useful for human action recognition, and the contextual dependencies themselves, are represented.

Let us now formalize the concept of context in visual recognition.

18.1.1 What is Context?

Human perception is adapted to a contextual world, where objects and actions never appear in isolation; it has been shown [32] that contextual information greatly helps in human visual recognition tasks. Despite this, visual analyses of human action have historically rarely taken contextual information into account (see earlier chapters in this volume). The same phenomenon can be observed with visual analyses of objects [10]. Divvala et al. [10] argue that one reason might be the lack of a clear definition of context in visual recognition.

In, arguably, the first principled discussion about context in Computer Vision, Strat [37] organizes types of context into three groups:

- *Physical context* including all information about the world that is independent of the camera/sensor.
- *Photogrammetric context* including information about the camera/sensor and time and position of data acquisition.
- *Computational context* including information about the hardware used to process the images/sensor data.

The types of context given in our example above can all be regarded as physical, except information about the scene which also comprises time and place of data acquisition which is defined as photogrammetric context. Due to the rapid development in hardware capacity, computational context is nowadays not as relevant for activity recognition, other than in real-time applications with very limited computational power.

Divvala et al. [10] revisit the task of defining context in Computer Vision, particularly object detection in images. They organize object context into 10 groups:

- *Local pixel context* including image neighborhoods.
- *2D scene gist context* including global image statistics.
- *3D geometric context* including 3D scene layout, surfaces, and occlusions.
- *Semantic context* including event/activity depicted, object classes, scene category, and keywords.
- *Photogrammetric context* including internal camera parameters.
- *Illumination context* including lighting direction and shadow contrast.
- *Weather context* including information about wind speed, temperature, and season.
- *Geographic context* including GPS location, terrain type, and elevation.
- *Temporal context* including temporally nearby frames/images, videos of similar scenes, and time of capture.
- *Cultural context* including photographer and dataset bias, visual clichés.

Comparing with Strat's context categories, Divvala et al. have essentially removed the computational category and made a more fine-granular division of the physical and photogrammetric categories. The, now more specific, context classes are selected with detection of objects in images in mind.

While the data used in object detection are still images, action is most often recognized from temporal trajectories of human pose (in turn extracted from video). The cues relevant for action recognition essentially emanate from what Divvala et al. term 2D scene, 3D scene, semantic, and cultural context. We know of no example where photogrammetric context is used *directly* for action recognition, but one could imagine using such cues. Therefore, a category for photogrammetric context, similar to Strat's category with that name (i.e., corresponding to Divvala's local pixel, photogrammetric, illumination, weather, geographic and pixel-level temporal context) is also introduced. We suggest the following four groups of contextual cues for visual action recognition:

- *Object context* including the classes and states of objects interacting with the human during the course of the action. Object state here means position and velocity in the scene, as well as static and dynamic internal states such as color, weight, filling degree, articulation, etc.
- *Scene context* including scene category, topological scene layout, and metric scene properties, such as the presence and orientation of surfaces that the human can interact with in actions such as window cleaning or sitting.
- *Semantic context* including temporally proximal or concurrent actions, composite activities that the current action is part of, information from a speech modality,

and video captions or storylines. This category also includes expert and domain knowledge, often implemented as priors in the learning. Furthermore, it includes cultural context such as nationality of the human involved in the action; this is of relevance to the recognition of some actions, such as facial expressions.

- *Photogrammetric context* including information about the camera/sensor and time and position of data acquisition.

The first three categories correspond to the three types of context described in the example in the beginning of the chapter, and the fourth category correspond to a potentially interesting source of contextual information.

The scope of this chapter is contextual information in analysis of human actions. Nevertheless, there has recently been a significant interest in context for a number of recognition and estimation tasks. Examples are, to mention a few, scene context for motion estimation [1], scene context for human pose estimation [4, 24, 41], object context for human pose estimation [13, 17, 21, 35, 36, 40], action context for human pose estimation[19, 42], semantic context for object recognition [10, 14], and scene context for object recognition [39].

18.1.2 What Are the Advantages of Context?

What are then the advantages of using context in action recognition, apart from its biological motivation discussed above? There are two main advantages:

Context improves recognition   since more information—and information that can not be retrieved from the human pose data—is incorporated in the analysis.

> *Example* (Having breakfast)
> The action of pouring-coffee is highly defined by the coffee-pot, the coffee, the cup, and their respective state changes during the action. The human motion by itself is a much weaker cue to recognition; if the same forward-upward hand motion is observed with a tv-remote-control, it would signify a very different action.

Context makes semi-supervised learning easier   since additional views—largely independent of the human pose view—of the action state become available.

With view, we here mean a measurement of the action state. The measurement might be features retrieved from a video sequence of the action, such as hand or body pose, or the classes of objects visible in the images. Alternatively, it may be a storyline or a caption describing the action in words. It can also be the time of day, or the type of scene in which the action takes place.

With semi-supervised learning, we mean that the training data are not fully labeled—either in that some examples are not labeled, or in that examples are only partly labeled, e.g., with a high-level activity label but not with each individual action in the activity denoted.

It is possible to train a single view (non-contextual) classifier with partly labeled data using a generative approach, such as Expectation-Maximization (EM) [8]. However, multiple views have been shown [2] to greatly improve the learning, provided they give complementary information about the model state.

Multiple views also make it possible to train the classifier with partly labeled data using a discriminative learning approach, such as Co-Training [3].

18.2 Context in Human Action Recognition

We now review methods for contextual action recognition, found in the literature. Figure 18.1 provides an overview of recent efforts, organized according to the type of context employed in the recognition. No methods for including photogrammetric context are yet found in the literature, but this is a potentially interesting source of contextual information. An avenue of research in the future is thus to investigate how photogrammetric contextual information can be employed to enhance human action recognition.

The publications listed in Fig. 18.1 are discussed below, grouped in the same manner as in Fig. 18.1.

18.2.1 Object Context in Human Action Recognition

In early work, Mann and Jepson [28] use a force-dynamic bottom–up approach to describe the interaction between hands and objects in scenes. Both the hand and the object are modeled as objects, moving freely and imparting forces on other objects. Objects are tracked in the image, assigned properties like Grasper based on observations of collisions. However, the underlying process generating the video sequences is in general far too complex to be modeled deterministically. The increase in computing resources since 1998 has allowed the use of probabilistic methods, which are more powerful but also more computationally demanding.

Recognition of manipulation hand actions can be guided by knowledge about the objects manipulated. Wu et al. [44] represent kitchen activity solely in terms of the sequence of objects in contact with the hand during the activity. They learn a dynamic Bayesian network model that represents temporal sequences of actions and objects involved in the actions. Object and action classes in each frame are nodes in the network, while temporal contextual dependencies are modeled as edges between nodes. The features used for classification are RFID tags attached to the objects and the human hand.

Filipovych and Ribeiro [11] go a step further, allowing action context to influence the object recognition in parallel to the object-contextual action recognition. The

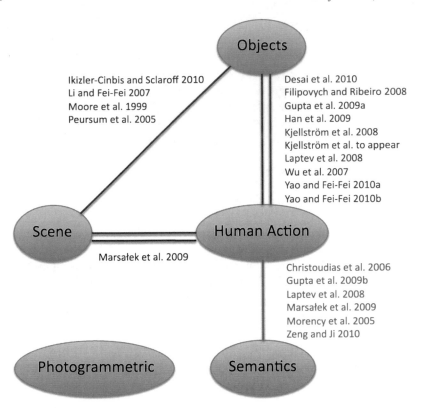

Fig. 18.1 Graphical representation of the different classes of context in human action recognition. Edges between two types of information correspond to methods using these two types of information for human action recognition. Edges of the same color between several types of information correspond to methods using all these types of information for human action recognition. The papers listed in font of the same color as an edge present methods using that type of context. Blue (Objects–Human Action) papers are described in Sect. 18.2.1. Purple (Scene–Human Action) papers are described in Sect. 18.2.2. Red (Objects–Scene–Human Action) papers are described in Sect. 18.2.3. Green (Semantics-Human Action) papers are described in Sect. 18.2.4. No papers employing photogrammetric context directly for human action recognition have been found. As discussed in the text, papers presenting combination of other types of cues for contextual recognition, such as Scene–Objects, Human Pose–Objects, Semantics–Scene, etc., are not included in this review

method learns primitive actor–object interactions such as grasp-cup, touch-spoon from video, representing static and dynamic properties of the object, the hand and the hand–object interaction in a Bayesian network, trained using the EM algorithm. To facilitate image feature extraction, a simplified setting with uniform background and camera view from above is used.

Along the same line, Gupta et al. [15] and Kjellström et al. [22, 23] recognize actions and objects in context of each other. The actions considered in these works are more high-level than the examples in [11], of the type pouring-from-pitcher. Actions are recognized from a sequence of human poses, while objects are detected in the image using a standard sliding window detector. Object action relationships are modeled using different types of graphical models, where actions and objects are represented in the nodes, and temporal and contextual dependencies are modeled as edges. Gupta et al. use a Bayesian directed graphical model to represent object–action relationships, while Kjellström et al. use an undirected graphical model. The main difference is that Gupta et al. segment manipulation action by detection of reaching motion, so that the observation of each action is a pre-segmented sequence of human poses, while Kjellström et al. instead incorporate the temporal segmentation into the recognition using a sliding window approach, so that the observation of an action at time t is the human poses in a temporal window around the time t. This leads to a more noisy action recognition process, but enables recognition of actions following each other, without any special delimiter actions such as reaching, putting down or picking up. Furthermore, Gupta et al. focus on upper-body or whole body actions while Kjellström et al. study hand manipulation actions. The method in [22] is presented in more detail in Sect. 18.3.

The work described here is related to the concept of Object–Action Complexes (OACs) [43] which models objects and actions as an inseparable entity. This philosophy is in turn related to the concept of affordances [12] where objects are understood in context of how they are used; both a `chair` and a `bench` can according to this theory be defined as `sittable`.

Laptev et al. [26] and Han et al. [18] address a slightly different problem, detection of object–action interactions such as `answer-phone` and `get-out-of-car` in a very demanding movie dataset, collected by Laptev et al. and also used in [29]. Laptev et al. represent a movie clip using a bag of spatio-temporal features (in a way similar to representing a text document as a bag of words, not considering word order). Movie clips are classified using an SVM-based [6] classifier. Han et al. use a slightly more specific scene descriptor that encodes feature presence/absence and also structural (spatial) relationships between object parts. Movie clips are classified using a kind of Bayesian classifier, developed by them. Both methods outperform other state-of-the-art action classification algorithms on standard action datasets, and Han et al. perform slightly better than Laptev et al. on the movie dataset. This way of modeling object context is profoundly different form the methods described above—object and action are here viewed as an inseparable entity (very similar in spirit to OACs), recognized together from spatio-temporal features.

The methods above all recognize action from video, i.e., sequences of images. Using contextual information it is also possible to recognize action from a single image, using contextual cues to compensate for the motion information not represented in the single snap-shot of the action. Yao et al. [45] present a new type of image representation called Grouplet, well suited to represent object–action interactions in still images. With this feature, they are able to capture subtle nuances like the difference between `playing-the-violin` and `holding-a-violin` in a single still image.

Another paper by the same authors [46] presents a method with an undirected graphical model (a random field model) that captures spatial relationships between the pose of a human and objects interacting with the human, in context of the action being performed. The action class, the object position and class, and the poses of all body parts of the human are represented in nodes of the graph, while spatial relationships and class dependencies are modeled in the edges of the graph. The action and pose context makes it possible to detect very small objects against cluttered background, while the action and object context makes it possible to estimate human pose from very sparse image evidence.

A similar method is presented by Gupta et al. [15], where a Bayesian (directed) graphical model is used instead of a random field model. These two papers show that, regardless of the type of graphical model, it is possible to recognize human action from very sparse evidence, a single image, if contextual information in the form of both spatial relationships and object and action class relationships are employed. This claim is supported by Desai et al. [9], who show that encoding such spatial relationships significantly improves recognition of objects and human actions.

18.2.2 Scene Context in Human Action Recognition

Another contextual cue to action recognition is the scene itself, as noted in the introduction. The underlying assumptions is that a certain type of object and a certain type of human action are more likely to be observed in some types of scenes than others. Marszałek et al. [29] present a method for simultaneous recognition of scene type and action from video. The method uses the same kind of features and classification methodology as in [26], but to recognize human action and scene in context of each other instead of human action and objects. It is evaluated with the challenging movie dataset also used in [18, 26].

Marszałek et al. note that the scene dependence is not equally strong for all actions; the action `lock-door` has a high scene correlation and the detection of this action will benefit greatly from scene context. However, the detection rate of the action `smile` cannot be expected to be improved by scene context.

We would like to add that the action `smile` on the other hand is highly correlated with semantic context, such as spoken language or movie scripts. One conclusion that can be drawn is that different actions are correlated with different contextual cues. We know of no examples in the literature where the types of contextual information to employ in the action recognition are learned from data. An important topic to investigate in the future is therefore how an action classifier could automatically select what different types of contextual information to take into account in the classification, depending on the type of actions investigated.

18.2.3 Object–Scene Context in Human Action Recognition

Li and Fei-Fei [27] present a method for recognition of events from single images, with image search as the main application. As with other algorithms employing scene context, the underlying assumption is that events take place in certain types of environment. Similarly, as noted above, the presence of specific objects (boat, car, etc.) and image areas (water, road, etc.) are strong cues to the type of event taking place. A directed graphical model with nodes representing image area labels, scene labels image layout, and event labels, is trained with a number of images labeled with image event. Image area labels are not given in training, but are treated as latent variables. Given a new unlabeled image, both the individual image parts labels and the global event depicted in the image can be inferred from the model.

Similarly, Ikizler-Cinbis and Sclaroff [20] use scene and object context to help recognition of human actions in video, with video search as the intended application. The main idea is to extract a dense and overlapping set of features from the image, object-, person-, and scene-centered, describing shape and motion. They then use a semi-supervised learning framework to associate bags of features (i.e., image regions) with action and object labels. This simultaneous segmentation and recognition approach is similar in spirit to work on simultaneous segmentation and recognition of objects in (single) images, e.g., [24].

Another aspect of the scene, which contains contextual information about objects and action, is its spatial layout. Early on, Moore et al. [30] provide a Bayesian framework for recognizing objects in a scene, and actions being performed on the objects. The main purpose of the system is to infer an object's class from human actions observed in connection with the object. The system tracks the hands, and registers collisions with detected objects in the scene. The classes of objects are inferred using a Naive Bayesian classifier from image-based evidence such as object color and shape, action based evidence such as the motion of the hand prior to and during collision with the object, and scene based evidence such as objects priorly in contact with the hand. A scene model is maintained with memory of locations and appearances of objects.

Peursum et al. [33] focus on surveillance scenes with wide angle, low resolution views. As with [30], human actions are used to aid scene segmentation and to infer object and scene region classes. A Bayes classifier is used to infer labels of different regions in the scene, based on object and human actions observed in connection to these regions. Object classes are in turn inferred from human actions in connection to the object, and human action classification is guided by contextual information about higher-level activities involving these actions and co-located objects.

18.2.4 Semantic Context in Human Action Recognition

Semantic annotations of the video provide powerful contextual cues to visual action recognition. Movie scripts are one type of annotation. The script of a movie can be viewed as an incomplete and noisy labeling of the actions and objects in the same movie. Laptev et al. [26] and Marszałek et al. [29] employ text classification techniques and temporal alignment of scripts and movies to automatically segment the video and retrieve action, object and scene labels.

Alternatively, the movie script can be seen as second modality, providing a noisy view of the movie content along with the video data. Replacing the script with spoken language registered in connection to the video sequence, is the idea of speech-contextual gesture recognition. The method of Morency et al. [31] employs contextual information from speech in head gesture recognition. Head gestures are heavily correlated with questions and points of turn-taking in a dialogue, which means that information from speech can be used to differentiate between casual head motion and communicative head gestures, like nodding.

Multiple modalities also enables semi-supervised learning. Christoudias et al. [5] address the learning of speech unit classifiers and gestures from partly labeled data. From two complementary data sources, audio and video, they use Co-Training [3] to iteratively label more and more of the unlabeled data with the respective data source, one at a time.

As stated in the introduction, one type of semantic context is structure inherent in the activity shown in the video. Methods for learning grammars from video, described in the previous chapter, make this information explicit. The grammatical structure can then be used as a contextual cue for action recognition in similar videos. One example from the literature is Gupta et al. [16], who present a method which discovers causal relationships between actions in a video. The retrieved relationships are used to generate a storyline, which can be regarded as a stochastic grammar (see the previous chapter of this volume) representing "explanations" of the series of actions in the video.

Another type of semantic context is domain knowledge, which can be used as a prior in training the action recognizer. Zeng and Ji [47] present a method to include prior domain knowledge when training probabilistic graphical models, making it possible to use less training data. Domain knowledge is represented as logic rules, constraining model parameters in different ways.

18.3 Example: A Contextual Object–Action Recognition Method

Let us now be more concrete, taking a method-level look at an approach to contextual simultaneous recognition of manipulation actions and the objects manipulated. The intended application is Robot learning from demonstration.

The reader is referred to a more in-depth presentation of the method in [22], along with a larger set of experiments. An early version of the method is described in [23]. As with [15], the method aims at using contextual information about objects to help action recognition, and contextual information about actions to help recognizing the objects involved in the action. The main difference to our approach is that they segment manipulation action by detection of reaching motion. We instead incorporate the temporal segmentation into the recognition using a temporal sliding window approach, described below. This enables us to recognize actions following each other, without any special delimiter actions such as reaching, putting down or picking up.

The features used for contextual object–action classification are first described in Sect. 18.3.1. The graphical model used to represent the object–action dependencies is then outlined in Sect. 18.3.2, followed by a description of how it can be used for simultaneous detection and temporal segmentation of actions and objects in Sect. 18.3.3. Section 18.3.4 describes experiments with the model.

18.3.1 Features for Classification

Extraction of object and action features could be done in a variety of ways depending on the purpose of the feature extraction (see earlier chapters in this volume). As opposed to many other action recognition applications, it is here necessary to obtain the location of the human hand to find the object or objects involved. Furthermore, it should be possible to recreate the recognized action with a robot, which means that the hand position, orientation and articulated pose should be retrievable from the action representation.

Object features   Different actions involve different number of objects. For example, the action pour involves two containers, one to pour from and one to pour to, while the action sit involves one piece of furniture. The object state o_t therefore encodes both the number and the classes of objects involved in the action at time t.

The object state is approximated by a vector $\mathbf{x}_t^o$ where each element is the detection probabilities for each object class, respectively. At this pre-processing stage, objects are categorized according to appearance into 6 semantic categories: book, magazine, hammer, box, cup, and pitcher. Section 18.3.3 describes how these object classes are grouped according to observed human use.

All objects of the known range of classes in the neighborhood of the hand are detected. We use sliding window detectors, one for each object class. The detector for a certain object class searches over image position, scale and height/width ratio in the image plane, in the vicinity of the human hand. The search limits for the sliding window detector in terms of window size, aspect ratio and offset from the human hand are learned from training data. Each window is classified as object or background using a two-class SVM [6]. Figure 18.2 shows example detections of the object classes book, magazine, box, and pitcher.

A representation similar to HOG [7] is used in the SVM classification. Gradient orientation $\mathbf{G}(\mathbf{W}) \in [0, \pi)$ is computed from an image window $\mathbf{W}$ as $\mathbf{G}(\mathbf{W}) = \arctan(\frac{\partial \mathbf{W}}{\partial y} / \frac{\partial \mathbf{W}}{\partial x})$ where x denotes downward (vertical) direction and y rightward (horizontal) direction in the image window. From $\mathbf{G}(\mathbf{W})$, a pyramid with L levels of histograms with different spatial resolutions are created; on each level l, the gradient orientation image is divided into $2^{L-l} \times 2^{L-l}$ equal partitions. A histogram with B bins is computed from each partition. In the SVM classification, a window $\mathbf{W}$ is represented by the vector $\mathbf{w}$ which is the concatenation of all histograms at all levels in the pyramid. The length of $\mathbf{w}$ is thus $B \sum_{l=1}^{L} 2^{2(L-l)}$. In our experiments in Sect. 18.3.4 we use $B = 4$ and $L = 4$.

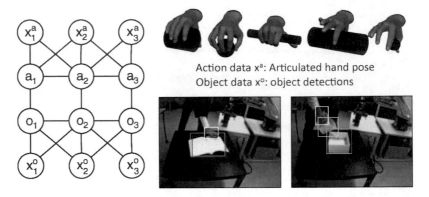

Fig. 18.2 Illustration of the object–action recognition method presented in [22]. Actions are simultaneously recognized and temporally segmented using a temporal sliding window approach with a factorial CRF (FCRF). In the temporal sliding window, $t = 1, 2, 3$ are three consecutive frames in the sequence. The sliding window is moved forward one frame at a time. The action and object recognition results at each frame are taken as a_2, o_2. The action data $\mathbf{x}_t^a$ are articulated hand poses, obtained using the method described in [35]. The object data $\mathbf{x}_t^o$ are object detections with associated probabilities in each frame t

In each classification step in the sliding window detection, each object class is treated separately. For each object class, a two-class SVM with an RBF kernel is trained with a set of feature vectors $\mathscr{D}^{\mathrm{fg}} = \{\mathbf{w}_i^{\mathrm{fg}}\}$ containing image bounding boxes with objects, and a set $\mathscr{D}^{\mathrm{bg}} = \{\mathbf{w}_i^{\mathrm{bg}}\}$ containing randomly chosen image windows. This basic object classifier is suitable for deformable objects, where the range of object appearances cannot easily be parameterized; the range of appearances spans a manifold with complex shape in the feature space. This manifold is non-parametrically represented using the SVM.

A sequence of object detections is denoted $\mathbf{x}^o = \{\mathbf{x}_t^o\}$, $t = 1, \ldots, T$, where $\mathbf{x}_t^o$ is a vector of detection probabilities for the 6 known object classes. Similarly, $\mathbf{o} = \{o_t\}$, $t = 1, \ldots, T$ denotes the corresponding object state, where o_t is an integer value, indicating the combination of objects involved in the action at time t.

Action features A human manipulation action is to a very large degree described by the articulated motion of the hand. We therefore use the hand pose reconstruction method in [35] to reconstruct and track the articulated motion of the hand in 3D.

The method is example based. In each time step, the hand is first segmented from the image using skin color. The appearance of the hand is compared to a large database (on the order of 10^5 examples) of synthetic hand views tagged with articulated pose and orientation. Temporal pose consistency is enforced in the reconstruction. Moreover, typical occlusions from objects in the hand are modeled by including object occlusions in some examples in the database.

Reconstruction examples can be seen in Fig. 18.2. The reconstruction is quite crude with angular errors of 10–20%. However, the method is functioning in real-time and is very robust to temporary tracking failure. Our intended application is to understand the relationship between objects and hand actions (e.g., grasps) performed on them on a semantic level. In other words, the object–action classification is intended for qualitative reasoning about which hand actions apply to which objects, rather than for learning precise hand motion from demonstration. Thus, speed and robustness in the hand reconstruction is more critical than accuracy, which makes the method described here suitable for our purposes.

To provide position invariance the global velocity of the hand is encoded, rather than the global position itself. A hand pose is thus defined by global velocity, global orientation, and joint angles. In a manner similar to the object feature extraction, the hand pose at time t is classified as being part of the actions open, hammer, pour, or as not involved in any particular action. A separate two-class SVM is trained for each type of action, rendering an open/none classifier, a hammer/none classifier, and a pour/none classifier.

In the following, a sequence of single-frame action classifications is denoted $\mathbf{x}^a = \{\mathbf{x}_t^a\}$, $t = 1, \ldots, T$, where $\mathbf{x}_t^a$ is a vector of classification probabilities for the three action classes. The corresponding action state is denoted $\mathbf{a} = \{a_t\}$, $t = 1, \ldots, T$, where a_t is an integer value indicating action class.

Correlation between object and action features The temporal classifier described in Sect. 18.3.2 models explicit semantic dependencies between manipulation actions and the manipulated objects. However, there are also dependencies on the feature level.

The shape of the hand encoded in $\mathbf{x}_t^a$ gives cues about the object as well, since humans grasp different types of objects differently, due to object function, shape, weight and surface properties. Similarly, the object detection results encoded in $\mathbf{x}_t^o$ is affected by the hand shape since the hand occludes the object in some cases. Furthermore, there are temporal dependencies: $\mathbf{x}_{t-1}^a$ and $\mathbf{x}_t^a$ are correlated as are $\mathbf{x}_{t-1}^o$ and $\mathbf{x}_t^o$. This correlation within the data is *implicit* and difficult to model accurately, but should be taken into account when modeling the simultaneous action–object recognition.

18.3.2 Classification of Object–Action Data

Since we can expect complex dependencies within our action data $\mathbf{x}^a$ and object data $\mathbf{x}^o$ over time, a discriminative classifier which does not model the data generation process is preferable over a generative sequential classifier like a HMM [34]. We thus employ CRFs [25] which are undirected graphical models that represent a set of state variables $\mathbf{y}$, distributed according to a graph $\mathcal{G}$, and conditioned on a set of measurements $\mathbf{x}$.

Let $C = \{\{\mathbf{y}_c, \mathbf{x}_c\}\}$ be the set of cliques in $\mathcal{G}$. Then

$$p(\mathbf{y}|\mathbf{x}; \theta) = \frac{1}{Z(\mathbf{x})} \prod_{c \in C} \phi_c(\mathbf{y}_c, \mathbf{x}_c; \Theta_c), \tag{18.1}$$

where $\phi(\cdot)$ is a potential function parameterized by Θ as

$$\phi_c(\mathbf{y}_c, \mathbf{x}_c; \Theta_c) = e^{\sum_k \Theta_{c,k} f_k(\mathbf{y}_c, \mathbf{x}_c)} \tag{18.2}$$

and $Z(\mathbf{x}) = \sum_{\mathbf{y}} \prod_{c \in C} \phi_c(\mathbf{y}_c, \mathbf{x}_c; \Theta_c)$ is a normalizing factor. The feature functions $\{f_k\}$ are given, and training the CRF means setting the weights Θ, e.g., using belief propagation [25].

Linear-chain CRF For linear-chain data (for example a sequence of object or action features and labels), $\mathbf{y} = \{y_t\}$ and $\mathbf{x} = \{\mathbf{x}_t\}$, $t = 1, \ldots, T$. This means that the cliques are the edges of the model, which gives

$$p(\mathbf{y}|\mathbf{x}; \Theta) = \frac{1}{Z(\mathbf{x})} \prod_{t=2}^{T} \phi_t(y_{t-1}, y_t, \mathbf{x}; \Theta_t) \tag{18.3}$$

with a potential function

$$\phi_t(y_{t-1}, y_t, \mathbf{x}; \Theta_t) = e^{\sum_k \Theta_{t,k} f_k(y_{t-1}, y_t, \mathbf{x})}. \tag{18.4}$$

Each state y_t can depend on the whole observation sequence $\mathbf{x}$—or any subpart of it, e.g. the sequence $\{\mathbf{x}_{t-\mathscr{C}}, \ldots, \mathbf{x}_{t+\mathscr{C}}\}$, $\mathscr{C}$ being the *connectivity* of the model.

Factorial CRF In Sect. 18.3.1 we argue that there are correlations between action observations $\mathbf{x}^a$ and object observations $\mathbf{x}^o$ implicit in the data. We make use of this correlation on the data level by not imposing a simplified model on the data generation process and instead using a discriminative classifier, CRF. However, there is also an *explicit*, semantic correlation between actions and objects on the label level. This correlation can be modeled using a factorial CRF (FCRF) [38]. Figure 18.2 shows an FCRF with two states, action class a_t and object class o_t, for three time steps $t = 1, 2, 3$. The cliques in this model are the within-chain edges $\{a_{t-1}, a_t\}$ and $\{o_{t-1}, o_t\}$, and the between-chain edges $\{a_t, o_t\}$. The probability of $\mathbf{a}$ and $\mathbf{o}$ is thus defined as

$$p(\mathbf{a}, \mathbf{o}|\mathbf{x}; \Theta) = \frac{1}{Z(\mathbf{x})} \prod_{t=1}^{T} \phi_t(a_t, o_t, \mathbf{x}; \Theta_t)$$

$$\times \prod_{t=2}^{T} \phi_{a,t}(a_{t-1}, a_t, \mathbf{x}; \Theta_{a,t}) \phi_{o,t}(o_{t-1}, o_t, \mathbf{x}; \Theta_{o,t}). \tag{18.5}$$

The weights Θ are obtained during training, e.g., using loopy belief propagation [38].

18.3.3 Object–Action Recognition using CRF:s

Using the approach described above, the actions and objects in a video sequence of human activity can be both temporally segmented and classified, using an FCRF in a sliding window manner over time.

An FRCF structure of length T and connectivity $\mathscr{C}$ is trained with object–action patterns $\mathscr{D} = \{(\mathbf{o}, \mathbf{x}^o, \mathbf{a}, \mathbf{x}^a)_i\}$, involving the three different action classes and six different object classes described above.

A new sequence $(\boldsymbol{\chi}^\omega, \boldsymbol{\chi}^\alpha)$ of length τ can now be segmented and classified using this model. For each time step $t = 2, \ldots, \tau - 1$, the pattern $(\boldsymbol{\chi}^\omega_{t-1}, \boldsymbol{\chi}^\omega_t, \boldsymbol{\chi}^\omega_{t+1}, \boldsymbol{\chi}^\alpha_{t-1}, \boldsymbol{\chi}^\alpha_t, \boldsymbol{\chi}^\alpha_{t+1})$ renders the classification ω_t, α_t.

Objects can also be ordered into affordance categories using correlation information extracted from the training data $\mathscr{D}^{\text{labels}} = \{(\mathbf{o}, \mathbf{a})_i\}$. This is represented with a correlation matrix $\mathbf{C}$ where element $\mathbf{C}_{ij}$ indicates the degree to which object class i can be used to perform action j.

18.3.4 Experiments

Experiments with the object and action feature extractors in [22] showed certain confusions between classes, which appeared to be intrinsic to the object and action classes themselves. For example, books and magazines cannot always be distinguished by appearance only. However, they afford slightly different ranges of actions, which means that the action observed in connection to the object can be used to constrain the object classification. Similarly, action classification can be constrained by the objects observed in the vicinity of the hand during action.

In the experiment described here, we trained and evaluated an FCRF (Sect. 18.3.3) with the 6 object classes and the three action classes mentioned above, in the 7 following combinations: open-book, open-magazine, open-box, hammer-with-book, hammer-with-hammer, pour-from-pitcher-into-box, and pour-from-pitcher-into-cup. Thus, an open action can only be observed together with either a book, a magazine or a box; a hammer action only together with a book or a hammer; a pour action only together with a box and pitcher or a cup and pitcher.

We collected a training set $\mathscr{D}_{\text{train}}$ consisting of sequences in which three different individuals performed all seven object–action combinations, using one object instance per object class. Each frame of the sequences were labeled with object (none, book, magazine, hammer, box, cup, pitcher, box+pitcher, or cup+pitcher) and action (none, open, hammer, or pour) ground truth. Only the frames with hand detections were used for training.

The evaluation set $\mathscr{D}_{\text{test}}$ consisted of a sequence where a fourth individual performed the same object–action combinations, using the same object instances. Only the frames with hand detections were used for evaluation. (The frames with no hand were automatically labeled as object none, action none.)

From each frame of each of the four sequences in $\mathscr{D}_{train}$ and $\mathscr{D}_{test}$, object features were extracted as described in Sect. 18.3.1. The 6 background/object classifiers were trained with images of a fifth person handling the object instances in the same way as in the training and evaluation sequences. Action features were also extracted as described in Sect. 18.3.1. The three background/action classifiers were trained on hand poses and velocities from the three training sequences.

An FRCF structure of length $T = 3$ and connectivity $\mathscr{C} = 1$ was trained with $n = 1471$ consecutive frames of object and action features from the training set $\mathscr{D}_{train}$. This FCRF can be expected to learn

1. allowed object–action combinations,
2. allowed temporal action transitions (in this dataset, only none-action and action-none),
3. typical errors in the per-frame object feature extraction,
4. typical errors in the per-frame action feature extraction.

To provide a baseline, two individual CRFs of length $T = 3$ and connectivity $\mathscr{C} = 1$ were trained with the same $n = 1471$ consecutive frames of object features and action features, respectively. The object CRF can be expected to learn aspect 3 above, and the action CRF can be expected to learn aspects 2 and 4; none of them capture aspect 1.

The object–action FCRF and the individual action and object CRFs were used to classify the evaluation sequence. The classification result is shown in Fig. 18.3.

First, it can be noted that many frames of the sequence contains an object but action none; in other words, the human is doing something else with the object than opening, hammering or pouring. In these frames, the object classification in the FCRF (Fig. 18.3, row 1) is not supported by more information than the classification in the separate object CRF (Fig. 18.3, row 2), since all combinations of objects and action none are present in the training data. In the remainder of the analysis, we therefore focus on the 184 frames where there is an open, hammer or pour action taking place (red blocks below the diagrams in Fig. 18.3, rows 3, 4).

From the results in Fig. 18.3 we can conclude that both object and action recognition are improved by the contextual information: For the frames with an action taking place, the separate CRFs have a correct object classification rate of 52% and a correct action classification rate of 46%. The FCRF, which takes contextual recognition into regard, has a correct object classification rate of 60% and a correct action classification rate of 58%.

However, from an application perspective we are not primarily interested whether each frame of an object–action combination are correctly classified; the main focus is instead on whether the action–object combination is detected and correctly classified at all. From this perspective, both the FCRF and the individual CRFs detected all 7 object–action combinations, i.e., classified some frames of each object–action combination as something other than object none, action none.

The classification of the detected object–action combination is here defined as the majority vote among the classifications in the frames of the detection. The FCRF (Fig. 18.3, rows 1, 3) detected the seven following object–action combi-

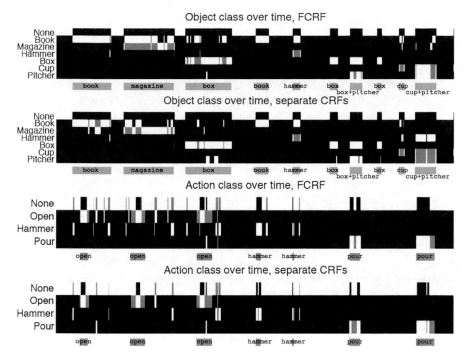

Fig. 18.3 Object–action classification over time. The depicted sequence contains seven object–action combinations: open-book, open-magazine, open-box, hammer-with-book, hammer-with-hammer, pour-from-pitcher-into-box, pour-from-pitcher-into-cup. Time on x axis, Classification on y axis. White block = (F)CRF classification during this time period. Grey block = classification ground truth during this time period. Ground truth object and action classifications are also indicated with blocks below each diagram

nations: open-book (correct), open-book (incorrect but allowed),[1] open-box (correct), hammer-with-book (correct), hammer-with-hammer (correct), pour-from-pitcher-into-box (correct), pour-from-pitcher-into- cup (correct). This concords with the findings in the experiments with the object feature extraction above: Books are often detected as magazines and vice versa (see also Fig. 18.2), and they both afford opening, which means that the contextual action information could not guide the object classification in the second object–action combination. The inclination to classify the magazine as book in Fig. 18.3, rows 1, 2 could be due to coincidences in the training and evaluation data—there were more images of books than magazines in the training data with the same orientation as the magazine in the evaluation data.

The two individual CRFs (Fig. 18.3, rows 2, 4) detected the seven following object–action combinations: open-book (correct), open-book (in-

---

[1]This object–action combination is allowed since it is observed in the training data; books and magazines both afford opening.

correct but allowed), open-box (correct), hammer-with-book (correct), hammer-with- hammer (correct), pour-from-pitcher-into-box (correct), pour-from-hammer (incorrect).[2] In the last combination, the object detection was inadequate by itself, but the contextual action information in the FCRF helped in inferring the correct object classes (Fig. 18.3, row 1). Furthermore, the actions are more accurately detected by the FCRF in the two last combinations (Fig. 18.3, row 3), than by the individual action CRF (Fig. 18.3, row 4). The reason is most certainly the contextual object information provided by the FCRF.

This shows that the FCRF is able to infer information about the object and action present in a frame, not immediately apparent from the present image information, from knowledge about which object–action combinations are commonly observed in other data. The many spurious detections, particularly of hammer actions, would pose problems to a learning from demonstration system employing the classification method. One way to address this problem is to increase the number of time steps in the FCRF, e.g., to use five or seven time steps instead of three. However, this increases the number of parameters to learn; a larger set of example sequences is then required to train the FCRF. Another measure to take is to improve the feature extractors, so that the FCRF is fed with cleaner data. This also requires much larger and more diverse datasets; more individuals, more object instances, more action instances performed by each individual.

18.4 Conclusions

This chapter has discussed the concept of context in action recognition, and identified four categories of contextual information, *object context*, *scene context*, *semantic context*, and *photogrammetric context*. As shown in Sects. 18.2 and 18.3, methods have been suggested to take the three first of these types of context into account in action recognition.

However, much remains to be done. Firstly, as discussed in Sect. 18.2, no efforts have been made to include photogrammetric contextual cues into the human action recognition. This is an interesting avenue of future research.

Furthermore, as discussed in Sect. 18.2.2, different actions are correlated to different contextual cues: While drink is highly correlated with liquid containers, lock-door has a high correlation with scenes in front of a house, and smile is to a higher degree correlated with semantic cues such as speech. A still unsolved issue is how to automatically determine which context to take into account in the recognition of different types of actions.

Another issue is that of benchmarking. Divvala et al. [10] noted that context rarely is employed in object detection and recognition, despite the obvious advan-

---

[2]This object–action combination is not allowed; hammers do not afford pouring.

tages of contextual recognition. As discussed in the introduction of this chapter, they suggested that one reason for this is the lack of common understanding of what context is. Moreover, they suggested that another reason might be the lack of benchmark datasets that would facilitate comparison of methods.

For action recognition, this is even more the case; the work presented in Sects. 18.2 and 18.3 contains virtually no systematic comparison of methods. We conclude that an integral issue for the contextual action recognition field is the collection of appropriate datasets for benchmarking.

We believe that a benchmark dataset for evaluating contextual action recognition methods should include:

- Action examples ranging from single, atomic actions, e.g., reaching, to semantically complex, composite activities, e.g., playing-soccer.
- Actions in which the human interacts with the scene, objects in the scene, and/or other humans.
- Actions involving one human, two humans and many humans.
- Actions involving the full body, upper body, lower body, and only hands.
- Action examples from many different domains and applications, such as learning from demonstration, visual surveillance and video retrieval.
- Actions with different types of semantic annotations, such as scripts, subtitles, spoken language in the video, information about geographic location, and captions and keywords.
- Other modalities, such as raw audio, 3D sensors, and passage detectors.
- Action captured by networks of sensors.
- Actions where the objects involved have been annotated in different ways, e.g., with ground truth 3D position, orientation, and image outline.
- Actions where the objects involved have sensors on them, e.g., pressure sensors.

Such efforts are under way, e.g., http://www.clsp.jhu.edu/workshops/ws10/groups/ stloavutva/, and will most certainly have a strong positive influence, promoting thoroughly evaluated, solid contributions in the contextual action recognition field.

18.4.1 Further Reading

Two interesting aspects of contextual recognition, only touched upon in this chapter, are multimodality and semi-supervised learning. More information on semi-supervised learning can be found in

- Chapelle, O., Schölkopf, B., Zien, A.: Semi-Supervised Learning. The MIT Press (2006)

The reader interested in multimodality is referred to

- Maragos, P., Potamianos, A., Gros, P. (eds.): Multimodal Processing and Interaction. Springer Series on Multimedia Systems and Applications, vol. 33 (2008)

References

1. Ali, S., Shah, M.: Floor fields for tracking in high-density crowd scenes. In: European Conference on Computer Vision (2008) [358]
2. Bickel, S., Scheffer, T.: Multi-view clustering. In: IEEE International Conference on Data Mining (2004) [359]
3. Blum, A., Mitchell, T.: Combining labeled and unlabeled data with co-training. In: Conference on Computational Learning Theory (1998) [359,364]
4. Brubaker, M.A., Sigal, L., Fleet, D.J.: Estimating contact dynamics. In: IEEE International Conference on Computer Vision (2009) [358]
5. Christoudias, C.M., Saenko, K., Morency, L., Darrell, T.: Co-adaption of audio-visual speech and gesture classifiers. In: International Conference on Multi-Modal Interface (2006) [364]
6. Cristianini, N., Shawe-Taylor, J.: An Introduction to Support Vector Machines. Cambridge University Press, Cambridge (2000) [361,365]
7. Dalal, N., Triggs, B.: Histograms of oriented gradients for human detection. In: IEEE Conference on Computer Vision and Pattern Recognition (2005) [365]
8. Dempster, A., Laird, N., Rubin, D.: Maximum likelihood from incomplete data via the EM algorithm. J. R. Stat. Soc. B **39**(1), 1–38 (1977) [359]
9. Desai, C., Ramanan, D., Fowlkes, C.: Discriminative models for static human–object interactions. In: Workshop on Structured Models in Computer Vision (2010) [362]
10. Divvala, S.K., Hoiem, D., Hays, J.H., Efros, A.A., Hebert, M.: An empirical study of context in object detection. In: IEEE Conference on Computer Vision and Pattern Recognition (2007) [356-358,372]
11. Filipovych, R., Ribeiro, E.: Recognizing primitive interactions by exploring actor-object states. In: IEEE Conference on Computer Vision and Pattern Recognition (2008) [359,360]
12. Gibson, J.J.: The Ecological Approach to Visual Perception. Lawrence Erlbaum Associates, Mahwah (1979) [361]
13. Gupta, A., Chen, T., Shen, F., Kimber, D., Davis, L.S.: Context and observation driven latent variable model for human pose estimation. In: IEEE Conference on Computer Vision and Pattern Recognition (2008) [358]
14. Gupta, A., Davis, L.S.: Beyond nouns: Exploiting prepositions and comparative adjectives for learning visual classifiers. In: European Conference on Computer Vision (2008) [358]
15. Gupta, A., Kembhavi, A., Davis, L.S.: Observing human–object interactions: Using spatial and functional compatibility for recognition. IEEE Trans. Pattern Anal. Mach. Intell. **31**(10), 1775–1789 (2009) [360,362,364]
16. Gupta, A., Srinivasan, P., Shi, J., Davis, L.S.: Understanding videos, constructing plots: Learning a visually grounded storyline model from annotated videos. In: IEEE Conference on Computer Vision and Pattern Recognition (2009) [364]
17. Hamer, H., Schindler, K., Koller-Meier, E., Van Gool, L.: Tracking a hand manipulating an object. In: IEEE International Conference on Computer Vision (2009) [358]
18. Han, D., Bo, L., Sminchisescu, C.: Selection and context for action recognition. In: IEEE International Conference on Computer Vision (2009) [361,362]
19. Herzog, D., Ude, A., Krüger, V.: Motion imitation and recognition using parametric hidden Markov models. In: IEEE-RAS International Conference on Humanoid Robots (2008) [358]
20. Ikizler-Cinbis, N., Sclaroff, S.: Object, scene and actions: Combining multiple features for human action recognition. In: European Conference on Computer Vision (2010) [363]
21. Kjellström, H., Kragić, D., Black, M.J.: Tracking people interacting with objects. In: IEEE Conference on Computer Vision and Pattern Recognition (2010) [358]
22. Kjellström, H., Romero, J., Kragić, D.: Visual object–action recognition: Inferring object affordances from human demonstration. Comput. Vis. Image Underst. (in press). doi:10.1016/j.cviu.2010.08.002 [360,361,364,366,369]

23. Kjellström, H., Romero, J., Martínez, D., Kragić, D.: Simultaneous visual recognition of manipulation actions and manipulated objects. In: European Conference on Computer Vision (2008) [360,364]
24. Kohli, P., Rihan, J., Bray, M., Torr, P.H.S.: Simultaneous segmentation and pose estimation of humans using dynamic graph cuts. Int. J. Comput. Vis. **79**(3), 285–298 (2008) [358,363]
25. Lafferty, J., McCallum, A., Pereira, F.: Conditional random fields: Probabilistic models for segmenting and labeling sequence data. In: International Conference on Machine Learning (2001) [367,368]
26. Laptev, I., Marszałek, M., Schmid, C., Rozenfeld, B.: Learning realistic human actions from movies. In: IEEE Conference on Computer Vision and Pattern Recognition (2008) [361,362]
27. Li, L., Fei-Fei, L.: What, where and who? Classifying events by scene and object recognition. In: IEEE International Conference on Computer Vision (2007) [362]
28. Mann, R., Jepson, A.: Towards the computational perception of action. In: IEEE Conference on Computer Vision and Pattern Recognition (1998) [359]
29. Marszałek, M., Laptev, I., Schmid, C.: Actions in context. In: IEEE Conference on Computer Vision and Pattern Recognition (2009) [361-363]
30. Moore, D.J., Essa, I.A., Hayes, M.H.: Exploiting human actions and object context for recognition tasks. In: IEEE International Conference on Computer Vision (1999) [363]
31. Morency, L., Sidner, C., Lee, C., Darrell, T.: Contextual recognition of head gestures. In: International Conference on Multimodal Interface (2005) [364]
32. Oliva, A., Torralba, A.: The role of context in object recognition. Trends Cogn. Sci. **11**(12), 520–527 (2007) [356]
33. Peursum, P., West, G., Venkatesh, S.: Combining image regions and human activity for indirect object recognition in indoor wide-angle views. In: IEEE International Conference on Computer Vision (2005) [363]
34. Rabiner, L.R.: A tutorial on hidden Markov models and selected applications in speech recognition. Proc. IEEE **77**(2), 257–286 (1989) [367]
35. Romero, J., Kjellström, H., Kragić, D.: Hands in action: Real-time 3d reconstruction of hands in interaction with objects. In: IEEE International Conference on Robotics and Automation (2010) [358,366]
36. Singh, V.K., Khan, F.M., Nevatia, R.: Multiple pose context trees for estimating human pose in object context. In: IEEE Conference on Computer Vision and Pattern Recognition (2010) [358]
37. Strat, T.M.: Employing contextual information in computer vision. In: ARPA Image Understanding Workshop (1993) [356]
38. Sutton, C., Rohanimanesh, K., McCallum, A.: Dynamic conditional random fields: Factorized probabilistic models for labeling and segmenting sequence data. In: International Conference on Machine Learning (2004) [368]
39. Torralba, A.: Contextual priming for object detection. Int. J. Comput. Vis. **53**(2), 169–191 (2003) [358]
40. Urtasun, R., Fleet, D.J., Fua, P.: Monocular 3D tracking of the golf swing. In: IEEE Conference on Computer Vision and Pattern Recognition (2005) [358]
41. Vondrak, M., Sigal, L., Jenkins, O.: The kneed walker for human pose tracking. In: IEEE Conference on Computer Vision and Pattern Recognition (2008) [358]
42. Wilson, A.D., Bobick, A.F.: Parametric hidden Markov models for gesture recognition. IEEE Trans. Pattern Anal. Mach. Intell. **21**(9), 884–900 (1999) [358]
43. Wörgötter, F., Agostini, A., Krüger, N., Shylo, N., Porr, B.: Cognitive agents – a procedural perspective relying on the predictability of object–action–complexes (OACs). Robot. Auton. Syst. **57**(4), 420–432 (2009) [361]
44. Wu, J., Osuntogun, A., Choudhury, T., Philipose, M., Rehg, J.M.: A scalable approach to activity recognition based on object use. In: IEEE International Conference on Computer Vision (2007) [359]
45. Yao, B., Fei-Fei, L.: Grouplet: A structured image representation for recognizing human and object intractions. In: IEEE Conference on Computer Vision and Pattern Recognition (2010) [361]

46. Yao, B., Fei-Fei, L.: Modeling mutual context of object and human pose in human–object interaction activities. In: IEEE Conference on Computer Vision and Pattern Recognition (2010) [361]
47. Zeng, Z., Ji, Q.: Knowledge based activity recognition with dynamic Bayesian network. In: European Conference on Computer Vision (2010) [364]

Chapter 19
Facial Expression Analysis

Fernando De la Torre and Jeffrey F. Cohn

Abstract The face is one of the most powerful channels of nonverbal communication. Facial expression provides cues about emotion, intention, alertness, pain, personality, regulates interpersonal behavior, and communicates psychiatric and biomedical status among other functions. Within the past 15 years, there has been increasing interest in automated facial expression analysis within the computer vision and machine learning communities. This chapter reviews fundamental approaches to facial measurement by behavioral scientists and current efforts in automated facial expression recognition. We consider challenges, review databases available to the research community, approaches to feature detection, tracking, and representation, and both supervised and unsupervised learning.

19.1 Introduction

An automatic analysis of the facial expressions of people are highly important for automatic understanding of humans, their actions and their behavior in general. Facial expression has been a focus of research in human behavior for over a hundred years [30]. It is central to several leading theories of emotion [38, 116] and has been the focus of, at times, heated debate about issues in emotion science. Facial expression figures prominently in research on almost every aspect of emotion, including psychophysiology [66], neural correlates [39], development [84], perception [2], addiction [47], social processes [52], depression [27] and other emotion disorders [118]. Facial expression communicates physical pain [100], alertness, personality and interpersonal relations [46]. Applications of facial expression analysis include marketing [107], perceptual user interfaces, human–robot interaction [98, 126, 145], drowsy driver detection [128], telenursing [29], pain assessment [79],

F. De la Torre (✉)
Robotics Institute, Carnegie Mellon University, Pittsburgh, PA 15213, USA
e-mail: ftorre@cs.cmu.edu

J.F. Cohn
Department of Psychology, University of Pittsburgh, Pittsburgh, PA 15260, USA
e-mail: jeffcohn@pitt.edu

T.B. Moeslund et al. (eds.), *Visual Analysis of Humans*,
DOI 10.1007/978-0-85729-997-0_19, © Springer-Verlag London Limited 2011

analyzing mother–infant interaction [45], autism [83], social robotics [6, 18], facial animation [72, 110] and expression mapping for video gaming [54] among others. A large number of examples are also provided in particular in Chaps. 22, 26 and 23.

In part because of its importance and potential uses as well as its inherent challenges, automated facial expression recognition has been of keen interest in computer vision and machine learning. Beginning with a seminal meeting sponsored by the US National Science Foundation [41], research on this topic has become increasingly broad, systematic, and productive. IEEE-sponsorship of international conferences (http://www.fg2011.org/), workshops, and a new journal in affective computing, among other outlets (e.g., IEEE journal System, Man, and Cybernetics and special issues of journals such as Image, Vision, and Computing Journal) speak to the vitality of research in this area. Automated facial expression analysis is critical as well to the emerging fields of Computational Behavior Science and Social Signal Processing.

Automated facial image analysis confronts a series of challenges. The face and facial features must be detected in video; shape or appearance information must be extracted and then normalized for variation in pose, illumination and individual differences; the resulting normalized features are used to segment and classify facial actions. Partial occlusion is a frequent challenge that may be intermittent or continuous (e.g., bringing an object in front of the face, self-occlusion from head turns, eyeglasses or facial jewelry). While human observers easily accommodate for changes in pose, scale, illumination, occlusion, and individual differences, these and other sources of variation represent considerable challenges for computer vision. Then there is the machine-learning challenge of automatically detecting actions that require significant training and expertise even for human coders. There is much good research to do.

We begin with a description of approaches to annotation and then review publicly available databases. Research in automated facial expression analysis depends on access to large, well-annotated, video data. We then review approaches to feature detection, representation, and registration, and both supervised and unsupervised learning of facial expression. We close with implications for future research in this area.

19.2 Annotation of Facial Expression

Two broad approaches to annotating facial expression are message–judgment and sign-based [25]. In the former, observers make inferences about the meaning of facial actions and assign corresponding labels. The most widely used approach of this sort makes inferences about felt emotion. Inspired by cross-cultural studies by Ekman [38] and related work by Izard [55], a number of expressions of what are referred to as basic emotions have been described. These include joy, surprise, anger, fear, disgust, sadness, embarrassment, and contempt. Examples of the first six are shown in Fig. 19.1. Message–judgment approaches tend to be holistic; that is, they typically combine information from multiple regions of the face, implicitly

Fig. 19.1 Basic facial expression phenotypes. 1, disgust; 2, fear; 3, joy; 4, surprise; 5, sadness; 6, anger. Figure reproduced with permission from [105]. © 2010 IEEE

acknowledge that the same emotion or cognitive state may be expressed in various ways, and they utilize the perceptual wisdom of human observers, which may include taking account of context. A limitation is that many of these emotions may occur infrequently in daily life and much human experience involves blends of two or more emotions. While a small set of specific expressions that vary in multiple regions of the face may be advantageous for training and testing, their generalizability to new image sources and applications is limited. Moreover, the use of emotion labels implies that posers are experiencing the actual emotion. This inference often is unwarranted, as when facial expression is posed or faked, and the same expression may map to different felt emotions. Smiles, for instance, occur in both joy and embarrassment [1].

In a sign-based approach, physical changes in face shape or texture are the descriptors. The most widely used approach is that of Ekman and colleagues. Their Facial Action Coding System (FACS) [40] segments the visible effects of facial muscle activation into "action units". Each action unit is related to one or more facial muscles. The Facial Action Coding System (FACS) is a comprehensive, anatomically based system for measuring nearly all visually discernible facial movement. FACS describes facial activity on the basis of 44 unique action units (AUs), as well as several categories of head and eye positions and movements. Facial movement is thus described in terms of constituent components, or AUs. Any facial event (for example, an emotion expression or paralinguistic signal) may be decomposed into one or more AUs. For example, what has been described as the felt or Duchenne smile typically includes movement of the zygomatic major (AU12) and orbicularis oculi, pars lateralis (AU6).

The FACS taxonomy was defined by manually observing graylevel variation between expressions in images and to a lesser extent by recording the electrical activity of underlying facial muscles [24]. Depending on which edition of FACS is used, there are 30 to 44 AUs and additional "action descriptors." Action descriptors are movements for which the anatomical basis is not established. More than 7000 AU combinations have been observed [104]. Figures 19.2 and 19.3 illustrate AUS from the upper and lower portions of the face, respectively. Figure 19.4 provides an example in which FACS action units have been used to label a prototypic expression of pain. Because of its descriptive power, FACS has become the standard for facial measurement in behavioral research and has supplanted use of message–judgment

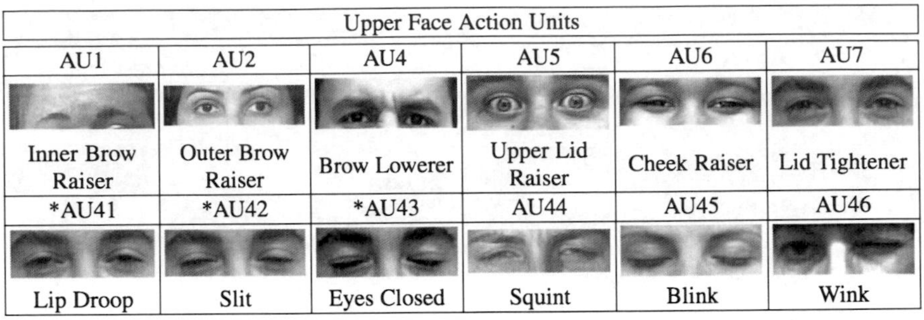

Upper Face Action Units
AU1
AU2
AU4
AU5
AU6
AU7
Inner Brow Raiser
Outer Brow Raiser
Brow Lowerer
Upper Lid Raiser
Cheek Raiser
Lid Tightener
*AU41
*AU42
*AU43
AU44
AU45
AU46
Lip Droop
Slit
Eyes Closed
Squint
Blink
Wink

Fig. 19.2 FACS action units (AU) for the upper face. Figure reproduced with permission from [24]

Lower Face Action Units
AU9
AU10
AU11
AU12
AU13
AU14
Nose Wrinkler
Upper Lip Raiser
Nasolabial Deepener
Lip Corner Puller
Cheek Puffer
Dimpler
AU15
AU16
AU17
AU18
AU20
AU22
Lip Corner Depressor
Lower Lip Depressor
Chin Raiser
Lip Puckerer
Lip Stretcher
Lip Funneler
AU23
AU24
*AU25
*AU26
*AU27
AU28
Lip Tightener
Lip Pressor
Lips Parts
Jaw Drop
Mouth Stretch
Lip Suck

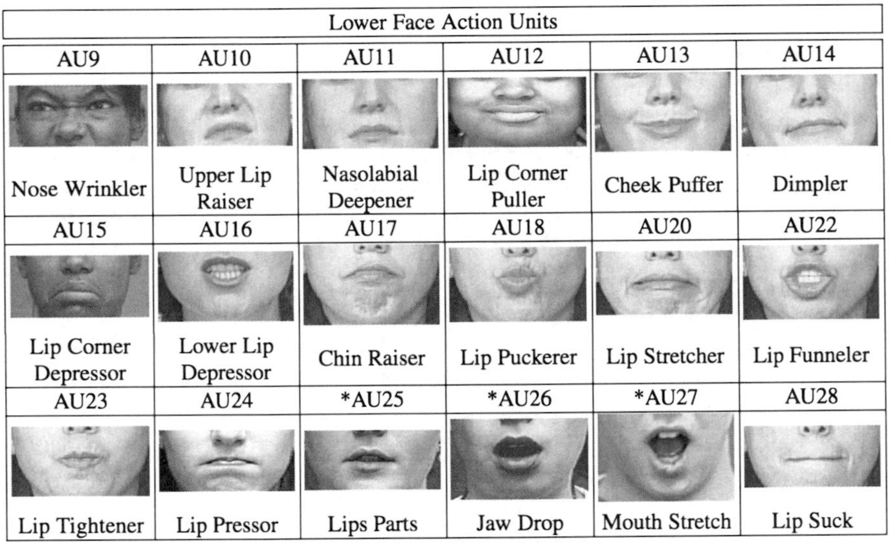

Fig. 19.3 Action units of the lower face. Figure reproduced with permission from [24]

AU 4: Brow lowering
AU 43: Closing eyes
AU 6: Cheek raising
AU 12: Pulling at corner lip
AU 7: Tightening of eyelids
AU 9: Wrinkling of nose
AU 10: Raising of upper lip
AU 25: Parting lips

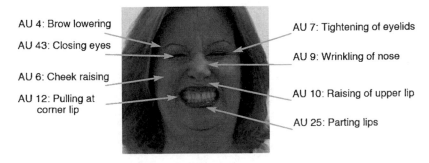

Fig. 19.4 An example of facial action units associated with a prototypic expression of pain. Figure reproduced with permission from [75]. © 2011 IEEE

Action Unit

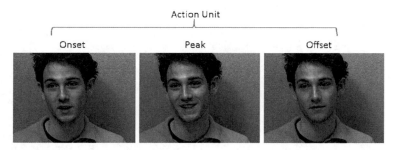

Onset   Peak   Offset

Fig. 19.5 FACS coding typically involves frame-by-frame inspection of the video, paying close attention to subtle cues such as wrinkles, bulges, and furrows to determine which facial action units have occurred and their intensity. Full labeling requires marking onset, peak and offset of the action unit and all changes in intensity. Full coding generally is too costly. *Left to right*, evolution of an AU 12 (involved in smiling), from onset, peak, to offset

approaches in automated facial image analysis. As well, FACS has become influential in the related area of computer facial animation. The MPEG-4 facial animation parameters [92] are derived from FACS.

Facial actions can vary in intensity, which FACS represents at an ordinal level of measurement. The original (1978) version of FACS included criteria for measuring intensity at three levels (X, Y, and Z). The more recent 2002 edition provides criteria for measuring intensity at five levels, ranging from A to E. FACS scoring produces a list of AU-based descriptions of each facial event in a video record. Figure 19.5 shows an example for FACS coding AU12 (Smile), where the onset, peak and offset are labeled.

For both message–judgment and sign-based approaches, the reliability of human coding has been a neglected topic in the automated facial expression recognition literature. With some exceptions, publicly available databases (Table 19.1) and research reports fail to provide information about inter-observer reliability or agreement. This is an important lack, in that inter-system agreement between manual and automated coding is inherently limited by intra-system agreement. If manual coding disagrees about the ground truth used to train classifiers, it is unlikely that classifiers will surpass them. Inter-system reliability can be considered in numerous ways [26]. These range from the precision of measurement of onsets, peaks, offsets, and changes in action unit intensity, to whether or not observers agree on action unit occurrence within some number of frames. More attention to reliability of coding would be useful in evaluating training data and test results. Sayette and Cohn [103] found inter-observer agreement varied among AU. Agreement for AU 7 (lower lid tightener) was relatively low, possibly due to confusion with AU 6 (cheek raiser). Some AU may occur too infrequently to measure reliably (e.g., AU 11). Investigators may want to consider pooling some AU to achieve more reliable units.

Agreement between human coders is better when temporal precision is relaxed. In behavioral research, it is common to expect coders to agree only within a $\frac{1}{2}$ second window. In automated facial image analysis, investigators typically assume exact agreement between classifiers and ground truth, which is a level of temporal precision beyond what may be feasible for many AU [24].

Table 19.1 Publicly available facial expression databases

Database	No. of Subjects	Elicitation	Imaging	Camera View	Labels	Requests
AR [85]	126	Posed	Static	Frontal Occlusion	Emotions	http://www2.ece.ohio-state.edu/~aleix/ARdatabase.html
Belfast	125	Interviews and TV	Video	Frontal	Emotion and dimensions	http://www.idiap.ch/mmm/corpora/emotion-corpus
Cohn–Kanade [58]	97	Posed	Video	Frontal	FACS AU	http://vasc.ri.cmu.edu/idb/html/face/facial_expression/
Cohn–Kanade+ [78]	123	Posed and Conversation	Video	Frontal and 15° to the side	FACS AU Emotion Landmarks	http://vasc.ri.cmu.edu/idb/html/face/facial_expression/
FABO	23	Posed	Video	Frontal	Emotion	http://research.it.uts.edu.au/cvrg/FABO.htm
GEMEP	10	Acted	Video	Frontal	Emotion	http://www.fg2011.org/fg.php?page=workshop
KDEF	70	Posed	Static	Five views		http://www.facialstimuli.com/index_files/Page369.htm
JAFFE [82]	10	Posed	Static	Frontal	Emotion	http://kasrl.org/jaffe.html
MMI [101, 124]	101	Posed Spontaneous	Static Video (5 min)	Frontal 90° to the side	FACS AU	http://emotion-research.net/toolbox/ toolboxdatabase.2006-09-28.5469431043
Face Database MPI [99]		Posed	Video	11 views at 18° intervals	FACS AU	http://vdb.kyb.tuebingen.mpg.de/
Multi-PIE [48]	337	Posed	Static	15 views 19 illuminations	Emotion Landmarks	http://www.multipie.org/
Prkachin–Solomon Pain [80]	129	Pain induction	Video	Frontal	AU Landmarks	http://www.pitt.edu/~jeffcohn/?K
Multi-PIE [64]	72	Posed	Static	Five views	Emotion	http://facedb.blogspot.com/2008/07/ short-description-of-database-set.html
RU-FACS [7]	100	Interview	Video (2 min)	Mostly frontal	FACS AU	http://mplab.ucsd.edu/grants/project1/research/ rufacs1-dataset.html
University of Texas Video Database [91]	284	Viewing videoclip	Video (10 minutes)	Frontal	Emotion	http://portal.acm.org/citation.cfm?id=1053716
Bosphorous	105	Posed	Static	3D	FACS AU Emotion	http://bosphorus.ee.boun.edu.tr/
BU-3DFE [132]	100	Posed	Static	3D	Emotion	http://www.cs.binghamton.edu/~lijun/Research/3DFE/ 3DFE_Analysis.html
BU-4DFE	101	Posed	Dynamic	3D	Emotion	http://www.cs.binghamton.edu/~lijun/Research/3DFE/ 3DFE_Analysis.html

19.3 Databases

The development of robust facial recognition algorithms requires well labeled databases of sufficient size that include carefully controlled variations of pose, illumination and resolution. Publicity available databases are necessary to comparatively evaluate algorithms. Collecting a high quality database is a resource-intensive task. The availability of public facial expression databases is important for the advancement of the field. Table 19.1 illustrates the characteristics of publicly available databases.

Most face expression databases have been collected by asking subjects to perform a series of expressions. These directed facial action tasks may differ in appearance and timing from spontaneously occurring behavior. Deliberate and spontaneous facial behavior are mediated by separate motor pathways, the pyramidal and extrapyramidal motor tracks, respectively. As a consequence, fine-motor control of deliberate facial actions is often inferior and less symmetrical than what occurs spontaneously. Many people, for instance, are able to raise their outer Brows spontaneously while leaving their inner brows at rest; few can perform this action voluntarily. Spontaneous depression of the lip corners (AU 15) and raising and narrowing the inner corners of the brow (AU 1+4) are common signs of sadness. Without training, few people can perform these actions deliberately, which incidentally is an aid to lie detection [36]. Differences in the temporal organization of spontaneous and deliberate facial actions are particularly important in that many pattern recognition approaches, such as HMMs, are highly dependent on the timing of the appearance change. Unless a database includes both deliberate and spontaneous facial actions, it will likely prove inadequate for developing face expression methods that are robust to these differences.

19.4 Facial Feature Tracking, Registration and Feature Extraction

Prototypical expression and AU detection from video are challenging computer vision and pattern recognition problems. Some of the most important challenges are: (1) non-frontal pose and moderate to large head motion make facial image registration difficult, (2) classifiers can suffer from over-fitting when trained with relatively few examples for each AU; (3) many facial actions are inherently subtle making them difficult to be model; (4) individual differences among faces in shape and appearance make the classification task difficult to generalize across subjects; (5) temporal dynamics of AUs are highly variable. These differences can signal different communicative intentions [62], levels of distress [9], and presents a challenge for detection and classification; (6) and the number of possible combinations of 40+ individual action units numbers in the thousands (more than 7000 action unit combinations have been observed [42]). To address these issues over the last 20 years, a large number of facial expression and AU recognition/detection systems have been

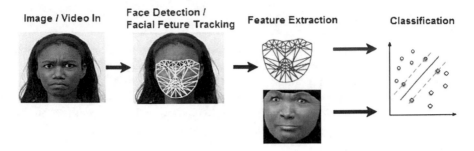

Fig. 19.6 Block diagram of our the CMU system. The face is tracked using an AAM; shape and appearance features are extracted, normalized, and output to a linear SVM for action unit or expression detection. Figure reproduced with permission from [78]. © 2010 IEEE

proposed. Some of the leading efforts include those at: Carnegie Mellon University [81, 108, 112, 142], University of California, San Diego [7, 68], University of Illinois at Urbana-Champaign [23, 129], Rensselaer Polytechnic Institute [117], Massachusetts Institute of Technology [43], University of Maryland [13, 131], Imperial College [59, 95, 123], IDIAP Dalle Molle Institute for Perceptual Artificial Intelligence [44], and others [82, 138].

Most facial expression recognition systems are composed of three main modules: (1) face detection, facial feature tracking and registration, (2) feature extraction and (3) supervised or unsupervised learning. Figure 19.6 illustrates an example of these three modules. In the following sections we will discuss each of these modules in more detail with emphasis in the current CMU system. For other systems see [44, 93, 113].

19.4.1 Facial Feature Detection and Tracking

Face detection is an initial step in most automatic facial expression recognition systems (see Chap. 5). For real-time, frontal face detection, the Viola and Jones [127] face detector is arguably the most commonly employed algorithm. See [137] for a survey of recent advances in face detection. Once the face is detected two approaches to registration are common. One performs coarse registration by detecting a sparse set of facial features (e.g., eyes) in each frame. The other detects detailed features (i.e. dense points around the eyes and other facial landmarks) in the video sequence. In this section we will describe a unified framework for the latter, which we refer to as Parameterized Appearance Models (PAMs). PAMs include the Lucas–Kanade method [74], Eigentracking [12], Active Appearance Models [28, 33, 34, 87] , and Morphable Models [14, 57], which have been popular approaches for facial feature detection, tracking and modeling faces in general.

PAMs are among the most popular methods for facial feature detection and face alignment in general. PAMs for faces build an appearance and/or shape representation from the principal components of labeled training data. Let $\mathbf{d}_i \in \Re^{m \times 1}$ (see an

Fig. 19.7 The figure shows the mean and first two modes of variation of 2D AAM shape **a** and appearance **b** variation and the mean and first two modes of 3D AAM shape. **c** Reconstructed face. Reproduced with permission from [88]

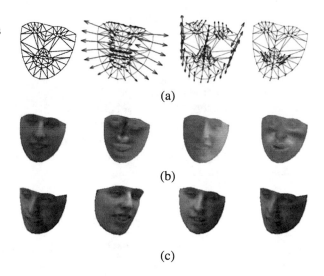

(a)

(b)

(c)

explanation of the notation[1]) be the ith sample of a training set $\mathbf{D} \in \Re^{m \times n}$ of n samples, where each vector $\mathbf{d}_i$ is a vectorized image of m pixels. In a training set, each face image is previously manually labeled with p landmarks. A $2p$-dimensional shape vector is constructed by stacking all (x, y) positions of the landmarks as $s = [x_1; y_1; x_2; y_2; \ldots; x_p; y_p]$. Figure 19.9a shows an example of several face images that have been labeled with 66 landmarks. Given the labeled training samples, Procrustes analysis [28] is applied to the shape vectors to remove two-dimensional rigid transformations. After removing rigid transformation with Procrustes, principal component analysis (PCA) is applied to the shape vectors to build a linear shape model. The shape model can reconstruct any shape on the training shape as the mean ($\mathbf{s}_0$) and linear combination of a shape basis ($\mathbf{U}^s$) (eigenvectors of the shape covariance matrix), that is, $\mathbf{s} \approx \mathbf{s}_0 + \mathbf{U}^s \mathbf{c}^s$, where $\mathbf{c}^s$ are the shape coefficients. $\mathbf{U}^s$ spans the shape space that accounts for identity, expression and pose variation in the training set. Figure 19.7a shows the shape mean and PCA basis. Similarly, after backwarping the texture to a canonical configuration, the appearance (normalized graylevel) is vectorized into an m-dimensional vector and stacked into the n columns of $\mathbf{D} \in \Re^{m \times n}$. The appearance model, $\mathbf{U} \in \Re^{m \times k}$ is computed by calculating the first k principal components [56] of $\mathbf{D}$. Figure 19.7b shows the mean appearance and the PCA basis. Figure 19.7c contains face images generated using the Active Appearance Model (AAM) by setting appropriate parameters of shape and texture.

Once the appearance and shape model have been learned from training samples (i.e., $\mathbf{U}$, $\mathbf{U}^s$ is known), alignment is achieved by finding the motion parameter $\mathbf{p}$ that

---

[1]Bold uppercase letters denote matrices (e.g., $\mathbf{D}$), bold lowercase letters denote column vectors (e.g., $\mathbf{d}$). $\mathbf{d}_j$ represents the jth column of the matrix $\mathbf{D}$. d_{ij} denotes the scalar in the row ith and column jth of the matrix $\mathbf{D}$. Non-bold letters represent scalar variables. $\mathrm{tr}(\mathbf{D}) = \sum_i d_{ii}$ is the trace of square matrix $\mathbf{D}$. $\|\mathbf{d}\|_2 = \sqrt{\mathbf{d}^T \mathbf{d}}$ designates Euclidean norm of $\mathbf{d}$.

best aligns the image w.r.t. the subspace $\mathbf{U}$ by minimizing:

$$\min_{\mathbf{c},\mathbf{p}} \left\| \mathbf{d}\big(\mathbf{f}(\mathbf{x},\mathbf{p})\big) - \mathbf{U}\mathbf{c} \right\|_2^2, \tag{19.1}$$

where $\mathbf{c}$ is the vector for the appearance coefficients. $\mathbf{x} = [x_1, y_1, \ldots, x_l, y_l]^T$ is the coordinate vector with the pixels to track. $\mathbf{f}(\mathbf{x},\mathbf{p})$ is the function for geometric transformation; the value of $\mathbf{f}(\mathbf{x},\mathbf{p})$ is a vector denoted by $[u_1, v_1, \ldots, u_l, v_l]^T$. $\mathbf{d}$ is the image frame in consideration, and $\mathbf{d}(\mathbf{f}(\mathbf{x},\mathbf{p}))$ is the appearance vector of which the ith entry is the intensity of image $\mathbf{d}$ at pixel (u_i, v_i). For affine and non-rigid transformations, (u_i, v_i) relates to (x_i, y_i) by:

$$\begin{bmatrix} u_i \\ v_i \end{bmatrix} = \begin{bmatrix} a_1 & a_2 \\ a_4 & a_5 \end{bmatrix} \begin{bmatrix} x_i^s \\ y_i^s \end{bmatrix} + \begin{bmatrix} a_3 \\ a_6 \end{bmatrix}. \tag{19.2}$$

Here $[x_1^s, y_1^s, \ldots, x_l^s, y_l^s]^T = \mathbf{x} + \mathbf{U}^s \mathbf{c}^s$. The affine and non-rigid motion parameters are $\mathbf{a}, \mathbf{c}^s$, respectively, and $\mathbf{p} = [\mathbf{a}; \mathbf{c}^s]$ a combination of both affine and non-rigid motion parameters. In the case of the Lukas–Kanade tracker [74], $\mathbf{c}$ is fixed to be one and $\mathbf{U}$ is the subspace that contains a single vector, the reference template which is the appearance of the tracked object in the initial/previous frame.

Given an unseen facial image $\mathbf{d}$, facial feature detection or tracking with PAM alignment algorithms optimize (19.1). Due to the high dimensionality of the motion space, a standard approach to efficiently search over the parameter space is to use gradient-based methods [5, 10, 12, 28, 31, 87]. To compute the gradient of the cost function given in (19.1), it is common to use Taylor series expansion to approximate:

$$\mathbf{d}\big(\mathbf{f}(\mathbf{x}, \mathbf{p} + \delta\mathbf{p})\big) \approx \mathbf{d}\big(\mathbf{f}(\mathbf{x}, \mathbf{p})\big) + \mathbf{J}_\mathbf{p}\mathbf{d}(\mathbf{p})\delta\mathbf{p}, \tag{19.3}$$

where $\mathbf{J}_\mathbf{p}\mathbf{d}(\mathbf{p}) = \frac{\partial \mathbf{d}(\mathbf{f}(\mathbf{x},\mathbf{p}))}{\partial \mathbf{p}}$ is the Jacobian of the image $\mathbf{d}$ w.r.t. to the motion parameter $\mathbf{p}$ [74]. Once linearized, a standard approach is to use the Gauss–Newton method for optimization [10, 12]. Other approaches learn an approximation of the Jacobian matrix with linear [28] or non-linear [71, 102] regression. Figure 19.9a shows an example of tracking 66 facial features with an AAM in the RU-FACS database [7].

19.4.2 Registration and Feature Extraction

After the face has been detected and the facial feature points have been tracked, the next two steps registration and feature extraction follow.

Registration: The main goal of registration is to normalize the image to remove 3D rigid head motion, so features can be geometrically normalized. 3D transformations could be estimated from monocular (up to a scale factor) or multiple cameras using structure from motion algorithms [51, 130]. However, if there is not much out of plane rotation (i.e. less than about 15 to 20 degrees) and the face is relatively far

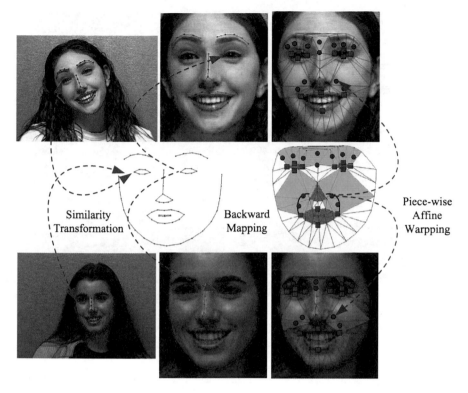

Fig. 19.8 Registration with two-step alignment. Figure reproduced with permission from [142]. © 2009 IEEE

away from the camera (assume orthographic projection), the 2D projected motion field of a 3D planar surface can be recovered with an affine model of six parameters. In this situation, simpler algorithms may be used to register the image to extract normalized facial features.

Following [108, 142] a similarity transform registers facial features with respect to an average face (see middle column in Fig. 19.8). To extract appearance representations in areas that have not been explicitly tracked (e.g. nasolabial furrow), we use a backward piece-wise affine warp with Delaunay triangulation. Fig. 19.8 shows the two step process for registering the face to a canonical pose for facial expression recognition. Purple squares represent tracked points and blue dots represent non-tracked meaningful points. The dashed blue line shows the mapping between the point in the mean shape and the corresponding points on the original image. Using an affine transformation plus backwarping, we can preserve the shape variation in appearance better than by geometric normalization alone. This two-step registration proves particularly important to detect low intensity AUs.

Geometric features: After the registration step, the shape and appearance features can be extracted from the normalized image. Geometric features contain information about shape and the locations of permanent facial features (e.g., eyes, brows,

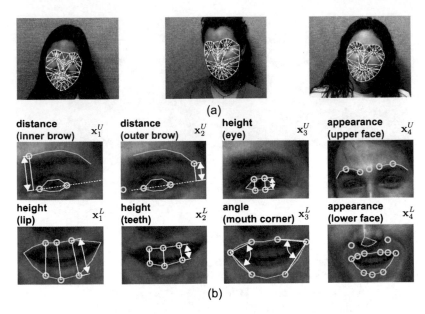

Fig. 19.9 a AAM fitting across different subjects. **b** Eight different features extracted from distance between tracked points, height of facial parts, angles for mouth corners, and appearance patches. Figure reproduced with permission from [144]. © 2010 IEEE

nose). Approaches that use only geometric features (or their derivatives) mostly rely on detecting sets of fiducial facial points [94, 96, 123], a connected face mesh or active shape model [20, 22, 61], or face component shape parametrization [113]. Some prototypical features include [108]: $\mathbf{x}_1^U$ the distance between inner brow and eye, $\mathbf{x}_2^U$ the distance between outer brow and eye, $\mathbf{x}_3^U$ the height of eye, $\mathbf{x}_1^L$ the height of lip, $\mathbf{x}_2^L$ the height of teeth, and $\mathbf{x}_3^L$ the angle of mouth corners, see Fig. 19.9b. However, shape features alone are unlikely to capture differences between subtle facial expressions or ones that are closely related. Many action units that are easily confusable by shape (e.g., AU 6 and AU 7 in FACS) can be discriminated by differences in appearance (e.g., furrows lateral to the eyes and cheek raising in AU 6 but not AU 7). Other AUs such as AU 11 (nasolabial furrow deepener), 14 (mouth corner dimpler), and 28 (inward sucking of the lips) cannot be detected from the movement of a sparse set of points alone but may be detected from changes in skin texture.

Appearance features: Represent the appearance (skin texture) changes and texture of the face, such as wrinkles and furrows. Appearance features for AU detection [3, 7, 50, 68, 111] outperformed shape only features for some action units, especially when registration is noisy see Lucey et al. [4, 77, 81] for a comparison.

Several approaches to appearance have been explored. Gabor wavelet coefficients are a popular approach. In several studies, Gabor wavelet coefficients outperformed optical flow, shape features, and Independent Component Analysis representations [3]. Tian [111, 113], however, reported that the combination of shape and appearance achieved better results than either shape or appearance alone. Recently,

Zhu et al. [142] have explored the use of SIFT [73] and DAISY [114] descriptors as appearance features. Given feature points tracked with AAMs, SIFT descriptors are first computed around the points of interest. SIFT descriptors are computed from the gradient vector for each pixel in the neighborhood to build a normalized histogram of gradient directions. For each pixel within a subregion, SIFT descriptors add the pixel's gradient vector to a histogram of gradient directions by quantizing each orientation to one of 8 directions and weighting the contribution of each vector by its magnitude. Similar in spirit to SIFT descriptors, DAISY descriptors are an efficient feature descriptor based on histograms. They are often used to match stereo images [114]. DAISY descriptors use circular grids instead of SIFT descriptors' regular grids; the former have been found to have better localization properties [89] and to outperform many state-of-the-art feature descriptors for sparse point matching [115]. At each pixel, DAISY builds a vector made of values from the convolved orientation maps located on concentric circles centered on the location. The amount of Gaussian smoothing is proportional to the radius of the circles. Donato [37] combined Gabor wavelet decomposition and independent component analysis. These representations use graylevel texture filters that share properties of spatial locality, independence, and have relationships to the response properties of visual cortical neurons. Zheng [138] investigated the use of two types of features extracted from face images for recognizing facial expressions. The first type is the geometric positions of a set of fiducial points on a face. The second type is a set of multi-scale and multi-orientation Gabor wavelet coefficients extracted from the face image at the fiducial points.

Other features: Other popular technique for feature extraction include more dynamic features such as optical flow [3], dynamic textures [21] and Motion History Images (MHIs) [16]. In an early exploration of facial expression recognition, Mase [86] used optical flow to estimate the activity in a subset of the facial muscles. Essa [43] extended this approach by using optic flow to estimate activity in a detailed anatomical and physical model of the face. Motion estimates from optic flow were refined by the physical model in a recursive estimation and control framework. The estimated forces were used to classify facial expressions. Yacoob and Davis [131] bypassed the physical model and constructed a mid-level representation of facial motion, such as a right mouth corner raise, directly from the optical flow. Ira et al. [22] implicitly recovered motion representations by building features such that each feature motion corresponded to a simple deformation of the face. MHIs were First proposed by Davis and Bobick [16]. MHIs compress the motion over a number of frames into a single image. This is done by layering the thresholded differences between consecutive frames one over the other. Valstar et al. [121] encoded face motion into Motion History Images. Zhao et al. [139] use volume Local Binary Patterns (LBPs), a temporal extension of local binary patterns often used in 2D texture analysis. The face is divided into overlapping blocks and the extracted LBP features in each block are concatenated into a single feature vector.

19.5 Supervised Learning

Supervised and more recently unsupervised approaches to action unit and expression detection have been pursued. In supervised learning event categories are defined in advance in labeled training data. In unsupervised learning no labeled training data are available and event categories must be discovered. In this section we discuss the supervised approach.

Early work in supervised learning sought to detect the six universal expressions of joy, surprise, anger, fear, disgust, and sadness; see Fig. 19.1. More recent work has attempted to detect expressions of pain [4, 69, 79], drowsiness, adult attachment [135], and indices of psychiatric disorder [27, 60]. Action unit detection remains a compelling challenge especially in unposed facial behavior. An open question is whether emotion and similar judgment-based categories are best detected by first detecting AU or by direct detection in which an AU detection step is bypassed. Work on this topic is just beginning [70, 79] and the question remains open.

Whether the focus is expression or AU, two main approaches have been pursued for supervised learning. These are (1) static modeling—typically posed as a discriminative classification problem in which each video frame is evaluated independently; and (2) temporal modeling—in which frames are segmented into sequences and typically modeled with a variant of DBNs (e.g. Hidden Markov Models, Conditional Random Fields).

19.5.1 Classifiers

In the case of static models, different feature representations and classifiers for frame-by-frame facial expression detection have been extensively studied. The pioneering work of Black and Yacoob [13] recognized facial expressions by fitting local parametric motion models to regions of the face and then feeding the resulting parameters to a nearest neighbor classifier for expression recognition. Tian et al. [111] made use of ANN classifiers for facial expression recognition. Barlett et al. [7, 8, 68] used Gabor filters in conjunction with AdaBoost feature selection followed by a Support Vector Machine (SVM) classifier. Lee and Elgammal [65] used multi-linear models to construct a non-linear manifold that factorizes identity from expression. Lucey et al. [76, 81] evaluated different shape and appearance representations derived from an AAM facial feature tracker, and an SVM for classification. Similarly, [139] made use of SVM.

More recent work has focused on incorporating the dynamics of facial expressions to improve performance (i.e. temporal modeling). De la Torre et al. [35] used condensation and appearance models to simultaneously track and recognize facial expression. Chang et al. [20] used a low-dimensional Lipschitz embedding to build a manifold of shape variation across several people and then used I-condensation to simultaneously track and recognize expressions. A popular strategy is to use HMMs to temporally segment expressions by establishing a correspondence between the action's onset, peak, and offset and an underlying latent state. Valstar and Pantic [123] used a combination of SVM and HMM to temporally segment and recognize AUs. Valstar and Pantic [94, 122, 125] proposed a system that enables fully automated robust facial expression recognition and temporal segmentation of onset, peak and offset from video of mostly frontal faces. Koelstra and Pantic [59] used Gentle-Boost classifiers on motion from a non-rigid registration combined with an HMM. Similar approaches include a nonparametric discriminant HMM from Shang and Chan [106], and partially observed Hidden Conditional Random Fields by Chang et al. [19]. For other comprehensive surveys see [44, 95, 113, 136]. Tong et al. [117] used DBNs with appearance features to detect facial action units in posed facial behavior. The correlation among action units served as priors in action unit detection. Ira et al. [22] used a BN classifiers for classifying the six universal expressions from video. In particular they used a Naive-Bayes classifiers and change the distribution from Gaussian to Cauchy, and use Gaussian Tree-Augmented Naive Bayes (TAN) classifiers to learn the dependencies among different facial motion features.

19.5.2 Selection of Positive and Negative Samples During Training

Previous research in expression and AU detection has emphasized types of registration methods, features and classifiers (e.g., [67, 97, 113, 134, 140]). Little attention has been paid to make efficiently use of the training data for assignment of video frames to positive and negative classes. Typically, assignment has been done in one of two ways. One is to assign to the positive class those frames that occur at the peak of each AU or proximal to it. Peaks refer to the maximum intensity of an action unit between the frame at which begins ("onset") and ends ("offset"). Negative class then is chosen by randomly sampling other AUs, including AU 0 or neutral. This approach suffers at least three drawbacks: (1) the number of training examples will often be small, which results in a large imbalance between positive and negative frames; and (2) peak frames may provide too little variability to achieve good generalization. These problems may be circumvented by following an alternative approach; that is to include all frames from onset to offset in the positive class. This approach improves the ratio of positive to negative frames and increases representativeness of positive examples. The downside is confusability of positive and negative classes. Onset and offset frames and many of those proximal or even further from them may be indistinguishable from the negative class. As a consequence, the number of false positives may dramatically increase. Moreover, how to make use of all negative samples in an efficient manner? Is there a better approach to selecting positive and negative training samples?

   In this section, we consider two approaches that have shown promise; one static and one dynamic. We illustrate the methods with particular classifiers and features, but the methods are not specific to the specific features or classifiers. As before, we distinguish between static and dynamic approaches. In the former, video frames are assumed to be independent. In the latter, first-order dependencies are assumed.

19.5.2.1 Static Approach

Recently, Zhu et al. [142] proposed an extension of cascade AdaBoost called Dynamic Cascade Bidirectional Bootstrapping (DCBB) to iteratively select positive samples and improve AU detection performance. In the first iteration, DCBB selected only the peaks and the two neighboring frames as positive frames, and randomly sample other AUs and non-AUs as negative samples. As in standard AdaBoost [127], DCBB defines the false positive target ratio, the maximum acceptable false positive ratio per cascade stage, and the minimum acceptable true positive ratio per each of the cascades. DCBB uses Classification and Regression Tree (CART) [17] as weak classifier. Once a cascade of peak frame detectors is learned in the first iteration, DCBB enlarges the positive set to increase the discriminative performance of the whole classifier. The new positive samples are selected after running the current classifier (learned in the previous iteration) in the original training data and selecting for the new positive training set the frames that were classified as positive. Recall that we have only trained with the peak frames in the first iteration. For more details see [142].

Figure 19.10 shows the improvement in the Receiver–Operator Characteristic (ROC) curve for testing data (subjects not in the training) using DCBB for three AUs (AU12, AU14, AU17). The ROC is obtained by plotting true positives ratios against false positives ratios for different decision threshold values of the classifier. In each subfigure there are five or six ROCs corresponding to alternative selection strategies: using only peak in the first step (same as standard Cascade AdaBoost), running three or four iterations in DCBB (spread x), and using all the frames between onset and offset (All+Boost). That is, there are three results shown using different positive training samples: 1) peak frames (first step); 2) all frames between onset and offset (All+Boost); and 3) iterations of DCBB (spread x). The first number between lines | denotes the area under the ROC, the second number is the size of positive samples in the testing dataset and separated by / is the size of negative samples in the testing dataset. The third number denotes the size of positive samples in training working sets and separated by / the total frames of target AU in training datasets. We can observe that the area under the ROC for frame-by-frame detection is improved gradually during each learning stage and the performance improves faster for some AU rather than others. Improvement rate appears to be influenced by the base rate of the AU. For AU14 and AU17, fewer potential training samples are available than for AU12.

Top of Fig. 19.11 shows the manual labeling for AU12 of the subject S015. We can see eight instances of AU12 with varying intensities ranging from A (weak) to E (strong). The strong AUs are represented by rectangles of height 4 and the weak ones with height 1. The remaining eight figures illustrates the sample selection process for each of the instances of the AU12. In the top right of each subfigure there is the corresponding AU instance number. The black curve in the bottom of the subfigures represents the similarity between the peak and the neighboring frames. The peak is the maximum of the curve. The positive samples in the first step are represented by green asterisks, in the second iteration by red crosses, in the third iteration by

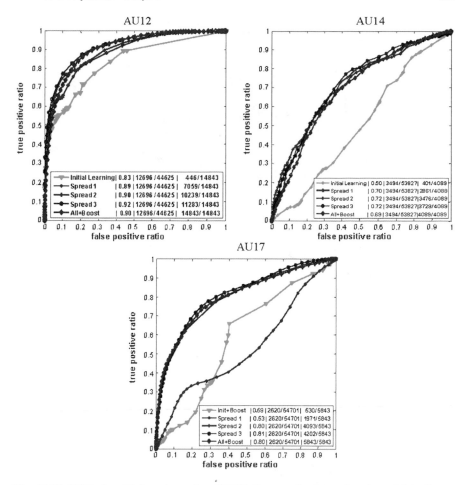

Fig. 19.10 ROCs for AU detection using DBCC: See text for the explanation of Init+Boost, spread x and All+Boost. Figure reproduced with permission from [142]. © 2009 IEEE

blue crosses, and in the final iteration by black circles. Observe that in the case of high peak intensity, subfigures 3 and 8 (top right number in the similarity plots), the final selected positive samples contain areas with low similarity values. However, when AU intensity is low, subfigure 7, the positive samples are only selected if they have a high similarity with the peak because otherwise we would select samples that will lead to many false positives. The ellipses and rectangles in the figures contain frames that are selected as positive samples, and correspond to strong and subtle AUs. The triangles correspond to frames between the onset and offset that are not selected as positive samples, and represent the ambiguous AUs.

Table 19.2 shows the area under the ROC for 14 AUs using DCBB and different set of features. The appearance features are based on SIFT descriptors. For all AUs the SIFT descriptor is built using a square of 48 × 48 pixels for twenty feature points for the lower face AUs or sixteen feature points for upper face. The shape

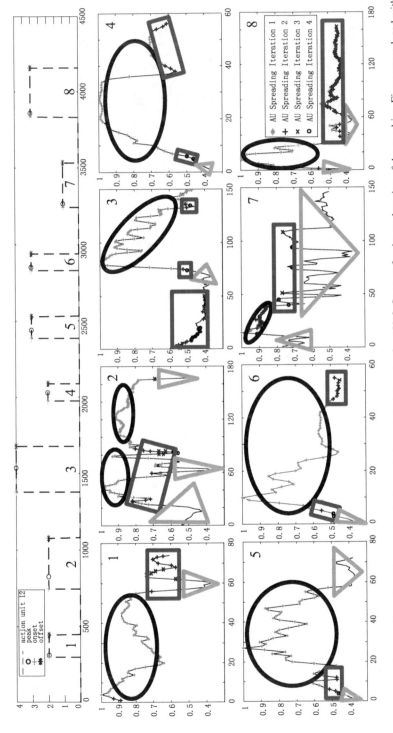

Fig. 19.11 The spreading of positive samples during each dynamic training step for AU12. See text for the explanation of the graphics. Figure reproduced with permission from [142]. © 2009 IEEE

Table 19.2 Area under the ROC for six different appearance and sampling strategies. AU peak frames with shape features and SVM (Peak+Shp+SVM), All frames between onset and offset with shape features and SVM (All+Shp+SVM), AU peak frames with appearance features and SVM (Peak+App+SVM), Sampling 1 frame in every 4 frames between onset and offset with PCA reduced appearance features and SVM (All+PCA+App+SVM), AU peak frames with appearance features and Cascade AdaBoost (Peak+App+Cascade Boost), DCBB with appearance features (DCBB)

	AU1	AU2	AU4	AU5	AU6	AU7	AU10	AU12	AU14	AU15	AU17	AU18	AU23
Peak+Shp+SVM	0.71	0.62	0.76	0.58	0.93	0.64	0.61	0.89	0.57	0.73	0.66	0.86	0.74
All+Shp+SVM	0.68	0.65	0.78	0.55	0.88	0.64	0.67	0.77	0.72	0.61	0.72	0.88	0.67
Peak+App+SVM	0.43	0.45	0.61	0.86	0.77	0.67	0.63	0.90	0.50	0.69	0.53	**0.95**	0.62
All+PCA+App+SVM	0.74	0.74	**0.85**	**0.89**	0.96	0.63	0.54	0.91	**0.82**	**0.86**	0.78	0.94	0.54
Peak+App+Cascade Boost	0.75	0.71	0.53	0.49	0.93	0.56	0.52	0.83	0.50	0.52	0.59	0.57	0.34
DCBB	**0.76**	**0.75**	0.76	0.77	**0.97**	**0.69**	**0.72**	**0.92**	0.72	**0.86**	**0.81**	0.86	**0.75**

features are the landmarks of the AAM. For more details see [142]. It is important to notice that the results illustrated in this section are obtained using a particular set of features and classifiers, but the strategy of positive sample selection in principle can be used with any combination of classifiers and features.

19.5.2.2 Dynamic Approach

Extensions of DBNs have been a popular approach for expression analysis [22, 106, 117, 123]. A major challenge for DBNs based on generative models such as HMMs is how to effectively model the null class (none of the labeled classes) and how to train effectively on all possible segments of the video (rather than independent features). In this section, we review recent work on a temporal extensions of a bag-of-words (BoW) model called kSeg-SVM [108] that overcomes these drawbacks. kSeg-SVM is inspired by the success of the spatial BoW sliding-window model [15] that has been used in difficult object detection problems. We pose the AU detection problem as one of detecting temporal events (segments) in time series of visual features. Events correspond to AUs, including all frames between onset and offset (see Fig. 19.12). kSeg-SVM represents each segment as a BoW; however, the standard histogram of entries is augmented with a soft-clustering assignment of words to account for smoothly varying signals. Given several videos with AU labeled events, kSeg-SVM learns the SVM parameters that maximize the response on positive segments (AU to be detected) and minimize the response in the rest of the segments (all other positions and lengths). Figure 19.12 illustrates the main idea of kSeg-SVM.

kSeg-SVM can be efficiently trained on all available video using the Structure Output SVM (SO-SVM framework) [119]. Recent research [90] in the related area of sequence-labeling has shown that SO-SVMs can out-perform other algorithms including HMM, CRF[63] and Max-Margin Markov Networks [109]. SO-SVMs

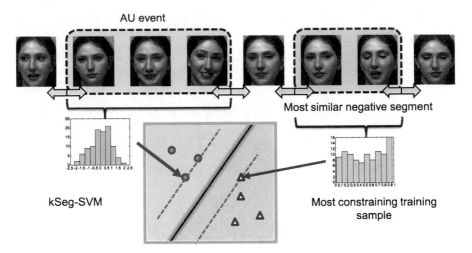

Fig. 19.12 During testing, the AU events are found by efficiently searching over the segments (position and length) that maximize the SVM score. During training, the algorithm searches over all possible negative segments to identify those hardest to classify, which improves classification of subtle AUs. Figure reproduced with permission from [108]. © 2009 IEEE

have several benefits in the context of AU detection: (1) they model the dependencies between visual features and the duration of AUs; (2) they can be trained effectively on all possible segments of the video (rather than on independent sequences); (3) they explicitly select negative examples that are most similar to the AU to be detected; and (4) they make no assumptions about the underlying structure of the AU events (e.g., i.i.d.). Finally, a novel parameterization of the output space is proposed to handle multiple AU event occurrences such that occur in long time series and search simultaneously for the k-or-fewer best matching segments in the time-series.

Given frame-level features, we will denote each processed video sequence i as $\mathbf{x}_i \in \mathbb{R}^{d \times m_i}$, where d is the number of features and m_i is the number of frames in the sequence. To simplify, we will assume that each sequence contains at most one occurrence of the AU event to be detected. For extensions to k-or-fewer occurrences see [108]. The AU event will be described by its corresponding onset to offset frame range and will be denoted by $\mathbf{y}_i \in \mathbb{Z}^2$. Let the full training set of video sequences be $\mathbf{x}_1, \ldots, \mathbf{x}_n \in \mathcal{X}$, and their associated ground truth annotations for the occurrence of AUs $\mathbf{y}_1, \ldots, \mathbf{y}_n \in \mathcal{Y}$. We wish to learn a mapping $f : \mathcal{X} \to \mathcal{Y}$ for automatically detecting the AU events in unseen signals. This complex output space contains all contiguous time intervals; each label $\mathbf{y}_i$ consists of two numbers indicating the onset and the offset of an AU:

$$\mathcal{Y} = \left\{ \mathbf{y} \mid \mathbf{y} = \emptyset \text{ or } \mathbf{y} = [s, e] \in \mathbb{Z}^2, 1 \le s \le e \right\}. \tag{19.4}$$

Table 19.3 Performance on the RU-FACS-1 dataset, ROC metric and F1 metric. Higher numbers indicate better performance, and best results are printed in bold

AU	Area under ROC					Max F1 score				
	SVM	HMM2	HMM4	BoW-kSeg	kSeg-SVM	SVM	HMM2	HMM4	BoW-kSeg	kSeg-SVM
1	**0.86**	0.85	0.83	0.52	**0.86**	0.48	0.43	0.39	0.13	**0.59**
2	0.79	0.71	0.62	0.45	**0.81**	0.42	0.42	0.18	0.14	**0.56**
6	0.89	**0.92**	**0.92**	0.69	0.91	0.50	0.62	**0.63**	0.28	0.59
12	0.94	0.94	**0.95**	0.77	0.94	0.74	0.76	0.77	0.61	**0.78**
14	**0.70**	**0.70**	0.69	0.56	0.68	0.20	0.18	0.12	0.17	**0.27**
15	**0.90**	0.86	0.85	0.49	**0.90**	0.50	0.26	0.25	0.04	**0.59**
17	**0.90**	0.76	0.85	0.51	0.87	0.55	0.38	0.28	0.06	**0.56**
24	**0.85**	0.83	0.67	0.52	0.73	0.15	**0.18**	0.05	0.04	0.08
1+2	0.86	0.67	0.77	0.46	**0.89**	0.36	0.31	0.31	0.12	**0.56**
6+12	0.95	**0.98**	**0.98**	0.69	0.96	0.55	**0.64**	0.63	0.28	0.62

The empty label $\mathbf{y} = \emptyset$ indicates no occurrence of the AU. We will learn the mapping f as in the structured learning framework [15, 120] as

$$f(\mathbf{x}) = \underset{\mathbf{y} \in \mathcal{Y}}{\text{argmax}}\, g(\mathbf{x}, \mathbf{y}), \tag{19.5}$$

where $g(\mathbf{x}, \mathbf{y})$ assigns a score to any particular labeling $\mathbf{y}$; the higher this value is, the closer $\mathbf{y}$ is to the ground truth annotation. For structured output learning, the choice of $g(\mathbf{x}, \mathbf{y})$ is often taken to be a weighted sum of features in the feature space:

$$g(\mathbf{x}, \mathbf{y}) = \mathbf{w}^T \varphi(\mathbf{x}, \mathbf{y}), \tag{19.6}$$

where $\varphi(\mathbf{x}, \mathbf{y})$ is a joint feature mapping for temporal signal $\mathbf{x}$ and candidate label $\mathbf{y}$, and $\mathbf{w}$ is the weight vector. Learning f can therefore be posed as an optimization problem:

$$\min_{\mathbf{w}, \boldsymbol{\xi}} \frac{1}{2} \|\mathbf{w}\|^2 + C \sum_{i=1}^{n} \xi_i,$$

$$\text{s.t. } \mathbf{w}^T \varphi(\mathbf{x}_i, \mathbf{y}_i) \geq \mathbf{w}^T \varphi(\mathbf{x}_i, \mathbf{y}) + \Delta(\mathbf{y}_i, \mathbf{y}) - \xi_i \; \forall \mathbf{y},$$

$$\xi_i \geq 0 \; \forall i. \tag{19.7}$$

Here, $\Delta(\mathbf{y}_i, \mathbf{y})$ is a loss function that decreases as a label $\mathbf{y}$ approaches the ground truth label $\mathbf{y}_i$. Intuitively, the constraints in (19.7) force the score of $g(\mathbf{x}, \mathbf{y})$ to be higher for the ground truth label $\mathbf{y}_i$ than for any other value of $\mathbf{y}$, and moreover, to exceed this value by a margin equal to the loss associated with labeling $\mathbf{y}$.

Table 19.3 shows the experimental results on the RU-FACS-1 dataset. As can be seen, kSeg-SVM consistently outperforms frame-based classification. It has the highest ROC area for seven out of 10 AUs. Using the ROC metric, kSeg-SVM appears comparable to standard SVM. kSeg-SVM achieves highest F1 score on nine out of 10 test cases. As shown in Table 19.3, BoW-kSeg performs poorly. There are two possible reasons for this. First, clustering is done with K-means, an unsupervised, non-discriminative method that is not informed by the ground truth labels. Second, due to the hard dictionary assignment, each frame is forced to commit to a single cluster. While hard-clustering shows good performance in the task of object-detection, our time-series vary smoothly, resulting in large groups of consecutive frames being assigned to the same cluster.

At this point, it is worth pointing out that until now, a common measure of classifier performance for AU detection has been area under the curve (i.e. ROC). In object detection, the common measure represents the relation between recall and precision. The two approaches give very different views of classifier performance. This difference is not unanticipated in the object detection literature, but little attention has been paid to this issue in facial expression literature. In pattern recognition and machine learning, a common evaluation strategy is to consider correct classification rate (classification accuracy) or its complement error rate. However, this assumes that the natural distribution (prior probabilities) of each class are known and balanced. In an imbalanced setting, where the prior probability of the positive class is significantly less than the negative class (the ratio of these being defined as the skew), accuracy is inadequate as a performance measure since it becomes biased toward the majority class. That is, as the skew increases, accuracy tends toward majority class performance, effectively ignoring the recognition capability with respect to the minority class. This is a very common (if not the default) situation in facial expression recognition setting, where the prior probability of each target class (a certain facial expression) is significantly less than the negative class (all other facial expressions). Thus, when evaluating performance of automatic facial expression recognizer, other performance measures such as precision (this indicates the probability of correctly detecting a positive test sample and it is independent of class priors), recall (this indicates the fraction of the positives detected that are actually correct and, as it combines results from both positive and negative samples, it is class prior dependent), F1-measure (this is calculated as 2*recall*precision/(recall + precision)), and ROC (this is calculated as P(x|positive)/P(x|negative), where P(x|C) denotes the conditional probability that a data entry has the class label C, and where a ROC curve plots the classification results from the most positive to the most negative classification) are more appropriate.

19.6 Unsupervised Learning

With few exceptions, previous work on facial expression or action unit recognition has been supervised in nature. Little attention has been paid to the problem of unsupervised temporal segmentation or clustering facial events prior to recognition. Essa and Pentland [43] proposed an unsupervised probabilistic flow-based method to describe facial expressions. Hoey [53] presented a multilevel BN to learn in a weakly supervised manner the dynamics of facial expression. Bettinger et al. [11] used AAMs to learn the dynamics of person-specific facial expression models. Zelnik-Manor and Irani [133] proposed a modification of structure-from-motion factorization to temporally segment rigid and non-rigid facial motion. De la Torre et al. [32] proposed a geometric-invariant clustering algorithm to decompose a stream of one person's facial behavior into facial gestures. Their approach suggested that unusual facial expressions might be detected through temporal outlier patterns. In recent work, Zhou et al. [143] proposed Aligned Cluster Analysis (ACA), an extension of spectral clustering for time series clustering and embedding. ACA was applied to discover in unsupervised manner facial actions across individuals that achieves moderate agreement with FACS. In this section, we briefly illustrate the applications of ACA for facial expression analysis, and refer the reader to [141, 143] for further details.

19.6.1 Facial Event Discovery for One Subject

Figure 19.13 shows the results of running unsupervised ACA on a video sequence of 1000 frames to summarize the facial expression of an infant into 10 temporal clusters. Appearance and shape features in the eyes and mouth, as described in Sect. 19.4.2, are used for temporal clustering. These 10 clusters provide a summarization of the infant's facial events. This visual summarization can be useful to automatically count the amount of time that the baby spends doing a particular facial expression (i.e. temporal cluster), such as crying, smiling or sleeping.

Extensions of ACA [143] can be used for facial expression indexing, given a sequence labeled by a user. Figure 19.14a on the left shows a frame of a sequence labeled by the user, and to the right there are six frames corresponding to six sequences returned by Supervised ACA (SACA). Next to the frames one can observe the matching score, which become higher the closer the retrieved sequence is to the user-specified sequence of facial expression.

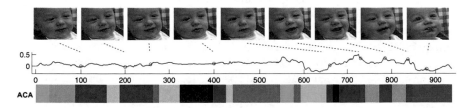

Fig. 19.13 Temporal clustering of infant facial behavior. Each color denotes a temporal unique cluster. Each facial gesture is coded with a different color. Observe how the frames of the same cluster correspond to similar facial expressions. Figure reproduced with permission from [108]. © 2010 IEEE

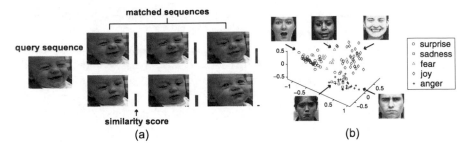

Fig. 19.14 **a** Facial expression indexing. The user specifies a query sequence and Supervised ACA returns six sequences with similar facial behavioral content as the video sequence selected by the user. **b** Three-dimensional embedding of 30 subjects with different facial expressions from the Cohn–Kanade database

ACA inherits the benefits of spectral clustering algorithms in that it provides a mechanism for finding a semantic low-dimensional embedding. In an evaluation, we tested the ability of unsupervised ACA to temporally cluster images and provide a visualization tool of several emotion-labeled sequences. Figure 19.14b shows the ACA embedding of 112 sequences from 30 randomly selected subjects from the Cohn–Kanade database [58]. The frames are labeled with five emotion labels: surprise, sadness, fear, joy and anger. The number of facial expressions varies across subjects. It is important to notice that, unlike traditional dimensionality reduction methods, each three-dimensional point in the embedding represents a video segment (of possibly different length) containing different facial expression. The ACA's embedding provides a natural mechanism for visualizing facial events and detecting outliers.

19.6.2 Facial Event Discovery for Sets of Subjects

This section illustrates the ability of ACA to discover dynamic facial events in the more challenging database RU-FACS [7] that contains naturally occurring facial behavior of multiple people. For this database the labels are AUs. We randomly selected 10 sets of 5 people and reported the mean clustering results and variance. The clustering accuracy is measured as the overlap between the temporal segmentation provided by ACA and the manually labeled FACS. ACA achieved an average accuracy of 52.2% in clustering the lower face and 68.8% in upper face using AUs labels. Figure 19.15a shows the results for temporal segmentation achieved by ACA on subjects S012, S028 and S049. Each color denotes a temporal cluster discovered by ACA. Figure 19.15 shows some of the dynamic vocabularies for facial expression analysis discovered by ACA. The algorithm correctly discovered smiling, with and without speech as different facial events. Visual inspection of all subjects' data suggests that the vocabulary of facial events is moderately consistent with human evaluation. More details are given in [143].

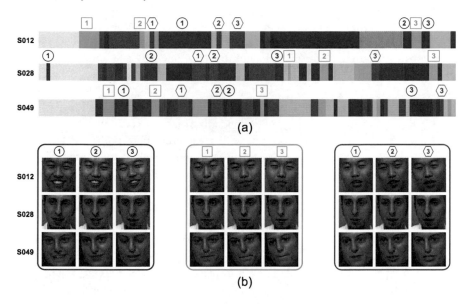

Fig. 19.15 a Results obtained by ACA for subjects S012, S028 and S049. **b** Corresponding video frames. Figure reproduced with permission from [108]. © 2010 IEEE

19.7 Conclusion and Future Challenges

Although many recent advances and successes in automatic facial expression analysis have been achieved, as described in the previous sections, many questions remain open, for which answers must be found. Few challenges remain such as (1) how to detect subtle AUs: more robust 3D models that effectively decouple rigid and non-rigid motion and better models that normalize for subject variability are needed to be researched. (2) More robust real-time systems for face acquisition, facial data extraction and representation, and facial expression recognition to handle head motion (both in-plane and out-of-plane), occlusion, lighting change, and low intensity expressions, all of which are common in spontaneous facial behavior in naturalistic environments; new 3D sensors such as structure light cameras or time-of-flight cameras can are a promising direction for real-time segmentation (3) most work on facial expression analysis has been done in the area of recognition (temporal segmentation is provided), and more specialized machine learning algorithms are needed for the problem of detection in naturally occurring behavior.

Because most investigators have used relatively limited datasets (with typically unknown reliability), the generalizability of different approaches to facial expression analysis remains unknown. With few exceptions, investigators have failed to report inter-observer reliability and the validity of the facial expressions they have analyzed. Approaches to facial expression analysis that have been developed in this way may transfer poorly to applications in which expressions, subjects, contexts, or image properties are more variable. In the absence of comparative tests on common data, the relative strengths and weaknesses of different approaches are difficult to determine. In particular, there is need for fully FACS coded databases with natural occurring behavior. Because intensity and duration measurements are critical, it is important to include descriptive data on these features as well.

Facial expression is one of several modes of nonverbal communication. The message value of various modes may differ depending on context and may be congruent or discrepant with each other. An interesting research topic is the integration of facial expression analysis with gesture, prosody, and speech. Combining facial features with acoustic features would help to separate the effects of facial actions due to facial expression and those due to speech-related movements.

At present, taxonomies of facial expression are based on FACS or other observer-based schemes. Consequently, approaches to automatic facial expression recognition are dependent on access to corpuses of FACS or similarly labeled video. This is a significant concern, in that recent work suggests that extremely large corpuses of labeled data may be needed to train robust classifiers. An open question in facial analysis is of whether facial actions can be learned directly from video in an unsupervised manner. That is, can the taxonomy be learned directly from video? And unlike FACS and similar systems that were initially developed to label static expressions, can we learn dynamic trajectories of facial actions? In our preliminary findings [143] on unsupervised learning using the using the RU-FACS database, agreement between facial actions identified by unsupervised analysis of face dynamics and FACS approached the level of agreement that has been found between independent FACS coders. These findings suggest that unsupervised learning of facial expression is a promising alternative to supervised learning of FACS-based actions. At least three benefits follow. One is the prospect that automatic facial expression analysis may be freed from its dependence on observer-based labeling. Second, because the current approach is fully empirical, it potentially can identify regularities in video that have not been anticipated by the top–down approaches such as FACS. New discoveries become possible. Three, similar benefits may accrue in other areas of image understanding of human behavior. Recent efforts by Guerra-Filho and Aloimonos [49] to develop vocabularies and grammars of human actions depend on advances in unsupervised learning. However, more robust and efficient algorithms that can learn from large databases are needed, as well as algorithms that can cluster more subtle facial behavior.

While research challenges in automated facial image and analysis remain, the time is near to apply these emerging tools to real-world problems in clinical science and practice, marketing, surveillance and human computer interaction.

Acknowledgements This work was partially supported by National Institute of Health Grant R01 MH 051435, and the National Science Foundation under Grant No. EEC-0540865. Thanks to Tomas Simon, Minh H. Nguyen, Feng Zhou, Simon Baker, Simon Lucey and Iain Matthews for helpful discussions, and some figures.

References

1. Ambadar, Z., Cohn, J.F., Reed, L.I.: All smiles are not created equal: Morphology and timing of smiles perceived as amused, polite, and embarrassed/nervous. J. Nonverbal Behav. **33**(1), 17–34 (2009) [379]
2. Ambadar, Z., Schooler, J.W., Cohn, J.F.: Deciphering the enigmatic face. Psychol. Sci. **16**(5), 403–410 (2005) [377]
3. Anderson, K., McOwan, P.W.: A real-time automated system for the recognition of human facial expressions. IEEE Trans. Syst. Man Cybern., Part B, Cybern. **36**(1), 96–105 (2006) [388,389]
4. Ashraf, A.B., Lucey, S., Cohn, J.F., Chen, T., Ambadar, Z., Prkachin, K.M., Solomon, P.E.: The painful face-pain expression recognition using active appearance models. Image Vis. Comput. **27**(12), 1788–1796 (2009) [388,390]
5. Baker, S., Matthews, I.: Lucas–Kanade 20 years on: A unifying framework. Int. J. Comput. Vis. **56**(3), 221–255 (2004) [386]
6. Bartlett, M., Littlewort, G., Fasel, I., Movellan, J.R.: Real time face detection and facial expression recognition: Development and applications to human computer interaction. In: CVPR Workshops for HCI (2003) [378]
7. Bartlett, M.S., Littlewort, G.C., Frank, M.G., Lainscsek, C., Fasel, I., Movellan, J.R.: Automatic recognition of facial actions in spontaneous expressions. J. Multimed. **1**(6), 22–35 (2006) [382,384,386,388,390,400]
8. Bartlett, M.S., Littlewort, G., Frank, M., Lainscsek, C., Fasel, I., Movellan, J.: Fully automatic facial action recognition in spontaneous behavior. In: AFGR, pp. 223–230 (2006) [390]
9. Beebe, B., Badalamenti, A., Jaffe, J., Feldstein, S., Marquette, L., Helbraun, E.: Distressed mothers and their infants use a less efficient timing mechanism in creating expectancies of each other's looking patterns. J. Psycholinguist. Res. **37**(5), 293–307 (2008) [383]
10. Bergen, J.R., Anandan, P., Hanna, K.J., Hingorani, R.: Hierarchical model-based motion estimation. In: European Conference on Computer Vision, pp. 237–252 (1992) [386]
11. Bettinger, F., Cootes, T.F., Taylor, C.J.: Modelling facial behaviours. In: BMVC (2002) [399]
12. Black, M.J., Jepson, A.D.: Eigentracking: Robust matching and tracking of objects using view-based representation. Int. J. Comput. Vis. **26**(1), 63–84 (1998) [384,386]
13. Black, M.J., Yacoob, Y.: Recognizing facial expressions in image sequences using local parameterized models of image motion. Int. J. Comput. Vis. **25**(1), 23–48 (1997) [384]
14. Blanz, V., Vetter, T.: A morphable model for the synthesis of 3D faces. In: SIGGRAPH (1999) [384]
15. Blaschko, M., Lampert, C.: Learning to localize objects with structured output regression. In: ECCV, pp. 2–15 (2008) [395,397]
16. Bobick, A., Davis, J.: The recognition of human movement using temporal templates. IEEE Trans. Pattern Anal. Mach. Intell. **23**(3), 257–267 (2001) [389]
17. Breiman, L.: Classification and Regression Trees. Chapman & Hall, London (1998) [392]
18. Bruce, V.: What the human face tells the human mind: Some challenges for the robot–human interface. In: IEEE Int. Workshop on Robot and Human Communication (1992) [378]
19. Chang, K.Y., Liu, T.L., Lai, S.H.: Learning partially-observed hidden conditional random fields for facial expression recognition. In: CVPR (2009) [391]
20. Chang, Y., Hu, C., Feris, R., Turk, M.: Manifold based analysis of facial expression. In: CVPR Workshops, p. 81 (2004) [388,390]
21. Chetverikov, D., Péteri, R.: A brief survey of dynamic texture description and recognition. In: Computer Recognition Systems, pp. 17–26 (2005) [389]
22. Cohen, I., Sebe, N., Cozman, F.G., Cirelo, M.C., Huang, T.S.: Learning Bayesian network classifiers for facial expression recognition using both labeled and unlabeled data. In: CVPR (2003) [388,389,391,395]
23. Cohen, I., Sebe, N., Garg, A., Chen, L.S., Huang, T.S.: Facial expression recognition from video sequences: Temporal and static modeling. Comput. Vis. Image Underst. **91**(1–2), 160–187 (2003) [384]

24. Cohn, J.F., Ambadar, Z., Ekman, P.: Observer-based measurement of facial expression with the facial action coding system. In: The Handbook of Emotion Elicitation and Assessment. Series in Affective Science. Oxford University Press, New York (2007) [379-381]

25. Cohn, J.F., Ekman, P.: Measuring facial action by manual coding, facial emg, and automatic facial image analysis. In: Handbook of Nonverbal Behavior Research Methods in the Affective Sciences, pp. 9–64 (2005) [378]

26. Cohn, J.F., Kanade, T.: Automated facial image analysis for measurement of emotion expression. In: The Handbook of Emotion Elicitation and Assessment, pp. 222–238 (2007) [381]

27. Cohn, J.F., Simon, T., Hoai, M., Zhou, F., Tejera, M., De la Torre, F.: Detecting depression from facial actions and vocal prosody. In: ACII (2009) [377,390]

28. Cootes, T.F., Edwards, G.J., Taylor, C.J.: Active appearance models. IEEE Trans. Pattern Anal. Mach. Intell. 23(6), 681–685 (2001) [384-386]

29. Dai, Y., Shibata, Y., Ishii, T., Hashimoto, K., Katamachi, K., Noguchi, K., Kakizaki, N., Ca, D.: An associate memory model of facial expressions and its application in facial expression recognition of patients on bed. In: ICME, pp. 591–594 (2001) [377]

30. Darwin, C.: The Expression of the Emotions in Man and Animals. Oxford University Press New York (1872/1998) [377]

31. De la Torre, F., Black, M.J.: Robust parameterized component analysis: theory and applications to 2d facial appearance models. Comput. Vis. Image Underst. 91, 53–71 (2003) [386]

32. De la Torre, F., Campoy, J., Ambadar, Z., Cohn, J.: Temporal segmentation of facial behavior. In: International Conference on Computer Vision (2007) [399]

33. De la Torre, F., Collet, A., Cohn, J., Kanade, T.: Filtered component analysis to increase robustness to local minima in appearance models. In: CVPR (2007) [384]

34. De la Torre, F., Vitrià, J., Radeva, P., Melenchón, J.: Eigenfiltering for flexible eigentracking. In: ICPR (2000) [384]

35. De la Torre, F., Yacoob, Y., Davis, L.: A probabilistic framework for rigid and non-rigid appearance based tracking and recognition. In: AFGR, pp. 491–498 (2000) [390]

36. DePaulo, B., Lindsay, J., Malone, B., Muhlenbruck, L., Charlton, K., Cooper, H.: Cues to deception. Psychol. Bull. 129(1), 74–118 (2003) [383]

37. Donato, G., Bartlett, M.S., Hager, J.C., Ekman, P., Sejnowski, T.J.: Classifying facial actions. IEEE Trans. Pattern Anal. Mach. Intell. 21(10), 979–984 (1999) [389]

38. Ekman, P.: An argument for basic emotions. Cogn. Emot. 6, 169–200 (1992) [377,378]

39. Ekman, P., Davidson, R.J., Friesen, W.V.: The Duchenne smile: Emotional expression and brain physiology II. J. Pers. Soc. Psychol. 58(2), 342–353 (1990) [377]

40. Ekman, P., Friesen, W.: Facial Action Coding System: A Technique for the Measurement of Facial Movement. Consulting Psychologists Press, Palo Alto (1978) [379]

41. Ekman, P., Huang, T.S., Sejnowski, T.J., Hager, J.C.: Final report to NSF of the planning workshop on facial expression understanding. Human Interaction Laboratory, University of California, San Francisco (1993) [378]

42. Ekman, P., Rosenberg, E.L.: What the Face Reveals: Basic and Applied Studies of Spontaneous Expression Using the Facial Action Coding System (FACS). Oxford University Press, London (2005) [383]

43. Essa, I.A., Pentland, A.P.: Coding, analysis, interpretation, and recognition of facial expressions. IEEE Trans. Pattern Anal. Mach. Intell. 19(7), 757–763 (2002) [384,389,399]

44. Fasel, B., Luettin, J.: Automatic facial expression analysis: a survey. Pattern Recognit. 36(1), 259–275 (2003) [384,391]

45. Forbes, E.E., Cohn, J.F., Allen, N.B., Lewinsohn, P.M.: Infant affect during parent–infant interaction at 3 and 6 months: Differences between mothers and fathers and influence of parent history of depression. Infancy 5, 61–84 (2004) [378]

46. Gatica-Perez, D.: Automatic nonverbal analysis of social interaction in small groups: A review. Image Vis. Comput. 27(12), 1775–1787 (2009) [377]

47. Griffin, K.M., Sayette, M.A.: Facial reactions to smoking cues relate to ambivalence about smoking. Psychol. Addict. Behav. **22**(4), 551 (2008) [377]
48. Gross, R., Matthews, I., Cohn, J.F., Kanade, T., Baker, S.: The cmu multi-pose, illumination, and expression (multi-pie) face database. Technical report, Carnegie Mellon University Robotics Institute, TR-07-08 (2007) [382]
49. Guerra-Filho, G., Aloimonos, Y.: A language for human action. Computer **40**, 42–51 (2007) [402]
50. Guo, G., Dyer, C.R.: Learning from examples in the small sample case: Face expression recognition. IEEE Trans. Syst. Man Cybern., Part B, Cybern. **35**(3), 477–488 (2005) [388]
51. Hartley, R., Zisserman, A.: Multiple View Geometry in Computer Vision. Cambridge University Press, Cambridge (2000) [386]
52. Hatfield, E., Cacioppo, J.T., Rapson, R.L.: Primitive emotional contagion. Emotion and Social Behavior **13**, 151–177 (1992) [377]
53. Hoey, J.: Hierarchical unsupervised learning of facial expression categories. In: IEEE Workshop on Detection and Recognition of Events in Video, pp. 99–106 (2002) [399]
54. Huang, D., De la Torre, F.: Bilinear kernel reduced rank regression for facial expression synthesis. In: ECCV (2010) [378]
55. Izard, C.E., Huebner, R.R., Risser, D., Dougherty, L.: The young infant's ability to produce discrete emotion expressions. Dev. Psychol. **16**(2), 132–140 (1980) [378]
56. Jolliffe, I.T.: Principal Component Analysis. Springer, New York (1986) [385]
57. Jones, M.J., Poggio, T.: Multidimensional morphable models. In: ICCV (1998) [384]
58. Kanade, T., Cohn, J.F., Tian, Y.: Comprehensive database for facial expression analysis. In: AFGR (2000) [382,400]
59. Koelstra, S., Pantic, M.: Non-rigid registration using free-form deformations for recognition of facial actions and their temporal dynamics. In: AFGR (2008) [384,391]
60. Kohler, C.G., Martin, E.A., Stolar, N., Barrett, F.S., Verma, R., Brensinger, C., Bilker, W., Gur, R.E., Gur, R.C.: Static posed and evoked facial expressions of emotions in schizophrenia. Schizophr. Res. **105**, 49–60 (2008) [390]
61. Kotsia, I., Pitas, I.: Facial expression recognition in image sequences using geometric deformation features and support vector machines. IEEE Trans. Image Process. **16**, 172–187 (2007) [388]
62. Krumhuber, E., Manstead, A.S., Cosker, D., Marshall, D., Rosin, P.: Effects of dynamic attributes of smiles in human and synthetic faces: A simulated job interview setting. J. Nonverbal Behav. **33**(1), 1–15 (2009) [383]
63. Lafferty, J., McCallum, A., Pereira, F.: Conditional random fields: Probabilistic models for segmenting and labeling sequence data. In: ICML (2001) [395]
64. Langner, O., Dotsch, R., Bijlstra, G., Wigboldus, D.H.J., Hawk, S.T., van Knippenberg, A.: Presentation and validation of the Radboud Faces Database. Cogn. Emot. **24**(8), 1377–1388 (2010) [382]
65. Lee, C., Elgammal, A.: Facial expression analysis using nonlinear decomposable generative models. In: IEEE International Workshop on Analysis and Modeling of Faces and Gestures, pp. 17–31 (2005) [390]
66. Levenson, R.W., Ekman, P., Friesen, W.V.: Voluntary facial action generates emotion-specific autonomic nervous system activity. Psychophysiology **27**(4), 363–384 (1990) [377]
67. Li, S., Jain, A.: Handbook of Face Recognition. Springer, New York (2005) [391]
68. Littlewort, G., Bartlett, M.S., Fasel, I., Susskind, J., Movellan, J.: Dynamics of facial expression extracted automatically from video. Image Vis. Comput. **24**(6), 615–625 (2006) [384, 388,390]
69. Littlewort, G.C., Bartlett, M.S., Lee, K.: Automatic coding of facial expressions displayed during posed and genuine pain. Image Vis. Comput. **12**(27), 1797–1803 (2009) [390]
70. Littlewort, G., Bartlett, M.S., Whitehill, J., Wu, T.F., Butko, N., Ruvulo, P., et al.: The motion in emotion: A cert based approach to the fera emotion challenge. In: Paper presented at the 1st Facial Expression Recognition and Analysis challenge 2011, 9th IEEE International Conference on AFGR (2011) [390]

71. Liu, X.: Generic face alignment using boosted appearance model. In: CVPR (2007) [386]
72. Lo, H., Chung, R.: Facial expression recognition approach for performance animation. In: International Workshop on Digital and Computational Video (2001) [378]
73. Lowe, D.: Object recognition from local scale-invariant features. In: ICCV (1999) [389]
74. Lucas, B., Kanade, T.: An iterative image registration technique with an application to stereo vision. In: Proceedings of Imaging Understanding Workshop (1981) [384,386]
75. Lucey, P., Cohn, J., Howlett, J., Lucey, S., Sridharan, S.: Recognizing emotion with head pose variation: Identifying pain segments in video. IEEE Trans. Syst. Man Cybern., Part B, Cybern. **41**(3), 664–674 (2011) [380]
76. Lucey, P., Cohn, J., Lucey, S., Sridharan, S., Prkachin, K.M.: Automatically detecting action units from faces of pain: Comparing shape and appearance features. In: CVPR Workshops (2009) [390]
77. Lucey, P., Cohn, J.F., Lucey, S., Sridharan, S., Prkachin, K.M.: Automatically detecting pain using facial actions. In: ACII (2009) [388]
78. Lucey, P., Cohn, J.F., Kanade, T., Saragih, J., Ambadar, Z., Matthews, I.: The extended Cohn–Kanade dataset (CK+): A complete dataset for action unit and emotion-specified expression. In: CVPR Workshops for Human Communicative Behavior Analysis (2010) [382,384]
79. Lucey, P., Cohn, J.F., Matthews, I., Lucey, S., Sridharan, S., Howlett, J., Prkachin, K.M.: Automatically detecting pain in video through facial action units. IEEE Trans. Syst. Man Cybern., Part B, Cybern. **PP**(99), 1–11 (2010) [377,390]
80. Lucey, P., Cohn, J.F., Prkachin, K.M., Solomon, P., Matthews, I.: Painful data: The UNBC-McMaster shoulder pain expression archive database. In: AFGR (2011) [382]
81. Lucey, S., Matthews, I., Hu, C., Ambadar, Z., De la Torre, F., Cohn, J.: AAM derived face representations for robust facial action recognition. In: AFGR (2006) [384,388,390]
82. Lyons, M., Akamatsu, S., Kamachi, M., Gyoba, J.: Coding facial expressions with gabor wavelets. In: AFGR (2002) [382,384]
83. Madsen, M., el Kaliouby, R., Eckhardt, M., Hoque, M., Goodwin, M., Picard, R.W.: Lessons from participatory design with adolescents on the autism spectrum. In: Proc. Computer Human Interaction (2009) [378]
84. Malatesta, C.Z., Culver, C., Tesman, J.R., Shepard, B., Fogel, A., Reimers, M., Zivin, G.: The Development of Emotion Expression During the First Two Years of Life. Monographs of the Society for Research in Child Development, pp. 97–136 (1989) [377]
85. Martinez, A.M., Benavente, R.: The AR face database. In: CVC Technical Report, number 24 (June 1998) [382]
86. Mase, K., Pentland, A.: Automatic lipreading by computer. Trans. Inst. Electron. Inf. Commun. Eng. **J73-D-II**(6), 796–803 (1990) [389]
87. Matthews, I., Baker, S.: Active appearance models revisited. Int. J. Comput. Vis. **60**(2), 135–164 (2004) [384,386]
88. Matthews, I., Xiao, J., Baker, S.: 2d vs. 3d deformable face models: Representational power, construction, and real-time fitting. Int. J. Comput. Vis. **75**(1), 93–113 (2007) [385]
89. Mikolajczyk, K., Schmid, C.: A performance evaluation of local descriptors. IEEE Trans. Pattern Anal. Mach. Intell. **27**(10), 1615–1630 (2005) [389]
90. Nguyen, N., Guo, Y.: Comparisons of sequence labeling algorithms and extensions. In: ICML (2007) [395]
91. O'Toole, A.J., Harms, J., Snow, S.L., Hurst, D.R., Pappas, M.R., Ayyad, J.H., Abdi, H.: A video database of moving faces and people. IEEE Trans. Pattern Anal. Mach. Intell. **27**(5), 812–816 (2005) [382]
92. Pandzic, I.S., Forchheimer, R.R. (eds.): MPEG-4 Facial Animation: The Standard, Implementation and Applications. Wiley, New York (2002) [381]
93. Pantic, M., Bartlett, M.S.: Machine analysis of facial expressions. In: Face Recognition, pp. 377–416 (2007) [384]
94. Pantic, M., Patras, I.: Dynamics of facial expression: Recognition of facial actions and their temporal segments from face profile image sequences. IEEE Trans. Syst. Man Cybern., Part B, Cybern. **36**, 433–449 (2006) [388,391]

95. Pantic, M., Rothkrantz, L.J.M.: Automatic analysis of facial expressions: The state of the art. IEEE Trans. Pattern Anal. Mach. Intell. **22**(12), 1424–1445 (2002) [384,391]
96. Pantic, M., Rothkrantz, L.J.M.: Facial action recognition for facial expression analysis from static face images. IEEE Trans. Syst. Man Cybern., Part B, Cybern. **34**(3), 1449–1461 (2004) [388]
97. Pantic, M., Sebe, N., Cohn, J.F., Huang, T.: Affective multimodal human–computer interaction. In: ACM International Conference on Multimedia, pp. 669–676 (2005) [391]
98. Pentland, A.: Looking at people: Sensing for ubiquitous and wearable computing. IEEE Trans. Pattern Anal. Mach. Intell. **22**(1), 107–119 (2000) [377]
99. Pilz, S.K., Thornton, I.M., Bülthoff, H.H.: A search advantage for faces learned in motion. Exp. Brain Res. **171**(4) 436–447 (2006) [382]
100. Prkachin, K.M., Solomon, P.E.: The structure, reliability and validity of pain expression: Evidence from patients with shoulder pain. Pain **139**(2), 267–274 (2008) [377]
101. Rademaker, R., Pantic, M., Valstar, M.F., Maat, L.: Web-based database for facial expression analysis. In: ICME (2005) [382]
102. Saragih, J., Goecke, R.: A nonlinear discriminative approach to AAM fitting. In: ICCV (2007) [386]
103. Sayette, M.A., Cohn, J.F., Wertz, J.M., Perrott, M.A., Parrott, D.J.: A psychometric evaluation of the facial action coding system for assessing spontaneous expression. J. Nonverbal Behav. **25**(3), 167–185 (2001) [381]
104. Scherer, K., Ekman, P.: Handbook of Methods in Nonverbal Behavior Research. Cambridge University Press, Cambridge (1982) [379]
105. Schmidt, K.L., Cohn, J.F.: Human facial expressions as adaptations: Evolutionary perspectives in facial expression research. Yearb. Phys. Antropol. **116**, 8–24 (2001) [379]
106. Shang, L.F., Chan, K.P.: Nonparametric discriminant HMM and application to facial expression recognition. In: CVPR (2009) [391,395]
107. Shergill, G.H., Sarrafzadeh, H., Diegel, O., Shekar, A.: Computerized sales assistants: The application of computer technology to measure consumer interest;a conceptual framework. J. Electron. Commer. Res. **9**(2), 176–191 (2008) [377]
108. Simon, T., Nguyen, M.H., De la Torre, F., Cohn, J.F.: Action unit detection with segment-based SVMs. In: Conference on Computer Vision and Pattern Recognition, pp. 2737–2744 (2010) [384,387,388,395,396,401]
109. Taskar, B., Guestrin, C., Koller, D.: Max-margin Markov networks. In: NIPS (2003) [395]
110. Theobald, B.J., Cohn, J.F.: Facial image synthesis. In: Oxford Companion to Emotion and the Affective Sciences, pp. 176–179. Oxford University Press, London (2009) [378]
111. Tian, Y., Kanade, T., Cohn, J.F.: Evaluation of Gabor-wavelet-based facial action unit recognition in image sequences of increasing complexity. In: AFGR (2002) [388,390]
112. Tian, Y., Kanade, T., Cohn, J.F.: Recognizing action units for facial expression analysis. IEEE Trans. Pattern Anal. Mach. Intell. **23**(2), 97–115 (2002) [384]
113. Tian, Y., Kanade, T., Cohn, J.F.: Facial expression analysis. In: Handbook of Face Recognition, Springer, Berlin (2008) [384,388,391]
114. Tola, E., Lepetit, V., Fua, P.: A fast local descriptor for dense matching. In: CVPR (2008) [389]
115. Tola, E., Lepetit, V., Fua, P.: Daisy: An efficient dense descriptor applied to wide baseline stereo. IEEE Trans. Pattern Anal. Mach. Intell. **99**(1) (2009) [389]
116. Tomkins, S.S.: Affect, Imagery, Consciousness. Springer, New York (1962) [377]
117. Tong, Y., Liao, W., Ji, Q.: Facial action unit recognition by exploiting their dynamic and semantic relationships. IEEE Trans. Pattern Anal. Mach. Intell. **29** 1683–1699 (2007) [384, 391,395]
118. Tremeau, F., Malaspina, D., Duval, F., Correa, H., Hager-Budny, M., Coin-Bariou, L., Macher, J.P., Gorman, J.M.: Facial expressiveness in patients with schizophrenia compared to depressed patients and nonpatient comparison subjects. Am. J. Psychiatr. **162**(1), 92 (2005) [377]
119. Tsochantaridis, I., Joachims, T., Hofmann, T., Altun, Y.: Large margin methods for structured and interdependent output variables. J. Mach. Learn. Res. **6**, 1453–1484 (2005) [395]

120. Tsochantaridis, I., Joachims, T., Hofmann, T., Altun, Y.: Large margin methods for structured and interdependent output variables. J. Mach. Learn. Res. **6**, 1453–1484 (2005) [397]
121. Valstar, M., Pantic, M., Patras, I.: Motion history for facial action detection in video. In: IEEE Int'l Conf. on Systems, Man and Cybernetics, pp. 635–640 (2005) [389]
122. Valstar, M.F., Pantic, M.: Fully automatic facial action unit detection and temporal analysis. In: CVPR (2006) [391]
123. Valstar, M.F., Pantic, M.: Combined support vector machines and hidden Markov models for modeling facial action temporal dynamics. In: ICCV Workshop on HCI (2007) [384,388, 390,395]
124. Valstar, M.F., Pantic, M.: Induced disgust, happiness and surprise: an addition to the mmi facial expression database. In: Proceedings of the EMOTION 2010 Workshop (2010) [382]
125. Valstar, M.F., Patras, I., Pantic, M.: Facial action unit detection using probabilistic actively learned support vector machines on tracked facial point data. In: CVPR Workshops (2005) [391]
126. van Dam, A.: Beyond wimp. IEEE Comput. Graph. Appl. **20**(1), 50–51 (2000) [377]
127. Viola, P., Jones, M.: Rapid object detection using a boosted cascade of simple features. In: CVPR (2001) [384,392]
128. Vural, E., Bartlett, M., Littlewort, G., Cetin, M., Ercil, A., Movellan, J.: Discrimination of moderate and acute drowsiness based on spontaneous facial expressions. In: ICPR (2010) [377]
129. Wen, Z., Huang, T.S.: Capturing subtle facial motions in 3d face tracking. In: CVPR (2008) [384]
130. Xiao, J., Baker, S., Matthews, I., Kanade, T.: Real-time combined 2D+3D active appearance models. In: CVPR (2004) [386]
131. Yacoob, Y., Davis, L.S.: Recognizing human facial expressions from long image sequences using optical flow. IEEE Trans. Pattern Anal. Mach. Intell. **18**(6), 636–642 (2002) [384,389]
132. Yin, L., Wei, X., Sun, Y., Wang, J., Rosato, M.J.: A 3d facial expression database for facial behavior research. In: AFGR (2006) [382]
133. Zelnik-Manor, L., Irani, M.: Temporal factorization vs. spatial factorization. In: ECCV (2004) [399]
134. Zeng, Z., Pantic, M., Roisman, G.I., Huang, T.S.: A survey of affect recognition methods: Audio, visual, and spontaneous expressions. IEEE Trans. Pattern Anal. Mach. Intell. **31**(1), 39–58 (2008) [391]
135. Zeng, Z., Hu, Y., Roisman, G.I., Wen, Z., Fu, Y., Huang, T.S.: Audio-visual emotion recognition in adult attachment interview. In: 8th International Conference on Multimodal Interfaces (2009) [390]
136. Zeng, Z., Pantic, M., Roisman, G.I., Huang, T.S.: A survey of affect recognition methods: Audio, visual, and spontaneous expressions. IEEE Trans. Pattern Anal. Mach. Intell. **31**(1), 31–58 (2009) [391]
137. Zhang, C., Zhango, Z.: A survey of recent advances in face detection. In: Technical Report, MSR-TR-2010-66 Microsoft Research (June 2010) [384]
138. Zhang, Z., Lyons, M., Schuster, M., Akamatsu, S.: Comparison between geometry-based and gabor-wavelets-based facial expression recognition using multi-layer perceptron. In: AFGR (2002) [384,389]
139. Zhao, G., Pietikainen, M.: Dynamic texture recognition using local binary patterns with an application to facial expressions. IEEE Trans. Pattern Anal. Mach. Intell. **29**(6), 915–928 (2007) [389,390]
140. Zhao, W., Chellappa, R.: Face Processing: Advanced Modeling and Methods. Academic Press, San Diego (2006) [391]
141. Zhou, F., De la Torre, F., Hodgins, J.: Aligned cluster analysis for temporal segmentation of human motion. In: IEEE Automatic Face and Gesture Recognition (2008) [399]
142. Zhu, Y., De la Torre, F., Cohn, J.F.: Dynamic cascades with bidirectional bootstrapping for spontaneous facial action unit detection. In: ACII (2009) [384,387,389,392-395]

143. Zhou, F., De la Torre, F., Cohn, J.: Unsupervised discovery of facial events. In: CVPR (2010) [399,400,402]
144. Zhou, F., De la Torre, F., Cohn, J.F.: Unsupervised discovery of facial events. In: Conference on Computer Vision and Pattern Recognition, pp. 2574–2581 (2010) [388]
145. Zue, V.W., Glass, J.R.: Conversational interfaces: Advances and challenges. Proc. IEEE **88**(8), 1166–1180 (2002) [377]

Chapter 20
Benchmarking Datasets for Human Activity Recognition

Haowei Liu, Rogerio Feris, and Ming-Ting Sun

Abstract Recognizing human activities has become an important topic in the past few years. A variety of techniques for representing and modeling different human activities have been proposed, achieving reasonable performances in many scenarios. On the other hand, different benchmarks have also been collected and published. Different from other chapters focusing on the algorithmic aspects, this chapter gives an overview of different benchmarking datasets, summarizes the performances of the-state-of-the-art algorithms, and analyzes these datasets.

20.1 Introduction

In the past few years, the problem of automatically recognizing human activities in videos has emerged as an important field and attracted many researchers in the vision community. The problem is challenging as in general, the videos could have been shot in an unconstrained environment where the camera could be moving, the background can be cluttered, or the camera view point can be different. All these factors already make recognition of human activities difficult, let alone possible occlusions or variations of activities different subjects perform. With that said, much progress has been made toward the automatic understanding of human activities. On one hand, many approaches (e.g. feature representations and modeling) have been proposed, which have addressed the problem to some degree. On the other hand, many benchmarks and datasets consisting of activity video sequences have been collected and published. Different from other chapters, which focus on activity representation and modeling, this chapter surveys different publicly available

H. Liu (✉) · M.-T. Sun
University of Washington, Seattle, WA 98195, USA
e-mail: hwliu@uw.edu

M.-T. Sun
e-mail: mts@uw.edu

R. Feris
IBM T.J. Watson Research Center, Hawthorn, NY 10532, USA
e-mail: rsferis@ibm.com

T.B. Moeslund et al. (eds.), *Visual Analysis of Humans*,   411
DOI 10.1007/978-0-85729-997-0_20, © Springer-Verlag London Limited 2011

benchmarks and summarizes the-state-of-art performances reported so far. Ideally, a
good benchmarking should approximate the realistic situations as much as possible
by incorporating video sequences with unrestricted camera motion, different scene
contexts, different degrees of background clutter and different camera perspectives.
It should also consist of video sequences with multiple subjects performing different activities in order to evaluate the robustness of activity recognition algorithms to
the intra-class variations of human activities. In what follows, we will also analyze
each dataset by these criteria. When summarizing the performances, we only report the best number achieved. The train/test split used in these works follow either
leave-one-out or leave-one-actor-out procedure. For the former, testing is done on
one sequence while training on the rest. For the latter, testing is done on sequences
performed by one actor while training on the rest. The performance is reported as
the average across the testing results.

20.2 Single View Activity Benchmarks with Cleaner Background

20.2.1 The KTH and the Weizmann Dataset

The KTH dataset [40] and the Weizmann dataset [10] are two widely used standard datasets, which consist of videos of different human activities performed by
different subjects. The KTH dataset is published by Schuldt et al. [40] in order to
benchmark their proposed motion features [40]. It contains six types of human activities (walking, jogging, running, boxing, hand waving, and hand clapping), which
are performed by 25 actors in four different scenarios, resulting in 600 sequences,
each with a spatial resolution of 160×120 pixels and a frame rate of 25 frames
per second. The other standard benchmark, the Weizmann dataset [10], contains 10
types of activities (walking, running, jumping, gallop sideways, bending, one-hand
waving, two-hand waving, jumping in place, jumping jack, and skipping), each performed by nine actors, resulting in 90 video sequences, each with a spatial resolution
of 180×144 pixels and a frame rate of 50 frames per second. The background is
static and clean with no camera motion. Each sequence is about three seconds long.

Since these datasets are originally published to validate proposed space–time features, they are easier compared with others as the background is cleaner and static,
the camera perspective is mostly frontal, and the camera motion is mostly still, although the KTH dataset contains a certain degree of camera zooming. Therefore,
they have been criticized for not being a realistic sampling of actions in the real
world. With that said, many researchers use them as a validation for newly proposed algorithms. Most state-of-the-art activity recognition algorithms have already
achieved higher than 90% accuracy on these two datasets. Below we summarize the
published results on both datasets in Tables 20.1 and 20.2. For these two datasets,
people typically use leave-one-actor-out evaluation. Hence, the training/testing split
is 24:1 for the KTH dataset and 8:1 for the Weizman dataset.

Table 20.1 Performances on the KTH dataset in average accuracy

Methods	Accuracy	Methods	Accuracy	Methods	Accuracy
Gilbert et al. [9]	95.7%	Cao et al. [4]	95.02%	Raptis et al. [35]	94.8%
Kovashka et al. [21]	94.5%	Brendel et al. [3]	94.2%	Liu et al [25]	94.16%
Han et al. [12]	94.1%	Liu et al. [26]	93.8%	Liu et al. [24]	93.43%
Yuan et al. [58]	93.3%	Bregonzio et al. [2]	93.17%	Wang et al. [51]	92.51%
Liu et al. [27]	92.3%	Leptev [23]	91.8%	Jhuang et al. [17]	91.7%
Fathi et al. [8]	90.5%	Yeffet et al. [57]	90.1%	Yao et al. [56]	87.8%
Ali et al. [1]	87.7%	Wang et al. [49]	87%	Messing et al. [31]	74%

Table 20.2 Performances on the Weizmann dataset in average accuracy

Methods	Accuracy	Methods	Accuracy
Wang et al. [51]	100%	Yeffet et al. [57]	100%
Fathi et al. [8]	100%	Tran et al. [44]	100%
Brendel et al. [3]	99.7%	Wang et al. [49]	97.2%
Bregonzio et al. [2]	96.66%	Satkin et al. [39]	95.76%
Lin et al. [24]	95.48%	Ali et al. [1]	95.2%
Chaudhry et al. [5]	94.4%	Jhuang et al. [17]	92.8%
Jiang et al. [18]	90%	Nieble et al. [32]	72.8%

20.2.2 The University of Rochester Activity of Daily Living Dataset

Messing et al. [31] publish an activity of daily living dataset. The dataset is created in order to approximate daily activities people might perform. The full list of activities is: answering a phone, dialing a phone, looking up a phone number in a telephone directory, writing a phone number on a white board, drinking a glass of water, eating snack chips, peeling a banana, eating a banana, chopping a banana, and eating food with silverware, all are ordinary activities people often perform. These activities are performed three times by five different people of different shapes, sizes, genders, and ethnicities, giving large appearance variations even for the same activity. The resolution is 1280 × 720 at 30 frames per second. Video sequences lasted between 10 and 60 seconds, ending when the activity was completed. Table 20.3 compares the performances on the University of Rochester activity of daily living dataset using different features. The evaluation follows the leave-one-actor-out procedure.

The evaluation consisted of training on all repetitions of activities by four of the five subjects, and testing on all repetitions of the fifth subjects activities. This leave-one-out testing was averaged over the performance with each left-out subject.

Table 20.3 Performances on the UR ADL dataset in average accuracy

	Methods	Recognition Accuracy
Messing et al. [31]	Velocity History	89%
Raptis et al. [35]	Tracklet	82.67%
Satkin et al. [39]	placeCityHOF + cropping	80%
Matikainen et al. [30]	Sequential Code Map + pairwise relation	70%

20.2.3 Other Datasets

Other than the aforementioned datasets, Tran et al. [44] compose a UIUC activity dataset, consisting of 532 high resolution (1024 × 768) sequences of 14 activities performed by 8 different actors with extensive repetition. Each sequence lasts for 10~15 seconds. They achieve an accuracy of 99.06% using the proposed metric learning method.

Another closely related source of datasets is the PETS (Performance Evaluation of Tracking and Surveillance) workshop [15], which releases high resolution surveillance footages every year. Portions of the released datasets are used as benchmarks for human activity recognition algorithms. For example, Ribeiro et al. [36] reported a 94% accuracy on the PETS04-CAVIAR dataset [13], which includes single person activities such as people fighting, walking or being immobile.

20.3 Single View Activity Benchmarks with Cluttered Background

20.3.1 The CMU Soccer Dataset and Crowded Videos Dataset

Different from the datasets introduced in previous section where the video sequences contain few or no background clutter, both the CMU soccer and CMU crowded video datasets are made to introduce cluttered background. In [7], Efros et al. record several minutes of a World Cup football game. The dataset consists of walking and running activities at different directions, giving a total of seven activities and around 5000 frames. Although the video sequences are recorded from TV programs, providing a resolution of 640 × 480, the dataset is challenging in that each human figure is only 30 pixels tall on average, and hence, fine-scale human pose estimation is not possible, making motion the only possible cue. Also, other moving humans from the background could also occlude the target subject. Table 20.4 summarizes the reported performance using leave-one-out procedure on this dataset. It suggests that putting a hierarchy or a generative model on the raw motion features could improve the performance by a 10% margin.

Ke et al. [19] collect video sequences of activities in crowded scenes to evaluate their proposed volumetric features, which are space–time templates for particular

Table 20.4 Performances on the soccer dataset in accuracy

	Methods	Accuracy
Wang et al. [50]	Motion descriptors + topic modeling	78.6%
Fathi et al. [8]	Mid-level motion descriptors	71%
Efros et al. [7]	Motion descriptors + nearest neighbor	67%

Table 20.5 Performances on the CMU crowded videos dataset in Area under ROC Curve (AU-ROC)

Actions/Methods	Ke et al. [19]	Brendel et al. [3]	Yao et al. [56]
Pick-up	0.47	0.60	0.58
One-hand wave	0.38	0.64	0.59
Push button	0.48	N.A.	0.74
Jumping jack	0.22	0.45	0.43
Two-hand wave	0.64	0.65	0.53

activities. These videos are recorded using a hand-held camera. Each activity is performed by three to six subjects, resulting in 110 activities of interest. The videos are downscaled to 160×120 in resolution. There is high variability in both how the subjects performed the activities and the background clutter. There are also significant spatial and temporal scale differences in the activities as well. Table 20.5 compares the performances of the state-of-the-art approaches. The performance gain of the latter two approaches comes from the incorporation of temporal features, for example, the time-series representation in [3]. Since these approaches are template-based, to test how well the templates generalize, the evaluation consists of training on sequences performed by one actor while testing on the rest.

20.3.2 The University of Maryland Gesture Dataset

Lin et al. [24] publish an UM gesture dataset consisting of 14 different gesture classes, which are a subset of the military signals. The gestures include "turn left", "turn right", "attention left", "attention right", "flap", "stop left", "stop right", "stop both", "attention both", "start", "go back", "close distance", "speed up" and "come near". The dataset is collected using a color camera with 640×480 resolution. Each activity is performed by three people for three times, giving 126 video sequences for training which are captured using a fixed camera with the person viewed against a simple, static background.

There are 168 video sequences for testing which are captured from a moving camera and in the presence of background clutter and other moving objects. Lin et al. [24] use the proposed prototype tree to achieve an accuracy of 91.07%. Brendel et al. [3] achieve 96.3% using time-series modeling while Tran et al. [44] achieve an 100% accuracy. Note that since this dataset focuses on military signals, it might not be a suitable benchmark for generic activity recognition.

20.4 Multi-view Benchmarks

The aforementioned benchmarks only provide video sequences from a single camera perspective. In real life, it might be desirable to have a multi-camera configuration, for example, in surveillance applications. In what follows, we introduce two datasets consisting of activities from different perspectives.

20.4.1 The University of Central Florida Sports Dataset

Rodriguez et al. [37] publish a dataset consisting of a set of actions collected from various sports which are typically featured on broadcast television channels such as BBC and ESPN. It contains over 200 video sequences at a resolution of 720 × 480 and consists of nine sport activities including diving, golf swinging, kicking, lifting, horseback riding, running, skating, swinging a baseball bat, and pole vaulting. These activities are featured in a wide range of scenes and viewpoints. Table 20.6 summarizes the published results using leave-one-out procedure on this dataset. Note that the space–time MACH filter [37] is a template matching approach. The low accuracy of its performance suggests that the model-based approach captures intra-class variability better when the camera view point varies.

Following the sports dataset, Yeffet et al. [57] publish a dataset of UFC videos from TV programs. UFC is a fighting sport similar to boxing. Therefore, the viewpoints and individual appearance vary differently and camera motion persists. In addition, two fighters act at the same time and could occlude each other. The dataset contains over 20 minutes of broadcast video, and two target activities are defined: the throw/take-down action and keen-kick action, two rarely occurred activities in UFC sport. Therefore, the dataset is versatile compared to other sports. One merit of this dataset is that the target activities are relevant to surveillance applications as these activities rarely occur and are similar to one person hitting another.

Table 20.6 Performances on the UCF sports dataset in average accuracy

	Methods	Recognition Accuracy
Kovashka et al. [21]	Hierarchical neighborhood feature	87.27%
Yeffet et al. [57]	Local trinity pattern feature	79.2%
Rodriguez et al. [37]	Space–time MACH filter	69%

Table 20.7 Performances on the multi-view dataset in average accuracy

*Result using information from all possible views

Methods	Accuracy
Weinland et al. [52]	91.11%*
Lv et al. [28]	80.06%
Tran et al. [44]	80%

20.4.2 The INRIA Multi-view Dataset

To the best of our knowledge, the multi-view dataset published by Weinland et al. [53] is the only known large scale multi-view dataset that provides synchronized video sequences from multiple cameras for each activity. They use multiple cameras to record 13 activities such as "walk", "sit down", "check watch", etc. Each activity is performed by multiple actors. The camera array provides five synchronized views at a resolution of 390 × 291 with a frame rate 23 frames per second. Each sequence lasts for a few seconds. Weinland et al. [52] demonstrate that by fusing views from multiple cameras, the accuracy can be greatly improved. Table 20.7 summarizes the performances reported so far. Note that Weinland et al. [52] use the information from all views while others, [28] and [44], use only one of the views. The evaluation follows the leave-one-actor-out procedure.

20.5 Benchmarks with Real World Footages

The datasets discussed thus far, except the UCF Sports Dataset, consist of video sequences where human actors perform different activities. Therefore, these datasets are made in a more controlled environment. In this section, we discuss datasets consisting of video sequences extracted from different real world sources, such as movies or the Internet. Since there is no limitation on how these video sequences should be made, these datasets are more difficult as the videos could contain occlusions, background clutters or could have been shot with different camera perspectives or motion.

20.5.1 The University of Central Florida Youtube Dataset

Liu et al. [26] collected video sequences from YouTube and made a dataset consisting of 11 activities, resulting in a total of 1168 sequences. These activities include basketball shooting (b_shooting), volleyball spiking (v_spiking), trampoline jumping (t_jumping), soccer juggling (s_juggling), horseback riding (h_riding), cycling, diving, swinging, golf swinging (g_swinging), tennis swinging (t_swinging), and walking (with a dog). Due to the diverse nature of video sources, these sequences contain significant camera motion, background clutters, and occlusions, variations

Table 20.8 Performances reported on the YouTube dataset in recognition accuracy

Methods/Actions	b_shooting	cycling	diving	g_winging	h_riding	s_juggling
Brendel et al. [3]	60.1%	79.3%	85.8%	89.8%	80.6%	59.3%
Liu et al. [27]	N.A.	N.A.	82%	86%	78%	60%
Ikizler-cinbis et al. [16]	48.48%	75.17%	95.0%	95.0%	73.0%	53.0%
Liu et al. [26]	53%	73%	81%	86%	72%	54%
Matikainen et al. [30]	N.A.	N.A.	N.A.	N.A.	N.A.	N.A.

Methods/Actions	swinging	t_swinging	t_jumping	v_spiking	walking	Mean
	61.7%	87.8%	88.3%	80.5%	82.7%	77.8%
	67%	76%	80%	80.2%	N.A.	76.1%
	66.0%	77.0%	93.0%	85.0%	66.67%	75.21%
	57%	80%	79%	73.3%	75%	71.2%
	N.A.	N.A.	N.A.	N.A.	N.A.	59%

in subject appearance, illumination and view point. Also, all the sequences are low-resolution videos (240 × 320) with a frame rate of 15 frames per second. Each activity is about 3∼5 seconds long. Table 20.8 summarizes the published results using the leave-one-out procedure on the YouTube dataset.

20.5.2 The Hollywood Dataset

In order to provide a realistic benchmarking in an unconstrained environment, Laptev et al. [22] initiates an effort by creating a dataset consisting of video sequences extracted from two episodes from the movie "Coffee and Cigarettes", providing a pool of examples for atomic actions, such as "drinking" and "smoking", where each atomic event ranges from 30 to 200 frames long, with a mean of 70 frames. They show on a ∼36000 frame test set that by combining both frame-based classifier and space–time based classifier improves the precision of action detection by a 30%∼40% margin given the same recall. Similarly, Rodriguez et al. [37] published a kissing/slapping dataset consisting of ∼200 sequences from several movies. They achieved ∼66% accuracy using a template-based approach.

Laptev et al. [23] later create a Hollywood-1 dataset by extracting eight different actions (answer phone, hug person, sit up, sit down, kiss, handshake, and stand up) from various movies. The dataset consists of ∼400 video sequences. Each sequence is about 50∼200 frames long with a resolution 240 × 500 and a frame rate of 24 frames per second. Using a combination of multi-scale flow and shape features, they achieve a 30%∼50% average precision for each action class. Marszałek et al. [29] subsequently create a Hollywood-2 dataset by augmenting Hollywood-1 to include up to twelve activities with a total of 600 K frames. The scene information is also

Table 20.9 Performances on Hollywood-1 datasets in average precision

Methods/Actions	AnswerPhone	GetOutCar	HandShake	HugPerson	Kiss	SitUp
Gilbert et al. [9]	47%	47%	45.6%	42.8%	72.5%	44.0%
Han et al. [12]	43.4%	46.8%	44.1%	46.9%	57.3%	38.4%
Sun et al. [43]	40%	42%	38%	42%	55%	40%
Leptev et al. [23]	32.1%	41.5%	32.3%	40.6%	53.3%	18.2%
Raptis et al. [35]	33.0%	27%	20.1%	34.5%	53.7%	19%
Yeffet et al. [57]	35.1%	32%	33.8%	28.3%	57.6%	13.1%

Methods/Actions	SitDown	StandUp	Mean
	84.6%	70.5%	56.8%
	46.2%	57.1%	47.5%
	50%	55%	47.1%
	38.6%	50.5%	38.4%
	27.4%	60%	34.3%
	36.2%	58.3%	N.A.

Table 20.10 Performances on Hollywood-2 datasets in average precision

Methods/Actions	AnswerPhone	DriveCar	Eat	FightPerson	GetOutCar	HandShake
Gilbert et al. [9]	40.2%	75%	51.5%	77.1%	45.6%	28.9%
Satkin et al. [39]	N.A.	N.A.	N.A.	N.A.	N.A.	N.A.
Han et al. [12]	15.57%	87.01%	50.93%	73.08%	27.19%	17.17%
Marszałek et al. [29]	10.7%	75%	28.6%	67.5%	19.1%	14.1%

HugPerson	Kiss	Run	SitDown	SitUp	StandUp	Mean
49.4%	56.6%	47.5%	62.0%	26.8%	50.7%	50.9%
N.A.	N.A.	N.A.	N.A.	N.A.	N.A.	43.48%
27.22%	42.91%	66.94%	41.61%	7.19%	48.6%	42.12%
13.8%	55.6%	56.6%	31.6%	14.2%	35.0%	35.1%

annotated. They achieve an average precision of 35.5% by incorporating the context, i.e. the scene information. Both the Hollywood-1 and Hollywood-2 datasets come with a clean training set and a test set of roughly equal size (about 200 sequences).

Overall, the Hollywood datasets pose a great challenge to activity recognition as the camera views are different from sequence to sequence, the background is cluttered, multiple subjects are present, occlusions occur very often, and the intra-class variability is large, making recognition hard. Tables 20.9 and 20.10 summarize reported performance on Hollywood-1 and Hollywood-2 datasets. As we see from the tables, there is still huge room for improvement. Gilbert et al. [9] is the current state-of-the-art by mining the spatial-temporal relationships between space–time interest points.

20.5.3 The Olympic Dataset

Recently, Niebles et al. [33] publish the Olympic Sports Dataset. The dataset contains 50 videos from each of the following 16 activities: high jump, long jump, triple jump, pole vault, discus throw, hammer throw, javelin throw, shot put, basketball layup, bowling, tennis serve, platform (diving), springboard (diving), snatch (weightlifting), clean and jerk (weightlifting) and vault (gymnastics). These sequences, obtained from YouTube, contain severe occlusions, camera movements, and compression artifacts. In contrast to other sport datasets such as the UCF Sports Dataset [37], which contains periodic or simple activities such as walking, running, golf swinging, ball kicking, the activities in the Olympic Dataset are longer and more complex. Niebles et al. [33] achieved an accuracy of 72% by modeling the temporal structure of these activities.

20.6 Benchmarks with Multiple Activities

The benchmarks introduced so far focus more on "activity recognition", i.e. video sequences in these datasets are typically pre-segmented and contain only one activity. It is desirable to have benchmarks with video sequences containing multiple activities for activity detection algorithms, i.e. finding out all possible activities in the video sequences, which is especially beneficial for surveillance applications. Uemura et al. [46] publish a Multi-KTH dataset, consisting of the same activities as the KTH dataset. The video sequences have a resolution of 640×480 and contain activities similar to the KTH dataset, except that one video sequence could contain multiple activities simultaneously and that the camera is constantly moving. By tracking space–time interest points, Uemura et al. [46] achieve an average precision of 65.4%, while Gilbert et al. [9] achieve 75.2% by data mining the space–time features. Table 20.11 summarizes the performances for each activity in terms of average precision.

In a similar setting to [19], Yuan et al. [58] publish an MSR-1 dataset containing 16 video sequences and having in total 63 actions: 14 hand clapping, 24 hand waving, and 25 boxing, performed by 10 subjects. Each sequence contains multiple

Table 20.11 Performances reported on the multi-KTH dataset in average precision

Methods/Actions	Clapping	Waving	Boxing	Jogging	Walking	Average
Gilbert et al. [9]	69%	77%	75%	85%	70%	75.2%
Uemura et al. [46]	76%	81%	58%	51%	61%	65.4%

types of actions. Some sequences contain actions performed by different people. There are both indoor and outdoor scenes. All of the video sequences are captured with cluttered and moving backgrounds. Each video is of low resolution, 320×240 and frame rate 15 frames per second. Their lengths are between $32 \sim 76$ seconds. An extended MSR-2 dataset consisting of 54 videos sequences is also available [4]. Yuan et al. [58] report a 57% recall and 87.5% precision.

Other than the aforementioned datasets, TRECVID [42] is an annual event detection challenge aiming at addressing realistic activity retrieval problems. The dataset is updated each year. It consists of videos from multiple surveillance cameras deployed at the London Gatwick airport. For example, for the 2009 challenge, the goal of the challenge was to detect several target events, including "ElevatorNoEntry", "OpposingFlow" (moving in the opposite direction), "PersonRuns", "Pointing", "CellToEar", "ObjectPut", "TakePicture", "Embrace", "PeopleMeet", and, "PeopleSplitUp". The dataset is challenging in that unlike the sequences in previous datasets where activities are repetitive, most of the target events in TRECVID are rare and subtle. For example, to detect the activity "CellToEar" or "PersonRuns" in unconstrained video sequences is extremely difficult. Also, the sequences always have cluttered background, which could also include moving people, resulting in complicated occlusion scenarios. The intra-class variations of each activity are also huge, since each person performs the same activity differently. The evaluation is done using the Detection Error Tradeoff (DET) curve, a trade off curve between miss rate and false alarm rate. The state of the art approach achieves only 90% miss rate while keeping the false alarm rate to 20 per hour. The miss rate drops to $\sim$80% while the false alarm rate is kept at 100 per hour, an indication of the difficulty of the dataset.

20.7 Other Benchmarks

Other than recognizing single subject kinematic activities, recently, researchers have tried to extend activity recognition to a broader context. For example, Prabhakar et al. [34] use temporal causality to detect activities that involve interactions among people. They evaluate their approach on a toy dataset consisting of sequences of ball playing activities ("roll-ball", "throw-ball", and "kick-ball") and a child play dataset [48] consisting of social games such as pattycake between an adult and a child, achieving 60%~70% accuracy. They also report results on the "HandShake" from the Hollywood dataset [29] for realistic evaluations. Another dataset that also involves human interactions is the PETS07-BEHAVE [14] dataset consisting of video sequences of 640×480 resolution. The activities include walking together, splitting, approaching, fighting, chasing, and so on.

Another category of activities that attracts many research works involves object manipulation. The recognition of object manipulation based activities finds its application, for example, in Programming by Demonstration in Robotics or flow optimization for factory workers. Experimental protocols for laboratory technicians and recipes for home cooks are also example tasks. Also, in object recognition, more and more context information are brought in to help recognizing the objects and the way an object is manipulated or held significantly constrained the category of the object. On the other hand, the object class also affects how it can be grasped or manipulated and the activities that can be performed on it.

Gupta et al. [11] collect a sports image dataset consisting of five activities: "Cricket bowling", "Croquet shot", "Tennis forehand", "Tennis serve", "Volleyball smash", each with 50 images. They report a 78.9% accuracy while recently, Yao et al. [55] achieve a recognition rate of 83.3% by jointly modeling activity, body pose and manipulated object.

Similarly, Yao et al. [54] publish an instrument playing dataset consisting of seven different musical instruments: bassoon, erhu, flute, French horn, guitar, saxophone, and violin. Each class includes ∼150 people-playing-musical-instrument images. They achieve an accuracy of 65.7% using their proposed Grouplet features, an extension of local interest point features to take into account neighboring relationships.

Kjellstrom et al. [20] collect the OAC (Object–Action-Complex) dataset. The dataset consists of 50 instances, each of three different action–object combinations: "look through binoculars", "drink from cup", and "pour from pitcher". The activities are performed by 10 subjects, 5 times each. The classes are selected so that two of the activities, "look through" and "drink from" are similar, while two of the objects, "cup"and "pitch" are similar as well. They report the best performance of 6% error rate by jointly inferring the activities and the manipulated object using a CRF.

Another closely related work is the HumanEva datasets [41]. These datasets contain video sequences of six simple activities performed by four~six subjects with motion sensors. Other than videos, the datasets also provide corresponding motion sensor values from the motion capture system in order to evaluate human pose estimation and articulated tracking algorithms.

Tables 20.12 and 20.13 summarize different properties, such as resolution, activities, degree of background clutter, of the major benchmarking datasets. We can see from the table, the numbers reported on the standard activity recognition datasets such as the KTH dataset [40] are saturated, mostly above 90%. On the other hand, there is still a huge room for improvement for realistic and multi-activity datasets, such as the Hollywood datasets [23, 29], the MSR dataset [58], or the TRECVID [42]. This suggests that more sophisticated methods are needed to address the problems of cluttered background or those of representing activities in finer scales.

20.8 Conclusions

In this chapter, we have covered the state-of-the-art benchmarking datasets for human activity recognition algorithms, ranging from standard KTH dataset [40] to realistic Hollywood dataset [23, 29] or TRECVID dataset [42]. To conclude, datasets such as the KTH dataset [40] or the Weizmann dataset [10] for which the state-of-the-art approaches have already achieved above 90% accuracy provide bench-

Table 20.12 Summary of all the datasets. "r" indicates that the dataset was made out of realistic videos. "v" indicates the dataset consists of video sequences with various perspectives. The performance is reported in average accuracy unless otherwise specified. The columns are dataset names, number of activities, number of actors, resolution of the videos (res.), and camera views

Dataset	activities	actors	res.	views
KTH [40]	6	25	160 × 120	frontal/side
Weizmann [10]	10	9	180 × 144	frontal/side
CMU Soccer [7]	7	r	30 × 30	side
CMU Crowded [19]	5	6	320 × 240	side/frontal
UCF Sports [37]	9	r	720 × 480	v
UR ADL [31]	10	5	1280 × 720	frontal
UM Gesture [24]	14	3	640 × 480	frontal
UCF Youtube [26]	11	r	240 × 320	v
Hollywood-1 [23]	8	r	240 × 500	v
Hollywood-2 [29]	12	r	240 × 500	v
MultiKTH [46]	6	5	640 × 480	side/frontal
MSR [58]	3	10	320 × 240	side/frontal
TRECVID [42]	10	r	640 × 480	v

marks in a more controlled environment, while the YouTube dataset [26], the Hollywood datasets [23, 29], and the TRECVID dataset [42] approximate realistic situations better, posing great challenges to human activity recognition algorithms. The datasets with videos containing multiple activities, such as the MSR dataset [58] provide suitable benchmarks for activity detection techniques, which are still few in its genre as most human activity recognition techniques assume pre-segmented video sequences. The properties of these major benchmarking datasets are summarized in both Tables 20.12 and 20.13. We hope that by summarizing the state-of-the-art numbers, people would be able to use them as a baseline and report improved numbers on top of them.

A dataset that is presently lacking is one that contains human actions with the information on the action context as well as on the objects that are involved in the actions. This need was also outlined in Chap. 18 where the reader may find a more detailed discussion.

20.8.1 Further Readings

We refer the interested readers to Turaga et al. [45] for generic topics about human activity recognition. For empirical methods and evaluation methodologies in Computer Vision, Henrik et al. [6] and Venkata et al. [47] both cover the design of experiments and benchmarks for various topics in Computer Vision. Interested readers could also see [38] and [59] for information about providing ground-truth labeling.

Table 20.13 Summary of all the datasets. "r" indicates that the dataset was made out of realistic videos. "v" indicates the dataset consists of video sequences with various perspectives. The performance is reported in average accuracy unless otherwise specified. The columns are dataset names, degree of background clutter (bg clutter), camera motion (c_motion), and the state-of-the-art performances

Dataset	bg clutter	c_motion	performances
KTH [40]	no	slightly	95.7% [9]
Weizmann [10]	no	no	100% [57]
CMU Soccer [7]	moderate	yes	78.6% [50]
CMU Crowded [19]	yes	yes	0.6 (AUROC) [56]
UCF Sports [37]	yes	no	87.27% [21]
UR ADL [31]	no	no	89% [31]
UM Gesture [24]	yes	yes	100% [44]
UCF Youtube [26]	yes	yes	77.8% (average precision) [3]
Hollywood-1 [23]	yes	yes	56.8% (average precision) [9]
Hollywood-2 [29]	yes	yes	50.9% (average precision) [9]
MultiKTH [46]	yes	yes	75.2% (average precision) [9]
MSR [58]	yes	yes	recall/precision: 57%/87.5% [58]
TRECVID [42]	yes	no	90% miss rate 20 false positives/hr

References

1. Ali, S., Shah, M.: Human action recognition in videos using kinematic features and multiple instance learning. IEEE Trans. Pattern Anal. Mach. Intell. **32**(2), 288–303 (2010) [413]
2. Bregonzio, M., Gong, S., Xiang, T.: Recognising action as clouds of space–time interest points. In: IEEE International Conference on Computer Vision and Pattern Recognition (CVPR) (2009) [413]
3. Brendel, W., Todorovic, S.: Activities as time series of human postures. In: IEEE European Conference on Computer Vision (ECCV) (2010) [413,415,418,424]
4. Cao, L., Liu, Z., Huang, T.: Cross-dataset action detection. In: IEEE International Conference on Computer Vision and Pattern Recognition (CVPR) (2010) [413,421]
5. Chaudhry, R., Ravichandran, A., Hager, G., Vidal, R.: Histograms of oriented optical flow and Binet–Cauchy kernels on nonlinear dynamical systems for the recognition of human actions. In: IEEE International Conference on Computer Vision and Pattern Recognition (CVPR) (2009) [413]
6. Christensen, H., Phillips, J.: Empirical Evaluation Methods in Computer Vision. World Scientific, Singapore (2002) [423]
7. Efros, A., Berg, A., Mori, G., Malik, J.: Recognizing action at a distance. In: IEEE International Conference on Computer Vision (ICCV) (2003) [414,415,423,424]
8. Fathi, A., Mori, G.: Action recognition by learning mid-level motion features. In: IEEE International Conference on Computer Vision and Pattern Recognition (CVPR) (2008) [413, 415]
9. Gilbert, A., Illingworth, J., Bowden, R.: Action recognition using mined hierarchical compound features. IEEE Transaction on Pattern Analysis and Machine Intelligence (PAMI) (2010) [413,419,420,424]
10. Gorelick, L., Blank, M., Shechtman, E., Irani, M., Basri, R.: Actions as space–time shapes. In: IEEE International Conference on Computer Vision (ICCV) (2005) [412,423,424]

11. Gupta, A., Kembhavi, A., Davis, L.: Observing human–object interactions: Using spatial and functional compatibility for recognition. IEEE Trans. Pattern Anal. Mach. Intell. **31**(10), 1775–1789 (2009) [422]
12. Han, D., Bo, L., Sminchisescu, C.: Selection and context for action recognition. In: IEEE International Conference on Computer Vision (ICCV) (2009) [413,419]
13. IEEE: Performance Evaluation of Tracking and Surveillance (2004) [414]
14. IEEE: Performance Evaluation of Tracking and Surveillance (2007) [421]
15. IEEE: Performance Evaluation of Tracking and Surveillance (2009) [414]
16. Ikizler-Cinbis, N., Sclaroff, S.: Object, scene and actions: Combining multiple features for human action recognition. In: IEEE European Conference on Computer Vision (ECCV) (2010) [418]
17. Jhuang, H., Serre, T., Wolf, L., Poggio, T.: A biologically inspired system for action recognition. In: IEEE International Conference on Computer Vision (ICCV) (2007) [413]
18. Jiang, H., Martin, D.: Finding actions using shape flows. In: IEEE European Conference on Computer Vision (ECCV) (2008) [413]
19. Ke, Y., Sukthankar, R., Hebert, M.: Event detection in cluttered videos. In: IEEE International Conference on Computer Vision (ICCV) (2007) [414,415,420,423,424]
20. Kjellström, H., Romero, J., Martínez, D., Kragić, D.: Simultaneous visual recognition of manipulation actions and manipulated objects. In: IEEE European Conference on Computer Vision (ECCV) (2008) [422]
21. Kovashka, A., Grauman, K.: Learning a hierarchy of discriminative space–time neighborhood features for human action recognition. In: IEEE International Conference on Computer Vision and Pattern Recognition (CVPR) (2010) [413,416,424]
22. Laptev, I., Perez, P.: Retrieving actions in movies. In: IEEE International Conference on Computer Vision (ICCV), pp. 1–8 (2007) [418]
23. Laptev, I., Marszałek, M., Schmid, C., Rozenfeld, B.: Learning realistic human actions from movies. In: IEEE International Conference on Computer Vision and Pattern Recognition (CVPR) (2008) [413,418,419,422-424]
24. Lin, Z., Jiang, Z., Davis, L.: Recognizing actions by shape-motion prototype trees. In: IEEE International Conference on Computer Vision (ICCV), pp. 444–451 (2009) [413,415,423]
25. Liu, J., Shah, M.: Learning human action via information maximization. In: IEEE International Conference on Computer Vision and Pattern Recognition (CVPR) (2008) [413]
26. Liu, J., Luo, J., Shah, M.: Recognizing realistic actions from videos in the wild. In: IEEE International Conference on Computer Vision and Pattern Recognition (CVPR) (2009) [413, 418,423,424]
27. Liu, J., Yang, Y., Shah, M.: Learning semantic visual vocabularies using diffusion distance. In: IEEE International Conference on Computer Vision and Pattern Recognition (CVPR) (2009) [413,418]
28. Lv, F., Nevatia, R.: Single view human action recognition using key pose matching and Viterbi path searching. In: IEEE International Conference on Computer Vision and Pattern Recognition (CVPR) (2007) [417]
29. Marszałek, M., Laptev, I., Schmid, C.: Actions in context. In: IEEE International Conference on Computer Vision and Pattern Recognition (CVPR) (2009) [418,421-423]
30. Matikainen, P., Hebert, M., Sukthankar, R.: Representing pairwise spatial and temporal relations for action recognition. In: IEEE European Conference on Computer Vision (ECCV) (2010) [414,418]
31. Messing, R., Pal, C., Kautz, H.: Activity recognition using the velocity histories of tracked keypoints. In: IEEE International Conference on Computer Vision (ICCV) (2009) [413,414, 423,424]
32. Niebles, J., Li, F.-F.: A hierarchical model of shape and appearance for human action classification. In: IEEE International Conference on Computer Vision and Pattern Recognition (CVPR) (2007) [413]
33. Niebles, J., Chen, C.-W., Li, F.-F.: Modeling temporal structure of decomposable motion segments for activity classification. In: IEEE European Conference on Computer Vision (ECCV) (2010) [420]

34. Prabhakar, K., Oh, S., Wang, P., Abowd, G., Rehg, J.: Temporal causality for the analysis of visual events. In: IEEE International Conference on Computer Vision and Pattern Recognition (CVPR) (2010) [421]

35. Raptis, M., Soatto, S.: Tracklet descriptors for action modeling and video analysis. In: IEEE European Conference on Computer Vision (ECCV) (2010) [413,414,419]

36. Ribeiro, P., Santos-Victor, J.: Human activity recognition from video: modeling, feature selection and classification architecture. In: International Workshop on Human Activity Recognition and Modelling (2005) [414]

37. Rodriguez, M., Ahmed, J., Shah, M.: Action mach: A spatio-temporal maximum average correlation height filter for action recognition. In: IEEE International Conference on Computer Vision and Pattern Recognition (CVPR) (2008) [416,418,420,423,424]

38. Russell, B., Torralba, A., Murphy, K.: Labelme: A database and web-based tool for image annotation. Int. J. Comput. Vis. 77(1–3), 157–173 (2008) [423]

39. Satkin, S., Hebert, M.: Modeling the temporal extent of actions. In: IEEE European Conference on Computer Vision (ECCV) (2010) [413,414]

40. Schuldt, C., Laptev, I., Caputo, B.: Recognizing human actions: A local SVM approach. In: International Conference on Pattern Recognition (ICPR) (2004) [412,422-424]

41. Sigal, L., Balan, A., Black, M.: Humaneva: Synchronized video and motion capture dataset and baseline algorithm for evaluation of articulated human motion. International Journal on Computer Vision (IJCV) 87(1–2) (2010) [422]

42. Smeaton, A., Over, P., Kraaij, W.: Evaluation campaigns and trecvid. In: ACM International Conference on Multimedia Information Retrieval (MIR) (2006) [421-424]

43. Sun, J., Wu, X., Yan, S., Cheong, L.-F., Chua, T.-S., Li, J.: Hierarchical spatio-temporal context modeling for action recognition. In: IEEE International Conference on Computer Vision and Pattern Recognition (CVPR) (2009) [419]

44. Tran, D., Sorokin, A.: Human activity recognition with metric learning. In: IEEE European Conference on Computer Vision (ECCV) (2008) [413,414,417,424]

45. Turaga, P., Chellappa, R.: Machine recognition of human activities: A survey. IEEE Trans. Circuits Syst. Video Technol. 18(11), 1473–1488 (2008) [423]

46. Uemura, H., Ishikawa, S., Mikolajczyk, K.: Feature tracking and motion compensation for action recognition. In: British Machine Vision Conference (BMVC) (2008) [420,423]

47. Venkata, S., Ahn, I., Jeon, D., Gupta, A., Louie, C., Garcia, S., Belongie, S., Taylor, M.: Sdvbs: The San Diego Vision Benchmark Suite (2009) [423]

48. Wang, P., Abowd, G., Rehg, J.: Quasi-periodic event analysis for social game retrieval. In: IEEE International Conference on Computer Vision (ICCV) (2009) [421]

49. Wang, Y., Mori, G.: Learning a discriminative hidden part model for human action recognitio. In: Advances in Neural Information Processing Systems (NIPS) (2008) [413]

50. Wang, Y., Mori, G.: Human action recognition by semilatent topic models. IEEE Trans. Pattern Anal. Mach. Intell. 31(10), 1762–1774 (2009) [415,424]

51. Wang, Y., Mori, G.: Max-margin hidden conditional random fields for human action recognition. In: IEEE International Conference on Computer Vision and Pattern Recognition (CVPR) (2009) [413]

52. Weinland, D., Boyer, E., Ronfard, R.: Action recognition from arbitrary views using 3d exemplars. In: IEEE International Conference on Computer Vision (ICCV) (2007) [417]

53. Weinland, D., Ronfard, R., Boyer, E.: Free viewpoint action recognition using motion history volumes. Computer Vision and Image Understanding (2006) [417]

54. Yao, B., Fei-Fei, L.: Grouplet: A structured image representation for recognizing human and object interactions. In: IEEE International Conference on Computer Vision and Pattern Recognition (CVPR) (2010) [422]

55. Yao, B., Fei-Fei, L.: Modeling mutual context of object and human pose in human–object interaction activities. In: IEEE International Conference on Computer Vision and Pattern Recognition (CVPR) (2010) [422]

56. Yao, B., Zhu, S.-C.: Learning deformable action templates from cluttered videos. In: IEEE International Conference on Computer Vision (ICCV) (2009) [413,415,424]

57. Yeffet, L., Wolf, L.: Local trinary patterns for human action recognition. In: IEEE International Conference on Computer Vision (ICCV) (2009) [413,416,419,424]
58. Yuan, J., Liu, Z., Wu, Y.: Discriminative subvolume search for efficient action detection. In: IEEE International Conference on Computer Vision and Pattern Recognition (CVPR) (2009) [413,420-424]
59. Yuen, J., Russell, B., Liu, C., Torralba, A.: Labelme video: Building a video database with human annotations. In: IEEE International Conference on Computer Vision (ICCV) (2009) [423]

Part IV
Applications

Chapter 21
Applications for Visual Analysis of People

Adrian Hilton

21.1 Introduction

Potential applications for the visual analysis of people in images and video are numerous. This has motivated this area as a central focus for research in computer
vision. Visual analysis of people forms a central element of applications ranging
from security and medicine through to the entertainment industries.

   This part presents reviews of the state-of-the-art for several application domains.
Review chapters are intended to introduce the problems related to analysis of people
for particular application domains. Adaption of the generic approaches introduced
in earlier parts is discussed together with techniques developed to address specific
problems. Application chapters also provide an insight into current progress and
open problems in these domains with guidance for further reading. This part provides reviews of nine different application areas of computer vision to the visual
analysis of people ranging from biometrics for security applications to visual reconstruction of movement for broadcast sports analysis. This is by no means an exhaustive list of the applications currently under investigation but provides an illustrative
cross-section of current progress and potential directions for future research.

   An overview of the application chapters included in this part is presented in Table 21.1. This table identifies the most relevant industry sectors for each application
and the primary techniques used for analysis of people introduced in earlier parts.
Table 21.1 shows the broad range of applications areas introduced in this part which
are of immediate relevance to the security, communication, entertainment and automotive industries. Visual analysis of people is also of relevance to other industries.
Other areas of current research include the biomechanical analysis of movement for
health and the measurement of body shape for fashion retail.

A. Hilton (✉)
Centre for Vision, Speech and Signal Processing, University of Surrey, Guildford, UK
e-mail: a.hilton@surrey.ac.uk

T.B. Moeslund et al. (eds.), *Visual Analysis of Humans*,
DOI 10.1007/978-0-85729-997-0_21, © Springer-Verlag London Limited 2011

Table 21.1 Overview of applications featured in this part, relevant industry and primary topics approaches used for visual analysis of people

Application	Industries	Tracking (Part I)	Pose Estimation (Part II)	Action Recognition (Part III)
Biometrics	Security	•	•	
Surveillance	Security	•		•
Pedestrian Analysis	Security	•		•
Human–Computer Interaction	Communication Entertainment	•	•	•
Social Signal Processing	Communication	•		•
Sign-Language Recognition	Communication	•		•
Sport TV	Entertainment	•		
Actor Reconstruction	Entertainment		•	
Driver Assistance	Automotive	•	•	

21.1.1 Security

Applications related to the security industry are a major area of interest for identity recognition, surveillance from CCTV for monitoring human activity and behaviour analysis to detect anomalous events. Given the widespread availability of video cameras in both public and private spaces the automated analysis of the vast quantities of footage has become increasingly important. Reliably analysing and detecting events in relatively low quality footage remains a challenging problem. Recent advances have increased robustness to the analysis of crowded scenes and the complexity of behaviour which can be handled. Two important advances in this area have been the introduction of spatio-temporal feature detectors for action recognition and the combination of video footage across cameras networks to facilitate large area surveillance.

Biometric analysis for identify recognition and verification is a field in its own right with problems such as face recognition attracting considerable interest due to the widespread potential for commercial exploitation. Visual biometrics range from iris and finger print analysis which achieve high-reliability in differentiating individuals but requires cooperation for image capture, through to gait analysis which can be used to differentiate people at a distance. Face recognition in uncontrolled environments is extremely challenging due to the variation in facial appearance with illumination and pose. To overcome these nuisance factors researchers have investigated solutions with active illumination and 3D measurement. This approach achieves improved performance in verification but requires subjects cooperation. Ultimately the challenge is to be able to recognise individuals at a distance from relatively uncontrolled imagery such as CCTV footage.

21.1.2 Communication

Understanding how humans communicate and interact is central to improving both person-to-person communication and human–computer interfaces. Visual analysis of individual behaviour, facial expression and gesture during social interaction also opens-up the possibility of developing improved man-machine interfaces for communication, entertainment, and the monitoring of health and wellbeing. Visual analysis of social interaction is a challenging problem which has only recently received significant interest due to the requirement for reliable automated algorithms for tracking of human face and body movements. As the performance of visual tracking improves it will be increasingly possible to develop human–computer interfaces which can interpret not only movement but the underlying expression of emotion. This will facilitate the development of interfaces which communicate with individuals in a more anthropocentric manner responding to both verbal and non-verbal cues.

One specific area of human gesture analysis is visual recognition of sign-language requiring interpretation of both face, hand and body movement as a multi-channel signal. Interpretation and understanding of sign-language requires the link between visual cues and their linguistic meaning to be established. Sign-language recognition has the potential to provide improved communication interfaces for man-machine communication and translation between sign and other languages. This remains a challenging open-problem although significant progress has been made in recent years. Recent introduction of low-cost depth sensors has allowed reliable real-time capture of whole-body motion for communication and interaction.

21.1.3 Entertainment

An important early application area for the visual analysis of people has been the entertainment industry. People form the central element of many forms of visual media. Film and TV are commonly centred on actor or presenter performance creating a demand for tools to track their motion to allow insertion of visual effects. Unlike other application domains where full automation is often the goal, in entertainment applications it is often acceptable and even desirable to have a human in the loop. This has allowed the early adoption of visual analysis algorithms which are not always 100% reliable on complex real-world scenes. In TV broadcast production 2D video analysis of sports events has exploited technologies for tracking of people in order to annotate captured video for improved presentation and analysis of events. A pre-requisite for visual analysis of people in this context is often through-the-lens calibration of the moving camera. Camera calibration and 2D player tracking can be used to locate players on the surface of a pitch or running track, analyse movement based on foot location or provide a visual comparison. Player tracking can also be exploited for performance analysis both for commentary and training.

Capture and analysis of actor performance is a central challenge. Optical marker-based motion capture systems, originally developed for biomechanical analysis of human movement, are now widely used in film and game production. Video-based reconstruction of human movement, without the attachment of markers, has considerable potential advantages, allowing capture of natural human movement and eliminating current restrictions on clothing or capture environment. This problem has attracted considerable interest in computer vision research over the past decade. However, current video-based solutions to reconstruction of skeletal motion do not yet approach the level of accuracy of marker-based technologies. An alternative approach investigated in recent research is reconstruction of actor performance as a 3D video using visual-hull or stereo reconstruction from multiple calibrated cameras in either a studio or outdoor environment. This approach allows free-viewpoint video replay rendering of novel virtual camera views achieving a visual quality comparable to the captured video. Methods for temporal registration of 3D video surface sequence have been developed to give a 4D spatio-temporal model of the scene dynamics. The resulting 4D model facilitates measurement and analysis of movement for action recognition or extraction of the underlying skeletal motion. This approach also forms the basis for production of interactive character models with realistic appearance for computer graphics applications.

21.1.4 Automotive

In the automotive industry there are a number of potential applications for visual analysis of people both for driver assistance and monitoring. Visual analysis of the scene surrounding the car can be used both for vehicle navigation and for detection of potential hazards such as people walking into the road. Equally cameras monitoring the driver can be used to detect drowsiness and monitor their actions to ensure safety. This is a challenging environment for computer vision due to the changing illumination and scenery outside the car. Ultimately such technologies will help in preventing accidents by alerting the driver to hazards, monitoring their behaviour and even taking evasive action.

21.2 Conclusion

These applications serve to illustrate the potential for the visual analysis of people across numerous varied domains. Improvements in reliability and robustness of visual analysis have enabled the development of systems which operate in real-world environments. A number of successful commercial applications of vision-based technologies have been demonstrated in security for monitoring CCTV footage and verification of identity, in communication for novel human computer interfaces, in entertainment for annotation and analysis of player movement and in cars to alert drivers to potential hazards. Visual analysis of people in general real-world scenes remains a challenging open-problem due to the diversity of appearance and dynamic changes in illumination conditions as well as the complexity of human movement. There remains significant potential for future advance leading to exploitation in a wide range of industries and applications. Important areas for future development include technologies for automatic monitoring of people in their home environment to support independent living with an ageing population, and the accurate measurement of movement from video to overcome the limitations of existing marker-based technologies for biomechanical assessment in health care and rehabilitation. Potential applications will continue to motivate visual analysis of people as an active area of computer vision research.

Chapter 22
Image and Video-Based Biometrics

Vishal M. Patel, Jaishanker K. Pillai, and Rama Chellappa

Abstract Biometrics deals with the problem of identifying individuals based on physiological or behavioral characteristics. Since many physical characteristics, such as face, iris, etc., and behavioral characteristics, such as voice, expression, etc., are unique to an individual, biometric analysis offers a reliable and natural solution to the problem of identity verification. In this chapter, we discuss image and video-based biometrics involving face, iris and gait. In particular, we discuss several recent approaches to physiological biometrics based on Sparse Representations and Compressed Sensing. Some of the most compelling challenges and issues that confront research in biometrics are also addressed.

22.1 Introduction

Biometrics refers to the physiological or behavioral characteristics of a person. Since many physical characteristics, such as face, and behavioral characteristics, such as voice, are unique to an individual, biometric analysis offers a reliable and natural solution to the problem of identity verification. In this chapter, we discuss image and video-based biometrics involving faces, iris and gait. In particular, we discuss several recent approaches to physiological biometrics based on (Sparse Representations (SR)) and (Compressed Sensing (CS)).

This chapter is broadly divided into four sections. The first section discusses image and video-based face recognition methods based on SR. In the second section, iris-based recognition is introduced. In particular, we discuss how some of the challenges in unconstrained iris recognition can be addressed with SR. Finally, a gait

V.M. Patel (✉) · J.K. Pillai · R. Chellappa
Department of Electrical and Computer Engineering, Center for Automation Research, University of Maryland, College Park, MD 20742, USA
e-mail: pvishalm@umiacs.umd.edu

J.K. Pillai
e mail: jsp@umiacs.umd.edu

R. Chellappa
e-mail: rama@umiacs.umd.edu

T.B. Moeslund et al. (eds.), *Visual Analysis of Humans*,
DOI 10.1007/978-0-85729-997-0_22, © Springer-Verlag London Limited 2011

recognition system is briefly described and some of the most compelling issues that confront research in biometrics are also addressed.

22.2 Face Recognition Techniques

Face recognition is concerned with identifying one or more persons from still images or video using a gallery of known faces [43]. Face recognition has a wide range of applications including surveillance, law enforcement and virtual reality. Compared to other biometrics systems such as fingerprint and palm print, a face biometric system has the advantage that facial images can be obtained from a distance without requiring cooperation of the subject. As a result, a face recognition system has to deal with significant appearance changes due to illumination and pose variations. Existing algorithms have reported high recognition rates in controlled scenarios, however, their performance degrades significantly in uncontrolled scenarios.

In recent years, SR [15, 40] and CS [6] have received a great interest in computer vision and biometrics. They have been successfully used for robust and secure physiological biometrics recognition such as face and iris. In this section, we discuss approaches to face recognition based on SR. We first briefly describe the traditional subspace-based approaches for face recognition.

22.2.1 Traditional Approaches

It has been observed that since human faces have similar overall configuration, the facial images can be described by a relatively low-dimensional subspace. Several dimensionality reduction methods such as PCA [35] and Linear Discriminant Analysis (LDA)/Fisher Linear Discriminant (FLD) [8, 16] have been proposed for the task of face recognition. In the case of PCA, the general strategy is to construct a set of images that provides the best approximation of the overall image dataset. The training set is then projected onto this subspace. To query a novel test image, it is projected onto this subspace and a training image whose projection that is closest to it is sought.

In the case of FLD, the original image set is separated into classes, one for each person. Let A be the collection of training images $\{A_i\}$, $i = 1, \ldots, N$ and μ be the mean of all the vectors. We divide A into C classes each corresponding to a person. Let N_j be the number of samples in class j and μ_j be the mean image of the jth class X_j. Then, the two scatter matrices, one between-class scatter S_B, another within-class scatter S_W are defined as

$$S_B = \sum_{j=1}^{C} N_j(\mu_j - \mu)(\mu_j - \mu)^T; \qquad S_W = \sum_{j=1}^{C} \sum_{x_k \in X_j} (x_k - \mu_j)(x_k - \mu_j)^T.$$

$$(22.1)$$

As can be seen from (22.1), S_B captures between-class variations and S_W captures within-class variations. The objective is to find a projection direction that minimizes the within-class scatter but maximizes the between-class scatter. This can be formulated as

$$W_{\text{opt}} = \underset{W}{\text{argmax}} \, \frac{|W^T S_B W|}{|W^T S_W W|}. \tag{22.2}$$

The solution set $\{w_i\}_{i=1}^m$ is obtained by solving the generalized eigenvalue problem $S_B w_i = \lambda_i S_W w_i$, $i = 1, \ldots, m$. For classification, the test image is first projected onto the subspace spanned by the computed projection vectors. The projection coefficients are then compared to all the stored vectors of labeled classes to determine the input class label.

In addition to these subspace-based methods, feature-based approaches such as elastic bunch graph matching [39], have also been quite successful for face recognition.

22.2.2 Sparsity Inspired Face Recognition

In recent years, the theories of SR and CS have emerged as powerful tools for efficiently processing data in non-traditional ways. This has lead to a resurgence in interest in the principles of SR and CS for physiological biometrics recognition [19, 30, 37, 41]. The idea is to create a dictionary matrix of the training samples as column vectors. The test sample is also represented as a column vector. Different dimensionality reduction methods are used to reduce the dimension of both the test vector and the vectors in the dictionary. One such approach for dimensionality reduction is random projections [20, 30]. Random projections, using a generated sensing matrix, are taken of both the dictionary matrix and the test sample. It is then simply a matter of solving an ℓ_1 minimization problem in order to obtain the sparse solution. Once the sparse solution is obtained, it can provide information as to which training sample the test vector most closely relates to.

Let each image be represented as a vector in $\mathbb{R}^n$, A be the dictionary (i.e. training set) and y be the test image. The Sparse Representation-based Classification (SRC) algorithm is as follows.

1. Create a matrix of training samples $A = [A_1, \ldots, A_C]$ for C classes, where A_i are the set of images of each class.
2. Reduce the dimension of the training images and a test image by any dimensionality reduction method. Denote the resulting dictionary and the test vector as $\tilde{A}$ and $\tilde{y}$, respectively.
3. Normalize the columns of $\tilde{A}$ and $\tilde{y}$.
4. Solve the following ℓ_1 minimization problem

$$\hat{\alpha} = \underset{\alpha'}{\text{argmin}} \, \| \alpha' \|_1 \quad \text{subject to} \quad \tilde{y} = \tilde{A} \alpha'. \tag{22.3}$$

5. Calculate the residuals

$$r_i(\tilde{y}) = \left\| \tilde{y} - \tilde{A}\delta_i(\hat{\alpha}) \right\|_2,$$

for $i = 1, \ldots, C$ where δ_i a characteristic function that selects the coefficients associated with the ith class.
6. Identify$(y) = \mathrm{argmin}_i\, r_i(\tilde{y})$.

The assumption made in this method is that given sufficient training samples of the kth class, $\tilde{A}_k$, any new test image y that belongs to the same class will approximately lie in the linear span of the training samples from the class k. This implies that most of the coefficients not associated with class k in $\hat{\alpha}$ will be close to zero. Hence, $\hat{\alpha}$ is a sparse vector. This algorithm can also be extended to deal with occlusions and random noise. Furthermore, a method of rejecting invalid test samples can also be introduced within this framework [41]. In particular, to decide whether a given test sample is a valid sample or not, the notion of Sparsity Concentration Index (SCI) has been proposed [41]. The SCI of a coefficient vector α is defined as

$$\mathrm{SCI}(\alpha) = \frac{\frac{C.\max \|\delta_i(\alpha)\|_1}{\|\alpha\|_1} - 1}{C - 1}. \tag{22.4}$$

SCI takes values between 0 and 1. SCI values close to 1 correspond to the case when the test image can be approximately represented by using only images from a single class. Thus, the test vector has enough discriminating features of its class and hence has high quality. If $\mathrm{SCI} = 0$, then the coefficients are spread evenly over all classes. Hence, the test vector is not similar to any of the classes and hence is of poor quality.

22.2.3 Face Recognition Across Illumination and Pose

There are a number of hurdles that face recognition systems have to overcome. One is designing algorithms that are robust to changes in illumination and pose; a second is that algorithms need to efficiently scale as the number of people enrolled in the system increases. In the SR-based approaches [19, 37, 41], the former mentioned challenge is met by collecting a set of images of each person that spans the space of expected variations in illumination. The SRC approach recognizes faces by solving an optimization problem over the set of images enrolled into the database. This solution trades robustness and size of the database against computational efficiency.

Recently, a dictionary-based face recognition (DFR) algorithm has been proposed in [28] that is robust to changes in illumination conditions. This method consists of two main stages. In the first stage, a dictionary is learned for each face class based on the given training examples, which minimizes the representation error with a sparseness constraint. In the second stage, a novel test image is projected onto the span of the elements in each learned dictionary. The resulting residual vectors are then used for classification. Furthermore, to handle changes in lighting conditions, a relighting approach based on a non-stationary stochastic filtering method [9] is

Fig. 22.1 Examples of the original images (*first column*) and the corresponding relighted images with different light source directions

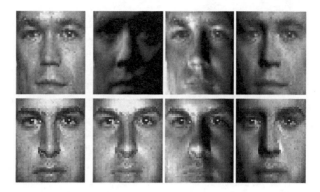

used to generate multiple images of the same person with different lighting. As a result, this algorithm has the ability to recognize human faces with good accuracy even when only a single or a very few images are provided for training. Figure 22.1 shows some relighted images and the corresponding input images [28].

Another way to address the problem of face recognition across illumination and pose variations is to characterize the set of images of an object under all possible combinations of pose and illumination. Recent results have showed that an image of a Lambertian object taken under any arbitrary illumination conditions can be approximately represented as a linear combination of the first nine spherical harmonic basis images [7]. Given an input image, if these spherical harmonic basis images can be estimated, then the face for which there exists a weighted combination of basis images that is the closest to the test face image determines the identity of the test image [42]. A 3D morphable model-based approach has also been proposed for the task of recognizing faces with varying illumination and pose [11].

Albedo estimation framework presented in [9] can be extended to deal with varying illumination and pose [10]. It is shown that 3D pose of the input face image is obtained as a byproduct of this algorithm. This method utilizes class-specific statistics of faces to iteratively improve albedo and pose estimates and does not require manually marked landmarks. Estimated albedo maps are then used for recognition.

22.2.4 Video-Based Face Recognition

Though face recognition research has traditionally been concentrated on recognition from still images, recently video-based face recognition has also gained a lot of interest. In video-based face recognition, one is faced with the challenge of how to exploit the available extra information from video. This can be done by one of the following approaches: using frame-based approach and fusing the results, extracting joint appearance and behavioral features from the video and modeling the temporal correlations explicitly to recognize the face.

A straightforward approach to use the extra information present in a video sequence is to fuse the results obtained by a 2D face classifier for each frame of the sequence. Here, the video sequence is viewed as an unordered set of images for both training and testing. During testing, each frame of the test video sequence independently votes for a particular identity for the test subject. Appropriate fusion techniques can then be applied to provide the final identity. The most frequently used fusion strategy in this case is majority voting [24]. The decision level fusion can also be applied where frame-level decisions are combined into a final decision. These approaches do not take advantage of the temporal information that is also present in the video sequence.

Several other methods have been proposed for extracting more descriptive appearance models from videos for recognition. A video sequence can be considered as a sequence of images sampled from an appearance manifold, which contains all possible appearances of the subject [23]. The complex nonlinear appearance manifold of each subject can be viewed by a collection of submanifolds. Submanifolds model the face appearances of each person in different poses. Each submanifold is approximated by a low-dimensional linear subspace. This low-dimensional subspace can be computed by PCA from the training video sequences. Given a video sequence, the temporal appearance variation is modeled as transitions between these subspaces and these can be learned directly from the training data. This method is robust to large appearance changes if sufficient 3D view variations and illumination variations are available in the training set. Furthermore, tracking can also be integrated into this framework by searching for a bounding-box on the test image that minimizes the distance of the cropped region to the learnt appearance manifold.

In a related work, [5] represents the appearance variations due to shape and illumination on human faces, using the assumption that the shape–illumination manifold of all possible illuminations and poses is generic for human faces. This in turn implies that the shape–illumination manifold can be estimated using a set of subjects exclusive of the test set. It was shown that the effects of face shape and illumination can be learnt using probabilistic principal component analysis (PCA) from a small, unlabeled set of video sequences of faces in randomly varying lighting conditions [5]. Given a novel sequence, the learnt model is used to decompose the face appearance manifold into albedo– and shape–illumination manifolds, producing the classification decision using robust likelihood estimation.

With the rapid development of 3D digital acquisition systems, 3D face data can be captured more quickly and accurately. The use of 3D information in face recognition has attracted great attention and various techniques have been presented in recent years. Since 3D face data contain explicit 3D geometry, more clues can be used to handle the variations of face pose, expression and aging. See [11, 21, 31, 38, 43] and references therein for details.

22.2.5 Face Recognition Experiments

To illustrate the effectiveness of the sparsity promoting methods for face recognition, we highlight some of the results presented in [28] on the extended Yale B

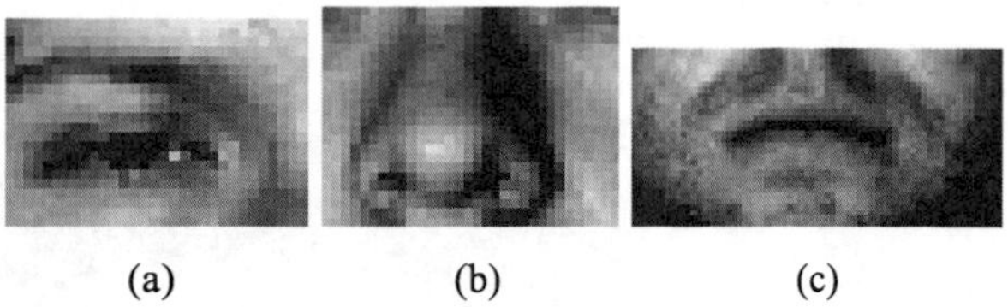

Fig. 22.2 Examples of partial facial features. **a** Eye **b** Nose **c** Mouth

(a)　　　　　　(b)　　　　　　(c)

Table 22.1 Recognition rates (in %) of different methods on the Extended Yale B database [28]

Method	DFR	SRC	NN	NS	SVM
Recognition Rate	99.17	98.1	90.7	94.1	97.7

Table 22.2 Recognition results with partial facial features [28]

Dimension	Right Eye	Nose	Mouth
	5,040	4,270	12,936
DFR	99.3%	98.8%	99.8%
SRC	93.7%	87.3%	98.3%
NN	68.8%	49.2%	72.7%
NS	78.6%	83.7%	94.4%
SVM	85.8%	70.8%	95.3%

dataset [17]. There are a total of 2,414 frontal face images of 38 individuals in the Extended Yale B dataset. These images were captured under various controlled indoor lighting conditions. They were manually cropped and normalized to the size of 192×168. We randomly selected 32 images per subject (i.e. half of the images) for training and the other half for testing. The maximum rank-1 recognition rates achieved by DFR, SRC, Nearest Neighbor (NN), Nearest Subspace (NS) and SVMs are summarized in Table 22.1. As can be seen from the table, even in the case of extreme illumination conditions, both the SRC and DFR methods perform well on this dataset.

Partial face features have been very popular in recovering the identity of human face [34, 41]. Examples of partial facial features are shown in Fig. 22.2. The rank-1 recognition results on partial facial features such as an eye, nose, and mouth are summarized in Table 22.2 on the same dataset. As can be seen from the table, DFR achieves recognition rates of 99.3%, 98.8% and 99.8% on eye, nose and mouth region, respectively, and it outperforms the other methods.

22.3 Iris-Based Personal Authentication

Iris recognition deals with using the patterns on the iris as a biometric for identification or verification. Iris is the colored region of the eye, which controls the amount of light entering the eye. It encloses the darker pupil and is surrounded by a white region called the sclera. Iris and the pupil are protected by a transparent membrane called the cornea. Figure 22.3 shows the different parts of the human eye.

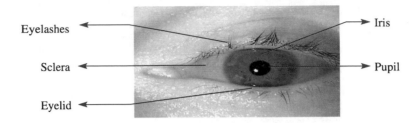

Fig. 22.3 Different parts of the eye

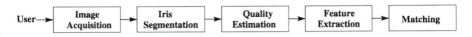

Fig. 22.4 Parts of an iris recognition system

The human iris typically has a rich set of patterns, which are believed to be formed randomly during the fetal development of the eye. The iris patterns are observed to differ for different individuals and remain stable for long periods of time, making it a good biometric. Iris-based human authentication deals with using these iris patterns to recognize individuals. It is a non-contact biometric, which is more hygienic than a contact biometric like finger print. Also it is protected from wear and tear by the cornea, which ensures its stability over years. However, an iris-based personal authentication system requires close proximity of the eye and a cooperative subject. When acquired correctly, iris-based biometric is highly accurate.

22.3.1 Components of an Iris Recognition System

A generic iris recognition system has five main components, as shown in Fig. 22.4. They are the acquisition unit, segmentation unit, quality estimation unit, feature extraction unit and the matching unit. Since the most well-known iris recognition system is the one by Daugman [14], we use it as an example to explain the different steps below.

The first step in an iris recognition system is the image acquisition, where the iris image of the user is obtained. Near infra-red illumination is normally used, as it reveals the detailed structure of the iris much better that visible light. Visible light gets absorbed by the melanin pigments on the iris where as the longer near infra-red radiations get reflected by them. After the image is obtained, the segmentation algorithm extracts the region of the image corresponding to the iris, for further processing. In Daugman's method, the inner and outer boundaries of the iris (known as the pupillary and limbic boundaries, respectively) are obtained by approximating them by circles and finding their parameters. Each of the boundaries is obtained for an image $I(x, y)$ by integrodifferential operators, which find the parameters (r, x_0, y_0) having the highest blurred partial derivatives in a circular arc of width ds along a circle of center (x_0, y_0) and radius r, given by

$$\max_{(r,x_0,y_0)} \left| G_\sigma(r) * \frac{\partial}{\partial r} \oint_{r,x_0,y_0} \frac{I(x, y)}{2\pi r} ds \right|,$$

where $G_\sigma(r)$ denotes a smoothing operator like the Gaussian with scale σ and $*$ denote convolution. After obtaining these boundaries, further processing is performed to remove the eye lids and eye lashes present in the iris region. To make the iris template invariant to changes in size, the extracted iris region is mapped to a normalized coordinate system, where the pupillary boundary is mapped to zero and the limbic boundary is mapped to 1. So any pixel in the new coordinate system is defined by an angle between 0 and 360 degrees and a radial coordinate from 0 to 1.

The quality estimation stage estimates the quality of the acquired iris sample and decides whether to further process the image for recognition or reject the sample. Energy of the high frequency Fourier coefficients can be used as a measure of blur in the acquired image. A blurred image will not have high frequency components and hence have lower energy in those coefficients.

If the acquired image is accepted by the quality estimation module, feature extraction unit computes features from the iris region, which capture the identity of the person. The texture patterns on the iris contain the information unique to each individual. To capture this, the extracted and normalized iris region is convolved with two-dimensional Gabor filters of the form

$$G(r, \theta) = \exp^{-i\omega(\theta-\theta_0)} \exp^{-\frac{(r-r_0)^2}{\alpha^2}} \exp^{-\frac{(\theta-\theta_0)^2}{\beta^2}},$$

where (r, θ) denote the polar coordinates. (r_0, θ_0) denote the location, ω the scale and (α, β) the width of the Gabor filter, respectively.

To improve the speed of matching, the extracted Gabor features are encoded into a binary vector. Each complex Gabor feature is represented by two bits—the first bit is 1 if the real part of the Gabor feature is positive and zero otherwise. Similarly the second bit capture the sign of the imaginary part of the Gabor feature. Normalized Hamming distance is then used as a measure of similarity between two iris images. It is defined as the fraction of the bits for which the two iris codes differ. The distance is computed only for those pixels for which both the iris codes are not occluded. To account for the in-plane rotation, the distance is computed for several rotations of the iris vector. The smallest among all those scores is used as the final similarity score.

The source code for a typical generic iris recognition system, similar to the one described above has been released by Masek et al. [26]. We refer the reader to [13] for an excellent survey of the recent efforts in iris recognition.

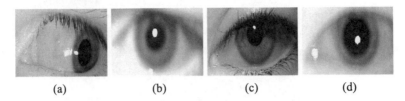

(a)   (b)   (c)   (d)

Fig. 22.5 Poorly acquired iris images from the ND dataset. Note that image **a** has specular reflections on the iris and is difficult to be segmented correctly due to the tilt and non-circular shape. Images **b** and **d** suffer from blurring, whereas image **c** is occluded by the shadow of the eyelids

22.3.2 Publicly Available Datasets

When the iris acquisition conditions are not constrained, many of the acquired iris images suffer from defocus blur, motion blur, occlusion due to the eyelids, specular reflections and off angle distortions. Numerous datasets are now available for the research community, containing varying degrees of these artifacts.

One of the earliest ones was the CASIA version 1 [1]. It contains 108 subjects and seven images per person. The images in the database are clean, without significant occlusion, blur or specular reflection on the iris. But the pupil has been edited in these images and replaced by a black region, which masks the specular reflections in the pupil region. A larger dataset containing some of the unedited images is now available under the name CASIA version 3 [1]. It has 1500 subjects and more than 2200 iris images.

Two large datasets have been collected by the University of Notre Dame for the Iris Challenge Evaluation (ICE) in 2005 and 2006. The ICE 2005 dataset [2] has 244 subjects and close to 3000 iris images in all. The ICE 2006 dataset [2] has 480 subjects and 60000 images in all. A super set of the ICE 2005 and ICE 2006 datasets is now available called the ND-IRIS-04-05 dataset [12] (ND dataset). It contains iris images with occlusion due to shadows and eyelids, blur due to motion of the subject and defocus, specular reflections and in-plane rotations. Some of these images are shown in Fig. 22.5. Gazed iris images with off angle distortions are available in the West Virginia University iris dataset [3].

22.3.3 Iris Recognition from Videos

Though research in iris recognition has been extremely active in the past decade, most of the existing results are based on recognition from still iris images. In many scenarios, multiple iris images of the test subject will be available. The distortions common in iris image acquisition like occlusion due to eyelids and eye lashes, blur, and specular reflections will differ in these different images. So by efficiently combining them, the performance could be improved.

One way of combining the information from multiple frames is by score level fusion. In this technique, the Hamming distances from the multiple images are combined to obtain a single score, which is used for matching. Different schemes like using log likelihood ratios, learning classifiers and taking the minimum or the mean scores are found to improve performance.

Temporal continuity in iris videos has also been used to improve performance [18]. This method averages the intensity values from the corresponding regions of the iris image in multiple frames. This averaging reduces the noise and there by improves performance. But averaging requires images to be well segmented and aligned, which may often not be possible in a practical iris recognition system. In the next section, we describe a quality-based matching score that gives higher weight to the evidence from good quality frames, yielding superior performance even when some of the video frames are poorly acquired.

22.3.4 Sparsity-Based Iris Recognition

Some of the challenges in unconstrained iris recognition have been addressed recently using the ideas of sparse representations and random projections [30]. This method provides a unified framework for image quality estimation, recognition and privacy in iris biometrics. The block diagram of the method is given in Fig. 22.6.

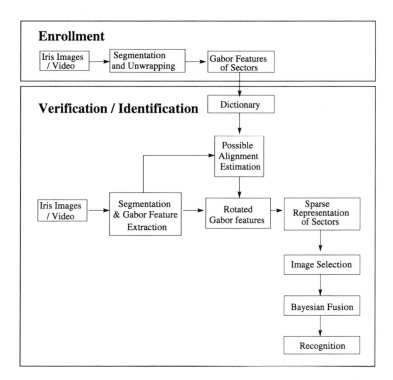

Fig. 22.6 A block diagram illustrating the sparsity-based image selection and recognition algorithm

The iris region is segmented using existing techniques and are divided into different sectors. Each sector is recognized separately using the ideas of sparse representations introduced in Sect. 22.2.2. Here the Gabor features obtained from the sectors form the columns of the dictionary. SCI is used as a quality measure for each sector. Sectors with low SCI values are rejected.

A Bayesian fusion technique is then employed to combine the results from the remaining sectors, based on their quality. Let $\mathbf{C}$ be the set of possible class labels and M be the number of sectors retained after rejection. Let $d_1, d_2, \ldots, d_M$ be the class labels of the retained sectors. The final class label is given by

$$\tilde{c} = \operatorname*{argmax}_{c \in \mathbf{C}} \mathrm{CSCI}(c), \tag{22.5}$$

where

$$\mathrm{CSCI}(c_l) = \frac{\sum_{j=1}^{M} \mathrm{SCI}(d_j) . \delta(d_j = c_l)}{\sum_{j=1}^{M} \mathrm{SCI}(d_j)}. \tag{22.6}$$

CSCI of a class is the sum of the SCI values of all the sectors identified by the classifier as belonging to that class. Therefore, the optimal estimate is the class having the highest CSCI. Thus higher weighting is given to the labels predicted by the better quality sectors when compared to the rest. To address the issue of in-plane rotation in the test iris image, the same formulation is extended by including sectors obtained after rotating the test iris image. When test videos are available, the sectors of the different frames of the video are combined based on their quality in a similar manner.

The performance of the algorithm is compared to a nearest neighbor (NN)-based recognition algorithm and the Masek's implementation on the ND dataset, in Table 22.3. When the test images are well acquired, the sparsity-based method obtained a recognition rate of 99.15% when compared to 98.33% for the NN and 97.5% for the Masek's method. The table also compares the performance in the presence of various distortions in the test image like blur, occlusion and segmentation errors. Observe that the recognition performance on poorly acquired images are higher when the sparsity-based image selection and recognition method is used.

In Fig. 22.7, the iris images having the lowest SCI values in the ND dataset are displayed. As can be observed, images with low SCI values suffer from high amounts of distortion.

Table 22.3 Recognition rate on ND dataset

Image Quality	NN	Masek's Implementation	Sparsity-based Method
Good	98.33	97.5	99.15
Blurred	95.42	96.01	98.18
Occluded	85.03	89.54	90.44
Seg. Error	78.57	82.09	87.63

Fig. 22.7 Iris images with low SCI values in the ND dataset. Note that the images in **a**, **b** and **c** suffer from high amounts of blur, occlusion and segmentation errors, respectively

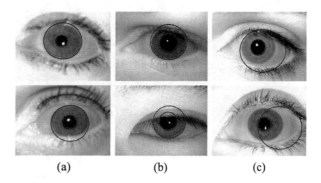

(a)   (b)   (c)

22.4 Gait-Based Recognition

Gait refers to the style of walking of an individual. Studies in psychophysics indicate that humans have the capability of recognizing people from even impoverished displays of gait, indicating the presence of identity information in gait. It is interesting, therefore, to study the utility of gait as a biometric. In fact the nature of shape changes of the silhouette of a human provides significant information about the activity performed by the human, as well as reveals the idiosyncratic movements of an individual.

Apart from providing information about the activity being performed, the manner of shape changes provides valuable insights regarding the identity of the object. Gait-based human identification is an area that has attracted significant attention due to its potential applications in remote biometrics.

The sensor for a gait-based biometric system is a video camera capturing videos of human subjects walking within its field-of view. The raw sensor video is then processed to extract relevant features which can then be used for recognition. The procedure for obtaining shapes from the video sequence is illustrated in Fig. 22.8. If the acquisition conditions are expected to be controlled and favorable then the quality of the video will enable extracting features such as joint angles from the images captured using one or more video cameras. In more typical uncontrolled settings, the features extracted could either be background subtracted binary images, silhouettes, shapes or width vectors—all examples of features capturing the extent of the human body to differing amounts of detail. During the training phase, several such sequences of each individual in the gallery are collected and the appropriate features are then stored in the database. During the test phase, each test sequence is compared with the training sequences available in the database and the similarity is used in order to perform person authentication. See [22, 25, 27, 32, 33, 36] for details on various gait recognition methods.

22.4.1 Results on the USF Database

We consider the problem of gait-based person identification, in which our goal is to identify the individual from a video sequence of the individual walking. Given a

Fig. 22.8 Illustration of the sequence of shapes obtained during a walking cycle. Each frame in the video is processed to obtain a pre-shape vector. These vectors lie on a complex hyper-spherical manifold. Image courtesy [36]

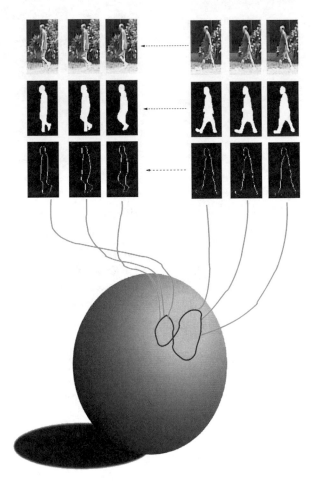

video sequence, we first perform background subtraction to extract the silhouette of the human. We then uniformly sample points on the outer contour of the silhouette to obtain the pre-shape vector. The USF database [29] consists of 71 people in the gallery. Several covariates, such as camera position, shoe type, surface and time, were varied in a controlled manner to design a set of challenge experiments [29]. The results are evaluated using cumulative match score[1](CMS) curves. The results for the seven experiments on the USF database are shown in Fig. 22.9 [36].

22.5 Conclusion

A number of challenges and issues confront biometrics recognition involving faces, iris and gait. Below we list a few.

---

[1] Plot of percentage of recognition vs. rank.

Fig. 22.9 Cumulative Match Scores using Dynamic Time Warping on shape space [36]

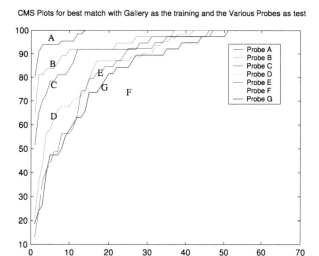

CMS Plots for best match with Gallery as the training and the Various Probes as test

Pose and illumination variations still remain one of the biggest challenges for face recognition. Most of the approaches that can handle facial pose require manual labeling of several landmark locations in the face, which is an impediment to realizing a completely automatic face recognition system. Another issue that needs to be addressed is robustness to low resolution and blurred images. Standard face recognition methods work well if the images or videos are of high quality, but usually fail when enough resolution is not available. A lot of work is still needed to handle the other sources of variations such as expressions, make-up, and aging.

The topic of multi-modal biometrics has gained strong interest in recent years [4]. In this approach, multiple biometrics data (either coming from the same sensing device or from different sources) are fused together and processed with a single matching algorithm or with several concurrent algorithms. The scores produced by different algorithms can be also fused to produce a single matching score for identification. Can SR- and CS-based methods offer better solutions for multi-modal biometric fusion?

In a practical iris recognition system, the acquired image could be of low quality due to motion, partial cooperation or the distance of the user from the scanner. Robust iris recognition in an unconstrained acquisition environment with limited user cooperation is an open research problem. Other areas requiring further research include protecting the privacy of the users without compromising security, improving recognition performance when the user is wearing contacts or glasses, and handling people with medical conditions like cataract, glaucoma etc. which could affect the iris signatures.

Since gait-based person identification often occurs without any particular viewpoint, view-invariance of the feature extracted from the video is another important challenge. This will ensure that recognition performance is robust to changes in the viewpoint of the camera. Another challenge for automated gait-based biometrics is that of changing illumination conditions in the scene. In order to be robust to changing illumination conditions, background subtraction is typically performed on the raw videos before the video data is used in a recognition algorithm. Another important issue is the variability in the clothing, shoe type and the surface on which the individuals walk.

Another area of current research is in generating secure biometrics signatures, known as cancelable biometrics [30].

Acknowledgements This work was partially supported by a MURI Grant N00014-08-1-0638 from the Office of Naval Research.

References

1. Casia iris image dataset. http://www.cbsr.ia.ac.cn/Database.htm [446]
2. Iris challenge evaluation data. http://iris.nis.gov/ice/ [446]
3. West Virginia university iris dataset. http://www.citer.wvu.edu/off_axis_angle_iris_dataset_collection_release1 [446]
4. Nandakumar K., Ross, A., Jain, A.K.: Handbook of Multibiometrics. Springer, New York (2006) [451]
5. Arandjelovic, O., Cipolla, R.: Face recognition from video using the generic shape–illumination manifold. Comput. Vis. Image. Underst. 27–40 (2006) [442]
6. Baraniuk, R.: Compressive sensing. IEEE Signal Process. Mag. **24**(4), 118–121 (July 2007) [438]
7. Basari, R., Jacobs, D.: Lambertian reflectance and linear subspaces. IEEE Trans. Pattern Anal. Mach. Intell. **25**(2), 218–233 (2003) [441]
8. Belhumeur, P.N., Hespanha, J.P., Kriegman, D.J.: Eigenfaces vs. fisherfaces: Recognition using class-specific linear projection. IEEE Trans. Pattern Anal. Mach. Intell. **19**(7), 711–720 (1997) [438]
9. Biswas, S., Aggarwal, G., Chellappa, R.: Robust estimation of albedo for illumination–invariant matching and shape recovery. IEEE Trans. Pattern Anal. Mach. Intell. **29**(2), 884–899 (March 2009) [440,441]
10. Biswas, S., Chellappa, R.: Pose-robust albedo estimation from a single image. In: Proc. IEEE Conference on Computer Vision and Pattern Recognition (2010) [441]
11. Blanz, V., Vetter, T.: Face recognition based on fitting a 3d morphable model. IEEE Trans. Pattern Anal. Mach. Intell. **25**(9), 1063–1074 (2003) [441,442]
12. Bowyer, K.W., P.J., Flynn: The nd-iris-0405 iris image dataset. Notre Dame CVRL Technical Report [446]
13. Bowyer, K.W., Hollingsworth, K., Flynn, P.J.: Image understanding for iris biometrics: A survey. Comput. Vis. Image Underst. **110**(2), 281–307 (2008) [445]
14. Daugman, J.: High confidence visual recognition of persons by a test of statistical independence. IEEE Trans. Pattern Anal. Mach. Intell. **15**, 1148–1161 (1993) [444]
15. Elad, M.: Sparse and Redundant Representations: From Theory to Applications in Signal and Image Processing. Springer, New York (2010) [438]
16. Etemad, K., Chellappa, R.: Discriminant analysis for recognition of human face images. J. Opt. Soc. Am. A **14**(8), 1724–1733 (1997) [438]
17. Georghiades, A.S., Belhumeur, P.N., Kriegman, D.J.: From few to many: Illumination cone models for face recognition under variable lighting and pose. IEEE Trans. Pattern Anal. Mach. Intell. **23**(6), 643–660 (June 2001) [443]
18. Hollingsworth, K.P., Bowyer, K.W., Flynn, P.J.: Image Averaging for Improved Iris Recognition. Lecture Notes in Computer Science, vol. 5558 (2009) [447]

19. Huang, J., Huang, X., Metaxas, D.: Simultaneous image transformation and sparse representation recovery. In: Proc. IEEE Conference on Computer Vision and Pattern Recognition, pp. 1–8 (2008) [439]
20. Pillai, J., Patel, V.M., Chellappa, R., Ratha, N.K.: Towards a practical face recognition system: Robust registration and illumination by sparse representation. In: Proc. IEEE International Conference on Acoustics, Speech and Signal Processing, pp. 1838–1841 (2010) [439]
21. Chang, K., Bowyer, K.W., Flynn, P.: A survey of approaches and challenges in 3d and multi-model 3d+2d face recognition. Comput. Vis. Image Underst. **101**, 1–15 (2006) [442]
22. Kale, A., Sundaresan, A., Rajagopalan, A., Cuntoor, N., Chowdhury, A.R., Kruger, V., Chellappa, R.: Identification of humans using gait. IEEE Trans. Image Process. **13**(9), 1163–1173 (2004) [449]
23. Lee, K., Ho, J., Yang, M., Kriegman, D.J.: Visual tracking and recognition using probabilistic manifolds. Comput. Vis. Image. Underst. **99**(3), 303–331 (2005) [442]
24. Liu, X., Chen, T., Thornton, S.M.: Eigenspace updating for non-stationary process and its application to face recognition. Pattern Recogn. **36**(9), 1945–1959 (September 2003) [442]
25. Liu, Z., Sarkar, S.: Improved gait recognition by gait dynamics normalization. IEEE Trans. Pattern Anal. Mach. Intell. **28**(6), 863–876 (June 2006) [449]
26. Masek, L., Kovesi, P.: MATLAB Source Code for a Biometric Identification System Based on Iris Patterns. The University of Western Australia, Perth (2003) [445]
27. Nixon, M., Tan, T., Chellappa, R.: Human Identification Based on Gait. Springer, New York (2006) [449]
28. Patel, V.M., Wu, T., Biswas, S., Chellappa, R., Phillips, P.J.: Dictionary-based face recognition. UMIACS Tech. Report, UMIACS-TR-2010-07/CAR-TR-1030, University of Maryland, College Park (July 2010) [440-443]
29. Phillips, P.J., Sarkar, S., Robledo, I., Grother, P., Bowyer, K.: The gait identification challenge problem: Data sets and baseline algorithm. In: Proceedings of the 16th International Conference on Pattern Recognition (2002) [450]
30. Pillai, J.K., Patel, V.M., Chellappa, R., Ratha, N.K.: Secure and robust iris recognition using random projections and sparse representations. Pattern Anal. Mach. Intell. **33**(9), 1877–1893 (September 2010) [439,447,452]
31. Queirolo, C.C., Silva, L., Bellon, O.R.P., Segundo, M.P.: 3d face recognition using simulated annealing and the surface interpenetration measure. IEEE Trans. Pattern Anal. Mach. Intell. **32**(2), 206–219 (2010) [442]
32. Robledo, I., Sarkar, S.: Statistical motion model based on the change of feature relationships: Human gait-based recognition. IEEE Trans. Pattern Anal. Mach. Intell. **25**(10), 1323–1328 (October 2003) [449]
33. Sarkar, S., Phillips, P.J., Liu, Z., Robledo, I., Grother, P., Bowyer, K.: The human id gait challenge problem: Data sets, performance. IEEE Tran. Pattern Anal. Mach. Intell. **27**(2), 162–177 (February 2005) [449]
34. Sinha, P., Balas, B., Ostrovsky, Y., Russell, R.: Face recognition by humans: Nineteen results all computer vision researchers should know about. Proc. IEEE **94**(11), 1948–1962 (2006) [443]
35. Turk, M., Pentland, A.: Eigenfaces for recognition. J. Cogn. Neurosci. **3**(1), 71–86 (1991) [438]
36. Veeraraghavan, A., Chowdhury, A.R., Chellappa, R.: Matching shape sequences in video with an application to human movement analysis. IEEE Trans. Pattern Anal. Mach. Intell. **27**(2), 1896–1909 (December 2005) [449-451]
37. Wagner, A., Wright, J., Ganesh, A., Zhou, Z., Ma, Y.: Towards a practical face recognition system: Robust registration and illumination by sparse representation. In: Proc. IEEE Conference on Computer Vision and Pattern Recognition, pp. 597–604 (June 2009) [439]
38. Wang, Y., Liu, J., Tang, X.: Robust 3d face recognition by local shape difference boosting. IEEE Trans. Pattern Anal. Mach. Intell. **32**(10), 1858–1870 (2010) [442]
39. Wiskott, L., Fellous, J.M., Kruger, N., von der Malsburg, C.: Face recognition by elastic bunch graph matching. IEEE Trans. Pattern Anal. Mach. Intell. **19**(7), 775–779 (1997) [439]

40. Wright, J., Ma, Y., Mairal, J., Sapiro, G., Huang, T.S., Yan, S.: Sparse representation for computer vision and pattern recognition. Proc. IEEE **98**(6), 1031–1044 (June 2010) [438]
41. Wright, J., Yang, A.Y., Ganesh, A., Sastry, S.S., Ma, Y.: Robust face recognition via sparse representation. IEEE Trans. Pattern Anal. Mach. Intell. **31**(2), 210–227 (2009) [439,440,443]
42. Zhang, L., Samaras, D.: Face recognition from a single training image under arbitrary unknown lighting using spherical harmonics. IEEE Trans. Pattern Anal. Mach. Intell. **28**(3), 351–363 (2006) [441]
43. Zhao, W., Chellappa, R., Phillips, P.J., Rosenfeld, A.: Face recognition: A literature survey. ACM Comput. Surv. **35**, 399–458 (December 2003) [438]

Chapter 23
Security and Surveillance

Shaogang Gong, Chen Change Loy, and Tao Xiang

Abstract Human eyes are highly efficient devices for scanning through a large quantity of low-level visual sensory data and delivering selective information to one's brain for high-level semantic interpretation and gaining situational awareness. Over the last few decades, the computer vision community has endeavoured to bring about similar perceptual capabilities to artificial visual sensors. Substantial efforts have been made towards understanding static images of individual objects and the corresponding processes in the human visual system. This endeavour is intensified further by the need for understanding a massive quantity of video data, with the aim to comprehend multiple entities not only within a single image but also over time across multiple video frames for understanding their spatio-temporal relations. A significant application of video analysis and understanding is intelligent surveillance, which aims to interpret automatically human activity and detect unusual events that could pose a threat to public security and safety.

23.1 Introduction

There has been an accelerated expansion of CCTV surveillance in recent years, largely in response to rising anxieties about crime and its threat to security and safety. Substantial numbers of surveillance cameras have been deployed in public spaces ranging from transport infrastructures (e.g. airports, underground stations), shopping centres, sport arenas to residential streets, serving as a tool for crime reduction and risk management. Conventional visual surveillance systems rely heavily on human operators to monitor activities and determine the actions to be taken upon the occurrence of an incident, e.g. tracking a suspicious target from one camera to another camera or alerting relevant agencies to areas of concern.

S. Gong (✉) · C.C. Loy · T. Xiang
Queen Mary University of London, London, E1 4NS, UK
e-mail: sgg@eecs.qmul.ac.uk

C.C. Loy
e-mail: ccloy@eecs.qmul.ac.uk

T. Xiang
e-mail: txiang@eecs.qmul.ac.uk

T.B. Moeslund et al. (eds.), *Visual Analysis of Humans*,
DOI 10.1007/978-0-85729-997-0_23, © Springer-Verlag London Limited 2011

Unfortunately, many actionable incidents are simply mis-detected in such a manual system due to inherent limitations from deploying solely human operators eyeballing CCTV screens. Mis-detections could be caused by (1) excessive number of video screens to monitor, (2) boredom and tiredness due to prolonged monitoring, (3) lack of a priori and readily accessible knowledge for what to look for, (4) distraction by additional responsibilities such as other administrative tasks [24]. As a result, surveillance footages are often used merely as passive records or as evidence for post-event investigations. Mis-detections of important events can be perilous in critical surveillance tasks such as border control or airport surveillance. Technology providers and end-users recognise that manual process alone is inadequate to meet the need for screening timely and searching exhaustively colossal amount of video data generated from the growing number of cameras in public spaces. To fulfil such a need, video content analysis paradigm is shifting from a fully human operator model to a machine-assisted and automated model.

In the following, we describe applications and the latest advances in automated visual analysis of human activities for security and surveillance. Section 23.2 outlines some of the most common technologies in the market, and highlights technical challenges that limit the use and growth of video analytics software. Section 23.3 discusses state of the art video analytics techniques, which may help in advancing current security and surveillance applications.

23.2 Current Systems

There is a surge in demand in the last few years for automated video analysis technologies. This trend is persisting[1][2], mainly driven by the government initiatives and strong demands from retail and transportation sectors[3]. Increasing number of CCTV solutions are made available with some degree of automated analytic capabilities by suppliers from large-scale system integrators to small and medium enterprise (SME) software developers including IBM, Bosch, Pelco, GE Security, Honeywell, Siemens, ObjectVideo, IOImage, Aimetis, Sony, Panasonic, Nice, AgilityVideo, March Network, Mate, Ipsotek, Citilog, Traficon, and BRS Labs [22, 25].

Current video analytics find applications in various areas. For instance, IBM assists the Chicago City in laying out city-wide video analytics system based on the IBM Smart Surveillance Solution (S3) to detect suspicious activity and potential public safety concerns [14]. The City of Birmingham, Alabama also sets up a surveillance system equipped with artificial neural network-based analytic software

---

[1] Frost and Sullivan estimates that the video surveillance software market will reach $670.7 million annually by 2011 [21].

[2] The growing interest on video analytics is also evident from various industrial focus conferences such as the IMS Video Content Analysis Conferences (http://www.imsconferences.com).

[3] Research conducted by the British Industry Security Association demonstrated that video analytics technologies are deployed by the transport and retail sectors most frequently (http://www.bsia.co.uk/aboutbsia/cctv/O5E926740891).

developed by the BRS Labs to detect suspicious and abnormal situations. Besides street-level surveillance, video analytics also find wide applications in the transport sector. For example, the Bosch Intelligent Video Analysis (IVA) software is employed at the Athens International Airport [10]. For border control, the Video Early Warning (VEW) software developed by ObjectVideo is used along the US border to locate suspicious individual or vehicles attempting to cross into the country [50]. Other government and commercial deployment of video analytics include installations of the IOImage video analytics software at the Israeli parliament, and the Aimetis VE Series at Volkswagen Sachsen.

Security has been the dominant driver for the development and deployment of video analytics solutions. Some common applications are:

1. **Intruder detection** often implies tripwire detection or fence trespassing detection, which alerts an operator if an intruder is detected crossing a virtual fence[4]. The underlying algorithm involves the extraction of foreground objects using background subtraction, followed by examining whether the foreground objects overlap with a pre-defined region in an image space. This application is useful to ensure perimeter control for sensitive and restricted areas such as limited-access buildings or train track areas, e.g. BRS Labs AISight[5].
2. **Unattended object detection** aims to ignore items attended by nearby person and only triggers an alarm when an item is deposited in a controlled area longer than a pre-defined time period, e.g. Honeywell video analytics[6].
3. **Loitering detection** aims to detect persons who stay in a controlled area for an extended period of time. This is often achieved by tracking an individual and recording the time stamps of appearance and disappearance of the person. Loitering detection is useful in bringing about attention on suspicious behaviour in advance to an actual security breach or intrusion, e.g. MarchNetworks Video-Sphere[7].
4. **Tailgating detection** aims to detect illegal follow-through behaviour at access control points, e.g. doorways. It relies on individual tracking in conjunction with an access control system. Alert is generated for an immediate review by security personnel if multiple persons enter a restricted area while only one of them is authorised by the access control system, e.g. Mate video analytics[8].
5. **Crowd management** software monitors and collects statistics on the crowd volume by measuring the foreground occupancy level in a video. It can be used

---

[4]A set of real-world datasets and alarm definitions are released as the Image Library for Intelligent Detection Systems (i-LIDS), a UK government Home Office Scientific Development Branch (HOSDB) benchmark for video analytics systems [63], which has also been adopted by the US National Institute of Standards and Technology (NIST).

[5]http://www.brslabs.com/index.php?id=79

[6]http://www.honeywellvideo.com/support/library/videos/

[7]http://www.marchnetworks.com/Products/Video-and-Data-Analytics/

[8]http://mateusa.net/

at transportation hubs and shopping malls to avoid overcrowding situations, e.g. NiceVision Video Analytics[9].

These applications provide some practical and useful solutions. Nevertheless, their effectiveness and success depend largely on rather stringent operational conditions in carefully controlled environments. There are growing concerns on the viability of using such analytics in real-world scenarios especially in unconstrained crowded public spaces. In particular, existing technologies for video content analysis largely rely on Video Motion Detection (VMD), hard-wired rules, and object-centred reasoning in isolation (i.e. object segmentation and tracking) with little if any context modelling. Such systems often suffer considerably high false alarm rate due to the changes in visual context, such as different weather conditions and gradual object behaviour drift over time. In addition, fully automated analysis of video data captured from public spaces is often intrinsically ill-conditioned due to large (and unknown) variations in video image quality, resolution, imaging noise, diversity of pose and appearance, and severe occlusion in crowded scenes. As a result, those systems that rely on hard-wired hypotheses and location-specific rules are likely to break down unexpectedly giving frequent false alarms, requiring elaborative re-configuration and careful parameter tuning by specialists, making system deployment non-scalable and hugely expensive. In the worst-case scenario, installed expensive video analytics systems are abandoned or otherwise infrequently used due to excessive operational burden and intolerable level of false alarms.

23.3 Emerging Techniques

Addressing the limitations of current systems demands more robust and intelligent computer vision solutions. In this section, we discuss several emerging video analysis techniques, which could help to remedy the problems with the existing video analytics technologies. We first highlight the recent developments in single view-based video analysis techniques, ranging from gauging individual intent (Sect. 23.3.1) to analysing crowd behaviour (Sect. 23.3.2). We then discuss the use of multiple cameras for cooperative monitoring of complex scenes (Sect. 23.3.3). Finally, we look into how one could exploit contextual information (Sect. 23.3.4) and learn from human feedback (Sect. 23.3.5) to facilitate more robust and smarter surveillance.

23.3.1 Intent Profiling

Psychological studies [15, 16] suggest that one's intention can be perceived from the microexpressions and incomplete motion cues. The findings have inspired the development of automated surveillance system to interpret human intent for making

---

[9]http://www.nice.com/video/analytics

      (a)   (b)   (c)

Fig. 23.1 **a** Facial expression, **b** head pose, and **c** gait may be used as behavioural cues to reveal human intention (images from [6, 52, 60])

rapid and anticipatory detection of deceptive intention from visual observations. For instance, the US Department of Homeland Security undertakes an initiative to develop automated capabilities for the Future Attribute Screening Test (FAST)[10] in order to link behavioural cues such as subtle changes in facial temperature to a variety of hidden emotions, and thereby spotting people being deceptive or planning for hostile acts.

Various computer vision studies have examined the possibility of inferring human emotion and intent based on temporal analysis of visual cues such as facial expression, head pose, body pose, and gait (see Fig. 23.1). In facial expression analysis [67], most systems extract either geometric-based [17] or appearance-based facial features, e.g. Gabor wavelets or LBP [60], to recognise prototypic emotional expressions, such as anger or fear. Different from facial expressions, the head pose of a person may reveal one's focus of attention. Popular head pose estimation methods [47] include holistic template-based approaches, i.e. classifying a pose direction based on the appearance of the entire face image, or local feature set-based approaches, i.e. corresponding facial landmarks such as eyes and lips to a set of trained poses. Recent studies have attempted to estimate head pose in low-resolution images [8] as well as crowded surveillance videos [52]. In addition to head pose, body posture configuration [46] and gait [49] may also play an important role in human intent inference. In particular, by tracking the body posture of a person over time, we may discover angry or aggressive-looking postures, indicating threatening intentions. A common strategy to articulated body pose estimation is to exploit the mapping of kinematically constrained object parts to a pictorial structure for the appearance of body parts [20]. As opposed to body posture inference, gait analysis typically models the characterisation of periodic motion and spatio-temporal patterns of human silhouettes. Recent studies on gait analysis have been focusing on coping with variations caused by various covariate conditions (e.g. clothing and view angle) [6], and distinguishing abnormal walking styles (e.g. walking with objects attached to the legs) [55].

---

[10]http://www.nature.com/news/2011/110527/full/news.2011.323.html

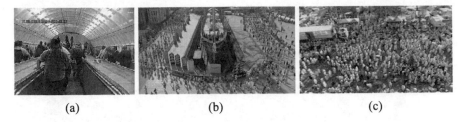

(a)   (b)   (c)

Fig. 23.2 A crowded scene may be structured (**a** and **b**) where crowd motion is almost direction-ally coherent over time, or unstructured (**c**) where the motion of the crowd at any given location is multi-modal. Object tracking in crowded scenes is very challenging due to severe inter-object occlusion, visual appearance ambiguity, and complex interactions among objects

Gauging one's intent is challenging because behavioural cues are often incomplete, vary from person to person, and may last only a fraction of time. In addition, an image-based analysis such as facial expression recognition becomes difficult given low-resolution video images captured from crowded public scenes. For accurate and robust intent inference, it is not only necessary to analyse the low-level imagery features and their inter-correlation, but also critical to model the high-level visual context, i.e. correlations among facial expression, head pose, body pose, and gait as well as their relationships with other entities in a scene.

23.3.2 Crowded Scene Analysis

Crowded scene analysis is indispensable in most surveillance scenarios since most video analyses, e.g. intent profiling, have to be carried out in unconstrained and crowded environments (see Fig. 23.2). Crowded scene analysis can be categorised into three main problems: (1) crowd density estimation and people counting, (2) tracking in crowd, and (3) behaviour recognition in crowd. There exist commercial applications that support crowd density estimation for overcrowding detection, such as the solutions developed by iOmniscient and VideoIQ. However, commercial systems for tracking and behaviour analysis in crowded public scenes are almost non-existent. The main reason is that most existing commercial solutions generally rely on object-centred representation with little if any context modelling. Specifically, they generally assume reliable object localisation and detection as well as smooth object movement. These assumptions are often invalid in real-world surveillance settings characterised by severe inter-object occlusions due to excessive number of objects in crowded scenes (Fig. 23.2). In this section, we focus our discussion on recent advances on behaviour analysis in crowded scenes, adopting a non-trajectory-based representation. Tracking in crowd will be discussed in Sect. 23.3.4. Readers are referred to [32] for a review on crowd density estimation.

One of the key problems in crowd behaviour understanding is *action detection*, which aims to detect specific action, e.g. fighting or falling down in a crowded scene (Fig. 23.3a). The problem of action detection in crowd is largely unresolved as

(a)   (b)

Fig. 23.3 Examples of crowded scene analysis: **a** Action detection in crowd, an example of detection of 'standing' action in a busy underground station. **b** Crowd analysis involving multiple objects, a police car breaks a red light and turns right through opposing traffic. Here the right flow of the other traffic is a typical action, as is the left flow of the police car. However, their conjunction (forbidden by the traffic lights) is not (images from [28, 62])

compared to the extensively studied action classification problem in well-defined environments [53]. Specifically, unlike action classification that assumes availability of pre-segmented single action sequence with fairly clean background, action detection in crowd does not assume well-segmented action clips. A model needs to search for an action of interest that can be overwhelmed by a large numbers of background activities in a cluttered scene. Existing approaches [33, 75] typically construct a set of action templates based on a single sample per action class. These templates are then used for matching given an unseen clip. The models may not be able to cope with large intra-class variations since only one sample per action class is used for a model. The intra-class variations can be captured using large numbers of training actions, but requiring manual annotations that can be time-consuming and unreliable. To generate sufficient training data without laborious manual annotation, different approaches have been proposed, e.g. the use of a multiple instance learning framework [29], a greedy k-nearest neighbour algorithm for automated annotation of positive training data [62], and a transfer learning framework [12] to generalise action detection models built from a source dataset to a new target dataset. For the detection strategy, most existing studies perform action detection by using sliding 3D search windows [29, 62]. This searching method, however, can be computationally prohibitive due to the enormous search space. This problem is addressed by Yuan et al. [76] using a 3D branch and bound searching method.

Beyond action recognition that focuses on the behaviour of individuals, another important research area is crowd analysis, which aims to derive a collective understanding of behaviours and interactions of multiple objects co-exist in a common space (see Fig. 23.3b). Conventional methods [27, 51] often start with individual tracking in the scene. Owing to the unreliability of tracking caused by extensive clutter and dynamic occlusions in crowded scenes, increasing numbers of studies approach the problem using a holistic representation to avoid explicit object seg-

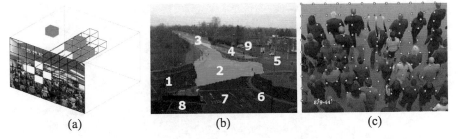

Fig. 23.4 After computing low-level activity features such as optical flow, there are different approaches to represent activity patterns. For example, **a** decomposition into local fixed-size spatio-temporal volumes, **b** decomposition into regions, each of which encapsulates location specific activities that differ from those observed in other regions, and **c** overlay of particles on the optical flow fields (images from [35] (original video sequence is courtesy of Nippon Telegraph and Telephone Corporation) [40, 44]), ((a, c) ©2009 IEEE)

mentation and tracking. In particular, recent studies tend to represent activity patterns using pixel-level features, including foreground pixel changes [7, 66], optical flow [28, 37], texture [42], and gradients of pixel intensities [35]. To construct a holistic representation given low-level pixel-based features, a model decomposes the scene and represents local activities as local fixed-size spatio-temporal volumes of features [28, 34, 35, 44, 70] (Fig. 23.4a). There are also studies [40, 66] that decompose a scene into different regions, which are semantically relevant to the activity dynamics and structural knowledge of a scene (Fig. 23.4b). Alternatively, motivated by the studies on fluid dynamics, the notions of particle flow [3] and streak flow [45] are also exploited (Fig. 23.4c). These studies overlay a cloud of particles over optical flow fields and subsequently learn the dynamics and interactive forces of these moving particles for crowd segmentation [3, 45] and abnormal crowd behaviour detection [44, 45, 73].

Given a representation of localised activity patterns, activity modelling is further considered for learning the space–time dependencies between local activities. To that end, suitable statistical learning models include DBNs [35], MRFs [34], and Probabilistic Topic Models (PTMs) [28, 37, 70]. Among them, PTMs such as LDAs [9] and HDP-based topic models [64] have gained increasing popularity. The PTMs are essentially bag of words models that perform clustering by concurrency. Specifically, local visual activities and video clips are often treated analogously as 'words' and 'documents'. Each video clip may be viewed as a mixture of various 'topics', i.e. a cluster of co-occurring words in different documents. In general, PTMs are less demanding computationally and less sensitive to noise in comparison to DBNs due to the bag of words representation. This advantage, however, is gained at the expense of throwing away explicit temporal dependencies between local activities. Different solutions have been proposed to address this shortcoming, e.g. by introducing additional Markov chain to a topic model for modelling explicit temporal dependencies [28].

Fig. 23.5 Partial observations of activities observed from different camera views: A group of people (highlighted in green boxes) get off a train [Cam 8, frame 10409] and subsequently take an upward escalator [Cam 5, frame 10443] which leads them to the escalator exit view [Cam 4, frame 10452]. Note that the same objects exhibit drastic appearance variations due to changes in illumination, camera viewpoint, and the distance between the objects and the cameras

23.3.3   Cooperative Multi-camera Network Surveillance

Multi-camera surveillance is another important and emerging research topic. In complex public scenes, multiple-camera network systems are more commonly deployed than single-camera systems. Specifically, disjoint cameras with non-overlapping field of view (FOV) are more prevalent, due to the desire to maximise spatial coverage in a wide-area scene whilst minimising the deployment cost. Most existing commercial applications for activity understanding and unusual event detection are designed for single-camera scenarios. Very few working systems are available for interpreting activity patterns across networked multiple disjoint camera views for global analysis and a coherent holistic situational awareness.

In this section, we highlight some efforts that have been made in the last few years by the computer vision community towards developing multi-camera video analytics, focusing on multi-camera object tracking and activity analysis.

Object tracking across camera views is a major research topic due to its potential usefulness in visual surveillance, e.g. monitoring long-term activity patterns of targeted individuals. Current solutions mostly achieve inter-camera tracking by matching the visual appearance features and motion characteristics, e.g. speed, of a target object across views. The appearance features are often extracted from the entire individual body since biometric features such as facial appearance is no longer reliable under typical surveillance viewing conditions. Inter-camera tracking, also known as *person re-identification*, aims to associate individuals observed at diverse locations in a camera network. Compared to multi-camera object tracking, methods devised for person re-identification generally ignore the temporal constraints across views and match objects based solely on appearance features. Due to the disparities in space, time, and viewpoint among disjoint cameras over different physical locations, objects travelling across such camera views often undergo drastic appearance variations (Fig. 23.5). To remedy the problem, different strategies have been proposed, including the mapping of colour distribution from one camera to another using a brightness transfer function [30, 54], exploiting contextual information extracted from surrounding people to resolve ambiguities [78], and computing more robust image features through incremental learning [23], boosting [26], or exploiting asymmetry/symmetry principles [19].

Robustness and accuracy in inter-camera tracking and person re-identification cannot be achieved ultimately by matching imagery information alone. It is essential to formulate and model knowledge about inter-camera relationships as contextual constraints in assisting object tracking and re-identification over significantly different camera views [13, 66]. The problem of inferring the spatial and temporal relationships between cameras is often known as *camera topology inference* [43, 68], which involves the estimation of camera transition probabilities, i.e. how likely an object exiting a camera view would reappear in another camera view, and a inter-camera time delay distribution, i.e. travel time needed to cross a blind area. Recent studies on topology inference have been focusing on disjoint camera networks. A common strategy for learning the topology of a disjoint camera network is by matching individual object's visual appearance or motion trends. This is essentially similar to the multi-camera object tracking and the person re-identification tasks as discussed above. Once object correspondences are established using a large amount of observations, it would be straightforward to infer the paths and transition time distributions between cameras. However, without having to solve the correspondence problem explicitly, which is often non-trivial in itself, another popular strategy applicable to disjoint cameras is to infer inter-camera relationship through searching for a consistent temporal correlation from population activity patterns (rather than individual whereabouts) across views [43, 66, 68]. For example, Makris et al. [43] present an unsupervised method that accumulates evidence from a large set of cross-camera entrance/exit events, so as to establish a transition time distribution. A peak in the transition time distribution essentially implies a connection between the two camera views.

Global activity analysis across multiple camera views is another emerging problem to be solved, in which the goal is to build an activity model for understanding activities captured by multiple cameras holistically, e.g. performing unusual event detection in a global context. Performing global activity analysis in a public space through multiple cameras is non-trivial, especially with non-overlapping inter-camera views, in which global activities can only be observed partially with different views being separated by unknown time gaps. A straightforward approach to activity understanding and unusual event detection in multiple disjoint cameras is to reconstruct the global path taken by an object by merging its trajectories observed in different views, followed by conventional single-view trajectory analysis [77]. With this approach, one must address the camera topology inference problem [43, 68] and the trajectory correspondence problem [30], both of which are still far from being solved. Wang et al. [71] propose an alternative trajectory-based method that bypasses the topology inference and correspondence problems by proposing a LDA-based co-clustering model. However, this model cannot cope with busy scenes and it is limited to capturing only co-occurrence relationships among activity patterns. In contrast to the trajectory-based approaches, Loy et al. [65] developed a method that automatically infers the unknown time-delayed dependencies between local activities across views without relying on explicit object-centred segmentation and tracking. This technique is particularly useful in coping with low-quality public scene surveillance videos featuring severe inter-object occlusion therefore improving robustness and accuracy in multi-camera unusual event detection and object re-identification.

23.3.4 Context-Aware Activity Analysis

Visual surveillance in public spaces is challenging due to severe occlusion, visual appearance variation, and temporal discontinuity. These factors contribute collectively in making visual observations noisy and incomplete, resulting in their interpretations ill-defined and ambiguous. To overcome this problem, a model needs to explore and discover extra knowledge about behavioural context from visual data. Activities in a public space are inherently *context-aware*, exhibited through implicit physical and social constraints imposed by the scene layout and correlated activities (and shared spaces) of other objects both in the same camera view and other views. Strong psychophysical evidence [5, 58] suggests that visual contexts, which encompass spatio-temporal relations of an object with its surroundings, are crucial for establishing a clear comprehension of a scene. Current commercial video analytics solutions have yet to embrace visual context modelling whilst significant efforts have been made by the computer vision research community.

Object tracking in crowded public spaces is one of the application areas that can benefit greatly from visual context modelling. Various techniques have been proposed following this idea. For instance, tracking-by-detection [11, 72] exploits human or body part detection as categorical contextual information for more reliable tracking. There are also studies that exploit contextual information around a target object both spatially and temporally to facilitate more robust long-term tracking [48, 74]. In another study, Ali and Shah [4] exploit scene structure and behaviour of the crowd to assist appearance-based tracking in structured crowded scenes. The work is extended by Rodriguez et al. [56] and Kratz et al. [36] to unstructured crowded scenes, whereby tracking of individuals is aided by leveraging the contextual knowledge learned from typical multi-modal crowd motions (Fig. 23.6a). Visual context is also beneficial for resolving ambiguities from inter-camera tracking or person re-identification. For instance, Zheng et al. [78] embed contextual visual knowledge extracted from surrounding people into supporting descriptions for matching people across disjoint and distributed multiple views (Fig. 23.6b).

Visual context learning can also facilitate the detection of subtle unusual events otherwise undetectable in complex public scenes. For example, Li et al. [39] yield robust detection of unusual events with subtle visual difference but contextually incoherent. This system models both behaviour spatial and correlation context in a single wide-area camera view to provide situational awareness for where a behaviour may take place and how it is affected by other objects co-existing in the scene. Beyond a single-camera view, activity understanding and unusual event detection in a multiple camera network can also benefit from the visual context learning [65, 66].

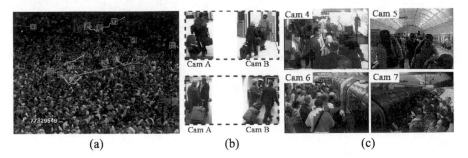

(a)   (b)   (c)

Fig. 23.6 Visual context learning can benefit various surveillance tasks: **a** Tracking in crowd by leveraging the context learned from typical crowd motions, **b** arbitrating ambiguities in person re-identification tasks by exploiting the visual context extracted from surrounding people and objects, and **c** global unusual event detection in multiple disjoint cameras by learning a global dependency context (images from [56, 65, 78]), ((a) ©2009 IEEE)

In particular, collective partial observations of an inferred global activity (not visually observable directly in a common space) are correlated and inter-dependent in that they take place following a certain temporal order even though with uncertain temporal gaps. Consequently, discovering the time-delayed correlations or dependencies between a set of visually disjoint partial observations can help to establish plausible and coherent visual context beyond individual camera views that facilitates more robust activity understanding (Fig. 23.6c).

23.3.5 Human in the Loop

A primary goal of a visual surveillance system is to detect genuine unusual events whilst ignoring distractors. Most unusual event detection methods [34, 44, 70] employ an outlier detection strategy, in which a model is trained using normal events through unsupervised one-class learning. Events that deviate statistically from the resulting normal profile are deemed unusual. This strategy offers a practical way of bypassing the problems of imbalanced class distribution and inadequate unusual event training samples. However, the outlier detection strategy may subject to a few inextricable limitations as pointed out by Loy et al. [41]. Specifically, without human supervision, unsupervised methods have difficulties in detecting subtle unusual events that are visually similar to a large numbers of normally behaving objects co-existing in a scene. In addition, surveillance video of public spaces are highly cluttered with large number of nuisance distractors, often appearing visually similar to genuine unusual events of interest. Relying on information extracted from imagery data alone is computationally difficult to distinguish a genuine unusual event from noise. The usefulness of machine detected events can benefit from further examination using human expert knowledge. From statistical model learning perspective, constructing a model that encompasses 'all' normal events is inherently difficult. Given limited (and often partial) observation, some outlying regions of a normal class may be falsely detected as being unusual (and of interest) if no human feedback is taken into account for arbitrating such false alarms.

To overcome this inherent limitation of unsupervised learning from incomplete data, other sources of information need be exploited. Human feedback is a rich source of accumulative information that can be utilised to assist in resolving ambiguities during class decision boundary formation. An attractive approach to learn a model from human feedback is by employing an *active learning* strategy [59]. Active learning aims to follow a set of predefined query criteria to select the most critical and informative point for human feedback on labelling verification. This strategy for active selection of human verification on some but not all machine detected events allows a model to learn quickly with far fewer samples compared to passive random labelling strategy. Importantly, it helps in resolving ambiguities of interest when lacking visual distinctiveness, leading to more robust and accurate detection of subtle unusual events.

There have been very few active learning systems proposed for activity understanding and unusual event detection. Sillito and Fisher [61] formulate a method to harnesses human feedback on-the-fly for improving unusual event detection performance. Specifically, human approval is sought if a newly observed instance deviates statistically from the learned normal profile. If the suspicious instance is indeed normal, it will be included in the re-training process, or else it will be flagged as anomaly. In a more recent study, Loy et al. [41] propose a stream-based multi-criterion model for active learning from human feedback. In particular, the model makes a decision on-the-fly on whether to request human verification on unsupervised detection. The model selects adaptively two active learning criteria, likelihood criterion and uncertainty criterion, to achieve (1) discovery of unknown event classes and (2) refinement of classification boundary. The system shows that active learning helps in resolving ambiguities in detecting genuine unusual events of interest, leading to a more robust and accurate detection of subtle unusual events compared to the conventional outlier detection strategy.

23.4 Conclusion

Current video surveillance technologies mostly suffer a high false alarm rate, oversensitive to visual context changes due to hard-wired rules, and poor scalability to crowded public scenes. Emerging techniques can help in mitigating some of these problems. In particular, video analytics can benefit from recent development in computer vision research for intent profiling, non-trajectory-based representation in crowded scene analysis, multi-camera network cooperative activity monitoring, visual context modelling, and human-in-the-loop learning. There are other notable emerging trends in both algorithm and hardware development, which can also improve visual analytics for surveillance and security.

Robust and transfer video analysis aim to construct computer vision algorithms learning adaptively over long duration of time and across locations in order to cope with weather conditions, large environmental changes (e.g. different seasons in a calendar year), camera changes, and transitions of activity dynamics. Knowledge learned in a particular scene can be transferred selectively to new scenes without the need to invoke a new learning process from the beginning again.

Multi-sensor surveillance aims to exploit information from multiple heterogeneous sensors for collaborative analysis. Utilising different visual devices can be of benefit, including a combination of pan-tilt-zoom (PTZ) cameras, thermal cameras, stereo cameras, time-of-flight cameras, or wearable cameras. Non-visual sensors such as audio sensors, positioning sensors, and motion sensors can also be integrated into such a heterogeneous system in order to assist surveillance tasks, e.g. cooperative object detection and tracking using multiple active PTZ cameras [18] and wearable cameras [2].

On-the-fly variable level-of-detail content search can benefit from recent proliferation on high-resolution and low-cost cameras. Activity- and behaviour-based focus of attention can be developed to facilitate capabilities for dynamic sensing of visual content at variable level of details for on-the-fly automatic searching of interesting events and object in high-resolution, face recognition, and expression analysis from long distance in a crowded space. This can be exploited by either the deployment of selective high-resolution cameras or massively deployed random forest of redundant low-cost cameras. The use of higher resolution videos also demands tractable and specialised algorithms that are able to run in individual camera nodes, e.g. on a field-programmable gate array (FPGA) in a camera, to share the computational loads of the centralised processing server.

23.4.1 Further Reading

Interested readers are referred to the following further readings:

- [25] for a general overview of the video surveillance market, the architecture of a surveillance system, and the technology status of video analytics.
- [38, 69] for surveys on action and activity recognition.
- [32] for a survey on crowd analysis.
- [1, 31] for system perspectives on multiple camera activity analysis.
- [57] for trends on surveillance hardware development.

References

1. Aghajan, H., Cavallaro, A. (eds.): Multi-camera Networks: Principles and Applications. Elsevier, Amsterdam (2009) [468]
2. Alahia, A., Vandergheynsta, P., Bierlaireb, M., Kunt, M.: Cascade of descriptors to detect and track objects across any network of cameras. Comput. Vis. Image Underst. **114**, 624–640 (2010) [468]
3. Ali, S., Shah, M.: A Lagrangian particle dynamics approach for crowd flow segmentation and stability analysis. In: IEEE Conference on Computer Vision and Pattern Recognition, pp. 1–6 (2007) [462]

4. Ali, S., Shah, M.: Floor fields for tracking in high density crowd scenes. In: European Conference on Computer Vision, pp. 1–24 (2008) [465]
5. Bar, M.: Visual objects in context. Nat. Rev. Neurosci. **5**, 617–629 (2004) [465]
6. Bashir, K., Xiang, T., Gong, S.: Gait recognition without subject cooperation. Pattern Recogn. Lett. **31**(13), 2052–2060 (2010) [459]
7. Benezeth, Y., Jodoin, P.-M., Saligrama, V., Rosenberger, C.: Abnormal events detection based on spatio-temporal co-occurrences. In: IEEE Conference on Computer Vision and Pattern Recognition, pp. 2458–2465 (2009) [462]
8. Benfold, B., Reid, I.: Guiding visual surveillance by tracking human attention. In: British Machine Vision Conference (2009) [459]
9. Blei, D.M., Ng, A.Y., Jordan, M.I.: Latent Dirichlet allocation. J. Mach. Learn. Res. **3**, 993–1022 (2003) [462]
10. Bosch: Athens International Airport (2001) http://www.boschsecurity.co.uk/ [457]
11. Breitenstein, M.D.: Visual surveillance – dynamic behavior analysis at multiple levels. PhD thesis, ETH Zurich (2009) [465]
12. Cao, L., Liu, Z., Huang, T.S.: Cross-dataset action detection. In: IEEE Conference on Computer Vision and Pattern Recognition, pp. 1998–2005 (2010) [461]
13. Chen, K.-W., Lai, C.-C., Hung, Y.-P., Chen, C.-S.: An adaptive learning method for target tracking across multiple cameras. In: IEEE Conference on Computer Vision and Pattern Recognition, pp. 1–8 (2008) [464]
14. IBM Corporation: Command, Control, Collabo-rate: Public Safety Solutions from IBM. Solution Brief (2009) [456]
15. Ekman, P.: Facial expressions of emotion: New findings, new questions. Psychol. Sci. **3**(1), 34–38 (1992) [458]
16. Ekman, P., Friesen, W.V.: Unmasking the Face, 2nd edn. Consulting Psychologists Press, Palo Alto (1984) [458]
17. Essa, I.A., Pentland, A.P.: Coding, analysis, interpretation, and recognition of facial expressions. IEEE Trans. Pattern Anal. Mach. Intell. **19**(7), 757–763 (1997) [459]
18. Everts, I., Sebe, N., Jones, G.A.: Cooperative object tracking with multiple PTZ cameras. In: International Conference on Image Analysis and Processing, pp. 323–330 (2007) [468]
19. Farenzena, M., Bazzani, L., Perina, A., Cristani, M., Murino, V.: Person re-identification by symmetry-driven accumulation of local features. In: IEEE Conference on Computer Vision and Pattern Recognition, pp. 2360–2367 (2010) [464]
20. Felzenszwalb, P.F., Huttenlocher, D.P.: Pictorial structures for object recognition. Int. J. Comput. Vis. **61**(1), 55–79 (2005) [459]
21. Frost & Sullivan: Video Surveillance Software Emerges as Key Weapon in Fight Against Terrorism. http://www.frost.com/ [456]
22. Frost & Sullivan: Eyes on the Network – Understanding the Shift Toward Network-based Video Surveillance in Asia (2007). http://www.frost.com/prod/servlet/market-insight-top.pag?docid=100416385 [456]
23. Gilbert, A., Bowden, R.: Incremental, scalable tracking of objects inter camera. Comput. Vis. Image Underst. **111**(1), 43–58 (2008) [464]
24. Gill, P.M., Spriggs, A., Allen, J., Hemming, M., Jessiman, P., Kara, D., Kilworth, J., Little, R., Swain, D.: Control room operation: findings from control room observations. Home office online report 14/05, Home Office (2005) [456]
25. Gouaillier, V., Fleurant, A.-E.: Intelligent video surveillance: Promises and challenges. Technological and commercial intelligence report, CRIM and Technôpole Defence and Security (2009) [456,468]
26. Gray, D., Tao, H.: Viewpoint Invariant Pedestrian Recognition with an Ensemble of Localized Features. In: European Conference on Computer Vision, pp. 262–275 (2008) [464]
27. Hongeng, S., Nevatia, R., Brémond, F.: Video-based event recognition: Activity representation and probabilistic recognition methods. Comput. Vis. Image Underst. **96**(2), 129–162 (2004) [461]

28. Hospedales, T., Gong, S., Xiang, T.: A Markov clustering topic model for mining behaviour in video. In: IEEE International Conference on Computer Vision, pp. 1165–1172 (2009) [461, 462]

29. Hu, Y., Cao, L., Lv, F., Yan, S., Gong, Y., Huang, T.S.: Action detection in complex scenes with spatial and temporal ambiguities. In: IEEE International Conference on Computer Vision (2009) [461]

30. Javed, O., Shafique, K., Shah, M.: Appearance Modeling for Tracking in Multiple Non-overlapping Cameras. In: IEEE Conference on Computer Vision and Pattern Recognition, pp. 26–33 (2005) [463]

31. Javed, O., Shah, M.: Automated Multi-camera Surveillance: Theory and Practice. Springer, New York (2008) [468]

32. Junior, J.C.S.J., Musse, S.R., Jung, C.R.: Crowd analysis using computer vision techniques. IEEE Signal Process. Mag. **27**, 66–77 (2010) [460,468]

33. Ke, Y., Sukthankar, R., Hebert, M.: Event detection in crowded videos. In: IEEE International Conference on Computer Vision, pp. 1–8 (2007) [461]

34. Kim, J., Grauman, K.: Observe locally, infer globally: A space–time MRF for detecting abnormal activities with incremental updates. In: IEEE Conference on Computer Vision and Pattern Recognition, pp. 2921–2928 (2009) [462,466]

35. Kratz, L., Nishino, K.: Anomaly detection in extremely crowded scenes using spatio-temporal motion pattern models. In: IEEE Conference on Computer Vision and Pattern Recognition, pp. 1446–1453 (2009) [462]

36. Kratz, L., Nishino, K.: Tracking with local spatio-temporal motion patterns in extremely crowded scenes. In: IEEE Conference on Computer Vision and Pattern Recognition, pp. 693–700 (2010) [465]

37. Kuettel, D., Breitenstein, M.D., Gool, L.V., Ferrari, V.: What's going on? Discovering spatio-temporal dependencies in dynamic scenes. In: IEEE Conference on Computer Vision and Pattern Recognition, pp. 1951–1958 (2010) [462]

38. Lavee, G., Rivlin, E., Rudzsky, M.: Understanding video events: A survey of methods for automatic interpretation of semantic occurrences in video. IEEE Transactions on Systems, Man, and Cybernetics, Part C: Applications and Reviews **39**(5), 489–504 (2009) [468]

39. Li, J., Gong, S., Xiang, T.: Global behaviour inference using probabilistic latent semantic analysis. In: British Machine Vision Conference, pp. 193–202 (2008) [465]

40. Li, J., Gong, S., Xiang, T.: Scene segmentation for behaviour correlation. In: European Conference on Computer Vision, pp. 383–395 (2008) [462]

41. Loy, C.C., Xiang, T., Gong, S.: Stream-based active unusual event detection. In: Asian Conference on Computer Vision (2010) [466,467]

42. Mahadevan, V., Li, W., Bhalodia, V., Vasconcelos, N.: Anomaly detection in crowded scenes. In: IEEE Conference on Computer Vision and Pattern Recognition (2010) [462]

43. Makris, D., Ellis, T., Black, J.: Bridging the Gaps Between Cameras. In: IEEE Conference on Computer Vision and Pattern Recognition, pp. 205–210 (2004) [464]

44. Mehran, R., Oyama, A., Shah, M.: Abnormal crowd behaviour detection using social force model. In: IEEE Conference on Computer Vision and Pattern Recognition, pp. 935–942 (2009) [462,466]

45. Mehran, R., Moore, B.E., Shah, M.: A streakline representation of flow in crowded scenes. In: European Conference on Computer Vision (2010) [462]

46. Moeslund, T.B., Hilton, A., Krüger, V.: A survey of advances in vision-based human motion capture and analysis. Comput. Vis. Image Underst. **104**(2), 90–126 (2006) [459]

47. Murphy-Chutorian, E., Trivedi, M.M.: Head pose estimation in computer vision: A survey. IEEE Trans. Pattern Anal. Mach. Intell. **31**(4), 607–626 (2009) [459]

48. Nguyen, H.T., Ji, Q., Smeulders, A.W.M.: Spatio-temporal context for robust multitarget tracking. IEEE Trans. Pattern Anal. Mach. Intell. **29**(1), 52–64 (2007) [465]

49. Nixon, M.S., Tan, T., Chellappa, R.: Human Identification Based on Gait. Springer, New York (2005) [459]

50. ObjectVideo: Hardening U.S. Borders (2003). http://www.objectvideo.com/ [457]

51. Oliver, N., Rosario, B., Pentland, A.: A Bayesian computer vision system for modeling human interactions. IEEE Trans. Pattern Anal. Mach. Intell. **22**(8), 831–843 (2000) [461]
52. Orozco, J., Gong, S., Xiang, T.: Head pose classification in crowded scenes. In: British Machine Vision Conference (2009) [459]
53. Poppe, R.: A survey on vision-based human action recognition. Image Vis. Comput. **28**(6), 976–990 (2010) [461]
54. Prosser, B., Gong, S., Xiang, T.: Multi-camera matching using bi-directional cumulative brightness transfer functions. In: British Machine Vision Conference (2008) [463]
55. Ran, Y., Zheng, Q., Chellappa, R., Strat, T.M.: Applications of a simple characterization of human gait in surveillance. IEEE Trans. Syst. Man Cybern., Part B, Cybern. **40**(4), 1009–1020 (2010) [459]
56. Rodriguez, M., Ali, S., Kanade, T.: Tracking in unstructured crowded scenes. In: IEEE International Conference on Computer Vision (2009) [465,466]
57. Schneiderman, R.: Trends in video surveillance give DSP an apps boost [special reports]. IEEE Signal Process. Mag. **27**(6), 6–12 (2010) [468]
58. Schwartz, O., Hsu, A., Dayan, P.: Space and time in visual context. Nat. Rev., Neurosci. **8**, 522–535 (2007) [465]
59. Settles, B.: Active learning literature survey. Technical report, University of Wisconsin-Madison (2010) [467]
60. Shan, C., Gong, S., McOwan, P.W.: Facial expression recognition based on local binary patterns: A comprehensive study. Image Vis. Comput. **27**(6), 803–816 (2009) [459]
61. Sillito, R.R., Fisher, R.B.: Semi-supervised learning for anomalous trajectory detection. In: British Machine Vision Conference (2008) [467]
62. Siva, P., Xiang, T.: Action detection in crowd. In: British Machine Vision Conference (2010) [461]
63. Team, i.: Imagery library for intelligent detection systems (i-LIDS); a standard for testing video based detection systems. In: Annual IEEE International Carnahan Conferences Security Technology, pp. 75–80 (2006) [457]
64. Teh, Y., Jordan, M., Beal, M., Blei, D.: Hierarchical Dirichlet processes. J. Am. Stat. Assoc. **101**(476), 1566–1581 (2006) [462]
65. Loy, C.C., Xiang, T., Gong, S.: Modelling activity global temporal dependencies using time delayed probabilistic graphical model. In: IEEE International Conference on Computer Vision, pp. 120–127 (2009) [464-466]
66. Loy, C.C., Xiang, T., Gong, S.: Time-delayed correlation analysis for multi-camera activity understanding. Int. J. Comput. Vis. **90**(1), 106–129 (2010) [462,464,465]
67. Tian, Y.-L., Kanade, T., Cohn, J.F.: Facial Expression Analysis. Springer, New York (2005). Chap. 11 [459]
68. Tieu, K., Dalley, G., Grimson, W.E.L.: Inference of non-overlapping camera network topology by measuring statistical dependence. In: IEEE International Conference on Computer Vision, pp. 1842–1849 (2005) [464]
69. Turaga, P., Chellappa, R., Subrahmanian, V.S., Udrea, O.: Machine recognition of human activities – A survey. IEEE Trans. Circuits Syst. Video Technol. **18**(11), 1473–1488 (2008) [468]
70. Wang, X., Ma, X., Grimson, W.E.L.: Unsupervised activity perception in crowded and complicated scenes using hierarchical Bayesian models. IEEE Trans. Pattern Anal. Mach. Intell. **31**(3), 539–555 (2009) [462,466]
71. Wang, X., Tieu, K., Grimson, W.E.L.: Correspondence-free activity analysis and scene modeling in multiple camera views. IEEE Trans. Pattern Anal. Mach. Intell. **32**(1), 56–71 (2010) [464]
72. Wu, B., Nevatia, R.: Detection and tracking of multiple, partially occluded humans by Bayesian combination of edgelet based part detectors. Int. J. Comput. Vis. **75**(2), 247–266 (2007) [465]
73. Wu, S., Moore, B.E., Shah, M.: Chaotic invariants of Lagrangian particle trajectories for anomaly detection in crowded scenes. In: IEEE Conference on Computer Vision and Pattern Recognition, pp. 2054–2060 (2010) [462]

74. Yang, M., Wu, Y., Hua, G.: Context-aware visual tracking. IEEE Trans. Pattern Anal. Mach. Intell. **31**(7), 1195–1209 (2008) [465]
75. Yang, W., Wang, Y., Mori, G.: Efficient human action detection using a transferable distance function. In: Asian Conference on Computer Vision (2009) [461]
76. Yuan, J., Liu, Z., Wu, Y.: Discriminative subvolume search for efficient action detection. In: IEEE Conference on Computer Vision and Pattern Recognition, pp. 2442–2449 (2009) [461]
77. Zelniker, E.E., Gong, S., Xiang, T.: Global Abnormal Behaviour Detection Using a Network of CCTV Cameras. In: IEEE International Workshop on Visual Surveillance (2008) [464]
78. Zheng, W., Gong, S., Xiang, T.: Associating groups of people. In: British Machine Vision Conference (2009) [463,465,466]

Chapter 24
Predicting Pedestrian Trajectories

Stefano Pellegrini, Andreas Ess, and Luc Van Gool

Abstract Pedestrians do not walk randomly. While they move toward their desired destination, they avoid static obstacles and other pedestrians. At the same time they try not to slow down too much as well as not to speed up excessively. Studies coming from the field of social psychology show that pedestrians exhibit common behavioral patterns. For example the distance at which one individual keeps himself from others is not uniformly random, but depends on the acquaintance level of the individuals, the culture and other factors. Our goal here is to use this knowledge to build a model that probabilistically represents the future state of a pedestrian trajectory. To this end, we focus on a stochastic motion model that caters for the possible behaviors in an entire scene in a multi-hypothesis approach, using a principled modeling of uncertainties.

24.1 Introduction

The behavioral patterns that regulate pedestrian interactions have been studied in the field of social psychology for a long time [5, 7, 12]. We know from several studies that these patterns are subject to variation that depend on culture, gender and other factors. Nevertheless, to a certain extent it is possible to exploit this knowledge by the means of models for pedestrian motion prediction whose goal is not only that of describing, but also and moreover, of synthesizing and predicting. These kinds of model have been used in different fields, such as in Computer Graphics [9, 11], Social Science [8, 15, 17] and Robotics [10, 19, 20]. Recently, interest in these models rose also in Computer Vision. Traditionally, Computer Vision researchers have resorted to using a simple constant-velocity assumption for pedestrians, especially

S. Pellegrini (✉) · A. Ess · L. Van Gool
ETH Zürich, Zürich, Switzerland
e-mail: stefpell@vision.ee.ethz.ch

A. Ess
e-mail: aess@vision.ee.ethz.ch

L. Van Gool
e-mail: vangool@vision.ee.ethz.ch
KU Leuven, Leuven, Belgium

T.B. Moeslund et al. (eds.), *Visual Analysis of Humans*,
DOI 10.1007/978-0-85729-997-0_24, © Springer-Verlag London Limited 2011

in applications such as tracking. Recently, however, more advanced models, often inspired by social simulations, received considerable attention. Antonini et al. [2] were one of the first to use a behavioral motion prior in a tracker, using a Discrete Choice Model to select the next position for each pedestrian. Ali and Shah [1] use scene-specific "floor field" models to make tracking in extremely crowded situations tractable. Pellegrini et al. [14] builds the motion prior on the assumption that each subject predicts the other pedestrians' trajectories with a simple linear extrapolation, calculating the next velocity based on this prediction. [18] focus on learning the parameters of a space-continuous time-discrete model that is optimized with a gradient-descent technique. Outside the area of tracking, Mehran et al. [13] use the social force model to detect abnormal behavior in crowded scenes.

When scene-specific knowledge is not available, a microscopic model (handling pedestrians separately) is usually preferred over a macroscopic one (focusing on a crowd's behavior, rather than its individual members). Microscopic models usually account for interactions among individuals, destinations, and desired velocities. However, accurately modeling a pedestrian's future path in a deterministic way is almost impossible: on the one hand, the observed information is incomplete, either because it is invisible to the camera (but visible to the pedestrian in the scene), or because it is part of a pedestrian's individual preferences (some people like to walk in the shade, others do not). On the other hand, model complexity is limited by computational power and inclusion of further elements should be handled with care. One element that could be considered is the grouping relationship among individuals. While already included in human motion models [8], grouping has not been properly tested for prediction purposes. In this chapter, we will present some preliminary result for the group classification task. Together with grouping, one could consider adding gender, body size, age and other similar factors. Instead of modeling more and more factors, an alternative approach is that of making the model more robust. A probabilistic motion model is robust to fluctuations in the behavioral patterns of the modeled pedestrians.

In the following, we show how a stochastic motion model can handle situations as those depicted in Fig. 24.1, where the two possible evading trajectories seem equally likely. We will use the stochastic formulation of the Linear Trajectory Avoidance (LTA) model [14], referred to as Stochastic LTA (sLTA). sLTA uses the same energy potential formulation as the original sLTA model, but within a Gibbs measure to turn the potential into a probability.

One specific question that is then addressed is the usability of the motion model for tracking. In [14], it has already been shown that a motion prior has better predictive power than linear extrapolation and that a tracker can benefit from its use in situations where the observation is unreliable (e.g., during occlusions). Here, we investigate this issue further by conducting a set of systematic experiments using an appearance-based tracker.

After briefly introducing the basic motion model (LTA) in Sec. 24.2, we present its stochastic extension in Sec. 24.3. Experiments are presented in Sec. 24.4, before concluding in Sec. 24.5.

Fig. 24.1 When moving through a scene, a person takes a variety of factors into account, such as steering clear of other people. In many cases, the prediction of the motion cannot be well described by a deterministic algorithm: In the above example the pedestrian on the *left hand side* could either evade the group by going on its left or right side, as indicated by the yellow lines. We therefore propose a stochastic, simulation-based motion model that can deal with the uncertain future motion of a pedestrian

24.2 LTA, a Pedestrian Motion Model

LTA linear trajectory avoidance is a simulation-based motion model [14]. It predicts a pedestrian's velocity[1] $\mathbf{v}_i^t$ based on the previous positions $\mathbf{x}_j^{t-1}$ and the velocities $\mathbf{v}_j^{t-1}$ of all the N pedestrians j in the scene, as well as on the pedestrians' desired destinations $\mathbf{r}_j$ and desired speeds u_j, and on the static obstacles represented by an obstacle map $\mathbf{O}$.[2] The state at time t for a subject i is given by its position and velocity $[\mathbf{x}_i^t, \mathbf{v}_i^t]$ while the joint state of all the subjects at time t is given by $\mathbf{S}^t = [\mathbf{x}_1^t, \mathbf{v}_1^t, \ldots, \mathbf{x}_N^t, \mathbf{v}_N^t]$. We call such a joint state a *world model* and we note that each subject is represented by a single state vector per timestep and therefore there is a single world model at each instant t in LTA.

Similar to other simulation-based motion models, LTA represents various social factors as energy functions. The interaction that a subject i *feels* from the other subjects is modeled as

$$I_i\left(\mathbf{v}_i^t; \mathbf{S}^{t-1}\right) = \sum_{\substack{j=1 \\ j \neq 0}}^{N} q_{ij} \exp\left(-\frac{d_{ij}^{*2}(\mathbf{v}_i^t; \mathbf{v}_j^{t-1}, \mathbf{x}_i^{t-1}, \mathbf{x}_j^{t-1})}{2\sigma_d^2}\right), \qquad (24.1)$$

where q_{ij} is a weighting factor, and d_{ij}^* is the smallest distance over time between subjects i and j if subject i keeps on moving with velocity $\mathbf{v}_i^t$ and subject j with velocity $\mathbf{v}_j^{t-1}$. σ_d is a free parameter. Note that the smaller the distance $d_{ij}^*(\mathbf{v}_i^t)$ the higher the interaction energy.

---

[1] As in physics, we use the term velocity for a two-dimensional motion vector, as opposed to the scalar value speed.

[2] To reduce notational complexity, we will omit the dependency on u, $\mathbf{r}$, $\mathbf{O}$ in the rest of the chapter. These values do not change in the time window of the prediction and are assumed to be known.

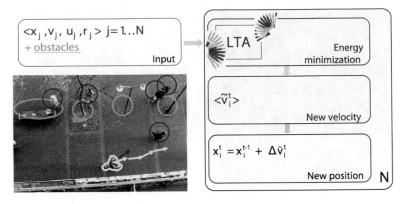

Fig. 24.2 Principle of LTA: given the state of the current image (red: pedestrians, green: obstacles), every pedestrian is simulated in turn, assuming a simple path-planning behavior of each individual. After finding the most probable velocity for each pedestrian (in a deterministic fashion), their position is updated in parallel. Here, we extend the deterministic behavior with a stochastic one, to account for the uncertainty of a person's future motion

While interacting with other pedestrians, each subject walks to a desired destination and with a desired speed. These two factors are modeled as

$$L_i\left(\mathbf{v}_i^t\right) = \left(u_i - \left\|\mathbf{v}_i^t\right\|\right)^2, \tag{24.2}$$

$$D_i\left(\mathbf{v}_i^t\right) = -\frac{(\mathbf{r}_i - \mathbf{x}_i) \cdot \mathbf{v}_i^t}{\|\mathbf{r}_i - \mathbf{x}_i\| \left\|\mathbf{v}_i^t\right\|}, \tag{24.3}$$

for the speed and the destination, respectively. All these *social* factors are included into an energy potential for each subject

$$E\left(\mathbf{v}_i^t; \mathbf{S}^{t-1}\right) = I_i\left(\mathbf{v}_i^t; \mathbf{S}^{t-1}\right) + \lambda_1 L_i\left(\mathbf{v}_i^t\right) + \lambda_2 D_i\left(\mathbf{v}_i^t\right), \tag{24.4}$$

where λ_1 and λ_2 are free parameters that need to be set. Taking the minimum of this potential yields a pedestrian's next *desired* velocity $\hat{\mathbf{v}}_i^t$ that is used to update the model.[3]

The procedure is repeated for each pedestrian independently in parallel, and illustrated in Fig. 24.2. While in [14] we show that taking into account these social factors improves prediction and object tracking performance compared to a

---

[3]In the original model, the desired velocity is linearly filtered for smoothness (see (14) in [14]). Here, we use an equivalent energy potential that includes already the same smoothing, by introducing a simple coordinate transformation:

$$E\left(\mathbf{v}^t; \mathbf{S}^{t-1}\right) = E_{\text{LTA}}\left(\frac{\mathbf{v}^t - \alpha * \mathbf{v}^{t-1}}{1 - \alpha}; \mathbf{S}^{t-1}\right),$$

where E_{LTA} is the formulation of the energy given in [14]. Note that this is an entirely equivalent formulation, but it has the advantage of being more compact.

constant-velocity model, there are two main problems with the formulation: firstly, deterministically choosing the minimum of the energy function cannot account for the multiple options a pedestrian can choose from when walking onto other people. Therefore, a deterministic instantiation of the model sometimes commits big errors when avoiding oncoming pedestrians on the wrong side. Secondly, uncertainty propagation is handled only empirically.

To this end, we propose an improved version of LTA, extending it to handle the uncertainty in a still approximate but more principled manner. Above all, rather than representing the output of the algorithm with only a single value, we will extend it to handling multiple choices for each pedestrian.

24.3 Stochastic LTA

To account for the uncertain future motion of a pedestrian, we extend LTA in a multi-hypothesis fashion. We term the new model sLTA. We still assume that a pedestrian, at each time step t, makes a decision for his next velocity based on its past observations of the environment. As opposed to standard LTA, however, we allow multiple *hypotheses* $[\mathbf{x}_{ih}^t, \mathbf{v}_{ih}^t]$ with $h \in \{1, \ldots, H^N\}$ to represent the state of subject i at time t. By using a mixture of Gaussians to model the subject state, we can associate a *weight* and an *uncertainty* to each hypothesis. We model therefore the distribution over the state for each subject as

$$p\left(\mathbf{x}_i^t, \mathbf{v}_i^t\right) = \sum_{h=1}^{H^t} w_h \mathcal{N}\left(\mathbf{x}_i^t; \boldsymbol{\mu}_{ih}^t, \boldsymbol{\Sigma}_{ih}^t\right). \tag{24.5}$$

At time t the distribution $p(\mathbf{S}^t)$ over the world models can be factorized as

$$p\left(\mathbf{S}^t\right) = \prod_{i=1}^{N} p\left(\mathbf{x}_i^t, \mathbf{v}_i^t\right). \tag{24.6}$$

Therefore also $p(\mathbf{S}^t)$ is a mixture of Gaussians

$$p\left(\mathbf{S}^t\right) = \sum_{m=1}^{M^t} w_m \mathcal{N}\left(\mathbf{S}^t; \boldsymbol{\mu}_{\mathbf{S}_m}^t, \boldsymbol{\Sigma}_{\mathbf{S}_m}^t\right), \tag{24.7}$$

with $M^t = (H^t)^N$. In order to account for multiple velocity *choices* for each subject, we move toward a stochastic formulation of (24.4). Based on the energy potential formulation, we define the posterior probability of a pedestrian's velocity $p(\mathbf{v}_i^t | \mathbf{S}^{t-1})$ as a Gibbs measure, for each pedestrian as

$$p\left(\mathbf{v}_i^t | \mathbf{S}^{t-1}\right) = e^{-\omega E(\mathbf{v}_i^t; \mathbf{S}^{t-1})} / Z, \tag{24.8}$$

where Z is a normalization constant and ω is a free parameter that will be discussed later.

Rather than working directly with (24.8), we fit to (24.8) a mixture of Gaussians,

$$p\left(\mathbf{v}_i^t | \mathbf{S}^{t-1}\right) \approx \sum_{k=1}^{K} w_k \mathcal{N}\left(\mathbf{v}_i^t; \tilde{\mathbf{v}}_{ik}^t, \tilde{\mathbf{\Psi}}_{ik}^t\right), \tag{24.9}$$

where w_k, $\tilde{\mathbf{v}}_{ik}^t$ and $\tilde{\mathbf{\Psi}}_{ik}^t$ are estimated from (24.8), as discussed next. In (24.9) each mixture component represents a choice of subject i for the next velocity.[4] This mixture could be fit with standard methods such as Expectation Maximization or iterative function fitting techniques. However, to keep the system applicable to real-time scenarios, we opt to use the following heuristic to estimate the mixture parameters.

1. Discretize the distribution of (24.8). The number of components K of the mixture is decided by counting the local maxima in the discretized distribution.
2. Run a BFGS maximization for each mode to refine the mode estimate. These mode estimates are assumed to be the locations of the means $\tilde{\mathbf{v}}_{ik}^t$ of the mixture components, with $k \in \{1, \ldots, K\}$.
3. Compute the gradient in the central point of each cell of the discretized distribution of (24.8). Assign the cell to the mode with the smallest angle between the gradient vector and the vector originating from the cell center and ending in the mode. Be this mode k. Estimate the covariances $\tilde{\mathbf{\Psi}}_{ik}^t$ by fitting a Gaussian distribution to the central points of the cells assigned to the mode.
4. The weight w_k of each mode is computed for each component independently, by setting the kth component's mode of the mixture equal to the energy at that point

$$w_k = \frac{\exp(-\omega E(\tilde{\mathbf{v}}_{ik}^t))/Z}{\mathcal{N}(\tilde{\mathbf{v}}_{ik}^t; \tilde{\mathbf{v}}_{ik}^t, \tilde{\mathbf{\Psi}}_{ik}^t)}. \tag{24.10}$$

These weights are finally normalized so that their sum is one (therefore, the equality in (24.10) does not necessarily hold anymore (see also Fig. 24.3).

This is obviously a rough estimate of the parameters, which will become worse the less the Gaussians are separated. Nevertheless, it turned out to be sufficient for our purposes (see Fig. 24.3 for an example fit). In Sec. 24.5, we explain why the algorithm is robust in this respect.

We are ultimately interested in the probability $p(\mathbf{x}_i^t, \mathbf{v}_i^t)$ of the state for a subject i at time t. From (24.5) we know that it is a mixture of Gaussians, but we need to find an explicit formula for the mixture parameters. We can write the state distribution as

---

[4]We assumed that K and N are time independent and the same for all the subjects. This need not to be the case. However, we drop the dependencies for the sake of readability. The generalization is straightforward.

Fig. 24.3 The energy
potential is brought into an
analytical form by fitting a
mixture of Gaussians using a
fast approximate method (see
text)

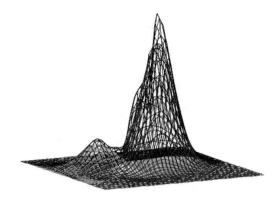

$$p\left(\mathbf{x}_i^t, \mathbf{v}_i^t\right) = \int p\left(\mathbf{x}_i^t, \mathbf{v}_i^t, \mathbf{S}^{t-1}\right) d\mathbf{S}^{t-1} \tag{24.11}$$

$$= \int p\left(\mathbf{x}_i^t | \mathbf{v}_i^t, \mathbf{x}_i^{t-1}\right) p\left(\mathbf{v}_i^t | \mathbf{S}^{t-1}\right) p\left(\mathbf{S}^{t-1}\right) d\mathbf{S}^{t-1}. \tag{24.12}$$

Note that we already have an approximation for $p(\mathbf{v}_i^t | \mathbf{S}^{t-1})$ from (24.9). For
$p(\mathbf{x}_i^t | \mathbf{v}_i^t, \mathbf{x}_i^{t-1})$, by modeling the update of the position as the linear process

$$\mathbf{x}_i^t = \mathbf{x}_i^{t-1} + \Delta \mathbf{v}_i^t + \boldsymbol{\gamma} \quad \text{with } \gamma \sim \mathcal{N}(\mathbf{0}, \Gamma), \tag{24.13}$$

we can write

$$p\left(\mathbf{x}_i^t | \mathbf{x}_i^{t-1}, \mathbf{v}_i^t\right) = \mathcal{N}\left(\mathbf{x}_i^t; \mathbf{x}_i^{t-1} + \Delta \mathbf{v}_i^t, \Gamma\right). \tag{24.14}$$

Finally, we can use (24.9), (24.14) and (24.7), to write

$$p\left(\mathbf{x}_i^t, \mathbf{v}_i^t\right) \approx \sum_{m=1}^{M^t} \sum_{k=1}^{K} w_{mk} \mathcal{N}\left(\mathbf{x}_i^t; \boldsymbol{\mu}_{imk}^t, \boldsymbol{\Sigma}_{imk}^t\right), \tag{24.15}$$

where

$$\boldsymbol{\mu}_{imk}^t = \begin{bmatrix} \mu_{\mathbf{x}_{im}}^{t-1} + \Delta \tilde{\mathbf{v}}_{imk}^t \\ \tilde{\mathbf{v}}_{imk}^t \end{bmatrix}, \tag{24.16}$$

$$\boldsymbol{\Sigma}_{imk}^t = \begin{bmatrix} \Gamma + \Delta^2 \tilde{\Psi}_{imk}^t + \boldsymbol{\Sigma}_{imk}^{t-1} & \Delta \tilde{\Psi}_{imk}^t \\ (\Delta \tilde{\Psi}_{imk}^t)^T & \tilde{\Psi}_{imk}^t \end{bmatrix}. \tag{24.17}$$

(The complete derivation of this approximation is given in Appendix A.) As (24.5)
shows, the distribution over the subject position has the form of a mixture of Gaussians with $M^{t-1}K = H^t$ components. As a consequence of (24.15) and (24.6) the
distribution over the world models has now $(M^t K)^N$ mixture components. This will

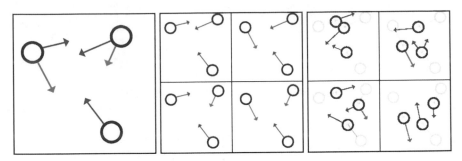

Fig. 24.4 A toy illustration of the state evolution. A red circle represents a subject position and the arrows show the subject velocities. For each subject, a circle together with one of the corresponding arrows represents a single hypothesis. Uncertainties and hypotheses weights are not shown. *Left*: the state at time $t-1$. *Center*: the *world models* at time $t-1$. Each world model is a 3-tuple in the Cartesian product of the subject state hypotheses. *Right*: the state at time t after the propagation from the previous time step. The position is updated with (24.14) while the new velocities are computed with (24.9). Note the growth in the number of subject hypotheses

be the number of world models in the next iteration. This clearly leads to a combinatorial explosion of the number of state mixture components, or world models. Figure 24.4 shows an example of this process. To prevent this from happening, we limit the maximum number of world models to a value $\hat{M}$. If the splitting process at a certain time step generates more than $\hat{M}$ world models, the most likely $\hat{M}$ are used, while the others are discarded. Further, we limit the combinatorial explosion in (24.15) by pruning the mixture components when $w_{mk} < \varepsilon = 0.1$. Since the value of w_{mk} decreases with time because of the splitting, at a certain point the splitting ceases.

Note that in the special case when $\hat{M} = 1$, the model is deterministic and almost the same as the original LTA. The main difference is that in the original LTA, the next velocity $\hat{\mathbf{v}}$ was computed with a gradient descent over the energy potential E_{LTA}, while now the heuristic just described is used.

Note also that this general approach of handling multiple possible world states is conceptually similar to multi-hypothesis tracking [16], in which each world corresponds to a possible data association between trajectories and observations.

24.3.1 Why not a Particle Filter Framework?

Equation (24.8) could be easily used in a particle filter framework as a propagation function (see Fig. 24.5). It is reasonable to expect that the results, for a sufficient number of particles, are more accurate than those obtained with an approximation by a mixture of Gaussians. However, there are at least two reasons why to refrain from taking this approach.

The first reason is related to computational requirements. Since we want to represent the interactions between subjects, the state space cannot be easily factored into

Fig. 24.5 Particle filter experiment: when simulating a person (yellow circle) given the other people (green circles) using a particle filter embodiment of the model, multiple modes (red particles) form naturally. While both options of steering clear of the oncoming persons are found, such a solution is computationally prohibitive (see text)

independent particle filters. The state should rather be represented jointly by the positions and velocities of all the subjects. With the ensuing rapidly growing state dimension, the number of particles increases exponentially. For each particle, the basic LTA procedure should be evaluated for each subject, which is computationally prohibitive. In contrast, in our formulation the LTA procedure is only invoked for each mode of the mixture.

Even if a particle filter were computationally feasible, we believe that the commonly used resampling stage [3] introduces a higher logic that we assume a pedestrian not to have in the LTA model: if a mode of the sampled distribution happens to die out at some point, e.g. due to higher likelihood of the other modes in the re-sampling stage, the history of the particles belonging to the cloud until that point is meaningless. Once an alternative has been created, it cannot cease to exist simply because, a posteriori, other alternatives are more suited. This would imply that pedestrians predict their complete possible future trajectories in advance, even with information that is unavailable to them at present, and then choose the feasible ones. This assumption is not part of the LTA model and also does not seem to be realistic.

24.3.2 Training

For training the underlying LTA, we employ the procedure described in [14], using the training set provided by the authors. The parameters for the stochastic version then remain the same, we inspect the effect of the remaining free parameters ($\hat{M}$, ω) in the experiments section.

24.4 Experiments

As noted before, a pedestrian motion model has a multitude of uses. For instance, in robotics, its predictions can be used for path-planning purposes. Alternatively, the model output can help improving data association in a tracking context when appearance is unreliable. In the following, we first evaluate the sLTA model by itself, comparing its prediction capabilities for different parameter settings. After that we show our preliminary results for the group classification task. We finally show the application of the model in a tracking experiment, highlighting the importance of a good motion model in data association. For these experiments, we use annotated data provided by the authors of [9]. The video shows part of a shopping street from an oblique view. A homography from image to ground plane was estimated using four manually clicked points on the footpath to transfer image to world coordinates. Standing and erratically moving people were marked; for these, a simple extrapolation is used. As destinations we chose two points far outside the left and right image borders, which holds for most subjects. Static obstacles (i.e., the building and the parked car) were also annotated.

24.4.1 Prediction

To test the prediction capabilities of our model, we evaluate on a subsequence of about 3 minutes @ 2.5 fps, containing 86 trajectories annotated with splines. We simulate all the subjects in parallel. Note that this is different from the prediction experiment in [14], where each subject was simulated in turn, while using the ground truth positions and velocities of all the others. Starting one simulation every 1.2 seconds with a prediction horizon of 4.8 seconds yields ≈ 200 simulations. To highlight the importance of using multiple modes, as well as the effect of the parameter ω, we run multiple simulations over all subjects, varying both the maximum number of world models $\hat{M}$, as well as the free parameter ω. For each simulation, we report the negative log-likelihood $\log p(GT|\hat{M}, \omega)$ of $\hat{M}$ and ω based on the ground truth trajectories GT, Fig. 24.6. As can be seen, increasing the number of world models, and therefore of modes, always improves the prediction result, irrespective of the chosen ω: this indicates that even with multiple modes, the model is conservative enough as not to allow completely improbable predictions. The parameter ω relates to how certain each hypothesis is. When ω is zero, the probability is uniform, while for bigger values of ω, the uncertainty around each mode decreases. Figure 24.6 shows a small yet interesting positive correlation between the value of ω and $\hat{M}$. This can be interpreted saying that when increasing the number of world models, less uncertainty per mode is *allowed*.

Fig. 24.6 Negative log-likelihood (vertical axis) while changing the number of world models $\hat{M}$ and free parameter ω. Increasing $\hat{M}$ always improves the result

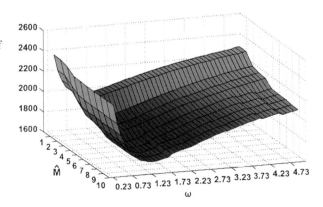

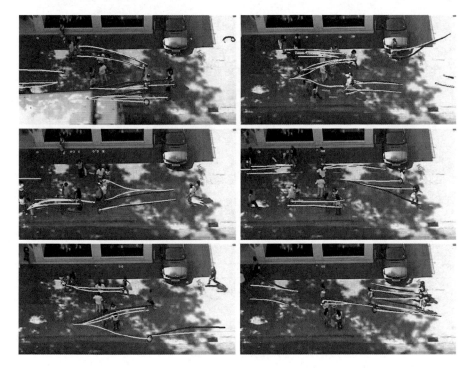

Fig. 24.7 Example extrapolations. The possible paths for a given person are shown in yellow, with blue circles indicating the σ-confidence of the fitted Gaussians. Note that the model operates in ground-plane coordinates, the lines and circles thus correspond to people's feet. Also note that all the subjects are simulated in parallel

Some example images when using 10 modes are shown in Fig. 24.7. Red lines indicate the ground truth, yellow lines indicate the predicted path of a person, blue circles correspond to the standard deviation of the fitted Gaussians at the respective end positions. Green lines indicate the linear extrapolations of people that are standing or moving erratically, white boxes the set of used obstacle points. Please note that the model operates in ground-plane coordinates, hence all drawings correspond to people's feet in the image. For each image, we show the final image after 4 s of extrapolation. As can be seen, the model manages to find the correct extrapolation for almost all persons in one of its modes, while keeping the number of modes at a minimum. Multiple possibilities can be especially seen when people are walking toward other groups of people.

In the deterministic setting ($\hat{M} = 1$), extrapolations in easy situations remain the same (Fig. 24.8(left); these images correspond to the left column of Fig. 24.7). In more difficult situations, only the stronger mode remains, which can either be correct (middle) or wrong (bottom). Thus, from a prediction point of view, it is indeed beneficial to use multiple modes in a stochastic fashion. Finally, Fig. 24.8, right column, shows some typical failures of the model. These are not all failures in the hard sense, as the stochastic options often also includes the correct solution: in the

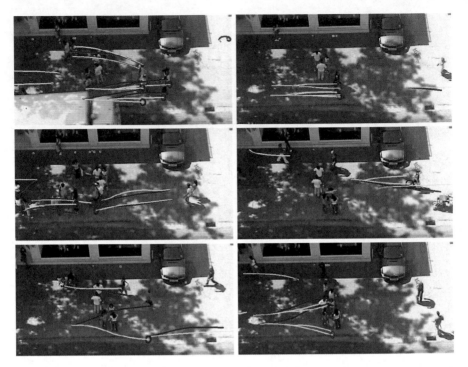

Fig. 24.8 *Left column*: Extrapolations when just using one mode, corresponding to a deterministic model. (see text). *Right column*: Typical failures of the: (*Top, middle*) unnecessary splittings can occur due to other wrong extrapolations, but are handled in the multi-hypothesis framework. (*Bottom*) without the knowledge of people walking in groups, wrong extrapolations can occur. (See text for details)

top-right image, the model splits too much because it is unsure what to do with two persons walking with each other in a group, but slightly changing positions to each other. It splits, but keeps the correct hypothesis. In the middle image, another person is wrongly extrapolated (green line in middle of image), causing a split, but the correct hypothesis is also kept. In the bottom-right image, the lower extrapolation is wrong, with the correct solution (going above the standing group) not identified: this is a special case of the first case, where two people walking in a group feel repulsion rather than staying together. The first and the third cases suggest that implementing the notion of groups would alleviate such problems. In the next subsection we will investigate this question further.

24.4.2 Group Classification

As we have seen in Fig. 24.8 some problems arise because no notion of people walking in a group is used in the current implementation of the model. Although they seem to represent a significant aspect of social walking, groups have largely

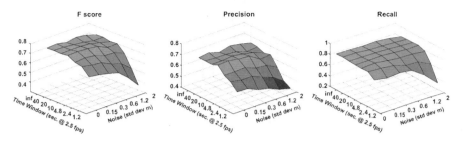

Fig. 24.9 Group classification results. *From left to right* we report Fscore, precision and recall for different time windows and noise values. Noise values refer to standard deviation of the Gaussian noise (in meters) and the time window is measured in seconds (at 2.5 frames per second)

been ignored. Probably one reason is that the knowledge of whether two people belong to the same group or not is not directly available in the image, but requires further processing. Here, we want to show some preliminary studies on the group classification task in order to suggest the amount of effort that is required for such a task and the results that one might expect. We will use only a proximity clue to perform the classification. In detail, we will look at the distances among pair of subjects across time, and try to answer the question whether the two subjects belong to the same group or not. Let us call d_{ij}^t the Euclidean distance among two subjects i and j at time t. If, starting from t, we concatenate d_{ij}^t in a vector over time, let us say over a time window of l time steps, we get $\mathbf{d}_{ij}^{t,l} = [d_{ij}^t, \ldots, d_{i,j}^{t+l-1}]$. If the time window is longer than the subject trajectories, the vector $\mathbf{d}_{ij}$ is opportunely trimmed to the shortest of the two trajectories.

Instead of using directly the whole $\mathbf{d}_{ij}^{t,l}$, we will use simple features extracted from it. The feature vector used for the group classification task is

$$\left[\text{mean}\big(\mathbf{d}_{ij}^{t,l}\big), \text{max}\big(\mathbf{d}_{ij}^{t,l}\big), \text{min}\big(\mathbf{d}_{ij}^{t,l}\big), \text{std\_dev}\big(\mathbf{d}_{ij}^{t,l}\big), \text{length}\big(\mathbf{d}_{ij}^{t,l}\big) \right]. \qquad (24.18)$$

We used an off-the-shelf SVM library [4] to perform the classification. For the evaluation, we performed a 20-fold cross-validation on the ETH dataset [14], and we averaged the results for F score, precision and recall. We repeated the same experiment for different values of the time window l and for changing Gaussian noise added to the $\mathbf{d}$ vector. The results are reported in Fig. 24.9. As one can see, the proximity alone, based on simple statistics over time, is already a powerful clue for the classification task. As one might expect, the results degrade rather quickly with a shorter time window l, but already after $\sim$5 seconds the precision of the classification reaches $\sim$70%.

These preliminary results suggest that grouping might be included in the model with a reasonable effort. For instance, an attraction potential [8] could be added to the interaction term of LTA when two people belong to the same group. Furthermore, other clues could be used together with proximity. For example one could try to figure out whether two subjects are talking or at least looking at each other. Further investigation is clearly required to better understand costs and potentialities of including this aspect in a pedestrian motion model. While future work will be dedicated to analyzing grouping in more details, in the tracking experiments of the next section we will only consider the basic stochastic model, without including group relationships.

24.4.3 Tracking

To explore the effect of a stochastic motion prior on tracking performance, we present the following experiment: for each person, and for increasing time horizons, we perform a Normalized Cross Correlation (NCC)-based template matching between a subject in a reference frame and its possible location in a later frame. The chosen motion model defines the search radius for the matching; the solution is found as the peak NCC-response, weighted by the motion models' uncertainty. The error in distance between this solution and the ground truth is accumulated for all persons and by starting the tracking every 1.2 seconds. As the model is trained in steps of 0.4 seconds (10 frames), we also keep this spacing for the experiment.

This experiment should highlight the advantage of a good motion model: a correct search region should prevent the tracker from drifting by guiding the data association. Instead of including the model into a complicated tracker, where many side-effects can influence the result, we keep the experiment as simple as possible to see the real merit of a motion model.

We specifically compare a simple Brownian motion model with a constant-velocity one, as well as different instantiations of sLTA. For the experiment, we use templates of 30×30 pixels on people's head positions. As an additional baseline, we use an adaptive tracker based on online boosting [6] that uses *all* intermediate frames (as opposed to steps of 10 frames). In the given sequences, purely appearance-based matching is especially tricky due to low contrast, cast shadows, and interlacing and compression artifacts. The motion model uncertainty is chosen as follows: for the Brownian model, the uncertainty is assumed uniform in the search region (which is bounded by a statistic on the maximum walking speed); for the constant-velocity one, we use a single Gaussian centered around the prediction (we plot results for two choices of the uncertainty); for sLTA, the mixture of Gaussians as introduced above is used. In this systematic experiment, velocities are inferred from the past frame's ground-truth. While this does not reflect the actual tracking application, it still allows for a fair comparison between the different models, and their (ideal) influence on appearance-based tracking.

Figure 24.10a plots the mean error in meters for all approaches. We furthermore report the number of actual tracking errors (deviation from ground truth >0.5 m) in Fig. 24.10b. For increasing frame gaps, an uninformed motion model makes tracking virtually impossible ("Brownian", mean error not plotted in (a) due to large error). For small time horizons, the result of a constant-velocity model ("Const. vel.") is virtually the same as with any more advanced model, as small motions can be sufficiently approximated by a linear extrapolation. However, for increasing

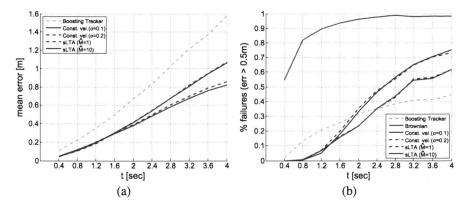

Fig. 24.10 a Mean error (in meters) of tracking using different motion models, for increasing frame gaps. **b** Number of tracking failures (error >0.5 m) using different motion models, for increasing frame gaps

time horizons, the positive effect of sLTA becomes more pronounced. This is also in line with other researchers' results [14], who mainly observed an effect of a strong motion model in cases of missing data, e.g.due to occlusion.

As an additional baseline, we show the result of purely appearance-based tracker, which uses *all* available intermediate frames while learning the model of the appearance ("Boosting Tracker"). Using all available data from the image produces fewer hard failures, still, the high mean error indicates that when the tracker starts drifting, it's totally lost. We therefore believe a strong motion model to be important for tracking.

Accounting for a pedestrian's future motion in a probabilistic manner, i.e., using $\hat{M} = 10$ instead of $\hat{M} = 1$, does not seem to have a considerable effect on tracking performance: both the mean error and the fraction of tracking errors seems to only improve slightly when allowing multiple modes. The important thing to note here is that in the presented sequence, there is only a limited number of "splittings" in general, and only in a fraction of these, the deterministic model chooses the wrong mode. While the effect thus seems limited, this still means that in such cases, the tracker would fail and lose an object for multiple seconds, searching in the wrong location. Employing a stochastic model therefore definitely helps in extreme situations, which can also be expected more frequently in more crowded scenarios.

24.5 Conclusion

This chapter presented a stochastic simulation-based motion model for pedestrians. The probabilistic formulation is based on using the LTA energy function in a Gibbs measure. Then, by using a multi-hypothesis approach with uncertainty propagation, a set of possible future world states is obtained. To achieve a good compromise between accuracy and tractability, we fit a Gaussian mixture model to the Gibbs measure. Although the fitting is rather approximate, we found it to work well in our experiments. This is due to the fact that the actual choices of pedestrians seem to be limited to one or two, for each timestep. Therefore the potential will have only one or two modes. Furthermore, the modes corresponding to alternatives of a choice for a pedestrian, tend to separate apart with time. This allows us to *wait* for the modes to be well separated before fitting the mixture (when their distance is below an empirical threshold, we group them and consider them as a single mode).

In our prediction experiments, we showed that the log-likelihood of the prediction increases considerably as we go from a deterministic instantiation to a stochastic one, showing the benefits of such a non-deterministic solution.

For tracking, a clear advantage over simpler motion models was demonstrated, the effect of a stochastic model is, however, not as pronounced as expected. While more complicated scenes would probably show an advantage of using a probabilistic formulation, this difference is only present at higher frame gaps, which could be e.g. due to occlusion. Generally, it thus seems that the prediction would be more suited to tasks in, e.g., robot navigation, where safety is a crucial issue.

Future work will therefore study the application of the model to robot navigation. Furthermore, we plan to explore the grouping behavior between pedestrians. In Sect. 24.4 we showed some preliminary experiments on grouping and we concluded that good results are already achieved with very little effort. Further investigation in this direction will shed some light on the potentialities of using groups as part of a motion prediction model.

Appendix A: Derivation of the marginal probabilities

In this appendix we are going to show a derivation for $p(\mathbf{x}_i^t, \mathbf{v}_i^t)$, and $p(\mathbf{x}_i^t)$.

We start by factorizing the probability of the state $\mathbf{S}^t$

$$p(\mathbf{S}^t) = \prod_{i=1}^{N} p(\mathbf{x}_i^t, \mathbf{v}_i^t). \tag{24.19}$$

Now, we can assume that $p(\mathbf{x}_i^0, \mathbf{v}_i^0)$ is initially given as a mixture of Gaussians (possibly with a single component). To show, by induction, that the marginal $p(\mathbf{x}_i^t, \mathbf{v}_i^t)$ will have the form of a mixture of Gaussians, we assume that at time $t - 1$ the distribution $p(\mathbf{x}_i^{t-1}, \mathbf{v}_i^{t-1})$ is already a mixture of Gaussians and prove that this is sufficient for $p(\mathbf{x}_i^t, \mathbf{v}_i^t)$ to have the same form.

For the moment, the fact that the each factor of (24.19) is a mixture of Gaussians, say with H^t component, means that $P(\mathbf{S}^t)$ will be itself a mixture of Gaussians with $M^t = (H^t)^N$ components

$$p(\mathbf{S}^t) = \prod_{i=1}^{N} \sum_{k=1}^{H^t} w_{ih} \mathcal{N}\left(\mathbf{x}_i^t, \mathbf{v}_i^t; \boldsymbol{\mu}_{ih}^t, \boldsymbol{\Sigma}_{ih}^t\right) \tag{24.20}$$

$$= \sum_{m=1}^{M^t} w_m \mathcal{N}\left(\mathbf{S}^t; \boldsymbol{\mu}_{\mathbf{S}_m}^t, \boldsymbol{\Sigma}_{\mathbf{S}_m}^t\right), \tag{24.21}$$

where we use a mapping function $\phi : \{1, \ldots, H\}^N \to \{1, \ldots, M\}$ from each N-tuple in the Cartesian product of the h indices to a single m and we define $w_m = w_{1h_1} w_{2h_2} \cdots w_{3h_3}$. $\boldsymbol{\mu}_{ih}^t$ and $\boldsymbol{\Sigma}_{ih}^t$ are the mean and the covariance matrix for the hth component of the mixture for subject i at time t, and $\boldsymbol{\mu}_{\mathbf{S}_m}^t$ and $\boldsymbol{\Sigma}_{\mathbf{S}_m}^t$ are the mean and the covariance matrix for the joint state $\mathbf{S}^t$. Note that $\boldsymbol{\mu}_{\mathbf{S}_m}^t$ is obtained by simply concatenating the $\boldsymbol{\mu}_{ih_i}^t$ for each subject, and the covariance matrix $\boldsymbol{\Sigma}_{\mathbf{S}_m}^t$ is a block diagonal matrix with blocks $\boldsymbol{\Sigma}_{ih_i}^t$. Also, note that the ϕ mapping describes the possible world models for the set of subjects, as in each component of the mixture in (24.21) there is a single component h_i selected from the mixture $p(\mathbf{x}_i^t, \mathbf{v}_i^t)$.

Now let us see how to derive a single marginal $p(\mathbf{x}_i^t, \mathbf{v}_i^t)$:

$$p\left(\mathbf{x}_i^t, \mathbf{v}_i^t\right) = \int p\left(\mathbf{x}_i^t, \mathbf{v}_i^t | \mathbf{S}^{t-1}\right) p\left(\mathbf{S}^{t-1}\right) d\mathbf{S}^{t-1} \tag{24.22}$$

to meet real-time requirements, here we simplify the mixture of Gaussians in (24.21) by substituting each normal distribution with a Dirac function:

$$p\left(\mathbf{S}^{t-1}\right) \approx \sum_{m=1}^{M^{t-1}} w_m \delta\left(\mathbf{S}_m^{t-1} - \boldsymbol{\mu}_{\mathbf{S}_m}^{t-1}\right), \tag{24.23}$$

so that we can rewrite the integral in (24.22) as

$$p\left(\mathbf{x}_i^t, \mathbf{v}_i^t\right) = \sum_{m=1}^{M^{t-1}} w_m p\left(\mathbf{x}_i^t, \mathbf{v}_i^t | \boldsymbol{\mu}_{\mathbf{S}_m}^{t-1}\right). \tag{24.24}$$

By this approximation, we retain the mean and weight of the mixture components, but we discard the covariances. We will compensate for this in the empirical covariance that we will introduce later on. Continuing with the derivation we have

$$p\left(\mathbf{x}_i^t, \mathbf{v}_i^t\right) = \sum_{m=1}^{M^{t-1}} w_m p\left(\mathbf{x}_i^t | \mathbf{v}_i^t, \boldsymbol{\mu}_{\mathbf{S}_m}^{t-1}\right) p\left(\mathbf{v}_i^t | \boldsymbol{\mu}_{\mathbf{S}_m}^{t-1}\right) \tag{24.25}$$

$$= \sum_{m=1}^{M^{t-1}} w_m \mathcal{N}\left(\mathbf{x}_i^t; \boldsymbol{\mu}_{\mathbf{x}_{im}}^{t-1} + \boldsymbol{\Delta v}_i^t, \Gamma\right) \sum_{k=1}^{K} w_k \mathcal{N}\left(\mathbf{v}_i^t; \tilde{\mathbf{v}}_{imk}^t, \tilde{\boldsymbol{\Psi}}_{imk}^t\right) \tag{24.26}$$

$$= \sum_{m=1}^{M^{t-1}} \sum_{k=1}^{K} w_m w_k \mathcal{N}\left(\mathbf{x}_i^t; \boldsymbol{\mu}_{\mathbf{x}_{im}}^{t-1} + \boldsymbol{\Delta v}_i^t, \Gamma\right) \mathcal{N}\left(\mathbf{v}_i^t; \tilde{\mathbf{v}}_{imk}^t, \tilde{\boldsymbol{\Psi}}_{imk}^t\right) \tag{24.27}$$

$$= \sum_{m=1}^{M^{t-1}} \sum_{k=1}^{K} w_{mk} \mathcal{N}\left(\mathbf{x}_i^t, \mathbf{v}_i^t; \boldsymbol{\mu}_{imk}^t, \boldsymbol{\Sigma}_{imk}^t\right), \tag{24.28}$$

where

$$\boldsymbol{\mu}^t_{imk} = \begin{bmatrix} \mu^{t-1}_{\mathbf{x}_{im}} + \boldsymbol{\Delta}\tilde{\mathbf{v}}^t_{imk} \\ \tilde{\mathbf{v}}^t_{imk} \end{bmatrix}, \tag{24.29}$$

$$\boldsymbol{\Sigma}^t_{imk} = \begin{bmatrix} \Gamma + \Delta^2 \tilde{\Psi}^t_{imk} & \Delta\tilde{\Psi}^t_{imk} \\ (\Delta\tilde{\Psi}^t_{imk})^T & \tilde{\Psi}^t_{imk} \end{bmatrix} \tag{24.30}$$

and where we define $w_{mk} = w_m w_k$. So we show that $p(\mathbf{x}^t_i, \mathbf{v}^t_i)$ has a mixture of Gaussian form with $H^t = M^{t-1}K$ components. As we noted above, because of the approximation in (24.23), we are discarding the uncertainty information included in the covariance matrix $\boldsymbol{\Sigma}^{t-1}_S$. We can partly compensate for this by appropriately modifying the covariance $\boldsymbol{\Sigma}^t_{mk}$. In particular, we modify (24.30) by adding the position covariance at the previous time step as

$$\boldsymbol{\Sigma}^t_{imk} = \begin{bmatrix} \Gamma + \Delta^2 \tilde{\Psi}^t_{imk} + \boldsymbol{\Sigma}^{t-1}_{imk} & \Delta\tilde{\Psi}^t_{imk} \\ (\Delta\tilde{\Psi}^t_{imk})^T & \tilde{\Psi}^t_{imk} \end{bmatrix}. \tag{24.31}$$

Note that the velocity components of the covariance are in fact discarded, but we partially account for this in the empirical setting of Γ.

Finally, let us derive $p(\mathbf{x}^t_i)$ as

$$p(\mathbf{x}^t_i) = \int p(\mathbf{x}^t_i, \mathbf{v}^t_i) \, d\mathbf{v}^t_i \tag{24.32}$$

$$= \sum_{m=1}^{M} \sum_{k=1}^{K} w_{mk} \mathcal{N}(\mathbf{x}^t_i; \mu^{t-1}_{\mathbf{x}_{im}} + \boldsymbol{\Delta}\tilde{\mathbf{v}}^t_{imk}, \Gamma + \Delta^2 \tilde{\Psi}^t_{imk} + \boldsymbol{\Sigma}^{t-1}_{imk}), \tag{24.33}$$

where we made use of the marginalization property of the Gaussian distribution.

References

1. Ali, S., Shah, M.: Floor fields for tracking in high density crowd scenes. In: ECCV (2008) [474]
2. Antonini, G., Martinez, S.V., Bierlaire, M., Thiran, J.P.: Behavioral priors for detection and tracking of pedestrians in video sequences. Int. J. Comput. Vis. **69**, 159–180 (2006) [474]
3. Arulampalam, M.S., Maskell, S., Gordon, N., Clapp, T.: A tutorial on particle filters for online nonlinear/non-Gaussian Bayesian tracking. IEEE Trans. Signal Process. **50** (2002) [481]
4. Chang, C.-C., Lin, C.-J.: LIBSVM: A Library for Support Vector Machines (2001). Software available at http://www.csie.ntu.edu.tw/~cjlin/libsvm [485]
5. Freedman, J.L.: Crowding and Behavior (1975) [473]
6. Grabner, H., Bischof, H.: On-line boosting and vision. In: CVPR (2006) [486]
7. Hall, E.T.: The Hidden Dimension. Garden City (1966) [473]
8. Helbing, D., Molnár, P.: Social force model for pedestrian dynamics. Phys. Rev. E **51**(5), 4282–4286 (1995) [473,474,485]

9. Lerner, A., Chrysanthou, Y., Lischinski, D.: Crowds by example. In: EUROGRAPHICS (2007) [473,482]
10. Luber, M., Stork, J.A., Tipaldi, G.D., Arras, K.O.: People tracking with human motion predictions from social forces. In: 2010 IEEE International Conference on Robotics and Automation, pp. 464–469. IEEE, New York (May 2010) [473]
11. Massive Software: Massive (2010) [473]
12. McPhail, C., Wohlstein, R.T.: Using film to analyze pedestrian behavior. Sociol. Methods Res. 10(3), 347–375 (1982) [473]
13. Mehran, R., Oyama, A., Shah, M.: Abnormal crowd behavior detection using Social Force model. In: CVPR (2009) [474]
14. Pellegrini, S., Ess, A., Schindler, K., Gool, L.V.: You'll never walk alone: Modeling social behavior for multi-target tracking. In: ICCV (2009) [474-476,481,482,485,487]
15. Penn, A., Turner, A.: Space syntax based agent simulation. In: Pedestrian and Evacuation Dynamics (2002) [473]
16. Reid, D.B.: An algorithm for tracking multiple targets. IEEE Trans. Autom. Control 24(6), 843–854 (1979) [480]
17. Schadschneider, A.: Cellular automaton approach to pedestrian dynamics – theory. In: PED (2001) [473]
18. Scovanner, P., Tappen, M.: Learning pedestrian dynamics from the real world. In: ICCV (2009) [474]
19. Trautman, P., Krause, A.: Unfreezing the robot: Navigation in dense, interacting crowds. In: IROS (2010) [473]
20. Ziebart, B.D., Ratliff, N., Gallagher, G., Mertz, C., Peterson, K., Andrew, J., Martial, B., Anind, H., Dey, K., Srinivasa, S.: Planning-based Prediction for Pedestrians (2009) [473]

Chapter 25
Human–Computer Interaction

Dennis Lin, Vuong Le, and Thomas Huang

Abstract   This chapter focuses on looking at users to build more intuitive and friendly interfaces. We will cover two general types of input modalities: tracking of the head and eyes, and tracking of the hand, especially of the fingers. Head pose and eye–gaze estimation are useful in allowing the computer to understand the direction of the user's focus. We will provide an overview of the many techniques that researchers have applied to this task. We will also consider the automated analysis of hand and finger gestures. These are more active modalities, designed to communicate and issue commands to the computer. We will provide a taxonomy of gestures in the context of human–computer interaction and survey the field of techniques. Finally, we will discuss possible applications of these input modalities. In general, we conclude that existing systems are not yet mature, but that there is great potential for future research.

25.1 Introduction

Once we have computers that look at people it is natural for us to wish for computers that respond to what they see. In this chapter we will discuss vision problems that have immediate applications to interface design and human–computer interaction. We will consider two body parts commonly used in nonverbal communication, the head and the hands.

The first part of the chapter will discuss systems for head and eye–gaze estimation. Head pose estimation has applications in meeting annotation, navigating large displays, and driver safety. It is usually accomplished with normal cameras both near and far away from the user. Eye–gaze estimation provides a finer-grain result. It is

D. Lin (✉) · V. Le · T. Huang
Beckman Institute, University of Illinois at Urbana-Champaign, 405 North Mathews Avenue,
Urbana, IL 61801, USA
e-mail: djlin@ifp.uiuc.edu

V. Le
e-mail: vuongle2@ifp.uiuc.edu

T. Huang
e-mail: huang@ifp.uiuc.edu

T.B. Moeslund et al. (eds.), *Visual Analysis of Humans*,
DOI 10.1007/978-0-85729-997-0_25, © Springer-Verlag London Limited 2011

used to help psychologists understand how humans parse a scene and as an input device for the disabled. It is also an important component in most auto-stereoscopic 3D systems. These systems usually require controlled illumination and special cameras, and as such, they have not been adopted by the general populace. Thus, there is room for developing robust systems that require less exotic setups.

The second part will survey gesture recognition. This is a tempting target of research because it is such a natural form of communication. It is highly desirable to be able to communicate with a machine without having to fumble with input devices such as a keyboard or a mouse. Gesture recognition can be especially useful in situations like clean rooms, public displays, and mobile applications where traditional devices add weight or maintenance requirements. We find, however, that gesture recognition is still at an early stage of research, and additional techniques and/or computing power are going to be needed to produce a robust system.

The ultimate goal of these systems is to provide the ability to actually command a machine in some way. As we will show, most of the techniques that we outlined in the chapter are not sufficiently robust for everyday use. However, it is sometimes possible to overcome the limitations of the underlying technology through the clever application of user interface design. In the final section we will look at some successes (and failures) in this arena.

25.2 Head and Eye–Gaze Tracking

We begin our discussion on human–computer interaction by considering the head and eyes. Directly connected to our brain, the head provides an informative source of nonverbal (and verbal) information. We will not consider the subject of facial emotion recognition as that was already covered in Chap. 19. Instead, we will cover two more indirect bits of information gleaned from looking at the user: head pose direction and eye–gaze direction. These two are useful for inferring the user's attention. Head tracking is less accurate but can be accomplished using normal cameras from relatively far away. Tracking the eyes specifically, however, is necessary to determine the exact Point of Gaze (PoG) of the user. Usually, it requires specialized equipment and closely placed cameras to observe this level of detail, although there is research on more flexible methods.

25.2.1 Head Pose Estimation

The purpose of a head tracker is to identify the position and orientation of the user's head. As an input modality, head motion is useful because it is a large voluntary motion. Unlike the eye, which unconsciously saccades[1], the user has very good

---

[1] A saccade is a quick, simultaneous movement of both eyes in the same direction.

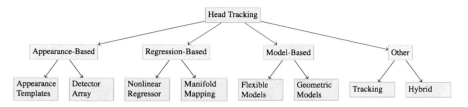

Fig. 25.1 Techniques for head pose estimation

control over head pose. The large size makes tracking the head possible from distant cameras. Obtaining a good estimate, however, is still an open problem, with no clear technique winning out over the rest. A good overview of the state of the art can be found in the survey article [29]. We will follow a slightly modified taxonomy (Fig. 25.1) from that work.

25.2.1.1 Appearance-Based Techniques

One naive attempt at pose estimation is to use *appearance templates* [31]. These try to infer the head pose directly from imagery without much concern for the understanding of any structure. Instead, these methods compare the input image to a database of labeled exemplars. The output of the estimator is simply the label of the closest-matching exemplar. This transforms the pose estimation problem into a database lookup problem. One big drawback of this method is that often the same face in different poses appear more similar than different faces in the actual pose. That is, a database search is likely to return an image of a person that looks like the query rather than a person in the same pose. As a result, a robust system will need either a very large (possibly impractical) database or a robust distance metric that can separate out the pose differences from identity differences.

Another way of overcoming the pose-versus-identity problem is to apply machine learning. The general approach is to train a *detector array* [19] of classifiers, one for each pose. Hopefully, the classifier will home in on the appearance variations caused by pose changes. A disadvantage of this technique is that it requires working with large numbers of classifiers. This can mean a high computation burden, both in training and evaluation.

25.2.1.2 Regression-Based Techniques

Instead of training many different classifiers, it may be preferable to train a single regressor. There are two general ways of doing this. One is to use a *nonlinear regressor*—a machine learning system such as a support vector regressor [23] or a neural network [12]. The hope is that the system will be able to automatically capture the essences of the pose variation. Another way is to consider that the final output only has a few (up to three) dimensions and to explicitly create a mapping between the high-dimensional image space and the low-dimensional pose space. There are a variety of ways of achieving the *manifold mapping*, including [kernelized] PCA, Isomap, LDA, and Locally Embedded Analysis (LEA) [10]. The advantages and drawbacks vary depending on the method. Some methods cannot apply the mapping to new points not in the training set and thus require a separate approximation technique. Many techniques do not look at the labels of the training set and as a result, their output may not directly correspond to pose angles.

25.2.1.3 Model-Based Techniques

The techniques listed so far have taken the face image and directly computed the pose angles. In contrast, the *flexible models* approach is generative. These systems have an internal model of what faces should look like. When presented with a test case, it tries to morph its internal model to match the input image. Two examples of this technique are Elastic Graph Matching (EGM) and AAM [46]. These models are conceptually attractive because they encode very explicit knowledge of how faces should appear. However, the matching process often proves computationally expensive.

Another approach to head pose estimation is to mirror what psychologists believe humans do. Human perception appears to rely on understanding facial symmetry and looking at the various parts of the face. These *geometric methods* [11] rely on finding the positions of key points such as the mouth corners and pupils. These methods are simple and can be reliable. However, they require accurate detection and localization of the various face parts, and thus are susceptible to occlusion. The existing works have concentrated on corner features and thus are likely to suffer during rapid motion where tracking can be lost. An interesting approach might be to use more robust parts detectors, although in some sense this simply pushes the detection problem down a level.

25.2.1.4 Other Techniques

Instead of detecting the head pose from a single image, a *tracking*-based approach tries to produce estimates for all frames of a video. One simple tracking approach is to estimate the minor shifts in adjacent frames. By integrating the shifts, it is possible to produce an overall estimate. Other trackers contain or learn a rigid model of the head [28] and uses it to estimate the head motion. In both cases trackers usually require good initialization and may require reinitialization when the tracking fails.

Finally, it is possible to combine one or more of the approaches above to from a *hybrid* method. A simple example [28] is to combine a tracker with one of the other methods for initialization and reinitialization. These methods can unify the strengths of their underlying components while hiding some of the weaknesses.

25.2.1.5 Discussion

There are a multitude of existing methods for head tracking. Unfortunately, no single technique has gained prominence for "solving" the head pose estimation problem. Instead, researchers that need head position data usually use magnetic, ultrasonic, or Infra-Red (IR) trackers attached to the head. Because of the large inter-user variation, the trend appears to be moving away from appearance-based methods. Rather, modern systems build more sophisticated face models, either explicitly or implicitly through regression. For real-time applications, the ideal solution will likely involve an element of tracking. Thus, the ultimate system for head-based computer interfaces is probably a hybrid one. Readers interested in creating said ultimate system are encouraged to peruse [29] for further details.

25.2.2 Eye–Gaze Estimation

When visually attending to objects, users usually point their head in roughly the right direction and then makes fine adjustments with their eyes. Therefore, together with head pose estimation, detecting direction of the eyes is an essential part for accurate PoG estimation. In this section, different approaches for detecting the visual attention of the eyes are summarized following the taxonomy drawn from [17] and [27].

25.2.2.1 Feature-Based Techniques

The gaze direction of an eye can be determined by the configuration of its parts. Feature-based techniques explore this configuration by analyzing the eye image details such as pupil position and glint[2]. These constitute the most common family of methods for gaze estimation.

Since the eye is a specular object, many of the apparent features are affected by the position of the light source. In an attempt to control this variable, many systems use active lighting provided by IR illuminators. These provide high contrast images, are not affected by normal lighting, and are invisible to humans. In these systems, one or more IR emitters are pointed at the eye and IR-compatible cameras are used to capture the images of the gazing eye. These images can then be analyzed either by regression models or geometric models.

In the regression models, the displacement between the glint and the pupil is used as observed data, and the gaze direction is estimated as the dependent variable. The model can be as simple as a polynomial of first or second order such as ones introduced in [26, 45]. These models usually cannot handle nonlinear variations such as those caused by head movement. More intricate models, such as those based on

---

[2]Glints are the specular reflections of the eye's parts from light sources.

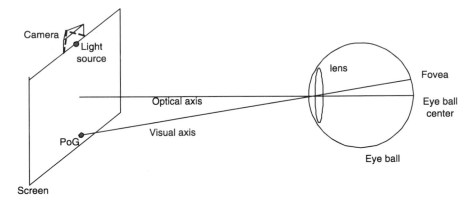

Fig. 25.2 Typical configuration of a gaze estimation system with one light source and one camera. PoG is estimated as the intersection of visual axis with the object

neural networks [21], can claim better performance despite head movement. However, the improvement is usually not significant. SVMs and GP interpolation with more complicated feature obtained by using more than one light sources and cameras are also proposed to find the mapping from eye features to the PoG on the screen [16, 50].

Implicitly modeling the dependence between the eye image features and the PoG, regression-based methods suffer heavily from head pose variation. Some authors [32, 33, 37] proposed using additional cameras for pose estimation and then modifying the model accordingly. This hybrid method of augmenting the regression model with another kind of model which explicitly represents the relation between head pose and PoG is called the 3D geometrical model.

In these approaches the 3D geometric structures of the eye, head, camera, and gazed objects are reconstructed, and the gaze direction vector is revealed by geometrical calculations. The typical configuration is depicted in Fig. 25.2. The position of the pupil is detected from the image. Given the global geometry of the head, eye ball center and fovea position are estimated from physiological knowledge and Euclidean measurements. The desired vector is either the optical axis or the visual axis of the eye. The former is defined by connecting the eye ball center to the pupil center and is a simple geometric computation. The latter is the vector connecting the fovea to the cornea center. This vector more accurately represents what the eye is seeing.

Needing full models of the scene, these methods depend heavily on calibration and face the problems of 3D reconstruction from 2D images. In the simplest systems, with one single calibrated camera and one light source, it is possible to reconstruct the PoG with some accuracy by using assumptions about properties of the eyes gleaned from the population average [33]. However, to improve results, some methods use more light sources and cameras [32], and others use personal calibration points. More cameras and more light sources seem to be necessary to compensate for head movements, both for 3D geometry reconstruction and for dealing with missing glints caused by occlusion [37]. Some multi-camera systems use several wide-angle cameras to cover large changes in head pose and other cameras with smaller fields of view to capture high-resolution eye images [4].

25.2.2.2 Appearance-Based Techniques

Using eye features for gaze detection is straightforward; however, the technique may be prone to errors because it depends heavily on feature detection. Moreover, there may be other features that affect the PoG but are ignored in the models. Approaching the problem from another point of view, appearance-based techniques look for a holistic model which can map the input image to a point on the screen. The basic idea is to do gaze prediction on a low-dimensional manifold determined by high dimension image data. One example of performing the nonlinear regression is to use LLE [41]. In this way the appearance models will not have to solve the reconstruction problem explicitly.

Nevertheless, there are two main drawbacks of appearance-based methods. First, in order to estimate multiple variations in system configuration, they require a much larger number of calibration points. This is not very convenient in some types of applications. Second, they do not have an efficient strategy to improve head pose invariance. The drawbacks make these methods not as commonly used as feature-based methods.

25.2.2.3 Natural Light Techniques

While methods using IR light sources are prominent, natural light-based techniques have the advantage of not requiring an IR emitter and receiver. They are also able to work outdoors without interference from other infra-red sources. These methods are mostly feature-based with a single [14], with multiple [44], or with stereo [24] cameras. In comparison with IR-based solutions, they need some adjustments or preprocessing steps to overcome the instability and low quality of the images. The natural light methods yield lower accuracy and are more sensitive to head pose. Also, it is difficult to use glint information because a sufficiently bright spot light causes the pupil to contract and makes the user uncomfortable.

25.2.2.4 Discussion

We have looked at the variation of the techniques used in gaze estimation, either feature-based or appearance-based, using IR or visible light and with different hardware configurations. Among them, feature-based methods dominate others. Within this class the methods involving fully calibrated systems based on 3D models of the eye such as [13] are the ones trusted the most for their relatively good accuracy and efficiency in session calibrations. This method, using one camera and many light sources, is used in some commercial systems.

Despite an abundance of approaches with well crafted configurations, there are
still many problems that future gaze estimators need to overcome. Beside the difficulty of head pose change, various kinds of interferences such as glasses and re-
fraction can compromise the systems. Some methods require complicated session
calibration and some are restricted to a particular hardware setup. A better understanding of the underlying cognitive and perceptual mechanisms of eye movement,
along with advanced image processing and better hardware may be the solution to
the current drawbacks.

25.3 Gesture Recognition

Another visual mode of human communication is gesturing. Humans gesture naturally as they interact with each other, and the ability to analyze these motions should
help us to understand each other and to work with machines. A solid hand tracking
system could also serve as a first step toward automatic sign language recognition.
However, since sign language will be covered in Chap. 27, we focus on other applications in this section.

In trying to understand gesture recognition, it is important to understand gestures. A taxonomy of human motion for the purpose of Human–Computer Interaction (HCI) was presented in [34] and is recreated in Fig. 25.3. This ontology classifies all intentional motion as a "gesture." Useful gestures are then classified into
two forms. One is *manipulative*, or gestures designed to perform an action such as
turning a knob or flipping a switch. Understanding these gestures is important for
creating realistic virtual environments and other similar interfaces. Since gestures
are performed in 3D, they are a natural way of expressing rotations and translations
that would otherwise require several control dials with a mouse.

The other class, the *communicative* gestures, are more abstract. These are in turn
divided into *acts* and *symbols*. In an act, the gesture itself is the message. This can
include *mimetic* actions, such as pantomiming the swinging of a hammer. Although
they are perhaps more natural than referential symbol gestures, they exhibit a significant amount of variation, subtlety, and complexity. As a result, understanding the
full range of mimetic acts can be as complex as understanding sign language, and it

Fig. 25.3 A taxonomy of
hand gestures for the purpose
of HCI

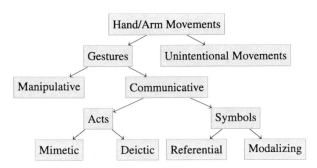

is difficult to imagine a computer interface composed of only mimetic actions. *Deictic* actions, on the other hand, are arguably the most commonly targeted form of gestures. These are the pointing gestures used to select items. Their simple mapping to existing User Interface (UI) paradigms such as the mouse make them a natural focus for interface design. At the same time, this is an area that is well served by traditional input devices, and a competing gesture system must clear a high bar in reliability and accuracy to be useful.

Symbols are the most abstract group in the taxonomy. The many signs in American Sign Language (ASL) that are arbitrary mappings from gestures to concepts fall into the class of *referential* symbols. For a less ambitious gesture recognition project, referential symbols can also apply to a much smaller subset of ASL such as finger spelling. It also represents other simple but abstract recognition problems, such as drawing out digits in the air. *Modalizing* symbols, in contrast, are gestures used in conjunction with another modality, usually speech. One example would be a speaker saying "I want a box about this big" and using his hands to indicate the approximate size. The transcript of the conversation is incomplete if it does not also note the information contained in the gesture. As such, these gestures are essential in multimodal input systems. However, by the same token, they are not a useful target in gesture-only systems.

At the risk of sounding tautological, the choice of which gestures to analyze heavily influences the design of a gesture-based interface. However, there has been relatively little study as to how these choices affect technical performance. One exception is [39]. Those embarking on a new project will be well advised to spend some time looking over this work and the taxonomy to consider which gestures to target.

25.3.1 Hand Gestures

In hand tracking, the emphasis is on understanding the location of the hand(s) relative to the body and not on trying to extract the shape of the hands themselves. The focus in this area of research has been to segment and recognize discrete gestures from the continuous motion.

In general, papers that focus on understanding gestures, such as [5, 47] take for granted the ability to track the hands. Most systems use an ad hoc approach based on skin color segmentation. Some systems use a static skin color model; others use a face detector to find the face and then assume that the face and hand have the same color distribution. Some systems also use motion as a supplemental cue. These systems usually distinguish among the blobs using simple rules. Generally, the face is considered to be the uppermost/largest blob. The left and right hands are distinguished by their relative locations. These simple techniques do not cover more complex cases, such as when the hands cross or if the user is wearing short sleeves. One system [1] compensates for these deficiencies by maintaining multiple hypotheses and resolving ambiguities at a higher level. In addition to the location, a hand tracker sometimes computes additional features like the area and higher moments to aid the recognition process.

Once potential hand locations are found, the next task is to extract semantic information from the motions. Extracting deictic information is relatively straight-forward. This involves either simply mapping the hand position to the screen or performing more sophisticated analysis accounting for the direction and orientation of the head [30]. Extracting symbolic information usually involves some kind of dynamic model such as HMMs, DBNs [40], or dynamic programming. One inter-esting aspect of the system in [1] is that it explicitly models subgestures, gestures that are prefixes of other gestures. For example, the gesture of drawing a "5" may be considered a prefix of drawing an "8." Simpler ways of segmenting gestures into pieces for recognition include looking for sharp changes in velocity or for pauses in the motion.

In summary, hand gesture recognition generally follows the path of sign language analysis. In this way, it is somewhat less about vision and more akin to speech recognition. Most of the emphasis is about understanding the semantic structure of the symbolic motion in its context.

25.3.2 Finger Gestures

A more sophisticated analysis of gestures requires understanding something about the position of the fingers within the hand. This is necessary for fine manipulative gestures, and it is also needed for symbols derived from hand shape rather than hand motion. Unfortunately, accurately locating and tracking the fingers is a diffi-cult challenge. One major issue is that the hand has a very large number of (approx-imately 20) Degrees of Freedom (DoF). Also, the fingers are relatively light masses driven by large muscles in the forearm, making them capable of rapid acceleration. This makes using dynamic models difficult.

The following sections present a brief overview of finger tracking techniques, summarized in Fig. 25.4. An interested reader may also look at a 2007 survey [9] of high DoF hand trackers.

25.3.2.1 Appearance-Based Techniques

Appearance-based systems for finger tracking parallel the appearance-based sys-tems for head pose estimation. The general idea of this technique is to build up a

Fig. 25.4 Techniques for finger tracking

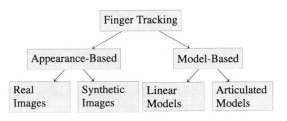

collection of images of the hand in different configurations. Then, recognizing the positions of the fingers becomes a database search problem. Using different metrics, the camera image is compared against the training images, and the pose information is read off the label associated with the best match.

Building a large corpus of training images for hand pose tracking is unfortunately extremely difficult. However, there are a few examples which use *real hand images* for training. One system is described in [42]. This system was trained on video of 24 hand shapes drawn from ASL. This work is also somewhat unique in that it uses a bank of classifiers to distinguish the 24 shapes rather than using a database lookup. Another system using actual hand images for training is [49], although this work only has a database of eight signs and five views. This system uses Locality Sensitive Hashing (LSH) as an acceleration technique for its database. Both of these systems have less than a thousand examples in their training databases. This severely restricts both the number of signs and global rotations that can be recognized. Labeling the hand images can also be difficult. Both systems were designed to recognize specific gestures; it would be almost impossible to label the exact angles of the joints from training photographs.

Faced with the logistical challenge of collecting live hand images, researchers have resorted to generating *synthetic images* using computer graphics. For example, the system in [3] has a database of 107,328 images (4,128 views of 26 different hand poses). It is also notable in that it uses an approximation of the full chamfer distance of edges as its similarity metric. Given two sets A and B, and an underlying distance metric d (usually the Euclidean distance), the chamfer distance $d_{\text{cfr}}(A, B)$ is given by:

$$d_{\text{cfr}}(A, B) = d_{\text{half-cfr}}(A, B) + d_{\text{half-cfr}}(B, A), \tag{25.1}$$

where

$$d_{\text{half-cfr}}(A, B) = \sum_{a \in A} \min_{b \in B} d(a, b). \tag{25.2}$$

In short, the directed chamfer distance $d_{\text{half-cfr}}(A, B)$ is the average distance from a point in A to its closest point in B. Note that although it is commonly referred to as a "distance," $d_{\text{cfr}}(A, B)$ is not a metric. This measure appears to give a much more reliable result over simply counting the number of different pixels (Euclidean distance in the image space) because it strongly penalize mismatches that are very far away.

A more recent version of that system [35] uses a slightly smaller database consisting of 80,640 images (4032 views of 20 hand poses). Another work which used pregenerated templates is [38]. This system uses both color and edge likelihoods for matching. It uses a half-chamfer distance to match the edges, but it also takes into account the direction of the edge in the measurement. It can track global motion (six DoF) using 16,055 templates. For another sequence, it can track eight DoF (six DoF global and two local) using 35,000 templates.

Appearance-based techniques have the advantage of being able to see the entire space of hand shapes in the beginning. Thus, it is possible to design acceleration structures for searching that space. However, acquiring and labeling a very large number of real hand images is impractical. Using synthesized images removes that burden. Even then, the exponential explosion in the number of possible shapes in the high-dimensional space puts a limit on the number of DoF that these systems can handle.

25.3.2.2 Model-Based Techniques

An alternative approach is to try to understand the space of possible hand shapes, and to use that information to perform a search. The approaches in this section are more varied. Some try to perform analyses on portions of the hand image to infer the finger location. Many propose hypothetical hand configurations and compare them with the camera image. Theoretically, because model-based systems are not restricted to a set of training images, they should be more flexible and user-independent. The models are likely to be simpler than appearance-based techniques, however, because they need to be generated "on-the-fly."

Linear models are the often the simplest to apply. In introducing the use of particle filtering to computer vision, [20] includes an example of tracking a hand over a cluttered background. For this system, the palm remains parallel to the image plane and is allowed to translate and rotate. As such, the problem was essentially reduced from 3D and 2D, and it is possible to model the hand shape as a 12-dimensional space. Two of the dimensions deal with in-plane translation. The remaining ten were trained using PCA and handle the hand shape and in-plane rotations. The system could track the hand for 500 frames in a cluttered scene. The system described in [18] also uses PCA to model the hand shapes. However, this system works in 3D and factors in textures instead of simply looking for contours. The advantage of using linear models is that it becomes very easy to compute the shape given the model parameters. However, it is an awkward technique for representing the inherently nonlinear nature of articulated motion, and more recent works have moved on to other approaches.

Given the structure of the hand, it is natural to carry a full kinematic model into the tracking system. In other words, these techniques generate an *articulated model* that can represent the motions at each of the joints. One of the oldest systems covered in this survey is the DigitEyes system [36], which uses two cameras and can track a full 27 DoF. This system produces wireframe-like "link" and "tip" models. To handle occlusion, the researchers developed a sophisticated technique of deciding which phalanx is in front of the other. This system is too slow to run in real time, but can track two fingers (nine DoF) where one occluded the other for 80 frames.

More modern systems have evolved from the rule-based predecessors to a more general framework. For example, the system described in [6] uses a structured light camera to extract a 3D image of the hand. This gives it enough information to fit a 26 DoF model using stochastic meta-descent. An even more sophisticated model is used in [8]. This model consists of 1000 facets, 22 articulation (hand pose) parameters, and 51 morphological (hand shape) parameters. It can handle lighting and texture, but not shadows. It tracked the same sequences as those in [38], achieving good results with full 22 local DoF. Note that the system in [38] could only handle two local DoF. This suggests an advantage to using model-based systems for tracking complex hand motion, although it is not clear what the price in speed might be.

The main advantage of the model-based approach is flexibility. A sufficiently general model can adapt to the hand shape of the user, and can more easily handle a wide range of motion. However, the computation costs for these models can be prohibitive, especially for real-time applications.

25.3.3 Discussion

As with the other vision problems posed in this chapter, there are no clear and robust solutions for the gesture recognition problem. Increased computational capacity is slowly improving the situation. Larger memory capacity means that is possible to fit bigger databases for the appearance-based approaches. Faster processing means that it will become possible to run the sophisticated model-based systems in real time. However, the curse of dimensionality means that computation power alone may not be sufficient in taming the problem. One exciting possibility is the commercial success of 3D sensors, such as the Microsoft Kinect. Designed for gaming, it can already handle a wide array of whole-body gestures. Extending this technology to the more delicate finger gestures will enable the possibility of sophisticated high-bandwidth interfaces.

25.4 Conclusion

Although the vision-based approaches described in this chapter have not yet matured to the point of common usage, researchers have developed experimental interfaces based on head and hand gestures. In this section, we consider some examples in the use of these modalities. Many of the systems were designed to overcome the limitations of the underlying technical approach, and they are partially successful in hiding the flaws. However, there is still a long road to a friendly, useful interface.

The most common approach for turning head pose information into user input is to emulate a mouse in some way. There are basically two modes of operation for this: "nose-pointer" and "joystick." In the former, the absolute position (and/or orientation) of the head determines the pointer location. In the latter, the head pose is used to shift the pointer. Usually there is a nonlinear transfer function to allow for both rapid motion and fine manipulation. In a very small scale study, [43] found that the nose-pointer mode is faster, but that the joystick mode is more accurate. Beyond mouse emulation, the head can be used to signal ascent or dissent by the means of nods and head shakes. A user study in [25] found that users liked these gestures when working with dialog boxes but disliked them for scrolling through a document. This suggests that head gestures can be a natural supplement to some interactions, but care must be taken in interface design.

In contrast to head trackers, there are a variety of IR-based eye tracking solutions available for purchase today. These are designed as an input modality for the disabled and for research, allowing scientists to understand what parts of a page draw the eye. However, they have not seen much use in the general populace. Part of the problem is the cumbersome nature of such devices and the potential calibration troubles. Another aspect is the difficulty of actually performing actions using only gaze input. The standard method of using gaze is to simulate a mouse. The user moves the mouse by looking at different locations and can simulate a mouse-click by dwelling at a particular location. This, however, can lead to the "Midas touch" problem, where simply looking for the option to select will cause it to execute. Thus, the dwell time has to be set to a large value (over 400 ms) making the input slow and tedious.

This problem can be alleviated by adopting methods from traditional UI design. For example, one study [22] shows that pie menus, which arrange the options in a circle around a central point, are much easier to navigate than traditional linear menus. Another method is to use a "fly-through" approach of constantly zooming in toward the point of fixation. Under this paradigm, the fixated object grows as the user continues to look at it, giving him time to avert his eyes if he finds that he is looking at the wrong thing. However, the study in [15] indicates that the overall speed of this system is only comparable to a traditional dwell-based keyboard.

More promising is the prospect of fusing eye–gaze information with traditional modalities. One classic example is the MAGIC system documented in [48]. This system warps the mouse cursor to where the user is looking in order to reduce hand movement. Fine grain selection is still performed manually with the mouse. A more modern example of this is found in [2], which combines a head tracker with a multiple-monitor system. However, this user study is perhaps more informative as a word of caution. Because the authors' head tracking system can find only rough gaze direction, their implementation only warped the mouse cursor from one monitor to another and did not alter the location of the cursor within a monitor. As a result, the system works against a user that is trying to perform a small jump that crosses a monitor boundary. Thus, the researchers found that the overall time require to perform the task actually increased over the baseline system without a head tracker. As this example shows, the traditional keyboard and mouse have proven to be highly reliable and fast input modalities; those who seek to improve on them have a high bar to clear.

For the hand, there has been a dearth of interfaces that actually interpret symbolic gestures. Usually, systems use some form of didetic gestures to emulate a mouse. One small study [7] found that using these pointing gestures was three times slower than using a mouse. The authors of the study blame the discrepancy on the fact that using the gestures requires moving the whole arm while operating a mouse only necessitates wrist motions.

In summary, head and gaze interfaces have to improve significantly if they are to find common usage among the general populace. They are hampered by limitations in the underlying technology. There also seem to be fundamental limitations in these modalities. The amount of bandwidth available seems to be limited in a user's gaze, and training the user to perform complex gestures may be unnatural. That said, technology and techniques continue to improve, and there is promise in using these tracking techniques as a supplement to traditional input.

25.4.1 Further Reading

Interested readers may wish to peruse some old works on interface design:

- Bolt, R.A.: "Put-that-there": Voice and gesture at the graphics interface. In: SIGGRAPH '80: Proceedings of the 7th Annual Conference on Computer Graphics and Interactive Techniques, pp. 262–270. ACM, New York (1980)
- Kelley, J.F.: An iterative design methodology for user-friendly natural language office information applications. ACM Trans. Inf. Syst. Secur. 2(1), 26–41 (1984)

References

1. Alon, J., Athitsos, V., Yuan, Q., Sclaroff, S.: A unified framework for gesture recognition and spatiotemporal gesture segmentation. IEEE Trans. Pattern Anal. Mach. Intell. 31(9), 1685–1699 (2009) [501,502]
2. Ashdown, M., Oka, K., Sato, Y.: Combining head tracking and mouse input for a GUI on multiple monitors. In: CHI '05: CHI '05 Extended Abstracts on Human Factors in Computing Systems, pp. 1188–1191. ACM, New York (2005) [506]
3. Athitsos, V., Sclaroff, S.: Estimating 3d hand pose from a cluttered image. In: Computer Vision and Pattern Recognition, vol. 2, pp. 432–439 (June 2003) [503]
4. Beymer, D., Flickner, M.: Eye gaze tracking using an active stereo head. In: Computer Vision and Pattern Recognition, 2003. Proceedings. 2003. IEEE Computer Society Conference on, vol. 2, pp. 451–458 (June 2003) [499]
5. Bowden, R., Windridge, D., Kadir, T., Zisserman, A., Brady, M.: A linguistic feature vector for the visual interpretation of sign language. In: Pajdla, T., Matas, J. (eds.) Computer Vision – ECCV 2004. Lecture Notes in Computer Science, vol. 3021, pp. 390–401. Springer, Berlin (2004) [501]
6. Bray, M., Koller-Meier, E., Schraudolph, N.N., Van Gool, L.: Fast stochastic optimization for articulated structure tracking. Image Vis. Comput. 25(3), 352–364 (2007). Articulated and Non-rigid motion [504]
7. Cabral, M.C., Morimoto, C.H., Zuffo, M.K.: On the usability of gesture interfaces in virtual reality environments. In: CLIHC '05: Proceedings of the 2005 Latin American Conference on Human–Computer Interaction, pp. 100–108. ACM, New York (2005) [506]
8. de La Gorce, M., Paragios, N., Fleet, D.J.: Model-based hand tracking with texture, shading and self-occlusions. In: Computer Vision and Pattern Recognition, 2008. CVPR 2008. IEEE Conference on, pp. 1–8 (23–28 June 2008) [505]
9. Erol, A., Bebis, G., Nicolescu, M., Boyle, R.D., Twombly, X.: Vision-based hand pose estimation: A review. Comput. Vis. Image Underst. 108(1–2), 52–73 (2007) [502]

10. Fu, Y., Huang, T.S.: Graph embedded analysis for head pose estimation. In: Automatic Face and Gesture Recognition, 2006. FGR 2006. 7th International Conference on, pp. 6–8 (April 2006) [496]

11. Gee, A., Cipolla, R.: Determining the gaze of faces in images. Image Vis. Comput. **12**(10), 639–647 (1994) [496]

12. Gourier, N., Hall, D., Crowley, J.: Estimating face orientation using robust detection of salient facial features. In: Proceedings of Pointing 2004, ICPR, International Workshop on Visual Observation of Deictic Gestures, pp. 17–25 (2004) [495]

13. Guestrin, E.D., Eizenman, M.: General theory of remote gaze estimation using the pupil center and corneal reflections. IEEE Trans. Biomed. Eng. **53**, 1124–1133 (2006) [499]

14. Hansen, D.W., Pece, A.E.C.: Eye tracking in the wild. Comput. Vis. Image Underst. **98**, 155–181 (2005) [499]

15. Hansen, D.W., Skovsgaard, H.H.T., Hansen, J.P., Møllenbach, E.: Noise tolerant selection by gaze-controlled pan and zoom in 3d. In: ETRA '08: Proceedings of the 2008 Symposium on Eye Tracking Research & Applications, pp. 205–212. ACM, New York (2008) [506]

16. Hansen, D.W., Hansen, J.P., Nielsen, M., Johansen, A.S., Stegmann, M.B.: Eye typing using Markov and active appearance models. In: Applications of Computer Vision, 2002. (WACV 2002). Proceedings. Sixth IEEE Workshop on, pp. 132–136 (2002) [498]

17. Hansen, D.W., Ji, Q.: In the eye of the beholder: A survey of models for eyes and gaze. IEEE Trans. Pattern Anal. Mach. Intell. **32**(3), 478–500 (2010) [497]

18. Heap, T., Hogg, D.: Towards 3d hand tracking using a deformable model. In: Automatic Face and Gesture Recognition, 1996, Proceedings of the Second International Conference on, Killington, VT, pp. 140–145 (14–16 October 1996) [504]

19. Huang, J., Shao, X., Wechsler, H.: Face pose discrimination using support vector machines (SVM). In: Pattern Recognition, 1998. Proceedings. Fourteenth International Conference on, vol. 1, pp. 154–156 (August 1998) [495]

20. Isard, M., Blake, A.: Condensation – conditional density propagation for visual tracking. Int. J. Comput. Vis. **29**(1), 5–28 (1998) [504]

21. Ji, Q., Zhu, Z.: Eye and gaze tracking for interactive graphic display. In: Proceedings of the 2nd International Symposium on Smart Graphics. SMARTGRAPH '02, pp. 79–85. ACM, New York (2002) [498]

22. Kammerer, Y., Scheiter, K., Beinhauer, W.: Looking my way through the menu: the impact of menu design and multimodal input on gaze-based menu selection. In: ETRA '08: Proceedings of the 2008 Symposium on Eye Tracking Research & Applications, pp. 213–220. ACM, New York (2008) [506]

23. Li, Y., Gong, S., Sherrah, J., Liddell, H.: Support vector machine based multi-view face detection and recognition. Image Vis. Comput. **22**(5), 413–427 (2004) [495]

24. Matsumoto, Y., Ogasawara, T., Zelinsky, A.: Behavior recognition based on head pose and gaze direction measurement. In: Intelligent Robots and Systems, 2000 (IROS 2000). Proceedings. 2000 IEEE/RSJ International Conference on, vol. 3, pp. 2127–2132 (2000) [499]

25. Morency, L.-P., Darrell, T.: Head gesture recognition in intelligent interfaces: The role of context in improving recognition. In: IUI '06: Proceedings of the 11th International Conference on Intelligent User Interfaces, pp. 32–38. ACM, New York (2006) [506]

26. Morimoto, C.: Pupil detection and tracking using multiple light sources. Image Vis. Comput. **18**(4), 331–335 (2000) [497]

27. Morimoto, C.H., Mimica, M.R.M.: Eye gaze tracking techniques for interactive applications. Comput. Vis. Image Underst. **98**(1), 4–24 (2005). Special Issue on Eye Detection and Tracking [497]

28. Murphy-Chutorian, E., Trivedi, M.M.: Hyhope: Hybrid head orientation and position estimation for vision-based driver head tracking. In: Intelligent Vehicles Symposium, 2008 IEEE, pp. 512–517 (June 2008) [496]

29. Murphy-Chutorian, E., Trivedi, M.M.: Head pose estimation in computer vision: A survey. IEEE Trans. Pattern Anal. Mach. Intell. **31**(4), 607–626 (2009) [495,497]

30. Nickel, K., Stiefelhagen, R.: Pointing gesture recognition based on 3d-tracking of face, hands and head orientation. In: Proceedings of the 5th International Conference on Multimodal Interfaces. ICMI '03, pp. 140–146. ACM, New York (2003) [502]
31. Niyogi, S., Freeman, W.T.: Example-based head tracking. In: Automatic Face and Gesture Recognition, 1996. Proceedings of the Second International Conference on, pp. 374–378 (October 1996) [495]
32. Ohno, T.: One-point calibration gaze tracking method. In: Proceedings of the 2006 Symposium on Eye Tracking Research & Applications. ETRA '06, p. 34. ACM, New York (2006) [498]
33. Ohno, T., Mukawa, N., Yoshikawa, A.: Freegaze: A gaze tracking system for everyday gaze interaction. In: Proceedings of the 2002 Symposium on Eye Tracking Research & Applications. ETRA '02, pp. 125–132. ACM, New York (2002) [498]
34. Pavlovic, V.I., Pavlovic, V.I., Sharma, R., Huang, T.S.: Visual interpretation of hand gestures for human–computer interaction: a review. IEEE Trans. Pattern Anal. Mach. Intell. **19**(7), 677–695 (1997) [500]
35. Potamias, M., Athitsos, V.: Nearest neighbor search methods for handshape recognition. In: PETRA '08: Proceedings of the 1st International Conference on PErvasive Technologies Related to Assistive Environments, pp. 1–8. ACM, New York (2008) [503]
36. Rehg, J.M.: Visual analysis of high DOF articulated objects with application to hand tracking. PhD thesis, Carnegie Mellon University (1995) [504]
37. Shih, S.-W., Wu, Y.-T., Liu, J.: A calibration-free gaze tracking technique. In: Pattern Recognition, 2000. Proceedings. 15th International Conference on, vol. 4, pp. 201–204 (2000) [498]
38. Stenger, B., Thayananthan, A., Torr, P.H.S., Cipolla, R.: Model-based hand tracking using a hierarchical Bayesian filter. IEEE Trans. Pattern Anal. Mach. Intell. **28**, 1372–1384 (2006) [503,505]
39. Stern, H., Wachs, J., Edan, Y.: A method for selection of optimal hand gesture vocabularies. In: Sales Dias, M., Gibet, S., Wanderley, M., Bastos, R. (eds.) Gesture-Based Human–Computer Interaction and Simulation. Lecture Notes in Computer Science, vol. 5085, pp. 57–68. Springer, Berlin (2009) [501]
40. Suk, H.-I., Sin, B.-K., Lee, S.-W.: Recognizing hand gestures using dynamic Bayesian network. In: Automatic Face Gesture Recognition, 2008. FG '08. 8th IEEE International Conference on, pp. 1–6 (17–19 September 2008) [502]
41. Tan, K.-H., Kriegman, D.J., Ahuja, N.: Appearance-based eye gaze estimation. In: Proceedings of the Sixth IEEE Workshop on Applications of Computer Vision. WACV '02, Washington, DC, p. 191. IEEE Comput. Soc., Los Alamitos (2002) [499]
42. Tomasi, C., Petrov, S., Sastry, A.: 3d tracking = classification + interpolation. In: Computer Vision, 2003. Proceedings. Ninth IEEE International Conference on, Nice, France, pp. 1441–1448 (13–16 October 2003) [503]
43. Tu, J., Tao, H., Huang, T.: Face as mouse through visual face tracking. Comput. Vis. Image Underst. **108**(1–2), 35–40 (2007). Special Issue on Vision for Human–Computer Interaction [505]
44. Wang, J.-G., Sung, E., Venkateswarlu, R.: Estimating the eye gaze from one eye. Comput. Vis. Image Underst. **98**, 83–103 (2005) [499]
45. White, Jr. K.P., Hutchinson, T.E., Carley, J.M.: Spatially dynamic calibration of an eye-tracking system. IEEE Trans. Syst. Man Cybern. **23**(4), 1162–1168 (1993) [497]
46. Xiao, J., Baker, S., Matthews, I., Kanade, T.: Real-time combined 2d+3d active appearance models. In: Computer Vision and Pattern Recognition, 2004. CVPR 2004. Proceedings of the 2004 IEEE Computer Society Conference on, vol. 2, pp. 535–542 (June 27 – July 2 2004) [496]
47. Yang, M.-H., Ahuja, N.: Recognizing hand gesture using motion trajectories. In: Computer Vision and Pattern Recognition, p. 472 (1999) [501]
48. Zhai, S., Morimoto, C., Ihde, S.: Manual and gaze input cascaded (magic) pointing. In: CHI '99: Proceedings of the SIGCHI Conference on Human Factors in Computing Systems, pp. 246–253. ACM, New York (1999) [506]

49. Zhou, H., Lin, D.J., Huang, T.S.: Static hand gesture recognition based on local orientation histogram feature distribution model. In: Computer Vision and Pattern Recognition Workshop, 2004 Conference on, p. 161 (2004) [503]
50. Zhu, Z., Ji, Q., Bennett, K.P.: Nonlinear eye gaze mapping function estimation via support vector regression. In: Pattern Recognition, 2006. ICPR 2006. 18th International Conference on, vol. 1, pp. 1132–1135 (2006) [498]

Chapter 26
Social Signal Processing: The Research Agenda

Maja Pantic, Roderick Cowie, Francesca D'Errico, Dirk Heylen, Marc Mehu,
Catherine Pelachaud, Isabella Poggi, Marc Schroeder,
and Alessandro Vinciarelli

Abstract The exploration of how we react to the world and interact with it and each other remains one of the greatest scientific challenges. Latest research trends in cognitive sciences argue that our common view of intelligence is too narrow, ignoring a crucial range of abilities that matter immensely for how people do in life. This range of abilities is called social intelligence and includes the ability to express and recognise social signals produced during social interactions like agreement, politeness, empathy, friendliness, conflict, etc., coupled with the ability to manage them in order to get along well with others while winning their cooperation. Social Signal Processing (SSP) is the new research domain that aims at understanding and modelling social interactions (human-science goals), and at providing computers with similar

M. Pantic (✉)
Computing Dept., Imperial College London, London , UK
e-mail: m.pantic@imperial.ac.uk

M. Pantic · D. Heylen
EEMCS, University of Twente, Enschede, The Netherlands

R. Cowie
Psychology Dept., Queen University Belfast, Belfast, UK

F. D'Errico · I. Poggi
Dept. Of Education, University Roma Tre, Rome, Italy

M. Mehu
Psychology Dept., University of Geneva, Geneva, Switzerland

C. Pelachaud
CNRS, Paris, France

M. Schroeder
DFKI, Saarbrucken, Germany

A. Vinciarelli
Computing Science Dept., University of Glasgow, Glasgow, UK
e-mail: vincia@dcs.gla.acvi.uk
IDIAP Research Institute, Martigny, Switzerland

T.B. Moeslund et al. (eds.), *Visual Analysis of Humans*,
DOI 10.1007/978-0-85729-997-0_26, © Springer-Verlag London Limited 2011

abilities in human–computer interaction scenarios (technological goals). SSP is in its infancy, and the journey towards artificial social intelligence and socially aware computing is still long. This research agenda is twofold, a discussion about how the field is understood by people who are currently active in it and a discussion about issues that the researchers in this formative field face.

26.1 Introduction

The exploration of how human beings react to the world and interact with it and each other remains one of the greatest scientific challenges. Perceiving, learning, and adapting to the world are commonly labelled as intelligent behaviour. But what does it mean being intelligent? Is IQ a good measure of human intelligence and the best predictor of somebody's success in life? There is now a growing research in cognitive sciences, which argues that our common view of intelligence is too narrow, ignoring a crucial range of abilities that matter immensely for how people do in life. This range of abilities is called social intelligence [1, 3, 17, 116] and includes the ability to express and recognise social signals like turn taking, agreement, politeness, empathy, friendliness, conflict, etc., coupled with the ability to manage them in order to get along well with others while winning their cooperation. There is no common definition for the concept of social signal (as explained in Sect. 26.2), and the definition that we adopt in this document refers to social signals as to signals produced during social interactions, that either play a part in the information and adjustment of relations and interactions between agents (human and artificial), or provide information about the agents. Social signals are manifested through a multiplicity of non-verbal behavioural cues including facial expressions, body postures and gestures, vocal outbursts like laughter, etc. (Fig. 26.1), which can be automatically analysed by technologies of signal processing (as discussed in Sect. 26.3), or automatically generated by technologies of signal synthesis (as talked about in Sect. 26.4).

When it comes to computers, however, they are socially ignorant [95]. Current computing devices do not account for the fact that human–human communication is always socially situated and that discussions are not just facts but part of a larger social interplay. However, not all computers will need social intelligence and none will need all of the related skills humans have. The current-state-of-the-art categorical computing works well and will always work well for context-independent tasks like making plane reservations and buying and selling stocks. However, this kind of computing is utterly inappropriate for virtual reality applications as well as for interacting with each of the (possibly hundreds) computer systems diffused throughout future smart environments (predicted as the future of computing by several visionaries such as Mark Weiser [128]) and aimed at improving the quality of life by anticipating the users needs. Computer systems and devices capable of sensing agreement, inattention, or dispute, and capable of adapting and responding in real-time to these social signals in a polite, non-intrusive, or persuasive manner, are likely to be perceived as more natural, efficacious, and trustworthy. For example,

Fig. 26.1 Manifestations of social signals include a variety of non-verbal behavioural cues including facial expressions, body postures/gestures, vocal outbursts like laughter, etc.

in education, pupils' social signals inform the teacher of the need to adjust the instructional message. Successful human teachers acknowledge this and work with it; digital conversational embodied agents must begin to do the same by employing tools that can accurately sense and interpret social signals and social context of the pupil, learn successful context-dependent social behaviour, and use a proper socially adept presentation language (e.g., see [93]) to drive the animation of the agent. The research area of machine analysis and employment of human social signals to build more natural, flexible computing technology goes by the general name of Socially Aware Computing as introduced by [94, 95].

Although the importance of social signals in everyday life situations is evident, and in spite of recent advances in machine analysis and synthesis of relevant behavioural cues like gaze exchange, blinks, smiles, head nods, crossed arms, laughter, expressive prosody, and similar [83, 89, 90, 112, 132], the research efforts in machine analysis and synthesis of human social signals like attention, empathy, politeness, flirting, (dis)agreement, etc., are still tentative and pioneering efforts. Nonetheless, the importance of studying social interactions and developing automated systems of social signals analysis from audiovisual recordings is indisputable. It will result in valuable multimodal tools that could revolutionise basic research in cognitive and social sciences by raising the quality and shortening the time to conduct research that is now lengthy, laborious, and often imprecise. The first results in the field attest that social interactions and behaviours, although complex and rooted in the deepest aspects of human psychology, can be analysed automatically with the help of computers (for extensive overview of the past research in the field of automatic analysis of social signals, see [125]). In fact, the pioneering contributions in Social Signal Processing (SSP) [32, 60, 94] have shown that social signals, typically described as so elusive and subtle that only trained psychologists can recognise them [45], are actually evident and detectable enough to be captured through sensors like microphones and cameras, and interpreted through analysis techniques like machine learning and statistics. At the same time, and as outlined above, tools for social signal synthesis in Human–Computer Interaction (HCI) form a large step ahead in realising naturalistic, socially aware computing and interfaces, built for humans, based on models of human behaviour. For example, combining synthetic speech with laughter influences the perception of social bonds [119]. Similarly, facial expressions influence a human user's evaluation of an Embodied Conversational Agent [105]. Contingency of signals has a key role in creating rapport between human user and virtual agent [46]. Politeness cues [127] and empathic expressions [83] are perceived as more appropriate in interactive scenarios.

SSP [95, 96, 124, 125] is the new research and technological domain that aims at providing computers with the ability to sense and understand human social signals. SSP is in its initial phase and the first step is to define the field and discuss issues facing the researchers in the field. This article attempts to achieve this. In Sect. 26.2, an overview of the relevant terminology defined by the related human-science fields is provided. Next, in the absence of a uniquely accepted definition of social signals, a working definition of social signals is introduced. In Sects. 26.3 and 26.4, challenging issues facing researchers in automatic social signal analysis and synthesis are summarised. Section 26.5 summarises the key goals of the SSP research overall, lists a number of issues that are of importance for the field but are still debated, and discusses the relevant ethical issues. Section 26.6 concludes the paper.

26.2 Social Signals: Terminology, Definition, and Cognitive Modelling

In order to anchor their discipline in the rich conceptual background developed in the behavioural sciences, SSP researchers are faced with the difficult task of defining a theoretical framework within which they will research the phenomena social signals they are eager to automatically detect, interpret, and synthesise. The major issue here is the diversity of conceptual ideas proposed about social signals and behaviour. Disciplines that dealt with the study of human psychological phenomena (mental states and behaviour) developed a myriad of ideas, definitions, and methods for the study of the same subject, human communication. In itself, this may be seen as a strength more than a weakness because having multiple approaches increases the potential for a good understanding of the complexities of human behaviour. However, this diversity may become a problem when people of different traditions come to work together on interdisciplinary research topic (such as SSP).

The increasing specialisation that characterises most scientific disciplines can be a barrier to inter-disciplinarity, for it can hinder communication between scholars. For communication to be successful, one has to use terms that will be understood by various researchers working in the field. In an attempt to achieve this, we describe here the different approaches adopted by the human sciences to study social signals. Section 26.2.1 presents a (non-exhaustive) glossary of concepts generated by different fields (ethology, social psychology, linguistics, semiotics, ...) to study communication. We present commonalities and differences between these approaches, so that scholars who are not familiar with the different disciplines can have a clearer idea of what the different positions are. The goal of this exercise is not to create a common definition for the concept of social signal because it would deny the specificities of each field and would constitute, for some, a loss of conceptual clarity. As SSP is a multi-disciplinary venture, our aim is to avoid the creation of a monolithic view that is unlikely to be adopted by the scientific community at large, or that may block the development of new ideas or research projects. Instead, our goal is to expose the diversity and be aware of it. However, as a definition of the studied phenomena is needed, and in the absence of a uniquely accepted definition of social signals, Sect. 26.2.2 introduces a working definition of social signals.

26.2.1 Terminology

Tables 26.1, 26.2, 26.3 and 26.4 present a (non-exhaustive) glossary of SSP-relevant concepts generated by different fields (ethology, social psychology, linguistics, semiotics, etc.) to study communication.

The main stream of research in animal and human communication acknowledges that signals convey information and/or meaning to a receiver. Although this could be considered as a commonality between all approaches, a critical analysis of research findings and theoretical developments in ethology suggest that the principles that are applied to the study of human language should not necessarily apply to the study of animal signals [102] or to some aspects of human non-verbal behaviour [87]. In other words, the strong semantic component of human language may not necessarily be shared by other channels of communication. For this reason, the ethological definition of signals includes the possibility that they do not carry information.

Different disciplines adopt different ways of defining a signal. For example, ethologists define signals by their properties or nature, and by their function of influencing a perceiver's behaviour or internal state (e.g. [78]). On the other hand, [100] define a social signal by its content (signals that have a social content, like a social attitude, a social emotion, etc.). In social psychology, scholars tend to use the term indicator, sign, signal, and display interchangeably (e.g. [18, 68]), without specifying what they mean by the terms indicator, sign, signal, or display. We assume that this lack of specificity implies that these authors endorse a general dictionary definition of the word, their goal being to study the eliciting circumstances

Table 26.1 Definitions of important ethology concepts for social signal processing

Ethology	
Signal	An act or structure that affects the behaviour (or internal state) of another organism, which evolved because of that effect, and which is effective because the receiver's response has also evolved [78]. A signal may [78] or may not [102] convey reliable information
Cue	A feature of the world, animate or inanimate, that can be used by individuals as a guide to future action [54]
Display	Behaviour pattern that has been modified in the course of evolution to convey information [6]. Displays are usually constituted of several components, like cues and signals
Handicap	A signal whose reliability is ensured because its cost is greater than those required to efficiently convey the information [131]. The signal may be costly to produce, or have costly consequences [122]
Index	A signal whose intensity is causally related with the information that is being signalled and that cannot be faked [77]. Indices are equivalent to performance based signals [38]
Minimal-cost symbol	A signal whose reliability does not depend on its cost (different from a handicap) and which can be made by most members of a population (different from an index) [78]
Icon	A signal which form is similar to its meaning
Symbol	A signal whose form is unrelated to its meaning, e.g. conventional signal [48]

and information content of particular behaviour patterns rather than to develop different concepts for non-verbal communication. Other authors, however, decided to use other terms than signals to describe specific categories of non-verbal behaviour [37].

The variety in definitions may be partly explained by the use of different methodologies and the different empirical questions that have driven research activities in different fields. For example, ethology has always focused on the adaptive significance of behavioural patterns for the organisms displaying them and the selective pressures responsible for the evolution of signals [34, 57]. Psychological science, however, has always placed a greater interest in discovering the significance or meaning of a particular behaviour in the mind of perceivers (for a critic, see [87]). Finally, linguistic has been mostly preoccupied by the role of signals in the regulation of discourse and social interactions among members of conversational groups [31, 52]. The diversity in research methods and theoretical interests led scholars to use different terms to describe the same thing, or the same term to describe different ideas. By no means should this signify that one approach has more authority than the other, or that a research question is more relevant than another. The only drawback is that this state of affair may create confusion in scholars who are interested in social signals but are not familiar with the human and behavioural sciences. We hope that the overview provided here is helpful in that direction.

Table 26.2 Definitions of important psychology concepts for social signal processing

Psychology	
Cue	Stimulus which serves as a sign or signal of something else, the connection having previously been learned [130]
Indicator	No clear definition for non-verbal indicator, seems to be used in a loose fashion to reflect a connection between non-verbal behaviour and some underlying dimension
Signal	No precise definition of signal in social psychology, though some authors seem to imply that signals are intentionally communicative [36]. The category seems to include all non-verbal behaviours or morphological structure that convey information to a receiver [100]
Social signal	Communicative or informative signal that, either directly or indirectly, conveys information about social actions, social interactions, social emotions, social attitudes and social relationships [100]
Sign	Refers to an act that is informative but that was not necessarily produced to communicate information [36]
Emblem	Non-verbal act which has a direct verbal translation that is well-known by all members of a group, class, or culture [33, 37]
Illustrator	Movement directly tied to speech that illustrates what is said verbally [33, 37]
Regulator	Act that maintains and regulates the conversation between two or more individuals [37]
Manipulator	Act that represents adaptive efforts to satisfy bodily needs, actions, to manage emotions, to develop interpersonal contacts, or to learn instrumental activities (see also adaptor in [37])
Emotional expression	Non-verbal act that is specific to a particular emotion [35, 117], or to an underlying emotional dimension [110]
Distal cues	Externalisation of stable traits or transient states, can be motor expression or physical appearance [16, 109]
Proximal percept	Mental representation resulting from the perceptual process of distal cues [16, 109]

Although we can see that research domains mostly differ in the detailed elaborations they made with regards to the nature of signals, their function, and their informative value, a few features and principles used to describe signals are shared among the different fields. First, some acts are considered functionally or intentionally communicative (e.g. signals, emblems, communicative signals); whereas others are simply considered as informative (cues, signs, informative signals), suggesting that information can be derived from them although they have not evolved, or are not intended, for communication1. Most theories also recognise the existence of signals which meaning follows social conventions: symbols, conventional signals, and emblems. The iconic act also seems to meet agreement in the different fields, as it is defined by everyone as an act which meaning is defined by its form. Finally, the importance of multi-modality is also recognised by all fields of research [2, 4, 91]. Commonalities of this sort make collaborations between dis-

Table 26.3 Definitions of important concepts for processes involved in the production and perception of social signals

Processes involved in the production and perception of social signals

Code	Principle of correspondence between the act and its meaning [37]. The code can be intrinsic, extrinsic, and iconic
Encoding	The process, taking place in the signaller, of relating the distal cue and its meaning. Transfer of information in one domain (e.g. thoughts, stances) to another domain (muscular contraction, blood concentration, …)
Decoding	The process taking place in the perceiver of relating the proximal percept to a semantic category or some other form of representation

Linguistics and semiotics

Turn taking	The order in which the participants in a conversation speak one after the other The fulfilment or violation of turn-taking rules in a conversation provides cues about its cooperative or competitive structure [31, 106]
Backchannel	Feedback and comments provided by listeners during face-to-face conversation, through short verbalisations and non-verbal signals, showing how they are engaged in the speakers' dialogue (HUMAINE glossary)

Table 26.4 Definitions of miscellaneous important concepts for social signal processing

Miscellaneous

Context	All the cues present in the physical and social environment of a perceiver as well as perceiver's characteristics that surrounds the signal
Information (Information theory)	Any physical property of the world that reduces uncertainty in the individual that perceives it [114]
Meaning	The meaning of something is what it expresses or represents (Cambridge Advanced learner's dictionary)
Ground truth	A term, with origins in cartography and aerial imaging, used to describe data that can be taken as definitive, and against which systems can be measured. Its application to emotion is controversial, since it is highly debatable whether emotions as they normally occur are things about which we can have definitive knowledge (HUMAINE glossary)

ciplines possible and create bridges that are necessary for inter-disciplinary research.

26.2.2 Working Definition of Social Signals

As a definition of the studied phenomena is needed, and in the absence of a uniquely accepted definition of social signals, we provide here a working definition of what 'social signals' are. Social signal: Let us first define what a 'signal' is. A signal is a perceivable stimulus PS a behaviour, a morphological trait, a chemical trace produced by an Emitter E. The Emitter E can be an individual or a group of people, a virtual character, an animal, or a machine. The signal is received by some Receiver R, who may interpret the signal and draw some information I from it (the signal's meaning), whether E really intended to convey I or not. Taking this into account, we may define a 'social signal' as follows. A social signal is a signal that provides information about 'social facts', i.e., about social interactions, social emotions, social attitudes, or social relations.

We can further distinguish between informative and communicative signals. A communicative signal is a signal that the Emitter produces in order to convey a particular meaning (see the Speech Acts perspective: [24, 47, 99]), while an informative signal is a signal from which the Receiver draws some meaning even if the Emitter did not intend to convey it (see the Semiotic perspective: [92]). Let us explain these notions by means of an example.

Suppose that during a lunch break there is a group of children talking in a circle, where one of them is slightly outside of the circle. A prediction can be made that the child outside of the circle is at risk of being bullied or being dropped out from the group. The spatial positioning of children is a social signal that conveys information about the social relation between the child in question and the other children, without any of the children being aware that they convey this information. This signal is not a communicative signal, but an informative signal. Furthermore, a distinction can be made between direct and indirect signals. Since social signals are produced (and understood) in context, information coming from the context may combine with the literal meaning of the signals (for a study on the literal meaning of behavioural signals, see [99]) to introduce, through inferential processes, further 'indirect meanings' of the displayed signals that differ from context to context. Let us explain this by means of an example.

Suppose that two people, A and B, sit together and both appear to be sad. This is not a social signal, just the fact that both people express the same emotion. However, if by showing sadness A wants to tighten her bond with B, then her display of sadness is an information signal representing an indirect social signal of her bond to B. Taking these notions into account, we can redefine the definition of 'social signals' as follows. A social signal is a communicative or informative signal that, either directly or indirectly, provides information about 'social facts', that is, about social interactions, social emotions, social evaluations, social attitudes, or social relations.

Hence, we define social signals as communicative and informative signals that concern 'social facts', namely, social interaction, social emotions, social evaluations, social attitudes and social relations. However, there is no strict definition of these notions. In what follows, we propose tentative definitions of these notions. Social interactions: Social interaction is a specific event in which an agent A performs some social actions directed at another agent that is actually or virtually present. Social interactions may be mediated by communicative and informative signals. Typical communicative signals in social interactions are backchannel signals such as head nods, which inform the recipient that her interaction partner is following and understanding her ([55]; Fig. 26.2).

Social emotions: A clear distinction can be made between individual and social emotions. The latter can be defined as an emotion that an Agent A feels toward and Agent B. Happiness and sadness are typical examples of individual emotions we can be happy or sad on our own; our feelings are not directed to any other person. On the other hand, admiration, envy, and compassion are typical examples of social emotions we have these feelings toward another person. Signals revealing individual emotions of a person and those communicating social emotions both include facial expressions, vocal intonations and outbursts, body gestures and postures, etc. However, if a behavioural cue like a frown is displayed as a consequence of an individual emotion, then this cue is a behavioural signal but not a social signal. It is a social signal only if it displayed in order to communicate a social emotion. In addition, a signal of empathy (e.g., patting a companion on the shoulder to convey that we share his sadness, Fig. 26.2) is a social signal. A typical signal associated with empathy is mimicry. However, mimicry is not always unconscious, which is typical for sincere empathy, but can be deliberately displayed in order to gain acceptance or approval. In the latter case, mimicry does not convey empathy. Studying the role and the effects of both deliberate and unconscious mimicry is a challenge facing the researchers in the field.

Social evaluation: Social evaluation of a person relates to assessing whether and how much the characteristics of this person comply with our standards of beauty, intelligence, strength, justice, altruism, etc. We judge other people because based on our evaluation we decide whether to engage in a social interaction with them, what types of social actions to perform, and what relations to establish with them. Typical signals shown in social evaluation are approval and disapproval, at least when it comes to the evaluator (e.g., Fig. 26.2). As far as the evaluated person is concerned, typical signals involve those conveying desired characteristics such as pride, self-confidence, mental strength, etc., which include raised chin, erected posture, easy and relaxed movements, etc.

Social attitudes: The notion of attitude has been widely investigated in Social Psychology. Social attitude can be defined as the tendency of a person to behave in a certain way toward another person or a group of people. Social attitudes include cognitive elements like beliefs, evaluations, opinions, and social emotions. All these elements determine (and are determined by) preferences and intentions [41].

Agreement and disagreement can be seen as being related to social attitudes. If two persons agree then this means that they have similar opinions, which usually entails an alliance, a commitment to cooperation, and a mutually positive attitude. In contrast, if two persons disagree, this typically implies conflict, non-cooperation, and mutually negative attitude. Typical signals of agreement and disagreement are head nods and head shakes, smile, lip wipe, crossed arms, wagging a hand, etc. [12, 13].

Fig. 26.2 'Social Facts' (from *top left, counter clock wise*): social emotions (compassion and empathy), social attitudes (approval and disapproval), social relations (dominance), and social relations (confederates)

Persuasion is also closely linked to social attitudes; it is a kind of social influence aimed at changing other people's attitudes towards a certain issue, by changing their opinions and evaluations about the target issue, and gaining agreement for the view he or she defends. Typical signals used in persuasion are persuasive words, gestures, gaze patterns, postures, as well as appropriate self-presentation aimed at eliciting the desired social evaluations. Social relations: A social relation is a relation between two (or more) persons in which these persons have common or related goals, that is, in which the pursuit, achievement, or thwarting of a goal of one of these persons determines or is determined in some way by the pursuit, achievement, or thwarting of a goal of the other involved person. Hence, not every relation is a social relation. Two persons sitting next to each other in a bus have a physical proximity relation, but this is not a social relation, although one can arise from it [19, 40]. We can have many different kinds of social relations with other people: dependency, competition, cooperation, love, exploitation, etc.

Exchange Theory [58, 67] has attempted to describe all relations including love and friendship in terms of costs and benefits. According to this theory, a person stays in a relation until it is a satisfying relation. The factors influencing this satisfaction are: rewards (material and symbolic rewards computed in terms of costs and benefits), evaluation of possible alternatives (that affects commitment), and investment (of time, effort and resources). Several critics have challenged this view as being too close to classical utilitarianism, which does not account for the difference between material and symbolic rewards and rules out altruism [57]. Different typologies of relations have been proposed in terms of criteria like public vs. private, cooperation vs. competition, presence vs. absence of sexual relations, social-emotional support oriented vs. task oriented (e.g., [7]). However, defining the notion of social relation and drawing a typology of social relations, such that they are conceptually sound while being useful for analysis and understanding of social signals, is yet to be attained. Also, assessing how social relations, social attitudes, social emotion, and social interaction overall, affect subsequent social relations is another challenge facing the researchers in the field.

Social relations can be established not only with a single person, but with a group. Within group relations, particular challenges concern the definition and description of mechanisms of power, dominance, and leverage [22, 73]. This relates to: (i) the allocation, change, and enhancement of power relations (e.g., through alliance, influence, and reputation), (ii) the interaction between gender and power relations, and (iii) the nature of leadership and the role of charisma in it. Clearly, all these issues are context and culture dependent. Typical signals revealing social relations include the manner of greeting (saying 'hello' first signals the wish for a positive social relation, saluting signals belong to a specific group like the army), the manner of conversing (e.g., using the word 'professor' signals submission), mirroring (signalling wish to have a positive social relation, or displaying 'typical' group's behaviour), spatial positioning (e.g., making a circle around a certain person distinguishes that person as the leader, touching another person indicates either affective relation or dominance, e.g., Fig. 26.2), etc. For group relationships, the manner of dressing, cutting one's hair, and mirroring, are the typical signals revealing whether a person belongs to a specific group or not. The emblems on the cloths, how elaborate is a hair dress or a crown, and the spatial arrangement of the members of the group are the typical signals revealing the status and the rank (i.e., power relations) of different members of the group.

26.3 Machine Analysis of Social Signals

Non-verbal behaviours like social signals cannot be read like words in a book [69, 103]; they are not always unequivocally associated to a specific meaning (although in general they are; [99]) and their appearance can depend on factors that have nothing to do with social behaviour. For example, some postures correspond to certain social attitudes, but sometimes they are simply comfortable [108]. Similarly, physical distances typically account for social distances, but sometimes they are simply the effect of physical constraints [53]. Moreover, as mentioned above, the same signal can correspond to different social behaviour interpretations depending on context and culture [118], although many advocate that social signals are natural rather than cultural [113]. In other words, social signals are intrinsically ambiguous, high-level semantic events, which typically include interactions with the environment and causal relationships.

Fig. 26.3 Behavioural cues typical of disagreement (*clockwise from top left*): Forefinger raise, forefinger wag, hand wag, and hands scissor [12]. These cues can be recognise with state-of-the-art human–action-recognition techniques like that proposed by [85]

An important distinction between the analysis of high-level semantic events and the analysis of low-level semantic events like the occurrence of an individual behavioural cue like the blink, is the degree to which the context, different modalities, and time, must be explicitly represented and manipulated, ranging from simple spatial reasoning to context-constrained reasoning about multimodal events shown in temporal intervals. However, despite a significant progress in automatic recognition of audiovisual behavioural cues underlying the manifestation of various social signals (e.g., see Fig. 26.3), most of the present approaches to machine analysis of human behaviour are neither multimodal, nor context-sensitive, nor suitable for handling longer time scales [89, 90, 132]. In turn, most of the social signal recognition methods reported so far are single-modal, context-insensitive and unable to handle long-time recordings of the target phenomena [125, 126].

Social interactions: Social interactions have been mostly studied in the context of small group meetings. The early works on automatic analysis of meetings [79] have been mainly aimed at recognising who says what (speaker diarisation and speech recognition) or who does what and when (tracking, movement analysis and action recognition); other aspects of social interactions like interaction cohesion, conversational context, and conversational patters, have not been studied. Arguably

the best-known group doing research towards such a deep analysis of social interactions is that led by Daniel Gatica-Perez. Relevant studies include the overview
of the past work on non-verbal analysis of social interactions in small groups [44],
automatic recognition of conversational context [64], and interaction cohesion estimation [59].

Social emotions: Whilst the state of the art in machine analysis of basic emotions such as happiness, anger, fear and disgust, is fairly advanced, especially when
it comes to analysis of acted displays recorded in constrained lab settings [132], machine analysis of social emotions such as empathy, envy, admiration, etc., is yet to be
attempted. Although some of social emotions could be arguably represented in terms
of affect dimensions—valence, arousal, expectation, power, and intensity—and pioneering efforts towards automatic dimensional and continuous emotion recognition
have been recently proposed ([39, 50, 82] see also [49], for a survey of the past work
in the field), a number of crucial issues need to be addressed first if these approaches
to automatic dimensional and continuous emotion recognition are to be used with
freely moving subjects in real-world scenarios like patient-doctor discussions, talk-
shows, job interviews, etc. In particular, published techniques revolve around the
emotional expressions of a single subject rather than around the dynamics of the
emotional feedback exchange between two subjects, which is the crux in the analysis of any social emotions. Moreover, the state of the art techniques are still unable
to handle natural scenarios such as incomplete information due to occlusions, large
and sudden changes in head pose, and other temporal dynamics typical of natural
facial expressions [132], which must be expected in human–human interaction scenarios in which social emotions occur.

Social evaluations: Only recently, efforts have been reported towards automatic
prediction of social evaluations including personality and beauty estimation. Automatic attribution of personality traits, in terms of the 'Big Five' personality
model, has been attempted based on non-verbal cues such as prosody [74], proxemics (Zen et al., 2010), position in social networks [86], and fidgeting [97]. Automatic facial attractiveness estimation have been attempted based on the facial shape
[51, 66, 111] as well as based on facial appearance information encoded in terms
of Gabor filters responses [129]. However, the research in this domain is still in
its very first stage and many basic research questions remain unanswered including exactly which features (and modalities) are the most informative for the target
problem.

Social attitudes: Similarly to social emotions and social evaluations, automatic
assessment of social attitudes has been attempted only recently and there are just
a few studies on the topic. These works include studies on automatic assessment
of agreement and disagreement in political debates based on non-verbal cues like
prosody, head and hand gestures [13, 14], analysis of turn-taking order in conflicts
[123], and work on detection of politeness and efficiency in a cooperative social
interaction [15].

Social relations: In contrast to other types of social signals, social relations roles, i.e., behavioural patterns associated to expectations of interaction participants [9] have attracted a surge of interest from signal processing research community. A number of relevant works have focused on recognition of roles in constrained settings like news and talks shows [10, 101, 107], while other works have attempted to recognise roles associated to norms expressed as beliefs and preferences like social and functional roles in meetings [98]. The social relation that has been extensively investigated is dominance. Dominance is a personality trait, often intertwined with the social role an individual plays, that makes an individual have a higher influence on the outcomes of a discussion [63]. Typically adopted approaches towards automatic recognition of social relations are based on the analysis of turn-taking structure, i.e. who talks when and how much. This is in line with the findings of Conversation Analysis, showing that regularities in turn-taking account for social phenomena [106]. As turns are organised in sequences, the most effective and most frequently applied techniques are probabilistic models like HMMs (including layered HMMs, Factorial HMMs, etc.), Hidden CRFs, DBNs and similar.

Given the current state of the art in automatic analysis of social signals, the focus of future research efforts in the field should be on addressing various basic research questions and on tackling the problem of context-constrained analysis of multimodal behavioural signals shown in temporal intervals. As suggested by [89, 90], the latter should be treated as one complex problem rather than a number of detached problems in human sensing, context sensing, and human behaviour understanding.

More specifically, there are a number of scientific and technical challenges that we consider essential for advancing the state of the art in machine analysis of human behaviour like social signals. Modalities: Which behavioural channels such as the face, the body and the tone of the voice, are minimally needed for realisation of robust and accurate human behaviour analysis? Does this hold independently of the target communicative intention (e.g., social interactions/emotions/relations) to be recognised? No comprehensive study on the topic is available yet. What we know for sure, however, is that integration of multiple modalities (at least facial and vocal) produces superior results in human behaviour analysis when compared to single-modal approaches. Numerous studies have theoretically and empirically demonstrated this (e.g., see the literature overview by [104], for such studies in psychology, and the literature overview by [132], for such studies in automatic analysis of human behaviour). It is therefore not surprising that some of the most successful works in SSP so far use features extracted from multiple modalities (for an extensive overview of the past works, see [125]). However, other issues listed above are yet to be investigated. Also, note that some studies in the field indicate that the relative contributions of different modalities and the related behavioural cues to judgement of displayed behaviour depend on the targeted behavioural category and the context in which the behaviour occurs [104].

Fusion: How to model temporal multimodal fusion which will take into account temporal correlations within and between different modalities? What is the optimal level of integrating these different streams? Does this depend upon the time scale at which the fusion is achieved? What is the optimal function for the integration? More specifically, most of the present audiovisual and multimodal systems in the field perform decision-level data fusion (i.e., classifier fusion) in which the input coming from each modality is modelled independently and these single-modal recognition results are combined at the end. Since humans display audio and visual expressions in a complementary and redundant manner, the assumption of conditional independence between audio and visual data streams in decision-level fusion is incorrect and results in the loss of information of mutual correlation between the two modalities. To address this problem, a number of model-level fusion methods were proposed that make use of the correlation between audio and visual data streams, and relax the requirement of synchronisation of these streams [132]. However, how to model multimodal fusion on multiple time scales and how to model temporal correlations within and between different modalities is yet to be explored.

Fusion and context: Do context-dependent fusion of modalities and discordance handling, which are typical for fusion of sensory neurons in humans, pertain in machine context sensing? Note that context-dependent fusion and discordance handling were never attempted within an automated system. Also note that while W4 (where, what, when, who) is dealing only with the apparent perceptual aspect of the context in which the observed human behaviour is shown, human behaviour understanding is about W5+ (where, what, when, who, why, how), where the why and how are directly related to recognising communicative intention including social signals, affect, and cognitive states of the observed person. Hence, SSP is about W5+. However, since the problem of context-sensing is extremely difficult to solve, especially for a general case (i.e., general-purpose W4 technology does not exist yet; [88, 90]), answering the why and how questions in a W4-context-sensitive manner when analysing human behaviour is virtually unexplored area of research. Having said that, it is not surprising that context-dependent fusion is truly a blue-sky research topic.

Technical aspects: Most methods for human sensing, context sensing, and human behaviour understanding work only in (often highly) constrained environments. Noise, fast movements, changes in illumination, etc., cause them to fail. Also, many of the methods in the field do not perform fast enough to support interactivity. Researchers usually choose for more sophisticated processing rather than for real-time processing. The aim of future efforts in the field should be the realisation of more robust, real-time systems, if they are to be deployed in anticipatory interfaces and social-computing technology defused throughout smart environments of the future.

26.4 Machine Synthesis of Social Signals

Automatic synthesis of social signals targets a human observer's or listener's perception of socially relevant information. While it may be true that much of social behaviour goes unnoticed [45], it appears that social signals still have an effect in terms of unconscious perception [61] without being able to say exactly say why, we either consider a person trustworthy, competent, polite, etc., or not. In automatic behaviour synthesis, the aim is thus to create this perception by timely generating suitable signals and behaviours in a synthetic voice, facial expressions and gestures of an Embodied Conversational Agent (ECA). For a comprehensive overview of works on social signal generation on virtual agents, see [126]. Above we defined social signals as communicative and informative signals that concern 'social facts' including social interaction, social emotions, social evaluations, social attitudes and social relations. The work on synthesis has considered each of these dimensions. We highlight some typical examples.

Social interactions: The prime appearance of virtual humans is as embodied conversational agents, most often referred to as ECAs [20]. The research regarding ECAs is concerned primarily with investigating social interaction in the form of face-to-face conversations that exhibit all the layers of interaction: natural language understanding and generation in combination with non-verbal signals [21], conversation management such as turn-taking and backchannelling [11, 56, 65, 71], and all the other social dimensions that will be mentioned next.

Social emotions: In many scenarios, the recognition and expression of emotions through a virtual humans face [83, 84] and voice [112] or any other form of non-verbal behaviour is very important. Besides the dimension of expression, the synthesis research community has devoted much energy in defining and implementing computational models of behaviours that underlie the decisions of the choice of emotional expression. For an overview see [75].

Social evaluations: The computational models of emotions, based on appraisal models typically contain variables that deal with the evaluation of the human interlocutor and the situation the agent is in. On the other hand, many studies dealing with the evaluation of virtual humans [105] consider the other side of the coin: the question of how the agent is perceived by the human. This can pertain to any of the behaviours exhibited by the agent and any dimension. For instance, [115] consider how different turn-taking strategies evoke different impressions, [29] and [26] consider the effect of wrinkles, just to give two extreme examples of behaviours and dimensions of expression that have been related to social evaluation.

Social attitudes: Several applications of virtual humans aim at changing attitudes of the user. This often takes the form of coaching applications. Bickmore's agent Laura, a fitness instructor, is a prime example [8]. Other relevant work is the treatment of politeness and related expressions (for instance by [28] and [84], Fig. 26.4).

Social relations: The Laura agent was one of the first agents that was extensively studied in a longitudinal study. One of the major research interests in developing the agent for this study was modelling the long-term relations that might develop between the agent and the user over the course of repeated interactions. This involved

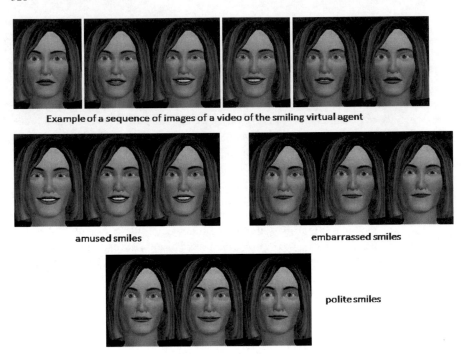

Example of a sequence of images of a video of the smiling virtual agent

amused smiles   embarrassed smiles

polite smiles

Fig. 26.4 A variety of smiles of a virtual agent (Ochs et al., 2010)

modelling many social psychological theories on relationships formation and friendship. Currently, there is a surge of work on companion agents and robots [23, 70, 72]. However, how to generate suitable behavioural signals is by no means clear, mainly due to the following two reasons. Firstly, too little is known about the types of socially relevant information conveyed in everyday human-to-human interactions, as well as about the signals and behaviours that humans naturally use to convey them. A first step in this direction would be to acknowledge the complexity of the phenomena, as has been done for emotion-related communication [30]. Then, different contexts and effects could be studied based on suitable data, and the findings could be described in terms of explicit markup language [76] or in terms of statistical, data-driven models. Secondly, it is not self-evident that synthetic agents should behave in the same way as humans do, or that they should exhibit faithful copy of human social behaviours. On the contrary, evidence from the cartoon industry [5] suggests that, in order to be believable, cartoon characters need to show strongly exaggerated behaviour. This suggests further that a trade-off between the degree of naturalness and the type of (exaggerated) gestural and vocal expression may be necessary for modelling a believable ECA's behaviour. In addition, a number of aspects of social signals are particularly relevant and challenging when it comes to synthesis of human-like behaviour.

Continuity: Unlike traditional dialogue systems, in which verbal and non-verbal behaviour is exhibited only when the system has the 'turn', socially aware systems need to be continuous in terms of non-verbal behaviour to be exhibited. In any socially relevant situation, social signals are continuously displayed, and lack of such displays in an automatic conversational system is interpreted as social ignorance [125]. The omission of social signals, typical for today's technology, is a social signal in itself, indicating the lack of social competence. Yet, continuous synthesis of socially appropriate social signals is yet to be attempted. Complex relations between social signals' form and meaning: As explained above, relationships between social signals and their meaning are intrinsically complex. Firstly, the meaning of various signals is often not additive: when signals with meanings x and y are shown at the same time, the meaning of this complex signal may not be derivable from x and y alone. In addition, context plays a crucial role for the choice and interpretation of social signals. For example, environmental aspects such as the level of visibility and noise influence the choice of signals to be shown. On the other hand, societal aspects such as the formality of the situation and previously established roles and relations of the persons involved, and individual aspects such as the personality and affective state influence not only the choice of signals to be shown but the interpretation of the observed signals as well. Hence, context-sensitive synthesis of human behaviour is needed but it still represents an entirely blue-sky research topic. Timing: Social signals are not only characterised by the verbal and non-verbal cues by means of which they are displayed but also by their timing, that is, when they were displayed in relation to the signals displayed by other communicators involved in the interaction. Thus, social signals of an ECA need to be produced in anticipation, synchrony, or response to the actions of the human user with whom the character engages in the social interaction. This requires complex feedback loops between action and perception in real-time systems. This is another entirely unexplored, yet highly relevant, research topic.

Consistency: In general, it appears that human users are very critical when it comes to the consistency of a virtual character [62]. This relates to the challenge of multimodal synchronisation, that is, to timing between facial expression, gesture, and voice conveying a coherent and appropriate message. Research on this aspect is still ongoing there is no consensus on whether multimodal cues need to be fully synchronised, whether the redundancy of information coming from multiple cues is required, or whether it is also possible for one modality to compensate for the lack of expressiveness in other modalities (e.g., [27]). Consistency may also play a role in Mori's notion of an 'uncanny valley' [81]—a robot that looks like a human but does not behave like one is perceived as unfamiliar and 'strange'. Similarly, behaviour that may be consistent with a photo-realistic character may not be perceived as natural for a cartoon-like character, and vice versa. Technical aspects: While it will take decades to fully understand and be able to synthesise various combinations of social signals that are appropriate for different contexts and different ECAs, we expect that it will soon be possible to model some limited but relevant phenomena. One example could be a model of politeness taking into account various modalities that, for a given ECA in a given context, contribute individually and jointly to the perception of a polite or rude behaviour (e.g., see the work by [28]).

There is an obvious relevance for applications: just like their human models, service robots/ECAs should exhibit polite behaviour, whereas rescue robots should be able to insist on security-related requests. However, even when it is clear what signals and behaviours to generate, a practical challenge remains: current technology still lacks flexible models of expressivity and it usually does not operate in real-time. Expressive synthetic speech, for example, is a research topic that despite two decades of active research is still somewhat in its infancy [112]. Existing approaches are either capable of domain-specific natural-sounding vocal expressivity for a small number of possible expressions, or they achieve more flexible control over expressivity but of lower quality. Similarly, fully naturalistic movements of virtual agents can be attained when human movements recorded using motion capture technology are played back [80], but movements generated based on behaviour markup language tend to look less natural [42]. These problems are not specific to synthesis of social signals, and they do not form insurmountable obstacles to research; however, they slow down the research, by making it substantially more time-consuming to create high-quality examples of the targeted expressions. Given the above-mentioned importance of timing, the lack of real-time systems impedes the realisation of timely appropriate social behaviours. Even a slight delay in the analysis and synthesis of signals hinders dynamic adaptation and synchrony that are crucial in social interaction. Furthermore, the technological limitations pose serious difficulties for exploitation of research results in end-user applications, where fast adaptation to new domains is an important requirement. Therefore, enhancing the existing technology remains an important challenge facing the researchers in the field, independently of whether the aim is to develop socially adapt ECAs or robots with no need of social awareness.

26.5 Summary and Additional Issues

Based on the enumeration of goals and challenges facing the researchers in the SSP domain as discussed in the previous chapters, the goals of the SSP research overall can be summarised under three headings: Technological goals, human science goals, and practical impact goals.

Technological goals:
- To develop systems capable of detecting and interpreting behavioural patterns that carry information about human social activity (analysis).
- To develop systems capable of synthesising behavioural patterns that carry socially significant information to humans (synthesis).
- To develop systems capable of spotting patterns of the user's behaviour that carry socially significant information to synthesise appropriate behaviours in an interaction with the user (system responsiveness).
- To develop sophisticated tools for instrumenting human science research.

Human science goals:

- To develop theories regarding the use of social signals during human–human interactions that can inform artificial agent behaviour, and can inform human–computer interactions.
- To contribute to the human science literature by modifying current theories and proposing new theories informed by the computational research in SSP.
- To create databases suitable for the analysis of human–human interactions, and suitable for training synthesis systems.
- To develop representational systems that describe human social behaviour and cognition in ways that are appropriate to technological tasks (such as labelling databases).
- To develop methods of measuring & evaluating social interactions (human/human and human/machine).

Practical impact goals: Application of the research on SSP is not restricted to a narrowly predefined set of issues like the ones listed above. It aims to address practical problems in a range of areas. Natural application areas include artificial agents and companions, human–computer interfaces, ambient intelligence, assisted living, entertainment, education, social skills training, and multimedia indexing. Applications have the important advantage of linking the effectiveness of detection/synthesis of social signals to the reality. For example, one of the earliest applications was the prediction of the outcome in transactions recorded at a call centre, and the results show that the number of successful calls can be increased by around 20% by stopping early the calls that are not promising [17]. Defining a set of promising real-world applications could not only have a positive impact on the eventual deployment of the technology, but could also provide benchmarking procedures for the SSP research, one of the best means to improve the overall quality of a research domain as extensively shown in fields where international evaluations take place every year (e.g., video analysis in TrecVid; Smeaton et al., 2006).

The key challenge: Based on the discussion so far, it should be clear that SSP research meets a specific challenge arising from the nature of the research it requires a strong collaboration between human sciences and technology research. This challenge should not only be achievable, but should be considered paramount to the success of SSP research.

Besides the challenges discussed in the previous sections, there are a number of issues with a significant bearing on the character of the field that are still a matter of debate. Although they have not been decisively resolved, the profile of technological activities in the field implies that it tilts towards a particular kind of balance. Key examples are the following.

- *Should linguistic information be included?* From a human science standpoint, language is the social signal par excellence, and should obviously be included. Technologically, there is an obvious motive to avoid it. To wit, findings in basic research like those reported by [43] and [3] indicate that linguistic messages are rather unreliable means to analyse human behaviour, and it is very difficult to anticipate a person's word choice and the associated intent in affective and socially situated expressions. In addition, the association between linguistic content and behaviour (e.g. emotion) is language-dependent and generalising from one language to another is very difficult to achieve.

• *Naturalness vs. artificiality*: Research in some related areas (e.g., affective computing) has relied heavily on data from actors or laboratory tasks, because naturalistic data and the related ground truth is too difficult to acquire. In return, some critics imply that only research on totally natural data is of any value. The balance implicit in the SSP research is that naturalness is a matter of degree, especially when it comes to learning the behaviour-synthesis models. Simulation is acceptable and, probably, in some cases practically necessary, so long as the signs in question are actually being used in an appropriate kind of interaction. Although such acted data can be used to learn how to synthesise certain behaviours, deliberately displayed data should be avoided when it comes to training machine learning methods for automatic analysis of social signals. Increasing evidence suggests that deliberate or posed behaviour differs in appearance and timing from that which occurs in daily life [25, 88, 120, 121]. Approaches that have been trained on deliberate and often exaggerated behaviours may fail to generalise up to the complexity of expressive behaviour found in real-world settings.

• *What are the appropriate validity criteria*? Research in computer science, especially in computer vision and pattern recognition, insists that data should be associated with a clear ground truth. In SSP that leads to very difficult demands asking, for instance, what a person really felt or intended in a particular situation. A common alternative is to require high inter-rater agreement. That, too, is problematic, because it is a feature of some social signals that different people 'read' them in different ways. The balance implicit in SSP is that the appropriate test depends on the actual application.

An additional challenging issue that has not been discussed so far relates to the fact that SSP deals with issues that are ethically sensitive. As a result, SSP has a range of ethical obligations. Many are standard, but some are not. Obligations that are shared with many other fields include: avoiding distress, deception and other undesirable effects on participants in studies, maintaining the confidentiality and where appropriate anonymity of participants involved in the research, avoiding the development of systems that could reasonably be regarded as intrusive, and limiting opportunities for abuse of the systems that they develop (e.g., through licensing arrangements). Particular obligations arise from the combination of complexity and sensitivity that is associated with social signals. The general requirement is sensitivity to the ways that social communication can affect people. Applying that to specific cases depends on intellectual awareness of individual issues (personality, age, etc.), of cultural issues (norms, specific signs, etc.), and of general expectations (what is disturbing, humiliating, etc.). Communicating about the area to non-experts raises particular issues. People are prone to systematic misunderstanding of SSP-type systems, so that they rely on them when they ought not to, fear them when they have no need to, and so on. Obligations relevant to offsetting are honesty (i.e., ensuring that what is said about a system is true), modesty (i.e., taking pains to ensure that its limitations as well as its achievements are understood), and public education (i.e., trying to equip people with the background knowledge to grasp what a particular system might or might not be able to do).

26.6 Conclusion

Social Signal Processing (SSP) [95, 96, 124, 125] is the new research and technological domain that aims at providing computers with the ability to sense and understand human social signals. SSP is in its initial phase and the first step is to define the field and discuss issues facing the researchers in the field, which we attempted to achieve in this article.

Despite being in its initial phase, SSP has already attracted the attention of the technological community: the MIT Technology Review magazine identifies reality mining (one of the main applications of SSP so far), as one of the ten technologies likely to change the world (Greene, 2008), while management experts expect SSP to change organisation studies like the microscope has changed medicine a few centuries ago [17]. What is more important is that the first results in the field attest that social interactions and behaviours, although complex and rooted in the deepest aspects of human psychology, can be analysed and synthesised automatically with the help of computers [125, 126]. However, although fundamental, these are only the first steps, and the journey towards artificial social intelligence and socially aware computing is still long.

Acknowledgements   This work has been funded in part by the European Community's 7th Framework Programme [FP7/20072013] under grant agreement no. 231287 (SSPNet).

References

1. Albrecht, K.: Social Intelligence: The New Science of Success. Wiley, New York (2005) [512]
2. Allwood, J.: Cooperation and flexibility in multimodal communication. In: Bunt, H., Beun, R. (eds.) Cooperative Multimodal Communication. Lecture Notes in Computer Science, vol. 2155, pp. 113–124. Springer, Berlin (2001) [517]
3. Ambady, N., Rosenthal, R.: Thin slices of expressive behavior as predictors of interpersonal consequences: A meta-analysis. Psychol. Bull. **111**(2), 256–274 (1992) [512,531]
4. Bänziger, T., Scherer, K.: Using actor portrayals to systematically study multimodal emotion expression: The GEMEP corpus. In: Paiva, A., Prada, R., Picard, R. (eds.) Affective Computing and Intelligent Interaction. Lecture Notes in Computer Science, vol. 4738, pp. 476–487. Springer, Berlin (2007) [517]
5. Bates, J.: The role of emotion in believable agents. Commun. ACM **37**(7), 122–125 (1994) [528]
6. Beer, C.G.: What is a display? Am. Zool. **17**(1), 155–165 (1977) [516]
7. Berscheid, E., Reis, H.T.: Attraction and close relationships. In: Lindzey, G., Gilbert, D.T., Fiske, S.T. (eds.), The Handbook of Social Psychology, pp. 193–281. McGraw-Hill, New York (1997) [522]
8. Bickmore, T.W., Picard, R.W.: Establishing and maintaining long-term human–computer relationships. ACM Trans. Comput.–Hum. Interact. **12**(2), 293–327 (2005) [527]
9. Biddle, B.J.: Recent developments in role theory. Annu. Rev. Sociol. **12**, 67–92 (1986) [525]
10. Bigot, B., Ferrane, I., Pinquier, J., Andre-Obrecht, R.: Detecting individual role using features extracted from speaker diarization results. Multimedia Tools Appl. 1–23 (2011) [525]

11. Bonaiuto, J., Thórisson, K.R.: Towards a neurocognitive model of realtime turntaking in face-to-face dialogue. In: Knoblich, G., Wachsmuth, I., Lenzen, M. (eds.), Embodied Communication in Humans and Machines. Oxford University Press, London (2008) [527]
12. Bousmalis, K., Mehu, M., Pantic, M.: Spotting agreement and disagreement: A survey of nonverbal audiovisual cues and tools. In: Proceedings of the International Conference on Affective Computing and Intelligent Interfaces Workshops, vol. 2 (2009) [520,523]
13. Bousmalis, K., Mehu, M., Pantic, M.: Agreement and disagreement: A survey of nonverbal audiovisual cues and tools. Image Vis. Comput. J. (2012) [520,524]
14. Bousmalis, K., Morency, L., Pantic, M.: Modeling hidden dynamics of multimodal cues for spontaneous agreement and disagreement recognition. In: IEEE International Conference on Automatic Face and Gesture Recognition (2011) [524]
15. Brunet, P.M., Charfuelan, M., Cowie, R., Schroeder, M., Donnan, H., Douglas-Cowie, E.: Detecting politeness and efficiency in a cooperative social interaction. In: International Conference on Spoken Language Processing (Interspeech), pp. 2542–2545 (2010) [524]
16. Brunswik, E.: Perception and the Representative Design of Psychological Experiments. University of California Press, Berkeley (1956) [517]
17. Buchanan, M.: The science of subtle signals. Strateg. Bus. **48**, 68–77 (2007) [512,531,533]
18. Burgoon, J.K., Le Poire, B.A.: Nonverbal cues and interpersonal judgments: Participant and observer perceptions of intimacy, dominance, composure, and formality. Commun. Monogr. **66**(2), 105–124 (1999) [515]
19. Byrne, D.: The Attraction Paradigm. Academic Press, New York (1971) [521]
20. Cassell, J., Sullivan, J., Prevost, S., Churchill, E.: Embodied Conversational Agents. MIT Press, Cambridge (2000) [527]
21. Cassell, J., Vilhjálmsson, H.H., Bickmore, T.W.: BEAT: The behavior expression animation toolkit. In: ACM International Conference on Computer Graphics and Interactive Techniques (SIGGRAPH'01), pp. 477–486 (2001) [527]
22. Castelfranchi, C.: Social power: A missed point in DAI, MA and HCI. In: Demazeau, Y., Mueller, J.P. (eds.) Decentralized AI, pp. 49–62. North-Holland, Elsevier (1990) [522]
23. Cavazza, M., de la Camara, R.S., Turunen, M.: How was your day?: A companion ECA. In: Proceedings of the 9th International Conference on Autonomous Agents and Multiagent Systems: volume 1 – Volume 1. AAMAS '10, pp. 1629–1630. International Foundation for Autonomous Agents and Multiagent Systems, Richland (2010) [528]
24. Cohen, P., Levesque, H.: Performatives in a rationally based speech act theory. In: Annual Meeting of the Association of Computational Linguistics, Pittsburgh, pp. 79–88 (1990) [519]
25. Cohn, J., Schmidt, K.: The timing of facial motion in posed and spontaneous smiles. Int. J. Wavelets Multiresolut. Inf. Process. **2**(2), 121–132 (2004) [532]
26. Courgeon, M., Buisine, S., Martin, J.-C.: Impact of expressive wrinkles on perception of a virtual character's facial expressions of emotions. In: Proceedings of the 9th International Conference on Intelligent Virtual Agents. IVA '09, pp. 201–214. Springer, Berlin (2009) [527]
27. de Gelder, B., Vroomen, J.: The perception of emotions by ear and by eye. Cogn. Emot. **14**(3), 289–311 (2000) [529]
28. de Jong, M., Theune, M., Hofs, D.H.W.: Politeness and alignment in dialogues with a virtual guide. In: International Conference on Autonomous Agents and Multiagent Systems, pp. 207–214 (2008) [527,529]
29. de Melo, C., Gratch, J.: Expression of emotions using wrinkles, blushing, sweating and tears. In: International Conference on Intelligent Virtual Agents (2009) [527]
30. Douglas-Cowie, E., Devillers, L., Martin, J.C., Cowie, R., Savvidou, S., Abrilian, S., Cox, C.: Multimodal databases of everyday emotion: Facing up to complexity. In: International Conference on Spoken Language Processing (Interspeech), pp. 813–816 (2005) [528]
31. Duncan, S.: Some signals and rules for taking speaking turns in conversations. J. Pers. Soc. Psychol. **23**(2), 283–292 (1972) [516,518]
32. Eagle, N., Pentland, A.: Reality mining: sensing complex social signals. J. Pers. Ubiquitous Comput. **10**(4), 255–268 (2006) [514]

33. Efron, D.: Gesture and Environment. King's Crown Press, New York (1941) [517]
34. Eibl-Eibesfeldt, I.: Human Ethology. Aldine De Gruyter, New York (1989) [516]
35. Ekman, P.: Are there basic emotions? Psychol. Rev. 99(3), 550–553 (1992) [517]
36. Ekman, P.: Should we call it expression or communication? Innov. Soc. Sci. Res. 10(4), 333–344 (1997) [517]
37. Ekman, P., Friesen, W.: The repertoire of nonverbal behavior: Categories, origins, usage and coding. Semiotica 1(1), 49–98 (1969) [516-518]
38. Enquist, M.: Communication during aggressive interactions with particular reference to variation in choice of behaviour. Anim. Behav. 33(4), 1152–1161 (1985) [516]
39. Eyben, F., Wollmer, M., Valstar, M.F., Gunes, H., Schuller, B., Pantic, M.: String-based audiovisual fusion of behavioural events for the assessment of dimensional affect. In: IEEE International Conference on Automatic Face and Gesture Recognition (FG'11) (2011) [524]
40. Festinger, L., Schachter, S., Back, K.: Social Pressures in Informal Groups: A Study of Human Factors in Housing. Stanford University Press, Palo Alto (1950) [521]
41. Fishbein, M., Ajzen, I.: Belief, Attitude, Intention, and Behavior: An Introduction to Theory and Research. Addison-Wesley, Reading (1975) [520]
42. Foster, M.E.: Comparing rule-based and data-driven selection of facial displays. In: Proceedings of the Workshop on Embodied Language Processing, pp. 1–8 (2007) [530]
43. Furnas, G.W., Landauer, T.K., Gomez, L.M., Dumais, S.T.: The vocabulary problem in human-system communication. Commun. ACM 30(11), 964–971 (1987) [531]
44. Gatica-Perez, D.: Automatic nonverbal analysis of social interaction in small groups: a review. Image Vis. Comput. 27(12), 1775–1787 (2009) [524]
45. Gladwell, M.: Blink: The Power of Thinking Without Thinking. Little, Brown and Co., New York (2005) [514,526]
46. Gratch, J., Wang, N., Gerten, J., Fast, E., Duffy, R.: Creating rapport with virtual agents. In: International Conference on Intelligent Virtual Agents, pp. 125–138 (2007) [514]
47. Grice, H.P.: Meaning. Philosoph. Rev. 66, 377–388 (1957) [519]
48. Guilford, T., Dawkins, M.S.: What are conventional signals? Anim. Behav. 49, 1689–1695 (1995) [516]
49. Gunes, H., Pantic, M.: Automatic, dimensional and continuous emotion recognition. Int. J. Synthet. Emot. 1(1), 68–99 (2010) [524]
50. Gunes, H., Pantic, M.: Dimensional emotion prediction from spontaneous head gestures for interaction with sensitive artificial listeners. In: International Conference on Intelligent Virtual Agents (2010) [524]
51. Gunes, H., Piccardi, M.: Assessing facial beauty through proportion analysis by image processing and supervised learning. Int. J. Human–Comput. Stud. 64, 1184–1199 (2006) [524]
52. Hadar, U., Steiner, T., Rose, F.C.: Head movement during listening turns in conversation. J. Nonverbal Behav. 9(4), 214–228 (1985) [516]
53. Hall, E.T.: The Silent Language. Doubleday, New York (1959) [522]
54. Hasson, O.: Cheating signals. J. Theor. Biol. 167, 223–238 (1994) [516]
55. Heylen, D.: Challenges ahead: Head movements and other social acts in conversations. In: International Conference on Intelligent Virtual Agents (2005) [520]
56. Heylen, D., Bevacqua, E., Pelachaud, C., Poggi, I., Gratch, J.: Generating Listener Behaviour. Springer, Berlin (2011) [527]
57. Hinde, R.: The concept of function. In: Baerends, G., Manning, A. (eds.), Function and Evolution in Behaviour, pp. 3–15. Clarendon Press, Oxford (1975) [516,522]
58. Homans, G.C.: Social Behavior: Its Elementary Forms. Harcourt Brace, Orlando (1961) [521]
59. Hung, H., Gatica-Perez, D.: Estimating cohesion in small groups using audio-visual nonverbal behavior. IEEE Trans. Multimedia, Special Issue on Multimodal Affective Interaction 12(6), 563–575 (2010) [524]
60. Hung, H., Jayagopi, D., Yeo, C., Friedland, G., Ba, S., Odobez, J.M., Ramchandran, K., Mirghafori, N., Gatica-Perez, D.: Using audio and video features to classify the most dominant person in a group meeting. In: International Conference Multimedia (2007) [514]

61. Hyman, S.E.: A new image for fear and emotion. Nature **393**, 417–418 (1998) [527]
62. Isbister, K., Nass, C.: Consistency of personality in interactive characters: Verbal cues, non-verbal cues, and user characteristics. Int. J. Human–Comput. Stud. **53**, 251–267 (2000) [529]
63. Jayagopi, D., Hung, H., Yeo, C., Gatica-Perez, D.: Modeling dominance in group conversations from non-verbal activity cues. IEEE Trans. Audio, Speech Language Process. **17**(3), 501–513 (2009) [525]
64. Jayagopi, D., Kim, T., Pentland, A., Gatica-Perez, D.: Recognizing conversational context in group interaction using privacy-sensitive mobile sensors. In: ACM International Conference on Mobile and Ubiquitous Multimedia (2010) [524]
65. Jonsdottir, G.R., Thorisson, K.R., Nivel, E.: Learning smooth, human-like turntaking in re-altime dialogue. In: Proceedings of the 8th international conference on Intelligent Virtual Agents, pp. 162–175. Springer, Berlin (2008) [527]
66. Kagian, A., Dror, G., Leyvand, T., Meilijson, I., Cohen-Or, D., Ruppin, E.: A machine learning predictor of facial attractiveness revealing human-like psychophysical biases. Vis. Res. **48**, 235–243 (2008) [524]
67. Kelley, H.H., Thibaut, J.: Interpersonal Relations: A Theory of Interdependence. Wiley, New York (1978) [521]
68. Keltner, D.: Signs of appeasement: Evidence for the distinct displays of embarrassment, amusement and shame. J. Pers. Soc. Psychol. **68**(3), 441–454 (1995) [515]
69. Knapp, M.L., Hall, J.A.: Nonverbal Communication in Human Interaction. Harcourt Brace, New York (1972) [522]
70. Koay, K.L., Syrdal, D.S., Walters, M.L., Dautenhahn, K.: Five weeks in the robot house. In: International Conference on Advances in Computer–Human Interactions (2009) [528]
71. Kopp, S., Stocksmeier, T., Gibbon, D.: Incremental multimodal feedback for conversational agents. In: International Conference on Intelligent Virtual Agents (2007) [527]
72. Leite, I., Mascarenhas, S., Pereira, A., Martinho, C., Prada, R., Paiva, A.: Why can't we be friends? – an empathic game companion for long-term interaction. In: International Conference on Intelligent Virtual Agents (2010) [528]
73. Lewis, R.L.: Beyond dominance: the importance of leverage. Q. Rev. Biol. **77**(2), 149–164 (2002) [522]
74. Mairesse, F., Walker, M.A., Mehl, M.R., Moore, R.K.: Using linguistic cues for the automatic recognition of personality in conversation and text. J. Artif. Intell. Res. **30**, 457–500 (2007) [524]
75. Marsella, S., Gratch, J., Petta, P.: Computational Models of Emotions. Oxford University Press, Oxford (2010) [527]
76. Martin, J., Abrilian, S., Devillers, L., Lamolle, M., Mancini, M., Pelachaud, C.: Levels of representation in the annotation of emotion for the specification of expressivity in ECAs. In: International Conference on Intelligent Virtual Agents (2005) [528]
77. Maynard-Smith, J., Harper, D.G.: Animal signals: Models and terminology. J. Theor. Biol. **177**, 305–311 (1995) [516]
78. Maynard-Smith, J., Harper, D.G.: Animal Signals. Oxford University Press, Oxford (2003) [515,516]
79. McCowan, I., Gatica-Perez, D., Bengio, S., Lathoud, G., Barnard, M., Zhang, D.: Automatic analysis of multimodal group actions in meetings. IEEE Trans. Pattern Anal. Mach. Intell. **27**(3), 305–317 (2005) [523]
80. Moeslund, T.B., Hilton, A., Krüger, V.: A survey of advances in vision-based human motion capture and analysis. Comput. Vis. Image Underst. **104**, 90–126 (2006) [530]
81. Mori, M.: The uncanny valley. Energy **7**, 33–35 (1970) [529]
82. Nicolaou, M., Gunes, H., Pantic, M.: Output-associative RVM regression for dimensional and continuous emotion prediction. In: IEEE International Conference on Automatic Face and Gesture Recognition (2011) [524]
83. Och, M., Niewiadomski, R., Pelachaud, C.: Expressions of empathy in ECAs. In: International Conference on Intelligent Virtual Agents (2008) [513,514,527]

84. Ochs, M., Niewiadomski, R., Pelachaud, C.: How a virtual agent should smile? morphological and dynamic characteristics of virtual agent's smiles. In: International Conference on Intelligent Virtual Agents (IVA'10) (2010) [527]
85. Oikonomopoulos, A., Patras, I., Pantic, M.: Discriminative space–time voting for joint recognition and localization of actions. In: International ACM Conference on Multimedia, Workshops (ACM-MM-W'10) (2010) [523]
86. Olguin, D., Gloor, P., Pentland, A.: Capturing individual and group behavior with wearable sensor. In: AAAI Spring Symposium (2009) [524]
87. Owren, M.J., Bachorowski, J.A.: Reconsidering the evolution of nonlinguistic communication: The case of laughter. J. Nonverbal Behav. **27**(3), 183–200 (2003) [515,516]
88. Pantic, M.: Machine analysis of facial behaviour: Naturalistic and dynamic behaviour. Philos. Trans. R. Soc. Lond. B, Biol. Sci. **364**, 3505–3513 (2009) [526,532]
89. Pantic, M., Pentland, A., Nijholt, A., Huang, T.: Human computing and machine understanding of human behavior: A survey. LNAI **4451**, 47–71 (2007) [513,523,525]
90. Pantic, M., Pentland, A., Nijholt, A., Huang, T.: Human-centred intelligent human–computer interaction (HCI2): How far are we from attaining it? Int. J. Auton. Adapt. Commun. Syst. (IJAACS) **1**(2), 168–187 (2008) [513,523,525,526]
91. Partan, S.R., Marter, P.: Communication goes multimodal. Science **283**(5406), 1272–1273 (1999) [517]
92. Peirce, C.C.: Collected Chapters. Cambridge University Press, Cambridge (1931–1935) [519]
93. Pelachaud, C., Carofiglio, V., Carolis, B.D., de Rosis, F., Poggi, I.: Embodied contextual agent in information delivering application. In: International Conference on Autonomous Agents and Multiagent Systems, pp. 758–765 (2002) [513]
94. Pentland, A.: Social dynamics: Signals and behavior. In: International Conference Developmental Learning (2004) [513,514]
95. Pentland, A.: Socially aware computation and communication. IEEE Comput. **38**(3), 33–40 (2005) [512-514,533]
96. Pentland, A.: Social signal processing. IEEE Signal Process. Mag. **24**(4), 108–111 (2007) [514,533]
97. Pianesi, F., Mana, N., Cappelletti, A.: Multimodal recognition of personality traits in social interactions. In: International Conference on Multimodal Interfaces, pp. 53–60 (2008) [524]
98. Pianesi, F., Zancanaro, M., Not, E., Leonardi, C., Falcon, V., Lepri, B.: Multimodal support to group dynamics. Pers. Ubiquitous Comput. **12**(3), 181–195 (2008) [525]
99. Poggi, I.: Mind, Hands, Face and Body: Goal and Belief View of Multimodal Communication. Weidler, Berlin (2007) [519,522]
100. Poggi, I., D'Errico, F.: Cognitive modelling of human social signals. In: Social Signal Processing Workshop, in Conjunction with International Conference on Multimedia (2010) [515,517]
101. Raducanu, B., Gatica-Perez, D.: Inferring competitive role patterns in reality TV show through nonverbal analysis. Multimedia Tools Appl. (2010) [525]
102. Rendall, D., Owren, M.J., Ryan, M.J.: What do animal signals mean? Anim. Behav. **78**(2), 233–240 (2009) [515]
103. Richmond, V.P., McCroskey, J.C.: Nonverbal Behaviors in Interpersonal Relations. Allyn & Bacon, Needham Heights (1995) [522]
104. Russell, J.A., Bachorowski, J.A., Fernandez-Dols, J.M.: Facial and vocal expressions of emotion. Annu. Rev. Psychol. **54**(1), 329–349 (2003) [525]
105. Ruttkay, Z., Pelachaud, C.: From Brows to Trust: Evaluating Embodied Conversational Agents. Kluwer Academic, Norwell (2004) [514,527]
106. Sacks, H., Schegloff, E.A., Jefferson, G.: A simplest systematics for the organization of turn taking for conversation. Language **50**(4), 696–735 (1974) [518,525]
107. Salamin, H., Favre, S., Vinciarelli, A.: Automatic role recognition in multiparty recordings: Using social affiliation networks for feature extraction. IEEE Trans. Multimedia **11**(7), 1373–1380 (2009) [525]

108. Scheflen, A.E.: The significance of posture in communication systems. Psychiatry **27**, 316–331 (1964) [522]
109. Scherer, K.R.: Personality inference from voice quality: The loud voice of extroversion. Eur. J. Soc. Psychol. **8**(4), 467–487 (1978) [517]
110. Scherer, K.R.: What does facial expression express? In: Strongman, K.T. (ed.) International Review of Studies of Emotion, vol. 2, pp. 139–165. Wiley, New York (1992) [517]
111. Schmid, K., Marx, D., Samal, A.: Computation of face attractiveness index based on neoclassic canons, symmetry and golden ratio. Pattern Recogn. **41**, 2710–2717 (2008) [524]
112. Schröder, M.: Expressive Speech Synthesis: Past, Present, and Possible Futures. In: Tao, J., Tan, T. (eds.) Affective Information Processing, pp. 111–126. Springer, Berlin? (2009) [513, 527,530]
113. Segerstrale, U., Molnar, P.: Nonverbal Communication: Where Nature Meets Culture. Lawrence Erlbaum Associates, Lawrence (1997) [522]
114. Shannon, C.E., Weaver, W.: The Mathematical Theory of Information. University of Illinois Press, Champaign (1949) [518]
115. ter Maat, M., Heylen, D.: Turn management or impressions management? In: International Conference on Intelligent Virtual Agents, pp. 467–473 (2009) [527]
116. Thorndike, E.L.: Intelligence and its use. Harper's Mag. **140**, 227–235 (1920) [512]
117. Tomkins, S.S.: Consiousness, Imagery and Affect vol. 1. Springer, Berlin (1962) [517]
118. Triandis, H.C.: Culture and Social Behavior. McGraw-Hill, New York (1994) [522]
119. Trouvain, J., Schröder, M.: How (not) to add laughter to synthetic speech. Lect. Notes Comput. Sci. **3068**, 229–232 (2004) [514]
120. Valstar, M.F., Gunes, H., Pantic, M.: How to distinguish posed from spontaneous smiles using geometric features. In: International Conference Multimodal Interfaces, pp. 38–45 (2007) [532]
121. Valstar, M.F., Pantic, M., Ambadar, Z., Cohn, J.F.: Spontaneous vs. posed facial behaviour: Automatic analysis of brow actions. In: International Conference Multimodal Interfaces, pp. 162–170 (2006) [532]
122. Verhencamp, S.L.: Handicap, Index, and Conventional Signal Elements of Bird Song. In: Edpmark, Y., Amundsen, T., Rosenqvist, G. (eds.) Animal Signals: Signalling and Signal Design in Animal Communication, pp. 277–300. Tapir Academic Press, Trondheim (2000) [516]
123. Vinciarelli, A.: Capturing order in social interactions. IEEE Signal Process. Mag. **26**(5), 133–137 (2009) [524]
124. Vinciarelli, A., Pantic, M., Bourlard, H., Pentland, A.: Social signal processing: State-of-the-art and future perspectives of an emerging domain. In: International Conference Multimedia, pp. 1061–1070 (2008) [514,533]
125. Vinciarelli, A., Pantic, M., Bourlard, H.: Social signal processing: Survey of an emerging domain. Image Vis. Comput. **27**(12), 1743–1759 (2009) [514,523,525,529,533]
126. Vinciarelli, A., Pantic, M., Heylen, D., Pelachaud, C., Poggi, I., D'Errico, F., Schröder, M.: Bridging the gap between social animal and unsocial machine: A survey of social signal processing. IEEE Trans. Affect. Comput. (2012, in press) [523,527]
127. Wang, N., Johnson, W.L., Rizzo, P., Shaw, E., Mayer, R.E.: Experimental evaluation of polite interaction tactics for pedagogical agents. In: International Conference Intelligent User Interfaces, pp. 12–19 (2005) [514]
128. Weiser, M.: The computer for the 21st century. Sci. Am. Special Issue on Communications, Computers, and Networks **265**(3), 95–104 (1991) [512]
129. Whitehill, J., Movellan, J.: Personalized facial attractiveness prediction. In: IEEE International Conference on Automatic Face and Gesture Recognition (2008) [524]
130. Woodworth, R.S.: Dynamics of Behavior. Holt, New York (1961) [517]
131. Zahavi, A.: Mate selection: selection for a handicap. J. Theor. Biol. **53**, 205–214 (1975) [516]
132. Zeng, Z., Pantic, M., Roisman, G.I., Huang, T.H.: A survey of affect recognition methods: Audio, visual and spontaneous expressions. IEEE Trans. Pattern Anal. Mach. Intell. **31**(1), 39–58 (2009) [513,523-526]

Chapter 27
Sign Language Recognition

Helen Cooper, Brian Holt, and Richard Bowden

Abstract This chapter covers the key aspects of sign-language recognition (SLR), starting with a brief introduction to the motivations and requirements, followed by a précis of sign linguistics and their impact on the field. The types of data available and the relative merits are explored allowing examination of the features which can be extracted. Classifying the manual aspects of sign (similar to gestures) is then discussed from a tracking and non-tracking viewpoint before summarising some of the approaches to the non-manual aspects of sign languages. Methods for combining the sign classification results into full SLR are given showing the progression towards speech recognition techniques and the further adaptations required for the sign specific case. Finally the current frontiers are discussed and the recent research presented. This covers the task of continuous sign recognition, the work towards true signer independence, how to effectively combine the different modalities of sign, making use of the current linguistic research and adapting to larger more noisy data sets.

27.1 Motivation

While automatic speech recognition has now advanced to the point of being commercially available, automatic Sign Language Recognition (SLR) is still in its infancy. Currently all commercial translation services are human based, and therefore expensive, due to the experienced personnel required.

SLR aims to develop algorithms and methods to correctly identify a sequence of produced signs and to understand their meaning. Many approaches to SLR incorrectly treat the problem as gesture recognition. So research has thus far focussed

H. Cooper (✉) · B. Holt · R. Bowden
University of Surrey, Guildford, GU2 7XH, UK
e-mail: H.M.Cooper@surrey.ac.uk

B. Holt
e-mail: B.Holt@surrey.ac.uk

R. Bowden
e-mail: R.Bowden@surrey.ac.uk

T.B. Moeslund et al. (eds.), *Visual Analysis of Humans*,
DOI 10.1007/978-0-85729-997-0_27, © Springer-Verlag London Limited 2011

on identifying optimal features and classification methods to correctly label a given sign from a set of possible signs. However, sign language is far more than just a collection of well specified gestures.

Sign languages pose the challenge that they are multi-channel; conveying meaning through many modes at once. While the studies of sign language linguistics are still in their early stages, it is already apparent that this makes many of the techniques used by speech recognition unsuitable for SLR. In addition, publicly available data sets are limited both in quantity and quality, rendering many traditional computer vision learning algorithms inadequate for the task of building classifiers. Due to the expense of Human translation and the lack of translation tools, most public services are not translated into sign. There is no commonly used, written form of sign language, so all written communication is in the local spoken language.

This chapter introduces some basic sign linguistics before covering the types of data available and their acquisition methods. This is followed by a discussion on the features used for SLR and the methods for combining them. Finally the current research frontiers and the relating work is presented as an overview of the state of the art.

27.2 Sign Linguistics

Sign consists of three main parts: Manual features involving gestures made with the hands (employing hand shape and motion to convey meaning), Non-Manual Features (NMFs) such as facial expressions or body posture, which can both form part of a sign or modify the meaning of a manual sign, and Finger spelling, where words are spelt out gesturally in the local verbal language. Naturally this is an oversimplification, Sign language is as complex as any spoken language, each sign language has many thousands of signs, each differing from the next by minor changes in hand shape, motion, position, non-manual features or context. Since signed languages evolved alongside spoken languages, they do not mimic their counterparts. For instance, British Sign Language (BSL) grammatical structure loosely follows the sequence of time-line, location, subject, object, verb and question. It is characterised by topic-comment structure where a topic or scene is set up and then commented on [10]. It uses its own syntax which makes use of both manual and non-manual features, simultaneous and sequential patterning and spatial as well as linear arrangement.

Signs can be described at the sub-unit level using phonemes.[1] These encode different elements of a sign. Unlike speech they do not have to occur sequentially, but can be combined in parallel to describe a sign. Studies of ASL by Liddell and Johnson [67] model sign language on the movement-hold system. Signs are broken into sections where an aspect is changing and sections where a state is held steady. This

---

[1]Sometimes referred to as visemes, signemes, cheremes or morphemes. Current linguistic usage suggests phonemes is the accepted term.

is in contrast to the work of Stokoe [102] where different components of the sign are described in different channels; the motion made by the hands, the place at which the sign is performed, the hand shapes, the relative arrangement of the hands and finally the orientation of both the hands and fingers to explain the plane in which the hands sit. Both of these models are valid in their own right and yet they encode different aspects of sign. Within SLR both the movement-hold, sequential information from Liddell and Johnson and the parallel forms of Stokoe are desirable annotations.

Below are described a small subset of the constructs of sign language. There is not room here to fully detail the entire structure of the language, instead the focus is on those that pose significant challenges to the field of SLR.

1. *Adverbs modifying verbs*; signers would not use two signs for 'run quickly' they would modify the sign for run by speeding it up.
2. *Non-Manual Features (NMFs)*; facial expressions and body posture are key in determining the meaning of sentences, e.g. eyebrow position can determine the question type. Some signs are distinguishable only by lip shape, as they share a common manual sign.
3. *Placement*; pronouns like 'he', 'she' or 'it' do not have their own sign, instead the referent is described and allocated a position in the signing space. Future references point to the position, and relationships can be described by pointing at more than one referent.
4. *Classifiers*; these are hand shapes which are used to represent classes of objects, they are used when previously described items interact. e.g. to distinguish between a person chasing a dog and vice versa.
5. *Directional verbs*; these happen between the signer and referent(s), the direction of motion indicates the direction of the verb. Good examples of directional verbs are 'give' and 'phone'. The direction of the verb implicitly conveys which nouns are the subject and object.
6. *Positional signs*; where a sign acts on the part of the body descriptively. e.g. 'bruise' or 'tattoo'.
7. *Body shift*; represented by twisting the shoulders and gaze, often used to indicate role-shifting when relating a dialogue.
8. *Iconicity*; when a sign imitates the thing it represents, it can be altered to give an appropriate representation. e.g. the sign for getting out of bed can be altered between leaping out of bed with energy to a recumbent who is reluctant to rise.
9. *Finger spelling*; where a sign is not known, either by the signer or the recipient, the local spoken word for the sign can be spelt explicitly by finger spelling.

Although SLR and speech recognition are drastically different in many respects, they both suffer from similar issues; co-articulation between signs means that a sign will be modified by those either side of it. Inter-signer differences are large; every signer has their own style, in the same way that everyone has their own accent or handwriting. Also similar to handwriting, signers can be either left hand or right hand dominant. For a left handed signer, most signs will be mirrored, but time line specific ones will be kept consistent with the cultural 'left to right' axis. While it is not obvious how best to include these higher level linguistic constructs of the language, it is obviously essential, if it is true, that continuous SLR is to become reality.

27.3 Data Acquisition and Feature Extraction

Acquiring data is the first step in a SLR system. Given that much of the meaning in sign language is conveyed through manual features, this has been the area of focus of the research up to the present as noted by Ong and Ranganath in their 2005 survey [88].

Many early SLR systems used datagloves and accelerometers to acquire specifics of the hands. The measurements (x, y, z, orientation, velocity etc.) were measured directly using a sensor such as the Polhemus tracker [115] or DataGlove [57, 108]. More often than not, the sensor input was of sufficient discriminatory power that feature extraction was bypassed and the measurements used directly as features [35]. While these techniques gave the advantage of accurate positions, they did not allow full natural movement and constricted the mobility of the signer, altering the signs performed. Trials with a modified glove-like device, which was less constricting [46], attempted to address this problem. However, due to the prohibitive costs of such approaches, the use of vision has become more popular. In the case of vision input, a sequence of images are captured from a combination of cameras (e.g. monocular [129], stereo [50], orthogonal [97]) or other non-invasive sensors. Segen and Kumar [94] used a camera and calibrated light source to compute depth, and Feris et al. [32] used a number of external light sources to illuminate a scene and then used multi-view geometry to construct a depth image. Starner et al. [98] used a front view camera in conjunction with a head mounted camera facing down on the subject's hands to aid recognition. Depth can also be inferred using stereo cameras as was done by Munoz-Salinas et al. [76] or by using side/vertical mounted cameras as with Vogler and Metaxas [111] or the Boston ASL data set [79]. Most recently the Microsoft Kinect™ has offered an affordable depth camera which has made depth a viable option for more researchers. However, at present there are no data sets available and as such the results are limited. There are several projects which are creating sign language data sets; in Germany there is the DGS-Korpus dictionary project collecting data across the country over a 15 yr period [21] or the similar project on a smaller scale in the UK by the BSL Corpus Project [11]. However, these data sets are directed at linguistic research, whereas the cross domain European project DictaSign [22] aims to produce a multi-lingual data set suitable for both linguists and computer vision scientists.

Once data have been acquired they are described via features; the features chosen often depend on the elements of sign language being detected.

27.3.1 Manual Features

Sign language involves many features which are based around the hands, in general there are hand shape/orientation (pose) and movement trajectories, which are similar in principle to gestures. A survey of gesture recognition was performed by Mitra and Acharya [74] giving an overview of the field as it stood in 2007. While many gesture recognition techniques are applicable, Sign language offers a more complex challenge than the traditionally more confined domain of gesture recognition.

27.3.1.1 Tracking Based

Tracking the hands is a non-trivial task since, in a standard sign language conversation, the hands move extremely quickly and are often subject to motion blur. Hands are deformable objects, changing posture as well as position. They occlude each other and the face, making skin segmented approaches more complex. In addition as the hands interact with each other, tracking can be lost, or the hands confused. In early work, the segmentation task was simplified considerably by requiring the subjects to wear coloured gloves. Usually these gloves were single coloured, one for each hand [56]. In some cases, the gloves used were designed so that the hand pose could be better detected; employing coloured markers such as Holden and Owens [49] or different coloured fingers [47]. Zhang et al. [128] made use of multicoloured gloves (where the fingers and palms of the hands were different colours) and used the hands geometry to detect both position and shape. Using coloured gloves reduces the encumbrance to the signer but does not remove it completely. A more natural, realistic approach is without gloves, the most common detection approach uses a skin colour model [4, 52] where a common restriction is long sleeves. Skin colour detection is also used to identify the face position such as in [122]. Often this task is further simplified by restricting the background to a specific colour (chroma keying) [51] or at the very least keeping it uncluttered and static [97]. Zieren and Kraiss [130] explicitly modelled the background which aids the foreground segmentation task. Depth can be used to allow simplification of the problem. Hong et al. [50] and Grzeszcuk et al. [39] used a stereo camera pair from which they generated depth images which were combined with other cues to build models of the person(s) in the image. Fujimura and Liu [34] and Hadfield and Bowden [41] segmented hands on the naive assumption that hands will be the closest objects to the camera.

It is possible to base a tracker solely on skin colour as shown by Imagawa et al. [52] who skin segmented the head and hands before applying a Kalman filter during tracking. Han et al. [43] also showed that the Kalman filter enabled the skin segmented tracking to be robust to occlusions between the head and hands, while Holden et al. [48] considered snake tracking as a way of disambiguating the head from the hands. They initialised each snake as an ellipse from the hand position on the previous frame, using a gradient based optical flow method and shifted the ellipse to the new object position, fitting from that point. This sort of tracker tends to be non-robust to cluttered or moving backgrounds and can be confused by signers wearing short sleeved clothes. Akyol and Alvarado [1] improved on the original colour based skin segmented tracker, by using a combination of skin segmentation and MHIs to find the hands for tracking. Awad et al. [4] presented a face and hand tracking system that combined skin segmentation, frame differencing (motion) and predicted position (from a Kalman filter) in a probabilistic manner. These reduced the confusion with static background images but continued to suffer problems associated with bare forcarms.

Micilotta and Bowden [72] proposed an alternative to colour segmentation, detecting the component parts of the body using Ong and Bowden's detector [86] and using these to infer a model of the current body posture, allowing the hand positions to be tracked across a video sequence. Buehler et al. implemented a robust tracker, which used labelled data to initialise colour models, head/torso detector and HOG pictorial descriptors. It used the distinctive frames in a sequence in much the same way that key frames are used in video encoding, they constrained adjacent frames and as such several passes could be made before the final trajectory is extracted. An alternative to this is the solution proposed by Zieren and Kraiss [130] who tracked multiple hypotheses via body modelling, disambiguating between these hypotheses at the sign level. These backward/forward methods for determining the hand trajectories offer accurate results, at the cost of processing time. Maintaining a trajectory after the hands have interacted also poses a problem. Shamaie and Sutherland [95] tracked bi-manual gestures using a skin segmentation based hand tracker, which calculated bounding box velocities to aid tracking after occlusion or contact. While adaptable to real time use, it suffers from the same problems as other colour only based approaches. Dreuw et al. used dynamic programming to determine the path of the head and hands along a whole video sequence, avoiding such failures at the local level [24] but negating the possibility of real-time application.

The desire for tracked data means that the Kinect™ device has offered the sign recognition community a short-cut to real-time performance. Doliotis et al. have shown that using the Kinect™ tracking in place of their previous skin based results boosts performance from 20% to 95% on a complex data set of ten number gestures [23]. In the relatively short time since its release several proof of concept demonstrations have emerged. Ershaed et al. have focussed on Arabic sign language and have created a system which recognises isolated signs. They present a system working for 4 signs and recognise some close up handshape information [29]. At ESIEA they have been using Fast Artificial Neural Networks to train a system which recognises two French signs [117]. This small vocabulary is a proof of concept but it is unlikely to be scalable to larger lexicons. One of the first videos to be uploaded to the web came from Zafrulla et al. and was an extension of their previous Copy-Cat game for deaf children [124]. The original system uses coloured gloves and accelerometers to track the hands, this was replaced by tracking from the Kinect™. They use solely the upper part of the torso and normalise the skeleton according to arm length. They have an internal dataset containing 6 signs; 2 subject signs, 2 prepositions and 2 object signs. The signs are used in 4 sentences (subject, preposition, object) and they have recorded 20 examples of each. They list under further work that signer independence would be desirable which suggests that their dataset is single signer but this is not made clear. By using a cross validated system they train Hidden Markov Models (HMMs) (Via the Georgia Tech Gesture Toolkit [71]) to recognise the signs. They perform 3 types of tests, those with full grammar constraints getting 100%, those where the number of signs is known getting 99.98% and those with no restrictions getting 98.8%. Cooper et al. have also extended their previous work [18] to use the 3D tracking capabilities of the Kinect™ [19]. By employing hard coded sign phonemes for both motion and location they show results on two data sets of 20 Greek and 40 German signs respectively. They use sequential pattern boosting [84], which combined with the robust phoneme features, produces a solution capable of signer independent recognition. This system has been received some evaluation by the Deaf community, the preliminary results of which are shown in [27].

27.3.1.2 Non-tracking Based

Since the task of hand tracking for sign language is a non-trivial problem, there has been work where signs are detected globally rather than tracked and classified. Wong and Cippola [118] used PCA on motion gradient images of a sequence, obtaining features for a Bayesian classifier. Zahedi et al. investigated several types of appearance based features. They started by using combinations of down-sampled original images, multiplied by binary skin-intensity images and derivatives. These were computed by applying Sobel filters [126]. They then combined skin segmentation with five types of differencing for each frame in a sequence, all are down sampled to obtain features [127]. Following this, their appearance based features were combined with the tracking work of Dreuw et al. [24] and some geometric features in the form of moments. Creating a system which fuses both tracking and non-tracking based approaches [125]. This system is able to achieve 64% accuracy rates on a more complex subset of the Boston data set [79] including continuous sign from three signers. Cooper and Bowden [16] proposed a method for sign language recognition on a small sign subset that bypasses the need for tracking entirely. They classified the motion directly by using volumetric Haar-like features in the spatio-temporal domain. They followed this by demonstrating that non-tracking based approaches can also be used at the sub-unit level by extending the work of [56] to use appearance and spatio-temporal features [15].

The variability of the signers also introduces problems, the temporal inconsistencies between signs are a good example of this. Corradini [20] computed a series of moment features containing information about the position of the head and hands before employing Dynamic Time Warping (DTW) to account for the temporal difference in signs. Results are shown on a small data set of exaggerated gestures which resemble traffic controls. It is unclear how well the DTW will port to the challenge of natural, continuous SLR.

27.3.1.3 Hand Shape

In systems where the whole signer occupies the field of view, the resolution of video is typically not high enough, and the computing power not sufficient for real time processing, so details of the specific hand shape tend to be ignored, or are approximated by extracting geometric features such as the centre of gravity of the hand blob. Using datagloves the hand shape can be described in terms of joint angles and more generically finger openness as shown by Vogler and Metaxas [110]. Jerde et al. combined this type of information with the known constraints of movement of the hands, in order to reduce the complexity of the problem [55]. Others achieved good results using vision based approaches. Ong and Bowden presented a combined hand detector and shape classifier using a boosted cascade classifier [83]. The top level of which detects the deformable model of the hand and the lower levels classified the hand shape into one of several image clusters, using a distance measure based on shape context. This offers 97.4% recognition rate on a database of 300 hand shapes. However, the hand shapes were assigned labels based on their shape context similarity. This means that the labels did not necessarily correspond to known sign hand shapes, nor did a label contain shapes which are actually the same, only those which look the same according to the clustering distance metric. Coogan and Sutherland [14] used a similar principle when they created a hierarchical decision tree, the leaf nodes of which contained the exemplar of a hand shape class, defined by fuzzy k-means clustering of the Eigenspaces resulting from performing PCA on the artificially constructed training images. Using gloved data to give good segmentation of the hands allowed Pahlevanzadeh et al. to use a generic cosine detector to describe basic hand shapes [90] though the system is unlikely to be tractable. Fillbrandt et al. used 2D appearance models to infer 3D posture and shape of the hands [33]. Each appearance model is linked to the others via a network which encodes the transitions between hand shapes, i.e. a model is only linked to another model if the transition between them does not require passage through another model. They tested their solution on a subset of hand shapes and postures but comment that for SLR a more complex model will be required. Hamada et al. used a similar transition principle [42], they matched the part of the hand contour which is not affected by occlusion or background clutter. These methods, while producing good results, require large quantities of labelled data to build accurate models. Liu and Fujimura [69] analysed hand shape by applying a form of template matching that compared the current hand outline to a gradient image of a template using a Chamfer Distance. Athitsos and Sclaroff used a method for matching binary edges from cluttered images, to edges produced by model hand shapes [3]. Each of the possibilities was given a quantitative match value, from which they computed a list of ranked possible hand shapes for the input image. While the method worked well for small angles of rotation it did not perform so well when large variations were introduced. This is unsurprising given the appearance based approach used. Stenger et al. [100] employed shape templates in a degenerate decision tree, which took the form of a cascaded classifier to describe the position of the hands. The posture of the hands could then be classified using a set of exemplar templates, matched using a nearest neighbour classifier. The use of a decision tree improved scalability over previous individual classifier approaches but results in the entire tree needing to be rebuilt should a new template need to be incorporated. Roussos et al. [93] employ an Affine-invariant Modelling of hand Shape-Appearance images, offering a compact and descriptive representation of the hand configuration. The hand-shape features extracted via the fitting of this model are used to construct an unsupervised set of sub-units.

Rezaei et al. used stereo cameras to reconstruct a 3D model of the hand [92]. They computed both loose point correspondences and 3D motion estimation, in order to create the full 3D motion trajectory and pose of the hands. In contrast

Guan et al. [40] used multiple cameras, not to create a 3D model, but instead for a contour based 2D matching approach, they then fused results from across each of the cameras. Oikonomidis et al. use the Kinect™ to acquire real-time depth information about the hand pose [82]. They then optimise the hand model parameters using a variant of Particle Swarm Optimization in order to match the current pose to a model. When using GPU coding they show promising results and are able to achieve frame rates of 15 fps. While this model fitting approach can give the parameters of the hand accurately it requires a further step to extract a known sign hand shape.

27.3.2 Finger Spelling

Manual features are also extended to finger spelling, a subset of sign language. Recognising finger spelling requires careful description of the shapes of the hands and for some languages the motion of the hands.

Isaacs and Foo [53] worked on finger spelling using wavelet features to detect static hand shapes. This approach limited them to non-dynamic alphabets. Liwicki and Everingham also concentrated on BSL finger spelling [70]. They combined HOG features with a HMM to model individual letters and non-letters. This allowed a scalable approach to the problem; unlike some of the previous work by Goh and Holden [37], which combined optical flow features with an HMM but which only encoded the co-articulation present in the data set lexicon. Jennings [54] demonstrates a robust finger tracking system that uses stereo cameras for depth, edges and colour. The system works by attempting to detect and track the finger using many different approaches and then by combining the approaches into a model, and the model which best explains the input data is taken as the solution. The approaches (or channels) are edges from four cameras, stereo from two and colour from one; seven channels in total. The channels are combined using Bayesian framework that reduces to a sum of squared differences equation. Stenger et al. [101] presented a model-based hand tracking system that used quadrics to build the underlying 3D model from which contours (handling occlusion) were generated that could be compared to edges in the image. Tracking is then done using an Unscented Kalman Filter. Feris et al. [32] generated an edge image from depth which is then used to generate a scale and translation invariant feature set very similar to Local Binary Patterns. This method was demonstrated to achieve high recognition rates, notably where other methods failed to discriminate between very similar signs.

Recently, Pugeault and Bowden have exploited the Kinect™ to create a real-time, interactive American Sign Language (ASL) finger spelling system [91]. Using a combination of both depth and colour streams the hand is segmented and Gabor features extracted. A random forest learnt to distinguish between letter hand shapes, gaining an average of 75%. They address the ambiguity between certain hand shapes with an interface allowing the user to choose between plausible letters.

27.3.3 Non-manual Features

In addition to the manual features, there is a significant amount of information contained in the non-manual channels. The most notable of these are the facial expressions, lip shapes (as used by lip readers), as well as head pose which was recently surveyed by Murphy-Chutorian and Trivedi. [78] Little work has currently been performed on body pose, which plays a part during dialogues and stories.

Facial expression recognition can either be explicitly construed for sign language, or a more generic human interaction system. Some expressions, described by Ekman [26], are culturally independent (fear, sadness, happiness, anger, disgust and surprise). Most non-sign related expression research has been based on these categories, resulting in systems which do not always transfer directly to sign language expressions. In this field Yacoob and Davies used temporal information for recognition. They computed optical flow on local face features, to determine which regions of the face move to create each expression [119]. This reliance solely on the motion of the face works well for isolated, exaggerated expressions but will be easily confused by mixed or incomplete expressions as found in the real world. In contrast Moore and Bowden worked in the appearance domain. They used boosted classifiers on chamfer images to describe the forms made by a face during a given expression [75]. Reported accuracies are high but the approach is unlikely to be scalable to larger data sets due to its classifier per expression architecture.

Other branches of emotion detection research use a lower level representation of expression, such as Facial Action Coding System (FACS) [68]. FACS is an expression encoding scheme based on facial muscle movement. In principle, any facial expression can be described using a combination of facial action units (AUs). Koelstra et al. [60] presented methods for recognising these individual action units using both extended MHIs and non-rigid registration using free-form deformations, reporting accuracies over 90%.

Recently the non-sign facial expression recognition community has begun work with less contrived data sets. These approaches are more likely to be applicable to sign expressions, as they will have fewer constraints, having been trained on more natural data sets. An example of this is the work by Sheerman-Chase et al. who combined static and dynamic features from tracked facial features (based on Ong's facial feature tracker [85]) to recognise more abstract facial expressions, such as 'Understanding' or 'Thinking' [96]. They note that their more complex data set, while labelled, is still ambiguous in places due to the disagreement between human annotators. For this reason they constrain their experiments to work on data where the annotators showed strong agreement.

Ming and Ranganath separated emotions and sign language expressions explicitly. Their work split these into lower and upper face signals [73]. The training data were separated by performing Independent Component Analysis (ICA) on PCA derived feature vectors. This was then compared to results from Gabor Wavelet Networks. They showed that while the networks out performed the component analysis, this was only the case for high numbers of wavelets and as such, the required processing time was much higher.

Nguyen and Ranganath then tracked features on the face using a Kanade–Lucas–Tomasi Feature Tracker, commenting on the difficulties posed by inter-signer differences. They proposed a method to cluster face shape spaces from probabilistic PCA to combat these inconsistencies [80]. In later work, they combined this with HMMs and an ANN to recognise four sign language expressions [81]. They concentrate mainly on the tracking framework as a base for recognition, resulting in scope for further extensions to the work at the classification level.

Vogler worked on facial feature tracking within the context of SLR [105–107]. Vogler and Goldstein approach the explicit problem of sign language facial expressions, using a deformable face model [105, 106]. They showed that by matching points to the model and categorising them as inliers or outliers, it is possible to manage occlusions by the hands. They propose that tracking during full occlusion is not necessary, but that instead a 'graceful recovery' should be the goal. This is an interesting and important concept as it suggests that when the signer's mouth is occluded it is not necessary to know the mouth shape. Instead they believe that it can be inferred by the information at either side, in a similar manner to a human observer. While the theory is correct, the implementation may prove challenging.

Krinidis et al. used a deformable surface model to track the face [62]. From the parameters of the fitted surface model at each stage, a characteristic feature vector was created, when combined with Radial Basis Function Interpolation networks it can be used to accurately predict the pan, tilt and roll of the head. Ba and Odobez used appearance models of the colour and texture of faces, combined with tracking information, to estimate pose for visual focus of attention estimation [5]. They learn their models from the Prima-Pointing database of head poses, which contains a wide range of poses. Bailey and Milgram used the same database to present their regression technique, Boosted Input Selection Algorithm for Regression (BISAR) [6]. They combined the responses of block differencing weak classifiers with an ANN. They boosted the final classifiers by rebuilding the ANN after each weak classifier is chosen, using the output to create the weights for selection of the next weak classifier.

Some signs in BSL are disambiguated solely by the lip shapes accompanying them. Lip reading is already an established field, for aiding speech recognition or covert surveillance. It is known that human lip readers rely heavily on context when lip reading and also have training tricks, which allow them to set a baseline for a new subject, such as asking them questions where the answers are either known or easily inferred. Heracleous et al. showed that using the hand shapes from cued speech (where hand gestures are used to disambiguate vowels in spoken words for lip readers) improved the recognition rate of lip reading significantly [45]. They modelled the lip using some basic shape parameters, however it is also possible to track the lips, as shown by Ong and Bowden who use rigid flocks of linear predictors to track 34 points on the contour of the lips [87]. This is then extended to include HMMs to recognise phonemes from the lips [63].

27.4 Recognition

While some machine learning techniques were covered briefly in Sect. 27.3.1.3, this section focusses on how they have been applied to the task of sign recognition. The previous section looked at the low level features which provide the basis for SLR. In this section it is shown how machine learning can create combinations of these low level features to accurately describe a sign, or a sub-unit of sign.

27.4.1 Classification Methods

The earliest work on SLR applied ANNs. However, given the success enjoyed by HMMs in the field of speech recognition, and the similarity of the problem of speech recognition and SLR, HMM based classification has dominated SLR since the mid 90's.

Murakami and Taguchi [77] published one of the first papers on SLR. Their idea was to train an ANN given the features from their dataglove and recognise isolated signs, which worked even in the person independent context. Their system failed to address segmentation of the signs in time and is trained at a sign level, meaning that it is not extendible to continuous recognition. Kim et al. [59] used datagloves to provide x,y,z coordinates as well as angles, from which they trained a Fuzzy Min Max ANN to recognise 25 isolated gestures with a success rate of 85%. Lee et al. [64] used a Fuzzy Min Max ANN to recognise the phonemes of continuous Korean Sign Language (KSL) with a vocabulary of 131 words as well as fingerspelling without modelling a grammar. Waldron and Kim [115] presented an isolated SLR system using ANNs. They trained a first layer ANN for each of the four sub-unit types present in the manual part of ASL, and then combined the results of the first layer in a second layer ANN that actually recognises the isolated words. Huang et al. [51] presented a simple isolated sign recognition system using a Hopfield ANN. Yamaguchi et al. [120] recognised a very small number of words using associative memory (similar to ANNs). Yang et al. [122] presented a general method to extract motion trajectories, and then used them within a Time Delay Neural Network (TDNN) to recognise ASL. Motion segmentation is performed, and then regions of interest were selected using colour and geometry cues. The affine transforms associated with these motion trajectories were concatenated and used to drive the TDNN which classifies accurately and robustly. They demonstrated experimentally that this method achieved convincing results.

HMMs are a technique particularly well suited to the problem of SLR. The temporal aspect of SLR is simplified because it is dealt with automatically by HMMs [89]. The seminal work of Starner and Pentland [98] demonstrated that HMMs present a strong technique for recognising sign language and Grobel and Assan [38] presented a HMM based isolated sign (gesture) recognition system that performed well given the restrictions that it applied.

Vogler and Metaxas [108] show that word-level HMMs are SLR suitable, provided that the movement epenthesis is also taken into consideration. They showed how different HMM topologies (context dependent vs. modelling transient move-ments) yield different results, with explicit modelling of the epenthesis yield-ing better results, and even more so when a statistical language model is intro-duced to aid classification in the presence of ambiguity and co-articulation. Due to the relative disadvantages of HMMs (poor performance when training data are insufficient, no method to weight features dynamically and violations of the stochastic independence assumptions), they coupled the HMM recogniser with mo-tion analysis using computer vision techniques to improve combined recognition rates [111]. In their following work, Vogler and Metaxas [109] demonstrated that Parallel Hidden Markov Models (PaHMMs) are superior to regular HMMs, Facto-rial HMMs and Coupled HMMs for the recognition of sign language due the in-trinsic parallel nature of the phonemes. The major problem though is that regular HMMs are simply not scalable in terms of handling the parallel nature of phonemes present in sign. PaHMMs are presented as a solution to this problem by mod-elling parallel processes independently and combining output probabilities after-wards.

Kim et al. [58] presented a KSL recognition system capable of recognising 5 sentences from a monocular camera input without a restricted grammar. They made use of a Deterministic Finite Automaton (DFA) to model the movement-stroke back to rest (to remove the epenthesis), and recognise with an DFA. Liang and OuhY-oung [65] presented a sign language recognition system that used data captured from a single DataGlove. A feature vector was constructed that comprised posture, position, orientation, and motion. Three different HMMs were trained, and these are combined using a weighted sum of the highest probabilities to generate an overall score. Results were good on constrained data but the method is unlikely to gener-alise to real-world applications.

Kadous [57] presented a sign language recognition system that used instance based learning k-Nearest Neighbors (KNNs) and decision tree learning to classify isolated signs using dataglove features. The results were not as high as ANN systems or HMM based systems, therefore given the relatively simple nature of the task it suggests that recognition using instance based learning such as KNN may not be a suitable approach.

Fang et al. [30] used a cascaded classifier that classified progressively one or two hands, hand shape and finally used a Self-Organizing Feature Map (SOFM)/HMM to classify the words. The novelty of their approach was to allow multiple paths in the cascaded classifier to be taken, allowing for 'fuzziness'. Their approach was fast and robust, delivering very good classification results over a large lexicon, but it is ill-suited to a real-life application.

Other classifiers are suitable when using alternative inputs such as Wong and Cippola [118], who used a limited data set of only 10 basic gestures and require rel-atively large training sets to train their Relevance Vector Machine (RVM). It should also be noted that their RVM requires significantly more training time than other vector machines but in return for a faster classifier which generalises better.

27.4.2 Phoneme Level Representations

Work in the field of sign language linguistics has informed the features used for detection. This is clearly shown in work which classifies in two stages; using first a sign sub-unit layer, followed by a sign level layer. This offers SLR the same advantages as it offered speech recognition. Namely a scalable approach to large vocabularies as well as a more robust solution for time variations between examples.

The early work of Vogler and Metaxas [108] borrowed heavily from the studies of sign language by Liddell and Johnson [67], splitting signs into motion and pause sections. While their later work [109], used PaHMMs on both hand shape and motion sub-units, as proposed by the linguist Stokoe [102]. Work has also concentrated on learning signs from low numbers of examples. Lichtenauer et al. [66] presented a method to automatically construct a sign language classifier for a previously unseen sign. Their method works by collating features for signs from many people then comparing the features of the new sign to that set. They then construct a new classification model for the target sign. This relies on a large training set for the base features (120 signs by 75 people) yet subsequently allows a new sign classifier to be trained using one shot learning. Bowden et al. [9] also presented a sign language recognition system capable of correctly classifying new signs given a single training example. Their approach used a 2 stage classifier bank, the first of which used hard coded classifiers to detect hand shape, arrangement, motion and position sub-units. The second stage removed noise from the 34 bit feature vector (from stage 1) using ICA, before applying temporal dynamics to classify the sign. Results are very high given the low number of training examples and absence of grammar. Kadir et al. [56] extended this work with head and hand detection based on boosting (cascaded weak classifiers), a body-centred description (normalises movements into a 2D space) and then a 2 stage classifier where stage 1 classifier generates linguistic feature vector and stage 2 classifier uses Viterbi on a Markov chain for highest recognition probability. Cooper and Bowden [15] continued this work still further with an approach to SLR that does not require tracking. Instead, a bank of classifiers are used to detect phoneme parts of sign activity by training and classifying (AdaBoost cascade) on certain sign sub-units. These were then combined into a second stage word-level classifier by applying a first order Markov assumption. The results showed that the detection rates achieved with a large lexicon and few training examples were almost equivalent to a tracking based approach.

Alternative methods have looked at data driven approaches to defining sub-units. Yin et al. [123] used an accelerometer glove to gather information about a sign, before applying discriminative feature extraction and similar state tying algorithms, to decide sub-unit level segmentation of the data. Kong et al. [61] and Han et al. [44] have looked at automatic segmentation of the motions of sign into sub-units, using discontinuities in the trajectory and acceleration, to indicate where segments begin and end, these are then clustered into a code book of possible exemplar trajectories using either DTW distance measures, in the case of Han et al. or PCA features by Kong et al.

27.5 Research Frontiers

There are many facets of SLR which have attracted attention in the computer vision community. This section serves to outline the areas which are currently generating the most interest due to the challenges they propose. While some of these are recent topics, others have been challenging computer vision experts for many years. Offered here is a brief overview of the seminal work and the current state of the art in each area.

27.5.1 Continuous Sign Recognition

The majority of work on SLR has been focussed on recognising isolated instances of signs, this is not applicable to a real-world sign language recognition system. The task of recognising continuous sign language is complicated primarily by the problem that in natural sign language, the transition between signs is not clearly marked because the hands will be moving to the starting position of the next sign. This is referred to as the *movement epenthesis* or co-articulation (which borrows from speech terminology). Both Vogler [108] and Gao et al. [36] modelled the movement epenthesis explicitly. Gao et al. [36] used datagloves and found the end points and starting points of all signs in their vocabulary. Clustering these movement transitions into three general clusters using a temporal clustering algorithm (using DTW), allowed them to recognise 750 continuous sign language sentences with an accuracy of 90.8%. More recently, Yang et al. [121] presented a technique by which signs could be isolated from continuous sign data by introducing an adaptive threshold model (which discriminates between signs in a dictionary and non-sign patterns). Applying a short sign detector and an appearance model improved sign spotting accuracy. They then recognise the isolated signs that have been identified.

27.5.2 Signer Independence

A major problem relating to recognition is that of applying the system to a signer on whom the system has not been trained. Zieren and Kraiss [130] applied their previous work to the problem of signer independence. Their results showed that the two problems are robust feature selection and interpersonal variation in the signs. They have shown that their system works very well with signer dependence, but recognition rates drop considerably in real-world situations. In [114] Von Agris et al. presented a comprehensive SLR system using techniques from speech recognition to adapt the signer features and classification, making the recognition task signer independent. In other work [112], they demonstrated how three approaches to speaker adaptation in speech recognition can be successfully applied to the problem of signer adaptation for signer independent sign language recognition. They contrasted a PCA based approach, a maximum likelihood linear regression approach and a MAP estimation approach, and finally showed how they can be combined to yield superior results.

27.5.3 Fusing Multi-modal Sign Data

From the review of SLR by Ong and Ranganath [88], one of their main observations is the lack of attention that non-manual features has received in the literature. This is still the case several years on. Much of the information in a sign is conveyed through this channel, and particularly there are signs that are identical in respect of the manual features and only distinguishable by the non-manual features accompanying the sign. The difficulty is identifying exactly which elements are important to the sign, and which elements are coincidental. For example, does the blink of the signer convey information valuable to the sign, or was the signer simply blinking? This problem of identifying the parts of the sign that contains information relevant to the understanding of the sign makes SLR a complex problem to solve. Non-manual features can broadly be divided into Facial Features which may consist of lip movement, eye gaze and facial expression; and Body Posture, e.g. moving the upper body forward to refer to the future, or sideways to demonstrate the change of the subject in a dialogue. While, as described in section 27.3.3, there has been some work towards the facial features, very little work has been done in the literature regarding the role of body posture in SLR. The next step in the puzzle is how to combine the information from the manual and non-manual streams.

Von Agris et al. [113] attempted to quantify the significance of non-manual features in SLR, finding that the overall recognition rate was improved by including non-manual features in the recognition process. They merged manual features with (facial) non-manual features that are modelled using an AAM. After showing how features are extracted from the AAM, they presented results of both continuous and isolated sign recognition using manual features and non-manual features. Results showed that some signs of Deutsche Gebärdensprache/German sign language (DGS) can be recognised based on non-manual features alone, but generally the recognition rate increases by between 1.5% and 6% upon inclusion of non-manual features. In [114], Von Agris et al. present a comprehensive sign language recognition system using images from a single camera. The system was developed to use manual and non-manual features in a PaHMM to recognise signs, and furthermore, statistical language modelling is applied and compared.

Aran et al. [2] compared various methods to integrate manual features and non-manual features in a sign language recognition system. Fundamentally they have identified a two step classification process, whereby the first step involves classifying based on manual signs. When there was ambiguity, they introduced a second stage classifier to use non-manual signs to resolve the problem. While this might appear a viable approach, it is not clear from sign language linguistics that it is scalable to the full SLR problem.

27.5.4 Using Linguistics

The task of recognition is often simplified by forcing the possible word sequence to conform to a grammar which limits the potential choices and thereby improves recognition rates [9, 48, 98, 116]. N-Gram grammars are often used to improve recognition rates, most often bi-gram [35, 47, 89] but also uni-gram [7]. Bungeroth and Ney [13] demonstrated that statistical sign language translation using the Bayes rule is possible and has the potential to be developed into a real-world translation tool. Bauer et al. [8] presented a sign language translation system consisting of a SLR module which fed a translation module. Recognition was done on word-level HMMs (high accuracy rate, but not scalable), and the translation was done using statistical grammars developed from the data.

27.5.5 Generalising to More Complex Corpora

Due to the lack of adequately labelled data sets, research has turned to weakly supervised approaches. Several groups have presented work aligning subtitles with signed TV broadcasts. Farhadi and Forsyth [31] used HMMs with both static and dynamic features, to find estimates of the start and end of a sign, before building a discriminative word model to perform word spotting on 31 different words over an 80000 frame children's film. Buehler et al. [12] used 10.5 hours of TV data, showing detailed results for 41 signs with full ground truth, alongside more generic results for a larger 210 word list. They achieve this by creating a distance metric for signs, based on the hand trajectory, shape and orientation and performing a brute force search. Cooper and Bowden [17] used hand and head positions in combination with data mining to extract 23 signs from a 30 minute TV broadcast. By adapting the mining to create a temporally constrained implementation they introduced a viable alternative to the brute force search. Stein et al. [99] are collating a series of weather broadcasts in DGS and German. This data set will also contain the DGS glosses which will enable users to better quantify the results of weakly supervised approaches.

27.6 Conclusion

SLR has long since advanced beyond classifying isolated signs or alphabet forms for finger spelling. While the field may continue to draw on the advances in gesture recognition the focus has shifted to approach the more linguistic features associated with the challenge. Work has developed on extracting signs from continuous streams and using linguistic grammars to aid recognition. However, there is still much to be learnt from relevant fields such as speech recognition or hand writing recognition. In addition, while some have imposed grammatical rules from linguistics, others have looked at data driven approaches, both have their merits since the linguistics of most sign languages are still in their infancy.

While the community continues to discuss the need for including non-manual features, few have actually done so. Those who have [2, 113] concentrate solely on the facial expressions of sign. There is still much to be explored in the field of body posture or placement and classifier (hand-shape) combinations.

Finally, to compound all these challenges, there is the issue of signer independence. While larger data sets are starting to appear, few allow true tests of signer independence over long continuous sequences. Maybe this is one of the most urgent problems in SLR that of creating data sets which are not only realistic, but also well annotated to facilitate machine learning.

Despite these problems recent uses of SLR include translation to spoken language, or to another sign language when combined with avatar technology [25, 114]. Sign video data once recognised can be compressed using SLR into an encoded form (e.g. Signing Gesture Markup Language (SiGML) [28]) for efficient transmission over a network. SLR is also set to be used as an annotation aid, to automate annotation of sign video for linguistic research, currently a time-consuming and expensive task.

27.6.1 Further Reading

Recommendations for further reading on sign-language recognition include: [88, 103, 104].

Acknowledgements This research was supported by funding from the European Community's Seventh Framework Programme (FP7/2007-2013) under grant agreement no 231135 – DictaSign.

References

1. Akyol, S., Alvarado, P.: Finding relevant image content for mobile sign language recognition. In: Procs. of IASTED Int. Conf. on Signal Processing, Pattern Recognition and Application, pp. 48–52, Rhodes, Greece (3–6 July 2001) [543]
2. Aran, O., Burger, T., Caplier, A., Akarun, L. A belief-based sequential fusion approach for fusing manual signs and non-manual signals. Pattern Recognit. Lett. **42**(5), 812–822 (2009) [554,556]
3. Athitsos, V., Sclaroff, S.: Estimating 3D hand pose from a cluttered image. In: Procs. of CVPR, vol. 2, Madison WI, USA (June 2003) [546]
4. Awad, G., Han, J., Sutherland, A.: A unified system for segmentation and tracking of face and hands in sign language recognition. In: Procs. of ICPR, Hong Kong, China, pp. 239–242 (August 2006) [543]
5. Ba, S.O., Odobez, J.M.: Visual focus of attention estimation from head pose posterior probability distributions. In: Procs. of IEEE Int. Conf. on Multimedia and Expo, pp. 53–56 (2008) [549]
6. Bailly, K., Milgram, M.: Bisar: Boosted input selection algorithm for regression. In: Procs. of Int. Joint Conf. on Neural Networks, pp. 249–255 (2009) [549]

7. Bauer, B., Hienz, H., Kraiss, K. Video-based continuous sign language recognition using statistical methods. In: Procs. of ICPR, Barcelona, Spain, vol. 15, pp. 463–466 (September 2000) [555]

8. Bauer, B., Nießen, S., Hienz, H.: Towards an automatic sign language translation system. In: Procs. of Int. Wkshp: Physicality and Tangibility in Interaction: Towards New Paradigms for Interaction Beyond the Desktop, Siena, Italy (1999) [555]

9. Bowden, R., Windridge, D., Kadir, T., Zisserman, A., Brady, M.: A linguistic feature vector for the visual interpretation of sign language. In: Procs. of ECCV, Prague, Czech Republic. LNCS, pp. 390–401, Springer, Berlin (11–14 May 2004) [552,555]

10. British Deaf Association: Dictionary of British Sign Language/English. Faber & Faber, London (1992) [540]

11. BSL Corpus Project. Bsl corpus project site (2010) [542]

12. Buehler, M., Everingham, P., Zisserman, A.: Learning sign language by watching TV (using weakly aligned subtitles). In: Procs. of CVPR, Miami, FL, USA, pp. 2961–2968 (20–26 June 2009) [555]

13. Bungeroth, J., Ney, H.: Statistical sign language translation. In: Procs. of LREC: Wkshp: Representation and Processing of Sign Languages, Lisbon, Portugal, pp. 105–108 (26–28 May 2004) [555]

14. Coogan, T., Sutherland, A.: Transformation invariance in hand shape recognition. In: Procs. of ICPR, Hong Kong, China, pp. 485–488 (August 2006) [546]

15. Cooper, H., Bowden, R.: Large lexicon detection of sign language. In: Procs. of ICCV: Wkshp: Human–Computer Interaction, Rio de Janeiro, Brazil, pp. 88–97 (16–19 October 2007) [545,552]

16. Cooper, H., Bowden, R.: Sign language recognition using boosted volumetric features. In: Procs. of IAPR Conf. on Machine Vision Applications, Tokyo, Japan, pp. 359–362 (16–18 May 2007) [545]

17. Cooper, H., Bowden, R.: Learning signs from subtitles: A weakly supervised approach to sign language recognition. In: Procs. of CVPR, Miami, FL, USA, pp. 2568–2574 (20–26 June 2009) [555]

18. Cooper, H., Bowden, R.: Sign language recognition using linguistically derived sub-units. In: Workshop on the Representation and Processing of Sign Languages: Corpora and Sign Languages Technologies, Valetta, Malta, (17–23 May 2010) [544]

19. Cooper, H., Ong, E.-J., Bowden, R.: Give me a sign: An interactive sign dictionary. Technical report, University of Surrey (2011) [544]

20. Corradini, A.: Dynamic time warping for off-line recognition of a small gesture vocabulary. In: Procs. of ICCV: Wkshp: Recognition, Analysis, and Tracking of Faces and Gestures in Real-Time Systems, Vancouver, BC, pp. 82–90. IEEE Comput. Soc., Los Alamitos (9–12 July 2001) [545]

21. DGS-Corpus. Dgs-corpus website (2010) [542]

22. DictaSign Project. Dictasign project website (2010) [542]

23. Doliotis, P., Stefan, A., Mcmurrough, C., Eckhard, D., Athitsos, V.: Comparing gesture recognition accuracy using color and depth information. In: Conference on Pervasive Technologies Related to Assistive Environments (PETRA) (May 2011) [544]

24. Dreuw, P., Deselaers, T., Rybach, D., Keysers, D., Ney, H.: Tracking using dynamic programming for appearance-based sign language recognition. In: Procs. of FGR, Southampton, UK, pp. 293–298 (10–12 April 2006) [544,545]

25. Efthimiou, E., Fotinea, S.-E., Vogler, C., Hanke, T., Glauert, J., Bowden, R., Braffort, A., Collet, C., Maragos, P., Segouat, J.: Sign language recognition, generation, and modelling: A research effort with applications in deaf communication. In: Procs. of Int. Conf. on Universal Access in Human–Computer Interaction. Addressing Diversity, San Diego, CA, USA, vol. 1, pp. 21–30, Springer, Berlin (19–24 July 2009) [556]

26. Ekman, P.: Basic emotions. In: Dalgleish, T., Power, T. (eds.) The Handbook of Cognition and Emotion, pp. 45–60. Wiley, New York (1999) [548]

27. Elliott, R., Cooper, H., Ong, E.-J., Glauert, J., Bowden, R., Lefebvre-Albaret, F.: Search-by-example in multilingual sign language databases. In: ACM SIGACCESS Conference on Computers and Accessibility (ASSETS): Sign Language Translation and Avatar Technology, Dundee, UK (23 October 2011) [545]

28. Elliott, R., Glauert, J., Kennaway, J., Parsons, K.: D5-2: SiGML Definition. ViSiCAST Project working document (2001) [556]

29. Ershaed, H., Al-Alali, I., Khasawneh, N., Fraiwan, M.: An arabic sign language computer interface using the Xbox Kinect. In: Annual Undergraduate Research Conf. on Applied Computing, Dubai, UAE (May 2011) [544]

30. Gaolin, F., Gao, W., Debin, Z.: Large vocabulary sign language recognition based on fuzzy decision trees. IEEE Trans. Syst. Man Cybern., Part A, Syst. Hum., **34**(3), 305–314 (2004) [551]

31. Farhadi, A., Forsyth, D.: Aligning ASL for statistical translation using a discriminative word model. In: Procs. of CVPR, New York, NY, USA, pp. 1471–1476 (June 2006) [555]

32. Feris, R., Turk, M., Raskar, R., Tan, K., Ohashi, G.: Exploiting depth discontinuities for vision-based fingerspelling recognition. In: Procs. of CVPR: Wkshp, Washington, DC, USA vol. 10, IEEE Comput. Soc., Los Alamitos (June 2004) [542,547]

33. Fillbrandt, H., Akyol, S., Kraiss, K.-F.: Extraction of 3D hand shape and posture from image sequences for sign language recognition. In: Procs. of ICCV: Wkshp: Analysis and Modeling of Faces and Gestures, Nice, France, pp. 181–186 (14–18 October 2003) [546]

34. Fujimura, K., Liu, X.: Sign recognition using depth image streams. In: Procs. of FGR, Southampton, UK, pp. 381–386 (10–12 April 2006) [543]

35. Gao, W., Ma, J., Wu, J., Wang, C.: Sign language recognition based on HMM/ANN/DP. Int. J. Pattern Recognit. Artif. Intell. **14**(5), 587–602 (2000) [542,555]

36. Gao, W., Fang, G., Zhao, D., Chen, Y.: Transition movement models for large vocabulary continuous sign language recognition. In: Procs. of FGR, Seoul, Korea, pp. 553–558 (17–19 May 2004) [553]

37. Goh, P., Holden, E.-J.: Dynamic fingerspelling recognition using geometric and motion features. In: Procs. of ICIP, pp. 2741–2744 (2006) [547]

38. Grobel, K., Assan, M.: Isolated sign language recognition using hidden Markov models. In: Procs. of IEEE Int. Conf. on Systems, Man, and Cybernetics, Orlando, FL, USA, vol. 1, pp. 162–167 (12–15 October 1997) [550]

39. Grzeszcuk, R., Bradski, G., Chu, M.H., Bouguet, J.Y.: Stereo based gesture recognition invariant to 3d pose and lighting. In: Procs. of CVPR, vol. 1 (2000) [543]

40. Guan, H., Chang, J.S., Chen, L., Feris, R.S., Turk, M.: Multi-view appearance-based 3D hand pose estimation, p. 154 [547]

41. Hadfield, S., Bowden, R.: Generalised pose estimation using depth. In: Procs. of ECCV Int. Wkshp: Sign, Gesture, Activity, Heraklion, Crete (5–11 September 2010) [543]

42. Hamada, Y., Shimada, N., Shirai, Y.: Hand shape estimation under complex backgrounds for sign language recognition. In: Procs. of FGR, Seoul, Korea, pp. 589–594 (17–19 May 2004) [546]

43. Han, J., Awad, G., Sutherland, A.: Automatic skin segmentation and tracking in sign language recognition. IET Comput. Vis. **3**(1), 24–35 (2009) [543]

44. Han, J.W., Awad, G., Sutherland, A.: Modelling and segmenting subunits for sign language recognition based on hand motion analysis. Pattern Recognit. Lett. **30**(6), 623–633 (2009) [552]

45. Heracleous, P., Aboutabit, N., Beautemps, D.: Lip shape and hand position fusion for automatic vowel recognition in cued speech for French. IEEE Signal Process. Lett. **16**(5), 339–342 (2009) [549]

46. Hernandez-Rebollar, J.L., Lindeman, R.W., Kyriakopoulos, N.: A multi-class pattern recognition system for practical finger spelling translation. In: Procs. of IEEE Int. Conf. on Multimodal Interfaces, p. 185. IEEE Comput. Soc., Los Alamitos (2002) [542]

47. Hienz, H., Bauer, B., Karl-Friedrich, K.: HMM based continuous sign language recognition using stochastic grammars. In: Procs. of GW, Gif-sur-Yvette, France, pp. 185–196. Springer, Berlin (17–19 March 1999) [543,555]

48. Holden, E.J., Lee, G., Owens, R.: Australian sign language recognition. Mach. Vis. Appl. **16**(5), 312–320 (2005) [543,555]
49. Holden, E.J., Owens, R.: Visual sign language recognition. In: Procs. of Int. Wkshp: Theoretical Foundations of Computer Vision, Dagstuhl Castle, Germany. LNCS, vol. 2032, pp. 270–288. Springer, Berlin (12–17 March 2000) [543]
50. Hong, S., Setiawan, N.A., Lee, C.: Real-time vision based gesture recognition for human-robot interaction. In: Procs. of Int. Conf. on Knowledge-Based and Intelligent Information & Engineering Systems: Italian Wkshp: Neural Networks, Vietri sul Mare, Italy. LNCS, vol. 4692, p. 493. Springer, Berlin (12–14 September 2007) [542,543]
51. Huang, C.-L., Huang, W.-Y., Lien, C.-C.: Sign language recognition using 3D Hopfield neural network. In: Procs. of ICIP, vol. 2, pp. 611–614 (23–26 October 1995) [543,550]
52. Imagawa, K., Lu, S., Igi, S.: Color-based hands tracking system for sign language recognition. In: Procs. of FGR, Nara, Japan, pp. 462–467 (14–16 April 1998) [543]
53. Isaacs, J., Foo, J.S.: Hand pose estimation for American sign language recognition. In: Procs. of Southeastern Symposium on System Theory, Atlanta, GA, USA, pp. 132–136 (March 2004) [547]
54. Jennings, C.: Robust finger tracking with multiple cameras. In: Procs. of ICCV: Wkshp: Recognition, Analysis, and Tracking of Faces and Gestures in Real-Time Systems, Corfu, Greece, pp. 152–160 (21–24 September 1999) [547]
55. Jerde, T.E., Soechting, J.F., Flanders, M.: Biological constraints simplify the recognition of hand shapes. IEEE Trans. Biomed. Eng. **50**(2), 265–269 (2003) [545]
56. Kadir, T., Bowden, R., Ong, E.J., Zisserman, A.: Minimal training, large lexicon, unconstrained sign language recognition. In: Procs. of BMVC, Kingston, UK, pp. 939–948 (7–9 September 2004) [543,545,552]
57. Kadous, M.W.: Machine recognition of Auslan signs using PowerGloves: Towards large-lexicon recognition of sign language. In: Procs. of Wkshp: Integration of Gesture in Language and Speech (1996) [542,551]
58. Kim, J.B., Park, K.H., Bang, W.C., Kim, J.S., Bien, Z.: Continuous Korean sign language recognition using automata based gesture segmentation and hidden Markov model. In: Procs. of Int. Conf. on Control, Automation and Systems, pp. 822–825 (2001) [551]
59. Kim, J.-S., Jang, W., Bien, Z.: A dynamic gesture recognition system for the Korean sign language (KSL). IEEE Trans. Syst. Man Cybern., Part B, Cybern. **26**(2), 354–359 (1996) [550]
60. Koelstra, S., Pantic, M., Patras, I.: A dynamic texture-based approach to recognition of facial actions and their temporal models. IEEE Trans. Pattern Anal. Mach. Intell. **32**(11), 1940–1954 (2010) [548]
61. Kong, W.W., Ranganath, S.: Automatic hand trajectory segmentation and phoneme transcription for sign language. In: Procs. of FGR, Amsterdam, The Netherlands, pp. 1–6 (17–19 September 2008) [552]
62. Krinidis, M., Nikolaidis, N., Pitas, I.: 3-d head pose estimation in monocular video sequences using deformable surfaces and radial basis functions. IEEE Trans. Circuits Syst. Video Technol. **19**(2), 261–272 (2009) [549]
63. Lan, Y., Harvey, R., Theobald, B.-J., Ong, E.-J., Bowdenn R.: Comparing visual features for lipreading. In: Procs. of Int. Conf. Auditory-visual Speech Processing, Norwich, UK (2009) [549]
64. Lee, C.-S., Bien, Z., Park, G.-T., Jang, W., Kim, J.-S., Kim, S.-K.: Real-time recognition system of Korean sign language based on elementary components. In: Procs. of IEEE Int. Conf. on Fuzzy Systems, vol. 3, pp. 1463–1468 (1–5 July 1997) [550]
65. Liang, R.H., Ouhyoung, M.: A real-time continuous gesture recognition system for sign language. In: Procs. of FGR, Nara, Japan, pp. 558–567 (14–16 April 1998) [551]
66. Lichtenauer, J., Hendriks, E., Reinders, M.: Learning to recognize a sign from a single example. In: Procs. of FGR, Amsterdam, The Netherlands, pp. 1–6 (17–19 September 2008) [552]
67. Liddell, S.K., Johnson, R.E.: American sign language: The phonological base. Sign Lang. Stud. **64**, 195–278 (1989) [540,552]

68. Lien, J.-J.J., Kanade, T., Cohn, J., Li, C.-C.: Automated facial expression recognition based on FACS action units. In: Procs. of FGR, Nara, Japan, pp. 390–395 (14–16 April 1998) [548]
69. Liu, X., Fujimura, K.: Hand gesture recognition using depth data. In: Procs. of FGR, Seoul, Korea, pp. 529–534 (17–19 May 2004) [546]
70. Liwicki, S., Everingham, M.: Automatic recognition of fingerspelled words in British sign language. In: Procs. of CVPR, Miami, FL, USA, pp. 50–57 (20–26 June 2009) [547]
71. Lyons, K., Brashear, H., Westeyn, T.L., Kim, J.S., Starner, T.: GART: The gesture and activity recognition toolkit. In: Procs. of Int. Conf. HCI, Beijing, China, pp. 718–727 (July 2007) [544]
72. Micilotta, A., Bowden, R.: View-based location and tracking of body parts for visual interaction. In: Procs. of BMVC, Kingston, UK, pp. 849–858 (7–9 September 2004) [543]
73. Ming, K.W., Ranganath, S.: Representations for facial expressions. In: Procs. of Int. Conf. on Control, Automation, Robotics and Vision, vol. 2, pp. 716–721 (2002) [548]
74. Mitra, S., Acharya, T.: Gesture recognition: A survey. IEEE Trans. Syst. Man Cybern., Part C, Appl. Rev. **37**(3), 311–324 (2007) [542]
75. Moore, S., Bowden, R.: Automatic facial expression recognition using boosted discriminatory classifiers. In: Procs. of ICCV: Wkshp: Analysis and Modeling of Faces and Gestures, Rio de Janeiro, Brazil, (16–19 October 2007) [548]
76. Munoz-Salinas, R., Medina-Carnicer, R., Madrid-Cuevas, F.J., Carmona-Poyato, A.: Depth silhouettes for gesture recognition. Pattern Recognit. Lett. **29**(3), 319–329 (2008) [542]
77. Murakami, K., Taguchi, H.: Gesture recognition using recurrent neural networks. In: Procs. of SIGCHI Conf. on Human factors in computing systems: Reaching through technology, pp. 237–242. ACM, New York (1991) [550]
78. Murphy-Chutorian, E., Trivedi, M. M.: Head pose estimation in computer vision: A survey. IEEE Trans. Pattern Anal. Mach. Intell. **31**(4), 607–626 (2009) [548]
79. Neidle, C.: National centre for sign language and gesture resources (2006) [542,545]
80. Nguyen, T.D., Ranganath, S.: Towards recognition of facial expressions in sign language: Tracking facial features under occlusion. In: Procs. of ICIP, pp. 3228–3231 (12–15 October 2008) [549]
81. Nguyen, T.D., Ranganath, S.: Tracking facial features under occlusions and recognizing facial expressions in sign language. In: Procs. of FGR, Amsterdam, The Netherlands, pp. 1–7 (17–19 September 2008) [549]
82. Oikonomidis, I., Kyriazis, N., Argyros, A.A.: Efficient model-based 3D tracking of hand articulations using Kinect. In: Procs. of BMVC, Dundee, UK (August 29 – September 10 2011) [547]
83. Ong, E.-J., Bowden, R.: A boosted classifier tree for hand shape detection. In: Procs. of FGR, Seoul, Korea, pp. 889–894 (17–19 May 2004) [546]
84. Ong, E.-J., Bowden, R.: Learning sequential patterns for lipreading. In: Procs. of BMVC, Dundee, UK (August 29 – September 10 2011) [544]
85. Ong, E.-J., Bowden, R.: Robust facial feature tracking using shape-constrained multiresolution selected linear predictors. IEEE Trans. Pattern Anal. Mach. Intell. **33**(9), 1844–1859 (September 2011). doi:10.1109/TPAMI.2010.205 [548]
86. Ong, E.-J., Bowden, R.: Detection and segmentation of hand shapes using boosted classifiers. In: Procs. of FGR, Seoul, Korea, (17–19 May 2004) [543]
87. Ong, E.-J., Bowden, R.: Robust lip-tracking using rigid flocks of selected linear predictors. In: Procs. of FGR, Amsterdam, The Netherlands (17–19 September 2008) [549]
88. Ong, S.C.W., Ranganath, S.: Automatic sign language analysis: A survey and the future beyond lexical meaning. IEEE Trans. Pattern Anal. Mach. Intell. **27**(6), 873–891 (2005) [542, 554,556]
89. Ouhyoung, M., Liang, R.-H.. A sign language recognition system using hidden Markov model and context sensitive search. In: Procs. of ACM Virtual Reality Software and Technology Conference, pp. 59–66 (1996) [550,555]
90. Pahlevanzadeh, M., Vafadoost, M., Shahnazi, M.: Sign language recognition. In: Procs. of Int. Symposium on Signal Processing and Its Applications, pp. 1–4 (12–15 February 2007) [546]

91. Pugeault, N., Bowden, R.: Spelling it out: Real-time ASL fingerspelling recognition. In: Consumer Depth Cameras for Computer Vision (CDC4CV), Barcelona, Spain (7–11 November, 2011) [547]

92. Rezaei, A., Vafadoost, M., Rezaei, S., Daliri, A.: 3D pose estimation via elliptical Fourier descriptors for deformable hand representations. In: Procs. of Int. Conf. on Bioinformatics and Biomedical Engineering, pp. 1871–1875 (16–18 May 2008) [546]

93. Roussos, A., Theodorakis, S., Pitsikalis, P., Maragos, P.: Hand tracking and affine shape-appearance handshape sub-units in continuous sign language recognition. In: Workshop on Sign, Gesture and Activity, 11th European Conference on Computer Vision (ECCV) (2010) [546]

94. Segen, J., Kumar, S.: Shadow gestures: 3D hand pose estimation using a single camera. In: Procs. of CVPR, vol. 1, Fort Collins, CO, USA (23–25 June 1999) [542]

95. Shamaie, A., Sutherland, A.: A dynamic model for real-time tracking of hands in bimanual movements. In: Procs. of GW, Genova, Italy, pp. 172–179 (15–17 April 2003) [544]

96. Sheerman-Chase, T., Ong, E.-J., Bowden, R.: Feature selection of facial displays for detection of non verbal communication in natural conversation. In: Procs. of ICCV: Wkshp: Human–Computer Interaction, Kyoto, Japan, pp. 1985–1992 (29 September – 2 October 2009) [548]

97. Starner, T., Pentland, A.: Real-time American sign language recognition from video using hidden Markov models. In: Procs. of Int. Symposium on Computer Vision, pp. 265–270 (21–23 November 1995) [542,543]

98. Starner, T., Weaver, J., Pentland, A.: Real-time American sign language recognition using desk and wearable computer based video. IEEE Trans. Pattern Anal. Mach. Intell. 20(12), 1371–1375 (1998) [542,550,555]

99. Stein, D., Forster, J., Zelle, U., Dreuw, P., Ney, H.: Analysis of the German sign language weather forecast corpus. In: Workshop on the Representation and Processing of Sign Languages: Corpora and Sign Language Technologies, Valletta, Malta, pp. 225–230 (May 2010) [555]

100. Stenger, B.: Template-based hand pose recognition using multiple cues. In: Procs. of ACCV, Hyderabad, India, vol. 2, pp. 551–561. Springer, Berlin (13–16 January 2006) [546]

101. Stenger, B., Mendonca, P.R.S., Cipolla, R.: Model-based 3D tracking of an articulated hand. In: Procs. of CVPR, Kauai, HI, USA, vol. 2 (December 2001) [547]

102. Stokoe, W.C.: Sign language structure: An outline of the visual communication systems of the American deaf. Stud. Linguist., Occas. Pap. 8, 3–37 (1960) [541,552]

103. Sutton-Spence, R., Woll, B.: The Linguistics of British Sign Language: An Introduction. Cambridge University Press, Cambridge (1999) [556]

104. Valli, C., Lucas, C.: Linguistics of American Sign Language: An Introduction. Gallaudet University Press, Washington (2000) [556]

105. Vogler, C., Goldenstein, S.: Analysis of facial expressions in American sign language. In: Procs. of Int. Conf. on Universal Access in Human–Computer Interaction, Las Vegas, Nevada, USA (2005) [549]

106. Vogler, C., Goldenstein, S.: Facial movement analysis in ASL. Universal Access in the Information Society 6(4), 363–374 (2008) [549]

107. Vogler, C., Li, Z., Kanaujia, A., Goldenstein, S., Metaxas, D.: The best of both worlds: Combining 3D deformable models with active shape models. In: Procs. of ICCV, Rio de Janeiro, Brazil, pp. 1–7 (16–19 October 2007) [549]

108. Vogler, C., Metaxas, D.: Adapting hidden Markov models for ASL recognition by using three-dimensional computer vision methods. In: Procs. of IEEE Int. Conf. on Systems, Man, and Cybernetics, Orlando, FL, USA, vol. 1, pp. 156–161 (12–15 October 1997) [542,550, 552,553]

109. Vogler, C., Metaxas, D.: Parallel hidden Markov models for American sign language recognition. In: Procs. of ICCV, Corfu, Greece, pp. 116–122 (21–24 September 1999) [551,552]

110. Vogler, C., Metaxas, D.: Handshapes and movements: Multiple-channel American sign language recognition. In: Procs. of GW, Genova, Italy, pp. 247–258 (15–17 April 2003) [545]

111. Vogler, C., Metaxas, D.: ASL recognition based on a coupling between HMMs and 3D motion analysis. In: Procs. of ICCV, Bombay, India pp. 363–369. IEEE Comput. Soc., Los Alamitos (4–7 January 1998) [542,551]

112. von Agris, U., Blomer, C., Kraiss, K.-F.: Rapid signer adaptation for continuous sign language recognition using a combined approach of eigenvoices, MLLR, and MAP. In: Procs. of ICPR, Tampa, Florida, USA, pp. 1–4 (8–11 December 2008) [553]

113. von Agris, U., Knorr, M., Kraiss, K.-F.: The significance of facial features for automatic sign language recognition. In: Procs. of FGR, Amsterdam, The Netherlands, pp. 1–6 (17–19 September 2008) [554,556]

114. von Agris, U., Zieren, J., Canzler, U., Bauer, B., Kraiss, K.-F.: Recent developments in visual sign language recognition. Univers. Access Inf. Soc. **6**(4), 323–362 (2008) [553,554,556]

115. Waldron, M.B., Kim, S.: Isolated ASL sign recognition system for deaf persons. IEEE Trans. Rehabil. Eng. **3**(3), 261–271 (1995) [542,550]

116. Wang, C., Gao, W., Shan, S.: An approach based on phonemes to large vocabulary Chinese sign language recognition. In: Procs. of FGR, Washington, DC, USA, pp. 411–416 (20–21 May 2002) [555]

117. Wassner, H.: Kinect + Reseau de Neurone = Reconnaissance de Gestes. http://tinyurl.com/5wbteug (May 2011) [544]

118. Wong, S.-F., Cipolla, R.: Real-time interpretation of hand motions using a sparse Bayesian classifier on motion gradient orientation images. In: Procs. of BMVC, Oxford, UK, vol. 1, pp. 379–388 (6–8 September 2005) [545,551]

119. Yacoob, Y., Davis, L.S.: Recognizing human facial expressions from long image sequences using optical-flow. IEEE Trans. Pattern Anal. Mach. Intell. **18**(6), 636–642 (1996) [548]

120. Yamaguchi, T., Yoshihara, M., Akiba, M., Kuga, M., Kanazawa, N., Kamata, K.: Japanese sign language recognition system using information infrastructure. In: Procs. of IEEE Int. Conf. on Fuzzy Systems, vol. 5, pp. 65–66 (20–24 March 1995) [550]

121. Yang, H.-D., Sclaroff, S., Lee, S.-W.: Sign language spotting with a threshold model based on conditional random fields. IEEE Trans. Pattern Anal. Mach. Intell. **31**(7), 1264–1277 (2009) [553]

122. Yang, M.-H., Ahuja, N., Tabb, M.: Extraction of 2D motion trajectories and its application to hand gesture recognition. IEEE Trans. Pattern Anal. Mach. Intell. **24**, 1061–1074 (2002) [543,550]

123. Yin, P., Starner, T., Hamilton, H., Essa, I., Rehg, J.M.: Learning the basic units in American sign language using discriminative segmental feature selection. In: Procs. of ASSP, Taipei, Taiwan, pp. 4757–4760 (19–24 April 2009) [552]

124. Zafrulla, Z., Brashear, H., Presti, P., Hamilton, H., Starner, T.: Copycat – Center for Accessible Technology in Sign. http://tinyurl.com/3tksn6s, http://www.youtube.com/watch?v=qFH5rSzmgFE&feature=related (2010) [544]

125. Zahedi, M., Dreuw, P., Rybach, D., Deselaers, T., Ney, H.: Geometric features for improving continuous appearance-based sign language recognition. In: Procs. of BMVC, Edinburgh, UK, pp. 1019–1028 (4–7 September 2006) [545]

126. Zahedi, M., Keysers, D., Deselaers, T., Ney, H.: Combination of tangent distance and an image based distortion model for appearance-based sign language recognition. In: Procs. of German Association for Pattern Recognition Symposium, Vienna, Austria. LNCS, vol. 3663, page 401, Springer, Berlin (31 August – 2 September 2005) [545]

127. Zahedi, M., Keysers, D., Ney, H.: Appearance-based recognition of words in American sign language. In: Procs. of IbPRIA, Estoril, Portugal, pp. 511–519 (7–9 June 2005) [545]

128. Zhang, L.G., Chen, Y., Fang, G., Chen, X., Gao, W.: A vision-based sign language recognition system using tied-mixture density HMM. In: Procs. of Int. Conf. on Multimodal interfaces, State College, PA, USA, pp. 198–204, ACM, New York (13–15 October 2004) [543]

129. Zieren, J., Kraiss, K.F., Non-intrusive sign language recognition for human computer interaction. In: Procs. of IFAC/IFIP/IFORS/IEA Symposium on Analysis, Design and Evaluation of Human Machine Systems (2004) [542]

130. Zieren, J., Kraiss, K.F., Robust person-independent visual sign language recognition. In: Procs. of IbPRIA, Estoril, Portugal, pp. 520–528 (7–9 June 2005) [543,544,553]

Chapter 28
Sports TV Applications of Computer Vision

Graham Thomas

Abstract This chapter focusses on applications of Computer Vision that help the sports broadcaster illustrate, analyse and explain sporting events, by the generation of images and graphics that can be incorporated in the broadcast, providing visual support to the commentators and pundits. After a discussion of simple graphics overlay on static images, systems are described that rely on calibrated cameras to insert graphics or to overlay content from other images. Approaches are then discussed that use computer vision to provide more advanced effects, for tasks such as segmenting people from the background, and inferring the 3D position of people and balls. As camera calibration is a key component for all but the simplest applications, an approach to real-time calibration of broadcast cameras is then presented. The chapter concludes with a discussion of some current challenges.

28.1 Motivation

Computer vision can be applied to many areas relating to sports broadcasting. One example is the automatic detection of highlights in sports programmes, for applications like navigation in video-on-demand services [16]. Techniques such as ball tracking can be used in the automatic annotation of sports videos [25]. However, this chapter focusses on applications that help the broadcaster illustrate, analyse and explain sporting events, by the generation of images and graphics that can be incorporated in the broadcast, providing visual support to the commentators and pundits.

Graphics is a key tool for the TV programme maker to help explain sporting events to viewers. Sports directors often refer to 'telling a story' to the viewer, and are keen to use the best tools available to bring out the key points in a clear, visually interesting and succinct way. Examples of current state-of-the art graphical analysis systems include tools for estimating the 3D trajectory and speed of tennis balls, or drawing virtual off-side lines across a football pitch. Other tools focus on providing views of the action in novel ways, without necessarily adding graphical

G. Thomas (✉)
BBC Research & Development, Centre House, 56 Wood Lane, London W12 7SB, UK
e-mail: graham.thomas@bbc.co.uk

T.B. Moeslund et al. (eds.), *Visual Analysis of Humans*,
DOI 10.1007/978-0-85729-997-0_28, © Springer-Verlag London Limited 2011

overlays. One example of such a tool is a system for allowing several heats of an event to be overlaid, synchronised in space and time, so that the performance of two downhill skiers can be compared visually. Other examples of tools that do not rely on graphical overlays include systems to generate novel views of a scene by producing close-ups from high-resolution still images, or by the use of 'free viewpoint' rendering techniques using images from multiple cameras.

Although such tools can be of great value to the broadcaster, they can also be highly relevant for sports trainers and in some cases to judges or referees. One example of this is the way in which the Hawk-Eye tennis system can now be called upon by players to determine whether a ball was in or out.

Some of the challenges in successfully applying computer vision techniques to applications in TV sports coverage are as follows.

- The environment in which the system is to be used is generally out of the control of the system developer, including aspects such as lighting, appearance of the background, clothing of the players, and the size and location of the area of interest. For many applications, it is either essential or highly desirable to use video feeds from existing broadcast cameras, meaning that the location and motion of the cameras is also outside the control of the system designer.
- The system needs to fit in with existing production workflows, often needing to be used live or with a short turn-around time, or being able to be applied to a recording from a single camera.
- The system must also give good value-for-money or offer new things compared to other ways of enhancing sports coverage. There are many approaches that may be less technically interesting than applying computer vision techniques, but nevertheless give significant added value, such as miniature cameras or microphones placed in a in cricket stump, a 'flying' camera suspended on wires above a football pitch, or a high frame-rate camera for super-slow-motion.

This chapter looks at some of the systems that have been developed to enhance the coverage of sports on TV. Section 28.2 starts by discussing simple graphics overlay on static images, and then moves on to describe tools that require calibrated cameras to insert graphics or to overlay content from other images. Section 28.3 looks at systems that use computer vision for more than just camera calibration, including applications involving segmenting people from the background, and inferring the 3D position of people and balls by using images from one or more cameras. As camera calibration is a key component for all but the simplest applications, Sect. 28.4 takes a closer look at how moving broadcast cameras can be calibrated in real time using the kind of image features typically found in sports coverage. Section 28.5 concludes the chapter with a discussion of some of the current challenges. The following chapter focusses on free-viewpoint video and its application to sports analysis.

28.2 Graphics and Analysis Systems that do not Rely on Computer Vision

28.2.1 Simple Graphics Overlay

Before looking at some applications using computer vision, it is worth looking at what can be done with simpler approaches that perform little or no image processing.

Some of the first systems that applied technology to sports analysis or visualisation did not use computer vision at all. Examples of such systems include the use of lasers and light sensors next to the lines on a tennis court, to detect when a ball just touches a line. Some of the first graphics systems, referred to as 'telestrators', provided a way for a sports pundit to draw on a frozen frame of video to highlight particular players or show the paths that they might take; these systems were simple drawing tools without any knowledge of the image content. Figure 28.1 shows an example of the kind of output a telestrator produces.

28.2.2 Graphics Overlay on a Calibrated Camera Image

Later systems introduced mechanical sensors on the camera mounting and lens to measure pan, tilt and zoom, which (together with off-line lens calibration to relate zoom ring position to focal length) allow graphics to be overlaid on moving video and remain registered to the background. By manually calibrating the position of the camera with respect to the scene, such systems can also generate graphics such as distance markings and off-side lines on a football pitch, which require knowledge of the pitch geometry and the camera pose. Such systems can be applied other sports such as swimming, running and long jump, adding lines to indicate world records

Fig. 28.1 Simple graphics overlay from a telestrator

or qualifying distances. Other virtual scene elements, such as virtual billboards or sponsor's logos, can also be added.

An interesting application of a system using mechanical camera sensors in conjunction with a separate set of cameras for object tracking is 'FoxTrax' [2]. This system is designed to render a graphical overlay on an ice hockey puck to improve its visibility. The puck has a set of infra-red LEDs embedded in it, which are picked up by an array of eight infra-red cameras looking down from the roof. The 3D position of the puck is computed by triangulation from these camera images, and a graphical overlay rendered to match the view of a broadcast camera fitted with sensors for pan, tilt and zoom. In addition to rendering a 'blue glow' over the puck, the system can also add a 'comet tail' to show the motion of the puck during periods of rapid acceleration.

The addition of some relatively simple image processing can allow graphics to appear as if drawn on the ground, and not on top of people or other foreground objects players, if the background is of a relatively uniform colour. For example, for football, a colour-based segmentation algorithm (referred to as a 'chromakeyer' by broadcast engineers) tuned to detect green can be used to inhibit the drawing of graphics in areas that are not grass-coloured, so that they appear behind the players. The fact that the chromakeyer will not generate a key for areas such as mud can actually be an advantage, as long as such areas are not large, as this adds to the realism that the graphics are 'painted' on the grass. Knowledge of the players' locations can be used to generate graphics such as distance lines to the goal or other players, such as the example shown in Fig. 28.2. Examples of this kind of system applied to American Football include the '1st an Ten™' line [19] and the 'First Down Line' [13].

Fig. 28.2 Example of virtual graphics overlaid on a rugby pitch [picture courtesy of Red Bee Media]

28.3   The Evolution of Computer Vision Systems for Sport

28.3.1   Analysis in 2D

Various interesting effects and analysis tools can be implemented using techniques to segment people or other moving objects from the background. For example, the motion of the segmented foreground person or object can be illustrated by overlaying a sequence of 'snapshots' on the background, to create a motion 'trail', allowing the recent motion of the foreground object or person to be seen. This produces a similar effect to that which can be achieved by illuminating the scene with a stroboscope and capturing an image using a camera with a long exposure. An early example of this was an analysis tool for snooker [21] which exploited the relatively benign nature of this sport (cameras are often static, and balls are easily segmented from the plain green background).

A more recent example of this kind of analysis tool [14] is often used to show movement in sports such as diving or ice skating. It is necessary to compensate for any pan/tilt/zoom of the camera, so that the segmented snapshots of the people are shown in the correct place; this is achieved using image analysis (see discussion in Sect. 28.4). This application is relatively benign to segmentation errors, which might result in the inclusion of parts of the background around the edges of a segmented person, as the person is overlaid on the background region from which they were originally extracted. By stitching together the background areas from a sequence of images and viewing this as one large image, it is possible to illustrate the entire movement of a person over a given period of time, as shown in Fig. 28.3. Where the person tends to occupy the same location over a period of time, such as an ice skater spinning around her axis, a set of successive images can be separated out and displayed on an arbitrary background, like a series of frames in a film.

An extension of this class of technique can be used to overlay the performance of several sports people during successive heats of an event, such as a downhill ski race [17]. This requires the calibration of the moving camera in a repeatable way, so that the background can be aligned from one heat to the next, and may also require the timing to be synchronised so that competitors are shown at the same time from the start of the heat. Figure 28.4 shows an example of this technique being used.

Fig. 28.3   An illustration of motion using a series of snapshots of the action [picture courtesy of Dartfish]

Fig. 28.4 Overlay of
successive heats of a ski
competition [picture courtesy
of Dartfish]

28.3.2 Analysis in 3D

The combination of foreground object segmentation and camera calibration can allow the approximate 3D positions of objects to be inferred, if some simple assumptions can be made. The segmentation of players on a pitch in an image from a calibrated camera can be used to infer their 3D position by assuming that the lowest
point of each silhouette (usually the feet) is in contact with they ground (usually
assumed to be planar). This simple approach can also be used to create a crude 3D
model of the scene [6], by placing the segmented players into a 3D model of a stadium, as textures on flat planes positioned at the estimated locations. An example of
this approach is shown in Fig. 28.5 [11]. This allows the generation of virtual views
of the game from locations other than those at which real cameras are placed, for
example to present a view of the scene that a linesman may have had when making
an off-side decision, or to provide a seamless 'fly' between an image from a real
camera and a fully virtual top–down view more suitable for presenting an analysis
of tactics.

The simple player modelling approach works well in many situations, but the
use of a single camera for creating the models restricts the range of virtual camera movement, with the planar nature of the players becoming apparent when the
viewing direction changes by more than about 15 degrees from that of the original
camera. Furthermore, overlapping players cannot easily be resolved. One solution
to these problems is to use pre-generated 3D player models, manually selected and
positioned to match the view from the camera. It can take a skilled operator several minutes to model such a scene, which is acceptable for a post-match analysis
programme but too slow for use in an instant replay. The player models also lack
realism. A multi-camera modelling approach (described in the following chapter)
provides an alternative.

One of the first commercially available multi-camera systems [8] based on computer vision was developed for tracking tennis balls in 3D. Although broadcast cameras were initially used to provide the images [12], the system is generally now deployed with a number of dedicated high-frame-rate synchronised cameras viewing

(a) Original image   (b) Virtual view

Fig. 28.5 Generation of a virtual view from a single camera image [picture courtesy of Red Bee Media]

Fig. 28.6 Analysis and prediction of cricket ball motion [picture courtesy of Hawk-Eye Innovations]

the tennis court [10], as there is no need to register the resulting 3D tracks to the images from the main broadcast cameras, and space is available around the court (often on the roof of the stands) to install them. Being static, they are easier to calibrate, interlace scanning can be avoided and short shutter times and higher frame rates can be used. There is a lot of prior knowledge about tennis that the system can use, including the size and appearance of the ball, its motion (once it is hit, its motion can be predicted using the laws of physics), and the area over which it needs to be tracked. The cameras and the geometry of the court can be accurately calibrated in advance. The system first identifies possible balls in each camera image, by identifying elliptical regions in the expected size range. Candidates for balls are linked with tracks across multiple frames, and plausible tracks are then matched between multiple cameras to generate a trajectory in 3D. The system is sufficiently accurate that it can be used by the referee to determine whether a ball lands in or out. It has now been used for other sports, for example in cricket, to predict the path that the ball would have taken if the batsman had not hit it, or if it had not turned when bouncing, as shown in Fig. 28.6. Other multi-camera analysis systems for balls in sporting events include [7].

Tracking the location of players is generally a more difficult task than tracking a ball: in sports such as football there are many people who will occlude each other from many viewpoints, and they tend to move erratically rather than following a

Fig. 28.7 Cameras installed
at a football ground for player
tracking [picture courtesy of
Prozone]

series of smooth paths as a bouncing ball does. The players usually need to be identified as well as tracked to produce useful statistics.

One approach is to use multiple static cameras distributed around the ground [15], although such an arrangement can be difficult and expensive to rig if the cameras are not left permanently installed. Commercial multi-camera player tracking systems tend to rely on a mixture of automated and manual tracking and player labelling. One such system [9] uses eight to ten cameras positioned at the corners of the pitch (see Fig. 28.7), connected via an IP link to a central control room, where the images are recorded. Events such as tackles and passes can be identified and logged manually live, and after the match the images are analysed semi-automatically to produce player positions at a rate of 10 Hz. The live data tend to be of most value to broadcasters, to provide statistics for live broadcast or web streaming, whilst the player position data can be analysed in-depth offline to provide insight into player performance for team coaches.

An alternative approach is to use two camera clusters [24], allowing stereo triangulation. It is also possible to use just one camera cluster, using the assumption that players are in contact with the pitch to derive 3D positions, and resolve occlusion problems by tracking players across multiple frames [20], although an operator is still needed to identify the players.

Tracking of the positions of limbs of athletes is a particularly challenging task. Marker-based motion capture systems are sometimes used during training, as these allow athlete motion to be captured to a very high accuracy of the order of a millimetre. For analysis of actual competitions, it is generally not possible to put markers or sensors onto athletes, so video analysis is the only possibility. Automated systems for tracking limbs from video are still the subject of research [5], as discussed in Chap. 9: *Model-Based Pose Estimation*. Manual systems, where an operator marks the positions of key points, can be used to provide interesting biomechanical information. Figure 28.8 shows an example in which the centre-of-mass of a triple-jumper is estimated from a manually fitted skeleton model, using information on the typical relative masses of each body part. The motion of the centre-of-mass can give

Fig. 28.8 Estimation of the centre-of-mass of a triple-jumper from limb positions

some insight into how the jumpers are performing, for example by showing whether they maximise the height of their centre-of-mass before jumping.

28.4 A Closer Look at Camera Calibration

Most of the applications above require accurate calibration of the camera, and in most cases this is a broadcast camera with a zoom lens, mounted on a pan/tilt head. Given the importance of having calibrated cameras, this section takes a closer look at how such cameras may be calibrated in real time in the context of a sports event.

One way in which camera calibration data can be derived is by performing an initial off-line calibration of the position of the camera mounting using surveying tools such as a theodolite or range-finder, and mounting sensors on the camera and the lens to measure the pan, tilt, and zoom. Figure 28.9 shows an example of a camera head equipped with sensors. However, this is costly and not always practical, for example if the cameras are installed and operated by another broadcaster and only the video feed itself is made available. The sensor data have to be carried through the programme production chain, including the cabling from the camera to the outside broadcast truck, recording on tape or disk, and transmission to the studio. Also, any system that relies on sensor data cannot be used on archive recordings.

A more attractive way of deriving calibration data is by analysis of the camera image. The lines on a sports pitch are usually in known positions, and these can be used to compute the camera pose. In some sports, such as football, the layout of some pitch markings (such as those around the goal) is fully specified, but the overall dimensions vary between grounds. It is thus necessary to obtain a measurement of the actual pitch. A minimum of four lines (which cannot all be parallel) must be visible to compute fully the camera pose, although fewer are needed if the camera position is already known.

Image processing methods based on identification of the pitch lines are now routinely used to derive camera tracking data for these kinds of sports application. An overview of one method used in commercial products for performing this task is given in Sect. 28.4.1. In some sports applications, there are insufficient lines visible

Fig. 28.9 A camera mounted on a pan/tilt head equipped with motion sensors

for this approach to be used, so an approach based on tracking areas of rich texture or other details such as corners may be used, as described in Sect. 28.4.2.

28.4.1 Tracking Camera Movement Using Pitch Lines

The process of estimating the camera pose using lines on a sports pitch can be broken down into the steps of estimating the position of the camera mounting (which is assumed to remain fixed), starting the tracker given a view of the pitch, and tracking from one image to the next at full video rate (50 Hz or 60 Hz). An overview of how these steps can be implemented is given in the following sections. A detailed description of this method is given in [23].

28.4.1.1 Estimating the Position of the Camera Mount

Most cameras covering events such as football generally remain in fixed positions during a match. Indeed, the positions can remain almost unchanged between different matches at the same ground, as the camera mounting points are often rigidly fixed to the stadium structure. It therefore makes sense to use this prior knowledge to compute an accurate camera position, which is then used as a constraint during the subsequent tracking process.

Estimating the position of a camera from a set of features in a single image can be a poorly constrained problem, particularly if focal length also needs to be estimated, as changes to the focal length have a very similar effect on the image to moving the camera along the direction of view. To improve the accuracy, multiple images can be used to solve for a common camera position value.

The pose computation method described in the following sections is used to compute the camera position, orientation and field-of-view, for a number of different camera orientations, covering a wide range of pan angles. The pose for all images is computed simultaneously, and the position is constrained to a common value for all

Fig. 28.10 Camera positions estimated from pitch lines in the image, using individual images

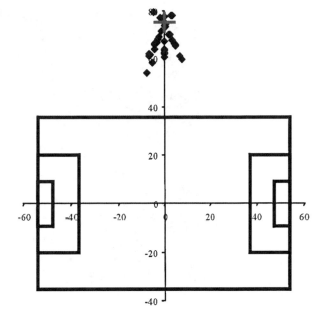

the images. This significantly reduces the inherent ambiguity between the distance of the camera from the reference features and the focal length. By including views of features in a wide range of positions (e.g. views of both goal areas), the uncertainty lies along different directions, and solving for a common position allows this uncertainty to be significantly reduced. The diamonds in Fig. 28.10 show the positions computed from approximately 40 individual images for a camera viewing a football pitch, indicating the range of uncertainty that using individual images produces. The points tend to lie along lines from the true camera position to the main clusters of features on the pitch (the goals and the centre circle). The cross shows the position optimised across all these images; note how this position is not simply the average of the individually measured positions.

The process described above can be repeated using images from all the cameras into whose feeds the production team are likely to want to add virtual graphics. For football, this is likely to include the camera on the centre line, the cameras in line with the two '18 yard' lines, and possibly the cameras behind the goals. The computed camera positions are then stored for future use.

28.4.1.2 Initialisation of the Camera Pose

Before the tracker can be run at full video rate, it is necessary to initialise it by determining which of the pre-calibrated camera positions the camera is at, and roughly what its values of pan, tilt and field-of-view are. This process needs to be carried out when the tracker is first started, and also whenever it loses track (for example if the camera briefly zooms in tightly to an area with no lines, or the video signal is cut

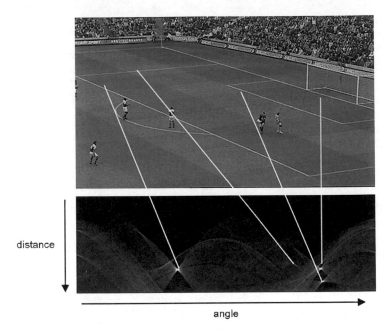

distance

angle

Fig. 28.11 Hough transform of lines as used for initialisation of camera pose

between cameras). It is usually possible to track from a so-called 'iso' feed (isolated signal from a single camera, rather than the output of the vision mixer that switches between cameras), so the tracker can maintain track even when the tracked camera is not on air. The challenge of the initialisation process is to locate pitch lines in the image and deduce which lines on the pitch they correspond to. The only prior knowledge available is the list of known camera positions, and the dimensions of the pitch.

The Hough transform is a well-known way of finding lines in an image. It maps a line in the image to a point (or accumulator "bin") in Hough space, where the two axes represent the angle of the line and the shortest distance to the centre of the image. If the camera pose is known roughly, it is possible to predict which peak in Hough space corresponds to which known line in the world, and hence to calibrate the camera. However, if the camera pose is unknown, the correspondence can be difficult to establish, as there may be many possible permutations of correspondences. Furthermore, if some lines are curved rather than straight, they will not give rise to a well-defined peak and are thus hard to identify. Figure 28.11 shows an example of a Hough transform of an image, operating on the output of the line detector described in the following section.

Rather than attempting to establish directly the correspondence between world lines and peaks in Hough space, the Hough transform can be used as a means to allow us to quickly establish a measure of how well the image matches the set of lines that would be expected to be visible from a given pose. A 'match value' for a set of lines can be obtained by adding together the set of bins in Hough space that correspond to the locations of the lines we would expect for this pose. Thus, to test for the presence of a set of N lines, it is only necessary to add together N values from the Hough transform, rather than examining all the pixels in the image that we would expect the lines to lie upon. By representing a curved line as a series of line segments, curves can also contribute to the match, even if they do not give rise to local maxima in the Hough transform. Although specific forms of Hough transform exist for circle or ellipse detection, the line segment approach allows both curves and lines to be handled in a single process.

This approach can be used in an exhaustive search process, to establish the match value for each pose that we consider. For each pre-determined camera position, and for the full range of plausible values of pan, tilt, and field-of-view, the match value can be calculated by summing the values in the bins in the Hough transform that correspond to the line positions that would be expected.

28.4.1.3 Frame-to-Frame Tracking of the Camera Motion

The tracking process uses the pose estimate from the previous image (or from the initialisation process), and searches a window of the image centred on each predicted line position for points likely to correspond to pitch lines. A straight line is fitted through each set of points, and an iterative minimisation process is used to find the values of pan, tilt, and focal length that minimise the distance in the image between the ends of each observed line and the corresponding line in the model when projected into the camera image.

28.4.2 Camera Tracking Using Areas of Rich Texture

For sports such as athletics, the camera image will generally show limited numbers of well-defined lines, and those that are visible may be insufficient to allow the camera pose to be computed. For example, lines on a running track are generally all parallel and thus give no indication of the current distance along the track, making pose computation impossible from the lines alone. For events such as long jump, the main area of interest (the sand pit) has no lines in it at all. Thus to accurately estimate the camera pose for the insertion of virtual graphics for these kinds of events, an alternative approach is needed.

The challenge is to be able to estimate the camera pose for these kinds of applications from the content of the image, without resorting to the use of mechanical sensors on the camera. This is a specific example of a problem known as Simultaneous Localization and Mapping (SLAM) (simultaneous location and mapping) [3], in which the pose of the camera and the 3D location of tracked image features are estimated as the camera moves. The general approach involves storing patches of image data centred on good feature points (such as corners), and matching

Fig. 28.12 Reference
features selected for camera
tracking on a triple-jump
event

these to the features seen in subsequent frames. From these observations, the pose
of the camera and the 3D location of the features can be estimated using techniques
such as an EKF.

In this application we need to be able to cope with significant changes in camera focal length, but can make use of the constraint that the camera is generally
mounted on a fixed point. This is in contrast to most implementations of SLAM,
which assume a fixed focal length camera but allow full camera movement. We also
need to be able to cope with a significant degree of motion blur, as motion speeds
of 20–30 pixels per field period are not uncommon with tightly zoomed-in cameras
covering sports events. The approach described in [4] is designed to meet these requirements. It uses a combination of fixed reference features to prevent long-term
drift (whose image texture is always that taken from the first frame in which the
feature was seen), and temporary features to allow non-static scene elements (such
as faces in the crowd) to play a useful part in the tracking process. The image features are assigned an arbitrary depth, as their depth cannot be determined from a
fixed viewpoint. Although it would be possible to treat the whole image as a single
texture and determine a homography that maps it to a stored panoramic reference
image (since the fixed position of the camera makes the 3D nature of the scene irrelevant), the presence of a large number of moving features (the athletes) makes
it advantageous to consider the image as a set of separate features, so that outlying features caused by athlete movement can be discarded using a technique such
as Random Sample Consensus (RANSAC). Figure 28.12 is an image from a triple-
jump event, showing the features that have been selected for tracking, with those
discarded due to athlete motion shown in red.

In order to obtain a calibration in a fixed world reference frame, the absolute
positions of some features in a selection of views can be specified by an operator,
and the system then refines the positions of all the fixed reference features to be
consistent with these, before storing the features for future use.

In situations where some lines are visible, such as that shown Fig. 28.12, it is
possible to use these in addition to the features centred on areas of image detail.
Further details of the algorithms used in this system, including the approach taken
to initialise the camera pose when tracking is first started, can be found in [4].

28.5 Conclusion

28.5.1 Camera Calibration

Camera calibration is difficult in uncontrolled scenes which typically have few features with accurately known 3D positions. Although lines on sports pitches are notionally in well-defined positions, pitches are rarely flat (being deliberately domed to improve drainage) and lines are often not painted in exactly the right positions. Techniques such as 3D laser scanning sometimes need to be used to build an accurate model of the environment which can then be used for camera calibration. When calibrating sparsely spaced cameras having a wide baseline, features in the scene can change their appearance significantly between camera viewpoints, making reliable feature matching between cameras difficult.

The use of zoom lenses on broadcast cameras inevitably makes intrinsic calibration more difficult. Lens distortion, image centre point and chromatic aberration can all vary as a function of both zoom and focus settings, and in the absence of data from lens sensors it can be difficult to accurately determine their values.

28.5.2 Segmentation, Identification and Tracking

Accurate segmentation of sportsmen can be very difficult given issues like motion blur, uncontrolled background and illumination, and aperture correction in the camera, yet accurate segmentation remains an important step in many sports analysis systems.

Automated identification and tracking of multiple players on a sports pitch remains difficult, particularly in the presence of occlusions. The value of player tracking data from a broadcaster's perspective may not justify the cost of using additional cameras or operators, although data such as distances that players have run, or 'heat maps' of team positions can provide some added value for post-match analysis, and are particularly useful for team coaches. Other tracking technologies such as RFID or ultra-wideband real-time location systems provide an alternative approach to vision-based tracking; although these can be used for gathering data during training, at present they are not acceptable for use during real events.

Issues such as self-occlusion, limited number of camera views, motion blur, and changing appearance over time make it difficult to track individual parts of sportsmen (such as feet and arms). This makes it hard to extract information that could be used for automated 3D modelling or generation of statistics such as stride length, or jump angle.

However, the current level of performance of camera calibration and segmentation is just about sufficient to allow multi-camera 3D reconstruction techniques to be applied, which are the subject of the next chapter.

28.5.3 Further Reading

There are several good textbooks available which give more insight into the area
of biomechanics for sports, mentioned briefly in Sect. 28.3.2. [1] is aimed at sports
students and coaches who need to use biomechanics as a part of their work. It gives
a clear explanation of many concepts and describes the relationship of biomechanics
to competitive sport. [18] is a more academic text aimed at researchers and biomedical engineering students. It provides an introduction to the experimental and numerical methods used in biomechanics research with many academic references. A
more in-depth discussion of the use of real-time virtual graphics in broadcast can be
found in [22].

Acknowledgements   Figures 28.2, 28.9, 28.10, 28.11 are reprinted from Chap. 5 of Advances in
Computers, Vol. 82, Graham Thomas, "Virtual Graphics for Broadcast Production", with permission from Elsevier.

References

1. Blazevich, A.: Sports Biomechanics: The Basics. Black, London (2007) [578]
2. Cavallaro, R.: The FoxTrax hockey puck tracking system. IEEE Comput. Graph. Appl. **17**(2),
   6–12 (1997) [566]
3. Davison, A., Reid, I., Molton, N., Stasse, O.: MonoSLAM: Realtime single camera SLAM.
   IEEE Trans. Pattern Anal. Mach. Intell. **29**(6), 1052–1067 (2007) [575]
4. Dawes, R., Chandaria, J., Thomas, G.A.: Image-based camera tracking for athletics. In:
   Proceedings of the IEEE International Symposium on Broadband Multimedia Systems
   and Broadcasting, BMSB 2009 (May 2009). Available as BBC R&D White Paper 181
   http://www.bbc.co.uk/rd/publications/whitepaper181.shtml [576]
5. del Rincon, J.M., Nebel, J.C., Makris, D., Urunuela, C.O.: Tracking human body parts using
   particle filters constrained by human biomechanics. In: BMVC08 (2008) [570]
6. Grau, O., Price, M., Thomas, G.A.: Use of 3-D techniques for virtual production. In: SPIE
   Conference on Videometrics and Optical Methods for 3D Shape Measurement, San Jose,
   USA (2001). Available as BBC R&D White Paper 033 http://www.bbc.co.uk/rd/publications/
   whitepaper033.shtml [568]
7. QuesTec Inc.: Real-time measurement, replay and analysis products for sports entertainment
   and digital replay. http://www.questec.com. Accessed 24/01/2011 [569]
8. Hawk-Eye   Innovations: Hawk-Eye   Tennis   Officiating   System.   http://www.
   hawkeyeinnovations.co.uk. Accessed 24/01/2011 [568]
9. Prozone Sports Ltd.: Prozone post-match analysis. http://www.prozonesports.com. Accessed
   24/01/2011 [570]
10. McIlroy, P.: Hawk-Eye: Augmented reality in sports broadcasting and officiating. In: ISMAR
    '08 Proceedings of the 7th IEEE/ACM International Symposium on Mixed and Augmented
    Reality, Washington, DC, USA. IEEE Comput. Soc., Los Alamitos (2008) [569]
11. Red Bee Media.: The Piero™ sports graphics system. http://www.redbeemedia.com/piero/.
    Accessed 10/10/2010 [568]
12. Owens, N.: Hawk-Eye tennis system. In: International Conference on Visual Information En-
    gineering (VIE2003), pp. 182–185. IEE Conference Publication No. 495 (2003) [568]
13. Orad: Trackvision First Down Line system. http://www.orad.co.il/products/trackvision-
    first-down-line-system. Accessed 24/01/2011 [566]
14. Prandoni, P.: Automated stroboscoping of video sequences. European Patent Specification
    EP1287518 B1 (2003) [567]

15. Ren, J., Xu, M., Orwell, J., Jones, G.A.: Multi-camera video surveillance for real-time soccer game analysis and reconstruction. In: Machine Vision and Applications. Springer, Berlin (2009) [570]
16. Ren, R., Jose, J.M.: General highlight detection in sport videos. In: Advances in Multimedia Modeling. Lecture Notes in Computer Science, pp. 27–38 (2000) [563]
17. Reusens, M., Vetterli, M., Ayer, S., Bergnozoli, V.: Coordination and combination of video sequences with spatial and temporal normalization. European patent specification EP1247255A4 (2007) [567]
18. Robertson, G., Caldwell, G., Hamill, J., Kamen, G., Whittlesey, S.: Research Methods in Biomechanics. Human Kinetics, Champaign (2004) [578]
19. Sportvision: 1st and Ten™ Line System. http://www.sportvision.com/foot-1st-and-ten-line-system.html. Accessed 24/01/2011 [566]
20. STATS: SportVU tracking technology. http://www.stats.com/sportvu.asp. Accessed 24/01/2011 [570]
21. Storey, R.: TELETRACK – a special effect. BBC Research Department Report 1984-10 (1984). Available as BBC R&D White Paper 033 http://www.bbc.co.uk/rd/publications/rdreport_1984_10.shtml [567]
22. Thomas, G.A.: Virtual Graphics for Broadcast Production. In: Advances in Computers, vol. 82. Elsevier, Amsterdam (2011) [578]
23. Thomas, G.A.: Real-time camera tracking using sports pitch markings. J. Real-Time Image Process. 2(2–3), 117–132 (2007). Available as BBC R&D White Paper 168 http://www.bbc.co.uk/rd/publications/whitepaper168.shtml [572]
24. TRACAB: TRACAB Image Tracking System. http://www.tracab.com/technology.asp. Accessed 24/01/2011 [570]
25. Yan, F., Christmas, W., Kittler, J.: Layered data association using graph-theoretic formulation with application to tennis ball tracking in monocular sequences. IEEE Trans. Pattern Anal. Mach. Intell. 30, 1814–1830 (2008) [563]

Chapter 29
Multi-view 4D Reconstruction of Human Action for Entertainment Applications

Oliver Grau

Abstract Multi-view 4D reconstruction of human action has a number of applications in entertainment. This chapter describes a selection of application areas that are of interest to the broadcast, movie and gaming industries. In particular, free-viewpoint video techniques for special effects and sport post-match analysis are discussed. The appearance of human action is captured as 4D data represented by 3D volumetric or surface data over time. A review of recent approaches identifies two major classes: 4D reconstruction and model-based tracking. The second part of the chapter describes aspects of a practical implementation of a 4D reconstruction pipeline. Implementations of the popular visual hull are discussed, as a building block in many free-viewpoint video systems.

29.1 Introduction

This chapter describes applications and approaches for capture and reconstruction of 4D appearance models of human action from multiple cameras. Then the use of these models in entertainment applications is outlined. Applications like free-viewpoint video aim to capture and reproduce the appearance of the human action as well as possible using a discrete number of multiple video streams.

A realistic synthesis of views from a continuum of new positions requires an underlining transformation model in order to generate these views from the captured video. This transformation can be formulated explicitly using a 3D geometrical description of the shape or by image-to-image correspondences between views. We refer to a representation that captures such human action as 4D model and use this term equivalent with *3D model of human action*. Another term often used in related literature is 3D video.

In the simplest case a 4D model is a sequence of 3D models, but it can also include temporally aligned 3D data. By analogy to the way that 3D reconstruction aims to generate a 3D model from multiple views we use the term 4D reconstruction

O. Grau (✉)
BBC Research & Development, 56 Wood Lane, London, UK
e-mail: Oliver.Grau@bbc.co.uk

T.B. Moeslund et al. (eds.), *Visual Analysis of Humans*,
DOI 10.1007/978-0-85729-997-0_29, © Springer-Verlag London Limited 2011

to describe the generation of a 4D model of action from multiple videos. A complementary approach is by using a model-based representation that usually fits a 3D shape model to captured data and then tracks motion over time.

There are a number of applications for 3D models of human action in entertainment. In particular the film industry increasingly makes use of 3D data to generate special effects using computer graphics methods [29]. The generated models employ a mix of different approaches, from completely manual to the use of laser scanning of static poses and motion capture techniques for the performance. In any case the effort in particular in the post-production phase is very high. The productions require the highest visual quality and high-end cinema productions dedicate a good proportion of the overall budget to the implementation of spectacular visual effects.

In broadcast production, budgets are on a much smaller scale. Furthermore, many productions are produced in real-time and broadcast immediately. Both requirements prohibit an extensive and therefore expensive post-production phase. Applications of 3D models of human action in broadcast require therefore methods that produce results without too much human intervention and a quick turnaround time or even real-time for live broadcast.

The production of video games is another domain that makes use of captured 3D human action. However, the data are used differently compared to applications in films and broadcast. The main difference lies in the fact that games always generate 'new' action on the fly, instead of just replaying captured action. This requires a different data representation. In practice the production process requires a lot of manipulation to achieve good visual results while keeping the amount of data and processing manageable on the end device.

29.2 Applications

Typical applications for 3D models of human action in broadcast and film are seeking to overcome the limitations of physical cameras. An important application is Free-Viewpoint Video (FVV) i.e. the freedom to chose a camera viewpoint independent from real camera positions. This enables a number of special effects.

The movie 'The Matrix' became famous for the *bullet time*™ effect. In this effect the action is stopped or slowed down and the camera viewpoint is then moved around the actors to explore the spatial domain. This effect was created with an array of cameras that synchronously capture a single image. The technique is also known as 'time slicing' and has been pioneered by a number of people including 19th-century photographer Eadweard J. Muybridge. Macmillan continued this work in the 1980s [1].

Kanade applied a similar technique to the US Superbowl, with 30 actively panning and tilting cameras known as the Eye Vision system [17]. An operator interactively defines the point of interest on the pitch and the cameras centre synchronously to this point. This gives the impression during replay that the virtual camera is rotating around this pivot point.

Fig. 29.1 Use of
free-viewpoint video to
visualise incidents in
sport [13]

Time slicing tries to explore the spatial domain by playing images captured at the same time, but from different cameras combined into a video sequence. Therefore the camera path is determined by the position of the real cameras and cannot be changed during replay. In contrast to that, FVV allows full control over the position of the virtual camera position at replay. In particular, camera positions or movements can be rendered that would be otherwise impossible to achieve with a real camera.

Another application of FVV is pre-visualisation for planning of shots. This is an issue for example when real and virtual scene content is mixed in a scene or if complicated camera movements are intended. With the help of FVV the interaction of the scene components and the camera path can be planned on the computer [9] and can reduce rehearsal and expensive on-set production time.

FVV can also be applied to visualise events or incidents. An important applica-tion is to generate new views from sport events, like football or rugby that enhance the coverage of such events. Since many players are involved and occlude each other in these sports it is usually hard to explain tactical aspects of key incidents from just fixed camera positions. FVV enables sport presenters to explore interesting incidents by moving to new viewpoints, like a virtual flight down to pitch level or overhead. This is a powerful tool to visualise spatial relationships between players and their tactics. An example[1] is depicted in Fig. 29.1.

3D data of action also have other uses, without directly generating new visual data. One example is the generation of additional data, like statistical information about speed and biometrical data of athletes. Another application area is the im-plementation of interaction between real actors and virtual scene components. In [11] an actor feedback system for the production of special effects is described. The feedback is provided with a view-dependent projection system. The head position is sensed in a non-intrusive way from a multi-camera system. The system computes a visual hull and finds the head position in the volumetric reconstruction. Moreover, the 3D data of the actor can be used to compute collisions with virtual components or 'virtual sensors'. This can then be used to trigger actions in a virtual world.

The remainder of this chapter focuses on free-viewpoint video applications, but the approaches discussed in the following sections can be applied to other appli-

---

[1]Result from the TSB *iview* project [12].

cations such as those discussed here. Where appropriate, requirements for specific applications will be mentioned.

29.3 Approaches

This section gives a brief overview of techniques to acquire a 4D model of human action. There are two general classes of approaches: *4D reconstruction* on one hand computes the geometry of the action without specific assumptions about the actors. On the other hand, *model-based tracking* usually starts with a 3D shape model and an articulated motion model and then determines motion parameters over time.

A further class of approaches are *image-based interpolation techniques*. These techniques do not compute an explicit 3D volumetric or surface representation of the scene, but synthesise new views directly from images. The techniques can be used to implement some spatio-temporal effects, including slow-motion [41] and interpolation between different camera views [33]. In the following we concentrate on the explicit approaches. Generally, there is no clear distinction between explicit and image-based methods, since sophisticated image-based methods use correspondences, like dense disparity maps, which can be regarded as an implicit 3D representation. On the other hand, the explicit model-based approaches also make use of image-based methods to generate high-quality synthesised views. For an overview on image-based approaches see, e.g. [34].

29.3.1 4D Reconstruction

Model-free 4D reconstruction does not make specific assumptions about the scene content. The most common approach is to reconstruct the shape of the scene independently for each time instant. Early approaches adopted well-known 3D reconstruction methods for that purpose, namely two-camera stereo matching that works best for cameras relatively close together, and silhouette-based computation for wide-baseline camera configurations. Both approaches are complementary.

Stereo reconstruction (or stereo vision) aims to find dense pixel correspondences between displaced camera views. The standard approach is window-based matching of (luminance) pixel values between views. Two-camera stereo matching (see for example [31] for an overview) has been used in early work. A number of methods have been developed to combine partial two-view stereo depth maps into a complete surface description, e.g. [19, 26]. Kanade built a half-dome studio system with 51 cameras, using stereo matching to provide a free-viewpoint experience [28]. Stereo vision usually produces poor results at object boundaries, since accurate matching is harder to achieve here.

Silhouette-based approaches rely on known camera parameters and segmentation of the foreground objects against background. In film and TV production, segmentation can sometimes be enforced by use of chroma-keying [35]. The object silhouettes and camera parameters are used to compute an approximation of the scene. Laurentini coined the term *visual hull* for this class of reconstruction, as it only represents a convex approximation of the visible object shape [21]. The visual hull (VH) can be computed very robustly and many 4D reconstruction approaches use it solely, or as an initial solution. A number of algorithms exist to compute the visual hull, Sect. 29.4.3.1 gives an overview. The visual hull shows a number of typical artefacts. The most important of these are 'phantom volumes'. These areas stay falsely occupied, because they are not visible as background against the object silhouettes. The fewer cameras that are used, the more likely phantom volumes are to appear.

Early work on free-viewpoint video has been implemented predominately based on visual hulls and extensions have been the subject of recent research. Many approaches were developed for controlled studio environments, using approximately 6–16 cameras [11, 25, 36, 47].

Recent work on 3D reconstruction (of static objects) is looking into improved multi-camera stereo methods. Particular progress was made by combining silhouette-based approaches with stereo matching (see, e.g., [15]). Further advances were made by applying global optimisation techniques, like graph-cuts, e.g. [7, 45]. See [32] for an overview. Some of the advanced methods are applied to 4D reconstruction problems. Starck for example combined stereo-matching with a visual-hull computation [36].

The focus of recent work on 4D reconstruction goes beyond simple concatenation of independently-generated 3D models. Approaches are looking into estimating dense or implicit correspondences of surface points over time. This would open up an number of new applications, like slow-motion, better compression of 4D content and extended editing capabilities. Dense correspondence can be established by matching surface points [37, 43]. Cagniart et al. presented a method to match 3D surfaces temporally based only on the geometry [3].

29.3.2 Model-Based Tracking

Model-based tracking is an approach to capture 3D human action by tracking motion. Early work targeting communication applications was using simple articulated 3D models, which were divided into partially-rigid components, for example for head-and-shoulder scenes. Kappei and others showed how 3D shape and motion for such models can be derived from monoscopic camera sequences [18, 20].

More recent work is making use of articulated models developed in computer graphics for animation and uses multi-camera set-ups to capture full body shape and motion [4, 46]. These approaches work in two stages.

1. An articulated shape and appearance model is initialised using a 3D modelling technique.
2. Tracking the action by estimating motion parameters from multiple images.

Both sub-tasks benefit from recent advances in 3D modelling and model-based markerless tracking. More recent work also demonstrates the ability to edit the character, i.e., the shape and appearance of the actor and the animation [44].

An advantage of the model-based tracking approach is that it uses only one 3D shape and appearance model that can be updated during the tracking. Therefore it uses only one 3D geometrical topology and only needs to update form and motion parameters over time. This separation of form and motion results in a compact set of parameters and is compatible with animation models used in post-production and gaming applications. On the other hand model-based approaches are quite limited in capturing local appearance or flexible shape changes, for example caused by moving cloth. Model-free 4D reconstruction is seen to have clear advantages here to capture more realistic shape and appearance of the action.

Another advantage of model-based approaches is the implicit surface definition and its known temporal transformation. That means that the position of surface points over time is known. As mentioned this temporal correspondence or alignment has to be determined for 4D reconstruction by matching.

29.4 A 4D Reconstruction Pipeline

This section describes the components of a 4D reconstruction system from a practical point of view. The application of 3D reconstruction in the entertainment industry raises a number of constraints that algorithms have to comply with: Firstly a system used in production must be easy to set up and run. Any elaborate calibration sessions or extensive parameter adjustment before or during operation must been kept to a minimum, otherwise there is the danger that this will cause disruption of the production process and keep expensive production crews idle. That means that suitable algorithms should have as few parameters as possible that need manual configuration, or ideally have a fully-automatic set-up process.

Another aspect is the processing speed of the system that either allows use under real-time conditions or with very short turnaround times. Therefore methods and algorithms selected for application in media processing should be fast and robust. This section describes a processing pipeline that has been developed and tested with respect to these requirements.

Figure 29.2 shows the modular groups and functional blocks of the system. The modular blocks are a logical grouping of functionalities. In practice functional blocks might be implemented across a number of IT components in a distributed system [6]. A challenge of such an implementation is the synchronisation of information and control of the data flow in a production environment.

The user interface controls the operational parameters of the system. This includes set-up of cameras and functional parameters. As many of these parameters have an impact on the visual quality of the synthesised images, the operator needs visual feedback at all stages of the processing pipeline.

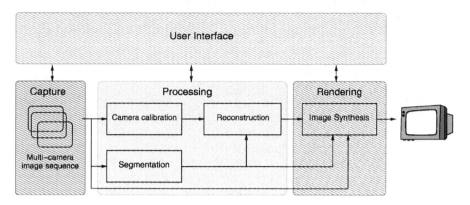

Fig. 29.2   Flow diagram of the processing pipeline

The capture component reads in the video stream from cameras.[2] Broadcast equipment traditionally uses a reference video signal to synchronise (or 'genlock') video sources such as cameras, and a time-code signal to allow recordings to be time-aligned. The use of time-code often requires extra connections or devices to embed the time signal in the video stream. An approach that avoids this by tight time synchronisation of the IT components is described in [6].

The processing module computes a 3D model of the scene. The functional blocks include camera calibration, segmentation of objects from the background and 3D reconstruction. These blocks will be described in more detail below.

The replay module renders the captured scene in real-time using the computed 3D model and the original camera images.

The system as implemented as a distributed system can operate in real-time. The implementation cited in [6] uses one server for two HD broadcast camera streams. The camera calibration (if cameras are moving) and segmentation is computed on these servers. Segmentation and camera parameters are then passed on to another server, which is collecting data and computes the 3D reconstruction. Some applications do not require real-time rendering (such as sport post-match analysis) or do not require the highest quality reconstruction, which is not feasible with real-time capable algorithms. In this case the images are stored locally on the capture servers and the processing is run at a later stage.

29.4.1 Camera Calibration

Camera calibration is a well studied problem. Most studio-based capture systems assume that the cameras are mounted statically and a calibration can be carried out

---

[2]This is called 'ingest' in broadcast.

once before the system is used. For this purpose chart-based calibration is a well-suited approach, see for example [42]. In less controlled environments, i.e. when a chart-based calibration is not possible for whatever reasons, structure-from-motion methods can be applied [14].

During production of broadcast programmes, camera parameters are typically changing all the time. A typical example is in sport coverage, where camera operators are permanently following the action by panning and tilting the camera and changing zoom and focus to capture close-ups. For these kind of scenarios the camera calibration has to estimate the camera parameters frame by frame. Although there are mechanical sensors available for broadcast cameras, a more flexible approach is to estimate camera parameters directly from the image information only. This would also increase the scope of the 3D-multi-view application, since it can be applied to image feeds without the need to get access to the cameras.

A suitable approach in sport applications is a line-based approach for the calibration of camera parameters against the pitch lines. This method is very fast, can be computed robustly in real-time on a PC and gives online updates of camera parameters for moving cameras [40]. An overview of this method was presented in Sect. 28.4 of Chap. 28.

29.4.2 Segmentation

The process of classifying the pixels of a digital image into foreground and background is called segmentation or matting (in the film industry) and keying (in broadcast). The result of this process is stored as the alpha channel of an image. The main application for keys or mattes is in compositing, for example to exchange the background of a scene with a different image.

A number of approaches have been developed to create a key or matte automatically. Chroma-keying is a long-established technique for special effects in film- and TV-productions (see [35] for an overview) and relies on the subject being filmed in front of a screen with known colour (usually blue or green). This technique is very robust, but limited to controlled environments.

Difference keying is another popular technique that works in two steps: First an image of the background (the background plate) is acquired. The alpha value is then estimated from the difference of an image with subject to the background plate.

More recent work is addressing keying of natural images, i.e. images with varying foreground and background colour. In order to solve the segmentation problem, the user is required to interactively provide hints in form of a tri-map or scribbles to indicate regions of foreground and background (see, e.g. [5, 16, 22, 30]). These techniques are applied to still images with recent extensions to video [2]. However, because these methods are computationally very expensive and require a lot of manual input, their use is usually restricted to offline applications.

For carrying out 3D reconstruction with a basic visual-hull algorithm only binary values {0, 1} are required. However, to achieve high-quality results in rendering, a continuous value of alpha in the interval [0, 1] is needed. These intermediate values for alpha occur for example in transparent objects or motion blur and in particular at the border of foreground objects when only a part of a pixel belongs to the object (mixed pixels). The continuous alpha values, together with pre-multiplied colour values are used by the image synthesis module that might need to blend textures from different cameras. The image + alpha format is accepted by most graphics systems, for example OpenGL. Pre-multiplied colour values represent the foreground colour of mixed pixels and can be obtained by solving the compositing equation:

$$C = \alpha F + (1 - \alpha)B \qquad (29.1)$$

with the combined colour C, foreground colour F and the background colour B.

This requires solving for both, α and background colour B. For more details see for example [16, 35].

29.4.2.1 Sport Broadcast

Applying free-viewpoint video FVV to outdoor broadcast, for example for post-match analysis, raises a number of problems not found in a controlled studio environment [12]. For the segmentation of players, colour-based methods such as chroma-keying against the green of football and rugby pitches have been considered. However, the colour of grass on pitches varies significantly. This is due to uneven illumination and anisotropic effects in the grass caused by the process of lawn-mowing in alternating directions. Under these conditions simple chroma-keying gives a segmentation that is too noisy to achieve a high-quality visual scene reconstruction. Difference keying can produce better results and is also able to segment pitch lines, logos and other markings of the background. The background model or 'background plate' can be created by either taking a picture of the scene without any foreground objects or, if this is not possible, the background plate can be generated by applying a temporal median filter over a sequence to remove moving foreground objects.

Broadcast cameras have a control known as aperture correction or sometimes 'detail'. The aperture correction is used to 'sharpen' an image and is one element that distinguishes the 'TV-look' from 'film-look'. Effectively the correction emphasises high-frequency image components and is therefore a high-boost filter. Figure 29.3 shows an example of a broadcast image. The image was taken during a rugby match with a Sony HDC-1500 high-definition camera.

A high level of aperture correction causes a significant colour shift to pixels close to luminance edges. As can be seen in the close-up on the right of Fig. 29.3, this can affect an area about 2–3 pixels around contour edges and leads to incorrect segmentation results using colour-based segmentation methods. The segmentation can be improved by compensating for the effects of the aperture correction. Figure 29.4 shows a close-up of results from a colour-based segmentation using the original image on the left, and after compensation for aperture correction on the right [10].

Fig. 29.3 Image of a sport scene from a broadcast camera (*left*) and detail (*right*)

Fig. 29.4 Detail of segmented broadcast picture before compensation for aperture correction (*left*) and after compensation (*right*)

29.4.3 Reconstruction

The reconstruction module computes a temporal geometric model of the action. For real-time applications and wide-baseline camera set-ups, methods based on visual-hull computation are generally used to compute a 3D reconstruction for each time instance.

Applications that require best visual quality and can afford offline processing may use more sophisticated reconstruction algorithms to extract temporally-consistent 4D data from the input data, as outlined in Sect. 29.3.

In this section we discuss aspects of visual-hull (VH) computation. The computation of the visual hull from 2D silhouettes is very robust, fast and well suited for modelling of human action. The computation of the visual hull, also known as shape-from-silhouette, is equivalent to an intersection of the back-projected 2D silhouettes (visual cones) in 3D. A number of approaches to compute this intersection have been suggested in the literature that differ in the underlying data structure and the processing.

29.4.3.1 Algorithms for Visual-Hull Computation

A basic implementation to compute the visual hull based on a volumetric data representation is described in Algorithm 1:

Algorithm 1 Basic volumetric visual-hull computation

---

  for all *voxel* in V_{def} **do**
    voxel := *true*
  end for
  for all *c* in *list of cameras* **do**
    for all *voxel* = *true* **do**
      fp = *FootPrintTest*(*c*, *voxel*)
      if *fp* = *AllZero* **then**
        voxel := *false*
      end if
    end for
  end for

This algorithm runs over all elements (voxels[3]) of a 3D array and projects each voxel into the 2D silhouette images and tests whether its footprint is on foreground or background. If the voxel footprint is on background it will be set to 'false'. From these volumetric data a surface description can be generated with an iso-surface extraction, for example using the marching cubes algorithm. Using a 3D array in this simple algorithm requires a high number of projections and footprint tests. To reduce this effort the use of hierarchical processing using octrees as a representation has been proposed [27, 38].

Matusik et al. describe an algorithm that synthesises new views of an object directly without generating a surface model. Their algorithm samples the object based on lines along the viewing frustum of the new view and computes a VH for this parametrisation [25]. Grau describes an algorithm to compute a surface model using sets of line segments [11].

Matsuyama et al. describe an algorithm that computes a VH by projecting the silhouette images into the volumetric space [23]. This is achieved with a 2D transformation into planes of a volumetric 3D array and intersection.

Another approach computes a surface description directly without going into an intermediate volumetric representation [24, 39]. These algorithms reproject the boundaries or edges of the 2D silhouettes using the inverse camera projection matrix and find the intersections in 3D to build up a polyhedral surface description.

Although the algorithms discussed above aim to compute the visual hull of an object, they all have different characteristics. The (classical) volumetric algorithms with iso-surface generation are very popular, because of their low complexity. On modern machines they are also fast to compute. Furthermore, they are very robust against segmentation errors. A typical problem is that the surface models look crude or rough. This is an aliasing artefact introduced by the iso-surface extraction on binary voxel values. Grau [8] analyses this problem and suggests super-sampling to enhance the accuracy of the reconstruction without increasing the complexity of the surface model.

---

[3] Volumetric elements.

Other algorithms, like the direct polyhedral surface computation are usually more complex, but run very fast. However, they are generally more sensitive to errors in the 2D silhouettes than the volumetric methods.

29.4.3.2 Alternative Computation Strategies

The visual hull only provides an approximation to the 3D shape of foreground objects, but systems with a high number of cameras under controlled conditions can produce visual results that meet the needs of some applications, like simple special effects in TV shows. However, some typical artefacts, like 'phantom volumes', become more pronounced when only a low number of cameras is used to capture the action. Another source of reconstruction errors comes from errors in the camera calibration. Several strategies have been developed to cope with the imperfections of VHs.

Erroneous camera calibration parameters are manifested by an erosion of the computed surface models. This can lead to loss of limbs of actors. More robustness against camera calibration errors can be achieved by over-estimating the visual hull. This results in a conservative visual hull (CVH) that is bigger than the object. Figure 29.5 shows an example of VH and CVH computed for a rugby game. The

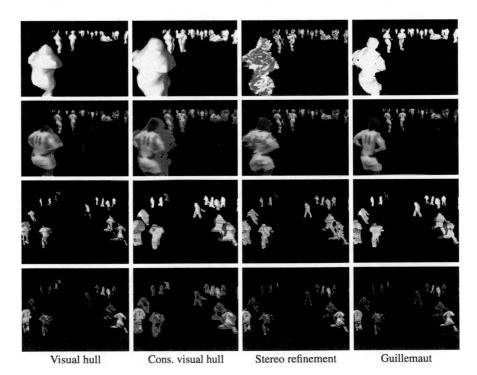

Visual hull   Cons. visual hull   Stereo refinement   Guillemaut

Fig. 29.5 Example of reconstruction results on rugby (*top*) and soccer (*bottom*) data from [13] (©IEEE 2010)

conservative effect can be achieved by dilating the 2D silhouettes. The amount of dilation should correspond to the maximal error (in pixels) of the camera calibration. During rendering, the camera images and the alpha channel from the segmentation are used to improve the shape of objects.

The VH or CVH can be used to initialise refinement methods. Guillemaut describes a method to compute a depth map per camera [13]. The process starts with an initial depth map derived from a VH. An algorithm formulated as a graph-cut problem then computes a refined depth map. Implicitly this method also computes a refined segmentation. Figure 29.5 compares results of this method with VH, CHV and stereo matching.

29.4.4 Rendering

The replay module uses the 3D models of the scene together with the original camera images to produce a novel view of the scene. Action captured and processed with model-based tracking, as described in Sect. 29.3.2 can often be rendered with standard animation software.

Action captured with 4D reconstruction approaches often uses specific rendering methods. Matusik et al. describe a direct image synthesis approach [25] that does not produce intermediate volumetric or surface geometry. Wuermlin et al. use point-based rendering as an alternative to a surface representation [47].

A method based on the use of surface geometry and view-dependent texture mapping can give good results: Three or more camera images are used and blended together. Cameras closer to the synthetic viewpoint get a higher weight. One option to achieve this is to use a simple formula based on the angle between the virtual camera, the real camera and the scene interest point.

The main advantage of view-dependent texture mapping is that it can mask many imperfections or errors in the reconstructed shape. Furthermore, appearance (including pecularities of surfaces) can be reproduced to a certain extent. The results in Figs. 29.1 and 29.5 are rendered using view-dependent texture mapping.

29.5 Conclusion

With recent advances in 3D and 4D reconstruction techniques, the use of these techniques in the entertainment industry is starting to emerge. The degree of operator input for these methods is dictated by production budgets and whether the programme is produced live or offline. The production pipeline described in the previous section was developed for use in broadcast, with a minimum of required user input and (potentially) allows real-time operation.

The method described here was based on the computation of visual hulls, mainly because of the requirement for real-time operation. The usefulness of this approach has been demonstrated for the visualisation of sport incidents. However, in this case the synthesised views are quite distant from the reconstructed objects.

For applications that require closer views of the action, for example in close-range studio set-ups, more sophisticated methods are required, as reconstruction errors become more disturbing. Advances in adaptation of global minimisation methods for 3D reconstruction as discussed earlier are also the most promising candidates to improve 4D reconstruction. Finally, a combination with temporal alignment methods will open new applications as the resulting 4D data sets will better fit the graphics production pipelines used in the entertainment industry.

References

1. Time slice films. http://www.timeslicefilms.com/ [582]
2. Bai, X., Wang, J., Simons, D., Sapiro, G.: Video SnapCut: Robust video object cutout using localized classifiers. In: ACM SIGGRAPH 2009 papers, pp. 1–11. ACM, New York (2009) [588]
3. Cagniart, C., Boyer, E., Ilic, S.: Probabilistic deformable surface tracking from multiple videos. In: ECCV 2010, pp. 326–339 (2010) [585]
4. Carranza, J., Theobalt, C., Magnor, M., Seidel, H.-P.: Free-viewpoint video of human actors. ACM Trans. Graph. **22**(3), 569–577 (2003) [585]
5. Chuang, Y.-Y., Curless, B., Salesin, D.H., Szeliski, R.: A Bayesian approach to digital matting. In: Proceedings of IEEE CVPR 2001, vol. 2, pp. 264–271. IEEE Comput. Soc., Los Alamitos (December 2001) [588]
6. Easterbrook, J., Grau, O., Schübel, P.: A system for distributed multi-camera capture and processing. In: Proc. of CVMP (2010) [586,587]
7. Furukawa, Y., Ponce, J.: Carved visual hulls for image-based modeling. Int. J. Comput. Vis. **81**(1), 53–67 (2009) [585]
8. Grau, O.: 3D sequence generation from multiple cameras. In: Proc. of IEEE, International Workshop on Multimedia Signal Processing 2004, Siena, Italy (September 2004) [591]
9. Grau, O.: A 3D production pipeline for special effects in TV and film. In: Mirage 2005, Computer Vision/Computer Graphics Collaboration Techniques and Applications, Rocquencourt, France. INRIA, Rocquencourt (March 2005) [583]
10. Grau, O., Easterbrook, J.: Effects of camera aperture correction on keying of broadcast video. In: Proc. of the 5th European Conference on Visual Media Production (CVMP) (2008) [589]
11. Grau, O., Pullen, T., Thomas, G.A.: A combined studio production system for 3-d capturing of live action and immersive actor feedback. IEEE Trans. Circuits Syst. Video Technol. **14**(3), 370–380 (2004) [583,585,591]
12. Grau, O., Thomas, G.A., Hilton, A., Kilner, J., Starck, J.: A robust free-viewpoint video system for sport scenes. In: Proc. of 3DTV-Conference, Kos island, Greece (May 2007) [583,589]
13. Guillemaut, J.Y., Kilner, J., Hilton, A.: Robust graph-cut scene segmentation and reconstruction for free-viewpoint video of complex dynamic scenes. In: Computer Vision, 2009 IEEE 12th International Conference on, pp. 809–816. IEEE Comput. Soc., Los Alamitos (2010) [583,592,593]
14. Hartley, R.I., Zisserman, A.: Multiple View Geometry in Computer Vision. Cambridge University Press, Cambridge (2000) [588]
15. Hernández Esteban, C., Schmitt, F.: Silhouette and stereo fusion for 3D object modeling. Comput. Vis. Image Underst. **96**(3), 367–392 (2004) [585]
16. Hillman, P., Hannah, J., and Renshaw, D.. Foreground/background segmentation of motion picture images and image sequences. IEE Proc., Vis. Image Signal Process. **152**(4), 387–397 (2005) [588,589]

17. Kanade, T., et al.: Eyevision at super bowl XXXV. Web (2001) [582]
18. Kappei, F., Liedtke, C.-E.: Ein verfahren zur modellierung von 3d-objekten aus fernsehbild-folgen. In: Mustererkennung 1987, 9. DAGM-Symposium, pp. 277–281 (1987) [585]
19. Koch, R.: Model-based 3-d scene analysis from stereoscopic image sequences. ISPRS J. Photogramm. Remote Sens. **49**(5), 23–30 (1994) [584]
20. Koch, R.. Dynamic 3-d scene analysis through synthesis feedback control. IEEE Trans. Pattern Anal. Mach. Intell. **15**(6), 556–568 (1993) [585]
21. Laurentini, A.: The visual hull concept for silhouette-based image understanding. IEEE Trans. Pattern Anal. Mach. Intell. **16**(2), 150–162 (1994) [585]
22. Levin, A., Lischinski, D., Weiss, Y.: A closed-form solution to natural image matting. IEEE Trans. Pattern Anal. Mach. Intell. **30**(2), 228–242 (2007) [588]
23. Matsuyama, T., Wu, X., Takai, T., Wada, T.: Real-time dynamic 3-d object shape reconstruction and high-fidelity texture mapping for 3-d video. IEEE Trans. Circuits Syst. Video Technol. **14**(3), 357–369 (2004) [591]
24. Matusik, W., Buehler, C., McMillan, L.: Polyhedral visual hulls for real-time rendering. In: Proc. of 12th Eurographics Workshop on Rendering, pp. 116–126 (2001) [591]
25. Matusik, W., Buehler, C., Raskar, R., Gortler, S.J., McMillan, L.: Image-based visual hulls. In: Akeley, K. (ed.) Siggraph 2000, Computer Graphics Proceedings, pp. 369–374. ACM Press, New York (2000) [585,591,593]
26. Okutomi, M., Kanade, T.: A multiple-baseline stereo. IEEE Trans. Pattern Anal. Mach. Intell. **15**(4), 353–363 (1993) [584]
27. Potmesil, M.: Generating octree models of 3D objects from their silhouettes in a sequence of images. Comput. Vis. Graph. Image Process. **40**, 1–29 (1987) [591]
28. Rander, P., Narayanan, P.J., Kanade, T.: Virtualized reality: Constructing time-varying virtual worlds from real world events. In: IEEE Visualization, pp. 277–284 (1997) [584]
29. Roble, D., Zafar, N.B.: Don't trust your eyes: Cutting-edge visual effects. vol. 42, pp. 35–41 (2009) [582]
30. Rother, C., Kolmogorov, V., Blake, A.: "GrabCut": Interactive foreground extraction using iterated graph cuts. ACM Trans. Graph. **23**(3), 309–314 (2004) [588]
31. Scharstein, D., Szeliski, R.: A taxonomy and evaluation of dense two-frame stereo correspondence algorithms. Int. J. Comput. Vis. **47**(1), 7–42 (2002) [584]
32. Seitz, S.M., Curless, B., Diebel, J., Scharstein, D., Szeliski, R.: A comparison and evaluation of multi-view stereo reconstruction algorithms. In: Computer Vision and Pattern Recognition, 2006 IEEE Comput. Soc. Conference on, vol. 1, pp. 519–528 (2006) [585]
33. Seitz, S.M., Dyer, C.R.: View morphing. In: Proceedings of the 23rd Annual Conference on Computer Graphics and Interactive Techniques, pp. 21–30. ACM, New York (1996) [584]
34. Shum, H.-Y., Kang, S.B., Chan, S.-C.: Survey of image-based representations and compression techniques. IEEE Trans. Circuits Syst. Video Technol. **13**(11), 1020–1037 (2003) [584]
35. Smith, A.R., Blinn, J.F.: Blue screen matting. In: SIGGRAPH '96: Proceedings of the 23rd Annual Conference on Computer Graphics and Interactive Techniques, pp. 259–268. ACM, New York (1996) [584,588,589]
36. Starck, J., Hilton, A.: Model-based multiple view reconstruction of people. In: Proc. of ICCV, pp. 915–922 (2003) [585]
37. Starck, J., Hilton, A.: Correspondence labelling for wide-timeframe free-form surface matching. In: Computer Vision, 2007. ICCV 2007. IEEE 11th International Conference on, pp. 1–8. IEEE Comput. Soc., Los Alamitos (2007) [585]
38. Szeliski, R.: Rapid octree construction from image sequences. CVGIP, Image Underst. **58**(1), 23–32 (1993) [591]
39. Franco, J.S., Boyer, E.: Exact polyhedral visual hulls. In: British Machine Vision Conference, pp. 329–338 (2003) [591]
40. Thomas, G.A.: Real-time camera pose estimation for augmenting sports scenes. In: Proc. of 3rd European Conf. on Visual Media Production (CVMP2006), London, UK, pp. 10–19 (November 2006) [588]
41. Thomas, G.A., Lau, H.Y.K.: Generation of high quality slow-motion replay using motion compensation. In: Proc. of International Broadcasting Convention (1990) [584]

42. Tsai, R.: A versatile camera calibration technique for high-accuracy 3D machine vision metrology using off-the-shelf TV cameras and lenses. IEEE J. Robot. Autom. 3(4), 323–344 (1987) [588]
43. Vedula, S., Baker, S., Rander, P., Collins, R., Kanade, T.: Three-dimensional scene flow. IEEE Trans. Pattern Anal. Mach. Intell. 27(3), 475–480 (2005) [585]
44. Vlasic, D., Baran, I., Matusik, W., Popović, J.: Articulated mesh animation from multi-view silhouettes. In: ACM SIGGRAPH 2008 papers, pp. 1–9. ACM, New York (2008) [586]
45. Vogiatzis, G., Esteban, C.H., Torr, P.H.S., Cipolla, R.: Multiview stereo via volumetric graph-cuts and occlusion robust photo-consistency. IEEE Trans. Pattern Anal. Mach. Intell. 29(12), 2241–2246 (2007) [585]
46. Weik, S., Wingbermühle, J., Niem, W.: Automatic creation of flexible antropomorphic models for 3D videoconferencing. In: Computer Graphics International, 1998. Proceedings, pp. 520–527. IEEE Comput. Soc., Los Alamitos (1998) [585]
47. Würmlin, S., Lamboray, E., Staadt, O.G., Gross, M.H.: 3D video recorder: A system for recording and playing free-viewpoint video. Comput. Graph. Forum 22, 181–193 (2003). Wiley Online Library [585,593]

Chapter 30
Vision for Driver Assistance: Looking at People in a Vehicle

Cuong Tran and Mohan Manubhai Trivedi

Abstract An important real-life application domain of computer vision techniques looking at people is in developing Intelligent Driver Assistance Systems (IDAS's). By analyzing information from both looking in and looking out of the vehicle, such systems can actively prevent vehicular accidents, improve driver safety as well as driver experience. Towards such goals, developing systems looking people in a vehicle (i.e. driver and passengers) to understand their intent, behavior, and states is needed. This is a challenging task which typically requires high reliability, accuracy, and efficient performance. Challenges also come from the dynamic background and varying lighting condition in driving scenes. However, looking at people in a vehicle also has its own characteristics which could be exploited to simplify the problem such as people typically sitting in a fixed position and their activities being highly related to the driving context. In this chapter, we give a concise overview of various related research studies to see how their approaches were developed to fit the specific requirements and characteristics of looking at people in a vehicle. From a historical point of view, we first discuss studies looking at head, eyes, and facial landmarks and then studies looking at body, hands, and feet. Despite lots of active research and published papers, developing accurate, reliable, and efficient approaches for looking at people in real-world driving scenarios is still an open problem. To this end, we will discuss some remaining issues for the future development in the area.

30.1 Introduction and Motivation

Automobiles were at the core of transforming lives of individuals and nations during the 20th century. However, despite their many benefits, motor vehicles pose a considerable safety risk. A study by World Health Organization mentions that annually, over 1.2 million fatalities and over 20 million serious injuries occur worldwide [28].

C. Tran (✉) · M.M. Trivedi
Laboratory for Intelligent and Safe Automobiles (LISA), University of California at San Diego, San Diego, CA 92037, USA
e-mail: cutran@ucsd.edu

M.M. Trivedi
e-mail: mtrivedi@ucsd.edu

T.B. Moeslund et al. (eds.), *Visual Analysis of Humans*,
DOI 10.1007/978-0-85729-997-0_30, © Springer-Verlag London Limited 2011

Fig. 30.1 Looking-in and
Looking-out of a vehicle [36]

Most roadway accidents are caused by driver error. A 2006 study sponsored by the
US Department of Transportation's National Highway Traffic Safety Administration concluded that driver inattention contributes to nearly 80 percent of crashes
and 65 percent of near crashes. Therefore in today's vehicles, embedded computing
systems are increasingly used to make them safer as well as more reliable, comfortable, and enjoyable to drive.

In vehicle-based safety systems, it is more desirable to prevent an accident (active
safety) rather than reduce the severity of injuries (passive safety). However, active-
safety systems also pose more difficult and challenging problems. To be effective,
such technologies must be human-centric and work in a "holistic" manner [34, 36].
As illustrated in Fig. 30.1, information from looking inside a vehicle (i.e. driver and
passengers), looking outside to the environment (e.g. looking at roads, other cars), as
well as vehicle sensors (e.g. measuring steering angle, speed) need to be taken into
account. In this chapter, we focus on the task of looking at people inside a vehicle
(i.e. driver and passengers) to understand their intent, behavior, and states. This task
is inherently challenging due to the dynamic driving scene background and varying
lighting condition. Moreover it also demands high reliability, accuracy, and efficient
performance (e.g. real-time performance for safety related applications). Obviously,
the fundamental computer vision and machine learning techniques looking at people, which were covered in previous chapters, are the foundation for techniques
looking at people inside a vehicle. However, human activity in a vehicle also has its
own characteristics, which should be exploited to improve the system performance
such as people typically sit in a fixed position and their activities are highly related
to the driving context (e.g. most of driver foot movements are related to pedal press
activity).

In the following sections, we provide a concise overview of several selected research studies focusing on how computer vision techniques are developed to fit the
requirements and characteristics of systems looking at people in a vehicle. We start
in Sect. 30.2 with a discussion of some criteria for categorizing existing approaches
such as their objective (e.g. to monitor driver fatigue or to analyze driver intent) or
the cueing information which is used (e.g. looking at head, eyes, or feet). Initially,

research studies in this area focus more on cues related to driver head like head pose, eye gaze, and facial landmarks which are needed to determine driver attention and fatigue state [3, 13, 14, 18, 20, 26, 30, 38]. Some selected approaches of this kind are covered in Sect. 30.3. More recently, beside these traditional cues, other parts of the body like hand movement, foot movement, or the whole upper body posture are also shown to be important for understanding people intent and behavior in a vehicle [6, 7, 19, 31, 33, 35]. We will talk about some selected approaches in this category in Sect. 30.4. Despite lots of active research, developing accurate, reliable, and efficient approaches for looking in a vehicle as well as combining them with looking-out information for holistic human-centered Intelligent Driver Assistance System (IDAS) are still open problems. Section 30.5 is a discussion of some open issues for the future development in the area, and finally we have some concluding remarks in Sect. 30.6.

30.2 Overview of Selected Studies

There are several ways to categorize related studies in the area depending on specific purpose. Figure 30.2 shows the basic steps of a common computer vision system looking at people. We see that approaches may use different types of input (e.g. monocular camera, stereo camera, camera with active infrared illuminators), extract different types of intermediate features, and aim to analyze different types of driver behavior or state. Beside these functional criteria, we can also categorize the approaches based on the fundamental techniques underlying their implementation at each step. With the goal of providing an overview of several selected research studies, we put them into a summary table (Table 30.1) with the following important elements associated with these approaches.

- Objective: What is the final goal of that study (e.g. to monitor driver fatigue, detect driver distraction, or to recognize driver turn intent)?
- Sensor input: Which type of sensor input is used (e.g. monocular, stereo, or thermal camera)?

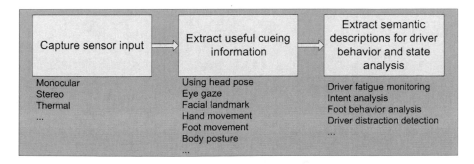

Fig. 30.2 Basic components of a system looking at people in a vehicle

Table 30.1 Overview of selected studies for looking at people in a vehicle

	Objective	Sensor input	Monitored body parts	Methodology and experimental evaluation
Grace et al. '98 [14]	Drowsiness detection for truck driver	Two PERCLOS [14] cameras	Eyes	Use illuminated eye detection and PERCLOS measurement. In-vehicle experiment
Smith et al. '03 [30]	Determination of driver visual attention	Monocular	Head eyes, and face features	Use appearance-based head and face features tracking. Model driver visual attention with FSM's. In-vehicle experiment
Ishikawa et al. '04 [18]	Driver gaze tracking	Monocular	Eyes	Use active appearance model to track the whole face. Then detect iris with template matching and estimate eye gaze. In-vehicle and simulation
Ji et al. '04 [20]	Driver fatigue monitoring and prediction	Two cameras with active infrared illuminators	Head, eye, facial landmarks	Combine illumination based and appearance-based techniques for eye detection. Fuse different information from head pose, eyes in a probabilistic fatigue model. Simulation experiment
Trivedi et al. '04 [35]	Occupant posture analysis	Stereo and thermal cameras	Body posture	Use head tracking to infer sitting posture. In-vehicle experiment
Fletcher et al. '05 [13]	Driver awareness monitoring	Commercial eye tracker	Eye gaze	Develop road sign recognition algorithm. Use epipolar geometry to correlate eye gaze with road scene for awareness monitoring. In-vehicle experiment
Veeraragha-van et al. '05 [37]	Unsafe driver activities detection	Monocular	Face and hands	Use motion of skin regions and a Bayesian classifier to detect some unsafe activities (e.g. drinking, using cellphone). Simulation experiment
Bergasa et al. '06 [3]	Driver vigilance monitoring	One camera w/illuminator	Head and eyes	Use PERCLOS, nodding frequency, blink frequency in a fuzzy inference system to compute vigilance level. In-vehicle experiment
Cheng and Trivedi '06 [6]	Turn intent analysis	Multi-modal sensors and maker-based motion capture	Head and hands	Use sparse Bayesian learning to classify turn intent and evaluate with different feature vector combination. In-vehicle experiment

(*continued on the next page*)

Table 30.1   (Continued)

	Objective	Sensor input	Monitored body parts	Methodology and experimental evaluation
Cheng et al. '06 [5]	Driver hand grasp and turn analysis	Color and thermal camera	Head and hands	Use optical flow head tracking and HMM based activity classifier. In-vehicle experiment
Ito and Kanade '08 [19]	Prediction of 9 driver operations	Monocular	Body	Track 6 marker points on shoulders, elbows, and wrists. Use discriminant analysis to learn Gaussian operation models and then Bayesian classifier. Simulation experiment
Doshi and Trivedi '09 [11]	Driver lane change intent analysis	Monocular	Head, eye	Use Relevance Vector Machine for lane change prediction (optical flow based head motion, manually labeled eye gaze). In-vehicle and simulation
Tran and Trivedi '09 [31]	Driver distraction monitoring	3 cameras	Head, hands	Combine tracked head pose and hand position using a rule-based approach. In-vehicle experiment
Murphy-Chutorian and Trivedi '10 [26]	Real-time 3D head pose tracking	Monocular	Head	Hybrid method combining static pose estimation with an appearance-based particle filter 3D head tracking algorithm. In-vehicle experiment
Wu and Trivedi '10 [38]	Eye gaze tracking and blink recognition	Monocular	Eye	Use two interactive Particle Filters to simultaneously track eyes and detect blinks. In-vehicle and lab experiment
Cheng and Trivedi '10 [7]	Driver & passenger hand determination	Monocular camera with illuminator	Hands	Use HOG feature descriptor and SVM classifier. In-vehicle experiment

- Monitored body parts: Which type of cueing feature is extracted (e.g. information about head pose, eye gaze, body posture, or foot movement)?
- Methodology and algorithm: The underlying techniques that were used
- Experiment and evaluation: How were the proposed approach evaluated? Was it actually evaluated in real-world driving scenario or indoor simulation?

In the next sections, we will review several selected methods focusing on how computer vision techniques were developed to fit the requirements and characteristics of systems looking at people in a vehicle. Based on the type of cueing information, we will discuss those approaches in two main categories which are approaches looking at driver head, face, and facial landmarks (Sect. 30.3) and approaches look-ing at driver body, hands, and feet (Sect. 30.4).

30.3 Looking at Driver Head, Face, and Facial Landmarks

Initial research studies looking at driver focused more on cues related to driver head like head pose, eye gaze, and facial landmarks. This kind of cueing features were shown to be important in determining driver attention and cognitive state (e.g. fa-tigue) [3, 13–15, 20]. Some example studies in this category are approaches for monitoring and prediction of driver fatigue, driver head pose tracking for monitor-ing driver awareness, eye tracking and blink recognition.

30.3.1 Monitoring and Prediction of Driver Fatigue

The National Highway Traffic Safety Administration (NHTSA) [27] has reported drowsy drivers as an important cause for fatal on road crashes and injuries in the U.S. Therefore, developing systems that actively monitor a driver's level of vigi-lance and alert the driver of any insecure driving conditions is desirable for accident prevention. Different approaches were used to tackle the problem such as assessing the vigilance capacity of an operator before the work is perform [9], assess the driver state using sensors mounted on the driver to measure heart rate, brain activity [39] or using vehicle embedded sensors information (e.g. steering wheel movements, accel-eration and braking profiles) [2]. Computer vision techniques looking at the driver could provide another non-intrusive approach to the problem. Research studies have shown that information such as the PERCLOS measurement introduced by Grace et al. [14] are highly correlated to fatigue state and can be used to monitor driver fatigue. Other head and face related features like eye blink frequency, eye move-ment, nodding frequency, facial expression have also been used for driver fatigue and vigilance analysis [3, 20].

We will take a look at a representative approach proposed by Ji et al. [20] for real-time monitoring and prediction of driver fatigue. In order to achieve the robust-ness required for in-vehicle applications, different cues including eyelid movement, gaze movement, head movement, and facial expression were extracted and fused in a Bayesian Network for human fatigue modeling and prediction. Two CCD cam-eras with active infrared illuminators were used. For eye detection and tracking, the bright pupil technique was combined with an appearance-based technique us-ing a SVM classifier to improve the robustness. This information of eye detection and tracking was then also utilized in their algorithm for tracking head pose with Kalman filter and using Gabor features to track facial landmarks around the mouth and eye regions.

The validation of the eye detection and tracking part as well as the extracted fa-tigue parameters and score were provided which showed some good results (e.g.

0.05% false-alarm rate and a 4.2% misdetection rate). However, it seems that the proposed approach was only evaluated with data from indoor environment. Therefore how this approach work with real-world driving scenarios with their challenges is still an open question.

30.3.2 Eye Localization, Tracking and Blink Pattern Recognition

Focusing on the task of robustly extracting visual cue information, a former member of our team Wu et al. proposed an appearance-based approach using monocular camera input for eye tracking and blink pattern recognition [38]. For better accuracy and robustness, a binary tree is used to model the statistical structure of the object's feature space. This is a kind of global to local representation in which each subtree explains more detailed information than its parent tree (useful to represent object with high-order substructures like eye image). After the eyes are automatically located, a particle filter-based approach is used to simultaneously track eyes and detect blinks. Two interactive particle filters were used, one for open-eye and one for close-eye. The posterior probabilities learned by the particle filters are used to determine which particle filter gives the correct tracks. This particle filter is then labeled as the primary one and used to reinitialize the other particle filter. The performance of both the blink detection rate and the eye tracking accuracy were evaluated and showed good results with various scenarios including indoor and in-vehicle data sequences as well as the FRGC (Face Recognition Grand Challenge) benchmark data for evaluation of tracking accuracy.

Also focusing on a robust eye gaze tracking system, Ishikawa et al. [18] proposed to track the whole face with AAMs for more reliable extraction of eye regions and head pose. Based on the extracted eye regions, a template matching method is used to detect iris and use that for eye gaze estimation. This approach was evaluated and showed promising results with a few subjects for both indoor and in vehicle video sequences.

30.3.3 Tracking Driver Head Pose

Head pose information is also a strong indicator of a driver's field of view and current focus of attention and typically is less noisy than eye gaze. Driver head-motion estimation has also been used along with video-based lane detection and the vehicle CAN-bus (Controller Area Network) data to predict the driver's intent to change lanes in advance of the actual movement of the vehicle [22]. Related works in head pose estimation can be roughly categorized into static head pose estimation methods which estimate head pose directly from the current still image, tracking methods which recover the global pose change of the head from the observed movement between video frames, and hybrid methods. A detailed survey of head pose estimation and tracking approaches can be found in [25]. Up to now, computational head pose estimation still remains a challenging vision problem, and there are no solutions that are both inexpensive and widely available. In [26], a former member of our team Murphy-Chutorian et al. proposed an integrated approach using monocular camera input for real-time driver head pose tracking in 3D. In order to overcome the difficulties inherent with varying lighting conditions in a moving car, a static head pose estimator using support vector regressors (SVRs) was combined with an appearance-based particle filter for 3-D head model tracking in an augmented reality environment.

For initial head pose estimation with SVRs, the Local Gradient Orientation (LGO) histogram, which is robust to minor deviations in region alignment, lighting, was used. The LGO histogram of a scale-normalized facial region is a 3D histogram $M \times N \times O$ in which the first two dimensions correspond to the vertical and horizontal positions in the image and the third to the gradient orientation. Based on the initial head pose estimation, an appearance-based particle filter in an augmented reality, which is a virtual environment that mimics the view space of a real camera, is used to track the driver head in 3D. Using an initial estimate of the head position and orientation, the system generates a texture-mapped 3-D model of the head from the most recent video image and places it into the environment. A particle filter approach is then used to match the view from each subsequent video frame. Though this operation is computationally expensive, it was highly optimized for graphic processing units (GPUs) in the proposed implementation to achieve real-time performance (tracking head at ~30 frames per second). Evaluation of this approach showed good results in real-world driving situations with drivers of varying ages, race, and sex spanning daytime and nighttime conditions.

30.4 Looking at Driver Body, Hands, and Feet

Beside cues from head, eyes, and facial features, information from other parts of the driver body like hand movement, foot movement, or the whole upper body posture also provides important information. Recently, there have been more research studies making use of such cues for better understanding of driver intent, behavior [6, 7, 31, 33].

30.4.1 Looking at Hands

Looking at driver hands is needed since it is an important factor in controlling the vehicle. However, it has not been studied much in the area of looking inside a vehicle. In [6], a sparse Bayesian classifier taking into account both hand position and head pose was developed for lane change intent prediction. Hand position was also used in a system assisting driver in "keeping hands on the wheel and eyes on the road" [31]. A rule-based approach with state machines was used to combine hand

Fig. 30.3 System for "keeping hands on the wheel and eyes on the road" [31]

position and head pose in monitoring driver distraction (Fig. 30.3). In [7], a former member of our team Cheng et al. proposed a novel real-time computer-vision system that robustly discriminates which of the front-row seat occupants is accessing the infotainment controls. The knowledge of who is the user-that is, driver, passenger, or no one-can alleviate driver distraction and maximize the passenger infotainment experience (e.g. the infotainment system should only provide its fancy options, which can be distracting, to the passenger but not the driver). The algorithm uses a modified histogram-of-oriented-gradients HOG feature descriptor to represent the image area over the infotainment controls and a SVM and median filtering over time to classify each image to one of the three classes with ~96% average correct classification rate. This rate was achieved over a wide range of illumination conditions, human subjects, and times of day.

30.4.2 Modeling and Prediction of Driver Foot Behavior

Beside hands, driver feet also has an important role in controlling the vehicle. In addition to information from embedded pedal sensors, the visual foot movement before and after a pedal press can provide valuable information for better semantic understanding of driver behavior, state, and style. They can also be used to gain a time advantage in predicting a pedal press before it actually happens, which is very important for providing proper assistance to driver in time critical (e.g. safety related) situations. However, there were very few research studies in analyzing driver foot information. Mulder et al. have introduced a haptic gas pedal feedback system for car-following [23] in which the gas pedal position was used to improve the system performance. A former member of our team McCall et al. [22] developed a brake assistance system, which took into account both driver's intent to brake (from pedal positions and the camera-based foot position) and the need to brake given the current situation.

Recently, our team has examined an approach for driver foot behavior analysis using a monocular foot camera input. The underlying idea is motivated by the fact that driver foot movement is highly related to the pedal press activity. After tracking the foot movement with an optical flow based tracking method, a 7-state HMM) for describing foot behavior was specifically designed for driving scenarios (Fig. 30.4). The elements of this driver foot behavior HMM are as follows.

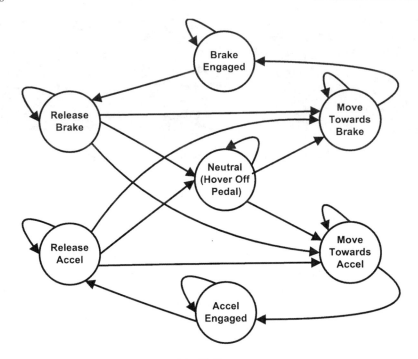

Fig. 30.4 Foot behavior HMM state model with 7 states

- *Hidden states*: We have 7 states $\{s_1, s_2, s_3, s_4, s_5, s_6, s_7\}$ including *Neutral, BrkEngage, AccEngage, TowardsBrk, TowardsAcc, ReleaseBrk, ReleaseAcc*. The state at time t is denoted by the random variable q_t.
- *Observation*: The observation at time t is denoted by the random variable O_t which has 6 components $O_t = \{p_x, p_y, v_x, v_y, B, A\}$ where $\{p_x, p_y, v_x, v_y\}$ are the current estimated position and velocity of driver foot. $\{B, A\}$ are obtained from vehicle CAN information which determine whether the brake and accelerator are currently engaged or not.
- *Observation probability distributions*: In our HMM model, we assume a Gaussian output probability distribution $P(O_t|q_t = s_i) = N(\mu_i, \sigma_i)$.
- *Transition matrix*: $A = \{a_{ij}\}$ is a 7×7 state transition matrix where a_{ij} is the probability of making a transition from state s_i to s_j, $a_{ij} = P(q_{t+1} = s_j|q_t = s_i)$.
- *Initial state distribution*: Assume an uniform distribution of the initial states.

Utilizing reliable information from the vehicle CAN data, an automatic data labeling procedure was developed for training and evaluating of the HMM model. The HMM model parameters Λ including the Gaussian observation probability distribution and the transition matrix are learned using a Baum–Welch algorithm.

The meaning of these estimated foot behavior states also connect directly to the prediction of actual pedal presses (i.e. when the foot is in the state *TowardsBrk* or *TowardsAcc*, we can predict a corresponding brake or acceleration press in near future). This approach was evaluated with data from a real-world driving testbed

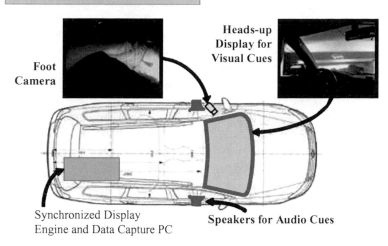

Fig. 30.5 Vehicle testbed configuration for foot analysis experiment

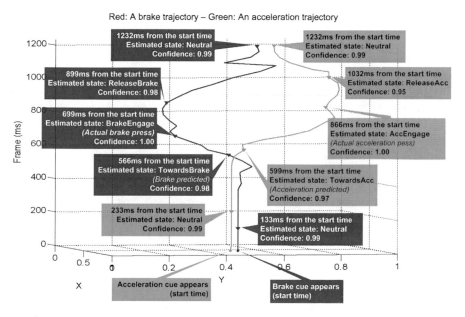

Fig. 30.6 Tracked trajectories of a brake (red) and an acceleration (blue). The labeled points show the outputs of the HMM based foot behavior analysis

(Fig. 30.5). An experimental data collection paradigm was designed to approximate stop-and-go traffic in which the driver will accelerate or brake depending on whether the stop or go cue is shown. Figure 30.6 visualizes the outputs of the approach for a brake and an acceleration example. Over all 15 experimental runs with 128 trials (a stop or go cue is shown) per run, a major part ~75% of the pedal presses can be predicted with ~95% accuracy at 133 ms prior to the actual pedal press. Regarding the misapplication cases (i.e. subjects were cued to hit a specific pedal but instead applied the wrong pedal), all of them were predicted correctly ~200 ms on average before the actual press, which is actually earlier than for general pedal press prediction. This indicates the potential of using the proposed approach in predicting and mitigating pedal errors which is one problem of recent interest to the automotive safety community [16].

30.4.3 Analyzing Driver Posture for Driver Assistance

The whole body posture is another cueing information that should be explored more in looking at people inside a vehicle. Figure 30.7 shows some possible ranges of driver posture movement which might have connection to driver state and intention. For example, leaning backward might indicate relax position, leaning forward indicates concentration. Driver may also change posture in preparation for some specific tasks such as moving head forward to prepare for a better visual check before lane change. In [19], Ito and Kanade used six marker points on shoulders, elbows, and wrists to predict nine driver operations toward different destinations including navigation, A/C, left vent, right vent, gear box, console box, passenger seat, glove compartment, and rear-view mirror. Their approach has been evaluated with different subjects in driving simulation with high prediction accuracy 90% and low false positive rate 1.4%. This approach, however, requires putting markers on the driver. In [8], Datta et al. have developed a markerless approach for tracking systems of articulated planes was also applied to track 2D driver body pose on these same simulation data. Though this approach has automated the tracking part, it still requires a manual initialization of the tracking model.

Beside looking at driver, looking at occupant posture is also important. In [35], our team investigated basic feasibility of using stereo and thermal long-wavelength infrared video for occupant position and posture analysis, which is a key requirement in designing "smart airbag" systems. In this investigation, our suggestion was to use head tracking information, which is easier to track, instead of more detailed

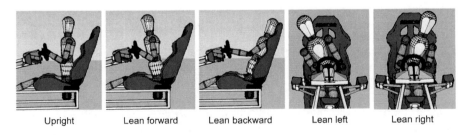

| Upright | Lean forward | Lean backward | Lean left | Lean right |

Fig. 30.7 Illustration of some possible range of driver posture movement during driving

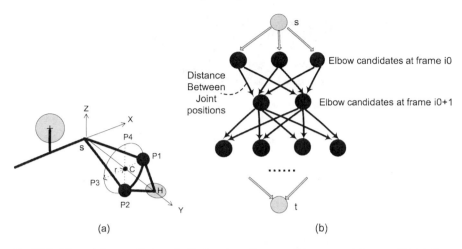

Fig. 30.8 Elbow joints prediction. (*Left*) Generate elbow candidates at each frames. (*Right*) Over a temporal segment, select the sequence of elbow joints that minimizes the joint displacement. By adding 2 pseudo nodes s and t with zero-weighted edges, this can be represented as a shortest path problem

occupant posture analysis for robust "smart airbag" deployment. However, for potential applications goes beyond the purpose of "smart airbag" such as driver attentiveness analysis and human-machine interfaces inside the car, we see we need to look at more detailed body posture of driver and occupant.

Our team has developed a computational approach for upper body tracking using the 3D movement of extremities (head and hands) [32]. This approach tracks a 3D skeletal upper body model which can be determined by a set of upper body joints and end points positions. To achieve robustness and real-time performance, this approach first tracks the 3D movements of extremities, including head and hands. Then using human upper body configuration constraints, movements of the extremities are used to predict the whole 3D upper body motion with inner joints. Since the head and hand regions are typically well defined and undergo less occlusion, tracking is more reliable and could enable us more robust upper body pose determination. Moreover by breaking the problem of high-dimensional search for upper body pose into two steps, the complexity is reduced considerably. The downside is that we need to deal with the ambiguity in inverse kinematics of upper body, i.e. there could be various upper body poses corresponding to the same head and hands positions. However, this issue is reduced in driving scenarios, since the driver typically sits in a fixed position. To deal with this ambiguity, the "temporal inverse kinematics" based on observation of dynamics of the extremities was used instead of just inverse kinematics constraints at each single frame.

Figure 30.8 briefly describes this idea with a numerical method to predict elbow joint sequences. Since the lengths of upper arm and lower arm are fixed, possible elbow joint positions with known shoulder joint position S and hand position H will lie on a circle. At each frame, the range of possible elbow joint (the mentioned circle) is determined and then quantized into several elbow candidates based on a distance

Fig. 30.9 Superimposed results of 3D driver body pose tracking using extremities movement

threshold between candidates (Fig. 30.8(left)). For a whole temporal segmentation, the selected sequence is the one that minimize the total elbow joint displacement. As shown in Fig. 30.8(right), this selection can be represented as a shortest path problem. Due to the layer structure of the constructed graph, a dynamic programming technique can be used to solve this shortest path problem in linear time complexity $O(n)$ where n is the number of frames in the sequence.

This approach was validated and showed good results with various subjects in both indoor and in vehicle environments. Figure 30.9 shows some example results of the 3D driver body pose tracking superimposed on input images for visual evaluation.

30.5 Open Issues for Future Research

Some related research studies have shown promising results. However, the development of accurate, reliable, and efficient approaches to looking at people in a vehicle for real-world driver assistance systems is still in its infancy. In this section, we will discuss some of the main issues that we think should be addressed for the future development in the area.

- Coordination between real-world and simulation testbeds: Simulation environments have the advantage of more flexibility in configuring sensors and designing experiment tasks for deeper analysis, which might be difficult and unsafe for implementing in real-world driving. However, the ultimate goal is to develop systems that work for real vehicle and there are always gaps between simulation environment and real world. Therefore in general a coordination between real-world driving and simulation environment is useful and should be considered in the development process.
- Looking at driver body at multiple levels: To achieve robustness and accuracy, a potential trend is to combine cues at multiple body levels since human body is a homogeneous and harmonious whole and behavior and states are generally expressed at different body levels simultaneously. However, we see that cueing information from different body parts have different characteristics and typically require different approaches to extract. Therefore how to develop efficient systems looking at driver body at multiple levels is still an open question.
- Investigating the role of features extracted from different body parts: Depending on the concerned behavior and/or cognitive state, features from some body parts may be useful, while others may not or may even be distracting factors. Moreover

for efficiency, only useful feature cues should be extracted. In [11], Doshi et al. from our team have done a comparative study on the role of head pose and eye gaze for driver lane change intent analysis. The results indicated that head pose, which is typically less noisy and easier to track than eye gaze, is actually a better feature for lane change intent prediction. In general, how to systematically do similar investigation for different feature cues and analysis tasks is desirable.

- Combining looking-in and looking-out: Some research studies have combined the output of looking-in and looking-out analysis for different assistance systems such as driver intent analysis [7, 10, 21], intelligent brake assistance [22], traffic sign awareness [13], driver distraction [17]. In [29], Pugeault and Bowden showed that information from a looking-out camera can be used to predict some driver actions including steering left or right, pressing accelerator, brake, or clutch. This implies that the contextual information from looking-out is also important to looking-in analysis of driver behavior and states. In general, both looking-in and looking-out information will be needed in developing efficient human-centered driver assistance systems [34, 36].

- Interacting with driver when needed: Generally, IDAS's need to have the ability to provide feedbacks to the user when needed (e.g. to alert driver in critical situations). However, these IDAS feedbacks must be introduced carefully to ensure that they do not confuse or distract the driver, thereby undermining their intended purpose. Generally, interdisciplinary efforts need investigation as to the effect of different feedback mechanisms including visual, audio, and/or haptic feedback [1].

- Learning individual driver models vs. generic driver models: It has been noted that individual drivers may act and respond in different ways under various conditions [4, 12, 24]. Therefore, it might be difficult to learn generic driver models that work well for all drivers. In order to achieve better performance, adapting the assistance systems to individual drivers based on their style and preferences has been needed. Murphey et al. [24] used the pedal press profile for classification of driver styles (i.e. calm, normal, and aggressive) and showed the correlation between these styles and the fuel consumption. In [12], our team has also studied some measures of driving style and their correlation with the predictability and responsiveness of the driver. The results indicated that "aggressive" drivers are more predictable than "non-aggressive" drivers, while "non-aggressive" drivers are more receptive of feedback from Driver Assistance Systems.

30.6 Conclusion

Looking at people in a vehicle to understand their behavior and state is an important area which plays a significant role in developing human-centered Intelligent Driver Assistance Systems. The task is challenging due to the high demand on reliability and efficiency as well as the inherent computer vision difficulty of dynamic background and varying lighting conditions. In this chapter, we provided a concise overview of several selected research studies looking at different body parts ranging from coarse body to more detailed levels of feet, hands, head, eyes, and facial landmarks. To overcome the inherent challenges and achieve the required performance, some high-level directions learned from those studies are as follows.

- Design techniques which are specific for in-vehicle applications utilizing the characteristics such as that a driver typically sits in a fixed position or driver foot movement is highly related to pedal press actions.
- Integrate cueing information from different body parts.
- Consider the trade-offs between the cues that can be extracted more reliably and the cues that seem to be useful but hard to extract.
- Make use of both dynamic information (body motion) and static information (body appearance).
- Make use of different input modalities (e.g. color cameras and thermal infrared cameras).

Despite lots of active studies, more research efforts are still needed to bring these high-level ideas into development of accurate, reliable, and efficient approaches for looking at people in a vehicle and actually improve the lives of drivers around the world.

30.6.1 Further Reading

Interested readers may consult the following references for a broad overview of research topic trends and research groups in the area of intelligent transportation systems.

- Li, L., Li, X., Cheng, C., Chen, C., Ke, G., Zeng, D., Scherer, W.T.: Research collaboration and ITS topic evolution: 10 years at T-ITS. IEEE Trans. Intell. Transp. Syst. (June 2010)
- Li, L., Li, X., Li, Z., Zeng, D., Scherer, W.T.: A bibliographic analysis of the IEEE transactions on intelligent transportation systems literature. IEEE Trans. Intell. Transp. Syst. (October 2010)

Acknowledgements   We thank the sponsorships of U.C. Discovery Program, National Science Foundation as well as industry sponsors including Nissan, Volkswagen Electronic Research Laboratory, and Mercedes. We also thank former and current colleagues from our Laboratory for Intelligent and Safe Automobiles (LISA) for their cooperation, assistance, and contributions: Dr. Kohsia Huang, Dr. Joel McCall, Dr. Tarak Gandhi, Dr. Sangho Park, Dr. Shinko Cheng, Dr. Steve Krotosky, Dr. Junwen Wu, Dr. Erik Murphy-Chutorian, Dr. Brendan Morris, Dr. Anup Doshi, Mr. Sayanan Sivaraman, Mr. Ashish Tawari, and Mr. Ofer Achlertheir.

References

1. Adell, E., Várhelyi, A.: Development of HMI components for a driver assistance system for safe speed and safe distance. In: The 13th World Congress and Exhibition on Intelligent Transport Systems and Services ExCel London, United Kingdom (2006) [611]

2. Artaud, P., Planque, S., Lavergne, C., Cara, H., de Lepine, P., Tarriere, C., Gueguen, B.: An on-board system for detecting lapses of alertness in car driving. In: The 14th Int. Conf. Enhanced Safety of Vehicles (1994) [602]

3. Bergasa, L.M., Nuevo, J., Sotelo, M.A., Barea, R., Lopez, M.E.: Real-time system for monitoring driver vigilance. IEEE Trans. Intell. Transp. Syst. **7**(1), 63–77 (2006) [599,600,602]

4. Burnham, G.O., Seo, J., Bekey, G.A.: Identification of human drivers models in car following. IEEE Trans. Autom. Control **19**(6), 911–915 (1974) [611]

5. Cheng, S.Y., Park, S., Trivedi, M.M.: Multiperspective and multimodal video arrays for 3d body tracking and activity analysis. Comput. Vis. Image Underst. (Special Issue on Advances in Vision Algorithms and Systems Beyond the Visible Spectrum) **106**(2–3), 245–257 (2007) [601]

6. Cheng, S.Y., Trivedi, M.M.: Turn-intent analysis using body pose for intelligent driver assistance. IEEE Pervasive Comput. **5**(4), 28–37 (2006) [599,600,604]

7. Cheng, S.Y., Trivedi, M.M.: Vision-based infotainment user determination by hand recognition for driver assistance. IEEE Trans. Intell. Transp. Syst. **11**(3), 759–764 (2010) [599,601, 604,605,611]

8. Datta, A., Sheikh, Y., Kanade, T.: Linear motion estimation for systems of articulated planes. In: IEEE Conference on Computer Vision and Pattern Recognition (2008) [608]

9. Dinges, D., Mallis, M.: Managing fatigue by drowsiness detection: Can technological promises be realized? In: Hartley, L. (ed.) Managing Fatigue in Transportation, Elsevier, Oxford (1998) [602]

10. Doshi, A., Trivedi, M.M.: Investigating the relationships between gaze patterns, dynamic vehicle surround analysis, and driver intentions. In: IEEE Intelligent Vehicles Symposium (2009) [611]

11. Doshi, A., Trivedi, M.M.: On the roles of eye gaze and head pose in predicting driver's intent to change lanes. IEEE Trans. Intell. Transp. Syst. **10**(3), 453–462 (2009) [601,611]

12. Doshi, A., Trivedi, M.M.: Examining the impact of driving style on the predictability and responsiveness of the driver: Real-world and simulator analysis. In: IEEE Intelligent Vehicles Symposium (2010) [611]

13. Fletchera, L., Loyb, G., Barnesc, N., Zelinsky, A.: Correlating driver gaze with the road scene for driver assistance systems. Robot. Auton. Syst. **52**(1), 71–84 (2005) [599,600,602,611]

14. Grace, R., Byrne, V.E., Bierman, D.M., Legrand, J.M., Davis, R.K., Staszewski, J.J., Carnahan, B.: A drowsy driver detection system for heavy vehicles. In: Digital Avionics Systems Conference, Proceedings, The 17th DASC, The AIAA/IEEE/SAE (1998) [599,600,602]

15. Hammoud, R., Wilhelm, A., Malawey, P., Witt, G.: Efficient realtime algorithms for eye state and head pose tracking in advanced driver support systems. In: IEEE Conference on Computer Vision and Pattern Recognition (2005) [602]

16. Healey, J.R., Carty, S.S.: Driver error found in some Toyota acceleration cases. In: USA Today (2010) [608]

17. Huang, K.S., Trivedi, M.M., Gandhi, T.: Driver's view and vehicle surround estimation using omnidirectional video stream. In: IEEE Intelligent Vehicles Symposium (2003) [611]

18. Ishikawa, T., Baker, S., Matthews, I., Kanade, T.: Passive driver gaze tracking with active appearance models. In: The 11th World Congress on Intelligent Transportation Systems (2004) [599,600,603]

19. Ito, T., Kanade, T.: Predicting driver operations inside vehicles. In: IEEE International Conference on Automatic Face and Gesture Recognition (2008) [599,601,608]

20. Ji, Q., Zhu, Z., Lan, P.: Real time non-intrusive monitoring and prediction of driver fatigue. IEEE Trans. Veh. Technol. **53**(4), 1052–1068 (2004) [599,600,602]

21. McCall, J., Wipf, D., Trivedi, M.M., Rao, B.: Lane change intent analysis using robust operators and sparse Bayesian learning. IEEE Trans. Intell. Transp. Syst. **8**(3), 431–440 (2007) [611]

22. McCall, J.C., Trivedi, M.M.: Driver behavior and situation aware brake assistance for intelligent vehicles. Proc. IEEE **95**(2), 374–387 (2007) [603,605,611]

23. Mulder, M., Pauwelussen, J.J.A., van Paassen, M.M., Mulder, M., Abbink, D.A.: Active deceleration support in car following. IEEE Trans. Syst. Man Cybern., Part A, Syst. Hum. **40**(6), 1271–1284 (2010) [605]

24. Murphey, Y.L., Milton, R., Kiliaris, L.: Driver's style classification using jerk analysis. In: IEEE Workshop on Computational Intelligence in Vehicles and Vehicular Systems (2009) [611]

25. Murphy-Chutorian, E., Trivedi, M.M.: Head pose estimation in computer vision: A survey. IEEE Trans. Pattern Anal. Mach. Intell. **31**(4), 607–626 (2009) [604]

26. Murphy-Chutorian, E., Trivedi, M.M.: Head pose estimation and augmented reality tracking: An integrated system and evaluation for monitoring driver awareness. IEEE Trans. Intell. Transp. Syst. **11**(2), 300–311 (2010) [599,601,604]

27. NHTSA: Traffic safety facts 2006 – a compilation of motor vehicle crash data from the fatality analysis reporting system and the general estimates system. In: Washington, DC: Nat. Center Stat. Anal., US Dept. Transp. (2006) [602]

28. Peden, M., Scurfield, R., Sleet, D., Mohan, D., Hyder, A.A., Jarawan, E., Mathers, C.: World report on road traffic injury prevention: Summary. In: World Health Organization, Geneva, Switzerland (2004) [597]

29. Pugeault, N., Bowden, R.: Learning pre-attentive driving behaviour from holistic visual features. In: The 11th European Conference on Computer Vision (2010) [611]

30. Smith, P., Shah, M., Lobo, N.V.: Determining driver visual attention with one camera. IEEE Trans. Intell. Transp. Syst. **4**(4), 205–218 (2003) [599]

31. Tran, C., Trivedi, M.M.: Driver assistance for keeping hands on the wheel and eyes on the road. In: IEEE International Conference on Vehicular Electronics and Safety (2009) [599, 601,604,605]

32. Tran, C., Trivedi, M.M.: Introducing 'XMOB': Extremity movement observation framework for upper body pose tracking in 3d. In: IEEE International Symposium on Multimedia (2009) [609]

33. Tran, C., Trivedi, M.M.: Towards a vision-based system exploring 3d driver posture dynamics for driver assistance: Issues and possibilities. In: IEEE Intelligent Vehicles Symposium (2010) [599,604]

34. Trivedi, M.M., Cheng, S.Y.: Holistic sensing and active displays for intelligent driver support systems. IEEE Comput. **40**(5), 60–68 (2007) [598,611]

35. Trivedi, M.M., Cheng, S.Y., Childers, E., Krotosky, S.: Occupant posture analysis with stereo and thermal infrared video: Algorithms and experimental evaluation. IEEE Trans. Veh. Technol. (Special Issue on In-Vehicle Vision Systems) **53**(6), 1698–1712 (2004) [599,600,608]

36. Trivedi, M.M., Gandhi, T., McCall, J.: Looking-in and looking-out of a vehicle: Computer-vision-based enhanced vehicle safety. IEEE Trans. Intell. Transp. Syst. **8**(1), 108–120 (2007) [598,611]

37. Veeraraghavan, H., Atev, S., Bird, N., Schrater, P., Papanikolopoulos, N.: Driver activity monitoring through supervised and unsupervised learning. In: IEEE Conference on Intelligent Transportation Systems (2005) [600]

38. Wu, J., Trivedi, M.M.: An eye localization, tracking and blink pattern recognition system: Algorithm and evaluation. ACM Trans. Multimedia Comput. Commun. Appl. **6**(2) (2010) [599,601,603]

39. Yammamoto, K., Higuchi, S.: Development of a drowsiness warning system. J. Soc. Automot. Eng. Jpn. (1992) [602]

Glossary

3D video 3D surface sequence without temporally coherent structure. 581

4D model 3D surface sequence with temporally coherent structure and known temporal correspondence. 581

AAM Active Appearance Model. 385, 386, 389, 390, 395, 399, 496, 554, 603

action primitive Action primitives are considered to be building blocks out of which complex actions or activities are composed. In that sense, action primitives are similar to phonemes out of which utterances are composed. Other terms exist also, like *actemes*, etc. 281, 283–285

ANN Artificial Neural Networks (ANNs) is the umbrella term for a large class of machine learning techniques, among them Multi-Layer Perceptrons, Convolutional Neural Networks, and Kohonen Self-Organizing Maps. Their commonalities are to formulate machine learning problems in terms of networks of "artificial neuron" units (input, output, and intermediate hidden ones) that are connected via activation links with learned weights and a, typically non-linear, activation function. 40, 73, 78, 339, 390, 549–551

ARMA Auto Regressive Moving Average Model: Given a time series of data the ARMA model is a tool for understanding and, perhaps, predicting future values in this series. The model consists of two parts, an autoregressive (AR) part and a moving average (MA) part. 48, 305

ASL American Sign Language. 501, 503, 540, 542, 547, 550

BFGS Broyden–Fletcher–Goldfarb–Shanno (BFGS) is an approximation of Newton's method for solving nonlinear optimization problems. 478

BN Bayesian network. 299, 339, 391, 399

body frame The body frame is a frame of reference fixed at the moving body. 147

BSL British Sign Language. 540, 542, 547, 549

CCTV Closed-Circuit TeleVision. 110, 432, 455, 456

CFG Context-Free Grammar. 298, 299, 345

CRBM A Conditional Restricted Boltzmann Machine is an extension of an RBM designed to model time series data. 189, 190

T.B. Moeslund et al. (eds.), *Visual Analysis of Humans*,
DOI 10.1007/978-0-85729-997-0, © Springer-Verlag London Limited 2011

CRF Conditional Random Field: A discriminative probabilistic graphical model. 62, 213, 286, 338, 339, 345, 346, 367, 368, 370–372, 395, 422, 525

CS Compressed Sensing. 437–439, 451

DBN Dynamic Bayesian network. 286, 299, 326, 390, 391, 395, 462, 502, 525

DFA Deterministic Finite Automaton. 551

DGS Deutsche Gebärdensprache/German sign language. 554, 555

discriminative model Discriminative models typically model a conditional distribution of target outputs given a set of inputs. Discriminative models differ from generative models in that they do not allow one to generate samples from the joint distribution over inputs and outputs (and/or hidden variables). Discriminative models are particularly well suited for input–output tasks such as classification or regression. 132, 190, 228, 271, 334, 345

DoF Degrees of Freedom. 502–505

DP Dynamic Programming. A combinatorial algorithm for optimizing decomposable objective functions recursively. 206, 211

DPM Deformable Part-based Model. 57, 59, 65

DTW Dynamic Time Warping, a technique for temporal alignment of sequences. 545, 552, 553

EGM Elastic Graph Matching. 496

EKF The Extended Kalman Filter is a Kalman filter where the state update and measurement equations do not need to be linear functions of the state. 17, 21, 576

EM In statistics, an Expectation–Maximization algorithm is a method for finding maximum likelihood or maximum a posteriori (MAP) estimates of parameters in statistical models, where the model depends on unobserved latent variables. 35, 159, 337

filtering distribution The filtering distribution is a distribution of the form $p(X_k|Y_0, Y_0, \ldots, Y_k)$. 173

FLD Fisher Linear Discriminant. 438

forward kinematics Given an articulated body parameterized by joint angles $\Theta \in Q$, the forward kinematics is defined as the mapping from the vector of joint angles to the position and orientation of the body segment $\mathbf{G}_{sb} : Q \to SE(3)$. 147, 265

FVV Free-Viewpoint Video allowing a user to interactively change the viewpoint by rendering novel virtual views of a scenes which are different from the real camera viewpoint. 582, 583, 589

generative model Generative models are models capable of generating (synthesizing) observable data. Generative models are able to model joint probability distributions over the input, output and hidden variables in the model. During inference generative models are often used as an intermediate step in forming conditional distribution of interest. Generative models, in contrast to discriminative models, provide a full probabilistic model over all variables, whereas a discriminative model provides a model over the target output variable(s) conditioned on the input variables. 132–134, 153, 190, 228, 270, 283, 284, 334–336, 338, 339, 345

Gibbs sampling Gibbs sampling is used for statistical inference on graphical models which proceeds by sequentially sampling a single variable holding all others fixed. 207, 315, 316, 318

gimbal lock Gimbal lock is the loss of one of the three DoF of a rotation parameterized by either Euler angles or three concatenated revolute joints. It occurs when two of the axes of rotation align and therefore one degree of freedom is lost. 142, 143, 149

GMM Gaussian Mixture Model: see also mixture of Gaussians. 336–338

GP A Gaussian Process is a continuous stochastic process defined on a real-valued domain (e.g., time). It defines a Gaussian distribution over functions, and is fully characterized by a mean function and a covariance function. In addition any realization at a finite set of points in the domain (e.g., time instants) forms a multivariate Gaussian density. 179, 180, 182, 185, 186, 344, 498

GPDM A Gaussian Process Dynamical Model is an extension of the GPLVM to handle high-dimensional time series data. In addition to the probabilistic generative mapping from latent positions to the observation in the GPLVM, it includes a dynamical model that models the temporal evolution of the data in terms of a latent dynamical model. 182–186

GPLVM A Gaussian Process Latent Variable Model is a probabilistic generative model that is learned from high-dimensional data. It can be used as a probabilistic dimensionality reduction, where the latent variables capture the structure (latent causes) of the high-dimensional training data. It is a generalization of probabilistic PCA to nonlinear mappings. 178–186, 189, 190, 230, 338, 344

graph cuts Graph Cuts (or, more precisely, s-t mincut) is a popular technique for energy minimization problems, as used in Markov Random Fields and Conditional Random Fields. s-t mincut reduces the energy minimization problem to the well-known max-flow problem in graphs, for which efficient augmenting path algorithms exist that are optimized for the grid-like connectivity structures that predominantly occur in images. Graph cuts can be shown to yield a globally optimal solution for submodular energies with binary labels. For multi-label problems, approximate solutions can be obtained by several extension techniques, such as alpha extension or alpha–beta swapping. 60, 62

HamNoSys The Hamburg Notation System, used by linguists to annotate sign language data at the sub-unit level. *see also* SiGML

HCI Human–Computer Interaction. 500, 514

HDP Hierarchical Dirichlet Process. 314, 316, 317, 322, 329, 462

Hessian matrix Matrix of second-order partial derivatives of a function of several variables. It describes the local curvature of a function. Suppose a function

$f : \mathbf{R}^n \mapsto \mathbf{R}, \; f(x_1, x_2, \ldots, x_n)$ then

$$
\mathbf{H}_f = \begin{bmatrix}
\dfrac{\partial^2 f}{\partial x_1^2} & \dfrac{\partial^2 f}{\partial x_1 \, \partial x_2} & \cdots & \dfrac{\partial^2 f}{\partial x_1 \, \partial x_n} \\[2ex]
\dfrac{\partial^2 f}{\partial x_2 \, \partial x_1} & \dfrac{\partial^2 f}{\partial x_2^2} & \cdots & \dfrac{\partial^2 f}{\partial x_2 \, \partial x_n} \\[2ex]
\vdots & \vdots & \ddots & \vdots \\[2ex]
\dfrac{\partial^2 f}{\partial x_n \, \partial x_1} & \dfrac{\partial^2 f}{\partial x_n \, \partial x_2} & \cdots & \dfrac{\partial^2 f}{\partial x_n^2}
\end{bmatrix}
$$

is the Hessian matrix. 165, 237

HMM A Hidden Markov Model (HMM) is a graphical model in which the system being modeled is assumed to be a Markov process with unobserved (hidden) states. An HMM can be considered as the simplest dynamic Bayesian network. 47, 73, 286, 291, 292, 297, 299, 336–339, 341, 345, 347, 367, 383, 390, 391, 395, 502, 525, 544, 547, 549–551, 555, 605, 606

HOG Histograms of Oriented Gradients: Common gradient-based descriptor for an image. 56, 57, 59, 65, 201, 202, 215, 244, 268, 365, 544, 547, 605

homogeneous coordinates Homogeneous coordinates are a system of coordinates used in projective geometry with applications in computer vision and computer graphics. Rigid transformation of points and vectors have a simpler representation in those coordinates than in the typical Euclidean coordinates. Let us define the following notation:
Homogeneous coordinates of a point $\mathbf{p} \in \mathbf{R}^3$ are $\bar{\mathbf{p}} = [\mathbf{p} \; 1]$.
The homogeneous coordinates of a vector $\mathbf{v} \in \mathbf{R}^3$ are $\bar{\mathbf{v}} = [\mathbf{v} \; 0]$.
The homogeneous coordinates of a rigid motion $\mathbf{g} = (\mathbf{R}, \mathbf{t})$ are $\mathbf{G}_{sb} = \begin{bmatrix} \mathbf{R}_{sb[3 \times 3]} & \mathbf{t}_{s[3 \times 1]} \\ \mathbf{0}_{[1 \times 3]} & 1 \end{bmatrix}$. Thereby, if we can transform a point by a rigid motion $\mathbf{g}$ with simple matrix multiplication $\bar{\mathbf{p}}(1) = \mathbf{G}\bar{\mathbf{p}}(0)$. 141

homography A homography is an invertible transformation from the real projective plane to the projective plane that maps straight lines to straight lines. 46

ICA Independent Component Analysis. 548, 552

ICP Iterative Closest Point is an algorithm to align or register two sets of points. The algorithm iterates the following steps: (i) collect correspondences from the two sets of points by the nearest neighbor criterion, (ii) estimate the transformation between both sets. (iii) transform the points with the computed transformation. This procedure is iterated until convergence. 157

IDAS Intelligent Driver Assistance Systems. 599, 611

image contour Image contour features are edge features that are on the outer extremity of the object. In other words, it is a sub-set of edge features on the outline of the object (as opposed to internal edge features). 154

image edge Image edges are defined as pixels in the image where there exists a discontinuities in the pixel brightness. Image edges are common features used in vision as they are easy to compute and are largely invariant to lighting. 154, 172

image likelihood Given an observed image (or images), I, the image likelihood, $p(I|x)$, measures the probability of that image(s) being observed given a set of input parameters x. 133, 161, 205, 241

image mosaicing Stitching several overlapping images on a surface, e.g. a plane to construct a combined image. 46

image silhouette Image silhouette corresponds to a binary image where pixels that are 0 are assumed to be part of the background and pixels that have value of 1 are part of the foreground object of interest. Binary image features are most often obtained through the process of background subtraction. 154

inverse kinematics Inverse kinematics is the process of determining the parameters (joint angles) of a parameterized articulated object in order to achieve a desired goal. Goals are configurations of position and/or orientation of typically end-effector segments (such as the hands). 265

IR Infra-Red. 497, 499, 506

ISM Implicit Shape Model. 58, 59, 61, 65

Isomap Isometric feature mapping. 240, 242, 496

Jacobian matrix Matrix of all first order derivatives of a vector- or scalar-valued function with respect to another vector. Suppose $\mathbf{F} : \mathbf{R}^n \to \mathbf{R}^m$ is given by $y_1(x_1, \ldots, x_n), \ldots, y_m(x_1, \ldots, x_n)$, then

$$
\mathbf{J_F} = \begin{bmatrix} \dfrac{\partial y_1}{\partial x_1} & \cdots & \dfrac{\partial y_1}{\partial x_n} \\ \vdots & \ddots & \vdots \\ \dfrac{\partial y_m}{\partial x_1} & \cdots & \dfrac{\partial y_m}{\partial x_n} \end{bmatrix}
$$

is the Jacobian matrix. 156

K-means A statistical clustering method which aims to partition observations into k clusters in which each observation belongs to the cluster with the nearest mean. 36

Kalman filter Kalman filter is an algorithm for efficiently doing exact inference in a linear dynamical system (LDS), where all latent and observed variables have a Gaussian (or multivariate Gaussian) distribution. 92, 93, 161, 173, 192, 543

KDE Kernel Density Estimation. 36, 37, 39, 40, 47

kinematic chain Parameterization commonly used to represent the motion of articulated figures. The orientation and position of an end-effector segment is determined by the orientation and position of the previous segment in the chain and an angular rotation about a joint axis. 140, 265

kinematic singularity In the context of human pose estimation a kinematic singularity refers to the fact that multiple configurations of joint angles result in the same human pose. 161

KNN k-Nearest Neighbor. 551

KSL Korean Sign Language. 550, 551

LBP Local Binary Pattern. 389, 459

LDA Linear Discriminant Analysis. 438, 464, 496

LDA Latent Dirichlet Allocation. 312–315, 317, 318, 322, 323, 326, 329, 462

LDS The term Linear Dynamical System is used to refer to a linear-Gaussian Markov process. In such a process the state evolution is modeled as a linear transformation plus Gaussian process noise. A first-order LDS on state $\mathbf{x}$, for matrix $\mathbf{A}$, is given by $\mathbf{x}_t = \mathbf{A}\mathbf{x}_{t-1} + \eta$ where η is a Gaussian random variable that is independent of $\mathbf{x}$ and IID through time. 174, 176, 187

LEA Locally Embedded Analysis. 496

level set Region-based level set methods are a popular technique for image segmentation and tracking. They minimize the energy functional by evolving a contour in the direction of the negative energy gradient using variational methods. In contrast to explicit approaches such as Snakes, level set methods define the contour of interest implicitly as the zero-level set of a continuous embedding function. This approach has several advantages, chief among them the ability to deal with topological changes of the segmented or tracked regions. 7, 60, 63

LGO Local Gradient Orientation. 604

LLE Locally Linear Embedding. 181, 185, 291, 499

LSH Locality Sensitive Hashing. 503

LTA Linear Trajectory Avoidance. 474, 475, 477, 480, 481, 485, 487

MAP In Bayesian statistics, a Maximum a Posteriori Probability (MAP) estimate is defined as a mode of the posterior distribution. 100, 160, 172, 182, 189, 347, 554

Markov process A Markov process (or Markov chain) is a time-varying stochastic process that satisfies the Markov property. An n-order Markov process, $(\mathbf{x}_1, \mathbf{x}_2, \mathbf{x}_3, \cdots)$, satisfies $p(\mathbf{x}_t \mid \mathbf{x}_1, \cdots, \mathbf{x}_{t-1}) = p(\mathbf{x}_t \mid \mathbf{x}_{t-1}, \cdots, \mathbf{x}_{t-n})$. That is, conditioned on the previous n states, the current state is independent of all other previous states. 161, 173, 174

MCMC Markov Chain Monte Carlo: A general framework for generating samples from a graphical model, of which Gibbs sampling is a popular special case. 95, 207, 239, 303, 315, 316

mean-shift Mean-shift is an interactive, non-parametric method for mode estimation in discrete data motivated by kernel density estimation. Starting from an initial location in feature space, mean-shift first applies a kernel function (i.e., a bounded function with non-negative profile and compact support) to the neighborhood around the current location and computes the weighted mean of all data points under the kernel's support. Then, it shifts the kernel to the new mean, hence the name. It can be shown that the mean-shift vector is proportional to the normalized density gradient; thus, mean-shift is guaranteed to converge to a nearby mode of the underlying density. The mean-shift idea can also be used to define a clustering technique. In this case, all data points are associated to the same cluster whose mean-shift windows converge to the same mode. 7, 39, 63, 92

MHI Motion History Image, a spatio-temporal object representation. 389, 543, 548

mixture of Gaussians A probability density function expressed as a convex combination of Gaussian distributions. 35, 201, 337, 478, 480, 486

ML Maximum likelihood estimation is a method for estimating parameters of a statistical model. For a fixed set of data and underlying statistical model, the method of maximum likelihood selects values of the model parameters that produce a distribution that gives the observed data the greatest probability (i.e., parameters that maximize the image likelihood function). 160, 212

MLN Markov Logic Networks. 83

MoCap Motion Capture: The process of recoding movement and translating that movement to a digital model. MoCap technology has numerous applications in entertainment, sports and medical applications. 131, 133, 262, 263

MRF A Markov Random Field, Markov network or undirected graphical model is a graphical model in which a set of random variables have a Markov property described by an undirected graph. 47, 62, 74, 292, 462

NCC Normalized Cross Correlation. 486

NMF Non-Manual Feature, part of sign language which does not involve the hands such as facial expressions, lip shapes, body pose etc. 540, 541

NN Nearest Neighbor. 443

NS Nearest Subspace. 443

optical flow Optical flow or optic flow is the pattern of apparent motion of objects, surfaces, and edges in a visual scene caused by the relative motion between an observer (an eye or a camera) and the scene. 48, 158, 172, 200, 291, 294–296, 304, 543, 547, 548

PaHMM Parallel Hidden Markov Model. 551, 552, 554, *see also* HMM

particle filter The particle filters, also known as sequential Monte Carlo methods (SMC), approximate the posterior filtering distribution with a set of typically weighted samples. 92, 93, 161, 163, 165, 166, 177, 189, 193, 211, 218, 480, 481, 603, 604

PbD see robot learning from demonstration. 336

PCA Principal Component Analysis is a method for dimensionality reduction, wherein high-dimensional data are projected onto a linear subspace with an orthogonal matrix. It can be formulated as the orthogonal linear mapping that maximizes the variance of projection in the subspace. Probabilistic PCA is a closely related latent variable model that specifies a linear-Gaussian generative process. 73, 153, 175–178, 181, 187, 240, 242, 291, 294, 342–344, 438, 442, 496, 504, 545, 546, 548, 549, 552, 553

PCP Percentage of Correctly estimated body Parts: Common error measure for 2D articulated pose estimation. According to PCP criterion a body part returned by the algorithm is considered correct if its endpoints lie within X% of the length of the ground-truth segment from their annotated locations; typically, $X = 50\%$. 257, 266, 268, 269

PERCLOS Percentage of Eye-Closure over time. 600, 602

PHMM A Parametric Hidden Markov Model (PHMM) is a HMM in which the observation density functions have a joint parameterization. As an example, to model a hand gesture "The fish was *this* big", one needs a single PHMM, while the fish size is given as a parameter. Using classical HMMs one would have to define an HMM for every fish size. 338

PID controller A Proportional–Integral–Derivative (PID) controller is a feedback controller that defines the error in a process as the difference between the measured value and the desired setpoint. The PID, then, attempts to minimize this error by adjusting the process inputs. 18, 20

Player/Stage Player is a device server that provides an interface to a variety of sensors and actuators using a TCP socket-based client–server model. Stage is a robot simulator; when used as a Player plug-in, Stage provides virtual Player robots which interact with simulated devices. For more information: http://playerstage.sourceforge.net/. 26, 27

pLSA Probabilistic Latent Semantic Analysis. 312–314, 324, 327

PoG Point of Gaze. 494, 497–499

posterior Posterior probability of a random event is the conditional probability once all the relevant evidence is taken into account. According to Bayesian statistical theory posterior can be expressed as a product of the prior and likelihood, i.e., $p(x|I) \propto p(I|x)p(x)$. 133, 161, 172

prior A prior probability measures the likelihood of an event before any observable data evidence is taken into account. 133

PTM Probabilistic Topic Model. 462

QP Quadratic Program: This is a convex optimization problem for which large-scale solvers exist. A support-vector machine SVM can be trained with a quadratic program. 214

RANSAC Random Sample Consensus, an iterative methods to estimate parameters of a model given a set of observations which includes outliers. 576

RBM A Restricted Boltzmann Machine is a bipartite, undirected, probabilistic graphical model. The graph comprises "visible" (observed) nodes (e.g., image pixels) and "hidden" (or latent) nodes. The basic RBM has binary random variables, but it has been extended to the real-valued case. The model is restricted in that no edges connect visible or hidden nodes to one another. Rather, all edges connect visible nodes to hidden nodes. Thus, conditioned on the hidden state, the visible variables are independent, and vice versa. This enables efficient learning and inference. 189, 190

rigging In computer graphics, given mesh representation of an articulated body, rigging is the process of inserting a skeleton with a bone hierarchy and skinning the mesh. Rigging is the standard way to animate characters or mechanical objects. 151

rigid body motion refers to the motion of a set of particles that move rigidly together i.e., the distance between any two points in the rigid body is constant over time. Therefore, the position of a rigid body is completely determined by the position of a reference point in the body and its orientation. 141

robot learning from demonstration In robot learning from demonstration, a robot learns how to perform a task by watching another agent (e.g., a human) perform the task, and then mapping the task from the performer's embodiment to its own embodiment. 364

RVM Relevance Vector Machine. 551

SGD Stochastic Gradient Descent: An on-line algorithm for optimizing objective functions defined on large training sets. 214

SGT A Situation Graph Tree is a hierarchical classification tool used to describe behaviors of agents in terms of spatio-temporal predicates. The tree contains a priori knowledge of the admissible behaviors in a defined domain. 14, 25, 26

shape context Shape context, a histogram of the relative position of points on a 2D shape contour used for shape matching. 546

SIFT Scale-Invariant Feature Transform: Common method for generating a sparse set of invariant keypoints and descriptors from an image. 56, 154, 158, 201, 230–232, 291, 293, 294, 389, 393

SiGML Signing Gesture Markup Language, allows sign language sequences to be defined in a form suitable for performance by an avatar. 556, *see also* HamNoSys

singularity In mathematics, a singularity is in general a point at which a given mathematical object is not defined, or a point where it fails to be well-behaved in some particular way. For a given function examples of singularities are points where the function is not defined or not differentiable. 142

skinning In computer graphics, given a surface mesh of the body and a skeleton, skinning is the process of binding skin to the skeleton bones. Every vertex in the mesh has to be assigned to one of the bones. It can be thought of as a segmentation of an articulated body in a number of rigid segments. 151

SLAM Simultaneous Localization and Mapping, a technique used for map building and updating in robotics and autonomous vehicles. 575, 576

SLDS A Switching Linear Dynamical System is a collection of N LDS models along with a discrete switching variable, $s \in \{1, \ldots, N\}$. The switching variable identifies which LDS should be active at each time step. As a probabilistic generative model, each LDS is a linear-Gaussian model, and on maintains a multinomial distribution for s. SLDS models are used to approximate nonlinear dynamical processes in terms of piecewise linear state evolution. 187, 190

SLR Sign Language Recognition. 539–542, 545, 546, 549, 550, 552–556

sLTA Stochastic Linear Trajectory Avoidance. 474, 477, 481, 486, 487

Sobel filter Sobel filter, a central difference image derivative operator. 545

SOFM Self-Organizing Feature Map. 551

spatial frame The spatial frame is an inertial frame of reference which is fixed to the environment. 147

SR Sparse Representations. 437–440, 451

SSP Social Signal Processing aims to understand and model social interactions (human-science goals), and to provide computers with similar abilities in human–computer interaction scenarios (technological goals). 514, 515, 525, 526, 530–533

statistical independence Two events are said to be statistically independent if occurrence of one event does not make the other event more or less probable. 133

SVD Singular Value Decomposition. 175

SVM Support Vector Machine: This is a linear classifier that is trained using a max-margin objective function. Extensions include nonlinear classifiers trained with kernel mappings, and "soft"-margin constraints using a hinge-loss objective. 55–57, 73, 77, 214, 338, 339, 348, 365–367, 443, 498, 602, 605

TDNN Time Delay Neural Network. 550, *see also* ANN

UI User Interface. 501, 506

wedge operator The wedge operator ($\wedge$) for a point or vector $\omega \in \mathbb{R}^3$ is defined as $(\omega)^\wedge = \begin{bmatrix} 0 & -\omega_3 & \omega_2 \\ \omega_3 & 0 & -\omega_1 \\ -\omega_2 & \omega_1 & 0 \end{bmatrix}$. Throughout the book, we will often use $\widehat{\omega}$ as a replacement for $\omega^\wedge$. The notation $\omega_{[\times]}$ is also commonly used in the computer vision literature to denote the wedge operator. Analogously the operator for the full *twist coordinates* $\xi \in \mathbb{R}^6$ is defined as $\widehat{\xi} = \begin{bmatrix} v \\ \omega \end{bmatrix}^\wedge = \begin{bmatrix} \widehat{\omega} & v \\ \mathbf{0} & 0 \end{bmatrix}$ and is used to construct the *twist action* $\widehat{\xi} \in se(3)$. 144, 145

Index

Printed by Publishers' Graphics LLC USA
SO20120316-006
2012